Historical Geography of India

Collection of Articles from the Indian Historical Quarterly

In 2 Vols.

These articles have been published in the Indian Historical Quarterly and the details of the articles is given below for reference:

Issue	Year of Pub.	Page Nos.	Page Nos. in the present book
Vol. 4 (1-4)	1928	228-233	1-5
Vol. 28 (1-4)	1952	205-214	7-15
Vol. 12 (1-4)	1936	511-517	17-22
Vol. 30 (1-4)	1954	332-338	23-29
Vol. 19 (1-4)	1943	214-224	31-43
Vol. 14 (1-4)	1938	388-391	45-48
Vol. 38 (1-4)	1962	98-110	49-60
Vol. 5 (3-4)	1929	659-665	61-67
Vol. 7 (1-2)	1931	245-253	69-76
Vol. 27 (1-4)	1951	215-238	77-101
Vol. 21 (1-4)	1945	297-314	103-122
Vol. 9 (1-2)	1933	470-478	123-131
Vol. 10 (1-4)	1934	642-664	133-156
Vol. 38 (1-4)	1962	303-326	157-178
Vol. 39 (1-4)	1963	38-58	179-197
Vol. 2 (1-4)	1926	345-350	199-204
Vol. 4 (1-4)	1928	694-701	205-212
Vol. 4 (1-4)	1928	339-346	213-220
Vol. 10 (1-4)	1934	541-550	221-230
Vol. 13 (1-4)	1937	703-704	231-232
Vol. 35 (1-4)	1959	254-258	233-236
Vol. 31 (1-4)	1955	293-322	237-261
Vol. 31 (1-4)	1955	1-31	263-291
Vol. 8 (1-2)	1932	332-341	191-200
Vol. 6 (1-4)	1930	1-30	201-224
Vol. 32 (1-4)	1956	286-289	225-228
Vol. 2 (3-4)	1926	698-709	229-238
Vol. 2 (3-4)	1926	495-508	239-250
Vol. 17 (1-4)	1941	196-206	251-262
Vol. 13 (1-4)	1937	610-616	263-268
Vol. 2 (3-4)	1926	657-662	269-274

Historical Geography of India

Collection of Articles from the Indian Historical Quarterly

Compiled by
P Mittal
Geeta Dua

Re-arranged with an Introduction by
Devendra Swarup

In 2 Vols.

Vol. 1

Originals
(an imprint of Low Price Publications)
Delhi-110052

Distributed by
D.K. Publishers Distributors (P) Ltd.
4834/24, Ansari Road, Darya Ganj,
New Delhi-110002
Phones: 51562573, 51562575, 51562578
e-mail: dkpd@del3.vsnl.net.in
visit us at: www.dkpd.com

Articles First Published in the Journal from 1925-1963
Collected and Published With an Introduction 2005

ISBN 81-88629-35-9 (Set)
ISBN 81-88629-36-7 (Vol. 1)

Published by
Originals
(an imprint of Low Price Publications)
A-6, Nimri Commercial Centre,
Near Ashok Vihar Phase-IV,
Delhi-110052
Phone: 27452453
e-mail: lpp@nde.vsnl.net.in
visit us at: www.lppindia.com

Printed at
D K Fine Art Press P Ltd.
Delhi-110052

PRINTED IN INDIA

Introduction

"A knowledge of space, no less than that of time, of geography, no less than that of chronology, is an indispensible prerequisite of any serious historical study." In fact, there can be no history without geography.

History of a people or civilization happens on the territory to which they belong or which they acquire through conquest or migration. Every historical event is connected with some place-name and therefore, when we read any ancient epic or modern book of history we come across names of rivers, mountains, towns, kingdoms, pilgrim centres, flora and fauna, climatic conditions etc. But many times we are not able to identify these place-names because, with the passage of time they have changed or new names have been superimposed upon them by foreign invaders and rulers. Here, historical geography comes to our help. It establishes a relation between ancient and modern place-names.

India is a vast country with a history going back to many millenia. Having passed through repeated foreign invasions, long periods of foreign rule and turbulence, she has been able to preserve a huge repository of literary, epigraphic and numismatic sources of its past. These sources are clothed in many classical and modern languages-Sanskrit, Pali, Prakrit, Tamil, Kannada, Telugu and other old regional languages. Besides these indigenous sources, the accounts of foreign invaders, travellers, scholars and ambassadors in their own ancient languages throw valuable light on our past. Sometimes we are puzzled to find the same place-name presented to us in different phonetic or linguist forms peculiar to different linguistic groups. So we find *Cholamandalam* transformed into *Coromandel*. Vedic river *Vitasta* being spelled as *Hydespes* by the Greek and Roman writers. Historical geography alone can unravel these puzzles. But it has been a very neglected subject in our country.

Some beginnings in the study of historical geography were made by Alexander Cunningham in the nineteenth century and were carried further by Indian scholars like Nundolal Dey, B C Law, D C Sircar and S B Chowdhary and some journals like Indian Antiquary and Indian Historical Quarterly conveyed their research articles, in a peace meal manner to interested readers. These journals ceased publication long back, therefore, much valuable and painstaking research done by the scholars of the old generation lies buried in their old files. Our best homage to the hallowed memory of these pioneers could be to compile and present their efforts to the inquisitive minds of the new generation. This book is a result of that craving.

The present book in two volumes presents 62 articles on the Historical Geography of India written by eminent scholars of the older generation. Their insightful wisdom and painstaking research reflected in these articles will guide us a correct understanding of the historical place-names connected with political as well as religious march of our civilizational history.

The articles have been arranged here is some topical order.

1. The first two articles penned down by H C Ray Chaudhuri and Vasudeva Sharan Agarwal respectively, clearly underline the importance and utility of the discipline called Historical Geography.

2. Subsequent articles present geographical data available in individual literary or epigraphic sources–such as Panini, Dharmashastras, Yadavapakasa, Agni Purana, Kalachuri inscriptions etc.

3. Next section brings together efforts by different scholars to identify and trace the history of specific historical places or pilgrimage centres. For example Sri Lanka of the Ramayana, Dwarka and Kurukshetra of the Mahabharata etc. These articles would show how scholars have strived to identify the location of an ancient place-name, and how they have sometimes arrived at quite different identifications.

4. In some articles the data about ancient ethnic groups or tribes such as ancient Tamils, Nagas, Chedis, Hunas, Yavanas, Kambojas etc. has been analysed.

5. Very useful data on fauna found in the Valmiki Ramayana and in the writings of Kalidasa has also been included in these volumes.

We hope that the material collected here will be found not only useful but inspiring for further reserarch in this important but neglected field of study.

Devendra Swarup

Contents

Plates

1

The Study of Ancient Indian Geography

H. C. Ray Chaudhuri

For an intelligent study of the history of any country, a thorough knowledge of its geography is indispensable. It is impossible for the student to follow the course of events unless he has accurate information about the precise location of the various places which figure prominently in the narrative. Besides, no scientific historian of a country can overlook the immense influence which its physical features exercise over the character of its people and their political destiny. If the above remarks are applicable to modern history, they apply with still greater force to the ancient history of a country like India with its references to tribes, territories, rivers, mountains and cities whose names have long passed out of current use. Indeed, in the case of India it is not merely the political historian who finds a knowledge of geography to be absolutely essential. The student of social history who reads about the distinctive usages of *Udicya, Śiṣṭadeśa* and *Dakṣiṇāpatha* in the Dharma Sūtras will find it difficult to follow the text unless he knows the exact signification of those terms. The student of literary history must learn to distinguish between *Gauḍa* and *Vidarbha, Mahārāṣṭra* and *Śūrasena,* to name only a few provinces which gave their names to distinct styles of poetic composition and different kinds of popular speech. More than the political, social and literary historian, the student of religion and mythology will feel at every step the need of a thorough acquiantance with the divine rivers and mountains which receive to this day the homage of the faithful, and those Dharma-kṣetras and Puṇya-sthānas which even now attract pilgrims from the remotest corners of the country. A knowledge of space, no less than that of time, of geography no less than that of chronology, is an indispensable prerequisite of a serious historical study. It is, therefore, needless to emphasise the necessity of the study of the historical geography of Ancient India.

The original materials for the study of ancient Indian geography are supplied principally from the following sources: –

(1) Indigenous texts on geography.

(2) Incidental references extracted from Indian works of a non-geographical character.

(3) Inscriptions and coins.

(4) Foreign accounts.

(1) Independent Indian treatises dealing with geography are by no means common. A list of such works is given by Mr. S.N. Majumdar Śāstrī in the Indian Antiquary, 1921, p.123. But they have not been sufficiently examined and it is difficult to say how many of them may be accepted as genuine. Compositions of a geographical character are, however, not unoften found embedded in the religious, legendary and astrological literature of ancient India. One of the earliest and most remarkable compositions of this type is the famous river hymn of the Ṛgveda (x, 75). Not less remarkable are the sections of the Atharvaveda (xix, 17, 1-9) and the Aitareya Brāhmaṇa (viii, 14) referring to the five-fold division of India. Fuller details are given in the two great epics, each of which contains a number of chapters which give a fairly accurate description of India with its territorial divisions. In the Rāmāyaṇic account, for instance, of the search parties of monkeys sent in quest of Sītā, given in four cantos (40–43) of the *Kiṣkindhyā kāṇḍa,* we have a detailed survey of the tribes, rivers, towns and hermitages of the five great regions of India. In the *Digvijaya* and *Tīrthayātrā* sections of the sister epic we have details of a similar character. More professedly geographical are the *Jambukhaṇḍavinirmāṇa Parva* (Mbh., vi, 5-9) of the Mahābhārata and the corresponding sections of the Purāṇas and the Kāvyamīmāṃsā styled *Jambudvīpavarṇana, Bhuvana-koṣa or Bhuvana-vinyāsa* and *Deśavibhāga.* Of the same type but of inferior value, is the *Kūrma-vibhāga* or *Kūrma-niveśa* section of Purāṇic and astrological works like the Mārkaṇḍeya Purāṇa (ch. 58), the Bṛhat-saṃhitā and the Parāśara Tantra.

As pointed out by Pargiter (J.R.A.S., 1984, p. 231) "there is plenty of the fabulous in Hindu geography, but it is confined, as a rule, to outside lands and the allusions to purely Indian topography are generally sober." The most serious difficulty in the way of utilising the Epic and Purāṇic accounts is the corruption of the texts. About a thousand years ago Alberuni complained (i, 238) "Such is the custom of the copyists and scribes in every nation. I cannot declare the students of the Purāṇas to be free from it, for they are not men of exact learning." The Bṛhat-saṁhitā is undoubtedly more free from textual corruption. The section called *Kūrma-vibhāga* correctly mentions *Mekalāmbaṣṭha* and *Puṇḍrotkala* while the corresponding passage of the Mārkaṇḍeya Purāṇa has *Mekhalāmuṣṭa* and *Purṇotkata*. But, as pointed out by Fleet, the Kūrma-vibhāga list "does not furnish materials for preparing an accurate map of ancient India. Mistakes in details can easily be shown, e.g. though Varāhamihira places Kaccha and Girinagara both in the southern division, he locates Raivataka in the south-west; whereas this mountain is quite close to Girinagara (Junagaḍh) and the Girnār mountain and is considerably to the south of Cutch,".

Descriptions of India, and Particulary of its central region, are also found in Buddhist literature. Of a slightly different character is the Jaina account of "Milikka" and "Āriya" lands found in the Pannavanā and other Upāṅgas (cf. the Mārkaṇḍeya passage 57, 15 "Tair vimiśrā janapadā mlecchāś cāryāś ca bhāgaśaḥ"). The name of the sixth Upāṅga called Jambuddvivapannatti, however, reminds us of the *Jambudvīpavarṇana* of the Brāhmaṇical texts.

(2) Besides long texts of a decidedly geographical character, Indian literature, both religious and secular, contains numerous isolated references to countries and cities, rivers and mountains, forests and deserts "which collectively amount to a considerable addition to geographical knowledge." Of special value are the references in the Jātakas, the Vinaya texts; the Aṅguttara Nikāya, the Sutta Nipāta, the Mahāgovinda Suttanta, the Dhammapada commentary, the Paramattha Jotikā, the Divyāvadāna, the Mahāvastu, the Jaina Sūtras, the early Tamil poems, the grammatical works of Pāṇini, Patañjali and Kramadīśvara, the Kāvyas of Kālidāsa and Daṇḍin, the Dharmasūtra of Bodhayana, the Dharmaśastra of Manu, the Arthaśastra of Kauṭilya, the Kāmaśāstra of Vātsyāyana, Nātyaśāstra of Bharata, the Siddhāntaśiromaṇi of Bhāskara and the Rājataraṅgiṇī of Kalhaṇa. Important information is also given in lexicographies like the Amarakoṣ a, the Abhidhānacintāmaṇi and the Abhidhānappadipikā.

(3) Inscriptions and coins constitute the third class of materials for ancient Indian geography. They are hardly less important to the student of Indian geography than to the student of Indian history. They not only afford us glimpses of the historical map of India in definite epochs, but supplement the information and advance the knowledge derived from literary sources. Who would ever have heard of the kingdoms of Satiyaputra and Ḍavāka, and the province of Vārakamaṇḍala, but for the inscriptions of Asoka and Samudragupta and the copper-plate grants of Dharmāditya, Gopacandra and Samācāradeva? Who would, again, have perceived the intimate connection between the city of Madhyamikā and the country of the Śibis but for certain coins discovered near Chitor?

(4) We now turn to the fourth and last class of materials viz. foreign accounts. Valuable information about India is given by numerous travellers, historians, geographers and even rulers of foreign nationalities. The name Hindu (Hidu) for instance is first met with in an inscription of a foreign potentate whose dominions extended from the Indus to the Ægean. If we omit the obscure references to Ophir and Sophir (Sovīra or Sauvīra?) in the Bible, the Persians are the earliest foreign people to leave an account of India. Mention is made of this country and some of its rivers and provinces in the Āvestā and inscriptions of Darius, the potentate to whom we have just referred.

The next foreign people who wrote about India are the Greeks. Writers of this nationality are valuable guides for a period covering about seven centuries from the time of Hekataios to that of Klaudios Ptolemaios. The officers of Alexander and his Seleukidan successors in particular have done much to illumine the darkness enveloping the ancient geography of Northern India, and particularly of the Land of the Five Rivers, the scene of the exploits of 'Philip's warlike son' and his Syrian and Bactrian successors. The Romans and their Greek subjects in Eqypt who navigated the Indian ocean and maintained commercial or diplomatic relations with this country in the early centuries of the Christian era, throw much light on the topography of the Western seaboard and the land of pepper, pearls and beryls in the Far South. The most valuable additions to our knowledge are made by the author of the Periplus of the Erythræan Sea and the Christian monk of Alexandria who bore the name of Kosmos Indikopleustes. The store of information gathered by the mariners of the period was evidently utilised by Strabo, Pliny and the compiler of the Peutingerian Tables.

But it is to the Chinese pilgrims, and particularly to Fa Hien, Song-yun, Yuan Chwang and I-tsing, that we are indebted for the most detailed information about the historic sites of the Indian interior and the countries under its cultural sway. It is a just observation of Cunningham that the pilgrimage of Yuan Chwang "forms an epoch of as much interest and importance for the ancient history and geography of India, as the expedition of Alexander the Great."

The last notable Chinese pilgrim to visit India was U-kong who travelled in the eighth century. It is fortunate that the time when the light from the Chinese records began to fail, light was vouchsafed from another source viz. the narratives of Muslim writers. Almost every Muslim observer from Sulaīman to Abul Fazl has something interesting to say about the topography of ancient (and not merely of mediæval) India. The greatest of the Islamic writers is perhaps Al-beruni whose

Tahqlq-i-Hind was written in 1030 A.D. The account of Al-beruni is valuable not only because it embodies the personal observations of an intelligent foreigner who actually visited this country, but also because it affords us a glimpse into the geographical texts of the Purāṇas available to him, which had already undergone much corruption in his day, i.e. as early as the eleventh century A.D.

The accounts of Muslim writers are supplemented by the records of mediæval European writers like Marco Polo. The Tibetan chroniclers (cf. Antiquities of Indian Tibet, p. 64) give little geographical information about the Indian interior that is not available elsewhere.

The known date of most of the foreign writers makes their evidences particularly interesting, and enables the geographer to note the changes in the map of India from age to age. The most serious defect of the non-Indian accounts is the distortion of names due either to the mis-bearing of the Indian sounds or the various transcriptions through which they have come down to us, which makes the work of identification particularly difficult. Another shortcoming which is most noticable in the work of Klandious Ptolemaios is the distortion of the shape of India. But this blemish must be shared by those indigenous writers who likened India to a lotus flower or compared its shape to that of a *Kūrma* or tortoise.

A list of poineers in the field of ancient Indian geographical studies is given by Mr. S. N. Majumdar Śāstrī in his edition of Cunningham's great work (pp. xviii). The following names deserve to be added to the list : –

Edward Thomas, Weber, Bühler, Burgess, Abbott, Holdich, Fleet, Oldham, Rhys Davids, Gerini, Stein, S. Lévi, Foucher, Hultzsch, Kanakasabhai, Pillay, Menon, A Barua, Nobin Chandra Das and Manomohan Chakravarti.

2

Ancient Indian Geography

V. S. Agarwala

The subject of ancient Indian geography is richly documented in the Sanskrit, Pāli and Prakrit literatures as well as the writings of the Greek, Chinese and Arab geographers. The information relating to the several aspects of geographical science like physical, political and commercial geography is indeed so vast that the subject merits a research dissertation planned on special lines. The original sources are in many languages, Sanskrit, Pāli, Prakrit, Greek, Latin, Chinese, Arabic, Persian, ancient Pahlavi, Avesta and the Indian regional languages. By patient gleaning of scattered information from innumerable sources and piecing the results together, it may be expected that a rich picture of Indian geographical knowledge would become available. A hundred years of Indian historical studies have remained without a proportionate advance in the knowledge of ancient Indian geography.

It is worth while to record here in a clarified manner the sources on this subject from the earliest times:

1. Vedic geography as depicted in the four Vedic Saṁhitās, especially the *Ṛgveda,* which acquaints us with the geography of north-western India about the beginning of the second millenium B.C. References to Gaṅgā, Sindhu, Sarasvatī and the rivers of the Punjab, especially to the Suṣomā or Sohan, a tributary of the Indus, to Marudvṛdhā, modern Maruvardhan flowing through Kashtawar in Kashmir, and to Suvāstu, modern Swat, are important landmarks of Vedic geography. Equally interesting is the mention of such names as Kamboja (ancient Pamir). Bālhīka (Balkh or Bactria), Mūjavanta (modern Munjan lying to the south of Oxus) and Gandhāra. These names tie down the Vedic hymns to a specific part of the country and give them a reality as nothing else does, for the geographical tradition in the form of place-names is most tenacious and almost indestructible. Such names as Kubhā (Kabul), Gomatī (Gomal), Krumu (Kurram), Yavyāvatī (Jhob), Bhalana (Bolan), Pakthana (Pakhtoon), Trikakut (Sulaiman mountain which was the source

of the famous salve known both in ancient and modern times),—are also unmistakable landmarks of Vedic geography, pointing to the area of extension of those peoples. The later Vedic literature including the secondary Saṁhitās, Brāhmaṇas, Upaniṣadas, Sūtras and Prātiśākhyas, is also rich in place-names and some of the important routes like the one from Gandhāra to Kuru-Pañcāla are mentioned there. *Le geographie et ethnographic Vedique* by Saint Martin was an excellent pioneer work, but an exhaustive study of Vedic geography as the firm basis of early Indian historical studies is needed.

2. Epics: *Rāmāyaṇa* and *Mahābhārata*. In the *Rāmāyaṇa* the route of Rāma's exile and of Vaśiṣṭha's messengers to Bharata in the Kekaya country (Salt range) require clarification. Prof. Pargiter devoted a special article to the geography of Rāma's exile, but the subject merits a fresh approach. The routes of the monkey army sent in quest of Sītā in the four directions, although preserving an important geographical document, seem to be a later addition made some time in the Gupta period when Indonesian geography of Yavadvīpa (Java) and Suvarṇadvīpa (Sumatra) became a vital reality for Indian navigators.

The *Mahābhārata* is the richest single source of ancient geography preserved in Sanskrit and old literature. Its most important chapters are those relating to Bhuvanakoṣa (Bhīṣmaparva, ch. 9), Tīrthayātrā (Vanaparva, chs. 80-88 and 89-153 describing the pilgrimage of Dhaumya and of Yudhiṣṭhira respectively, being a shorter and a longer version of a religious itinerary round the country), Pāṇḍavadigvijaya or conquest of the four regions, and the Upāyana-parva (Sabhāparva, chs. 25-32 and chs. 51-52), which incidentally provides a unique record of ancient economic geography with respect to the manufactured articles peculiar to each country. Apart from this material the *Mahābhārata* is a vast encyclopedia of geographical information of inestimable value. The epic information (Bhīṣmaparva, ch. 11) about the original homeland of the Śakas (Scythians) and Ṛṣikas (Yue-chi) in Central Asia including a number of old place-name is almost as important as that given by Herodotus and is of a kindred nature, pointing to its compilation some time about the fifth century B.C. when the Śakas still occupied the highlands of the Oxus and Central Asia.

3. Purāṇas: The mass of literature under this name treats the Bhuvanakoṣa or traditional account of ancient geography. *Tīrthas* or culture centres which were marked out during the course of Aryan colonisation of the country as sacred spots or focal points of diffusion and congregation; *Sthala-māhātmyas* (specific descriptions of local topography in much greater detail), and hundreds of special topics

bearing on Indian geography. The time range of Purāṇic compilation extends over about two thousand years and this literature undoubtedly preserves a unique record of the slow and steady process of land-settlement or "land taking," a cultural process of the highest sanctity by which the original ancestors planted themselves on land as 'children of the soil' and became welded and fused from epoch to epoch in an indivisible nationhood. The Purāṇas present the only record of the cultural unity that India achieved through the ages of which each stage was unfolded against a definite geographical background in the extensive river valleys, plains mountains and forests of India. Pargiter's edition of the Mārkaṇḍeya Purāṇa testifies to the richness of Purāṇic geography, of which the vast material still remains unworked. Dr. B.C. Law and Dr. D.C. Sircar have also made considerable contributors to the clarification of the Bhuvanakoṣa portions relating to the countries, mountains and rivers of India.

4. Paṇini's *Aṣṭādhyāyī* and grammatical literature. Pāṇini in his *sūtras* presents a rich picture of Indian geography discussed in my paper on "Geographical Data in the *Aṣṭādhyāyī* (*Journal of the U.P. Historical Society,* vol. XVI, pt. I, pp. 11-57). The material in the *Gaṇapāṭ ha* consists of important lists of place-names and tribal names comprising about a thousand items. This materical is only matched in importance and richness of recording by the information in the writings of the classical geographers of India. A comparative study of the two sources is likely to yield important results for the geography of the formative period of Indian history (B.C. 500- first century A.D.). The *Mahābhāṣ ya* of Patañjali and the *Kāśikā* have preserved in their own way a mass of evidence unknown from any other source.

5. Buddhist literature: Geographical evidence in the Pāli Tṛpiṭaka and its commentaries is available in the admirable *Dictionary of Pāli Proper Names* by Dr. Malalasekera. More important are the routes of Buddha's itinerary and those of his disciples both through north India and Gandhāra. We may also mention under the topic of Buddhist sources the Sanskritic texts of Buddhism compiled mostly between the first and the fifth century A.D., which although belonging to an altogether different epoch furnish highly important material relating to international routes connecting India with the adjacent countries and also Greater India. Prof. Paul Pelliot contributed an article of almost classical importance for the geography of Further India entitled 'Two Itineraries between China and India' (*BEFEO,* 1904, pp. 218 ff.). Mons. Przyluski has contributed a detailed account of North-West India according to the Vinaya of Mūla-Sarvāstivādins and connected texts

(*Journal Asiatique,* 1914, pp. 493-568). Dr. Sylvain Levi also made brilliant contributions to the geography of the Indian Archipelago (*Journal Asiatique,* 1921, pp. 332ff.) and to the geographical material of the *Bṛhatkathā* and the *Mahāniddesa*. His monograph on the geographical contents of the *Mahāmāyurī* (*JA.*, 1915) is a model of critical investigation of sources often discarded as valueless. It was presented by me in an English rendering for Indian readers (*Journal of the U.P. Historical Society,* vol. XV, pt. II, pp. 24-52). Dr. P.C. Bagchi, Çoedes (The Kingdom of Śrīvijaya, *BEFEO,* XVIII, 6, pp. 19 ff), Pelliot and Moens have written important papers based on Sanskrit and Chinese Buddhist sources of Indian geography.

6. Chinese Tripiṭakas: The vast body of this literature comprising about 2000 texts rendered into Chinese is still a sealed book, but many secular texts including some on Indian geography are preserved there. The *Fan-Fan-Yu* a geographical dictionary with Sanskrit and Chinese names in parallel columns published by D. Raghuvira is an instance of what may be expected. Even maps of old land-routes between India and China are preserved in the Chinese Tripiṭakas, as Dr. Bagchi kindly showed to me once.

7. Tibetan Buddhism: A large number of Sanskrit texts are preserved in Tibetan translations of the *Tanjur* and *Kanjur* collections, and Indian geography like other aspects of Indian culture is sure to benefit from an examination of these works.

8. Chinese travellers: Fa-hien, Yuan-Chwang, I-Tsing, Sung-Yun are classical names whose accounts of travels between China and India are priceless treasures as sources of Indian history and culture, and none the less of geography. The overland route from India to China through Afghanistan and Central Asia as may be mapped in the footsteps of the pilgrim Yuan-Chwang is a marval of human effort in forging international contacts under conditions of the utmost difficulty and risk. Beal, Watters and last of all Arther Walley in his latest book '*The Real Tripiṭaka and other Pieces*' which is a report on the travel of the Master of the Law, Dharmācārya Mokṣacārya Yuan-Chwang compiled from several sources, have made capital contributions to Indian geographical study through concentrated work on the Yuan-Chwang Saga. The importance of this Chinese source besides its accurate observation and truthful recording lies in the fact that its date is known with certainty as in the first half of the seventh century A.D. It provides corroborative evidence to Sanskritic sources of about the same period e.g. the geographical chapters in the *Bṛhatsaṁhitā* of Varāhamihira.

9. Classical Geographers of India, who accompanied Alexander and followed in his train for a period of more than five centuries have

left a vast body of literature, a class by itself, which is one of the richest sources of Indian economic, commercial and political geography. Ptolemy and Periplus treat of Indian geography frankly as a science, presenting a systematic treatment of high value. Jerini in his researches on Ptolemy's geography of eastern Asia and Prof. Renou in his new edition of Ptolemy's geography, and Schoff in his *Periplus* have done great service to Indian geographical studies. But the pioneer contribution of a monumental nature still unsurpassed, we owe to the labours of Prof. McCrindle whose six volumes of the classical sources of Indian geography are a valuable mine of knowledge about India.

10. Old Iranian sources: The inscriptions of Darius the Great, the Avesta and the Pahlavi texts and inscriptions also contribute an important chapter to the ancient geography of India, especially that relating to the North-West. Shri J.J. Modi has thrown welcome light on these sources in his writings.

11. Jain sources: The Jain canonical texts or the Aṅga literature with its commentaries, the subsequent Jain writings and the Apabhraṁśa literature together with the Prabandhas or historical essays which were a special literary feature of the medieval Jain authors, all these constitute a very important source of Indian geography. The material lies practically unworked upto now. There is also some literature on Tīrtha-yātras to the sacred places of the Jainas both in north and south India, of which none has been properly published. Similarly the Dūta-kāvyas following the model of Kālidāsa's *Meghadūta* treat of certain routes along which the messengers are supposed to travel across the length and breadth of the country. About seventy of these Saṁdeśa poems are known, of which the geographical study would repay the labours of any scholar. The colophons of Jain manuscripts both of Sanskrit, Prākrit and Apabhraṁśa are also replete with geographical information, as even a casual perusal of the *Jain-Pustaka-Praśasti-Saṅgraha* by Muni Jina Vijaya will show.

12. Sanskrit literature: The works of Kālidāsa, Bāṇa, Rājaśekhara, Varāhamihira, Kalhaṇa and a host of other important authors furnish geographical material of the first-rate value. The fourth and the thirteenth cantos of *Raghuvaṁśa* may be regarded as one of the most important chapters of ancient Indian geography, keeping in view a survey of the entire sub-continent and its adjacent countries in the Gupta age. Varāhamihira (6th centuty A.D.) deals in detail with the divisions of the country (*Bṛhatsaṁhitā*, chs. 14 and 16) noting about 300 names most of which are of certain value and known from contemporaneous sources and inscriptions. Dr. Fleet contributed a paper on this material in the *Indian Antiquary*. Rājaśekhara in his *Kāvya-*

Mīmāṁsā enumerates about 125 names of countries, rivers and mountains, and adds that for further information the reader should consult his bigger work, the Bhuvanakoṣa, of which unfortunately the text has not yet come to light. The author bases his accounts on the five principal divisions of India that were also known to Yuan-Chwang and other early writers, viz. Madhyadeśa, Pūrvadeśa, Dakṣiṇāpatha, Paścimadeśa and Uttarāpatha. Rājaśekhara also mentions the economic products of each region and directs that a poet should make himself familiar with these details about peoples and places in order to escape errors in his description.

Some of the Sanskrit lexicons of medieval times also note geographical details that have some corroborative value. It is surprising to find both the *Abhidhāna-cintāmaṇi* and the *Vaijayanti* explaining some obscure place-names of Pāṇinian geography, e.g. Pratyagratha (=Ahicchatrā), Bhaurika (=Samataṭa). The Āgamas and the Tantra works also contribute in their own way strings of geographical names in connection with the holy spots relating to several gods and goddesses. Dr. D.C. Sircar in his latest monograph on the 108 Śaktipīṭhas or centres of Śakti-worship has instituted a comparative and critical inquiry into their identification throwing a flood of light on old Indian geography. (*JRASB.*, 1948, pp. 1-108).

13. Arab geographers, ninth to the fourteenth centuryA.D. Arab geographers wrote extensively about India and of commerce between India and her neighbours on the west and the east. Their outlook was critical and scientific, dealing with the principal trade-routes, making inquiries about various places and their distances, and also collecting a great deal of original information about political and cultural conditions. During the tenth century we observe the development of a literary geographical school in Arabia which was to exert a lasting influence on succeeding generations of writers. Much of the commercial success of Arab traders depended on the critical geographical inquiries fostered under the geographer scientists of Arabia of the tenth century. Istakhri (950 A.D.), Ibn Haukal (975 A.D.), Al-Berūnī (973-1048 A.D.), Idrīsī (1154 A.D.), Damishqī (1325 A.D.) and Ibn-Batūtā (1355 A.D.) have made important contributions to the knowledge of Indian geography, especially to that of South India. Dr. G. Ferrand in two big volumes relating to the accounts of the voyages and the geographical texts by Arab authors on India and the Far East has rendered great service to the cause of Indian geographical studies, followed in this work by Dr. Muhammad Husayun Nainar of the Madras University in his book *Arab Geographer's Knowledge of Southern India* (1942).

14. Inscriptions: Perhaps the richest and the most authoritative source of Indian geography is contained in the many thousands of Indian Inscriptions ranging in date from the Mauryan period to the eighteen century. A complete concordance of all the geographical names with details about them on the basis of the thousands and thousands of published inscriptions from all over India would be constitute the eternal bed-rock of ancient Indian geography. It would be considered an achievement if accomplished by any Research Institute or University in India or abroad. Such a work was planned by the Kern Institute of Leyden but given up owing to the war. The inscriptions contain the names of the divisions of the country at various periods as they formed political units under particular dynasties and kings. This information is valuable for tracing the evolution of Indian political geography. Besides giving the names of countries, the inscriptions are also rich in other classes of geographical names e.g. mountains, rivers forming boundaries of kingdoms, capital cities, military encampments, trading emporia, and above all smaller administrative divisions. The land-grants form a class by themselves as mentioning the names of villages granted by the rulers to the donees. Such villages and even the names of hamlets are usually accompanied with information about their boundaries which separate them from other units. Sometimes single fields or pieces of land are mentioned together with their boundaries in sale-deeds which were executed by the secretariat officers in favour of the purchasers. All this acquaints us with the geographical material spread over the entire country in a surprisingly rich manner.

The above material is spread mainly over scores of research journals in which the inscriptions have been edited, e.g. *Epigraphia Indica, Indian Antiquary, Journal of the Bombay Branch of the Royal Asiatic Society, Journal of the Asiatic Society of Bengal,* and the *Reports of the Archaeological Survey* as well as *Reports on South Indian Epigraphy,* and the several volumes of the *Corpus of Indian Inscriptions* published under the Archaeological Survey. Fortunately most of these publications are equipped with detailed indexes of proper names and the work of preparing a geographical dictionary from this source will rather be found to be of less difficulty. It should, however, be remembered that a study of geography consists not merely in the indexing of names, howsoever important that may be, but in interpreting that material as a science contributing towards the elucidation of the political, physical, commercial, economic and ethnographical history of the land. Geography is the true bed-rock of historical knowledge and it is an undeniable fact that the study of Indian history will remain incomplete without a corresponding effort to tackle the problem of its geography.

Many authors and scholars have written on the subject of Indian geography both in the form of books, special studies and articles. A complete bibliography of the original sources and texts bearing on the subject, a list of all the geographical articles published in the journals and of textual studies must precede a comprehensive and planned study of Indian geography as envisaged above.

The information should be written down on separate cards, one for each entry. This card-index would be the first preliminary step leading to the completion of a period-wise geographical survey followed by volumes of Dictionary proper.

The scheme of an Indian Geographical Dictionary may be set forth as follows:

Volume 1.

(a) Introduction.

(b) Physical geography with complete descriptions of the mountains (Varṣa-parvata and Kula-parvata), river systems, deserts, plains, and the principal land and sea-routes, as well as seasons, plants, and animals.

(c) Period-wise survey of Indian geography from the point of view of its evolution:

- (i) Pre-historic geography and earliest land-settlement.
- (ii) Vedic and the later Vedic period.
- (iii) Epic and the Mahājanapada periods.
- (iv) Nanda empire to the Śuṅga empire.
- (v) North Indian geography from the first to the seventh century A.D.
- (vi) South Indian geography from the Āndhra to the Pallava period.
- (vii) Geography of Greater India and its routes :
  - (a) India, Inner-most Asia, Afghanistan, the Oxus region, Chinese Turkestan, and the land-route to China.
  - (b) Sea-routes, Burma, Siam, French Indo-China, Malaya, Java, Sumatra, Bali, Ceylon etc.
  - (c) India and the Western countries—Persia, Arabia, Syrian empire, Egypt, Africa, Greece, and the Roman empire.

(viii) Geography of the early medieval period (8th-9th century).

(ix) Geography of the late medieval period (10th-12th century).

(x) Geography of the Sultanate period.

(xi) Geography of the Mughal period.

Volumes II, III, IV and V.

Alphabetical Dictionary of Ancient Indian Geography.

3

Geographical Data in Pāṇini

Basudev Upadhyaya

No Ptolemy has given us a detailed and accurate geographical account of ancient India, but a minute study of the *Purāṇas* and *Pāṇini* reveals the fact how detailed and accurate the information of our ancestors was regarding parts of the Indian continent.

Alexander's men have mentioned some places of Afghanistan and the Punjab. By a study of Pāṇini's aphorisms we find that these are only corrupt forms of those ancient names mentioned by Pāṇini. The number of names of towns, villages, rivers and mountains, occurring in the *Aṣṭādhyāyī* of Pāṇini, is indeed very large. It would be difficult or even impossible to identify them all, but the positions and modern names of a good many of them can be determined, and in fact something has been done by S.N. Mazumdar in his Notes appended to Cunningham's *Geography.*[1]

The northern-most kingdom of Afghanistan, in ancient times, was known to some of the Greeks and Roman geographers by the name of Kapisene, and the Chinese traveller Hieun Tsang calls it, Kia-pi-she. Pāṇini mentions Kāpiśī in his sūtra कापिश्याः ष्फक् (IV. 2. 99) from which he derives कापिशायिनी the name of a grape and कापिशायन the name of a wine, manufactured from grapes and produced in the district. The country about Kabul is still remarkable for its fine grapes. So it is quite clear that Kapisene of Greek writers is no other but Kāpiśī of Pāṇini.[2]

Another province of Afghaniṣtan is called Fa-la-nu by Hieuen Tsang, and identified with the modern Vaneh or Wanneh by some, and with Bannu by Cunningham. The Sanskrit word corresponding to this is not known. Pāṇini, however, mentions a country named Varṇu in several places,[3] which is very likely the same as Hieuen Tsang's Fa-la-nu (*SNM.*, p. 679).

The river Suvāstu which is mentioned in Pāṇini's Sūtra सुवास्त्वादिभ्योऽण् (4. 2. 77) is the modern Swat, a branch of the Kābul river (*SNM.*, p. 678).

The position of the hill-fort of Aornos, in the capture of which, 'the warlike son of Philip displayed his martial vigour and military tactics and which has been beautifully described by Arrian, is still a matter of uncertainty. The Sanskrit name corresponding to it is quite unknown. Professor Wilson[4] traces it to the word Āvaraṇa 'enclosing', which, he thinks, forms the latter part of many names of cities. On the other hand Cunningham derives it from the name of a king, whom he calls Rājā-Vara but these identifications appear to be without any foundation. There is a Sūtra of Pāṇini वरणादिभ्यश्च (4. 2. 82) which means that the city in the neighbourhood of Varaṇā is called Varaṇā. Dr. Bhandarkar rightly thinks Varaṇā of Pāṇini is the original word maintains its existence in the corrupt form of Aornos of the Greeks.

Arachosia which was probably situated on the site of modern Herat is mentioned as a province of Afghanistan by Greek writers. A great controversy exists among scholars as regards its original name. Dr. Bhandarkar opines that there was a mountain named Ṛkṣoda in this province and the inhabitants were known as Ārkṣoda. Dr. Bhandarkar on the strength of the following aphorism आयुधजीविभ्यश्छ: पर्वते (4. 3. 91) of Pāṇini maintains that Ārkṣoda is the original word of Archosia of the Greeks. Seeing the phonetic resemblance of these two words, we can accept Dr. Bhandarkar's suggestion.

Greek writers have described the Malloi and the Oxydrakæ as two tribes of warriors. The Malloi tribe was living on the confluence of Rāvi and Indus and the Oxydrakæ in the midland of Rāvi and Vyās. A scholar of note traces the origin of the word Oxydrakæ from the word Kṣatriya. On the other hand, Dr. Bhandarkar is of opinion that these two words are derived from the words Mālavya and Kṣaudrakya respectively. Patañjali while commenting on the Sūtra जनपदशब्दात् क्षत्रियादञ् (4. 1. 168) mentions Mālavya and Kṣaudrakya as two confederacies.[5]

Now, we try to give an account of those cities and towns which have been identified by scholars with modern towns and villages and whose remains are still to be found on the site of their ancient sites.

Pāṇini mentions Kamboja as the name of a country in one of his Sūtras (कम्बोजाल्लुक्, 4. 1. 175). Scholars are of opinion that Kamboja was the ancient name of Afghanistan, at least of its northern part. According to Dr. Stein the eastern part of Afghanistan was Kamboja. Its capital was Dvārakā which should not be confused with Kṛṣṇa's Dvārakā in Gujerat. The Shia-posh tribe which now resides on the Hindukush mountain is said to have descended from the Kambojas.

In the Sūtra साल्वेयगान्धारिभ्यां च (4. 1. 169), Pāṇini refers to Gandhāra as the name of a country in which a Kṣatriya tribe called Gāndhāri was living. The country of Gandhāra lies along the Kabul river between the Khoaspes (Kunar river) and the Indus comprising the modern districts of Peshawar and Rawalpindi. Its capitals were in different ages Puruṣapura (modern Peshawar) and Takṣaśilā (modern Taxila). Ptolemy makes the Indus as the western boundary of Ganddāri (Gandhāra). Puṣ kalāvatī or Puṣkarāvatī was its most ancient capital, which the *Rāmāyaṇa* places in the Gandhāra-deśa. The modern town of Kandahar in Afghanistan still indicates that part of the country to which the ancient province of Gandhāra must have belonged.

Pāṇini gives us further information about the important cities of the Gandhāra province. They are Śalātura and Takṣaśilā. The name of Śalātura occurs in the Sūtra तूदीशलातुरवर्मतीकूचवाराड्ढक्छण्ढञ्यकः (4. 3. 94). This sacred city was the birth-place of Pāṇini himself, because the celebrated Sanskrit grammarian is mentioned by later Ācāryas as Śālāturīya (one born in Śalātura). This city existed even so late as the seventh century A.D., when it was shown with great reverence to Hieuen Tsang when he was crossing the frontier on his way to India from China. As regards the identification of Śalātura opinions differ. It has been identified by Cunningham with the village of Lahora to the North-West of Ohind in the Punjab. On the other hand Bühler identifies it with Lahul.

Pāṇini mentions the name of Takṣaśilā with that of Sindhudeśa in the Sūtra सिन्धुतक्षशिलादिभ्योऽणाञौ (4. 3. 93). The remains of Takṣaśilā are still to be found in the district of Rawalpindi in the Punjab. Cunningham places the site of the city near Shehdheri, one mile north-east of Kālā-kā-Serai between Attock and Rawalpindi where he found the ruins of a fortified city. Takṣaśilā was well known as a city in ancient times for its world-famous university. It is said that Pāṇini received his education at this great centre of learning.

Passing from Gandhāra we come to the province of the Punjab, the Madradeśa of ancient times. The country of Madra is referred to by Pāṇini in the Sūtra मद्रेभ्योऽञ् (4. 2. 108). This country was situated between the rivers Irāvati (Rāvi) and Candrabhāgā (Chenab). Madra was the kingdom of Śālva of the *Mahābhārata* and also of the king Aśvapati, father of the celebrated Sāvitrī, the wife of Satyavān. Some suppose that Madra was also called Vāhīka, which, however, appears to be only a part of Madradeśa. Hemacandra in his *Abhidhānacintamaṇi* calls it Ṭakkadeśa where the Ṭākkī language was most famous. Sākala which has been mentioned in the Sūtra संकलादिभ्यश्च (4. 2. 75) was the capital of Madradeśa. Cunningham identifies it with Sanglawala-Tiba in the district of Jhang in the Punjab. But this identification seems erroneous. Dr. Fleet rightly identifies it with Sialkote in the Lahore division in the Punjab. It is interesting to know that this was the birth-place of Sāvitrī. The town was important not only in the time of Pāṇini but continued to enjoy an undiminished supremacy and uninterrupted glory even in later centuries of Christian era as it was the capital of the Greek conqueror Menandar (2nd century B.C.) and of the Hūṇa kings Toramāṇa and Mihirakula (5th century A.D.)

From Madradeśa now we pass to the Kekaya country which is mentioned by Pāṇini in the Sutra केकयमित्रयुप्रलयानां यादेरिय: (7. 3. 2). It was a country situated between the Beas and the Sutlej. It was the kingdom of the father of Kaikeyī. Giribrajapura or Rājagiri was the capital of Kekaya, on the north of Beas, in the Punjab which has been identified by Cunningham with Jālālpura, the ancient name of which was Giriyak. Pāṇini does not omit mentioning the celebrated river of Kekaya. Vipāśā, the modern Beas and the Hypasis of the Greeks, is referred to by him in the Sūtra उदक च विपाश: (4. 2. 70).

Passing eastward we come to Kurudeśa which has been enumerated by Pāṇini in the Sūtra विभापा कुरुयुगन्धराभ्याम् (4. 2. 130). The ancient capital of this country was Hastināpura. Kurudeśa needs no detailed description because it was a famous country in ancient times.

Śālva (4. 2. 76) was also a country near Kurukṣetra known in ancient times by the name of Mātikavata. It was the kingdom of the father of Satyavān, the husband of celebrated Sāvitrī. It comprised portions of the modern territories of Jaipur, Jodhpur and Alwar.

Moving still eastward we reach the country of Pañcāla which is referred to by Pāṇini in the Sūtra न प्राच्यभर्गादियौधेयादिभ्य: (4. 1. 172). It was originally the country situated north-west of Delhi from the foot of the Himālayās to the river Chambal. But it was afterwards divided into north and south Pañcāla and was separated by the Ganges. The capital of the former was Ahicchatra and of the latter Kāmpilya. South Pañcāla was the kingdom of Rāja-Drupada whose daughter was Draupadī.

Leaving the countries of Madra and Pañcāla, we now come to the famous country of Kośala which has contributed a good deal to the annals of ancient India. The ancient Kośala was Oudh of modern times. It was divided into north Kośala and south Kośala. The capital of the latter was Kuśāvatī founded by Kuśa and the capital of the former was Śrāvasti. At the time of Buddha it was a powerful kingdom but in 300

B.C. it was absorbed into the kingdom of Magadha. Kālidāsa divides Kośala into north and south Kośala. The latter included the eastern part of the Central Provinces.

Magadha which is mentioned in the Sūtra द्वयञमगधकलिङ्गसूरमसादण् (4. 1. 100) is well known. It was one of the most famous and powerful kingdoms of ancient India.

The names of Aṅga and Vaṅga occur in the Sūtra न प्राच्यभर्गादियौधेयादिभ्य: (4. 1. 172). The country about Bhagalpur including Monghyr was known by the name of Aṅga in ancient times. It was one of the sixteen famous political divisions of India at the time of the Buddha. Its famous political divisions of India at the time of the Buddha. Its capital was Campā or Campāpuri. The western limit of its northern boundary, at one time, was the confluence of the Ganges and the Sarayū. It was the kingdom of Lomapāda of the *Rāmāyaṇa* and Karṇa of the *Mahābhārata*.

Kaliṅga is mentioned in one of his Sūtras द्वयञ्मगधकलिङ्गसूरमसासादण् (4. 1. 100). Kaliṅga (modern northern Sircars) was lying on the South of Orissa and north of Draviḍa on the border of the sea. According to Cunningham it was situated between the Godāvarī river on the south-west and the Gaoliya branch of the Indravatī on the north-west. According to Rapson it was between the Mahānadī and the Godāvarī. Its chief towns were Maṇipura and Rājapur. In the time of the *Mahābhārata* Orissa (*Utkala*) was included in Kaliṅga, but in the time of Kālidāsa these were two different provinces as he mentions them separately in his *Raghuraṃsa*: – उत्कलादृर्शितपथ: कलिङ्गाभिमुखो ययौ (Canto 4. 39). The country of Utkala was, however, to the north of Kalinga. The very word Utkala means north of Kaliṅga (उत्कालङ्ग). It comprised the modern province of Orissa. Chanduar, situated on the opposite side of Cuttack across the river was the ancient capital of Utkal under the Magadha kings.

Pāṇini mentions the name of Sindhu as a country, in the Sūtra सिन्धुतक्षशिलादिभ्योऽणञौ (4. 3. 93) which corresponds to the modern province of Sindh. According to Ptolemy the Ābhīras dwelt in the southern portion of Sindhu and the Muṣikas resided in the northern portion. After the death of Menandar who reigned over the Punjab, Kabul and Sindh from 140-110 B.C., *Mancs,* the Scythian king, conquered Sindh and expelled the Greeks.

The *Janapada* of Sauvīra is enumerated in the Sūtra स्त्रीषु सौवीरसाल्वप्रीक्षु (4. 2. 76). It has been identified by Cunningham with Eder, a district in the province of Gujerat. It was called Badari by the Buddhists, and was situated at the head of the gulf of Cambay. Sauvīra was the Sophir or Ophir of the Bible and Sovira at *Milinda-Pañho* where it is described as a sea-port. Dr. Rhys Davids places Sauvīra in his map to the north of Kathiawad and along the Gulf of Cutch.

The names of Avanti and Kunti occur in the Sutra अवन्तिकुन्तिकुरुभ्य एश्च (4. 1. 176). Avanti was a well-known kingdom in ancient India, famous for its enormous wealth and cultured people. Ujjayin was the capital of this noted kingdom and was famous for the pictursque temple of Mahākāla.

Kunti was also called Kunti-bhoja. It was an ancient town of Malava, where Kunti, the mother of Yudhiṣṭhira and his brothers was brought up by her adoptive father Kunti-bhoja, the king of Bhoja. It was situated on the bank of a small river called Aśvanadi on Aśvarathanadi.

The name of Vidarbha country is included in the term प्राच्य in the Sutra, न प्राच्यभर्गादियौधेयादिभ्यः (4. 1. 172), which comprised the modern province of Berar. It was the kingdom of Bhīṣmaka whose daughter Rukmiṇi was married to Kṛṣṇa. Its principal towns were Kuṇḍinagara and Bhojakaṭa. कुण्डिनगर or Vidarbhanagara its capital was evidently Bidar. The ancient country of Vidarba included the kingdom of Bhopal and Bhilsa to the north of the Narbada. Kuṇḍinanagara which has been beautifully described by Śrihatṣa in his Naiṣadhīyacarita (2. 73-105), was the birth-place of celebrated Damayantī, wife of king Nala.[6]

References

1. Cunningham's *Ancient Geography of India with intro. and* notes by S.N. Majumdar, Calcutta, 1924; henceforth abbreviated as SNM.
2. *SNM.*, pp. 671.
3. वर्णौ वुक् (4. 2. 103) सिन्धु तक्षशिलादिभ्योऽणञौ (4. 3. 93) सिन्धुगण comprises good many words one of which is वर्णु.
4. See Wilson's *Ariana Antiqua.*
5. The credit of suggesting these identifications for the first time goes to Dr. R. G. Bhandarkar. Vide *Ind. Ant.* vol. I (1872), pp. 21 ff. and his *Collected Works,* vol. I, ff. 102-107.
6. The writer is much indebted to Mr. Nanda Lal Dey in the preparation of this essay. His *Geographical Dictionary* has been of invaluable help.

4

Ancient Indian Geography

*as revealed in Dharma-sūtras**

Sures Chandra Banerji

The *Dharma-sūtras* contain some geographical material about the India of the times in which they were composed. We propose to collect here the geographical names under appropriate heads. It may be pointed out that some of the names, collected herein, have not been mentioned in such standard works as De's *Geographical Dictionary of Ancient and Medieval India* and Cunningham's *Ancient Geography.*

In this collection, we have set forth such information about the geographical names as can be gathered from the texts and the commentaries thereon.

The geographical names are arranged below in the English Alphabetical order under the following classes : –

A. Rivers.

B. Mountains and Hills.

C. Places in general.

A. Rivers

Candrabhāgā : Vi. 85.48

Its bank is regarded as very sacred for purposes of *śrāddha, japa, homa* and *tapas*.

Gaṅgāsāgara-saṃgama : Vi. 85.28

It serves the same purpose as the Candrabhāgā.

---

* The following abbreviations have been used in this paper: –

B – Baudhāyana or *Baudhāyana-dharmasūtra,* ed. A.C. Śāstrī.

V Vasiṣṭha or *Vāsiṣṭha-dharmaśāstra,* ed. Fuhrer, Bombay, 1883.

Vai – *Vaijayanti,* Nandapaṇḍita's comm. on *Viṣṇu-Smṛti*.

Vi – Viṣṇu or *Viṣṇu-Smṛti,* ed. Jolly, Calcutta, 1188.

Gaṅgā : B.I. 2.11; V.I. 12; Vi. 20.23, 85.10

Acc. to some, the region bet. Gaṅgā and Yamunā is called Āryāvarta (B., V.) (Also see Yamunā). Its bank is very sacred for purposes of *śrāddha, japa, homa* and *tapas*.

Godāvarī : Vi. 85.42

Its bank is sacred for *śrāddha, homa, japa* and *tapas*.

Gomatī : Vi. 85.43 Do

Īrāvatī : Vi. 85.49 Do

Jyotiṣā : Vi. 85.33 Do

[See Śoṇa]

Kumāra-dhārā : Vi. 85.25

Kāśmīra-deśe krauñca-parvate kumāra-
śakti-prahārena jala-dhārā nirgatāsti
Sā kumāra-dhārātasyām | *dakṣina-*
samudra iṣupāta-kṣetre vā. | Vai.

Mahā-gaṅgā : Vi. 85.23

Its bank is regarded as sacred for *śrāddha, japa, homa* and *tapas*.

Naḍantikā : Vi. 85.19 Do

(or Naḍintikā)

Narmadā : Vi. 85.8 Do

Phalgu: Vi. 85.22

'gayāstha' – Vai. Do

Sarayū : Vi. 85.32 Do

Sarasvatī : Vi. 85.27 Do

Śatadru : Vi. 85.47 Do

Śoṇa : Vi. 85.33

Acc. to Vai., the confluence of the Śoṇa and the Jyotiṣā (see *ante*) lies in the midst of the Vindhyas.

Its bank is sacred for *śrāddha, japa, homa* and *tapas*.

Vetravatī : Vi. 85.45 Do

Vitastā : Vi. 85.46 Do

Yamunā : B.I. 2.11; V.I. 12; Vi. 85.9

See Gaṅgā.

B. Mountains and hills

Amara-kaṇṭaka : Vi. 85.6.

It is sacred for the performance of *śrāddha, japa, homa* and *tapas*.

Himavat : B.I. 2.10; V.I. 8.

It constitutes the northern boundary of Āryāvarta, acc. to B. and V.

Kālaka-vana : B.I. 2.10, V.I. 8.

It constitutes the eastern boundary of Āryāvarta.

Mahālaya : Vi. 85.18.

It is sacred for *śrāddha, japa, homa* and *tapas*.

Pāriyātra : B.I. 2.10; V.I. 8.

1 A mountain-range (Bühler).

2 Western Vindhya range (MW) (For the variant 'pāripātra', see Bühler, SBE. XIV. p. 147, f.n.9).

It is the southern boundary of Āryāvarta.

Śrī-parvata : Vi. LXXXV. 34.

Dakṣiṇa-deśasthaḥ Śrīśailo mallikārjunasthānam-Vai.

A mountain in the Deccan, the place of Mallikārjuna (a symbol of Śiva).

Varāha : Vi. 85.7.

Varāhākāre parvata-viśeṣe-Vai.

On it *śrāddha, japa, homa* and *tapas* are commended.

Vindhya: V.I. 9.

The southern limit of Āryāvarta.

C. Places in general

Agastyāśrama. Vi. 85.29.

puṣkara-samipe sarasvatī-tīre

. . . . *dakṣiṇa-deśe svāmisthānevā*-Vai

It is a sacred place for *śrāddha, japa, homa* and *tapas*.

Aṅga : B.I. 2.14.

People of this place are of mixed castes.

Avanti : B.I. 2.14.

People of this place are said to be *saṃkīrṇa-yonayaḥ* (of mixed castes).

Āryāvarta[1] : B.I. 2.10-13; V.I. 8-15 Vi. 84.4

The extent of Āryāvarta, as described by B., is as follows: –

Bounded on the north by the Himavat, on the cast by the Kālaka-vana[2], on the south by the Pāriyātra[3] (or Pāripātra) and on the west by *adarśana* (the place where the river Sarasvati has dried up and disappeared. That the exact extent of the Āryāvarta was a matter of controversy, even at the time of composition of B., is clearly indicated by B's reference to the views of others according to which this tract of land lies between the Gaṅgā and the Yamunā. The Bhāllavins, referred to by B., described Āryāvarta as follows: –

paścāt sindhur visaraṇī sūryasyodayanaṃ puraḥ/

yāvat kṛṣṇo vidhāvati tāvaddhi brahmavarcasam//

We may, however, negatively form an idea of the extent of Āryāvarta, as conceived by B., by excluding those regions which have been declared unholy and a visit to which is said to render a man liable to expiation. The unholy places are as follows: –

Avanti, Aṅga, Magadha, Surāṣṭra,

Dakṣiṇāpatha, Upāvṛt, Sindhu, Sauvīra, Āraṭṭa,

Kāraskara, Puṇḍra, Vaṅga, Kaliṅga, Prānūna (B.I. 2.14-16)

It is not, however, clear whether or not these prohibited places were also included in Āryāvarta by B.

V's conception of Āryāvarta is the same as that of B. with the difference that the former reads *ādarśa* for *adarśana* read by the latter. The other views, given by V., are the same as those referred to by B. Acc. to Vi., Āryāvarta is the tract of land beyond the regions known as Mleccha-deśa. Mleccha-deśa is the name given by Vi. to those places where the caste-system does not prevail (Vi. 84.4).

Āraṭṭa : B.I. 2.15.

Entrance into this place is said to render one liable to expiation.

Ausaja : Vi. 85.52.

Śūrpākāraṃ dakṣiṇa-deśasthaṃ tīrtham-Vai. A place sacred for *śrāddha, japa, homa* and *tapas.*

Binduka : Vi. 85.12.

dakṣiṇa-deśastha-tīrtha-viśeṣaḥ-Vai. Sacred for *śrāddha, japa, homa* and *tapas.*

Bhṛgu-tuṅga : Vi. 85.16.

Amara-kaṇṭaka-samīpastho vindhyapādaḥ-Vai. Sacred for *śrāddha, japa, homa* and *tapas.*

Dakṣiṇāpatha : B.I. 2.14.

People of this place are branded as *saṅkīrṇa-yonayaḥ.*

Gaṅgādvāra : Vi. 85.28.

Sacred for *śrāddha, japa, homa* and *tapas.*

Gayā : Vi. 85.4, 66. Do

Kaliṅga : B.I. 2.15, 16.

Entrance into this region is said to render a man liable to expiation.

Kanakhala : Vi. 85.14.

Uttara-parvatastham tryambakastham vā-Vai.

Sacred for *śrāddha, japa, homa* and *tapas.*

Kaṇvāśrama : Vi. 85.30.

Mālinī-tīre-Vai.

Sacred for *śrāddha, japa, homa* and *tapas.*

Kāraskara : B.I. 2.15.

Entrance into this tract of land is said to render one liable to *prāyaścitta.*

Kālodaka : Vi. 85.35.

Yāmunas tīrtha-viśeṣaḥ-Vai.

Sacred for *śraddha, japa, homa* and *tapas.*

Kedāra : Vi. 85.17.

Uttara-parvatasthaḥ-Vai,

Sacred for *śrāddha, homa, japa* and *tapas.*

Kausikī : Vi. 85.31. Do

Kubjāmra : Vi.85.15. Do

Utkalu-deśasthaṃ gaṅgā-dvārasthaṃ vā-Vai.

Kuśāvarta : Vi. 85.11. Do

tryambaka-giristho godāvarī-prabhavaḥ-Vai.

Magadha : B.I. 2,14.

People of this place are said to be *saṅkīrṇa-yonayaḥ.*

Mātaṅga-vāpī : Vi. 85.38. Do

gayā-dakṣiṇa-bhāgasthā-Vai.

Mleccha-viṣaya : Vi. 84, 1, 2, 4.

Śrāddha in, even visit to, this region is condemned. Vi. defines Mleccha-deśa as the land where the caste-system does not prevail.

Nīla-parvata : Vi. 85.13.

It is sacred for purposes of *śrāddha, japa, homa* and *tapas.*

Naimiṣāraṇya : Vi. 85.28. Do

Pañca-nada : Vi. 85.51. Do

Kṛṣṇa-veṇā-tuṅgabhadrā koṇānāṃ pañcānāṃ nadīnāṃ samāhāradeśe-Vai.

Prabhāsa : Vi. 85.26. Do

dvārakā-samīpe-Vai.

Puṇḍra : B.I. 2.15.

A visit to this place renders one liable to expiation.

Prayāga : Vi. 85.28.

Sacred for *śrāddha, japa, homa* and *tapas*.

Prānūna : B.I. 2.15.

A visit to this tract of land renders one liable to expiation.

Puṣkara : Vi. 85.1

Sacred for *śrāddha, japa, homa* and *tapas*.

Saptārṣa : Vi. 85.39

A place for pilgrimage, according to Vai. Do

Śākambharī : Vi. 85.21. Do

Sindhu : B.I. 2.14; V.I. 15 Vi. 85, 50.

People of this region are branded as *saṃkīrṇa.yonayaḥ*. It is rather curious that Vi. reads it among the rivers whose banks are regarded as sacred for *śrāddha, japa, homa* and *tapas*.

Sugandhā : Vi. 85.20.

Saugandhika-nadī-samīpasthā—Vai.

Sacred for *śrāddha, japa, homa* and *tapas*.

Surāṣṭra : B.I. 2.15.

People of this region are said to be *saṅkīrṇa-yonayaḥ*.

Sauvīra : B.I. 2.14,15.

People of this place are like those of Surāṣṭra. Besides, entrance to this region is said to render one liable to *prāyaścitta*.

Trihalika-grāma : Vi. 85.24.

Śāla-grāmaḥ taṇḍulikāśrama ītī vā pāṭhaḥ—Vai.

Regarded as sacred for *śrāddha, japa, homa* and *tapas*.

Upāvṛt : B.I. 2.14.

People of this place are characterised as *Saṅkīrṇa-yonayaḥ*.

Uttara-mānasa : Vi. 85.36.

Kedārottara-parvatastham—Vai.

Sacred for *śrāddha, japa, homa* and *tapas*.

Vaḍavā : Vi. 85.37.

tīrtha-viśeṣo dakṣiṇa-deśasthaḥ—Vai.

Identification, given in the *Geographical Dictionary,* appears to be different .

Sacred for *śrāddha, japa, homa* and *tapas.*

Vaṅga : B.I. 2.15,16.

Sojourn to this place is said to render one liable to expiation.

Vārāṇasī : Vi. 85.28.

Sacred for *śrāddha, japa, homa* and *tapas.*

References

1. For a discussion on Āryāvarta, as conceived by authors of *Dharma-sūtras,* see Cunningham's *Ancient Geography,* pp. xi-xiii. This work however, does not take the *Viṣṇu-smṛti* into account.
2. Probably name of a mountain as suggested by Patañjali on II.4.10. Some would identify it with Prayāga (vide Cunningham, *op. cit.,* pp. XII. f.n.). Others would take it as the ancient name of the Rajmahal hills in Bihar (vide *Geographical Dictionary,* pp. 84).
3. Acc. to Bühler, name of a mountain identified by Monier Williams (*Skt-Eng. Dictionary*) as the western Vindhya range. It, however, appears to have been different from the Vindhyas.

5

Yādavaprakāsa on the Ancient Geography of India

D C Ganguly

Yādavaprakāśa was born in the village Tiruppuṭkuli or Gṛdhrasaras near Kāñcīpuram or Conjeeveram. He was the *Guru* (preceptor) of the great Vaiṣṇava teacher Rāmānujācārya. He is referred to by Hemacandra. He may be taken to have flourished in the second half of the eleventh century A.D. Dr. Gustav Oppert places his date in *c.* 1000 A.D.

Yādavaprakāśa has written a book on Sanskrit vocabulary, named *Vaijayantī.*[1] The *Deśādhyāya* in *Bhūmikāṇḍa* and *Purādhyāya* in *Pātālakāṇḍa* of the *Prayāyabhāga* of this work throw important light on the ancient geography of India. The book has hardly been noticed by the scholars working on this branch of Indology.

The *Vaijayantī* states that[2] there are six islands, *viz.*, Aṅgadvīpa, Yavadvīpa, Malayadvīpa, Śaṅkhadvīpa, Kuśadvīpa, and Varāhadvīpa. Prācya is to the south-east of Śarāvatī, and Udīcya is to the north-west of it (Śarāvatī). Madhya-deśa is in between them (Prācya and Udīcya). Āryāvarta, otherwise known as Brahmavedi, is between the Vindhya and the Himālaya.

Udīcya includes the following countries (janapada): Cīna (=Kharaṃbhara), Gandhāra (=Dihaṇḍa), Yavana (=Huruṣkara), Saṃbhāla (=Sūrasena), Laṃpāka (=Muruṇḍa), Tokṣāra (=Yugālika), Jālaṃdhara (=Trigarta) Hola (=Kharaṭī), Pratyagratha (=Ahicchatra), Tula (=Kalṃgaka), Ṭarka (in which is Bālhīka), Vāhīka (in which is Vālhika), Kāśmīra (in which is Kīra), Turuṣka (in which is Śākhi), Sindhu (in which is Dārada), Kumālaka (=Sauvīra), Yaudheya (=Nṛgālika), Pārada, Kiñja, Kolya and other places.

Prācya includes the janapadas: Mudgaraka (=Kuja), Prāgjyotiṣa (=Kāmarūpa and Prāgjālika), Videha, (=Tīrabhukti), Srāvastī (=Puraṃjaka) Rāḍhā (=Suhma), Puṇḍra (=Vareṃdrī), Bhaurika

(=Samataṭa), Aṅga (=Campā, Vaṅga (=Harikelī), Magadha (=Kīkaṭa), Andhra, Vrata, Sālva and others.

Dakṣiṇāpatha is the name of the country to the south of the Vindhya.

In it are the countries (deśa): Pāṇḍya (=Pāṃdiya), Kuntala (=Upahālaka), Cola (=Utpalāvarta), Mahārāṣṭra (=Daṇḍaka), Kerala, Kulya, Setuja, Kulakālaka, Iṣīka, Śabara, Āraṭṭa, and other countries.

Aparāṃta (also known as Pāścātya and Sūryāraka) includes Malada and other countries upto the Vindhya settlements. In it are the following: –

Malada (=Sthaura), Karūśa (=Bṛhadgṛha), Traipura (=Hahāla, Caidya, and Cedi), Daśārṇa (=Vedipara), Mālava (=Avanti), Mekala, Bhoja, Kośala and other countries.

Madhyadeśa includes the countries: Marava (=Daśeraka), Śālva (=Kārakutsīya, and whose six parts are Udumbara, Tilakhala, Mahākāra, Yugaṃdhara, Huliṃga, and Śaradaṃḍa), Kuntala, Kulya, Kaliṅga, Kāśi, Kosala, Mekala, Kusaṭa, Jāṃgala, Pṛthava (Pṛthu), Vṛka, and Paṭaccara.

Names of cities: Sāketa (=Ayodhyā and Kosalānandinī), Dvārakā (=Dvāravatī), Madhurā (=Madhūṣikā, Mathurā, Madhūpaghnā) situated in Śūrasena, Kauśa (=Kuśasthalī), Vārāṇasī (=Śivapurī, Vāraṇāsī, and Kāśikā), Mithilā (=Videha), Kanyākubja (=Mahodaya), Hastinī (=Hāstinapura, Nāgāhva, and Hastināpura), Khāṇḍavaprastha, Jayantipura (=Āhuka), Avantī (=Takṣaśilā), Kakundī (=Vāraṇāvata), Devīkoṭṭa (=Koṭivarsa), Māhiṣmatī (=Vṛkasthalī).

The above geographical observations of *Vaijayantī* may be compared with those made in Rājaśekhara's *Kāvyamīmāṃśā*[3] (*c.* A.D. 925), Hemacandra's *Abhidhānacintāmaṇi*[4] (*c.* A.D. 1150), Puruṣottamadeva's *Trikāṇḍaśeṣa*[5] (twelfth century), and in other contemporary and nearly contemporary works in order to estimate their value.

Āryāvarta-Brahmavedi. Rājaśekhara and Hemacandra mention that Āryāvarta is the country between the Himalaya and the Vindhya, and it extends from the eastern ocean to the western ocean.[6] Rājaśekhara elsewhere states[7] that the Narmadā is the boundary between the Āryāvarta and Dakṣiṇāpatha. According to Hemacandra Brahmavedi is the territory between the five Rāma lakes.[8] Bhuvaneśvar Inscription[9] of Bhaṭṭa-Bhavadeva states that Rāḍhā is situated in Āryāvarta.

Udīcya. According to *Vaijayantī* it extended from Ramnagar, in Rohilkhand (Ahicchatra), to Lamghan (Lampaka) in Afghanistan. It appears from the Ghoshrawa inscription of Devapāla that Udīcīpatha and Uttarāpatha are identical.[10] Rājaśekhara mentions Udīcya as one of the four quarters (*diśaḥ*). He places Uttarāpatha beyond Pṛthudaka, modern Pehoba, in the Karnal District, Punjab, and states that Śaka, Kekaya, Vokkāṇa, Hūṇa, Vāṇāyuja, Kāmboja, Vālhīka, Valhava, Limpāka, Kulūta, Kīra, Tangaṇa, Tuṣāra, Turuṣka, Barbara, Hurahūva, Hūhuka, Sahuḍa, Haṃsamārga, Ramaṭha, Karakaṇṭha etc., are situated in it.[11] Hemacandra agrees with Yādavaprakāśa in placing it to the north-west of Śarāvatī.[12] An inscription, dated 1107 A.D., relates that Banjsthana (Madhukarghar, in the Bundi State, Rajputana) lay in the extremity of Dakhin and Udīcya-deśa.[13]

Gāndhāra-Dihaṇḍa. Gāndhāra is mentioned in the Khalimpur inscription of Dharmapāla.[14]

Yavana-Huruṣkara. Yavana is referred to in the Khalimpur inscription of Dharmapāla. Rājaśekhara places Yavana country in Paścād-deśa.[15]

Sambhāla-Śūrasena. Śūrasena was the country in which Mathurā was situated.[16] Rājaśekhara refers to Śūrasena.[17]

Lampaka-Muruṇḍa. Hemacandra also states that Lampaka is Muruṇḍa.[18] Rājaśekhara seems to be referring to Lampaka as Limpaka.[19] Muruṇḍa is mentioned in the Allahabad Pillar Inscription of Samudragupta along with Daivaputra Sāhi Sahānuṣāhi and Śaka.[20] Lampaka is the modern Lamghan in Afghanistan.

Tokṣāra-Yugālika. Tokṣāra seems to be identical with Tuṣāra, mentioned by Rājaśekhara.[21] It is identified with upper Oxus valley, including Balkh and Badakshan.

Jalaṃdhara-Trigarta. Hemacandra agrees with *Vaijayantī* on this point. Puruṣottama mentions Trigartaka as another name of Ṭakka. An inscription from Baijnath states that Jālaṃdhara is identical with Trigarta.[22]

Pratyagratha-Ahicchatra. Vaijayantī finds support in Hemacandra.[23] It is identified with Ramnagar, in the Bareilly District.

Ṭarka-Bālhīka. Rājaśekhara refers to Ṭakka and Vālhika.[24] Hemacandra differs from Yādavaprakāśa. He states that Ṭakka is another name of Vāhīka, and Vālhīka is distinct from it.[25] Ṭakka is the country round Sialkot, in the Punjab. Puruṣottama mentions Bālhika and Trigartaka as different names of Ṭakka.[26]

Vāhīka-Vālhika. Rājaśekhara also distinguishes Vāhīka from Bālhika.[27] Hemacandra reports that Vālhika is an alternative form of Vālhīka.[28]

Kāśmīra Kīra. Rājaśekhara places Kīra in Uttarāpatha, and locates Kāśmīra elsewhere.[29] Puruṣottama mentions that Kīra is in Kāśmīra. Hemacandra states that Mādhumata, Sārasvata and Vikarṇika are the other names of Kāśmīra.[30] Kīra is identified with the Kangra valley, in the Punjab.

Turuṣka-Śākhi. Rājaśekhara refers to Turuṣka.[31] Hemacandra mentions Sākhi as the second name of the Turuṣka.[32] Puruṣottama states that Khaśa is same as Turuṣka.[33]

Sindhu-Dārada. Sindhu is to be located to the north of Kashmir, as the Dārada country was situated in it.

Kumālaka-Sauvīra. *Vaijayantī's* report is supported by Hemacandra.[34] It is identified with Multan.

Cīna-Kharaṃbhara, Hola-Kharaṭī, Tula-Kaliṅgaka, Yaudheya-Nṛgâlika, Pārada Kiñja, and Kulya are not mentioned by the authorities referred to above.

Prācya. *Vaijayantī's* statement regarding the location of Prācya agrees with Hemacandra.[35] Rājaśekhara mentions Prācya or Prācī as one of the four quarters, which includes the countries Aṅga, Vaṅga, Suhma, Brahma, Puṇḍra etc.[36] According to him Pūrva-deśa is beyond Vārāṇasi. In it are situated–Aṅga, Kaliṅga, Kosala, Tosala, Utkala, Magadha, Mudgara, Videha, Nepāla, Puṇḍra, Prāgjyotiṣa, Tāmaliptaka, Malada, Mallavartaka, Suhma, Brahmottara, etc.[37] Puruṣottama makes a confusion between Madhya-deśa and Pūrvadeśa.[38]

Mudgaraka-Kuja. Rājaśekhara mentions it as Mudgara.[39] It is to be identified with Mudgalagiri or Mudgagiri, modern Munghyr.[40]

Prāgjyotiṣa-Kāmarūpa-Prāgjālika. Rājaśekhara mentions Prāgjyotiṣ a as a country and Kāmarūpa as a mountain.[41] Hemacandra agrees with *Vaijayantī* that Kāmarūpa is another name of Prāgjyotiṣa.[42] Puruṣottama states that Prāgjyotiṣa is in Kāmarūpa.[43] Vaidyadeva's Kamauli plate mentions that Kāmarūpa-Maṇḍala is in Prāgjyotiṣa-Bhukti.[44]

Videha-Tīrabhukti. Rājaśekhara refers to the country of Videha.[45] Puruṣottama states that Nicchavi (Licchavi?) and Videha are the alternative names of Tīrabhukti.[46] Hemacandra mentions Videha as a city.[47] *Mañjuśrī Mūlakalpa* locates Tīrabhukti on the north bank of the Ganges.[48] A miniature label in a Nepal Mss. of the eleventh century lays down that Vaiśālī is situated in Tīrabhukti.[49]

Srāvastī-Puraṃjaka. Srāvastī is mentioned in the inscriptions of this period.

Rāḍhā-Suhma. Rājaśekhara refers to Suhma, and distinguishes it from Tāmaliptaka.[50] It is known from Hemacandra and Puruṣottama that Dāmalipta, Tāmaliptī, Tamālinī, Stambapū, Viṣṇugṛha, Velākūla, Tamālika are the other names of the city of Tāmalipta.[51] Daṇḍin in his *Dāśakumāracarita*[52] states that the city of Dāmalipa is situated in Rāḍhā. Dhoyī in his *Pavanadūta* mentions that Suhma is on the bank of the Ganges.[53] Nīlakaṇṭha in his commentary on *Mahābhārata* lays down that Suhma is identical with Rāḍhā.[54] The Sonpur grant[55] of Mahāśivagupta distinguishes Rāḍhā from Gauḍa. *Prabodhacandrodaya* and two inscriptions of the twelfth century state that Rāḍhā is in Gauḍa-deśa.[56]

Puṇḍra-Varendrī. The country of Puṇḍra formed a part of the Puṇḍravardhana-Bhukti, which included also Vaṅga and Samataṭa. The Silimpur inscription[57] states that the village Vālagrāma, the ornament of Varendrī, is situated in Puṇḍra. It is known from *Rāma-carita*[58] that the village Bṛhadvaṭu is the crest-jewel of Varendrī, and is attached to Puṇḍravardhanapura. It will follow from these sources that the country of Puṇḍravardhana was either identical with Varendrī or included it, in which was situated the city of Puṇḍravardhana. The *Karatoyā-māhātmya*[59] states that the people of Puṇḍra purified themselves by taking their bath in the Karatoyā. *Trikāṇḍaśeṣa*[60] mentions *Puṇḍrāḥ syur Varendrī Gauḍa nīvṛtih.* Some take it to mean—Puṇḍra is Varendrī and Gauḍa is Nīvṛti. *Mañjuśrī Mūlakalpa*[61] mentions Gauḍa and Puṇḍra side by side. But the above statement of *Trikāṇḍāśeṣa* may also be taken to mean that Varendrī, Gauḍa and Nīvṛti are the other names of Puṇḍra. Gauḍa cannot be taken to be distinct from Puṇḍra-Varendrī. *Rājataraṅgiṇī*[62] mentions that the city of Puṇḍravardhana was the seat of the king of Gauḍa. *Rāma-carita* mentions Varendrī as the paternal kingdom of Rāmapāla. It elsewhere mentions Rāmapāla as the king of Gauḍa.[63] The *Purāṇsarvasva*[64] states that Varendrī was situated in Gauḍa. The Kollagalu inscription.[65] dated A.D. 967, reports that Gadādhara was the crest-jewel of Gauḍa and the illuminator of Varendrī.

Bhaurika-Samataṭa. It is known from the Baghaura inscription[66] that the Tipperah District was in Samataṭa. *Mañjuśrī Mūlakalpa* states that Samotadya (Samataṭa ?) is to the east of Lohitya. The same authority elsewhere mentions Sāmataṭa and Sāmātaṭa.[67]

Vaṅga-Harikela. Vikrampur in the Dacca District and Ramasiddhi in the Sadar Sub-Division of the Bakharganj District were in Vaṅga.[68] So it may be assumed that the Dacca, Faridpur, and part of Bakarganj Districts were situated in Vaṅga. *Mañjuśrī Mūlakalpa* mentions that Vaṅgaka is to the east of Lauhitya. It elsewhere states that Vaṅga-deśa was on the bank of the Lauhitya.[69] Vaṅgaka is identical with Vaṅga. Jayamaṅgala in his commentary on Vātsyāyaṇa's *Kāmasūtra* places Vaṅga to the east of Lauhitya.[70] But in view of the fact that Vikrampur was to the west of Lauhitya, the above statement of *Mañjuśrī Mūlakalpa* and Jayamaṅgala cannot be accepted as correct.[71] *Matsya-Purāṇa*[72] reports that the Ganges passes by Kauśika, Magadha, Brahmottara, Vaṅga and Tāmralipta. Vaṅga may be taken to have been the country between the Ganges and the Meghna.

Harikela,[73] Harikelā,[74] Harikeli,[75] Harikella,[76] Harikelī[77] and Harikola[78] are synonymous terms. Yādavaprakāśa's statement that Harikelī is the same as Vaṅga finds support in Hemacandra.[79] Rāmpāl plate[80] of Śrīcandra seems to be corroborating the above statement of Yādavaprakāśa. The inscription states that Śrīcandra's father. Trailokyacandra, who was the king of Harikela, became the ruler of Candradvīpa. This suggests that Harikela was contiguous to Candradvīpa. Candradvīpa was situated in the southern part of the Bakarganj District. Śrīcandra was the ruler of Vaṅga, and he and his predecessors are not known to have ever held sway over the territory to the east of the Meghna. So the normal conclusion will be that Trailokyacandra, the king of Vaṅga-Harikela, annexed Candradvīpa to his kingdom.

Mañjuśrī-Mūlakalpa[81] refers to Vaṅga, Samataṭa, Harikela, Kalasamukha, and Carmaraṅga side by side. This may be taken to be distinguishing Vaṅga from Harikela. But *Mañjuśrī Mūlakalpa's* statements are not always reliable. It mentions Vidiśā, Mālava, and Daśārṇa side by side.[82] It will be wrong to assume that Vidiśā was distinct from Mālava and Daśārṇa.[83]

Aṅga-Campā. Rājaśekhara refers to Aṅga. Hemacandra mentions that Aṅga is indicated by Campā.[84] Both Hemacandra and Puruṣottama state that Mālinī is the other name of the (city) of Campā.[85] Aṅga is identified with Bhagalpur.

Magadha-Kīkaṭa. Hemacandra and Puruṣottama support *Vaijayantī.*[86] Rājaśekhara states that Magadha is to the east of Vārāṇasī.[87]

Andhra. An inscription[88] from the Andhra country calls Vijayāditya III, king of Andhra, as the king of Dakṣiṇāpatha. Allahabad inscription of Samudragupta also places Andhra in Dakṣiṇāpatha.[89]

Vaijayantī also places Salya in Madhyadeśa. Kuja and Vrata are not found mentioned in any contemporary record.

Dakṣiṇāpatha. Rājaśekhara places Dakṣiṇāpatha to the south of Māhiṣmatī. Countries, situated in it, are Mahārāṣṭra, Māhiṣaka, Aśmaka, Vidarbha, Kuntala, Krathakaiśika, Sūrpāraka, Kāñcī, Kerala, Kāvera, Murala, Vanavāsaka, Siṃhala, Coḍa, Daṇḍaka, Pāṇḍya, Pallava, Gaṅga, Nāsikya, Koṅkaṇa, Kollagiri, Kallara etc. It[90] included Mahendra mountain. A miniature label in a Mss. from Nepal of the eleventh century states that Kāñcīpura (Conjeeveram) is in Dakṣiṇāpatha.[91]

Kuntala-Upahālaka. Hemacandra supports *Vaijayantī.*[92]

Cola-Utpalāvarta. Cola is identical with Coḍa, mentioned by Rājaśekhara. According to the same authority Utpalāvatī is the name of a river in Dakṣiṇāpatha.[93] This river is the modern Vyapar, in the Tennevally District.

Mahārāṣtra-Daṇḍaka. Rājaśekhara distinguishes Mahārāṣṭra from Daṇḍaka.

Kerala. According to Hemacandra Oṇḍra is the same as Kerala.[94]

Kulya, Setuja, Kulakālaka, Iṣīka, and Āraṭṭa are not mentioned in the contemporary records. *Mahābhārata* places Āraṭṭa in the Punjab.[95]

Aparānta-Pāścātya-Sūryāraka. Rājaśekhara refers to Paścād-deśa, which lay beyond Devasabhā, and which included Devasabhā, Surāṣṭ ra, Daśeraka. Travaṇa, Bhṛgukaccha, Kacchīya, Ānarta, Arbuda, Brāhmaṇavāha, Yavana etc.[96]

Malada-Sthaura. Rājaśekhara places Malada in Pūrva-deśa.[97]

Karūśa-Bṛhadgṛha. Hemacandra and Puruṣottama support *Vaijayantī.*[98] Rājaśekhara mentions Bṛhadgṛha as the name of a mountain in Pūrva-deśa.[99]

Traipura-Hahāla-Caidya-Cedi. Hemacandra[100] mentions that Ḍāhala and Caidya are the other names of Tripura. According to Puruṣottama Caidya is the same as Ḍāhala.[101]

Daśārṇa-Vedipara. An inscription from Kalinjar mentions the Candella Paramārdi as the King of Daśārṇa.[102]

Mālava-Avanti. Hemacandra and Puruṣottama support *Vaijayantī.*[103] Kings of the Paramāra dynasty, who ruled from Dhārā and Ujjain, are mentioned as kings of Mālava[104] Kāmasūtra's commentator Jayamaṅgala, who flourished later than the fourteenth century, states that Āvantika, which is identical with Ujjayinī-deśa, is apara Mālava.[105] This had led some writers to suggest that Mālava proper is Daśārṇa. Jayamaṅgala's geographical knowledge is not perfect. It has already been noticed that he places Vaṅga to the east of Lauhitya. His remark on Mālava is to be rejected as it runs counter to the earlier authorities. Rājaśekhara mentions Mālava, Avanti and Vidiśā, and Mañjuśrī mentions Mālava, Vidiśā and Daśārṇa side by side.[106]

Bhoja. Bhoja is mentioned in the Khalimpur inscription of Dharmapāla.

Vaijayantī also places Mekala and Kosala in Madhya-deśa.

Madhya-deśa. Rājaśekhara states that Madhya-deśa lies between Uttarāpatha, Pūrva-deśa, Dakṣiṇāpatha and Paścād-deśa. It extends from the Himalaya to the Vindhya, and from Vinaśana to Prayāga.[107] Hemacandra agrees with Rājaśekhara in regard to the extent of Madhyadeśa.[108] Puruṣottama lays down that Kurukṣetra is Vinaśana.[109]

Vaijayantī differs from the above authorities and includes Kaliṅga and Kuntala in Madhyadeśa.

Marava-Daseraka. Hemacandra supports *Vaijayantī*.[110] Puruṣottama states that Marubhuva is an alternative name of Daśeraka.[111] Rājaśekhara places Daśeraka in Paścād-deśa. It is to be identified with Marwar.

Sālva-Kārakutsīya. Hemacandra supports *Vaijayantī*.[112]

Udumbara. Udumbara-Viṣaya, which was situated in the Kālañjara-Maṇḍala, has been mentioned in the Barah copper plate of the Pratihāra Bhoja.[113]

Rajaśekhara places Kaliṅga and Kosala in Pūrvadeśa and Mekala mountain in Dakṣiṇāpatha. Pārthaparākrama mentions the Cāhamāna Pṛthvīrāja III, as the king of Jāṅgala.[114]

Sāketa-Ayodhyā-Kosalānandinī. Hemacandra states that Kosala and Ayodhyā are also known as Sāketa.[115] According to Puruṣottama Ayodhyā, and Uttara-Kosala, and Sāketa indicate the same countries.[116] Candravati plate[117] of the Gāhaḍavāla Candradeva lays down that Ayodhyā is identical with Uttara-Kosala.

Dvāraka-Dvāravatī. Hemacandra supports *Vaijayantī*.[118] Puruṣottama states that Abdhinagarī is Dvāravatī, and Dvārakā is Vanamālinī.[119]

Madhurā-Madhuṣikā-Mathurā-Madhupaghna. Hemacandra reports that Madhurā and Madhupaghna are the other names of Mathurā.[120] According to Puruṣottama Mathurā is Madhupaghna.[121]

Vaijayantī distinguishes *Kauśa-Kuśasthalī* from *Kānyakubja-Mahodaya*. But Hemacandra mentions that Kānyakubja, Mahodaya, Kanyākubja, Gādhipura, Kauśa, and Kuśasthala are the alternative names.[122] According to Puruṣottama, Kuśasthala is Kānyakubja.[123]

Vārāṇasī-Śivapurī-Varaṇāsī-Kāśika. Hemacandra remarks that Kāśi, Vārāṇasī, Varāṇasī and Śivapurī are the different names.[124] Puruṣottama states that Vārāṇasī is Tīrtharāja.[125] *Mañjuśrī Mūlakalpa* and some Gāhaḍavāla inscriptions mention Kāśī as a city.[126] The Nanyaura plate of the Candella Dhaṅga refers to Kāśikā.[127]

Mithilā-Videha. Both Hemacandra and Puruṣottama support *Vaijayantī*.[128]

Hastinī-Hāstinapura-Nāgāhva-Hastināpura. Hemacandra mentions that Hāstinapura, Hastinīpura, Gajāhva, and Hastināpura are identical.[129] Puruṣottama remarks that Hastināpura and Gajāhva are the other names of Nāgāhva.[130]

Avantī-Takṣaśilā. Hemacandra reports that Viśālā, Avantī, and Puṣkaraṇḍinī are the other names of Ujjayanī.[131] *Vaijayantī* is not supported by any other authority.

Devīkoṭṭa-Kaṭivarṣa. Hemacandra[132] lays down that Koṭivarṣa, Bāṇapura, Devīkoṭa, Umāvana, and Śoṇitapura are identical. Puruṣottama agrees with Hemacandra except that he mentions Uṣāvana in place of Umāvanta.[133] Manahali grant of Madanapāla refers to Koṭivarsa-Viṣaya.[134] Koṭivarṣa is identified with Bangadh in the Dinajpur District, Bengal.

Māhiṣmatī-Vṛkasthalī. The Paramāra Devapāla granted lands from his camp at Māhiṣmatī, which is identified with Mandhata on the Narmada.[135] Rājaśekhara refers to Māhiṣmatī beyond which lay Dakṣiṇāpatha.[136]

Kakundī-Vāraṇāvata and Khāṇḍavaprastha are not mentioned elsewhere.

It will follow from the above discussion that Yādavaprakāśa's observations on the ancient geography of India are fairly accurate. It is interesting to note that some of the countries and their different names mentioned by him, do not find place in the works of his contemporaries. The importance of the *Vaijayantī* for the knowledge in ancient geography of India can hardly be overestimated.

References

1. Edited by Gustav Oppert, Ph.D., Madras, 1893.
2. *Ibid.*, p. 36.
3. Gaekwad Oriental Series, No. I.
4. Ed. S.V. Dharmapuri, *Yashovijaya.* Jaina Granthamāla (41), pp. 379 ff.
5. Ed. C.A. Seelakkandha. Bombay, 1916, pp. 30. The earliest reference to Puruṣottamadeva is that by Sarvānanda (1159 A.D.). For further discussion cf. Intro. XXII, *Kalpadrukośa, GOS.*, No. XLII.
6. *Kāvya.*, pp. 93.
7. *Bālarāmāyaṇa,* Act. VI.
8. *Abhi.*, pp. 379.
9. *Ins. Bengal,* 36.
10. *Gauḍalekhamālā,* 47, 49.
11. *Kāvya.*, 51, 94.
12. *Abhi.*, pp. 380.
13. Author's *History of the Paramāra Dynasty,* pp. 159.
14. *Gauḍalekhamālā,* pp. 14. *Cf.* Foucher, *L'Iconographie Bouddhique de l'Inde,* vol. I, pp. 193. Gandhārāmaṇḍala.
15. *Ibid., Kāvya.* 94. *Cf.* Yavana-pura. N. L. Dey, *Geo. Dic.*

16. *Vaijayantī*, pp. 37, v. 25.
17. *Kāvya.*, 8, 50.
18. *Abhi.*, p. 383.
19. *Kāvya.*, 94.
20. *Cll.*, 8.
21. *Kāvya.*, 94.
22. *Abhi.*, p. 382; *Trikāṇḍa.*, pp. 31; *El.*, I, 116, 117.
23. *Abhi.*, p. 383. The early Jaina literature states that Ahicchatra is in Jāṅgala (*IA.*, XX, 375). But Hemacandra makes it clear that Pratyagratha, otherwise called Ahicchatra, is distinct from Jāṅgala or Nirjala. (*Abhi.*, p. 380).
24. *Kāvya.*, pp. 51, 94.
25. *Abhi.*, pp. 382, 383.
26. *Trikāṇḍa.*, p. 31.
27. *Kāvya.*, p. 8.
28. *Abhi.*, p. 383.
29. *Kāvya*, pp. 94, 98.
30. *Abhi.*, p. 382. *Trikāṇḍa.*, p. 31.
31. *Kāvya.*, p. 94.
32. *Abhi.*, p. 383.
33. *Trikāṇḍa.*, p. 31.
34. *Abhi.*, p. 383.
35. *Abhi.*, p. 380.
36. *Kāvya*, pp. 94, 98.
37. *Kāvya*, p.94
38. *Trikāṇḍa*, p. 31.
39. *Kāvya.*, p. 93.
40. *Cf.* N. L. Dey's *Geo. Dictionary.*
41. *Kāvya.*, p. 93.
42. *Abhi.*, p. 381.
43. *Trikāṇḍa.*, p. 31.
44. *Gauḍalekhamālā*, p. 134.
45. *Kāvya.*, p. 93.
46. *Trikāṇḍa.*, p. 31.
47. *Abhi.*, p. 389.
48. T. Ganapati Sastri, p. 282.
49. Foucher, *Icono.*, I, p. 197.
50. *Kāvya.*, p. 93.

51. *Abhi.*, p. 391; *Trikāṇḍa.*, p. 31.
52. Ed. Jiv. and Vid. V. p. 244.
53. *JASB.*, 1905, pp. 45, 57.
54. Sabhā P., Ch. XXIX.
55. *JBORS.*, II, 45-49.
56. *Ins. Madras Presidency,* vol. I, p. 353; Cg. 248.
57. *El.*, XIII, 283.
58. *Kavi. Pr.*, V. i.
59. *Skanda Purāṇa.*
60. p. 31.
61. T. G. Sastri, p. 232.
62. *Gauḍa-rājāśrayam—nagaram Pauṇḍravardhanam*—B.K, IV, v. 421.
63. Ch. 1, vs. 38, 39; *Kavi. Pr.*, v. 11.
64. Aufrecht. *Cat.*, p. 87.
65. *El.*, XXI, 264.
66. *El.*, XVII.
67. T. Sastri, pp. 206, 232, 332.
68. *Ins. Bengal,* 130, 177.
69. T.G. Sastri, pp. 206, 325.
70. *Vaṅgā Lauhityāt purveṇa.*
71. The Jaina *Upāṅga Prajñāpana* mentions that Tāmralipti was situated in Vaṅga. The same authority again tells us that Koṭivarṣa was situated in Rāḍhā (*Koḍīvarisam va Lāḍhāya*) *IA.*, XX, 375. So no importance should be attached to the above statements of this authority.
72. Ch. 120, vs. 43-52, Baṅgavāsi ed., pp. 360.
73. Rampal Pl., *Ins. Beng.*, 4.
74. Chittagong Pl. of Kāntideva, *Modern Review,* 1922.
75. *Kalpadrukośa,* Gaek. Or. S., vol. I, No. XLII, pp. 7.
76. Foucher, *Iconographie Bouddhique l'lnde,* vol. I, pp. 200.
77. Hemacandra, *Abhi.*, 382; *Vaijayantī.*
78. Dacca University Mss.
79. *Abhi.*, pp. 382.
80. *Ins. Beng.*, pp. 4.
81. T.G. Sastri, pp. 232, 233.
82. *Ibid.*, 332.
83. I-tsing places Samataṭa in Eastern India, and states that Harikela is the eastern limit of Eastern India (Beal's *Life,* Intro, XXXI). This will place Harikela to the east of Comilla. *Kalpadrukośa,* (*op. cit.*,) a work of the

seventeenth century, states that Śrihaṭṭa is Harikeli. This finds support in a Dacca University Mss.of the same period. Another Mss. of Dacca University mentions Harikola and Śrīhaṭṭa as identical. (I am thankful to Mr. S. C. Banerji, M.A., of the Mss. Section of the D.U. Library for drawing my attention to the above statement of *Kalpadrukośa*.)

84. *Abhi.*, p. 382.
85. *Ibid.*, 300; *Trikāṇḍa*, 32.
86. *Abhi.*, 383; *Trikāṇḍa*. 31.
87. *Kāvya.*, p. 33
88. *South Indian Epigraphy*. 1938.
89. *CII.*, 8.
90. *Kāvya.*, p. 93.
91. Foucher, *Icon. Boud. Inde.*, I, p. 201.
92. *Abhi.*, 383.
93. *Kāvya.*, p. 93.
94. *Abhi.*, 383.
95. *Cf.* N. L. Dey's *Geo. Dic.*
96. *Kāvya.*, p. 94.
97. *Kāvya.*, p. 93; *cf.* N.L. Dey's *Geo Dic.*
98. *Abhi.*, 383; *Trikāṇḍa.*, p. 31.
99. *Kāvya.*, p. 93.
100. *Abhi.*, 381.
101. *Trikāṇḍa.*, p. 31.
102. Cunningham, *ASI.*, XXI, 37.
103. *Abhi.*, 381; *Trikāṇḍa*, 31.
104. Author's *History of the Paramāra Dynasty.*
105. *Vaṅgā Lauhityāt pūrveṇa/ Aṅga Mahānadyāḥ pūrveṇa/ Kaliṅgā Gauḍa-Viṣayāddakṣiṇena/ Vālhika deśyā Uttarāpathikāḥ/ Āvantikā Ujjayinī deśa bhavāḥ/ tā evāpara Mālavyaḥ/ paścima samudra samīpe Aparānta deśaḥ/ apara Mālava paścimena Lāṭa-Viṣayaḥ/ ...... Narmadā Karṇāṭa Viṣayayormadhye Mahārāṣṭra-Viṣaya/ ----*
106. *Kāvya.*, p. 9; T.G. Sastri.
107. *Kāvya.*, 94.
108. *Abhi.*, 379.
109. *Trikāṇḍa.*, 32.
110. *Abhi.*, 382.
111. *Trikāṇḍa.*, 31.
112. *Abhi.*, 382.

113. *EI.*, XIX, 15.
114. *Kāvya.*, Gaek. Or. S. No. IV. p. 3.
115. *Abhi.*, 389.
116. *Trikāṇḍa.*, 31.
117. *EI.*, XIV, 193.
118. *Abhi.*, 391.
119. *Trikāṇḍa.*, 32.
120. *Abhi.*, 390.
121. *Trikāṇḍa.*, 32.
122. *Abhi.*, 389.
123. *Trikāṇḍa.*, 32.
124. *Abhi.*, 389.
125. *Trikāṇḍa.*, 32.
126. T.G. Sastri, p. 642; *EI.*, IV, 124-128.
127. *IA.*, XVI, 203.
128. *Abhi.*, 389; *Trikāṇḍa.*, 32.
129. *Abhi.*, 390.
130. *Trikāṇḍa.*, 32.
131. *Abhi.*, 390 (Rājaśekhara mentions Hastināpura as a *janapada. Kāvya.*, p.8).
132. *Ibid.*, 390.
133. *Trikāṇḍa.*, 32.
134. *Gauḍalekhamālā,* p. 147.
135. *EI.*, IX, 103.
136. *Kavya,* 93.

6

Jambudvīpa-prajñapti-saṃgraha of Padmanandi

A. N. Upadhye

Indian cosmography is a subject by itself. Many Jaina texts, earlier and later,both in Prākrit and Sanskrit, treat this subject in an exhaustive manner giving many a minute detail. In the Ardhamāgadhī canon, works like *Sūrapaṇṇatti,* (Skt. Sūryaprajñapti), *Jambuddīva-paṇṇatti* (Skt. Jambudvīpa-prajñapti) and *Caṃdapaṇṇatti* (Skt. Candra-prajñapti) are devoted to this subject. An excellent account of Jaina cosmography is given by Dr. W. Kirfel in his work *Dic Kosmographie der Inder* (Bonn u. Leipzig, 1920, pp. 208-340). Many Śvetāmbara texts, both canonical and non-canonical, are used by him. Among the Digambara works Indravāmadeva's *Trailokyadīpikā* and Nemicandra's *Trailokyasāra* (Prākrit) are drawn upon. With the Digambaras *Tiloyapaṇṇatti* (Skt. Trilokaprajñapti) of Jadivasaha (Skt. Yativṛṣabha) and *Jambuddīvapaṇṇatti* (Skt. Jambudvīpa-prajñapti) of Paümaṇaṃdi (Skt. Padmanandi) are considered as the most important Prākrit works dealing with cosmography. So far as I know, no commentaries are available on these texts; and further the obscurity of the subject-matter and the unsatisfactory preservation of the text only heighten the difficulties of a student who wants to wade through the technical details of these works. From the linguistic point of view these two texts are very important, as they contain much additional matter for the student of Prākrit grammar. *Tiloyapṇṇatti* is being tentatively edited by me in the *Jaina Antiquary* (Arrah, Bihar); and I propose to discuss in this article some important details about *Jambuddīvapaṇṇatti,* a Ms. of which has just reached my hands.

The paper Ms., measuring 14 by 8½ inches, is a recent copy (Vaiśākha śu. 1, Saṃvat 1971), and belongs to the Ailaka Pannālala Digambara Jaina Pāṭhaśālā, Sholapur. It has 84 leaves in double folios. Though carefully copied in bold Devanāgarī script, there are scribal errors here and there.

The copyist calls it *Jambudvīpa-prajñapti,* but the actual title of the text, as mentioned in the colophons of various Uddeśas, is *Jambudvīpa-prajñapti-saṃgraha.* The word *saṃgraha* indicates that the author is compiling the contents from some earlier source, whose name was perhaps *Dīvasāgarapaṇṇatti,* as indicated by the following two verses:

दे वन्दिदूण सिरसा वोच्छामि जहा-कमेण जिण-दिट्ठं।
आयरियपरम्परया पण्णात्तिं दीव जलधीगं॥
अयारिय-परम्परया सायर-दीवाण तहा य पण्णत्ती।
संखेवेण समत्थं वोच्छामि जहाणुपुव्वीए॥

The contents are attributed to Mahāvīra; they were codified into texts by Gaṇadharas, and handed down by succeding teachers (I. 8 etc. & XIII. 141 etc.). Padmanandi says that he is writing down a summary of what was traditionally handed down:

आयरिय-परम्परेण य गंथत्थं चेव आगयं सम्मं।
उवसंहरित्थ लिहियं समासदो हि णायव्वं॥[1]

In all there are thirteen Uddeśas, and the total number of gāthās comes to 2426, as seen from the following table:

	Name of the Uddeśas:	No. of gāthās:
I.	उवघाय-पत्थावो[2]	74
II.	भरहेरावय-वंस-वण्णणो	210
III.	पव्वद-नदी-भोगभूमी-वण्णणो	246
IV.	महाविदेहाहियारे चत्तदेशो[3]	291
V.	महाविदेहाहियारे मन्दरगिरि-जिणभवण-वण्णणो	125
VI.	महाविदेहाहियारे देवकुरु-उत्तरकुरु-विण्णस-पत्थारो[4]	177
VII.	महाविदेहाहियारे कच्छाविजय-वण्णणो	152
VIII.	महाविदेहाहियारे पुव्वविदेह वण्णणो	198
IX.	महाविदेहाहियारे अवरविदेह वण्णणो	197
X.	लवण समुद्द वावण्णणो	102
XI.	वाहिर-उहार-दीव-दीसायर[5]-नरयगदि-सिद्धखेत्त-वण्णणो	365
XII.	जोइसलोय-वण्णणो	113
XIII.	पमाण-परिच्छेदो	176

The names of the Uddeśas, read in the light of Dr. Kirfel's account of Jaina cosmography, give a fair idea of the contents of the work. As far as I have seen, the whole work is written in gāthā metre; and the

Prākrit dialect used by Padmanandi is Jaina Śaurasenī. Now and then there are descriptions of some regions which remind us of the long compounds in the Ardhamāgadhī canon.

Though no date of the composition is mentioned, Padmanandi has supplied us with some information about his spiritual genealogy in the concluding verses. There was a great saint Vīranandi who was endowed with five Mahāvratas, pure in faith, possessed of knowledge and the merits of self-control and penance, free from attachment etc., heroic, full of five-fold conduct, kind to six classes of living beings, free from infatuation, and above pleasure and pain (XIII. 158-9). His great disciple was Balanandi, who was well-versed in the Sūtras and their interpretation,who was of deep wisdom, who abstained from scandalising others, who was free from attachment, and who was endowed with faith, knowledge and conduct (XIII. 160-1). And his disciple was Paümaṇaṃdi (Skt. Padmanandi), endowed with many a virtue, free from three Daṇḍas, pure with reference to three Śalyas, free from three Gāravas, who had reached the other end of Siddhānta, who was endowed with penances and other vows, who was devoted to faith, knowledge and conduct, and who was free from preliminary sins (XIII. 162-3). Padmanandi tells us that he received instructions in the scripture from Siri Vijaya (Sk. Śrīvijaya), also mentioned as Risi Vijaya (Skt. Ṛṣi Vijaya), who was a great monk of spiritual virtues and a great teacher of Paramāgama (XIII. 144-5, 164). There was a famous and learned monk Māghanandi; he had a well-disciplined and wise pupil Sakalacandra; his disciple was Śrīnandi; and it is for the sake of Śrīnandi that Padmanandi wrote this work. The work was written when Padmanandi was staying in Bārā-nayara, i.e. the town of Bārā, in the country of Pariyatra, the contemporary king of which was Śānti-bhūpāla[6] (*Vāra-nayarassa pahū naruttamo Sa[ṃ] tibhūpālo,* 166) who was respected by the sovereign king (Narapati), who was heroic, who was endowed with many religious virtues, and was devoted to Jainism. To state the bare facts in brief, Padmanandi was a monk, his immediate predecessor was Balanandi, the pupil of Vīranandi. He studied under Śrīvijaya, and composed or compiled this work for Śrīnandi, the disciple of Sakalacandra, the pupil of Māghanandi. The work was composed in the town of Bāra in the country of Pariyatra, when the contemporary chief was Śānti.

To commemorate the memory Winternitz who has so much obliged the students of Indian literature by his authoritative studies. I have just introduced this work to the students of Prākrit literature. An attempt to discuss the date and other details will be made at a later stage, as I am in search of some more Ms. material.

References

1. The line appears to be defective.
2. Is it *upodghāta-prastāvaḥ?*
3. The last word appears to be corrupt.
4. The last word looks like-*yacchāro* as well.
5. The reading is not satisfactory.
6. The Ms. reads Sati, apparently a scribal error for Saṃti – Śānti.

7

Place-Names in the Kalacuri Records*

R. K. Lal

It has already been shown[1] that in the earlier records (250-750 A.C.) of the Kalacuri-Cedi era, the place-names generally ended in Khēṭa, Padra, Padraka or Pallī. A change however, is noticed in the later records (850-1500 A.C.) wherein the names of the towns generally ended in Nagara or Pura and those of the villages in Grāma or Pāṭaka. Some localities were named after the member of the royal family or some important personality who founded them. If however, we limit ourselves to the records belonging to the different branches of the Kalacuris and their feudatories only, and study by analysis and classification the place-names occurring in them, many interesting facts come to light regarding the sources of their origin.

The place-names occurring in the records of the Kalacuris may be classified mainly from two points of views viz.

A. Semantic

B. Morphological

A. Viewed semantically, considerable number of place-names occurring in the records of the Kalacuris may be treated to be of popular origin describing various phenomena as follows;

I. Descriptive of actual or hypothetical geographical situation or landmark or environment; for example,

(a) Paṇḍartalāi[2] identified with modern Pendriā, 7 miles north-west of Sheorinārāyaṇ in Bilaspur district of Madhya Pradesh. It is noteworthy that a historical tank was actually built here by Āmaṇadeva I a scion of a collateral branch of the Kalacuri family in the year K-919. The place is also referred to in the Bilaigarh Plates of Pṛithvīdeva II, of Kalacuri year 896.

---

* Numbers mentioned in the footnotes of this article refer to the numbers of the Inscription in the Corpus Inscriptionum Indicarum:vol. IV, Inscription of the Kalacuri-chedi era, parts I and II, Ed. by V. V. Mirashi.

(b) Shaṭashaḍikā-Ghāṭa,[3] identified with Ālhā-Ghāṭ in Vindhya Pradesh. The inscription of Narasiṃha of Vikram year 1216, in which this place has been mentioned, is itself on a block of stone, about hundred yards from a large cave somewhere near the foot of Alha-ghāṭ which is one of the natural passes of the Vindhya hills by which Tons river finds its way from the table land of Rewa to the plain of the Gangā. Narasiṁhadeva constructed this ghāṭ and a temple of goddess Ambikā was built by him near the road leading to it.

(c) Kadambaguhā,[4] identified with modern Kadwāhā (six miles south of Terahi) by Dr. Kielhorn, was the seat of Śaivism in mediaeval times. It is also referred to in the Ranod inscription as the place of residence of spiritual ancestor of sage Puranadara. From the literal meaning of the name of this place it seems that with the cave dwellings of these sages it also probably abounded in Kadamba trees.

(d) Samudra Pāṭa,[5] identified with modern Samand Pipariā 4 miles south of Jabalpur, by its very meaning, indicates symbolically its extent just like sea.

(e) Vaṭagartikā,[6] modern Barhati, 10 miles west by south of Jabalpur probably points the presence of Vaṭa trees and holes or caves that might have existed there once.

(f) Vaṇārī,[7] indentified with Banāri near Janjgir in Bilaspur district, probably indicates a forest (Vana) that might have existed there once.

2. Descriptive of some old reminiscences as regards incident or commercial activity, for example;

(a) Daṇḍapura[8] (literally meaning the City of Punishment), is still unidentified. In the Koni Stone Inscription of Pṛithvīdeva II, verse 26 refers to the exploits of Puruṣottama, the Sarvādhikārin of Ratnadeva II. He is said to have punished Daṇḍapura by subduing it with fierce arm (दण्डपुरदण्डनचण्डबाहुः) He also threatened the lord of Daṇḍakabhukti.

(b) Vimānapura (literally meaning the City of Vehicle), Durlabhapura (lit. the city of Rarity), Lavaṇanagara (lit. the city of salt) and Saubhāgyapura (lit. the lucky City) have been referred to in the Bilhari stone Inscription of Yuvarājadeva II[9] in connection with celebration of a fair in honour of the deity of the temple of Nauhaleśvara (which Nohalā the queen of Yuvarājadeva construced). "The (inhabitants of) famous Tripurī, Saubhāgyapura, Lavaṇanagara, Durlabhapura, Vimānapura . . . shall bring guarded (to the monastery ?) the bull made of beautiful wood everyday (at the fair ?) of the god for the performance of religious rite" (verse 83). Probably all of these cities were in some way or other obliged to provide material for the daily needs of the temple in its smooth performance if religious rites and were named symbolically. It may also be that Vimānapura and Lavaṇanagara were famous for their commercial activity in vehicles and salt respectively and hence they were so named. Saubhāgyapura may remind us of some incident or success that somebody achieved there and from which the place was named.

3. Descriptive of caste or profession of the local resident; for example,

(a) Bamhaṇī,[10] modern Bamhani, 4 miles north east of Akaltarā in Bilaspur district, and Bramhapurī,[11] modern Bāhmangaon, 7 miles south by west of Gurgi near Rewa had probably big settlements of Brāhamaṇas to which the names point. It is interesting to note that the Kalacuri court of Ratanpur attracted Brāhmaṇas to migrate from such distant places as Soṇabhadra[12] in Uttar Pradesh and Kumbhaṭī[13] in Madhya Bharat.

(b) Ābhīrapallī[14] (unidentified as yet) similarly points to a settlement of Ābhīras (cowherds) from which the place seems to have derived its name. It is noteworthy that Ābhīras, during this period, rose in social status and like Huṇas were ranked amongst the best known Kṣatriya families.

(c) Nāgabala[15] (identified with modern Naigawān, 2 miles south of Bilhari in Jabalpur district), was most probably named after the settlement of Nāgas that might have existed there. Nāgas used to hold good positions during the Kalacuri reign, e.g. in the Chhōṭi Deori Stone Inscription of Śaṅkaragaṇa.[16] The illustrious Chuṭu Nāgaka has been stated to be in charge of the Viśaya of Kakandakuṭu.

(d) Similarly Kōṇiyānām (Vāṭaka),[17] identified with Kanhuvāḍī in Nasik district, was most probably a hamlet of the Koṇiyās.

(e) Vaṇiāpāṭaka[18] (identified with Bāonpār near Kahla in Gorakhpur district of U.P.) was probably named after the predominently merchant population there. This may very well be compared with the Vaṇiṅ-Nagara (Merchant town) referred to in the Anjaneri Plates of Caulukya Bhōgaśakti.[19]

4. Descriptive of some ancient legendary accounts; for example,

(a) Tripurī,[20] identified with modern village Tewar in Jabalpur district, was the place where, according to Āvantyakhaṇḍa of the Skanda Purāṇa the powerful demon Tripurā was defeated by Mahādeva, the presiding deity of Avantī. In the Bālarāmāyaṇa, Rājaśekhara ascribes the origin of Tripurī to the fall from the sky of a portion of the three cities of Tripurāsura burnt by Śiva (Bālarāmāyaṇa, Act. III, V. 38)

(b) Machkā-Sihavā[21] which is the same as modern Mechkā-Sihavā, a tract south of Dhamtari in Raipur district, seems to have been regarded as a piece of holy land since ancient times. Many legends regarding the origin of Sihāwā and Mechakā are still existing. According to one account, a certain king Siṅharāja of Jagannātha Purī, the ancestor of King Karṇa of lunar dynasty (referred to in the Sihāwa Stone. Inscription of Karṇarāja)[22] having become leper quitted that place and came to Sihāwā which was then merely a dense jungle. There he found a spring of water (still pointed out) in which he bathed and his leprosy was healed. He was then installed the king of place which was named Sihawa i.e. Siṅha + Avah (the comfort of Siṅha) from the relief that the king obtained there. Sihāwā is again the source of the sacred Mahānadī and is supposed to be the hermitage of Rishi Śhringin who is still worshipped there. Five miles away is the village Ratawa where Āngiras Rishi is said to have resided. Sage Mucukunda had his āśram in the village Machkā, about 20 miles distant. The place evidently derives its name from the Sage.[23] Apparently the tract formerly went by the name of Mechkāsihavā as we find it so mentioned in the Rajim Stone Inscription of Jagapāladeva.[24]

Some of the place-names whose origin is of learned aim at elegance any they seem to have been names after these: (1) Names of the local deities, (2) Names of distinguished personalities, (3) Names of animals, plants, flowers etc., and (4) Idea of dimension, extension etc.

1 Names of the local deities; for example,

(a) Nārāyaṇapura[25] (lit. the city of Nārāyaṇa) seems to have derived its name from God Viṣṇu of which it might have been a centre of worship. The place situated 20 miles south-west of Kharōd in Raipur district has the same name even now. A medieval temple of Viṣṇu is still existing there.

(b) Similarly Durga,[26] now the chief town of Durga district, seems to owe its name from the Goddess Durgā whose temple was constructed there by Gaṅgādhara the chief minister of Ratnadeva III. Cunningham however is of opinion that 'the very name, which means simply "the fort", would seem to point it out as having once been the principal fortified position in the southern half of Mahā-Kośala'. (Cunningham: Archaeological Survey Reports, vol. xvii, pp. 3, 4).

(c) Devagrāma[27] (lit. the village of God) (identified with Deogavān close to Khairha in Vindhya Pradesh) might have been so named because of its being the place of worship of some deity. A number of old wells, water reservoir and remains of old buildings are still existing here and this indicates it to be a centre of worship once.

(d) Similarly Devaparvata[28] (lit. the mountain of God) might have taken its name from the worship of some deity in the locality, most probably on the top of some local mountain. The place has not so far been identified. If however Dr. Mirashī's suggestion[29] identifying Vikarṇapura with modern Kōṭgaḍh, one and half mile to the north of Akaltarā (Bilaspur district) is accepted, Devaparvata at whose foot a very deep well was constructed by Vallabharāja, may be identified with modern Dalhā Pahār, about a mile further north of Kōṭgaḍh.

2. Names of the members of the royal family or men of high position; for example;

(a) Ratnapura,[30] founded in his personal name by Ratnadeva I, Kalacuri king of Ratanpur branch. The place has been identified with Ratanpur, 16 miles north of Bilaspur.

(b) Jājallapura,[31] the city founded by Jājalladeva of Ratanapur branch of the Kalacuri in his own name. The place is the same as modern Jānjgir, tahsil headquarter in Bilaspur district.

(c) Tejjalapura,[32] evidently founded in the name of Tejjaladeva a colleteral Kalacuri prince. The place is untraceable now, but most probably it was situated not far from Sheorinārāyaṇ in Bilaspur district.

(d) Gōsalapur, a village about 19 miles north-east of Jabalpur was evidently named after Gōsaladevī, the queen of Kalacuri Jayasiṁha of Tripurī.

(e) Karṇāvatī,[33] identified with modern Karaṇbel (a village about a mile from Tripurī in Jabalpur district) must have been named after Kalacuri Karṇa of Tripurī. Even the modern corruption of the name has "a double signification, retaining the memory of the founder in the first half and giving the distinguishing mark of the site in the second, there being a jungle of bel trees to supply leaves to the numerous Śiva liṅgas once shrined there"[34] It may be noted that Karṇapura is also the name of a ridge near Kārītalāi.

(f) Karṇatīrtha, probably a ghāṭ built after the name Karṇa at Allahabad where, after bathing in Gaṅgā and worshipping Śiva, he made grant of the village Chandpahā situated in the Kauśamba-pattalā.[35]

(g) Jagapālapura,[36] the city founded in his personal name by Jagapāla, the general of Pṛithvīdeva II of the Ratanpur branch of the Kalacuris. Jagapālapura may be suggested to be the same as modern Jagadalpur, the district town of Bastar. In the Rājim Stone Inscription of Pṛithvīdeva II, Jagapāla is said to have taken the strong forts of

Saharāgaḍha and Machakā-Sihavā and conquered the countries of Bhramaravadra, Kāntāra, Kusumabhōga, Kāndā-ḍoṅgara and Kākayara. In this newly acquired territory he is said to have established the town of Jagapālapura. According to Dr. Kielhorn Saharāgaḍha was the ancient name of modern Sāraṅgarh, formerly a feudatory state in Chattisgarh. Hiralal has identified Machkā-Sihawā with Mechkā-Sihavā, south of Dhamatarī (Hiralal : Inscription in C.P. and Berar, no. 178) Bhramaravadra has been identified with Bhramara Kōṭya Maṇḍala in the Baster district.[37] Kākyara is modern Kāṅker in the same district and Kāntāra may be the forest not far from it. Kāndā-Ḍōṅgara may be the southern portion of the former Bindrā-Nawāgarh Zamindari where a range of hills still goes by the name of Kāndā.

From the above identifications it is apparent that the "newly acquired territory" of Jagapala must have comprised a major portion of Bastar district and some part of the Raipur district. The new city of Jagapālapura founded in this region may therefore be no other than Jagadalpur which, at present, is the headquarter of Bastar district.

(h) Rāyapura,[38] identified with modern Raipur, the district town of Chattisgarh was most probably founded by Rai-Brahmadeva, a prince of the Junior branch of the Kalacuris which separated from the senior branch of Ratanpur. Rāyapura was the capital of this branch of the Kalacuris but Khalvāṭikā seems to have been their another capital as is evidenced from the Khalāri Stone Inscription of Haribrahmadeva V, year 1470. It is not certain whether, after separating from the main branch, the prince of this branch first settled at Khalāri or Raipur. If Khalāri was their first capital, it is possible that Rai Brahmadeva may have removed it to Raipur and named the latter after himself as Rāyapura.[39] Dr. V. V. Mirashi however is of opinion that Rāyapura (the Royal city) may have been founded by Rāmcandra, the predecessor of Brahmadeva.[40]

3. Names of certain animals, plants, flowers grains etc.; for example,

(a) Hastigrāma,[41] literally means the village of elephant.

(b) Makarapāṭaka,[42] has been named after Makara (i.e. crocodile). It has been identified with Magarmuhā, 4 miles to the west of Bherāghāṭ near Jabalpur. Its situation described in the record as "on the right bank of Narmadā in the land near the foot of the hills," probably points to the reason why it was so named.

(c) Sārasaḍōllaka[43] literally means the hamlet of Sārasa i.e. Indian crane (identified with Sarsi, 34 miles south by west of Candrehe).

(d) Bhramaravadra[44] (identified with modern Bhramarakoṭyamaṇḍala, central portion of Bastar) is named after Bhramara i.e. the large black bee.

(e) Kākyara[45] (modern Kāṅker, a former feudatory state in Chattisgarh) derives its name from Kāk i.e. crow.

(f) Kukkuṭa[46] (not yet identified) seems to be named after Kukkuṭa i.e. cock.

(g) Vaṭa nagara[47] (Vaḍner, Nasik Dist.), literally means the city of Vaṭa trees.

(h) Kusumabhōga[48] (modern Kusumurrā in Dhamatari Tahsil of Raipur district) literally means bhoga (sub-division of a Viśhaya) of flower.

(i) Khalvāṭikā,[49] (Khalāri in Raipur district) means a garden of Khalva (a liguminous plant).

(j) Taṇḍulapadraka[50] (identified with Tāndaljā in Baroda district) is named after Taṇḍula, meaning grain.

4. Idea of dimension, extent or position; for example,

(a) Bṛihannārikā,[51] literally meaning "the larger Naria" (identified with modern Nāriā, near Goraj in Baroda district) gives a vague idea of its dimensional position.

(b) Dīrghāśākhika,[52] literally meaning "long branched" (identified with Dighī near Kārītalāi in Jabalpur district) symbolically indicates the extent of the village.

(c) Antarpāṭa[53] (identified with Amaturrā near Kārītalāi in Jabalpur district) probably named in the sense of "Antardēśa" indicates the location of the village.

B. Viewed Morphologically, the place-names in the Kalacuri records may be classified into various types as follows: –

1. Names ending in "Nagara"; for example,

(a) Vaṭanagara[54] (identified with Vadner in Nasik district of Bombay).

(b) Lavaṇanagara[55] (not yet identified).

2. Names ending in "Pura"; for example,

(a) Ānandapura[56] (same as Ānand in Kaira district in Gujarat).

(b) Varelāpura[57] (identified with Barelā near Ratanpur in Bilaspur district).

(c) Sāṇṭhivapura[58] (same as Soṇṭhi, near Akaltarā-Bilaspur district).

(d) Rāyapura[59] (Raipur town in Chatisgarh); and many others.

3. Names ending in "Grāma"; for example,

(a) Rajōgrāma[60] (not yet identified).

(b) Nikhatīgrāma[61] (modern Naktauli near Kahla in Gorakhapur district).

(c) Devagrāma[62] (modern Dēogavān near Khaira in Vindhya Pradesh).

(d) Hastigrāma[63] (unidentified as yet).

4. Names ending in "Pāṭaka"; for example,

(a) Chhallipāṭka[64] (same as Chilhāri near Dhavala in Vindhya Pradesh).

(b) Dhaṅgaṭapāṭaka[65] (identified with Dungarhai near Bilhari in Jabalpur district).

(c) Khailapāṭaka[66] (identified with Khailwāra near Bilhari in Jabalpur district).

(d) Mahiāripāṭaka[67] (same as Mehdiā–Gorakhpur district).

(e) Asathīpāṭaka[68] (identified with Avasthi in Gorakhpur district).

(f) Duāripāṭaka[69] (unidentified as yet).

5. Names ending in "Padraka" for example;

(a) Nirguṇḍīpadraka[70] (probably modern Nagarvāḍā near Dabhoi)

(b) Taṇḍulapadraka[71] (Identified with Tandaljā near Sankheḍā in Baroda district etc.

6. Names ending in "Ḍōllaka"; for example,

(a) Sārasaḍōllaka (as above).

(b) Vakkaḍōllaka[72] (unidentified as yet).

7. Names ending in "Katin"; for example,

(a) Karīkatin[73] (Khurai, near Deori Maḍhā in Jabalpur district).

(b) Asekatin[74] (unidentified).

8. Names ending in "Hrada"; for example,

(a) Pāshāṇihrada[75] (identified with Saṇiadarī near Saṅkhhedā in Baroda district).

(b) Cakrahradī[76] (same as Cakadahi near Karitalai in Jabalpur district).

9. Names containing the element "Pundikā"; for example,

(a) Nāsapuṇḍikā[77] (unidentified).

(b) Pōṇḍikā[78] (unidentified).

10. Names containing the element "Vaḍa", for example

(a) Dhōṭṭavāḍa[79] (unidentified).

(b) Khāḍā[80] (identified with Karrā, near Ratanpur in Bilaspur district).

(c) Kaṇḍarvāḍa[81] (same as Kunda in Jabalpur district).

(d) Kumarī-Vaḍao[82] (identified with Kawarwārā near Goraj in Baroda district).

(e) Vaḍadā[83] (probaly the same as Badra in Baloda Bazar tahsil of the Raipur district).

(f) Avaḍachaṇa[84] (unidentified).

(g) Saḍaviḍa[85] (unidentified).

(h) Vāna-vaḍada[86] (identified with Balaudā in the Janjagir tahsil of Bilaspur district).

(i) Viḍā[87] (unidentified)

(j) Bhauḍā[88] (unidentified).

Morphological analysis made above makes it clear that the origin of the place-names in the Kalacuri records may be traced to two different sources, viz. Āryan source and Non-Āryan source.

All those place-names which have prefix of clearly Sanskritic origin or have as suffix Sanskrit words like Nagara, Pura, Grāma, Hṛada, Pāṭ, Kuṭu (corruption from Kūṭ), etc. belong to Āryan source.

Some names apparently containing elements foreign to Sanskrit seem to be of Non-Āryan origin. The reason of this is not far to seek when, as indicated above, we know that people of non-Āryan tribes like Ābhīras and Nāgas used to enjoy dignified position in the Kalacuri courts and they had some settlements within the Kalacuri empire. Mutual cultural influence was therefore natural. Place-names where non-Āryan influence is noticed are :

(a) Names containing the element Vāḍ (No. 10 above) whose basic element seems to be a bād. They are most probably of Austric origin (cf. Ho. barre), or they may be explained as having some connection with Dravidian Vaḍā or Kol Oṛak "house."[89] Probably this austric origin is responsible for some names contaning repetition Buḍubuḍū[90] (identified with Burubur near Pāli in Bilaspur district).

(b) Names containing the elements Īng, Aṅga, Puṇḍi etc. e.g. Khijjiṅga[91] (same as Khiching, capital of the Bhañjas), Kōsaṅga[92] (identified with modern Kosagin in former Churai Zamindari in Bilaspur district), Nāspuṇḍikā (as above), Pōṇḍika (as above) etc. They seem to be of Dravidian origin (cf. Ho. (Kol):Īng "Ī", Aṅga "Little", Puṇḍi "White" etc.[93])

(c) Names containing the elements Nāḍu, Uṇḍi, Iṇḍi etc. which seem to be of south Indian origin (cf. Telegu, Nāḍu "place" Tamil Unṭ i "Home") eg. Seṇāḍu[94] (identified with Sōnada near Kharōd in Bilaspur district), Nāmüṇḍī[95] (place unidentified) Khimmiṇḍi,[96] (identified with Kimeḍi Zamindari in Ganjam district) etc.

Many other place-names in the Kalacuri records which seem to be otherwise unexplained regarding their origin are still awaiting scholarly investigation.

References

1. V. V. Mirashi : *Corpus Inscriptionum Indiacarum,* vol. IV, part I, pages CXXXIII to CXXXVI.
2. No. 89 and 95.
3. No. 62.
4. No. 45.
5. Nos. 64.
6. No. 42.
7. No. 98.
8. No. 90.
9. No. 45.
10. No. 96.
11. No. 46.
12. No. 83.
13. No. 97.
14. No. 46.
15. No. 45.
16. No. 36.
17. No. 14.
18. No. 74.
19. No. 4.
20. No. 45.
21. No. 88.
22. '*Epigraphia Indica,* vol. IX, pp. 182 ff.
23. A.E. Nelson: *Raipur District Gazetteer,* p. 342.
24. Hiralal Inscriptions in C.P. and Berar, No. 178.

25. Nos. 90 and 100.
26. No. 100.
27. No. 56.
28. No. 95.
29. Mirashi, *Corpus Inscriptionum Indicarum,* Vol. IV, part II, pp. 431, 496, 501 and 503n.
30. No. 75.
31. No. 77.
32. No. 96.
33. No. 56.
34. *Epigraphia Indica,* vol. XII, p. 209.
35. No. 50.
36. No. 88.
37. *Epigraphia Indica,* vol. IX, p. 179.
38. No. 107.
39. *Raipur District Gazetteer.*
40. *Corpus Inscription Indicarum,* vol. IV part I, page cxxxi, f.n. 8.
41. No. 74.
42. No. 60.
43. No. 46.
44. No. 88.
45. No. 88.
46. No. 77.
47. No. 14.
48. No. 88.
49. No. 108.
50. No. 13.
51. No. 15.
52. No. 42.
53. No. 42.
54. No. 14.
55. No. 45.
56. No. 15.
57. No. 96.
58. No. 98.
59. No. 107.
60. No. 46.
61. No. 74.

62. No. 56.
63. No. 74.
64. No. 42.
65. No. 45.
66. *Ibid.*
67. No. 74.
68. *Ibid.*
69. *Ibid.*
70. No. 13.
71. *Ibid.*
72. No. 46.
73. No. 36.
74. *Ibid.*
75. No. 13.
76. No. 42.
77. No. 46.
78. *Ibid.*
79. No. 70.
80. No. 95.
81. No. 64.
82. No. 15.
83. No. 123.
84. No. 74.
85. No. 95.
86. No. 100.
87. No. 45.
88. No. 95.
89. S.K. Chatterjee in "Vedic Age" (Ed. R.C. Majumdar) p. 147 and K.P. Goswami: *Journal of the Deptt. of letters,* Calcutta University Vol. XXXIII, pp. 33-35.
90. No. 94.
91. No. 90.
92. No. 105.
93. W. W. Hunter *A Comparative Dictionary of the Non-Aryan Languages of India and High Asia* (1868).
94. No. 100.
95. No. 60.
96. No. 90.

8

Topography in the Purāṇas–

Puruṣottamakṣetra

S. B. Chaudhuri

Introduction

To the student of mythology and religion, a thorough acquaintance with the sacred rivers and mountains, Tīrthasthānas and Puṇyakṣetras of India, which even to this day attract pilgrims from the remotest parts of India, is but essential. A general knowledge of the topography of those places was perhaps sufficiently well-known in the days of the Purāṇas. We are often informed of the rivers and mountains of India, with description of the boundary of those Puṇyasthānas. We are often directed to undertake the journey to the kṣetra concerned by the southern side of a hill, pursuing a course along the north bank of a particular river, keeping a city in the left and a village in the right and so on. These topographical records are valuable for determining some unknown places of ancient Indian geography. Some of the Purāṇas which, to some extent, may be regarded as handbooks to the Puṇyasthānas are thus valuable as a source of the study of Ancient Indian geography, and also as tending to indicate the different stages in the evolution of Ancient Indian geography.

The Skanda Purāṇa and the Purāṇic Topography

In India, notices of Topography are essentially related to the description of Tīrthas; so the best specimen of Purāṇic topography. I believe, is to be found in the Skanda Purāṇa–a book as voluminous as the Mahābhārata, having not a single feature by which it can be called a Purāṇa; and if it is at all to be styled so, it can be called a "Tīrtha Purāṇa.". Indeed it is to be noted that the Skanda Purāṇa begins with the description of the Tīrtha places in a very systematic way and describes them one by one according to their geographical setting. For example, the Purāṇa after describing the Puruṣottamakṣetra passes through all the tīrthas of south-east and south-west coast of India, one by one, until the Prabhāsa-kṣetra (Book vii) is reached and in this way it appears that the Purāṇa has attempted to form a garland of Tīrthas. My references are therefore to Skanda Purāṇa, and I have utilised the materials of the other Purāṇas where necessary. I have attempted here only to show how far the topographical records involved in the description of the Puṇyasthānas and in the narration of the pilgrimage to those places, as contained in the Purāṇas, are in harmony with the position of the various rivers, mountains and cities which we know. Let us start with the Puruṣottamakṣetra.

The whole of the second canto to the second volume of the Skanda Purāṇa describes the māhātmya of the Puruṣottamakṣetra. Regarding the boundary of the kṣetra it is thus said in ii, 2, 1

Aho tat paramaṃ kṣetraṃ vistṛtaṃ daśayojanaiḥ

Tīrtharājasya salilād utthitaṃ bālukācitam 12

Nīlācalena mahatā madhyasthena virājitam 13

* * * * * *

Sāgarasyottaratīre mahānadyās tu dakṣiṇe

Sa pradeśaḥ pṛthivyāṃ hi sarvatīrthaphalapradaḥ 31

Puruṣottamakṣetra is therefore the tract of land which rises from the ocean and is bounded by it on the south and by the river Mahānadī on the north. This is ten yojanas in area. The river Mahānadī here certainly refers to the great river of Orissa on the north of Puri. It should be noticed that the eastern coast of India has taken a definite south-western bend from Puri, or near about that, so much so that the ocean, that is, the Bay of Bengal, surrounds Puri in the south, and, the Puruṣottamakṣ etra which extended in the south up to Puri thus stands on the north of the ocean (Sāgarasyottaratīre). But regarding the northern boundary of the kṣetra another statement is to be found in ii, 2, 12 where it is said,

Dakṣiṇasyodadhes tīre nīlācalavibhūṣitam

Daśayojanavistīrṇaṃ * * * 74

* * * * * *

Tasyottarasyāṃ vikhyātaṃ vanam ekāmrakāhvayam 77

The northern boundary of the kṣetra is said here to have been the Ekāmravana instead of the river Mahānadī. The Ekāmravana is the modern Bhuvaneśvara on the river Gandhavatī, some twenty miles to the south of Cuttack in Orissa (Brahma Purāṇa, 41). So it appears that Bhuvaneśvara was the northern boundary of the kṣetra and not the river Mahānadī. And as Cuttack is to some extent on the bank of the

Mahānadī.\ Bhuvaneśvara is thus twenty miles south of the river Mahānadī. So it follows that the area of the kṣetra is ten yojanas, when Mahānadi or Bhuvaneśvara is the northern boundary. This however is contradictory. Anyway leaving aside the question of the area of the kṣ etra, it can be reasonably supposed that the kṣetra at the time of the Skanda Purāṇa comprised the modern South Cuttack and Puri district of the Orissa division of the Bihar and Orissa Province.

Nīlācala

In both the passages quoted above it is said that in the interior of the kṣetra there was the Nīlācalaparvata. There are two ranges of hills of that name in Cuttack. In northern Cuttack, north of the river Mahānadī near Balasore, there is a group of picturesque rocky hills, while in the southern Cuttack along the shore there are several hills terminating in a chain of mountains. But as the Puruṣottamakṣetra, as shown above, comprised the southern Cuttack and Puri district, Nīlācala cannot be the hills of Northern Cuttack, but must be the hills of southern Cuttack running like a chain along the sea-shore. And to this effect we find other passages in the Purāṇa. Thus in ii, 2, 1, 34 it is said–

Sindhutīre tu yo brahman rājate Nīlaparvataḥ etc.

and again in ii, 2, 11, 128–

Dakṣiṇodadhitīre 'sti Nīlādriḥ kānanāvṛtaḥ.

All these imply the immediate neighbourhood of the sea to the Parvata, which more plauslbly refers to the hills of southern Cuttack, lying within the boundary of the kṣetra, and is nearer to the sea than the hills of northern Cuttack which has got no such vicinity to the sea. The distance of the Parvata from the sea is stated to be two (ii, 2, 3, 52-53) or three krośas (ii, 2, 4, 1). So also the area of the kṣetra is given as ten yojanas and five krośas (ii, 2, 3, 52; ii, 2, 4, 1). It is really difficult to make out anything from these contradictory statements.

Utkala, Uḍra, Orissa, Kaliṅga

The holy kṣetra seems to have been included within a country which they called Utkala, and which they described as being situated on the shore of the southern ocean. Thus it is said in ii, 2, 4:

Supuṇye cotkale deśe dakṣiṇārṇavatoraṇe

The southern ocean is the Bay of Bengal as has been found to be implied on many occasions and it is said that Utkala was on the shore of that sea. Utkala perhaps meant a greater unit than the kṣetra, roughly corresponding to the modern Orissa division of the Bihar and Orissa province. And this is implied in some verses also (ii, 2, 6, 26-7). The chapter begins with a query as to the location of the Puruṣottamakṣ etra, and it is held that the kṣetra lies in Utkaladeśa regarding which the following notice is given :

Sa eṣa deśapravara utkalākhyo dvijottamāḥ 26

Ṛṣikulyām samāsādya dakṣiṇodadhigāmīnīm

Svarṇa-rekhā mahānadyor madhye deśaḥ pratiṣṭhitaḥ 37

It is apparent here that Utkala comprised the country beginning from the river Ṛsikulyā which flows to the sea (Bay of Bengal) up to the river Suvarṇarekhā including the river Mahānadī. Ṛsikulyā is the modern river Rasikoila (Thorn. Gaz.) on which is situated Ganjam and which falls into the sea. The river Suvarṇarekhā, which is still called so, practically divides Bengal and Bihar & Orissa. Utkala therefore corresponded to the country beginning from Ganjam in the south up to the south-western confines of Bengal, i.e., roughly speaking, it corresponded to the modern Orissa division about as far north as the river Suvarṇarekhā on the confines of the Midnapur and Balasore districts. But what was Oḍra or Uḍra deśa? In ii, 2, 7, 23 it is said that Uḍradeśa lies on the shore of the ocean, where there is the Puruṣottamakṣetra. Evidently Utkala and Uḍra are here supposed to be the same country. The Brahma Purāṇa (28, 1) also says that Auḍra lies near to the sea and in other places (28, 9; 42, 6) it has been called Utkala; and further it is said (42, 35) that the famous Puruṣottama resides there. All these suggest that Utkala and Uḍra are the same country. But unless we know the boundary of Uḍra we cannot probably be sure of it. The Skanda Purāṇa records no boundary of Uḍra. The Brahma Purāṇa, however, says (28, 1-2) that Uḍra-deśa extended right up to Virāja-maṇḍala from the shore of the sea. The shore of the sea certainly refers to Puri and its adjoining places. Regarding Virāja-maṇḍala it is said that it was on the river Vaitaraṇī (92, 9). The Mahābhārata also repeats (Vana, 85, 6) that Virāja-kṣetra was on the river Vaitaraṇī. Virāja-maṇḍala is therefore modern Jaipur which stands on the northern bank of a river, which is still called Vaitaraṇī, flowing between the river Suvarṇarekhā on the north and Mahānadī on the south. It seems therefore that though Utkala was called Uḍra, yet there was much difference between the two. For, whereas Utkala extended from Ṛṣikulyā right up to the river Suvarṇarekhā, Uḍra only extended up to the river Vaitaraṇī on the confines of the Balasore and Cuttack districts from Puri. Uḍra, according to the Purāṇas, was therefore a much lesser unit than Utkala, though, of course, it was included within the country mentioned last.

Mr. Pargiter (Ancient Countries of Eastern India, JASB, 1897, p.103 f.) however arrives at an altogether different conclusion. He says that

Oḍra in ancient times occupied the western part of Midnapur and also other districts such as Manbhum, Singhbhum, etc., north of the river Kapiśā of Kālidāsa (Raghu, iv, 38-93), i.e., modern Cossye which flows through Midnapur. But it is really discouraging to think that the Purāṇa, which has preserved an accurate geography of the Puruṣottamakṣetra, should err and confuse in such a manner. The Uḍras are rarely alluded to in the Sanskrit literature, excepting in some passages of the Mahābhārata. It will also be acknowledged that it is the Oḍras, who have given their name to modern Orissa or Oḍradeśa as it is also called. It is also to be noticed that the Oriya or Oḍiya is spoken throughout Orissa and Ganjam district. All these connect Oḍra more with modern Orissa or Utkala than with Midnapur and its neighbouring districts. Again in the Bṛhat-saṃhitā of Varāhamihira where we find an elaborate list of the countries and people respectively belonging to the nine divisions, nowhere Uḍra and Utkala are mentioned as separate countries; on the other hand, Oḍra has been mentioned as a country (xiv, 5, 6, 7) and Utkala a people in the same division implying, thereby, that in the same country of Uḍra, the Utkalas lived. Mr. Pargiter gives no other reason, expect that if the country from Ganjam to the river Cossye were occupied by the Kaliṅgas and Utkalas, then the Oḍras must be pushed further up the river in Bengal. But there are no reasonable grounds to introduce the separate establishment of the Uḍras and the Utkalas; on the other hand, there is strong evidence in the Purāṇas, as we have seen, of their common establishment in one country, which is alternately described as Uḍradeśa or Utkaladeśa though, of course, Udra was a smaller unit than Utkala. But as the Purāṇas reflect almost the mediæval stage of Indian geography it might be said as Mr. Pargiter has carefully observed (p. 104) that in ancient times the Oḍras probably occupied some portions of Bengal near Midnapur, but afterwards they "pushed southward" and resided in the country from Ṛsikulyā to the river Suvarṇarekhā which they called Uḍradeśa or Utkaladeśa.

Kaliṅga

Then what was Kaliṅga? Rapson says that it was between the rivers Godāvarī and Mahānadī (Ancient India, p. 164). General Cunningham is of opinion that it was between the Godāvarī river on the south-west and the Gaoliya, branch of Indravatī river on the north-west (Anc. Geo., p. 516). Pargiter observes from some passages of the Mahābhārata (JASB, 1897, p. 98) that Kaliṅga began in the north from the river Vaitaraṇī; and in the west extended up to the Amarakaṇṭaka hills (Kurma Purāṇa, ii, 39, 9). That Kaliṅga lay in the south-east part of India is also admitted by Varāhamihira (Bṛhat-Saṃhitā, xiv, 8, 9, 10). But we have seen in the passages cited above that the whole country from Ṛṣikulyā up to the river Suvarṇarekhā was called Utkala. So we see that the testimony of the Mahābhārata and the Skanda Purāṇa is radically opposite. In Raghuvaṃśa, iv, 38-53 Kālidāsa seems to support the Mahābhārata. There he says that Raghu after crossing the river Kapisā or Cossye in Midnapur was received by the king of Utkala who took him to Kaliṅga, which has led Mr. Pargiter to conclude that Utkala roughly corresponded to the country from Cossye to Vaitaraṇī, and from Vaitaraṇī southwards the country was called Kaliṅga. It seems hazardous to draw an accurate boundary of these two countries, for most probably it is a fact that there was no sharp demarcation between these two countries, and that the same country which was called Kaliṅga in ancient times came to be termed both Utkala and Kaliṅga at a later period. The word Utkala appears to have been coined in comparatively modern times probably because both the Utkalas and Kaliṅgas belonged to the one and the same race ('Kal' is common). The country in a later period came to be termed both Utkala and Kaliṅga, and in fact, it is very often to be found in the Purāṇas, which reflect the mediæval stage of Indian geography, that the same country is called both Kaliṅga and Utkala, probably implying the possibility of drawing this conclusion that there was hardly any difference between the two, and if any difference between the two ever existed, it was probably very slight.

King Indradyumna's pilgrimage to Puri

In chapter 11 of the Skanda Purāṇa (ii, 2) is described the journey of the king Indradyumna of Mālava to Puruṣottamakṣetra. The king perhaps followed a route through the southern valley of the Tāptī, and it is said that he halted with his party in a certain forest called Dhātukandara on the bank of the river Citrotpalā Mahānadī. Now, the river Mahānadī, as we know, rising in a hill (Amarakaṇṭaka) of the Central Provinces flows northwards for a long distance, and then takes an eastern course. In course of its northern flow a river called Pain meets it near Rajim in the Raipur district of the Chatrishgarh division of the Central Provinces. The Mahānadī below its junction with Pain was called Citrotpalā or rather Citrotpalā of the Mārkaṇḍeya Purāṇa (Mārk. 57; Arch. Sur. R., vii, 155; xvii, 70). The Dhātukandara forest might be some hill of the Raipur district. It is natural therefore that this Citropalā Mahānadī intervened in the king's way to Orissa from Mālava. However the king crossed the river and so entered into the southern valley of the river Mahānadī; and it is said that there he was received by the king of Utkala, evidently implying that the boundary of the country over which the king of Utkala ruled extended in the west up to the river Mahānadī, in the Raipur district of the Central Provinces, where the Mahānadī was called Citropāla Mahānadī; and this seems to be more in consonance, if we regard Kaliṅga and Utkala as one and the same country, for the Kurma Purāṇa (ii, 39, 9; see ante. p. 9) says that Kaliṅga extended in the west up to Amarakaṇṭaka Parvata—a hill wherefrom the river Mahānadī has taken its rise. It appears, therefore, that Utkala extended from the river Suvarṇarekhā on the north to the river Ṛsikulyā on the south, and from Citropalā Mahānadī river of the C.P. on the west to the sea on the east.

However, the king with his party proceeded eastwards (ii, 2, 12) and then reached the Ekāmrakānana. Ekāmrakānana is Bhuvaneśvara and it is said that they crossed the river Gandhavahā, which is but too natural, for Ekāmrakānana was situated on that river. Here it is said that the king Indradyumna enquired about the distance of the kṣetra from that place. 'Kṣetra' here obviously means Puri, for Bhuvaneśvara, as we have seen, was included in the kṣetra. The king of Utkala replied that it was yet 3 yojanas. Three yojanas is perhaps equivalent to some 25 miles (JRAS, 1904, p. 83) which roughly speaking may be supposed to be 30 miles, the distance between Puri and Bhuvaneśvara.

So it seems that the topographical records of the skanda Purāṇa involved in the description of the Puruṣottamakṣetra evince a fairly good knowledgc of the compilers regarding the modern Orissa division of Bihar and Orissa province. It can be concluded that this geographical knowledge could hardly have been obtained except from an actual visit to that Tīrtha by some person.

9

Topography in the Purāṇas

Veṅkaṭācala

S. B. Chaudhuri

Veṅkaṭācala in the Skanda Purāṇa

In the Caitanya Caritamṛta (ii. 9) it is said that Caitanya after visiting Purī crossed the river Godāvarī, passed through various tīrthas, and subsequently, arrived at Veṅkaṭācala. Veṅkaṭācala appears to have been a very sacred place; it is worth while, therefore, to see what information the Skanda Purāṇa furnishes us with, regarding the location of that tīrtha. The first canto of the second volume (Viṣṇu Khaṇḍa) of the Skanda Purāṇa describes the māhātmya of Veṅkaṭācala. The identification of the hill, however, is not very difficult if the inaccuracies which have crept into the passages concerned are eliminated, but considerable difficulties seem to lie in the task of reconciling the present position of Veṅkaṭācala with the position given in our Purāṇa. Thus in ii, i, i, 43-44, 46 is given the topograhical details of Veṅkaṭācala as follows : –

> Hastiśailāduttarataḥ pañcayojanamātrataḥ,
> Suvarṇamukharī nāma nadīnāṃ pravarā nadī. 43
> Tasyā evottare tīre Kamalākhyaṃ sarovaraṃ,
> Tattīre Bhagavānāste Śukasya varado Hariḥ. 44
> Kamalākhya sarasa uttare kānanottame,
> Krośadvayārddhamātre tu haricandana-śobhite,
> Śrīveṅkaṭācalo nāma Vāsudevālayo mahān. 46

Here it is said that there is a śaila called Hastiśaila, on the north of which is a river called Suvarṇamukharī. On the north of that river is a sarovara called Kamala, on the north of which stands Śrī Veṅkaṭācala, seven yojanas in length and one yojana in height. That Veṅkaṭācala lay on the north of Kamala sarovara, on the south of which the river Suvarṇamukharī was flowing is made further clear in ii. 19 where it is said that one Raṅgadāsa, wishing to visit Veṅkaṭācala from Pāṇḍya country, arrived on the bank of the river Suvarṇamukharī where he bathed. He then crossed it (19) and came to the sacred Kamala sarovara where he again bathed and performed pūjās. He crossed it (20-21) and gradually advanced towards Veṅkaṭācala. All these clearly show that Veṅkaṭacala was situated on the north of Kamala sarovara, by the south of which flowed the river Suvarṇamukharī, keeping Hastiśaila on the south.

Hastiśaila is perhaps still to be found in modern Kālahasti, a small range of hills, an off-shoot of the Nagari hills, spreading from Kālahasti on the north to Candragiri on the south-west in the North Arcot district (Ep. Ind., vol. I, p. 368; vol. III, pp. 116, 240) of the Madras Presidency. On the north of this range of hills from Kāla-hasti to Candragiri still flows a river called Svarṇamukhī, which is undoubtedly the river Suvarṇamukharī of our Purāṇa (ii, i, 113). It can, therefore, be said that the Purāṇic Hastiśaila and Suvarṇamukharī are occupying the same position with regard to each other as they possibly occupied at the time of the Purāṇa. The river Suvarṇamukharī rising from the Velikond range (southern spurs) of the Madras Presidency flows in a north-eastern direction and falls into the Bay of Bengal. But somewhere at a place on the north of the modern Kāla-hasti railway station of the M. & S. M. Ry., it bifurcates and one branch flows first southwards by the western side of the Kāla-hasti railway station and then takes a south-western course by the northern side of the off-shoots of the Nagari Hills. Thus we see that the river Suvarṇamukharī or Svarṇamukhī flows by the north of Hastiśaila as stated in the Purāṇa.

But there are some inaccuracies regarding the course of the river. In ii. 1, 22, 33-4 of the Skanda Purāṇa it is said that Agastya Aśrama was on the bank of the river Suvarṇamukharī. Again in ii. 1, 33, 18 & 31 it is stated that the river originating from Agastya-śaila falls in Dakṣ iṇasāgara. Dakṣiṇasāgara refers to the Bay of Bengal as has been found in many cases, and so the river Suvarṇamukharī falls in the Bay of Bengal. The other statements of the Purāṇa, however, are highly improbable. There were many Agastya-Āśramas, but if it was the Āśrama of the Nasik division of the Bombay Presidency, it is not possible that the river Suvarṇamukharī flowed as the far as Bombay Presidency to meet the Agastya Āśrama. The river in question does not reach the western part of the North Arcot district, not to speak of the far western part of the Bombay Presidency. Agastya-Āśrama may also probably be the Agastya-Śaila, wherefrom the river originated as stated above. But Agastya-Śaila is the Agastyakūṭa mountain of the Tinnevelly district in the Madras Presidency. But this is also highly improbable for the river Suvarṇamukharī does not flow even beyond the Madras Presidency. These inaccuracies, which have crept into the Purāṇa, either through textual corruption or on account of the ignorance of the compilers, must be eliminated in order to find out the true position of the river. A similar mistake occurs again in ii, 1, 30, 24 where it is said that Bharadvāja-Āśrama was on the bank of Suvarṇamukharī. Evidently the river could not have flowed northwards up to Prayāg where the Āśrama was situated (*Rāmāyaṇa,* Ayodhyā k., ch. 54). Again in ii. 1, 34, 25f. it is said that the river Suvarṇamukharī after its confluence with the river Veṇā flowed northwards with great force by the side of many tīrthas, through many dense forests and through the Udakhala country, until its confluence with the river Vyagrapadā after which it flowed towards Vṛṣabhācala. There are various Veṇās but taking it to be the river Kṛṣ ṇā which is nearest to Svarṇamukhī, no such confluence can be found. The river (Svarṇamukhī) has not even joined the various southern branches of the river Penner which flows on the immediate north of it, not to speak of the far more northern river Kṛṣṇā and also the river Kālindī, with which a confluence of the river Suvarṇamukharī is also described (ch. 25). These are some of the inaccurancies which must be eliminated to find out the real course of the river. It is impossible to think of a river, which flowed through Tinnevelly, Nasik and Madras and at the same time extended up to the United Provinces to meet the river Yamunā.

Arjuna's pillgrimage

So the statement of the Purāṇa that Suvarṇamukharī flows by the north of Kālahasti is a geographical fact. It is said that on the north of the river Suvarṇamukharī was a sarovara called Kamala sarovara. About 3 miles to the north of the Suvarṇamukharī there is a town called Tirpadi or Tirpati or Tripati in the district of North-Arcot, 72 miles north-west of Madras, and at a short distance from the Renigunta Railway station of the M. & S. M. Ry. Between Tripati and the river Svarṇamukhī there are still about 32 ponds and large tanks, the most famous of which is Svāmī puṣkariṇī. It is therefore probable that one of these ponds was called Kamala in those days. It is said that on the north of that Sarovara lay Veṅkaṭācala. On the east of Tripati at a distance of about six miles there stands a range of mountains called Tirumala giri consisting of seven ranges, running from north to south and the northern range is called Veṅkaṭagiri. The Padma Puraṇa (Uttara kh., ch. 90) also mentions Veṅkaṭa hill. But it gives no topographical details. Veṅkaṭ agiri is also called Śeṣācala in the Purāṇas and nowadays it is also known as Śeṣādri (Ep. Ind., vol. III, p. 240). In the Skanda Purāṇa (ii, 1, 1, 51 f.) it is said that there are many tīrthas in Veṅkaṭācala such as Ākāśagaṅgā, Pāpanāśana, Kumāradhārikā, Pāṇḍava tīrtha. The Tīrthas are all to be found more or less near the Veṅkaṭagiri i.e. the first (north) range of the Tirumali hill, although Akāśagaṅga and Kumāradhārikā are now called Viradgaṅgā and Kumāravārikā. On the top of the Veṅkaṭagiri there is the celebrated image of Nārāyaṇa called Veṅkaṭeśvara or Bālāji Viśvanāth. It was also visited by Caitanya (Cai. Caritā. ii. 1) so it can be safely established that the first (northern) range of the Tirumali hill which is still called Veṅkaṭagiri is the Veṅkaṭ ācala of our Purāṇa situated on the north of Kamala sarovara. On the south of this hill is the river Svarṇamukhī (Suvarṇamukharī), flowing by the northern side of Kāla-hasti. So we see that the position of Veṅkaṭ ācala as described in the Purāṇa exactly coincides with the present position of the same hill; on the north of Veṅkaṭācala therefore flowed the river Penner which was known in ancient times as the river Pinākinī (Sewell's Arch. Surv. of S. India, vol. 1, pp. 123, 129). That in ancient times it occupied the very same position is corroborated by the following description of the journey of Arjuna from Indraprastha to Veṅkaṭācala (Skandapurāṇa, ii, i. 29): Arjuna first arrived at the river Bhāgīrathī, and then pursuing a course along her bank gradually passed through Gaṅgādvāra, Prayāg and Kāśikā, and arrived at the Dakṣiṇasāgara (39-40). He gradually advanced and by crossing on his way the famous river Mahānadī he came to the sacred place Puruṣottama and thence to Siṃhācala (41). Afterwards he came to the bank of the river Godāvarī, crossed it and after seeing the river Malāpahā on his way, arrived at the bank of the river Kṛṣṇā-Veṇī (42-44). He then came to Śri-parvata (45). After passing that Parvata he crossed the river Pinākinī and arrived at Veṅkaṭācala, the abode of Nārāyaṇa. After alighting from the highest peak of Veṅkaṭagiri, he advanced towards the river Suvarṇamukharī (48).

This survey of the position of Veṅkaṭācala from the north exactly coincides with the position of the same as surveyed from the south by the route of pilgrimage of Raṅgadāsa. Arjuna, it seems, started from Indraprastha i.e., modern Delhi and came to Gaṅgādvāra i.e., Māyāpurī, which included Hardwar (Mbh., Vana, 84). The Kur-P. also says (ii, 42) that Gaṅgādvāra and Haridvāra are identical. The Vāmana (4&34) and Liṅga Purāṇas also seem to testify to this (e.g. i, 100). So from Haridvāra, Arjuna pursued a course along the banks of the Ganges and came to Prayāg i.e., Allahabad and then came to Kāśikā i.e., Benares. From Kāśikā it is said that he arrived at a place close to Dakṣiṇasāgara, i.e. the Bay of Bengal.[1] Travelling southwards from that corner of India

Arjuna crossed the river Mahānadī and came to Puruṣottama Kṣetra i.e. Purī.[2] From Purī he came to Siṃhācala, a place (hill) which still now bears that ancient name.[3] To come to Veṅkaṭācala from Siṃhācala, he had to cross the river Godāvarī. Then it is said that he crossed one river Malāpahā and then the river Kṛṣṇā-Veṇī. Kṛṣṇā-Veṇī, must be the river Kṛṣṇā itself, which flows by the south of Godāvarī, and as such it must have intervened Arjuna's way. It appears therefore that the river Malāpahā lay between Godāvarī and Kṛṣṇā. It is probable that the river Muner which meets Kṛṣṇā at Kondapalli is the same as Malāpahā. It should be noticed that from Bezwada to the Sea, Kṛṣṇā, becomes wider and wider, and so perhaps Arjuna had to abandon the coastal route and go further up the river Kṛṣṇā to cross it which he could not do without crossing the river Muner which lies between Godavari and Kṛṣṇā. After crossing the river Muner or Malāpahā, he crossed the river Kṛṣṇa-Veṇā i.e. Kṛṣṇā, and then came to Śrīparvata and subsequently to the river Pinākinī. The river Pinākinī is the river Penner on the south of which Nellore is situated. Śrīparvata therefore might be a mountain on the north of Penner and south of Kṛṣṇā. On the immediate south side of the river Kṛṣṇā there is a Śaila called Śrī Śaila in the Karnal Country in the Balaghat ceded districts (De, Dict., p. 193). This Śrīśaila is also called Śrīparvata and Parwattam. Caitanya visited that hill (Ca-Ca. ii. 9). It was perhaps a sacred place and it is but natural that Arjuna would visit that hill, and more so because the parvata lay almost on his way to Veṅkaṭācala from the river Kṛṣṇā. Thus he passed through the Śrīparvata and then crossed the river Pinākinī or Penner. After that he arrived at Veṅkatācala which as shown above was on the south of the river Pinākini. It thus clearly follows that the topographical records contained in the description of Arjuna's pilgrimage evince a fairly good geographical knowledge of the compilers of the Skandapurāṇa.

Baladeva's pilgrimage to Veṅkaṭācala

We have further evidences regarding the corroboration of the present position of Veṅkaṭācala. In chapter 79 of the tenth canto of the Bhāgavata-purāṇa, is described a journey of Baladeva. It is said that Baladeva first arrived on the bank of the river Kauśikī and then went to that Sarovara wherefrom the river Sarayu has sprung. He then travelled along the banks of Sarayu and subsequently arrived of Prayāg. There he visited the Pulahā Āśrama. From that place he continued his journey, bathing on his way in the rivers Gomatī, Gaṇḍakī, Vipāśā and Śoṇa, till he arrived at Gayā where he performed Pitṛ worship. From Gayā he came to Gaṅgā Sāgara Saṅgama, whence he travelled southward and reached the Mahendra Parvata. From Mahendra Parvata he respectively passed through the rivers Sapta Godāvarī, Veṇā, Pampā and Bhīmarathī and then arrived at Śrīśaila. Travelling south from Śrīśaila he arrived at Veṅkaṭagiri.

The river Kauśikī is perhaps the river Kuśi or Kauśaki mentioned in the Rāmāyaṇa (Ādi, 34) and also in Var. P. (140). All the Purāṇas agree that the river has taken its rise from the Himālayas and so probably had a course through the United Provinces. It can be supposed therefore that the river Kauśikī of Baladeva was the river Kośi, which now flows through the Rāmpur state of the United Provinces. So from the Kośi river of Rāmpur, Baladeva started and arrived at the Sarovara, wherefrom the river Sarayu originates. The river rises in the mountain of Kumaun, but the traditional belief is that the river issues from the Mānasa Sarovara (Mbh., Anuśā., 155). So it seems that Baladeva went straight north from the river Kośi and arrived at the Mānasa Sarovara. From that lake he followed a course along the bank of Sarayu or Gogrā as it is called nowadays, and then came to Prayāg i.e. modern Allahabad. It is said that there he visited Pulahāśrama. The Var. P. says (143) that Pulahāśrama and Śālagrāma are one and the same place. According to Pad. P. (Pātāla. kh. 78) and Bhāg. P. (v. 7) Śālagrāma is placed near the source of the river Gandak where ṛṣi Pulaha performed asceticism. It is not reasonable to think that Baladeva travelled northwards as far as the slopes of the Himālayas from Prayāg and then again descended southwards to bathe in the river Gomatī which was his next halting station from the Pulahāśrama. The inclusion of Pulahāśrama in the list is therefore a textual corruption which should be eliminated. So it stands that from Allahabad, Baladeva marched along the northern bank of the river Ganges, and then reached probably Bhitri where the river Gomatī joins the Ganges, and crossed it after bathing there. From that place he continued his march for Gaṇḍakī. Gaṇḍakī is the present river Gaṇḍak which joins the Ganges flowing from the north, at Sonepur in the district of Muzaffarpur in Bihar. And so when it is said that Baladeva bathed in that river, it follows that after crossing the river Gomatī near Bhitri he journeyed through Ballia and Saran and then came to Sonepur, which seems to be the shortest way from Gomatī to Gaṇḍak. Probably, at Sonepur, Baladeva bathed in the river Gaṇḍak. It is said that he also bathed at Vipāśā. Vipāśā or the Beas or the Hyphasis of the Greeks is in the Punjab. This inclusion of Vipāśā in the list of therefore essentially a textual corruption like the Pulahāśrama which is placed near Allahabad. So if we omit Vipāśā from the list it stands that Baladeva after bathing in the river Gaṇḍak, bathed at Śoṇa, which was regarded as a sacred river and then marched straight east to Gayā. From Gayā he went to Gaṅgā Sāgara Saṅgama, which probably meant a place somewhere near the confluence of the Ganges with the sea, like Arjuna's Dakṣina Sagāra. So from Gayā, Baladeva probably marched southwest and arrived somewhere near the mouth of the Ganges in the Bay of Bengal and then followed a coastal route and reached the Mahendra Parvata. Mahendra Parvata was used by the ancient Indians as a sort of generic term denoting the whole range of hills extending from Orissa to the district of Madura. It probably meant the hill of Kaliṅga (see Raghuvaṃsa, vi, 54) and the Uttara-Naiṣadhacarita (canto XII, 24) also supports it. However, Baladeva arrived at Kaliṅga and then came to Sapta Godāvarī. It was a place of pilgrimage and is mentioned often in the Purāṇas (Pad., Svarga, 19). According to the Rājataraṅgiṇī, (bk. viii, s. 34449, Dr. Stein's trans., vol. ii, p. 271) it meant the modern Dowlaishwerani 6 miles to the south of Rajahmundry. We have seen Baladeva following a coastal route and so it is but natural that he would come to the mouth of Godāvarī, and cross it at Sapta Godāvarī or Dowlaishewerani as it was considered a sacred place. After crossing the river Godāvarī, it would have been the easiest route for Baladeva to cross the river Kṛṣṇā and come directly to Śriśaila which was to the immediate south of the river. But we have seen that Arjuna, after crossing the river Godāvari, avoided a strictly coastal route and so was entangled in the crossing of the river Malāpahā or the river Mener, before he could cross the river Kṛṣṇā. Baladeva also avoided a coastal route after crossing the river Godāvarī and came across the rivers Veṇā, Pampā, Bhīmarathī before he could reach Śriśaila. It appears therefore that Baladeva was entangled in the South-western route instead of following a strictly southern route. There are many Veṇās, one is Veṇī, a branch of the Kṛṣṇā itself (Padma, Uttara, 74) which rises in the Western Ghats. But it is impossible to think that Baladeva went as far as the Western Ghats to cross it in view of the fact that there are other Veṇās which lay near him.

There is another river called Veṇā or Veṇvā or Veṅgā or Veṇi-gaṅgā which is identified with the river Wain-Gaṅgā of Central Provinces, being a tributary of the river Godāvarī (Mbh., Vana, 85; Padma, Ādi, 3). It rises from the Vindhyāpada range. But we have seen that Baladeva arrived at the mouth of the Godāvarī and probably crossed it. So no longer perhaps it was possible for him to retrace his steps north-west up to the northern border of the Hyderabad State to meet the river Wain-Gaṅgā. Veṇā of Baladeva was therefore the Kṛṣṇā itself. Pampā has still retained that ancient name being a tributary of the river Tuṅgabhadrā. It flows by the side of Kampli in the district of Bellary (Bom. Gaz, vol. I, pt. II, p. 369). The river Bhīmarathī is the river Bhīmā of the Hyderabad State which joins Kṛṣṇā near about the Ḳistna railway station of the G.I.P. Ry. But it appears that the rivers are not placed in proper setting so far as their geographical position is concerned. For once Baladeva crosses the Veṇā, i.e., Kṛṣṇā and Pampā, than he comes to the Bellary district and then again reverts northwards as far as Kistnā to cross Bhīmā in the Hyderabad State, seems improbable specially in view of the fact that after crossing the river Pampā his aim was to go to Śrīśaila. The rivers might therefore be placed in this order, Bhīmarathī, Veṇā and Pampā. So it appears very certain that after crossing the river Godāvarī, Baladeva instead of following a strictly southern route journeyed westward through the Hyderabad State and arrived at the confluence of the rivers Bhīmā and Kṛṣṇā or Veṇā. Then he continued his march in a south-western direction through the Madras Presidency, by crossing the river Tuṅgabhadrā, which of course is not mentioned, and perhaps by the western side of the Anagundi hills. This took him to the Bellary district, and he was thus face to face with the river Pampā in order to go to Śrīśaila. Naturally, therefore, Baladeva crossed the river Pampā and probably took a direct eastern course which took him to Śrīśaila standing, as we have pointed out, on the south of the river Kṛṣṇā. Thus we see that Baladeva was entangled in a very round about course, only because he abandoned the coastal route. It is said that from Śrī-śaila he arrived at Veṅkaṭagiri and so from Śrīśaila Baladeva took a direct southern route and arrived at the first (northern) range of the Tirumalagiri which is called Veṅkaṭagiri. It thus clearly follows that the topographical records contained in this description of the journey of Baladeva, with the exception of some few textual corruptions, and the literary evidences adduced in this paper to locate Veṅkaṭācala from Hardwar on the one hand and Pāṇḍya on the other evince the fairly good geographical knowledge of the Hindus regarding the upper and middle portion of India.

References

1. Dakṣina Prayāga means the Triveṇī on the north of Hugli in Bengal (Bṛ-Dharma-P., i, 6; A. S.B., vol. VI, 1910, p. 613).
2. For a detailed topographical description of Purī, see Indian Historical Quarterly, Dec. 1929, p. 659.
3. A railway station of the B.N. Ry, some five miles to the north of Waltair, also bears this name.

10

Text of the Purāṇic List of Rivers

D. C. Sircar

Some time ago I edited a part of the geographical section common to some of the Purāṇas in a paper, entitled 'Text of the Purāṇic List of Peoples', published in *IHQ*, vol. XXI, pp. 297-314. A critical edition, on the same plan, of another part of the Purāṇic section in question is offered in the following pages. For introductory remarks and list of abbreviations, vide *op. cit.*, pp. 297-99.

Text

[Bmd, ch. 49, vv. 28-42; Krm, I, ch. 46 (ch. 47 in some versions), vv. 28-39; Mk, ch. 57 (ch. 54 in some versions), vv. 17-30; Mts, ch. 114, vv. 20-32; Vmn, ch. 13, vv. 20-33; Vy, ch. 45 (of Bk. I according to some versions; cf. also Sachau, *Alb. Ind.*, I, pp. 357-39), vv. 94-107.]

I

[1]पीयन्ते यैरिमा नद्यो[2] गङ्गा सिन्धुः सरस्वती[3] ।

1. The following line is omitted in Krm. A little independence as regards the other of enumeration of the rivers issuing from the Himavat (Himālaya) is noticed in Mk and, to a greater degree with deliberate omissions and commissions, in Vmn. Mk has—गङ्गा सरस्वती सिन्धुश्चन्द्रभागा तथा परा। यमुना च शतद्रुश्च वितस्तेरावती कुहुः ॥ गोमती धूतपापा (*c*—धृत०) च बाहुदा (*d*—ब०) सद्दशद्वती (*d*—च०)। विपाशा (*b*—०सा) देविका रङ्क्षुर्निश्चीरा गण्डको तथा ॥ कौशिकी चापगा विप्र हिमवत्पादनिःसृताः ॥ Vmn has —सरस्वती पञ्चरूपा कालिन्दी च हिरण्वती। शतद्रुश्चन्द्रिका नीला वितस्तेरावती कुहुः ॥ मधुरा हाररावी च उशीरा धातुकी (*b*—०त०) रसा। गोमती धूतपापा च बाहुदा सा दृषद्वती ॥ निःखरा गण्डकी चित्ता कौशिकी तु वधूसरा। सरयूश्च सलोहित्या (*b*—०लौ०) हिमवत्पादनिःसृताः ॥ Most of the Himalayan rivers are noticed by Alberuni, vide *infra*, note 15. Though he speaks of both Vy and Mts, possibly the names were quoted by him from the latter work with an amount of misunderstanding and confusion.

2. Vy, Bmd – [तैर्विमिश्रा जनपदा आर्यम्लेच्छाश्च (Vy*e*—०र्या०) नित्यश: ।] पीयन्ते यैरिमा नद्य:; Mts – [तैर्विमिश्रा जनपदा (*bc*—जा०) आर्या म्लेच्छाश्च सर्वत: ।] पिबन्ति बहुला नद्य:.

3. Vy. Bmd, Mts—गङ्गा सिन्धु: सरस्वती; Mk —गङ्गा सरस्वती सिन्धु: Omitted in Krm. Some Mts versions read the names of the rivers in the second case-ending. It is well known that the Gaṅgā is the Ganges and the Sindhu the Indus. The Sarasvatī rises in the Sirmur hills of the Sewalik range in the Himālayas and emerges into the plains at Ād-Badrī in the Ambala District, Panjab. It disappears once at Chalaur but reappears at Bhavanipur; then it disappears at Balchappar but again appears at Barakhera; next it is joined by the Mārkaṇḍa at Urnai near Pehoa and the united stream, still called Sarasvatī, ultimately falls into the Ghaggar which is now the name of the united streams of the Satlaj and the Beas but is believed to have borne the name Sarasvatī in ancient times. In the early Vedic period, the Sarasvatī probably flowed into the Arabian sea. Later literature speaks of its disappearance at Vinaśana (near modern Sirsa) in Kurukṣetra or Brahmārvarta (in the Eastern Punjab) which is described as the land between the Sarasvatī and the Dṛṣadvatī. Cf. दक्षिणेन सरस्वत्या उत्तरेण दृषद्वतीम् । ये वसन्ति कुरुक्षेत्रे ते वसन्ति त्रिविष्टपे ॥ (*Mbh*, III, 83, 204-05); सरस्वतीदृषद्वत्योर्देवनद्योर्यदन्तरम् । तं देवनिर्मितं देशं ब्रह्मावर्तं प्रचक्षते ॥ (*Manu*, II, 17). Vide *infra*, note 9.

शतद्रुश्चन्द्रभागा च[4] यमुना सरयूस्तथा[5] ॥
इरावती वितस्ता च[6] विपाशा देविका कुहू:[7] ।

4. Vy., Bmd, Krm, Mts—शतद्रु श्चन्द्रभागा च; cf. Vmn–शतद्रू श्चन्द्रिका नीला ।. The Śatadru is the modern Satlaj whose stream united with that of the Beas is called the Ghaggar. It is the Vedic Śutudri and the Zaradros or Hesydrus of the classical writers. The Chandrabhāgā is the modern Chenab which is the same as Asiknī of the Vedic literature and the Acesines of the classical authors. Ptolemy calls it Sandabala or Sandabal. The Nīlā referred to by Vmn reminds us of the name Nilāb applied by the early Muslim writers to a part of the river Indus (cf. Ray, *DHNI*, I, pp. 84).

5. Vy *a*, Mts *a*–यमुना सरयुस्तथा; Bmd, Vy *cde*, Mts *b*—यमुना सरयूस्तथा; Krm *a*—सरयु यमुना तथा; *bc*—सरयूर्यमुना तथा; Mts *c*, Vy *e* (v.l.)—यमुना शरयूस्तथा ।. The Yamunā is the modern Jumnā (Yamunā) joining the Ganges near Allahabad. The Sarayū is the modern Ghagra or Gogra on which the ancient city of Ayodhyā (near Fyzabad) is situated. It rises in the Kumaon hills and is called Sarayū, Ghagra or Devā after its junction with the Kālīnadī.

6. Vy., Bmd, Krm, Mts *a*—इरावती वितस्ता च; Mts *bc*—ऐरावती वितस्ता च. The Irāvatī or Airāvatī is the moderm Rāvī which was known to the classical writers as Hydraotes. The Vitastā is the modern Jhelam the upper course of which is still known by the old name. It was known to the classical writers as the Hydaspes or Bidaspes.

7. Vy *a,* Bmd—विपाशा देविका कुहुः; Krm, Mts *a,* Vy *cde* —विपाशा देविका कुहूः; Krm *b* (v. l.) विपाशा देविका कुहुः; Mts *bc* —विशाला देविका कुहूः। The Vipāśā is the modern Beas, called the Vipāś in earlier literature and the Hyphasis or Bipasis in the works of the classical writers. The Devikā is the modern Deeg, a tributary of the Rāvī. Another identification suggested by some writers is that with the Devā, a name applied to the lower course of the Sarayū. The Kuhū has been identified with the modern Kabul river, called Kubhā in the *Ṛgveda* and Kophen, Kophes or Koa by classical writers.

गोमती धूपपापा च[8] बाहुदा च दृषद्वती[9] ॥
[10]कौशिकी च तृतीया तु[11] निश्चीरा गण्डकी तथा[12] ।

8. Mk *abd,* Vy *abc,* Bmd, Krm, Vmn—गोमती धूतपापा च; Vy *de*—गोमती धुतपापा च; Mts—गोमती धौतपापा च; *Ms* c—गोमती धृतपापा च। The river Gomatī has to be identified with the Ṛgvedic Gomatī which is the modern Gomal a western tributary of the Indus, or with the modern Goomti which joins the Ganges below Benares. There is another river of this name in the Kangra District, Panjab. The Dhūtapāpā was a tributary of the Ganges in the Benares region. The name has been associated with Ahopāp on the Goomti, 18 miles south-west of Sultanpur in Oudh.

9. Mk *abc*—बाहुदा सद्दशद्वती, d– —बहुदा च द्दशद्वती; Vy, Bmd, Krm, Mts —बाहुदा च दृषद्वती; Krm *b* (v. l.) Vy *e* (v. l.)—बहुदा च दृषद्वती; Vmn बाहुदा सा दृषद्वती। The Bāhudā has been identified by some with the Dhavalā (modern Dhumela or Burha-Rāptī), a tributary of the Rāptī, and by others with the Ramganga that joins the Ganges near Kanauj. The river Dṛṣadvatī is usually identified with the Citang, Citrang or Cautang which runs parallel to the Sarasvatī; but some writers prefer its identification with the Rakshi that flows by the south-east of Thanesvar. The view of certain earlier writers identifying the Dṛṣadvatī with the Ghaggar seems to be unjustifiable.

10. The following two lines are contracted into one in Krm — कौशिकी लोहिनी (*b* [v. l.], c [v. l.]—लोहिता) चेति हिमवत्पादनिःसृताः। Vmn and Mk arrange the names rather independently.

11. Vy., Bmd—कौशिकी च तृतीया तु; Mts—कौशिकी तु तृतीया च। Pargiter suggests the emendation—कौशिकी करतोया तु or कौशिको च त्रिस्रोतास्तु। The Kauśikī is no doubt the modern Kosi which runs through Nepal and Tirhut and joins the Ganges below Patna; but originally the river seems to have passed through North Bengal to join the Brahmaputra. There is another Kosi (Kauśikī) which flows by Almora and Ramnagar in the north-western U.P. *Tṛtīyā* may be a mistake for Karatoyā the celebrated river of North Bengal. *Niścirā* seems also to be a mistake for *Trisrotas,* the Sanskrit name of the Teestā in North Bengal. Agn (ch. 116, 7) seems to locate the rivers Tṛtīyā and Niścirā in the Gayā region; but the evidence is doubtful, and, moreover, in that case, they can not be associated with the Himalayas. Cf. *infra,* note 12.

12. Mk, Vy, Bmd—निश्चीरा गण्डकी तथा; Mts—निश्चला गण्डकी तथा; Vmn—निःखरा गण्डकी चित्रा। For *Niścirā,* see remarks *supra,* note 11. The Gaṇḍakī (modern Gaṇḍak) is the famous tributary of the Ganges and joins the river near Sonepur (Hariharakṣetra) in the Muzaffarpur District, Bihar.

इक्षुर्लौहित्य इत्येता[13] हिमवत्पादनिःसृता[14] ॥[15]

13. Vy, Bmd—इक्षुर्लोहित इत्येताः; Mts *a*—इक्षुर्लोहितमित्येताः, *bc*—इक्षुर्लौहित्यमित्येता; *c* (v. l.)—चङ्कुं लोहितामित्येताः। The name Ikṣu may indicate the Ikṣumatī (modern Kālīnadī, a tributary of the Ganges); but the form *Caṅku* as well as *Raṅkṣu* (or *Vaṅkṣu*) in Mk probably suggests that it is no other than the Vakṣu or Oxus (Amu Darya); Cf. Kālidāsa's *Raghuvaṃśa,* IV, 67, in Vallabha's commentary. The Lohitya or Lauhitya is the same as the Brahmaputra.

14. Mk, Vy, Bmd, Krm, Vmn—हिमवत्पादनिःसृताः; Mts—हिमवत्पार्श्वनिःसृताः, *c* (v. l.)—दिवमाप्नोति याः स्मरन्।

15. The following rivers are mentioned by Alberuni (Sachau, *Alb. Ind.,* I, ch. 25) as issuing from the Himavat: 1. Sindh (Sindhu or Indus) or the river of Vaihand (ancient Udabhāṇḍa or Udahāṇḍa, modern Und near Attock), 2. Biyatta (Vitastā) or Jailam (Jhelam), 3. Candrabhāgā or Candrāha, 4. Biyāha (Vipāśā) to the west (sic. east) of Lahore, 5. Irāvatī to the east (sic. west) of Lahore, 6. Śatarudra or Śataldar (Śatadru or Satlaj), 7. Sarsat (Sarasvatī) flowing to the country of Sarsat (Sārasvata), 8. Jaun (Yamunā), 9. Gaṅgā, 10. Sarayū or Sarwa, 11. Devikā, 12. Kuhū, 13. Gomatī, 14. Dhūtapāpā, 15. Viśālā (cf. Mts *c, supra,* note 7), 16. Bāhudāsa (sic. Bāhudā, with *sa* prefixed to the next name in the text consulted; cf, *supra,* note 9), 17. Kauśikī, 18. Niścirā, 19. Gaṇḍakī, 20. Lohitā, 21. Dṛṣadvatī. Other names of this list appear to have been wrongly taken mostly from that of the rivers issuing

from the Pāriyātra (vide section II). They are: 22. Tāmrā Aruṇā (Tāmravarṇā ?), 23. Parṇāśā, 24. Vedasmṛti, 25. Vedāsinī or Vidāsinī (cf. *infra,* note 16), 26. Candanā, 27. Kāwanā (same as Kawini, tributary of the Sarwa ?), 28. Parā, 29. Carmaṇvatī, 30. Vidiśā, 31. Veṇumatī, 32. Śiprā that rises in the Pārivātra and passes by Ujain (Ujjayinī), 33. Karatoyā, 34. Shmāhina (cf. *infra,* notes 19, 33). Alberuni further says (*loc. cit.*, pp. 259 ff.), "In the mountains bordering on the kingdom of Kāyabish (Kāpiśa), i.e. Kābul, rises a river which is called the *Ghorvand* on account of its many branches. It is joined by several affluents: 1. The river of the pass of Ghūzak; 2. The river of the gorge of Panchīr (Panjshir falling into the Ghorvand), below the town of Parvān (about 8 miles to the north of Chārikar); 3-4. The river Sharvat and the river Sāva, which latter flows through the town of Lambagā (Lampāka), i.e. Lamghan; they join the Ghorvand at the fortress of Drūta; 5-6. The rivers Nūr and Kīrāt. —Swelled by these affluents, the Ghorvand (Kābul) is a great river opposite the town of Purshāvar (modern Peshāwar) being there called *the ford,* from a ford near the village of Mahanāra on the eastern banks of the river, and it falls into the river Sindh (Indus) near the castle of Bītūr, below the capital of al-Kandahār (Gandhāra), i.e. Vaihand (Und near Attock). —The river Biyatta (Vitastā), known as Jailam (Jhelam), from the city of this name on its western banks, and the river Candarāha (Candrabhāgā) join each other nearly fifty miles above Jahrāvār (which together with Mūltān comprised the ancient Sauvīra country; cf. *loc. cit.*, pp. 300, 302), and pass along west of Mūltān (which was originally known as Kāśyapapura, next as Haṃsapura, then as Vegapura, afterwards as Sāmbapura and ultimately as Mūlāsthāna; cf. the views of Utpala; *loc. cit.*, pp. 298). —The river Biyāh (Vipāśā) flows east of Mūltān, and joins afterwards the Biyatta (Vitastā) and Candarāha (Candrabhāgā). —The river Irāva (Irāvatī) is joined by the river Kaj which rises in Nagarkot in the mountains of Bhātul. Thereupon follows as the fifth the river Śatladar (Śatadru). —After these five rivers have united below Mūltān at a place called *Pañcanada,* i.e. the meeting place of the five rivers, they form an enormous watercourse... The Muslims call the river, after it has passed the Sindhī city Aror, as a united stream, the *river of Mihran.* Thus it extends ... ... enclosing in its course places like islands until it reaches al-Mansūra, situated between several of its arms, and flows into the ocean at two places, near the city of Loharānī, and more eastward in the province of Kacch at a place called *Sindhusāgara,* i.e. *the Sindh Sea.* —As the name *union of five rivers* (Pañcanada) occurs in this part of the world (the Panjab), we observe that a similar name is used also to the north of the above mentioned mountain chains (i.e. the mountain bordering on the kingdom of Kāyabish), for the rivers which flow thence towards the north after having united near Tirmidh and having formed the river of Balkh, are called the union of *seven rivers* (cf. *hapta-hindu* of the ancient Iranians). The Zoroastrians of Sogdiana (Bukhara region) have confounded these two things; for they say that the whole of the seven rivers is *Sindh,* and its upper course *Barīdīsh* ... The river Sarsati (Prabhāsa-Sarasvatī, mod. Raunakshi) falls into the sea at the distance of a bow-shot east of Somnāth. – The river Jaun Yamunā) joins the Ganges below Kanoj, which lies west of it. The united stream falls into the great ocean near Gaṅgāsāgara. – Between the mouths of the rivers Sarsati and Ganges is the mouth of the river Narmadā which descends from the eastern mountains, takes its course in a south-western direction and falls into the sea near the town of Bahroj (Broach) nearly sixty *yojana* east of Somnāth. – Behind the Ganges flow the rivers Rahab (modern Ramgaṅgā) and Kavīnī which join the river Sarva near the city of Bārī (to the east of the Ganges at a distance of three to four days' marches from Kanoj; cf. pp. 199)".

II

वेदस्मृतिर्वेदवती[16] वृत्रघ्नो सिन्धुरेव च[17]।
पर्णाशा चन्दना चैव[18] सदानीरा महो तथा[19]।
[20]पारा चर्मण्वती लूपी(?)[21] विदिशा वेत्रवत्यपि[22]।

16. Mk, Vy, Bmd, Krm – वेदस्मृतिर्वेदवती; Krm *b* (v. l.) *c* (v. l.) – वेदस्मृतिर्वेदरता; Mts – वेदस्मृतिर्बेत्रवती। The Vedasmṛti has been identified with the modern Besulā in Malwa. For the Vetravatī, vide *infra,* note 21.

17. Mk, Vy *acde,* Bmd, Mts, Vmn – वृत्रघ्नी सिन्धुरेव च; Krm – व्रतघ्नी त्रिदिवा तथा Vy *b* recognises Vṛtraghnī (cf. Vārtaghnī in Km.; modern Vātrak, a tributary of the Sabarmatī in Gujarāt) only. The Sindhu is no doubt the modern Kālīsindh, a tributary of the Jumna between the Chambal and Betwa.

18. Mk *abc* – वेण्वा सानन्दनी चैव, *d* – वेण्वा सानन्दना चैव, Vy *a,* Krm *ab* (v. l.) *c* (v. l.) – पर्णाशा चन्दना चैव; Bmd, Vy *cde,* Krm *bc* – वर्णासा चन्दना चैव; Mts – पर्णाशा नर्मदा चैव; Vmn *a* – पर्णाशा नन्दिनी चैव, *b* – पर्णासा नन्दिनी चैव; Vy *b* – पर्णाशा नन्दना चैव; Krm *b* (v. l.) *c* (v. l.) – पर्णासा बन्धना चैव, *b* (v. l.) – पर्णाशा बन्धना चैव। The Parṇāśā is no other than the modern Banās, a tributary of the Chambal, in Rajputana. *Candanā* is believed to have been another name of the Sabarmati.

19. Mk, Bmd, Vy *d* (v. l.)–सदानीरा मही—तथा; Vy *acde*–सतीरा महती तथा, *b*–सद्वानारा मदी तथा (sic), *c* (v. l.)– सदातीरा मही तथा; Krm *ab* (v. l.)–सदानीरा मनोरमा, *bc*– सचमर्ण्यवतो सुरा; Mts–काबेरी महती तथा; Vmn–पावनी च मही तथा। The Mahī is no doubt the river of that name rising in Malwa and draining itself in the Gulf of Cambay.

20. The following two lines have been contracted into one in Krm *bc*–विदिशा वेत्रवत्यपि पारियात्राश्रया: स्मृता, *b* (v. l.)–चर्मण्वती तथा सूर्या विदिशा वेत्रवत्यपि।

21. Mk *ac*–पारा चर्मण्वती तापो, *bd*–पारा चर्मण्वती नूपी; Bmd, Vy *acde*–पारा, चर्मण्वती चैव; Vy *b*– परा चर्मण्वती लूपा (?), *e* (v. l.)– पारा चर्मण्वती चैव; Krm–चर्मण्वती तथा द्दर्या, *b* (v. l.)– चर्मण्वती तथा सूर्या; Mts–पारा च धन्वती रूपा, *c* (v. l.)– पारा चर्मण्वती रूपा। The Pārā may be the same as the Pārvatī which rises in Bhopal and is a tributary of the Chambal, while Charmaṇvatī is no other than the Chambal itself. The Chambal is a well known tributary of the Jumna.

22. Mk. Vy *acde*, Bmd, Krm–विदिशा वेत्रवत्यपि; Mts–विदुषा वेणुमत्यपि; Vmn– विदिशा वेणुमत्यपि; Vy *b* recongnises Vidiśā only. The river Vidiśā is the modern Bes or Besali which falls into the Betwa near Besnagar (ancient Vidiśā-nagarī). The Vetravatī is the modern Betwa which is a tributary of the Jumna.

[23]शिप्रा ह्यवन्ती कुन्ती च[24] पारियात्राश्रया: स्मृता:[25] ॥

23. This line is omitted in Krm *a* and Vy *b*.

24. Mk *abc*–शिप्रा ह्यवर्णी च तथा; Vy *acde*, Bmd–शिप्रा ह्यवन्ती च तथा; Vy *e* (v. l.). Mk *d*– क्षिप्रा ह्यवन्ती च तथा; Mts– शिप्रा ह्यवन्ती कुन्ती च; Vmn– चित्रा ह्योघवती रम्या। The Siprā is mentioned in literature as the river on which the celebrated city of Ujjayinī (modern Ujjain in the old Gwalior state) was situated. The river Avantī rises near Mhow and flows into the Chambal. The Kuntī, otherwise called Aśvanadī or Aśvarathanadī, is a small tributary of the Chambal (see Dey, *Geog. Dict.*, s. v. *Kuntī-Bhoja*).

25. Mk *abc*, Bmd–पारिपात्राश्रया: स्मृता:; Vy, Mk *d* – परियात्राश्रया: स्मृता:; Mts–पारियात्राश्रिता: स्मृता:; Vmn–परियात्रोद्भवा: स्मृता:। Pāriyātra or Pāripātra was the name applied to the Western Vindhyas together with the Aravelly range.

III

[26]शोणो महानदी चैव[27] नर्मदा सुरसा किया[28]।
मन्दाकिनी दशार्णा च[29] चित्तकूटा तथैव च[30]॥

26. This line is omitted in Mts *ab.* For the first three lines, Krm reads rather freely–नर्मदा सुरसा शोणो दशार्णा च सहानदी। मन्दाकिनी चित्तकूटा तामसी च पिशाचिका॥

27. Vy, Bmd, Mts *c*–शोणो महानदश्चैव; Vmn– शोणो महानदी चैव। The Śoṇa is the celebrated Sone which rises in the Amarkaṇṭak range and drains itself into the Ganges not far from Patna. The ancient city of Pāṭaliputra stood on the junction of the Śoṇa and the Gaṅgā. The Mahānadī also rises from the same range and flows through Orissa into the Bay of Bengal..

28. Mk–नर्मदा सुरथाद्रिजा; Vy *acde*– नर्मदा सुमहा द्रुमा, *b*–नर्मदा सुरसा किर्वा (sic. क्रिया), *c* (v. l.) e (v.l.)– नर्मदा सुरहा द्रुमा; Bmd–नर्मदा सुवहा द्रुमा; Vmn–नर्मदा सुरसा क्रिया; Mts *c*– नन्दना सुकृशा क्षमा; cf. सुरसा शिवा in Grd, I, 55, 8. The Narmadā is the famous Narbadā (Nerbudda) which rises in the Amarkaṇṭak range and falls into the Arabian Sea.

29. Mk, Vy, Bmd, Mts, Vmn–मन्दाकिनी दशार्णा च। The Mandākinī (now called Mandākin) flows into the Paisuni near the Citrakūṭa hill, while the Daśārṇā is the modern Dhasan flowing past Saugor between the Betwa and the Ken.

30. Mk–चित्तकूटा तथापरा; Vy. Bmd, Mts–चित्तकूटा तथैव च; Vmn– चित्तकूटा हि देविका। The Citrakūṭā was either the same as the Mandākin or a part of it.

[31]तमसा पिप्पनश्रोणो[32] करमोदा पिशाचिका[33]।
चित्तोत्पला विपाशा च[34] मञ्जुला बालूवाहिनी[35]॥
[36]शुनी लज्जा शुक्रिमती[37] शकुली त्रिदिवा क्रमु:[38]।

31. This line is omitted in Krm. A little freedom is noticed in some texts as regards the order of the names in the following two lines. Mk has–चित्तोत्पला सतमसा करमोदा पिशाचिका। तथान्या पिप्पलि-श्रीणिर्विपाशा (*d*–पिप्पल०) वञ्जुला नदी॥ Mts has–तमसा पिप्पली श्येनी तथा चित्तोत्पलापि च। विमला चञ्चला चैव तथा च धूतवाहिनी॥ Vmn has–चित्तोत्पला वै तमसा करमोदा (*b*–०तोया) पिशाचिका। तथान्या पिप्पलश्रेणो विपाशा वञ्जुलावती॥

32. Vy *ade,* Bmd–तमसा पिप्पला श्रोणी; Mts–तमसा पिप्पली श्येणी; Vy *bc*–तमसा पिप्यला श्रोणी। The Tamasā is the modern Tons flowing into the Ganges below Allababad. The Pippalaśroṇī may be the modern Paisuni or Parsaroni which is a tributary of the Jumna running between the Ken and the Tons.

33. Mk—करमोदा पिशाचिका; Vy *acde,* Bmd, Vmn—करतोया पिशाचिका; Vy *b*—करमोदा पिशाबिका (sic. पिशाचिका)। Pargiter suggests the identification of the Karamodā with the modern Karamnāśā flowing into the Ganges above the Sone.

34. Vy *acde,* Bmd—नीलोत्पला विपाशा च; Krm, चित्रोत्पला विशाला च, *b* (v. l.), c (v.l.)— चित्रोत्पला विपाशा च; Vy *b*— चित्रपला (sic. चित्रोत्पला) महावेगा, *e* (v. l.)— चितोत्पला विपाशा च। The Citrotpalā is a branch of the Mahānadī in Orissa or the Mahānadī itself below its junction with the Pyri.

35. Vy *acde*—जम्बुला बालुवाहिनी, *bc* (v. l.)— वञ्जुला बालुवाहिनी; Bmd—जम्वूला बालुवाहिनी; Krm—मञ्जुला बालुवाहिनी, *b* (v. l.) *c* (v. l.)—मञ्जुला रत्नवाहिनी।

36. The following line is omitted in Krm.

37. Mk—सुमेरुजा शुक्रिमती; Vy *acde,* Bmd— सितेरजा शुक्रिमती; Vy *b* has Śuktimatī only, *c* (v. l.)—सितेरजा मुक्तिमती; Mts *a*— शुक्तिमती शुनी लज्जा, *bc*—शुक्तिमन्ती शुनी लज्जा; Vmn—सत्सन्तजा शुक्तिमती। The Śuktimatī is the modern Ken a tributary of the Jumna flowing through Bundelkhand. On its bank stood a city of the same name (Pali *Sotthivatī*) which was the ancient capital of the Cedi people.

38. Mk. *ab*—शकुली त्रिदिवा क्रमुः, *c*— शकुली त्रिदिवा क्रमः, *d*—सकुली त्रिदिवा क्रमुः; Vy *acde*— मक्रुणा त्रिदिवा क्रमात् , *c* (v. l.)—मक्षणा त्रिदिवा क्रमात्, *e* (v. l.)— मकणा त्रिदिवा क्रमा; Bmd— मक्षुणा त्रिदिवा क्रमात्; Mts *ab*— मुकुटा ह्रदिकापि च, *c*—मुकुटा ह्रादिकापि च; Vmn—चक्रिणी त्रिदिवा वसुः; Vy *b*—शक्रुणा त्रिदिवा क्रमात्। The Śakulī (Śakrulī ?) may be the Sakri which flows into the Śeonath, a tributary of the Mahānadī.

अक्षपादात् प्रसूतास्ता[39] नद्यो मणिनिभोदकाः[40] ॥[41]

39. Mk *ac* (v. l.) *d*—ऋक्षपादप्रसूता वै; *bc*—स्कन्धपादप्रसूता वै; Vy, Bmd—ऋक्षपादात् प्रसूतास्ता, Krm—ऋक्षवत्पादजा नद्यः; Mts *ac*—ऋक्षवन्त-प्रसूतास्ताः, *b*—ऋष्यवन्तप्रसूतास्ताः; Vmn—ऋक्षपादप्रसूता च। For the Ṛkṣavat, see below note 41.

40. Mk—तथान्या वेगवाहिनी; Vy, Bmd—नद्यो मणिनिभोदकाः; Krm—सर्वपापहरा नृणाम्; Mts—नद्योमलजलाः शुभाः; Vmn *a*—तथान्या बलवाहिनी, *b*—तथान्या वल्गुवाहिनी।

41. It is to be noted that the short list in section IX below wrongly speaks of some of these rivers as flowing not from the Ṛkṣavat but from the Vindhya. The name Ṛkṣavat was applied to a particular section of the range that was in a general sense called the Vindhya. While the

name Vindhya was loosely applied to the whole chain of hills running from Gujarat to the Gayā region and lying on both sides of the Narmadā, that of Ṛkṣavat, when especially mentioned in literature, is always associated with the central part of the Narmadā valley, of which Māhiṣmatī (either Māndhātā in the Nimār District of the Madhya Pradesh, or Maheśvar in the old Indore State) was the most important city and Daśārṇā (see note 29 above) a notable river. The Vindhya, when distinguished from the Ṛkṣavat, denotes the chain lying to the south of the Narmadā as suggested by Nīlakaṇṭha who explains the passage *Vindhy-arkṣavantāv=abhitaḥ* (i.e., 'lying between the Vindhya and the Ṛkṣavat') in the *Hv,* II, 38, 7 as *Vindhyasy=ottarata Ṛkṣavato dakṣiṇata ity=arthaḥ* (i.e., 'lying to the north of the Vindhya and to the south of the Ṛkṣavat'). Cf. Raychaudhuri, *Stud. Ind. Ant.,* pp. 128. The Puranic text quoted above (cf. note 39) would also suggest that the Ṛkṣavat was that part of the Vindhyan range which lies to the north of the Narmadā and runs from the Malwa region right up to the sources of that river as well as of the Mahānadī.

IV

[42]तापी पयोष्णी निर्विन्ध्या[43] शिप्रा च निषधावती[44] ।
वेण्वा वैतरणी चैव[45] शिनिबाहु; कुमुद्वती[46] ॥
तोया चैव महागौरी[47] दुर्गा चान्त:शिला तथा[48] ।

42. In some texts slight independence is noticed in the order of the names contained in this line. Mk has—शिप्रा (*d*—क्षिप्रा) पयोष्णी निर्विन्ध्या तापो सनिषधावती (*d*—च निषधावती); Vmn has—शिवा पयोष्णी निर्विन्ध्या तापी सनिषधावती।

43. Vy *abde* (v. l.), Bmd, Krm, Mts—तापी पयोष्णी निर्विन्ध्या; Vy *ce*—तापी पयोष्णी निर्वन्ध्या। The Tāpī, otherwise called Tāptī, is the celebrated river that flows into the Arabian Sea. The Payoṣṇī has been identified by some scholars with the Pain or Paingaṅgā which is a tributary of the Godāvarī. The Nirvindhyā is the modern Newuj, a tributary of the Chambal flowing between the Betwa and the Kālīsindh.

44. Vy *acde,* Bmd—मद्रा च निषधा नदी; Vy *b* — सिर्वा (sic. सिप्रा) च निषधा नदी; Krm— शीघ्रोदा च महानदी; Mts *a*— क्षिप्ता च ऋषभा नदी, *bc*— क्षिप्रा च ऋषभा नदी। Mk has *Śiprā* (*d*—*Kṣiprā*) and Vmn *Śivā* for *Madrā* (Bmd and Vy with the exception of *b*), *Śīghrodā* (Krm) and *Kṣiptā* or *Kṣiprā* (Mts).

45. Mk. *ac,* Vy *abce* (v. l.), Bmd, Krm *a*—वेण्वा वैतरणी चैव; Vy *de*—वेन्वा वैतरणी चैव; Krm *bc*—विन्ना वैतरणी चैव, *b* (v. l.) *c* (v. l.)—वेण्या वैतरणी चैव, चिन्ता वैतरणी चैव; Mts, Vmn *b*—वेणा वैतरणी चैव; Vmn *a*— वणा (sic. वेणा)

वैतरणी चैव; Mk *bd* वेण्या वैतरणी चैव । The Veṇvā may be the Waingaṅgā, a tributary of the Godāvarī. Pargiter thinks that Veṇvā is the Waingangā together with the Prānhitā. The Vaitaraṇī seems to be the celebrated river of that name flowing through Orissa into the Bay of Bengal.

46. Mk *abc*—सिनीबाली कुमुद्वती, *d*—सिनीवाली कुमुद्वती; Vy *acde*, Bmd—शितिबाहु कुमुद्वती; Krm—वलाका च कुमुद्वती; Mts—विश्वमाला कुमुद्वती; Vmn—सिनीबाहुः कुमुद्वती; Vy *b*—सिनिहाहुः कुमुद्वती, *e* (v. l.)— शिनिबाहुः कुमुद्वती।

47. Mk—करतोया महागौरी; Vy *a*—तोण्वा चैरमहागौरी; Vy *cde*, Bmd, Krm *a*, Mts— तोया चैव महागौरी; Vy *b*— तोबा (sic, तोया) चैव महागौरी; Krm *bc*—तथा चैव महागौरी; Vmn—तोया रेवा महागौरी; cf. ब्रह्माणीं च महागौरीं दुर्गामपि च भारत in *Mbh*, VI, 9, 33. The Brahmāṇī seems to be the same as the Brāhmaṇī river flowing through Orissa.

48. Mk *abc*—दुर्गा चान्तःशिरा तथा, *d*— दुर्गा चान्तःशिवा तथा; Vy, Bmd, Krm—दुर्गा चान्तःशिला तथा; Mts—दुर्गमा तु शिला तथा; Vmn— दुर्गन्धा वा शिला तथा; cf. दुर्गा चित्रशिलां चैव in *Mbh*, VI, 9, 30. It is to be noted that *Mbh* mentions Durgā once in relation to Mahāgaurī (*supra*, note 47) and again in connection with Citraśilā (sic. *c*=*Āntaḥśilā*) apparently due to confusion.

विन्ध्यपादप्रसूतास्ता[49] नद्यः पुण्यजलाः शुभाः[50] ॥[51]

49. Mk, Krm *a*, Mts—विन्ध्यपादप्रसूतास्ताः; Vy, Bmd, Vmn—विन्ध्यपादप्रसूताश्च; Krm *bc*— विन्ध्यपादप्रसूतास्तु । For the Vindhya, see note 47 above.

50. Mk, Vy, Bmd, Vmn—नद्यः पुण्यजलाः शुभाः; Krm—सद्यः पापहरा नृणाम्, *b* (v. l.) *c* (v. l.) सद्यः पुण्यजलाः शुभाः; Mts—सर्वाः शीतजलाः शुभाः, *c* (v. l.)—नद्यः शीतजलाः शुभाः ।

51. Note that the short list in Section IX below wrongly speaks of some of these rivers as flowing from the Ṛkṣavat and not from the Vindhya. Vide note 41 above.

V

गोदावरी भीमरथी[52] कृष्णा बेण्वा च वञ्जुला[53] ।
तुङ्गभद्रा सुप्रयोगा[54] बाह्या काबेरी चैव तु[55] ॥

52. Mk *abc*—गोदावरी भीमरथा; Vy, Bmd, Mts, Vmn, Mk *d*, Krm *c*—गोदावरी भीमरथी; Krm *ab*—गोदावरी भीमरक्षी । The Godāvarī, still known by its ancient name, rises in the Western Ghats and flows through the Deccan into the Bay of Bengal. The Bhīmarathī or Bhīmarathā is the modern Bhīmā which is a tributary of the Kṛṣṇā.

53. Mk *ac*–कृष्णवेण्वा तथा परा, *bd*– कृष्णा वेण्या तथा परा; Vy *acde*, Bmd–कृष्णा वैण्यथ बञ्जुला; Krm *a*–कृष्णा वेणा च वैश्यता, *bc*– कृष्णा वेणा च वश्यता, *b* (v. l.)– कृष्णा वर्णा च पासरी; Mts– कृष्णवेणी च वञ्जुला; Vmn *a*– कृष्णवेण्या सरिद्वती, *b*– कृष्णा वेण्या सरिद्वती; Vy *b*–कृष्णा वैण्या सवञ्जुला। The Kṛṣṇā is still known by its ancient name and flows from the Western Ghats through the Deccan into the Bay of Bengal. The Veṇvā is the modern Veṇā which is a tributary of the Kṛṣṇā, the combined stream of the two rivers being often mentioned as Kṛṣṇaveṇā or Kṛṣṇaveṇī. The Vañjulā is no other than the modern Mañjīrā which is a southern tributary of the Godāvarī.

54. Mk, Vy, Bmd, Mts–तुङ्गभद्रा सुप्रयोगा; Vmn–विशमद्री सुप्रयोगा। The Tuṅgabhadrā is a well known tributary of the Kṛṣṇā.

55. Mk–बाह्या काधेर्यथापगा; Vy *acde*, Bmd–काबेरी च तथापगा; Krm–काबेरी च द्विजोत्तमा:; Mts–बाह्या काबेरी चैव तु; Vmn– बाह्या काबेरिरेव च; Vy *b*–पाजय (sic. ब्राह्या) काबेरी चैव तु। The Kāverī is the celebrated holy river of the southernmost part of India. It is mentioned by the Greek geographer Ptolemy as Khaberos as rising from the Adeisathron mountain range.

दक्षिणापथनद्यस्तु[56] सह्यपादाद्विनि:सृता:[57] ॥

56. Mk abc–विन्ध्य (sic. सह्य०) पादविनिष्कान्ता, *db* (v. l.)– सह्यपाद-विनिष्कान्ता; Vy, Bmd, Mts *a*, Krm–दक्षिणापथनद्यस्तु; Mts *bc*–दक्षिणापथनद्यस्ता:; Vmn–एताश्चापि महानद्य:, *b*– दुग्धोदा नलिनी चैव वारिसेना कलखना। एतश्चापि महानद्य: । Sahya is the name applied to that part of the Western Ghats which lies to the north of the Travancore hills. For the spurious addition of a line in Vmn *b*, cf. similar additions in a different work discussed by me elsewhere (*JRASB.*, Letters, vol. XIV, pp. 44, note 3, pp. 45, note 5, etc.).

57. Mk–इत्येता: सरिदुत्तमा:; Vy, Bmd, Mts, Krm *bc*–सह्यपादद्विनि:सृता:; Krm *a*–सह्यपादविनि:सृता:; Vmn–सह्यपादविनिर्गता: ।

VI

कृतमाला ताम्रपर्णी[58] पुष्पजा चोत्पलावती[59] ।
[60]मलयाभिजाता नद्य:[61] सर्वा: शीतजला: शुभा:[62] ॥

58. Mk, Vy *a;* Krm *a,* Mts, Vmn–कृतमाला ताम्रपर्णी; Krm *bc*–ऋतुमाला ताम्रपर्णी; Bmd, Vy *bcde* (v. l.)–कृतमाला ताम्रवर्णा; Vy *e*– कृतमाला ताम्रवर्णी। The Kṛtamālā is no other than the modern Vaigai running past Madura (cf. *Caitanya-caritāmṛta,* ch. IX). The Tāmraparṇī is now known as Tāmbravari which combines its stream with the Chittar in the Tinnevelly District of Madras.

59. Mk – पुष्पजासूत्पलावती; Vy, Bmd, Krm *a* – पुष्पजात्युत्पलावती; Mts – पुष्पजा ह्युत्पलावती; Vmn – वञ्जुला चोत्पलावती; Krm. *b* – पुष्पवत्युत्पलावती, *c* – पुण्यवत्युत्पलावती।

60. The following line is omitted in Vmn together with the two lines in Section VII following. Thus the Vmn text would make the rivers mentioned in Section VI flow from the Śuktimat mountain (cf. Section VIII below) apparently through mistake.

61. Mk – मलयाद्रिसमुद्भताः, Vy – मलयाभिजातास्ता नद्यः; Bmd – मलयाभिजाता नद्यः; Krm – मलयान्निःसृता नद्यः; Mts *a* – मलयप्रसूता नद्यः; *bc* – मलयप्रसूता नद्यस्ताः। Malaya (derived from the Dravidian word *malai* meaning 'hill') was the name applied to the Travancore hills and the southernmost part of the Western Ghats.

62. Mk – नद्यः शीतजलास्त्विमाः; Vy, Bmd, Mts – सर्वाः शीतजलाः शुभाः; Krm – सर्वाः शीतजलाः स्मृताः।

VII

[63]त्रिसामा ऋषिकुल्या च[64] इक्षुला त्रिदिवा च या[65]।
[66]लाङ्गुलिनी वंशधरा[67] महेन्द्रतनयाः स्मृताः[68]॥

63. The following two lines, as a already indicated above (note 60), are omitted in Vmn and are represented in Krm by one line reading ऋषिकुल्या त्रिसामा च गन्धमादनगामिनी without any reference to the range from which the rivers spring. Thus the Krm text would wrongly represent the rivers mentioned in Section VII as issuing from the Śuktimat (see Section VIII).

64. Mk – पितृसोमर्षिकुल्या च; Vy *acd* – त्रिसामा ऋतुकुल्या च, *b* – त्रिसागा ऋषिकुल्या च, *e* – त्रिसामा ऋतुकूल्या च; Bmd – त्रिसामा ऋषिकुल्या च; Krm – ऋषिकुल्या त्रिसामा च; Mts – त्रिभागा ऋषिकुल्या च। The Ṛṣikulyā, still bearing its ancient name, flows into the Bay of Bengal near Berhampur on the Bengal-Nagpur Railway in the Ganjam District of Orissa.

65. Mk – इक्षुका त्रिदिवा च या; Vy *acde,* Bmd – इक्षुला त्रिदिवा च या; Mts – इक्षुका त्रिदिवाचला; Vy *b* – इक्षुला त्रिदिवायना। Cf. त्रिदिवामिक्षुलां क्रिमिम् in *Mbh,* VI, 9, 17.

66. Mts reads for this line rather freely – ताम्रपर्णी तथा मूली शवरा (*c* – शरवा) विमला तथा। महेन्द्रतनयाः सर्वा प्रख्याताः शुभगामिनीः॥ It may be noted that *śubha-gāminīḥ* does not suit the context; Cf. Pargiter, *op. cit.*, pp. 78ff.

67. Mk *ac*—लाङ्गलिनी वंशकरा, *bd*— लाङ्गूलिनी वंशकरा; Vy *abd,* Bmd—लाङ्गलिनी वंशधरा; Vy *ce*—लाङ्गूलिनी वंशधरा। The Lāṅgulinī is the modern Lāṅguliyā running past Chicacole (Śrīkākulam) in the District of that name in Madras. The Vaṁśadharā, which is still known by the old name, runs past Kalingapatam near Chicacole.

68. Mk—महेन्द्रप्रभवा: स्मृता:; Vy, Bmd— महेन्द्रतनया: स्मृता:। Mahendra was the name applied to the Eastern Ghats.

VIII

[69]ऋषिकुल्या कुमारी च[70] मन्दगा मन्दवाहिनी[71]।

69. Vmn contracts the two following lines into one—शुनी चैव सुदामा च शुक्तिमत्प्रभवास्त्विमा: (*b*—शक्तिमत्०) while Krm reads rather freely—क्षिप्रा (*b* v. l. —रूपा) पलासिनी चैव ऋषीका वंशधारिणी (*b* v. l., *c* v. l—बलकारिणी, रसकारिणी)। शुक्तिमत्पादसञ्जाता: सर्वपापहरा नृणाम्॥

70. Mk—ऋषिकुल्या कुमारी च; Vy *acde*— ऋषीका सुकुमारी च, *b*—ऋषीका सकुमारी च; Bmd—ऋषिका सुकुमारी च; Mts—काशिका सुकुमारी च। Cf. कुमारीमृषिकुल्याश्च in *Mbh,* VI, 9, 36, and note that in this case at least Mk seems to preserve the original reading (cf. note 91 below). Ray Chaudhuri's identification of Kumārī with the river of the same name in the Mānbhūm District in south Bihar seems to be quite probable in view of the plausibility of his identification of the *kula-parvata* called Śuktimat with the hills of eastern India extending from Chhattisgarh to the Santal Parganas (see note 73 below). The Ṛṣikulyā may be no other than the Koel in Chhota-Nagpur. Another Ṛṣikulyā is no doubt the Kiul, a tributary of the Ganges.

71. Mk. Vy *acde,* Bmd, Mts—मन्दगा मन्दवाहिनी; Vy *b*—बालुका मन्दवाहिनी; cf. Krm—गन्धमादनगामिनी and *Mbh,* VI, 9, 33—मन्दगां मन्दवाहिनीम्।

कूपा पलाशिनी चैव[72] शुक्तिमत्प्रभवा: स्मृता:[73]॥

72. Mk *abc,* Vy *e* (v. l.)—कृपा पलाशिनी चैव; Mk *c* (v. l.)—कृशा पलाशिनी चैव, *d*— कुशा पलाशिनी चैव; Vy *acde*—कूपा पलाशिनी चैव, *b*— किर्पा (sic. कृपा) पलासिनी चैव; Bmd—कुपा पलाशिनी चैव; Krm— क्षिप्रा पलाशिनी चैव; Mts— कृपा च पाशिनी चैव। Raychaudhuri identifies the Kūpā with the modern Kopā, a tributary of the Bāblā in Eastern India, and the Palāsinī with the modern Parās, a tributary of the Koel in Chhota-Nagpur.

73. Mk *abc,* Vy, Bmd—शुक्तिमत्प्रभवा: स्मृता:; Mk *d*— शुचिमत्प्रभवा: स्मृता:; Mts— शुक्तिमन्तात्मजास्तु ता:. The name of the Śuktimat is preserved in that of the Śakti hills in Raigarh, Madhya Pradesh, and possibly in

that of the Suktel river which joins the Mahānadī near Sonepur (Orissa). "The name Śuktimat was probably applied to the chain of hills that extends from Sakti in Raigarh, C.P., to the Dalma hills in Mānbhūm drained by the Kumārī and perhaps even to the hills in the Santal Parganas washed by the affluents of the Bāblā" (Raychaudhuri, *op. cit.*, pp. 120).

IX

[Vsn, II, ch. 3, vv. 9-13; Bmh, ch. 19, vv. 10-14; cf. Sv, Dharmasaṃhitā, ch. 34. vv. 9-12; Agn, ch. 118, vv. 6-8].

[74]शतद्रुश्चन्द्रभागाद्या[75] हिमवत्पादनिर्गताः[76] ।
वेदस्मृतिमुखाद्याश्च[77] पारियात्रोद्भवा मुने[78] ॥

74. This line is omitted in Sv and Agn.

75. Vsn, Bmh – शतद्रुचन्द्रभागाद्याः । (See note 4 above).

76. Vsn – हिमवत्पादनिर्गताः; Bmh – हिमवत्पादनिःसृताः (see note 14 above).

77. Vsn – वेदस्मृतिमुखाद्याश्च; Bmh – वेदस्मृतिमुखाश्चान्याः; Sv, Agn – वेदस्मृतिमुखा नद्यः । (See note 16 above).

78. Vsn – पारिपात्रोद्भवा मुने; Bmh, Sv – पारियात्रोद्भवा मुने; Agn – पारिपात्राद्भवास्तथा (See note 25 above).

[79]नर्मदासुरसाद्याश्च[80] नद्यो विन्ध्याद्रिनिर्गताः[81] ।
[82]तापीपयोष्णीनिर्विन्ध्याप्रमुखा ऋक्षसम्भवाः[83] ॥
[84]गोदावरीभीमरथीकृष्णवेण्यादिकास्तथा[85] ।
सह्यपादोद्भवा नद्यः स्मृताः पापभयापहाः[86] ॥
[87]कृतमाला ताम्रपर्णी प्रमुखा मलयोद्भवाः[88] ।
त्रिसामा ऋषिकुल्याद्या[89] महेन्द्रप्रभवाः स्मृताः[90] ॥

79. For the following line, Sv has – नर्मदासुरसाद्याश्च सन्त्यन्याश्च सहस्रशः । विन्ध्योद्भवा महानद्यः सर्वपापहराः शुभाः ॥ Agn has – विन्ध्याश्च नर्मदाद्याः स्युः सह्यात् (sic ऋक्षात्) तापी पयोष्णिका ।

80. Vsn – नर्मदासुरसाद्याश्च; Bmh – नर्मदासुरमाद्याश्च (See note 28 above).

81. Vsn – नद्यो विन्ध्याद्रिनिर्गताः; Bmh – नद्यो विन्ध्यविनिःसृताः । Note that the source of the Narmadā group of rivers is actually the Ṛkṣavat and not the Vindhya; vide note 41 above.

82. For the following line, Bmh has – तापीपयोष्णीनिर्विन्ध्याकावेरी-प्रमुखा नदीः । ऋक्षपादोद्भवा ह्येताः श्रुताः पापं हरन्ति याः ॥ For the wrong *vibhakti* in *nadīḥ,* see note 66 above. Note that the Tāpī and Kāverī are wrongly grouped together as rivers issuing from the Ṛkṣavat (see notes 43, 49, 55, 57 above). This line is omitted in Sv.

83. Vsn—तापीपयोष्णीनिर्विन्ध्याप्रमुखा ऋक्षसम्भवाः। Note that these rivers actually flow from the Vindhya and not from the Ṛkṣavat (see notes 41, 51 above).

84. For the following two lines, Sv has—गोदावरीभीमरथीतापीप्रमुखतोयगाः। विन्ध्याद्रिनिर्गताः पुण्याः स्नानात् पापभयापहाः॥ सह्यपादोद्भवा नद्यः कृष्णवेण्यादिकास्तथा॥

85. Vsn, Bmh—गोदावरी भीमरथी कृष्णवेण्यादिकास्तथा; Agn— गोदावरी भीमरथी कृष्णवेण्वादिकास्तथा।

86. Vsn, Bmh—सह्यपादोद्भवा नद्यः स्मृताः पापभयापहाः।

87. Agn has rather freely—मलयात् कृतमालाद्यास्त्रिसामाद्या महेन्द्रजाः। कुमाराद्याः शुक्तिमतो हिमाद्रेश्चन्द्रभागका॥

88. Vsn, Bmh—कृतमालाताम्रपर्णीप्रमुखा मलयोद्भवाः।

89. Vsn—त्रिसामा चार्ष्यकुल्याद्याः; Bmh— त्रिसान्ध्य ऋषिकुल्याद्याः; Sv—त्रियामा ऋषिकुल्याद्याः (See note 64 above).

90. Vsn, Bmh, Sv—महेन्द्रप्रभवाः स्मृताः (See note 68 above).

ऋषिकुल्याकुमार्यद्याः[91] शुक्तिमत्पादसम्भवाः[92] ॥[93]

91. Vsn, Sv—ऋषिकुल्याकुमार्याद्याः; Bmh— ऋषिकुल्याकुमाराद्याः (See note 70 above).

92. Vsn, Sv, Bmd—शुक्तिमत्पादसम्भवाः (See note 73 above).

93. Grd (I, ch. 56, 8-10) reads rather freely—वेदस्मृतिर्नर्मदा च वरदा सुरसा शिवा। तापी पयोष्णी सरयूः कावेरी गोमती तथा॥ गोदावरी भीमरथी कृष्णवेणी महानदी। केतुमाला ताम्रपर्णी चन्द्रभागा सरस्वती॥ ऋषिकुल्या च कावेरी मर्त्त्यगङ्गा पयस्विनी। विदर्भा च शतद्रुश्च नद्यः पापहराः शुभाः॥ Bgvt (V, ch. 19, section 17) has in prose—चन्द्रवशा ताम्रपर्णा अवटोदा कृतताला वैहायसी कावेरी वेण्वा पयस्विनी शर्करावर्त्ता तुङ्गभद्रा कृष्णवेण्वा भीमरथी गोदावरी निर्विन्ध्या पयोष्णी तापी रेवा सुरसा नर्मदा चर्मण्वती अन्ध्रः शोणश्च नदौ महानदी ववेदस्मृति ऋषिकुल्या त्रिसामा कौशिकी मन्दाकिनी यमुना सरस्वती दृशद्वती गोमती सरयुरोधवती षष्ठवती सप्तवती सुषोमा शतद्रुश्चन्द्रभागा मरुद्वृधा वितस्ता असिक्तो विश्वेति महानद्यः॥ Cf. Km (pp. 93-94) : (a) पूर्वदेश—शोणलौहित्यौ नदौ गङ्गाकरतोयाकपिशाद्याश्च नद्यः। (b) दक्षिणापथ—नर्मदातापीपयोष्णीगोदावरीकावेरीभैमरथीवेण्वाकृष्णवेण्वावञ्जुरातुङ्गभद्राताम्रपर्ण्युत्पलावती-रावणागङ्गाद्या इद्यः। (c) पश्चद्देश—सरस्वतीश्वभ्रवतीवार्तघ्नीमहीहिडिंवाद्या नद्यः। (d) उत्तरापथ—गङ्गासिन्धुसरस्वतीशतद्रु चन्द्रभागायमुनेरावतीवितस्ताविपाशाकुहूदेविकाद्या नद्य। For longer lists of rivers , see *Mbh,* VI, ch. 9, 14-36; *Varāha Purāṇa,* ch. 85, etc.

X

[Bmd, 51, vv. 40-60; Mts, ch. 121, vv. 39-51; Vy, ch. 47, vv. 38-48; cf. Sachau, *Alb. Ind.*, I, pp. 24-62.]

A

नद्याः स्रोतस्तु गङ्गायाः[94] प्रत्यपद्यत सप्तधा[95]।
नलिनी ह्लादिनी चैव[96] पावनी चैव प्रागगता[97]॥

94. Vy *adc,* Bmd—नद्याः स्रोतस्तु गङ्गायाः, *c*— नद्याः श्रोतस्तु गङ्गायाः; Mts—स्रोतांसि त्रिपथायास्तु। Note that Alberuni utilised in regard to this section the text of Mts; therefore here we shall have to speak of Mts *d* instead of Vy *b.* Thus Vy, when unspecified, would indicate here all the versions excepting Vy *b.*

95. Vy, Bmd—प्रत्यपद्यत सप्तधा; Mts—प्रत्यपद्यन्त सप्तधा।

96. Vy. Bmd, Mts *d*—नलिनी ह्लादिनी चैव; Mts *abc*—नलिनी ह्लादिनी चैव।

97. Vy *a*—पावनी चैव प्रागगता; Vy *cde*—पावनी चैव प्राग्गता; Mts—पावनी चैव प्राच्यगा।

सीता चक्षुश्च सिन्धुश्च[98] प्रतीचीं दिशमाश्रिताः[99]।
सप्तमी त्वनुगा तासां[100] दक्षिणेन भगीरथम्[101]॥
तस्माद्भागीरथी या सा[102] प्रविष्टा दक्षिणोदधिम्[103]॥

98. Vy, Mts, Bmd—सीता चक्षुश्च सिन्धुश्च।

99. Vy, Bmd—प्रतीचीं दिशमाश्रिताः; Mts—तिस्रस्ता वै प्रतीच्यगाः।

100. Vy, Mts—सप्तमी त्वनुगा तासां; Bmd—सप्तमी समानीता।

101. Vy *acd*—दक्षिणेन भागीरथीं; Vy *e,* Mts— दक्षिणेन भगीरथम्; Bmd—भगीरथमहात्मना।

102. Vy *a*—अस्माद् भागीरथी या सा, *cde,* Bmd— तस्माद् भागीरथी या सा; Mts—तस्माद् भागीरथी सा वै। For these seven rivers, cf. *Rāmāyaṇa* (I, 43, 11-14; 44, 6): विसमर्ज ततो गङ्गां हरो विन्दुसरः प्रति। तस्यां विसृज्यमानायां सप्तस्रोतांसि जज्ञिरे॥ ह्लादिनी पावनी चैव नलिनी च तथैव च। तिस्रः प्राचीं दिशं जग्मुर्गङ्गाः शिवजलाः शुभाः॥ सुचक्षुश्चैव सीता च सिन्धुश्चैव महानदी। तिस्रश्चैता दिशं जग्मुः प्रतीचीन्तु दिशं शुभाः॥ सप्तमी चान्वगात्तासां भगीरथरथन्तदा।.......त्रीन् पथो भावयन्तीति तस्मात् त्रिपथगा स्मृता॥ Of the seven streams, there is no difficulty about the identification of the Gaṅgā or Bhāgīrathī which is no other than the Ganges and of the Sindhu which is the Indus. The western stream Cakṣu is also apparently the same as Vakṣu or Vaṁkṣu, i.e., the Oxus or Amu Darya, while the second western river called Sītā may be no other than the Jaxartes or Syr Darya. As the eastern stream Hlādinī or Hrādinī is said to have

run through the country of the Kirātas, who were hill-men inhabiting the eastern Himālayas, this river may be tentatively identified with the upper Brahmaputra. Indradvīpa, through which the other eastern river called Pāvanī passed, is identified by some scholars with Burma (see note 167 below). This river may thus be tentatively identified with the Irawadi. See note 164 below on Vetrapatha and Śaṅkupatha (in Suvarṇabhūmi) through which the Pāvanī is said to have passed. The third eastern stream called Nalinī cannot be identified; but it is said to have entered into the sea in the Śaimi-*maṇḍala* which reminds us of Siam. [The name of Siam (Syāma-raṭṭha), which is unconnected with Sanskrit *śyāma,* is derived from that of a tribe called in Chinese *Sien,* Burmese *Shan,* Malayan *Syam,* Annamite *Xiem* and Cham *Syāṁ.*]. The Nalinī may thus be tentatively identified with the Salween or the Mekong. It must be remembered that the theory attributing the origin of all the seven rivers to the same lake in the Himālayas has to be regarded as a mere flight of fancy. The lists of countries washed by the rivers do not appear to be always accurate.

103. Vy. Mts *a,* Bmd—प्रविष्टा लवणोदधिम्; Mts *bc*—प्रविष्टा दक्षिणोदधिम्।

सप्तैता भावयन्तीह[104] हिमाह्वं वर्षमेव तु[105]।
प्रसूताः सप्त नद्यस्ताः[106] शुभा विन्दुसरोद्भवाः[107]।
नानादेशान् भावयन्त्यो[108] म्लेच्छप्रायांश्च सर्वशः[109]।
[110]उपगच्छन्ति ताः सर्वा[111] यतो वर्षति वासवः[112]॥

104. Vy. Bmd—सप्तैता भावयन्तीह; Mts—सप्त चैता प्लावयन्ति।

105. Vy. Bmd—हिमाह्वं वर्षमेवतु; Mts *a*—वर्षन्ति हिमसाह्वयम्, *bc*—वर्षं तु हिमसाह्वयम्। The Hima *varṣa* was otherwise called Haimavata or Bhārata *varṣa* (Bmd, I, 33, 55, etc.) lying between the Himālayas and the sea.

106. Vy, Bmd—प्रसूताः सप्त नद्यस्ताः; Mts— प्रसूताः सप्त नद्यस्तु।

107. Vy, Bmd, Mts—शुभा विन्दुसरोद्भवाः।

108. Vy *a*—नानादेशान् भावयन्तो, *d*— नानादेशान् भावयन्यो; Bmd, Vy *ce*—नानादेशान् भावयन्त्यो; Mts—तान् देशान् प्लावयन्ति स्म।

109. Vy, Mts, Bmd—म्लेच्छप्रायांश्च सर्वशः। cf. note 143 below.

110. The following line is omitted in Mts.

111. Vy, Bmd—उपगच्छन्ति ताः सर्वाः।

112. Vy, Bmd—यतो वर्षति वासवः।

B

सिरीन्ध्रान् कुकुरांश्चीनान्[113] वर्वरान् यवनान् शकान्[114]।
रुषाणांश्च कुणिन्दांश्च[115] अङ्गलोकवरांश्च यान्[116] ॥
कृत्वा द्विधा हिमवन्तं[117] सीतागात् पश्चिमोदधिम्[118] ॥

113. Vy – सिरीन्ध्रान् कुन्तलांश्चीनान्; Mts *abc* – सशैलान् कुकुरान् रौध्रान्; Bmd – सिरीन्ध्रान् कुकुरांश्चीनान्; Mts *d* – सलिलान् कर्स्तुबांश्चोनान्। For the Cīnas, see *List of Peoples,* note 31.

114. Vy – वर्वरान् यवसान् द्रुहान्; Bmd – वर्वरान् यवनान् द्रुहान्; Mts *ab* – वर्वरान् यवसान् खसान्, *c* – वर्वरान् यवनान् खसान्, v. l. – वर्वरान् यवनाञ्छकान्, *d* – वर्वरान् यवसान् ब्रहान्। For the Varvaras and Yavanas, see *List of Peoples,* notes 30 and 20.

115. Vy, Bmd – रुषाणांश्च कुणिन्दांश्च; Mts *abc* – पुलिकांश्च कुलत्थांश्च, *d* – पुष्करांश्च कुलतांश्च। For the Kuṇindas, see *L. P.,* note 22, although the people indicated here must have lived in Central Asia. The Ruṣūṇas were the people of Roshan in the Tadzhik Republic.

116. Vy, Bmd – अङ्गलोकवराश्च ये; Mts *abc* – अङ्गलोक्यान् वरांश्च यान्, *d* – मङ्गलकवरांश्च यान्। See *L. P.,* note 30.

117. Vy – कृत्वा द्विधा सिन्धुमरुं; Bmd – कृत्वा द्विधा सिन्धुमेरुं; Mts *abc* – कृत्वा द्विधा हिमवन्तं, *d* – कृत्वा द्विधा सङ्गवन्तं।

118. Vy, Bmd, Mts *d* – सीतागात् पश्चिमोदधिम्; Mts *abc* – प्रविष्टा दक्षिणोदधिम्।

C

अथ चीनमरूंश्चैव[119] तङ्गनान् सर्वशूलिकान्[120]।
साध्रांस्तुषारान् लम्पाकान्[121] पह्लवान् पारदान् शकान्[122] ॥
एतान् जनपदांश्चक्षुः[123] प्लावयन्ती गतोदधिम्[124] ॥

119. Vy, Bmd, Mts *ad* – अथ चीनमरूंश्चैव; Mts *bc* – अथ वीरमरूंश्चैव।

120. Vy *ac,* Bmd – तङ्गणान् सर्वमूलिकान्, *cd* – नङ्गणान् सर्वमूलिकान्, *e* (v. l.) – तङ्गणान् सर्वशूलिकान्; Mts *a* – कालिकांश्चैव चूलकान्, *bc* – कालिकांश्चैव शूलिकान् *d* – कालिकांश्चैव धूलिकान्। For the Taṅgaṇas and Cūlikas, see *L.P.,* notes 41 and 36. The correct reading of the last name may be *Cūlikān.*

121. Vy *ace* – सान्ध्रांस्तुषारांस्तम्पाकान्, *d* – साध्रांस्तुषारांस्तम्पाकान्; Mts *abc* – तुषारान् वर्वराकारान्, *d* – तुखारान् वर्वराकारान्; Bmd – साध्रांस्तुषारान् लम्पाकान्। For the Tuṣāras or Tukhāras and the Lampākas, see *L. P.,* note 31 and 35.

122. Vy *a* – पह्वान् दरदान् शकान्; Bmd, Vy *cde* – पह्लवान् दरदान् शकान्; Mts *abc* – पह्लवान् पारदान् शकान्, *d* – बारवाञ्चतान् (sic. पारदाञ्छकान्)। See *L. P.,* notes 19, 23.

123. Vy, Bmd, Mts – एतान् जनपदांश्चक्षुः ।

124. Vy *ac* (v. l.) *e* – प्लावयन्ती गतोदधिम्, *cde* (v. l.), Bmd – स्रावयन्ती गतोदधिम्; Mts – प्लावयित्वोदधिं गता ।

D

दरदांश्च सकाश्मीरान्[125] गान्धारान् औरसान् कुहून्[126] ।
शिवपौरान् इन्द्रमरून्[127] वसातींश्च विसर्जयान्[128] ॥

125. Vy, Bmd – दारदांश्च सकाश्मीरान्; Vy *e* (v. l.) – मरदांश्च सकाश्मीरान्; Mts *abc* – दरदोर्ज्जगुडांश्चैव, *d* – दरदजिन्दुतुन्दांश्च । See *L. P.*, notes 29, 41.

126. Vy, Bmd – गान्धारान् वरपान् ह्रदान्; Mts *abc* – गान्धारान् औरसान् कुहून्, *d* – गान्धारान् रूरसान् (sic. औरसान्) कूरान् । See *L. P.*, notes 20, 38. The Kuhus appear to have been the people inhabiting the valley of the Kuhu or Kabul river.

127. Vy, Bmd – शिवपौरान् इन्द्रहासान्; Mts – शिवपौरान् इन्द्रमरून् । The Śivapauras must have been the inhabitants of Śivapura, i.e. the modern Shorkot in the Jhang District of the Panjab.

128. Vy – वदातींश्च विसर्जयान्; Bmd – वसातींश्च विसर्जयान्; Mts *abc* – वसतीन् समतेजसम्, *d* – सबातीन् (sic. वसातीन्)... The Vasātis (Ossadioi of the Greeks) appear to have "occupied parts of the territory drained by the lower Acesines (Chenab) and situated between the confluence of that river with the Rāvī and the Indus respectively".

सैन्धवान् रन्ध्रकरकान्[129] भ्रमराभीररोमकान्[130] ।
शुनामुखांश्चोर्द्धमरून्[131] सिन्धुरेतान्निषेवते[132] ॥

129. Vy, Bmd – सैन्धवान् रन्ध्रकरकान्; Vy *a* (v. l.) – सैन्धवान् रन्ध्रवरकान्; Mts *abc* – सैन्धवानुर्वसान् वर्वान्, *d* – सैन्धवान् कुबतान् (sic. कूपथान्)...Other names in *Alb. Ind.* are Bahīmarvara, Mara, Mrūna and Sukurda which are apparently due to mistakes in the Arabic manuscripts of Alberuni's work consulted by Sachau. For the Saindhavas see *L. P.*, note 21 and for the variant readings of the other name, *ibid.*, note 24.

130. Vy – भ्रमराभीररोहकान्, *e* (v. l.) – भ्रमटाभीररोहकान्; Bmd – भ्रमराभीररोमकान्; Mts *abc* – कुगथान् भीमरोमकान् । *L. P.*, note 17 would suggest आभीरान् कालतोयकान् । But the Romakas may be the people of Rumā living probably near the Salt Range.

131. Vy Bmd – शुनामुखांश्चोर्द्धमनून्; Mts *abc* – शुनामुखांश्चोर्द्धमरून् ।

132. Vy – सिद्धचारणसेवितान्, *c* (v. l.), Mts *abc*, Bmd – सिन्धुरेतान्निषेवते ।

E

गन्धर्वान् किन्नरान् यज्ञान्[133] रक्षोविद्याधरोरगान्[134] ।
कलापग्रामकांश्चैव[135] तथा किंपुरुषान् खसान्[136] ॥

133. Vy, Mts, Bmd – गन्धर्वान् किन्नरान् यक्षान्। Alberuni explains the Gandharvas as musicians. These names originally indicated certain tribal peoples, although later they came to imply classes of mythical beings. The Kinnaras and Yakṣas were probably names applied to some Himālayan tribes, while Gandharva appears to have been the original name of the people later called Gandhāra (cf. *Rām.*, VII, 101, 11: तक्षं तक्षशिलायां तु पुष्कलं पुष्कलावते। गन्धर्वदेशे रुचिरे गान्धारविषये च सः ॥ etc.). The names however seem to have been used in the present context in the sense of the mythical tribes.

134. Vy, Bmd, Mts – रक्षोविद्याधरोरगान्। Alberuni explains the Uragas as those who creep on their breasts, i.e. the serpents. These three names, like those mentioned in note 133 above, originally indicated certain non-Aryan tribal peoples but were later used to indicate mythical tribes. They appear to be used in the present context in the mythical sense.

135. Vy, Bmd, Mts – कलापग्रामकांश्चैव। Alberuni explains Kalāpagrāma as the city of the most virtuous people.

136. Vy. Bmd – पारदान् सीगनान् खसान्, *e* (v. l.) – पारदांस्ताङ्गणान् खसान्; Mts *abc* – तथा किंपुरुषान् नरान्, *d* – तथा किंपुरुषान् खसान्। Alberuni explains the Khasas as mountaineers. The name Kimpuruṣa was originally applied to a Himālayan people but was later used to indicate a mythical tribe. The Khasas were a Himālayan tribe now represented by the Khakkas of Kashmir.

किरातांश्च पुलिन्दांश्च[137] कुरून् सभरतानपि[138] ।
पञ्चालकाशिमत्स्यांश्च[139] मगधाङ्गांस्तथैव च[140] ॥
ब्रह्मोत्तरांश्च वङ्गांश्च[141] ताम्रलिप्तांस्तथैव च[142] ।
एतान् जनपदानार्यान्[143] गङ्गा भावयते शुभा[144] ॥
ततः प्रतिहया विन्ध्ये[145] प्रविष्टा दक्षिणोदधिम्[146] ॥

137. Vy, Bmd, Mts – किरातांश्च पुलिन्दांश्च। Alberuni explains the Pulindas as hunters of the plains or robbers. For the Kirātas, see *L. P.*, note 15; the Pulindas were an aboriginal people inhabiting the Vindhyan region; but the name was later applied to Vindhyan mountaineers in general and still later to any aboriginal people. The meaning of *Kirāta,* originally a Himālayan tribe, was also similarly modified.

138. Vy, Bmd – कुरून् सभरतानपि; Mts – कुरून् वै भरतानपि। According to the epic and Purāṇic traditions, the Kurus and the Bharatas belonged to the same clan. For the Kurus, see *L. P.*, note 2.

139. Vy, Bmd – पञ्चालकाशिमत्स्यांश्च; Mts *a* – पञ्चालकौशिकान् मत्स्यान्, *bc* – पाञ्चालान् कौशिकान् मत्स्यान्, *d* – पाञ्चालान् कौषकान् मत्स्यान। See *L. P.*, notes 2, 6 and 7. But *Matsya* may be a mistake for *Vatsa* which was the name of the people inhabiting the Allahabad region.

140. Vy, Bmd, Mts *abc* – मगधाङ्गांस्तथैव च। Mts *d* omits *Aṅga*. See *L. P.*, notes 46 and 56.

141. Vy, Bmd, Mts *abc* – ब्रह्मोत्तरांश्च वङ्गांश्च; Mts *d* omits *Vaṅga*. See *L. P.*, notes 46 and 52.

142. Vy, Bmd, Mts – ताम्रलिप्तांस्तथैव च। See *L. P.*, note 55.

143. Vy, Bmd, Mts – एतान् जनपदान् आर्यान्। Cf. the reference here to *ārya* with *mleccha-prāyāṁś=cha sarvaśaḥ* in note 109 above.

144. Vy, Bmd – गङ्गा भावयते शुभान्; Mts, Vy *e* (v. l.) – गङ्गा भावयते शुभा।

145. Vy, Bmd, Mts – ततः प्रतिहता विन्ध्ये।

146. Vy, Bmd, Mts – प्रविष्टा दक्षिणोदधिम्।

F

ततश्च ह्लादिनी पुण्या[147] प्राचीनाभिमुखं ययो[148]।
प्लावयन्त्युपकानांश्च[149] निषादानपि सर्वशः[150]॥
धीवरानृषिकांश्चैव[151] तथा नीलमुखानपि[152]।
केकरानुष्ट्रकर्णांश्च[153] किराताऩपि चैव हि[154]॥
कालोदरान् विवर्णांश्च[155] कुशिकान् स्वर्गभूमिकान्[156]।
सा मण्डले समुद्रस्य[157] तिरोभूतानुपूर्वतः[158]॥

147. Vy – ततश्चाह्लादिनी पुण्या; Bmd – ततश्च ह्लादिनी पुण्या; Mts – ततस्तु ह्लादिनी पुण्या।

148. Vy *ac* – प्राचीनाभिमुखं ययौ; Mts *bc*, Vy *de* – प्राचीनाभिमुखी ययौ; Vy *e* (v. l.), Mts *a* – प्राचीनाभिमुखा ययौ; Bmd – प्राचीमाभिमुखी ययौ।

149. Vy, Bmd – प्लावयन्त्युपभोगांश्च; Mts *abc* – प्लावयन्त्युपकांश्चैव, *d* – प्लावयन्त्युपकानांश्च।

150. Vy, Bmd – निषादानाञ्च जातयः; Mts *abc* – निषादानपि सर्वशः, *d* – निषावानपि (sic.) सर्वशः।

151. Vy, Mts *abc* – धीवरानृषिकांश्चैव; Bmd – धीवरानृषकांश्चैव; Mts *d* – धीवरान् प्रिषकांश्चैव।

152. Vy, Bmd, Mts – तथा नीलमुखानपि।

153. Vy, Bmd – केरलानुष्ट्रकर्णांश्च; Vy *e* (v. l.) – केरलानोष्टकर्णांश्च; Mts *abc* – केकरान् एककर्णांश्च। *c* (v. l.) *d* – केकरान् उष्ट्रकर्णांश्च। Alberuni explains the Uṣṭrakarṇas as a people whose lips are turned like their ears possibly through a confusion of the word *uṣṭra* with *oṣṭha*.

154. Vy, Bmd, Mts – किराताननपि चैव हि।

155. Vy, Bmd – कालोदरान् विवर्णांश्च; Mts *abc* – कालञ्जरान् विवर्णांश्च, *c* (v. l.) – कालिन्दगतिकांश्चैव, *d* – कलीदरान् विवर्णांश्च। Alberuni explains Vivarṇa as the colourless people so called on account of their intensely black complexion.

156. Vy, Bmd – कुमारान् स्वर्णभूषितान्; Vy *e* (v. l.) – कुमारीस्वर्णभूषितान्; Mts *abc* – कुशिकान् स्वर्गभीमकान्, *c* (v. l.), *d* – कुशिकान् स्वर्गभूमिकान्, कुशिकान् पर्णभूमिकान्। Alberuni explains Svargabhūmi as a country like paradise.

157. Vy, Bmd, Mts – सा मण्डले समुद्रस्य।

158. Vy, Bmd – तारोभूतानुपूर्वतः; Mts *abc* – तीरे भूत्वा तु सर्वशः, *c* (v. l.) – तीरे भूत्वा चतुर्दश।

G

ततस्तु पावनी चैव[159] प्राचीमेव दिशं गता[160]।
कुपथान् प्लावयन्तीह[161] इन्द्रदुय्मप्रसरांस्यपि[162]॥
तथा खरपथांश्चैव[163] वेत्रशङ्कुपथानपि[164]।
मध्येनोद्यानकमरून्[165] कुथप्रावरणान् ययौ[166]॥
इन्द्रद्वीपसमुद्र तु[167] प्रविष्ठा लवणोदधिम्[168]॥

159. Vy, Bmd, Mts *d* – ततस्तु पावनी चैव, Mts *abc* – ततस्तु नलिनी चापि। Note that there is difference between the extant versions of Mts and those of Vy and Bmd, but that the Mts manuscript consulted by Alberuni supports Vy and Bmd.

160. Vy, Bmd – प्राचीमेव दिशं गता; Mts – प्राचीमेव दिशं ययौ।

161. Vy *acde* (v. l.), Bmd – अपथान् भावयन्तीह; Vy *e* – अपथान् प्लावयन्तीह; Mts – कुपथान् प्लावयन्ती सा। Alberuni explains Kupatha as a people who are far from sin. For names ending in *patha* or *mārga*, cf. Siddhapatha (*Rājatar.*, VIII, 557), the old name of the Sidau or Budil pass (14000 ft.) in Kashmir. See also note 164 below.

162. Vy, Bmd – इन्द्रद्युम्नसरोपि च; Mts – इन्द्रद्युम्नसरांस्यपि। Alberuni explains the passage as 'the cisterns of king Indradyumna'.

163. Vy, Bmd—तथा खरपथांश्चैव; Mts—तथा खरपथान् देशान्। Kharapatha reminds us of Ajapatha and Verāpatha, mentioned in the Buddhist *Niddesa* commentary, and the latter also by Ptolemy as Berabai which was not far from Takkola about the present istmus of Kra (cf. Majumdar, *Suvarṇadvīpa,* I, pp. 56-60; Lévi, *Etudes Asiatiques,* II, pp. 1-55). See note 164 below.

164. Vy, Bmd—इन्द्रशङ्कुपथानपि; Mts—वेत्रशङ्कुपथानपि। Śaṅkupatha is mentioned in the *Niddesa* commentary (cf. note 163 above) along with Verāpatha, Jaṇṇupatha, Ajapatha, Meṇḍhapatha, Chatrapatha, Vaṁśapatha, Śakuṇapatha, Muṣikapatha and Darīpatha. Vetrapatha (possibly called Vettādhāra or Vettācāra in the *Niddesa*) is mentioned in connection with Suvarṇabhūmi (the land beyond the eastern sea or the Bay of Bengal) in the *Bṛhatkathāślokasaṁgraha*. These extraordinary routes (passes ?) are also referred to in other early Indian works such as the *Vimāṇavatthu,* the *Tittira Jātaka,* the *Milindapañha,* Patañjali's comment on Pāṇini, V, 1, 77 and the *Gaṇapāṭha.* It has been suggested that the knowledge of the Far East exhibited by the *Niddesa* did not exist in India before the first century A.D. but that it is earlier than the third century A.D. The *Niddesa* list, with which the Purāṇic section under discussion may be contemporaneous, has been assigned to a date between the end of the first and the beginning of the third century A.D. Incidentally it may be pointed out that reference to knowledge of the Far East in the *Mahābhāṣya* points to a late date of the work in its present from as exactly suggested in *IHQ.,* XV, pp. 633 ff.

165. Vy *a*—मध्येनोद्याकमंराराान् *cde* (v. l.), Bmd—मध्येनोद्यानमस्कारान्; Vy *e*—मध्येनोद्यानमकरान्; Mts *abc*—मध्येनोज्जानकमरून्, *d*— मध्येनोद्यानमरूरान्।

166. Vy, Bmd, Mts *abc*—कुथप्रावरणान् ययौ; Mts *d*—कुशप्रावरणान् ययौ।

167. Vy, Bmd, Mts *a*—इन्द्रद्वीपसमुद्रे तु; Mts *bc*—इन्द्रद्वीपसमीपे तु, *c* (v. l.)—इन्द्रद्वीपसमुद्रान्ते। For the identification of Indradvīpa with Burma, see Cunningham, *Anc. Geog. Ind.,* ed. by Majumdar Sastri, pp. 751-52.

168. Vy, Bmd, Mts—प्रविष्टा लवणोदधिम्।

H

ततश्च नलिनी चागात्[169] प्राचीमाशां जवेन तु[170]।
तोमरान् भावयन्तीह[171] हंसमार्गान् सहूहुकान्[172]॥
पूर्वान् देशांश्च सेवन्ती[173] भित्त्वा सा बहुधा गिरीन्[174]।
कर्णप्रावरणांश्चैव[175] प्राप्य चाश्वमुखानपि[176]॥
सिक्ता पर्वतमरून् सा[177] गत्वा विद्याधरानपि[178]।
शैमिमण्डलकोष्ठे तु[179] प्रविष्टा सा महोदधिम्[180]॥

169. Vy, Bmd, Mts *d*—ततश्च नलिनी चागात्; Mts *abc*—ततस्तु पावनी प्रायात्। Note the differen000ce between the two versions; cf. note 159 above.

170. Vy, Bmd, Mts—प्राचीमाशां जवेन तु।

171. Vy *acde* (v. l.), Bmd—तोमरान् भावयन्तीह; Vy *e*—तोमरान् प्लावयन्तीह; Mts *abc*—तोमरान् प्लावयन्ती च, *d*—तामरान्, प्लावयन्ती च। See *L. P.*, note 40.

172. Vy *acd*—हंसमार्गान् सहूहुकान्, *c* (v. l.), Bmd— हंसमार्गान् बहूदकान्; Vy *e*—हंसमार्गान् सहूहुकान्; (sic.); Mts *abc*— हंसमार्गान् समूहकान्, *d*— हंसमार्गान् समूहुकान्। See *L. P.*, note 40.

173. Vy, Bmd, Mts *abc*—पूर्वान् देशांश्च सेवन्ती; Mts *d*—पूर्णान् देशांश्च सेवन्ती।

174. Vy, Bmd, Mts *d*—भित्त्वा सा बहुधा गिरीन्, Mts *abc*—भित्त्वा सा बहुधा गिरिम्।

175. Vy, Bmd—कर्णप्रावरणांश्चैव; Mts—कर्णप्रावरणान् प्राप्य। Alberuni explains *Karṇaprāvaraṇa* as a people whose ears used to fall down on their shoulders.

176. Vy, Bmd—प्राप्य चाश्वमुखानपि; Mts— गता साश्वमुखानपि। Alberuni explains *Aśvamukha* as a people with horse faces.

177. Vy, Bmd—सिकतापर्वतमरून्; Mts *abc*— सिक्ता पर्वतमेरुं सा, *d*— सिक्ता पर्वतमरुं सा। Alberuni explains *parvata-maru* as mountainous steppes.

178. Vy, Bmd—गत्वा विद्याधरान् ययौ; Mts—गत्वा विद्याधरानपि।

179. Vy—नेमिमण्डलकोष्ठे तु; Bmd—नेमिमण्डलमध्येन; Mts *ac*—शैमिमण्डलकोष्ठं तु, *b*— शौमिमण्डलकोष्ठं तु, *d*— रूमीमण्डलकोष्ठं तु। *Koṣṭhe* may be a mistake for *kacche*.

180. Vy, Bmd, Mts *d*—प्रविष्टा सा महोदपिम्; Mts *abc*—सा प्रविष्टा महत्सरः।

11

Text of the Puranic List of Peoples*

Dines Chandra Sircar

F. E. Pargiter made some interesting remarks in regard to the historical sections common to several of the Purāṇas. His views (cf. *The Purāṇa Text of the Dynasties of the Kali Age,* Oxford University Press, 1913, p. xxvi f.) may be summarised as follows. The *Bhv.* was the first Purāṇa to give an account of the dynasties of the Kali age and the *Mts, Vy* and *Bmd* got their accounts from it, though they as well as some other Purāṇas existed before the *Bhv.* Metrical accounts of the dynasties of North India grew up gradually, composed in ślokas in a literary Prakrit and recited by bards and minstrels. After the introduction of writing about the 7th century B.C., the accounts were composed and written down in or near Magadha in Māgadhī or Pāli. The *Bhv.* appropriated the Prakrit metrical accounts and converted the Prakrit ślokas into Sanskrit in the form of a prophecy uttered by Vyāsa. This reshaping was carried through generally but not yet completely, and revisions of the text with new inclusions were taking place from time to time. The account of the Andhras (Sātavāhanas) originally composed in North India and written in Kharoṣṭhī was incoporated into the text about the middle of the 3rd century A.D. The *Mts* borrowed the accounts from the *bhv* during the last quarter of the 3rd century. These *Bhv.* accounts which were still in Kharoṣṭhī and cannot now be traced in the extant text of the Purāṇa were revised during the first quarter of the 4th century and the revised text was borrowed by the *Vy* now represented by the Ms (*e* Vāyu of Pargiter) in the India Office Library. The text was revised again about the beginning of the second quarter of the 4th century and this version was adopted by the *Vy* and soon after by the *Bmd* (which may have copied from the *Vy*) and now constitutes their general versions. The *Vsn* next utilised the accounts about the end of the 4th century and condensed it in Sanskrit prose. About the 8th or the 9th century, the *Bgvt* (which in the main condensed the matter into new ślokas) drew its materials from the *Bmd* and more particularly from the *Vsn.* The *Grd* whose date is uncertain utilised the same materials but has a bald list of the kings in new Sanskrit ślokas. Since those times a quiet process of small emendation in details has been at work in these Purāṇas.

Some of the theories of Pargiter have been criticised. If we believe that the Brāhmī alphabet evolved out of the prehistoric Indus valley script, we should only speak of the growth of the popularity of writing and not of the introduction of writing about the 7th century B.C. The Andhras (Sātavāhanas) of the Deccan had nothing to do with the northwestern region of India where the Kharoṣṭhī script was prevalent; it is therefore difficult to believe that the historical accounts of this royal family were originally composed in northern (north-western ?) India and written in Kharoṣṭhī. The definite epochs suggested by Pargiter for the composition, revision or transmission of the particular texts are again no better than tentative. But from a study on the sections on cosmography and geography which are common to several of the Purāṇas, it appears that Pargiter is probably right as regards the chronological sequence of at least some of the Purāṇas with which he deals. As to the suggestion that the original of the historical sections of the Purāṇas was composed in Prakrit, we know that the theory has been contested by Keith (*JRAS.*, 1914, p. 1021 ff; 1915, p. 328 ff), though Winternitz (*HIL,* I, p. 524 n) seems to be inclined to agree with Pargiter. It is interesting to note that the geographical section exhibits Prakrit influence in such forms of the names as भरुकच्छ, वेदभ, ऋष्यवन्त, शुक्तिमन्ती, etc. It may be pointed out that the geographical sections, especially the list of *janapadas,* found in the *Bmd, Mk, Mts, Vmn* and *Vy* practically follow the same draft. The original draft seems to have been compiled for *Mts.* The *Vy* text appears to be the earliest copy from that of the *Mts.* The *Mk* probably copied the text from *Vy* at a slightly later date; but a little independence of the copyist in the arrangement of names in a few cases is noticed in this text. The *Bmd* furnishes us with a still later copy of the *Vy* text. The date of this copy is possibly not far removed from the time of Al-bīrūnī (*c.* 1030 A.D.) who is known to have consulted a Ms of *Vy* in giving a list of peoples after the Purāṇas. *Krm,* which like some other Purāṇas, copies the smaller draft of the *Janapada* list from the *Vsn,* has a fuller list of rivers probably after the *Vy.* The smaller drafts both of the list of peoples and of rivers appear to have been compiled from the bigger drafts in the *Mts* and *Vy* for the first time for the *Vsn.* Like that of the *Bmd,* the *Krm* text does not seem to be far removed in point of time from the date of Albīrūnī. The *Vmn* appears however to be the latest copy of the modified draft as found in the other texts. But in several cases the compiler of the *Vmn* shows a tendency to arrange the names rather independently, although in many cases he does not go much beyond the originals before him. The new readings introduced by later copyists of the original draft or its modifications appear to have been, in some cases, offered by way of improvement or correction, and it is sometimes difficult to determine the reading of the original draft. The fact however that even the late *Vmn* often leaves the mistakes of the other copies as they are probably points to the absence of any determined and persistent effort on the part of the copyists to deviate from the texts before them. It should be remembered that numerous mistakes had already crept into the *Vy* text as early as *c.* 1030 A.D. when Albīrūnī consulted a *Vy* Ms. The geographical section of the *Grd* exhibits considerable freedom, though it seems to have utilised the *Mk* section known as the *Kūrma-vibhāga*. The date of the *Grd* section seems to be close to that of the *Vmn,* as both add to the old description of the Kumārīdvīpa as पूर्व्वे किराता यस्यान्ते पश्चिमे यवनास्तथा, a new line placing the Turuṣkas in the north and Andhras in the south. As these Turuṣkas and Andhras appear to be no other than the Turkish Musalmans and the Kākatiyas respectively, the *Vmn* and *Grd* sections on geography could not possibly have been compiled much earlier than the 13th century. The *Sv* also contains the same reference.

Text

Mk. ch. 57 (ch. 54 in some versions), vv. 34-59; *Vy,* ch. 45, vv. 109-136, cf. Sachau, *Alb. Ind.*, I, pp. 299-300; *Bmd,* ch. 49, vv. 44-71; *Mts,* ch. 114, vv. 34-56; *Vmn,* ch. 13, vv. 36-58.

I

[1]तास्विमे कुरुपाञ्चाला:[2] शाल्वाश्चैव स-जाङ्गला:[3] ।
शूरसेना भद्रकारा[4] बोधा: सह-पटञ्चरा: (योधा: सह०, योधेया: स०)[5] ॥

1. The following two lines are omitted in Mk. Mbh (VI. 9, 39-40) however has—तत्रेमे कुरुपाञ्चाला: शाल्वा माद्रेय-जाङ्गला: । शूरसेना: पुलिन्दाश्च बोधा माला-स्तथैव च ॥ मत्स्या: कुशल्या: सौशल्या: कुन्तय: कान्ति-कोशला: । चेदि-मत्स्य-करूषाश्च भोजा: सिन्धु-पुलिन्दका: ॥ As to the janapadas of the Madhyadeśa, Vmn has rather freely—यत्स्था: (a—यस्या:) कुशूद्रा: किल कुण्डलाश्च (a—कण्ड०) पञ्चालकाश्चैव (a—०काश्च सह कौशिकैश्च । वृका: शका (a—शाका) बर्बर-कौरवाश्च कलिङ्ग-वङ्गाङ्ग जना-स्तथैते ॥ मर्मका मध्यदेशीया (a—०देशाबा) आभीरा: (a—अभीरा:) शाठ्यघानका: ॥

2. Mts—तास्विमे कुरुपाञ्चाला:; Vy, Bmd—तास्त्विमे कुरुपाञ्चाला: । For the Kuru country proper with its capitals at Hāstinapura in the present Meerut District and Indraprastha in the Delhi region, see PH, pp. 19-20, 113. For the Panchālas with their capitals at modern Rāmnagar in Bareilly Dist. and Kampil in Farrukhābād, ib, p. 114 f.

3. Vy, Bmd, Mts—शाल्वाश्चैव स-जाङ्गलाः ; Mbh—शाल्वा माद्रेय-जाङ्गलाः। For the six branches of the Śālva tribe, *Vj,* 1.3.I. 38-39. Jāṅgala is apparently the same as Kuru-Jāṅgala, see PH, p. 19 f. *Vj*—साल्वास्तु कारकुत्सी (Ac—क्षी) यास्तेषां त्वबयबाः परे। उदुम्बरास्तिलखला महा(द्र)कारा युगन्धराः। हु(भु)लिंगाः शरदण्डाश्च षट् साल्वावयवा इमे॥

Cf. the traditional verse referring to the constituting elements of the Sālva er Kārakukṣīya tribe that lived in the Panjab and adjoining regions of U.P. and Rajputana, quoted by grammarians, *Pre-Aryan and Pre-Dravidian in India,* p. 80.

4. Vy, Bmd, Mts—शूरसेना भद्रकाराः ; Mbh—शूरसेनाः पुलिन्दाश्च। The Bhadrakāras are apparently the same as the Madrakāras who were a branch of the Śālva tribe (supra, note 3) and inhabited the north eastern part of the Punjab or the adjoining regions. The Śūrasenas were a branch of the Yādavas and lived about Mathurā, PH, p. 117 f.

5. Vy *acde,* Bmd—बोधाः शतपथेश्वरैः ; Vy *b*—बोधाः सहपथेश्वरैः ; Mts—बाह्याः सहपटच्चराः ; Mbh— बोधाः मालास्तथैवच. The Paṭaccaras are known from Grd, I, 55, 11—पञ्चालाः कुरवो मत्स्या यौधेयाः सपटच्चराः। कुन्तयः शूरसेनाश्च मध्यदेशजनाः स्मृताः। For the Yodheya or Yaudheya tribe of Grd, PH, pp. 457-58.

मत्स्याः किराताः कुल्याश्च[6] कुन्तयः काशि-कोशलाः[7]।
आबन्ताश्च भुलिङ्गाश्च[8] मगधाश्चान्धकैः सह[9]॥
मध्यदेश्या जनपदाः[10] प्रायशोमी प्रकीर्त्तिताः[11]॥
[11] सह्यस्य उत्तरार्द्धे तु[12] यत्र गोदावरी नदी[13]।
पृथिव्यामिह कृतस्नायां[14] स प्रदेशो मनोरमः[15]॥

6. Vy *a*—वत्साः किसल्वाः कुल्याश्च, *b*—वत्साः किसद्याः कुल्याश्च, *c d e*—वत्साः किसष्णाः कुल्याश्च, *c* (v.l.) *e* (v.l.)—वत्साः किसष्टाः कुल्याश्च, *e* (v.l.) वत्साः किसज्याः कुल्याश्च; ; Bmd—वत्साः कुसट्टाः कुल्याश्च; Mk—मत्स्याश्चकूटाः कुल्याश्च; Mts— मत्स्याः किराताः कुल्याश्च। The first name is either Matsya (Jaipur-Alwar region) or Vatsa (Allahabad region). PH, pp. 111 f. Kirāta=Himalayan mountaineers; cf. the name of the Kirantis who once reigned over a large portion of Nepal. Kulya (adjective)=people belonging to a tribe.

7. Vy, Mk, Bmd, Mts—कुन्तलाः काशिकोशलाः ; Mts *c* (v.l.)—कुन्तयः काशिकोशलाः ; Mbh—कुन्तयः कान्तिकोशलाः. The reading कुन्तयः is supported by Grd, I, 55, 11 quoted supra, n. 5. The Kuntis were a branch of the Yādava tribe living apparently not far from the Mathurā region. The Kāśīs lived about Vārāṇasī (Benares). This Kośala is Uttara-Kossla with its capital at Ayodhyā (in the Fyzabad Dist). See PH. pp. 8 ff, 84 ff.

8. Mts – आवन्ताश्च कलिङ्गाश्च; Mk *a c* (v.l.) – अथर्वाश्च कलिङ्गाश्च, *b* – अथर्वाश्चार्कलिङ्गाश्च, *c* – अथवाश्चाकलिङ्गाश्च, *d* – अर्बुदाश्चार्कलिङ्गाश्च; *Bmd* – प्रथमाश्च कलिङ्गाश्च; Vy *ae* – अर्थपाश्च तिलङ्गाश्च, *cde* (v.l.) – अथ पार्श्वे तिलङ्गाश्च, *b* – अर्थयाश्वपु:लिङ्गाश्च (sic. अर्थपाश्च भुलिङ्गाश्च). The Bhuliṅgas were a branch of the Sālva tribe; cf. supra, note 3. The Āvantas are apparently the same as the Avantis who lived in West Malwa and had their chief city at Ujjain. PH, pp. 122-23.

9. Mk – मलकाश्च वृकैः सह; Bmd, Vy *acde* – मगधाश्च वृकैः सह, *b* – मषकाश्च वृकैः सह; Mts – मूकाश्चैवान्धकैः सह. Magadha = Patna and Gaya Districts of Bihār; PH. p. 94 ff. The Andhakas were a branch of the Yādava tribe and possibly lived originally not far from Mathurā. Later they appear to have migrated towards Kathiawar.

10. Mk – मध्यदेश्या जनपदाः ; Vy, Bmd, Mts – मध्यदेशा जनपदाः

11. Mk, Vy, Bmd – प्रायशोमी प्रकीतिताः ; Mts – प्रायशः परिकीर्तिताः

11a. The following lines including those referring to Govardhana are omitted in some of the *Vy* Mss. The verse is quoted in *Km*.

12. Vy *a* – सह्यस्य उत्तरार्द्धे तु, *cde* – सह्यस्य चोत्तरार्द्धे तु, *e* (v.l.) – सह्यस्य चोत्तरार्द्धं तु; Mk *a* – सह्यस्य चोत्तरे यस्तु, ; *bcd* – सहस्य चोत्तरे यास्तु; Bmd – सह्यस्य उत्तरान्ते तु। Sahya = the Western Ghats excluding the Travancore hills.

13. Mk, Vy, Bmd – यत्र गोदावरी नदी; Mts – तत्र गोदावरी नदी। The Puranic passage further refers to the holy place called Govardhana near Nasik on the Godāvarī river.

14. Vy, Bmd – पृथिव्यामिह कृत्स्नायां; Mk, Mts – पृथिव्यामपि कृत्स्नायां

15. Mk, Vy, Bmd, Mts – स प्रदेशो मनोरमः

II

वाह्लीका वाटधानाश्च[16] आभीराः कालतोयकाः[17] ।
अपरान्ताश्च (परान्ताश्चैव?) शू (क्षु?)द्राश्च[18] पह्लवाश्चर्मखण्डिकाः[19] ॥
गान्धारा यवनाश्चैव[20] सिन्धु-सौवीर-मद्रकाः[21] ।
शतद्रुजाः कुणिन्दाश्च[22] पारदा हारहूणका[23] ॥

16. Mk, Vy *ac*, Bmd, Mts, Vmn – वाह्लीका वाटधानाश्च, Vy *b* – वाह्लीका वाढवानाश्च, *de* (v.l.) – वाह्लीका वाढधानाश्च Valhīka = modern Balkh about the northern frontiers of Afghanistan.

17. Mk, Vy, Bmd, Mts – आभीराः कालतोयकाः ; Vmn *a* – अभीराः कालतोयदाः, *b* – अभिराः कालतोयदाः. For the Ābhīras who lived to the north of the Rajputana desert, see SS, p. 242 f. We may also think of Abiravān between Herat and Kandahar which may have been the original home of the Ābhīras.

18. Mk–अपरान्ताश्च शूद्राश्च, Vy *acde*, Bmd–अपरीताश्च शूद्राश्च; Vy *b* omits शूद्र; Mts *a*–पुरन्ध्राश्चैव शुद्राश्च, *bc*– पुरन्ध्राश्चैव शूद्राश्च, *c* (v.l.)–परान्धाश्चैव शूद्राश्च; Vmn–अपरान्तास्तथा शूद्रा: The Śūdras lived near the Ābhīras, SS, p. 242. Possibly we have to read परान्ताश्चैव in place of अपरान्ताश्च. As the Śūdras are mentioned below separately (note 27), we may possibly suggest Kṣ udra or kṣudraka, PH, p. 205.

19. Mk *ad*, Vy *de* (v.l.)–पह्लवाश्चर्मखण्डिका: ; Vy *acde*–पह्लवाश्चर्मखण्डिका: ; Mk *bc*, Bmd–पल्लवाश्चर्मखण्डिका: ; Mts–पल्लवाश्चात्तखण्डिका: ; Vmn–पल्लवाश्वसखेटका: Pahlava=the Pahlavis or Persians (Sasanians ?), Carmakhaṇḍika=people of Samarkand.

20. Mk *acd*, Vy, Bmd, Mts, Vmn–गान्धारा यवनाश्चैव; Mk *b*–गान्धारा गबलाश्चैव. Gandhāra=the Rawalpindi and Peshawar Districts, PH, p. 124 f. The ancient capitals of the country were Takṣaśilā and Puṣkalāvatī and Udabhāṇḍapura in the early medieval period. Yavana=Indo-Greek settlements in the north western part of the India and adjoining lands, cf. SS, p. 31.

21. Mk, Bmd, Mts *abe*–सिन्धुसौवीरमद्रका: ; Vy *acde*, Mts *c* (v.l.), Vmn–सिन्धुसौवीरभद्रका: ; Vy *b*–सिन्धुसौवीरमध्रका: । According to *alb. Ind.*, I, pp. 259-60, 300 Sauvīra was identical with Multān and Jahrawār which latter lay about fifty miles below the junction of the Jhelam and the Chenab.

22. Mk–शतद्रुजा: कलिङ्गाश्च; Vy *acde*–शकह्रदा: कुलिन्दाश्च; *e* (v.l.)–शका ह्रदा: कुणिन्दाश्च; Bmd–शका हूणा: कुलिन्दाश्च; Mts–शका द्रुह्या: पुलिन्दाश्च, *c* (v.l.)–शतद्रव(व:) पुलिन्दाश्च; Vy *b*– शकाद्रिहा ललित्ताश्च The ancient Kuṇindas are supposed to be represented by the modern Kunets of Kūlū and the Simla region; but they formerly appear to have extended into the Saharanpur and Ambala Districts where their coins have been discovered in large members. See Smith, *Cat.*, p. 161. Sātadruja=people of the Satlaj valley.

23. Bmd– पारदा हारहूणका: ; Mk–पारदा हारभूषिका: ; Vy *acde*–परिता हारपूरिका:; Mts–पारदा हारमूर्त्तिका:, *c* (v.l.)–परेता हारमूषिका:. Omitted in Vy *b*. The reading हारहूण is supported by Mbh, II, 32, 12, while Bs, XIV, 33. suggests हारहूर which is supported by Km. The Pāradas were the Parthians who lived in the Khorasan region. The Hārahūṇas or Hārahūras were probably a branch of the Huns who subjugated the whole land from Central Asia to Central India about the end of the 5th century A.D.

रमठाः कण्टकाराश्च[24] कैकेया दशमानकाः[25]।
क्षत्रियोपनिवेशाश्च[26] तथाशूद्रकुलानि च[27]॥
[28]काम्बोजा दरदाश्चैव[29] वर्वरा अङ्गलौकिकाः[30]।
चीनाश्चैव तुषाराश्च[31] बहुला बाह्यतो नराः[32]॥

24. Mk—माठरा बहुभद्राश्च, Vy *a*—रमठा रद्धकटकाः ; *cde*—रमटा रद्धकटकाः ; Bmd. रमणा रुद्धकटकाः ; Mts—रामठाः कण्टकाराश्च; Vmn— माठरोदकधाराश्च Omitted in Vy *b*.

25. Mk—कैकेया दशमालिकाः ; Bmd—केकषा दशमालिकाः ; Vy *ac*—केकया दशमाणिकाः, *de*—केकया दशमानिकाः ; Mts *a*—कैकेया दशमानकाः, *b*— कैकेया दशनामकाः, *c*—कैकेय्या दशनामकाः, *c* (v.l.)—कैकेय्या दशनामिकाः ; Vmn *a*—कैकेया दशमास्तथा, *b*— कैकेया दंशनास्तथा; Vy *e* (v.l.)— केशपा दशमाणिकाः Omitted in Vy *b*. For the Kekayas, PH, p. 52 ff.

26. Mk. Vy *acde,* Bmd— क्षत्रियोपनिवेशाश्च; Mts—क्षत्रियोपनिवेश्याश्च; Vmn—क्षत्रियाः प्रतिवैश्याश्च. Omitted in Vy *b.* For the Kṣatris, PH, p. 207.

27. Mk, Vy *acde,* Bmd—वैश्यशूद्रकुलानि च; Mts—वैश्याः शूद्रकुलानि च; Vmn— तथा शूद्रकुलानि च. Omitted in Vy *b.* See note 18 above.

28. The following two lines are omitted in Mts and partly in Vy *b*.

29. Mk, Vy *acde,* Bmd, Vmn—काम्बोजा दरदाश्चैव. The Kambojas probably lived in the land extending from the Rajauri valley in Kashmir to Kafiristan. The Daradas lived round Daratpurī in the upper valley of the Kishengaṅgā in northern Kashmir.

30. Mk *abc*—वर्वरा हर्षवर्द्धनाः ; Vy *acde*—वर्वराः प्रियलौकिकाः ; Mk *d*, Bmd—वर्वरा अंगलौकिकाः ; Vmn *a*—वर्वराश्चाङ्गलौकिकाः, *b*—वर्वराश्चाङ्गलोकिकाः. Aṅgaloka is also mentioned elsewhere in the Purāṇas; cf. List of Rivers, x. Varvara reminds one of Barbaricum, a port on the principal mouth of the Indus in the early centuries of the Christian era. But apparently the same people is also mentioned elsewhere; cf. List of Rivers, note 14.

31. Mk *ad*, Bmd, Vy *e* (v.l.)— चीनाश्चैव तुषाराश्च; Vy *acde*—पीनाश्चैव तुषाराश्च; Mk *bc*—चीनाश्चैव तुखाराश्च; Vmn— वेणाश्चैव तुषाराश्च. चीन=the Tibeto Chinese peoples. तुखार, तुषार—cf. Tukhāristān of the Arabs which included the old Bactria and indicated the mountainous country on both sides of the middle Oxus as far as Badakhshān, though the country to the south of the river was usually understood by the name (Wellhausen, *AKF,* tr. p. 430). *AA,* pp. 118-19.

32. Mk *abc*—बहुला बाह्यतो नराः ; Vy *acde*, MK *d*—पह्लवा बाह्यतोदराः ; Bmd— पह्लवाश्च क्षतोदराः ; Vmn—बहुधा बाह्यतो दराः ; Vy *b*— मल्लकोदराः (?), *c* (v.l.)—रत्नधाराः क्षतोदराः.

क्षत्रयोथ भरद्वाजा:[33] प्रस्थलाश्च दसेरका:[34]।
लम्पाकास्तल(श्चाब ?)गानाश्च[35] चूलिका जागुडै: सह[36]॥
[37]औपधा(औरसा ?)श्चानिभद्राश्च[38] किरातानाश्च जातय:[39]।
तोमरा हंसमार्गाश्च[40] काश्मीरास्तङ्गणास्तथा[41]॥
कुलूताश्चाहु(बाही ?)काश्चैव[42] ऊर्णा(हूणा ?) दर्वास्तथैव च[43]।
एते देशा उदीच्यास्तु[44] प्राच्यान् देशान् निबोधत[45]॥

33. Mk, vy *acde,* Bmd–आत्रेयाश्च भरद्वाजा: ; Mts *a*–क्षत्रयोथ भरद्वाजा:, *bc*–अत्रयोथ भरद्वाजा; Vmn–आत्रेया: सभरद्वाजा: ; Vy *b*–आत्रेयाश्च भरद्वका:

34. Mk *acd*–पुष्कलाश्च कशेरुका: ; *b*–पुष्कलाश्च कुशेरुका: ; Vy *acde,* Bmd–प्रस्थलाश्च कसेरुका: ; Mts–प्रस्थला: सदसेरका:, *c* (v.l.)–प्रस्थला: सहसौभका:; Vmn, Mk *c* (v.l.)–प्रस्थलाश्च दशेरका:. Both Prasthala and Puṣ kalāvataka are mentioned in the list of Vs, 16, 26, Rām, IV, 43, 11 locates Prasthala in the north, Puṣkala=people of Puṣklāvatī, modern Prang-Charsadda-Mir Ziyarat region near Peshwar. Daseraka=Maru, i.e. the Marwar region in Rajputana.

35. Mk–लम्पाका: शूलकाराश्च; Vy *acde,* Bmd–लम्पाकास्तनपाश्चैव; Mts *a*–लम्पाकास्तलनागाश्च, *bc*–लम्पाकास्तलगानाश्च, *c* (v.l.)–लम्पाकास्तङ्गणाश्चैव; Vy *e* (v.l.)–लम्पाकास्तानकाश्चैव, लम्पाकास्तनकाश्चैव, लम्पाकास्तनसाश्चैव, *b*–लम्पाकास्तालकूनाश्च. Lampāka=modern Laghman. The Āvagānas or Afghans are mentioned in Bs.

36. Mk–चुलिका जागुडै:सह; Vy *acde,* Bmd–पीडिका जुहुडै: सह; Vy *b*–सूलिकाजगरै: सह, *c* (v.l.)–चूडिका जुहुडै: सह; Mts–सैनिका: सह जाङ्गलै: ; Vmn–चूडिकास्तङ्गणै: सह । Jāguḍa=South Afghanistan with its capital at Ghazni.

37. The following three lines are omitted in Mts an Vy *b.*

38. Mk *a*–औपधाश्चालिभद्राश्च, *bd*–औपधाश्चानिमद्राश्च, *c*–औपधाश्चानिभद्राश्च; Vy *a*–अपसाश्चालिमद्राश्च; Bmd, Vy *cde*–अपगाश्चालिमद्राश्च; Vmn–अलसाश्चालिभद्राश्च. Aurasa=people of Urasā, modern Hazara Dist (Note 26 of List of Rivers).

39. Mk, Vy *acde*, Bmd, Vmn–किरातानाञ्च जातय:.

40. Mk–तामसा हंसमार्गाश्च; Vy *acde,* Bmd–तोमरा हंसमार्गाश्च; Vmn–तामसा कर्ममार्गाश्च. See note 110.

41. Mk *ac*, Vy *acde,* Bmd–काश्मीरास्तङ्गणास्तथा; Mk *b*–काश्मीरास्तुङ्गणास्तथा, *d*–काश्मीरास्तुमणास्तथा; Vmn– सुपार्श्वा गणकास्तथा. Kāśmīra=people of the upper Vitastā valley.

42. Mk—शूलिकाः कुहकाश्चैव; Vy *a*, Bmd—चुलिकाश्चाहुकाश्चैव; Vy *cde*—चूलिकाश्चाहुकाश्चैव; Vmn *a*—कुलूतो कुहिकाश्चूर्णाः, *b*— कुलूताः कुहिकाश्चूर्णा; Vy *e* (v.l.)— चूलिका बाहुकाश्चैव. For the Kulūtas, Allan, *Cat*, p. *c;* for the Bāhīkas, Sircar, *Sel. Ins.*, I, p. 276 n. (note 113).

43. Mk *ac*—जर्णादर्वास्तथैव च, *d*—ऊर्णादार्वास्तथैव च; Bmd, Mk *b*—ऊर्णादर्वास्तथैव च; Vmn— तूर्णपादाः सकुक्कुटाः ; Vy *acde*—पूर्णदर्वास्तथैव च. The reading suggested by another passage (note 113) is हूणादार्वा॰. The *Harṣacarita* places the Hūṇas in the Uttarāpatha apparently somewhere about the Western Panjab. Dārva=people of Dārvābhisāra which roughly comprised the Punch and Naoshera regions between the Jhelum and the Chenab.

44. Mk *abc*—एते देशा ह्युदीच्यास्तु, *d*—एते दशाह्युदीच्यास्तु; Vy *acde*, Bmd—एते देशाह्युदीच्याश्च; Mts— एते देशा उदीच्यास्तु. Vmn has rather freely— माण्डव्याः पानवीयाश्च उत्तरापथवासिनः

45. Vy *acde*, Bmd, Mts—प्राच्यान् देशान् निबोधत; Mk— प्राच्यान् देशान् निबोध मे

III

अङ्गा वङ्गा मुद्गरका[46] अन्तर्गिरिवहिर्गिरी[47] ।
[48]तथा प्रवङ्ग-वाङ्गेया[49] मलदा मल्लवर्त्तकाः[50] ॥
[51]ब्रह्मोत्तरा प्र(श्री ?)विजया [52]भार्गवाङ्गेय-मल्लकाः[53] ।
प्राग्ज्योतिषाश्च पौण्ड्राश्च[54] विदेहास्ताम्रलिप्तकाः[55] ॥
मल्ला मगध-गोनर्दाः[56] प्राज्या जनपदाः स्मृताः[57] ॥

46. Mk *abc*—अध्रारका मुदकराः ; *d*—अाध्रा वका मुद्गरकाः, *c* (v.l.)— अन्ध्रवाश्च मुद्गरकाः ; Vy *acde*, Bmd—अन्ध्रवाकाः सुजरकाः ; Vy *b*—अन्ध्रवाका मुद्रकरकाः ; Mts *ab*—अङ्गा वङ्गा मद्गुरकाः, *c*—अङ्गा वङ्गा भद्गुरकाः ; v.l. —अङ्गावङ्गा भद्रवकाः, अङ्गावङ्गा मद्गुरुकाः ; Vmn— अङ्गावङ्गा मद्गुरवाः. Aṅga and Vaṅga appear to have been separated from Āṅgeya and Vāṅgeya. Mudgaraka (modern Monghyr) is the same as Mudgara of Km and Mudgagiri of inscriptions. For Aṅga and Vaṅga, PH, pp. 91 f. SS. p. 30.

47. Mk *abc*—अन्तर्गिर्या वहिर्गिराः, *c* (v.l.)—अन्तर्गिरवहिर्गिराः ; Vy *acde*, Bmd, Mk *d*—अन्तर्गिरिवहिर्गिराः ; Mts—अन्तर्गिरिवहिर्गिरी; Vmn—स्वन्तर्गिरिवहिर्गिराः; Vy *b*— प्रान्तगिरवहिर्गिराः. Antargiri and Bahirgiri may be located towards the north of Prāgjyotiṣa (Assam) on the strength of Mbh, 11, 27, 1-3.

48. The line is omitted in Mts *ab*.

49. Mk *ac*—यथा प्रवङ्गारङ्गेयाः, *b*—तथा प्रवङ्गारङ्गेयाः ; *c* (v.l.)—तथा सवङ्गा वङ्गेयाः, *d*—तथा प्लवङ्गा रंगेयाः ; Vy *acde*—तथा प्रवंगवंगेयाः, *b*— तथा प्रथंगवंगेयाः; Bmd—तथा प्रवंगाा वङ्गाश्च; Vmn—तथा प्रवंगवाङ्गेयाः ; Mts *c*— ततः प्लवंगमातङ्गाः

50. Mk *abc*—मानदा मानवर्त्तिकाः, *c* (v.l.)—मालदा मालवर्त्तिकाः, *d*—मालदा मलवर्त्तिकाः ; Vy *acde*—मालदा मालवर्त्तिनः, *e* (v.l.)—मलदा मलवर्त्तिनः, मालवा मलवर्त्तिनः, *b*—मालवा मालवर्त्तिकाः ; Mts *c*—यमका मल्लवर्णकाः ; Bmd—मालदा मालवणिका; Vmn—मांसादा वलदन्तिकाः. The Maladas and Mallavartakas are also known from *Km;* cf. also note 95 below.

51. This Line is omitted in Vy *b.*

52. Mk *acd*—ब्राह्मोत्तराः प्रविजयाः ; Vy *acde.* Bmd, Vmn *a,* Mk *b*—ब्रह्मेत्तराः प्रविजयाः ; Vmn *b*— ब्रह्मोत्तराः प्राविजयाः, Mts *abc*—सुह्मोत्तराः प्रविजयाः, *c* (v.l.)—सह्मोत्तराः प्रविजयाः. The reading सुह्मोत्तर is not supported by Km which reads सुह्म (the ancient name of Rāḍha in south-west Bengal) and ब्रह्म or ब्रह्मोत्तर side by side. Brahmottara seems to be associated with the name of Burma which is derived from the the Mrama one of the three tribes that migrated into Burma and ultimately lent their name as a national designation to all Burmese. cf. List of Rivers, note 41. Śrīvijaya (modern Palembang in Sumatra) was the capital of the Śailendra emperors in the early medieval period. For a Barmhattar in Sarkar Satgaon, *AA*, p. 141.

53. Mk *abc*—भार्गवा ज्ञेयमल्लकाः, *d*—भार्गवा गेयमल्लकाः ; Vy *acde,* Bmd—भार्गवा गेयमर्थकाः ; Mts *abc*—मार्गवा गेयमालवाः ; *c* (v.l.)—भार्गवागेयमालवाः, भार्गवाश्चार्यगालवाः, मार्गवा ये च मालवाः ; Vmn *a*—भार्गवांगेयमर्यकाः, *b*—भार्गवांगेयमर्षकाः.

54. Mk—प्राग्ज्योतिषाश्च मद्राश्च; Vy—प्राग्ज्योतिषाश्च मुण्डाश्च; Bmd—प्राग्ज्योतिषाश्च पौण्ड्राश्च; Mts— प्राग्ज्योतिषश्च पुण्ड्रांश्च; Vmn—प्राग्ज्योतिषाः पृषध्राश्च. Prāgjuotiṣa=modern Gauhati Dist. of Assam and the adjoining region. Pauṇḍra=people of North Bengal with their city called पुण्ड्रनगर (later पुण्ड्रवर्द्धन) modern Mahāsthān in Bogra Dist.

55. Mk, Vy *acde,* Bmd, Mts, Vmn— विदेहास्ताम्रलिप्तकाः ; Vy *b*—आबिकास्ताम्रलिप्तिकाः. Videha=a people living in North Bihār and the adjoining region with their capital at Mithilā, modern Janakpur in the Nepalese Tarai. Tamraliptaka=people of the district round mod. Tamluk in south-west Bengal.

56. Mk *abc*—मल्ला मगधगोमन्ताः ; *d*—मल्ला मगधगोमेदाः ; Vy—माला मगधगोविन्दाः; Bmd—माला मगधगोनन्दाः ; Mts *a*—शाल्वमगधगोनर्द्राः, *bc*—शाल्वमागधगोनर्द्राः ; Vmn—माला मगधमानन्दाः For the Mallas, PH, p. 106 f. Note that Magadha was sometimes located in the Madhyadeśa (note 9) and sometimes in the Prācya. Vj which locates the Andhras

and Sālvas (cf. notes 46, 56) in East India apparently relied on erroneous texts of the Purāṇas. For Gonarda which beloned to East India only theoretically, see *JAHRS, IX.* i, p. 1ff.

57. Mk, Vy *a,* Bmd, Mts – प्राच्या जनपदाः स्मृताः ; Vmn – प्राच्या जनपदास्त्विमे; Vy *cde* – प्राच्यां जनपदाः स्मृताः.

IV

[58]अथापरे जनपदा[59] दक्षिणापथवासिनः[60] ।
पाण्ड्याश्च केरलाश्चैव[61] चालाः कुल्यास्तथैव च[62] ॥
सेतुका मूषिकाश्चैव[63] कुमारा वनवासकाः[64] ।
महाराष्ट्रा माहिषकाः[65] कलिङ्गाश्चैव सर्व्वशः[66] ॥
कावेराः सह चैषीका[67] आठव्याः शवराश्च ये[68] ॥

58. The following line is omitted in Vmn.

59. Mk, Vy, Bmd – अथापरे जनपदाः ; Mts – तेषां परे जनपदाः

60. Mk, Vy, Bmd, Mts – दक्षिणापथवासिनः

61. Mk *ac,* Vmn – पुण्ड्राश्च केरलाश्चैव; Mk *b* – पुण्ड्राश्च केवलाश्चैव; Vy, Bmd, Mts, Mk *d* – पाण्ड्याश्च केरलाश्चैव The Pāṇḍyas and Keraḷas lived about the Mādura-Ramnad-Tinnevelly region and Malabar respectively.

62. Mk *ac* – गोलाङ्गुलास्तथैव च, *b* – गोलाङ्गूलास्तथैव च, *d* – चोलाः कुत्यास्तथैव च; Vy, Bmd – चौल्याः कुल्यास्तथैव च; Mts – चोलाः कुल्यास्तथैव च; Vmn – चौडा कुल्याश्च राक्षस For the reading गोलाङ्गुल which seems to be a later emendation, see *Bs,* 16, 3. The Colas lived about the Tanjore and Trichinopoly districts of the Madras Presidency.

63. Mk – शैलूषा मूषिकाश्चैव; Vy, Bmd – सेतुका मूषिकाश्चैव; Mts – सेतुकाः सूतिकाश्चैव; Vmn – जानुका मूषिकादाश्च Setuka = people of Setybandha-Rāmeśvara. Mūṣika = probably the people living on the banks of the Musi now running by the town of Hyderabād (PH, p. 80).

64. Mk *abc* – कुसुमा नाम वासकाः, *d* – कुमारा वनवासकाः ; Vy *acde* – कुमना वनवासिकाः ; Bmd – कुनासा वानवासकाः ; Mts – कुपथा वाजिवासिकाः, *c* (v.l.) – कुपथा वाजिकाः शकाः, कुपथा वाजिकाशिकाः ; Vmn – कुमारादां महाशकाः ; Vy *b* – रुमना वनवासिका: The Vanavāsakas were the inhabitants of modern Banavasi in the North Kanara Dist. Kumāra = people of Cape Comorin?

65. Mk., Vy. Bmd, Vmn *a* – महाराष्ट्रा माहिषकाः ; Mts *a* – नवराष्ट्रा माहिषकाः; *bc* – नवराष्ट्रा माहिषिकाः ; Mk *d,* Vmn *b* – महाराष्ट्रा माहिषिकाः Mahārāṣṭra = modern Marāṭhā country. Māhiṣaka = people of the ancient Mahiṣaviṣaya in Mysore or of Māhiṣmatī on the Narmadā.

66. Mk, Vy, Bmd, Mts, Vmn—कलिङ्गाश्चैव सर्व्वशः ; Mts *c* (v.l.)—कपिलाश्चैव सर्व्वशः The Kalinga country originally comprised the present Puri and Ganjam Districts and the adjoining regions.

67. Mk—आभीराः सहवैशिक्याः ; Vy *abe* (v.l.), Bmd—आभीराः सह-चैषीकाः; Vy *cde*—अभीराः सहचैषीकाः ; Mts—कारूषाश्च सहैषीकाः, *c* (v.l.)—कावेराश्च सहोषीकैः; Vmn— आभीराः सहवैसक्याः These Ābhīras were probably those were coins and inscriptions have been discovered in Northern Mahārāṣṭra and the Konkan, Kāvera=people living on the Kāveri.

68. Mk *abc*—आढक्याः शवराश्च ये; Mk *d*, Vy *b*—आटव्याः शवराश्च ये; Vy *acde*, Bmd—आटव्याश्च वराश्च ये; Mts—आटव्याः शबरास्तथा, Vmn—आटव्याः शवराश्च ये Śrvara foresters=the Saoras of Ganjam and Vizagapatam.

पुलिन्दा विन्ध्यमूलीका(या)[69] विदर्भा दण्डकैः सह[70] ॥
[71]पौरिका मौलिका(?)श्चैव[72] अश्मका भोगवर्द्धनाः[73] ।
नै(ऋ ?)षिकाः कुन्तला अन्ध्रा[74] उद्भिदा नलकालिकाः (०लूपाः ?)[75] ॥
दाक्षिणात्याश्च वै देशा[76] अपरान्तान् निबोधत[77] ॥

69. Mk *abc*—पुलिन्दा विन्ध्यमौलेयाः, *d*— पुलिन्दा विन्ध्यमालेयाः ; Vy *ace*, Bmd—पुलिन्दा विन्ध्यमूलीकाः ; Vy *ad*—पुलिन्द्रा विन्ध्यमूलीकाः ; Mts— पुलिन्दा विन्ध्यपुषिकाः ; Vmn—पुलिन्दा विन्ध्यशौलेयाः. The reference is to the Pulindas of the Vindhya region.

70. Mk, Vy *bcde*, Mts *be*, Vmn *b*—वैदर्भा दण्डकैः सह; Vy *a*, Bmd, Mts *a*—विदर्भा दण्डकैः सह; Vmn *a*—वेदभो दण्डकैः सह The Prakritism in the form वेदभो is interesting to note. Vidarbha=modern Berar and the adjoining regions. Daṇḍaka is the old name of parts of the Maratha country including especially the Nasik Dist.

71. The following lines together with the first line of the next section are omitted in Mts.

72. Mk—पौरिका मौलिकाश्चैव; Vy *a*—पौनिका मौलिकाश्चैव, *cde*—पानिका मौनिकाश्चैव, *b* recognises मूलिक only : Bmd—शोलिका मौलिकाश्चैव Paurika=people of Purī in the Konkan. Maulika—cf. Mūlaka, the district round Paithan on the Godavari.

73. Mk, Vy *ab*, Bmd, Vmn *b*—अश्मका भोगवर्द्धनाः ; Vy *cde*—अस्मका भोगवर्द्धनाः; Vmn *a*—अलका भोगवर्द्धनाः Aśmaka was contiguous to Mūlaka and had its capital at Paudanya, identified by Raychaudhuri with Bodhan in the Hyderabad State. Bhogavardhan reminds us of Nānidivardhana and Nāgavardhana (Nagardhan in the Nāgpur Dist).

74. Mk *ac*—नैषिकाः कुन्तला अन्ध्राः, *b*—नैषिकाः कुन्तला अन्ध्राः *d*—नैषिकाः कुन्तला आन्ध्राः ; Vy *ace*—नैर्णिकाः कुन्तला अन्ध्राः, *b*—नैतिकाः कुन्तला अन्ध्राः ;

d– नैर्णिका: कुन्तला आन्ध्रा: ; Bmd – मैन्दिका: कुन्तला अन्ध्रा: ; Vmn – नैमिका: कुन्दला आन्ध्रा:. Kuntala = people of the district round Banavasi in the North Kanara Dist. Andhra people lived in the Andhrāpatha about the mouths of the Kistna and the Godāvarī. Originally they appear to have spread over large parts of Central and Northern Deccan. For the Ṛṣikas on the Kistna, see *Sel. Ins.*, I, p. 198 n.

75. Mk – उद्भिदा वनदारका:; Vy *acde*, Bmd – उद्भिदा नलकालिका:, *b* – उद्भिरा नलकालिका: ; Vmn *a* – उच्छिदा नलकारका:, उव्दिा नलकारका: । नलकालका: = ? नलकालूपा: = ? The Nalas and Ālupas. उद्भिद = ? आभीर The Ābhitas rules in the northern part of Mahārāṣṭra and the Koṅkan. See note 67.

76. Mk – दाक्षिणात्यास्त्वमी देशा: ; Vy, Bmd – दाक्षिणात्याश्च वै देशा: Vmn has rather freely – दाक्षिणात्या जनपदास्त्विमे शालकटांकट (*b* – ०कटंकट) Alb. wrongly recognises दाक्षिणात्य and वैदिश (sic. वै देशा:) as two *junapadas* of the South and refers to the following countries of the West as those belonging to the South.

77. Mk *abc* – अपरान्तान् निबोध मे; *d* – अपरांस्तान् निबोध मे; Vy, Bmd – अपरांस्तान् निबोधत.

V

[78]शूर्पारका: कोलवना[79] दुर्गास्तालीकटै: सह[80] ।
पुलेयाश्च सुरा(मुर?)लाश्च[81] रूपसास्तामसै: सह[82] ॥
[83]तथा तु रमिनश्चैव[84] सर्वे चैव कारस्करा:[85] ।
नासिक्याद्याश्च ये चान्ये[86] येचैवोत्तरनर्मदा:[87] ॥
भरु(भृगु)कच्छा: स-माहेया:[88] सह सारस्वतैरपि[89] ।
कच्छीयाश्च सुराष्ट्राश्च[90] आनर्त्ताश्चार्बुदै: सह[91] ॥
इत्येते अपरान्ताश्च[92] शृणुध्वं विन्ध्यवासिन:[93] ॥

78. The following line is omitted in Mts.

79. Mk – सूर्यारका: कालिबला: ; Vy *acd* – शूर्पाकारा: कोलवना:, *e* – सूर्पाकारा: कोलवना: ; Bmd, Vy *b* – शूर्पारका: कोलवना: ; Vmn – शूर्पारका वारिधाना: Sūrpāraka = Sopara not far from Bombay.

80. Mk *abc* – दुर्गाश्चानीकटै: सह, *d* – दुर्गाश्चामीकटै: सह; Vy *acde* – दुर्गा: कालीतकै: सह, *b* – दुर्गास्तिल्लीतकै: सह; Bmd – दुर्गा: कालीकटै: सह; Vmn – दुर्गास्तालीकटै: सह. The reading तालीकट is supported by *Bs,* XIV, 11 and Mbh, II, 31, 65 (where तालाकट is a mistake for तालीकट).

81. Mk – पुलिन्दाश्च सुमीनाश्च; Vy *acde,* Bmd – पुलेयाश्च सुरालाश्च; Vy *b* – पुलेयाश्च करालाश्च (?); Mts – कुलीयाश्च सिरालाश्च; Vmn – पुलीयाश्चासिनीलाश्च. For a river called मुरला in which the अपरान्त elephants sported, see *Sel.*

Ins., I p. 453 n. The Murala people is known to have come into contact with Pratihāra Mahīpāla I according to Rājaśekhara's *Bālabhārata* or *Pacanḍapānḍava* (N.S.P. ed., I. 7) and with Kalacuri Karṇa according to the Bheraghat inscription (*E.I.*, II, p. 11). Paramāra Sindurāja (C. 995-1010 A.D.) is represented in the *Navasāhasāṅkacarita* (X. 14-20) as having defeated the Muralas.

82. Mk – रूपपा: स्वापदै: सह; Vy *acde*, Bmd – रूपसास्तापसै: सह; Vmn – तापसास्तामसास्तथा; Vy *b* – रूपकास्तामसै: सह

83. Vmn has for the following two lines – कारस्करास्तु भमिनो नासिकान्ता: सुनर्मदा:

84. Mk – तथा कुरुमिनश्चैव; Vy *acde*, Bmd – तथा तु रसिताश्चैव; Mts – तथा तैत्तिरिकाश्चैव; Vy *b* – तथा तरूपणाश्चैव, *e* (v.l.) – तथा तु रमिनश्चैव

85. Mk – सर्वे चैव कठाक्षरा: ; Vy *b*, Mts, Mk *c* (v.l.) – सर्वे कारस्करास्तथा; Vy *acde* – सर्वे चैव परक्षरा:, *e* (v.l.) – सर्वे चैव परस्करा: ; Bmd – सर्वे चैवापराक्षरा:; cf. Vmn – कारस्करास्तु भमिन:. Mk *d* has, after this, the following additional lines – कारस्करा लोहजङ्घा वाजेया राजभद्रका: । तोसला: कोसलाश्चैव त्रैपुरा वैदिशस्तथा ॥ तुषारास्तम्बुराश्चैव सर्वे चैव करस्करा: ॥ The second of the three lines is taken out of the following section. The Kāraskaras are known from Baudh. D.S. I, 2, 14 – आरट्टान् कारस्करान् पुण्ड्रान् सौवीरान् वंगकलिंगान् प्राणूनानिति च गत्वा पुनस्तोमेन यजेत सर्वपृष्ठया वा ॥

86. Mk – नासिक्यावाश्च ये चान्ये; Vy, Bmd – नासिक्याद्याश्च ये चान्ये; Vy *e* (v.l.) – नासिकाद्याश्च ये चान्ये, नांसिकाद्याश्च ये चान्ये; Mts *a* – वासिकाश्चैव ये चान्ये, *bc* – बासिक्याश्चैव ये चान्ये.

87. Mk, Vy *b* – ये चैवोत्तरनर्मदा: ; Bmd, Mts, Vy *cde* (v.l.) – ये चैवोन्तरनर्मदा:; Vy *ae* – ये वै चान्तरनर्मदा:

88. Mk – भीरुकच्छा: समाहेया: ; Vy *acd* – भानुकच्छा: स-माहेया: ; Bmd, Mts, Vy *e* (v.l.) – भारुकच्छा: समाहेया: ; Vmn – दारुकच्छा: सुमाहेया: ; Vy *be* – भानुकच्छ्रा: समाहेया: The Prakritism in the form भारुकच्छ (Pali भरुकच्छ) for the Sanskritic भृगुकच्छ is interesting to note. Bhṛgukaccha = Broach. Māheya = people of the Mahi valley.

89. Mk, Vmn, Vy *b* – सह सारस्वतैरपि; Mts – सह सारस्वतैस्तथा, Vy *acde*, Bmd – सहसा शाश्वतैरपि Sārasvata = people of the Sarasvatī (Sarsuti) valley of the in the eastern Punjab or in Gujara (*AA*, p. 229).

90. Mk – काश्मीराश्च सुराष्ट्राश्च; Vy, Bmd – कच्छीयाश्च सुराष्ट्राश्च; Mts *a* – कच्छीकाश्चैव सौराष्ट्रा:, *bc* – काच्छीकाश्चैव सौराष्ट्रा: ; Vmn – वात्सीयाश्च सुराष्ट्राश्च Kacchīya = people of Cutch. Surāṣṭra = South Kathiawar.

91. Mk *acd,* Vmn–आवन्त्याश्चार्वुदैः सह, Mk *b*–अवन्त्याश्चार्वुदैः सह; Vy *acde* (v.l.)–अनर्त्ताश्चार्वुदेः सह; Bmd, Vy *e*–आनर्त्ताश्चार्वुदैः सह; Mts–आनर्त्ता अर्वुदैः सहः ; Vy *b*–अनर्त्ता हुदवुदैः (sic) सह Ānarta=district round Dvārakā. Arbuda=mod. Abu in Rajputana.

92. Mk, Vy *e* (v.l.)– इत्येते ह्यपरान्ताश्च; Vy *acde,* Bmd–इत्येते सम्परीताश्च; Mts–इत्येते अपरान्तास्तु. Vmn has rather freely– इत्येते पश्चिमामाशां स्थिता जानपदा जनाः

93. Mk *acd*–शृणु विन्ध्यनिवासिनः, *b*–शृणु विन्धनिवासिनः ; Vy *acde,* Bmd–शृणुध्वं विन्ध्यवासिनः ; Mts–शृणु ये विन्ध्यवासिनः

VI

[94]मलदाश्च कारूषाश्च[95] मेकलाश्चोत्कलैः सह[96] ।
उत्तमर्णा दशार्णाश्च[97] भोजाः किष्किन्धकैः सह[98] ॥
[99]तोशलाः कोशलाश्चैव[100] त्रैपुरा वैदिशास्तथा[101] ।
तुमुरास्तुम्बुराश्चैव (तुम्बानास्तुम्बवनाश्च ?)[102] पटवो निषधैः सह[103] ॥
[103*]अनूपास्तुण्डिकेराश्च[104] वीतिहोत्रा अवन्तयः[105] ।
एते जनपदाः सर्वे[106] विन्ध्यपृष्ठ-निवासिनः[107] ॥

94. Vy *b* omits several lines and makes the *janapadas* mentioned in the following two sections as those belonging to the West. See note 76.

95. Mk *a*– सरजाश्च करुषाश्च, *b*–सरजाश्च करूषाश्च; Vy *acde,* Bmd, Mts–मालवाश्च करूषाश्च; Vmn–कारूषाश्चैकलव्याश्च; Vy *b*–गलदाश्च करूषाश्च (note 50). The Mālavas (Malloi of the Greeks) lived on the lower Irāvatī (Ravī) in the Panjab in the fourth century B.C. Later they are found settled in Rajputana and ultimately they gave their name to modern Malawas in Central India. Kārūṣa, which is also called Bṛhadgṛha, is the same as the present Shahabad District of Bihar. The Maladas probably lived to the west of the Kārūṣas and to the east of Prayāga (Allahabad). Lama Tāranātha who locates a Mālava country near Prayāga seems to have confused the Maladas with the Mālavas of western India on the strength of erroneous Puranic passages quoted in the present note.

96. Mk–केरलाश्चोत्कलैः सह; Vy *ae*– रोकलाश्चोत्कलैः सह; Bmd, Mts, Vmn, Vy *bcd*–मेकलाश्चोत्कलैः सह The name Mekala is still preserved in that of the present Maikal range which is the connecting link between the Vindhyas and the Satpuras and stretches from the Khairagarh State in C.P. to the Rawah State (*SIA*. p. 134). Utkala was the western fringe of the Midnapore District and the adjoining parts of Orissa. The Mekalas lived near the Amarkantak hills.

97. The following line is wrongly placed in section V in Mk *d*.

98. Mk, Bmd, Vmn, Vy *d*—उत्तमर्णा दशार्णाश्च; Vy *ace*— उत्तमार्णा दशार्णाश्च, *b*—उत्तमर्णा बशार्णाश्च; Mts— औण्ड्रामाषा दशार्णाश्च. Daśārṇa formed parts of modern East Malwa (cf. the river of the same name) and the adjoining regions. It was also known as Ākara and had its capital at Vidiśā.

99. Mk—भोज्या: किष्किन्धकै: सह; Vy, Bmd, Mts—भोजा: किष्किन्धकै: सह; Vmn—गोप्ता किकरवै: सह. For the Bhojas, see *PH*, p. 76 ff.The Kiṣ kindhakas may be the people of Kekind, Jodhpur State (*INI*, Nos. 199, 1009) or of the Ramayanic Kiṣkindhā identified with the Raichur area of Hyderabad and the adjoining regions (*SIA*, p. 102). In any case, *Vindhya* is used in a wide sense.

100. Mk, Vmn *b*—तोशला: कोशलाश्चैव; Vy *acde*—तोसला कोसलाश्चैव; Bmd—तोसला: कौशलाश्चैव; Vmn *a*— तोशला शोकलाश्चैव; Mts *ac*—स्तोशला कोसलाश्चैव, *b*—स्तोशला कौसलाश्चैव; Vy *b*—recognises कोसल only. Both the names could be spelt either with the dental or with the palatal sibilant. Tosala was no doubt the district round the city of Tosalī (modern Dhauli, near Bhubaneswar in the Purī District, Orissa). In the early medieval period, the Tosala *janapada* is known to have been divided into Uttara-Tosala and Dakṣiṇa-Tosala. Kosala here is no doubt Dakṣiṇa-Kośala, identified with the modern Raipur-Bilaspur-Sambalpur region of the C.P. and Orissa. *PH*, pp. 252, 452.

101. Mk *a*—तैपुरा वैदिशस्तथा, *bcd*—त्रैपुरा वैदिशस्तथा; Vy—त्रैपुरा वैदिकास्तथा; Bmd, Mts— त्रैपुरा वैदिशास्तथा; Vmn—त्रैपुरा: खेल्लिशास्तथा The Traipuras were the people of Tripura or Tripurī, modernh Tewar in the Jubbulpore District. The Vaidiśas were the people of Vidiśa, modern Besnagar in the Gwalior State.

102. Mk *abc*—तुम्बुरास्तुम्बुलाश्चैव, *d*— तुम्बरास्तुम्बुलाश्चैव; Vy *acde*, Bmd— तुमुरास्तुम्बुराश्चैव; Mts *a*—तुमुरास्तम्बराश्चैव, *bc*—तुमुवास्तुम्बराश्चैव; Vmn—तुरगास्तुंबराश्चैव; Vy *b*—थर्पुरास्तुम्बुराश्चैव One of the names appears to be a mistake for तुम्बवन, modern Tumain in the Gwalior State. The other locality may be Tummāna (=Tumān), 45 miles north of Ratanpur in C.P.

103. Mk *a*—पटवो निषधै: सह, *bc*—पटवो नैषधै: सह, *d*— पटवी नैषधै: सह; Vy *acde*, Bmd—षट्सुरा निषधै: सह; Vy *e* (v.l.)—षट्सुरा: नैषधै: सह; Mts *ab*—पद्गमा निषधै: सह, *c*—पद्गमा नैषधै: सह; Vmn *a*—वहेला निषधै: सह, *b*—वहेला नैषधै: सह; Vy *b*—षत्तुमाना: पधै: सह. The Niṣadhas are associated with the Pāriyātra. They probably lived about Nalapura, modern Narwar in the Gwalior State.

103a. The following four lines are omitted in Vy *b.*

104. Mk *abcd*–अन्नजास्तुष्टिकाराश्च, *c* (v.l.)– अनूपास्तुण्डिकेशाश्च; Vy *acde,* Bmd, Vmn–अनूपास्तुण्डिकेराश्च; Vy *e* (v.l.)– अणुपास्तुण्डिकेराश्च; Mts–अरूपाः शौण्डिकेराश्च. Omitted in Vy *b.* Anūpa was on the Narmadā with the city of Māhīṣmatī (modern Māndhātā in the Nimār District, C.P.) as its capital. The Haihaya king Arjuna, son of Kṛtavīrya, ruled at Māhīṣmatī. Like the Bhojas, Vītihotras and Avantis mentioned in the section, the Tuṇḍikeras were a branch of the Haihayas. According to the Pūrāṇas (Mts, 43, 48-49; Vy, 94, 51-52; Bmh, 13, 203-04; Pdm, St. Kd., 12, 35-36; Hv, I, 33, 51-52), the Haihayas were subdivided into five clans, viz., Vītihotra (wrongly called वीरहोत्र and in some texts), Bhoja, Avanti, Tuṇḍikera (called कुण्डिकेर, and तौण्डिकेर and तुण्डकेर in some texts) and तालजङ्घ. It may be pointed out in this connection that Pargiter has (*AIS T,* p. 98, etc.) wrongly found the name of a Haihaya clan (शार्यात) in the word सञ्जाताः, असंख्याताः or सुजाताः (wrongly read in some texts as शार्याताः, सुरताः etc.). The Haihayas were themselves a branch of the Yādavas, See, e.g., Vsn, IV, ch. 11, section 1 ff.

105. Vy *acde,* Bmd–वीतिहोत्राह्यवन्तयः; Mk– वीरहोत्रा ह्यवन्तयः ; Mts–वीतिहोत्रा अवन्तयः ; Vmn– वीतिहोत्रास्त्ववन्तयः. Omitted in Vy *b.* The Avanti people lived in West Malwa.

106. Mk, Vy, Bmd–एते जनपदाः सर्वे; Mts–एते जनपदाः ख्याताः Vmn has rather freely– सुकेशा विन्ध्यमूलस्थास्त्विमे जनपदा स्थि (*b*–स्मृ)ताः

107. Mk, Vy, Bmd, Mts– विन्ध्यपृष्ठनिवासिनः.

VII

अतो देशान् प्रवक्ष्यामि[108] पर्वतश्रयिणश्च ये[109]।
निराहारा हंसमार्गाः[110] कुरवस्तङ्गणाः खसाः[111] ॥
कर्णप्रावरणाश्चैव[112] हूणा दार्वाः स-हूहुकाः[113]।
त्रिगर्त्ता मालवाश्चैव[114] किरातोस्तामसैः(०स्तोमरैः ?) सह[115] ॥

108. Mk, Vy *acde,* Bmd, Mts–अतो देशान् प्रवक्ष्यामि; Vmn–आद्यान् देशान् प्रवक्ष्यामः

109. Mk, Vy *acde,* Bmd, Mts–पर्वताश्रयिणश्च ये; Vmn–पर्वताश्रयिणस्तु ये

110. Mk–नोहारा हंसमार्गाश्च; Vy *acde,* Bmd–निगर्हरा हंसमार्गाः ; Mts–निराहाराः सर्वगाश्च; Vmn *a*–निराहारं हंसमार्गाः, *b*–निराहारा हंसमार्गाः The Haṃsamārgas of the Himalayan region are also known from another passage; cf. List of Rivers. note 72; also note 40 above.

111. Mk– कुरवो गुर्गणाः खसाः ; Vy *acde*–क्षुपणास्तङ्गणाः खसाः, *e* (v.l.)–कुणपास्तङ्गणाः खसाः, क्षुपणास्तङ्गणास्त्रसाः, क्षुपणास्तङ्गणाः खसाः ; Bmd–कुपथास्तङ्गणाः खसाः ; Mts–कुपथा अपथास्तथा; Vmn– कुपथास्तङ्गणाः खशाः These Kurus are doubtless the celebrated Uttarakurus living in the Himalayan region. The Tangaṇas and Khasa (identified with the modern Khakkas) lived about Kashmir. Mts, Vy and Bmd refer to a Himalayan locality called कुपथ or अपथ (cf. List of Rivers, Sec. X, n. 161).

112. Mk. कुन्तप्राबरणाश्चैव; Vy *acde*–कुशप्रावरणाश्चैव; Bmd, Vy *a*–कर्णप्रावरणाश्चैव; Mts. Vmn, Vy *e* (v.l.)–कुथप्रावरणाश्चैव. Both कुथप्रावरण and कर्णप्रावरण situated in the Himalayan region are elsewhere mentioned in Mts, Vy and Bmd (cf. List of Rivers, section X, n. 166 and 175). Rām. IV, 40, 25 locates कर्णप्रावरण in the eastern direction, probably in the eastern Himalayas.

113. Mk *a*–उर्णा दार्वाः सकृत्नकाः ; *bcd*– ऊर्णा दार्वाः सकृत्नकाः ; Vy *acde*–हूणा दर्वाः सहूदकाः ; Bmd– हूणदर्वाः बहूदकाः ; Mts *a*–उर्णादर्वाः समुद्गकाः, *bc*– ऊर्णा दर्वाः समुद्गकाः; Vmn– ऊर्णाः प्लुष्टाः सुहूहुकाः ; Vy *b*–हूणा दर्वाः सहूहकाः ; *e* (v.l.)–हूणा दर्वाः सुहूहुकाः, हूणा दर्वाः सहूहुकाः. For the Huṇas and Dārvas, see note 43 above. For the Hūhukas of the Himalayan region, see List of Rivers, note 72.

114. Mk *ac*, Vy–त्रिगर्त्ता मालवाश्चैव; Bmd–त्रिगर्त्ता मालयाश्चैव; Mts–त्रिगर्त्ता मण्डलाश्चैव Vmn has rather freely–त्रिगर्त्ताश्च किराताश्च तोमराः शशिखाद्रिकाः Mk *d*–त्रिगर्त्ता गालवाश्चैव Trigarta=modern Jalandhar region. For the *Sapta-mālava* or seven localities called Mālava, See *PH,* p. 492 n. Mālava in our text may be the same as the country of that name identified with the "cis-Sutlej districts of the Punjab together with some Himalayan territory".

115. Mk, Vy *acde,* Bmd– किरातास्तामसैः सह; Vy *b*–किरातास्तामरैः सह; Mts–किराताश्चामरैः सह Kirātas=Himalayan mountaineers; cf. the name of modern Kiranti, etc. The reading तोमर (for तामर) is supported by some passages; cf. List of Rivers, section X, n. 171. See also n. 40 above.

VIII

Condensed List

Vsn, II. ch. 3, vv. 14-17; Krm, I, ch. 46 (47 in some texts), vv. 41-44; Bmh, 21, 15-17

[115]*तास्विमे कुरु-पाञ्चाला[116] मध्यदेशादयो जनाः[117] ।

पूर्वदेशादिकाश्चैव[118] कामरूपनिवासिनः[119] ॥

पुण्ड्राः (पाण्ड्याः) कलिङ्गा मगधा (माहिषा)[120] दाक्षिणात्याश्च कृत्स्नशः[121]।
तथापरान्ताः सौराष्ट्राः[122] शूद्राभीरास्तथार्बुदाः[123]॥
मा(मे)रुका मालवाश्चैव[124] पारियात्रनिवासिनः[125]।
सौवीराः सैन्धवा हूणाः[126] शाल्वाः शाकलवासिनः[127]॥
मद्रारामा (द्रकारा?)स्तथाम्बष्ठाः[128] पारसीकादयस्तथा[129]॥

115a. This later list is very carelessly compiled and probably had some mistakes even in the original draft.

116. Vsn, Krm–तास्विमे कुरुपाञ्चालाः ; Bmd–तास्विमे कुरुपञ्चाल॰

117. Vsn, Krm Bmh–मध्यदेशादयो जनाः

118. Vsn, Krm, Bmh–पूर्वदेशादिकाश्चैव

119. Vsn, Kem, Bmh–कामरूपनिवासिनः

120. Vsn, Krm–पुण्ड्राः कलिङ्गा मगधाः ; Bmh–पौण्ड्राः कलिङ्गा मगधाः

121. Vsn, Krm–दाखिणात्याश्च कृत्स्नशः ; Bmh–दाक्षिणात्याश्च सर्वशः

122. Vsn–तथापरान्ताः सौराष्ट्राः ; Bmh–तथापरान्त्याः सौराष्ट्राः ; Krm–तथापरान्ताः सौराष्ट॰

123. Vsn. Bmh, Krm *ab* (v.l.)– शूद्राभीरास्तथार्वुदाः ; Krm *bc*–शूद्राहीनास्तथार्वुदाः

124. Vsn–कारूषा मालवाश्चैव; Krm *a*–मालका मालवाश्चैव, *b*–मालाका मलपाश्चैव, v.l.–मालका मलयाश्चैव *c*–मालका मलपाश्चैव; Bmh–मारुका मालवाश्चैव

125. Vsn. Krm *a*–पारिपात्रनिवासिनः ; Krm *b* (v.l.)–परियात्रनिवासिनः ; Krm *c*, Bmh–पारियात्रनिवासिनः

126. Vsn, Bmh–सौवीराः सैन्धया हूणाः ; Krm *b* (v.l.)–सौवीराः सैन्धवाकूणाः, *c* (v.l.)– सौवीराः सैन्धवाकृष्णाः ; Bmh–सोवीराः सैन्धवापस्त्राः

127. Vsn, Bmh–शाल्वाः शाकलवासिनः ; Krm *a*–शाल्वाः कान्यनिवासिनः, *b*–माल्या वाल्यानिवासिनः, v.l., *c* (v.l.)– शाल्वाः कल्पनिवासिनः

128. Vsn, Bmh–मद्रारामास्तथाम्बष्ठाः ; Krm *a*–मद्रारामास्तथैवान्ध्राः, *bc*–माद्रारामास्तथैवान्ध्राः

129. Krm–पारसीकास्तथैव च; Vsn, Bmh–पासीकादयस्तथा The Pārasīkas (persians) are not mentioned in the bigger list or in any early work.

Abbreviations

AA – *Ain-i-Akbari* tr. by Jarret, Vil. 11.

Ac – *Abhidhānacintāmaṇi*.

Bgvt – *Bhāgavata Purāṇa,* Baṅgabāsī Office, Calcutta.

Bhv – *Bhaviṣya Purāṇa.*

Bmd – *Brahmāṇḍa Purāṇa,* Baṅgabāsī Office, Calcutta.

Bmh – *Brahma Purāṇa,* Bangabāsī Office, Calcutta.

Bs – *Bṛhatsaṃhitā*–*a* Baṅgabāsī Office, Calcutta; *b* Restored text of the Ms consulted by Al Bīrūnī (c. 1030 A.D.).

Grd – *Garuḍa Purāṇa,* Baṅgabāsī Office, Calcutta.

Km – Rājaśekhara's *Kāvyamīmāṃsā,* G.O.S. ed., Baroda.

Krm – *Kūrma Purāṇa*–*a* Bangabāsī Office, Calcutta; *b* Bibliotheca Indica, RASB, Calcutta; *c* Baṅgabāsī Office, Calcutta; *d* Veṅkateśvar Press, Bombay.

Mbh – *Mahābhārata,* Baṅgabāsī Office, Calcutta.

Mk – *Mārkaṇḍeya Purāṇa*–*a* ed. M. C. Pal, Calcutta, 1890, *b* Bibliotheca Indica, RASB, Calcutta, 1862; *c* Baṅgabāsī Office, Calcutta; *d* Veṅkateśvar Press, Bombay.

Mts – *Matsya Purāṇa*–*a* Baṅgabāsī Office, Calcutta; *b* Veṅkateśvar Press, Bombay; *c* Ānandāśrama Press, Poona; *d* Restored text of the Ms. consulted by Al Bīrūnī (c. 1030 A.D.).

Pll. – *Political History of Ancient India* by H.C. Raychaudhuri, 1938.

Ram – *Rāmāyaṇa,* Nirṇayasāgar Press, Bombay.

SS – *The Successors of the Sātavāhanas* by D.C. Sircar, 1939.

Tks – Puruṣottama's *Trikāṇḍaśeṣa.*

Vj – Yādavaprakāśa's *Vaijauantī.*

Vmn – *Vāmana Purāṇa*–*a* ed. M. C. Pal, Calcutta, 1893; *b* Veṅkateśvar Press, Bombay.

Vy – *Vāyu Purāṇa* Baṅgabāsī Office, Calcutta; *b* Restored text of the Ms consulted by Al Bīrūnī (*c.* 1030 A.D.); *c* Bibliotheca Indica, RASB, Calcutta; *d* Veṅkateśvar Press, Bombay; *e* Ānandāśrama Press, Poona.

[Other editions of the works that have been consulted will be indicated later.]

12

The Study of Ancient Geography*

Agni- Purāṇa

Harihara V. Trivedi

Geographical materials, embodied in the Purāṇas, are not so meagre as those of history. The ancient Aryans belonged to a nomadic race and some of their wandering tribes did not definitely settle down till a very late period. Even in the Purāṇic age some of them travelled from place to place, being induced by the only aim of seeing the world.[1] In course of their wandering they passed through different countries, crossing various mountains and rivers. In those days India had established commercial intercourse with foreign lands,[2] and the growth of international trade necessitated a wide and accurate geographical knowledge.[3] Consequently her ancient inhabitants must have stored much valuable geographical materials in some treatises, now lost to us, or at least much information was orally handed down to succeeding generations, and ultimately embodied in the Purāṇas.

In the *Indian Antiquary* (XIV, pp. 319 ff.) Dr. Burgess suggested that lists of geographical names contained in the *Purāṇas, Itihāsas, Smṛtis* and other available sources of information should be prepared "as a means to the better elucidation of the ancient geography of India". He also gives the specimen of an alphabetical list of such names. Following his suggestion, Fleet, in a subsequent issue of the same Journal,[4] gives a list of topographical names contained in the *Bṛhat Saṃhitā* of Varāhamihira. After him J.E. Abbott gave a list of such names contained in the *Bhāgavata Purāṇa.*[5] After this, no further attempt was made in this direction.

In the following pages I propose to give an alphabetical list of topographical names as embodied in the *Agni Purāṇa.* All the various

---

* I must express my deep obligation to Dr. N. N. Law, the editor of this Journal not only for his valuable suggestions but also for the troubles that he has taken in revising this article.

readings have been put in the foot-notes. The text used by me is published by the Veṅkateśvara Press, Bombay; the figures of references are to its chapter and verse, indicated thus LIV. 14, LVI. 4. etc.

[Abbreviations used: – Bhā. = Bhāratavarṣa; Pl. = Plakṣa; Pu. = Puṣkara; Kr. = Krauñca; J. = Jambū; Śāl = Śālmala; D. = Dvīpa; Mt. = mountain; other abbreviations such as N. = North and S. = South are easily intelligible.]

The Topographical information contained in the Agni-Purāṇa:

A

Aṅga – A country in the S.E. of Bhā. LIV. 14.

Anutaptā – A river in the Pl. D., LVI. 4.

Andhakāraka[6] – A mt. in Kr. D., LVI. 13.

Andhra – A country and people in the S. of Bhā. LV. 6.

Abhīṣāha – A country in the N.E. of Bhā, LV. 20.

Abhrā[7] – A river in Kuśa- D., LVI. 11.

Amṛta – A river in Pl. D., LVI. 4.

Ambaṣṭha – A country in the S.W. of Bhā, LV. 16.

Aśmaka – A country in the S. of Bhā. LV. 15.

Aśvamukha[8] – A country in the N.W. of Bhā. LV. 18.

I

Ikṣu-samudra – (i) A sea surrounding Pl. D., LVI. 6.
(ii) A river in Śāka – D., LVI. 17.

Indra-Dvīpa – One of the nine parts of Bhā. LV. 4.

Ilāvṛta – One of the Varṣas; it is the middle portion of J.D., LIV. 12; LV. I.

U

Unnata – A mt. in Śāl. D., LVI. 6.

Ṛ

Ṛkṣa – One of the Kulācalas of J.D., LV. 7.

Ṛṣikulyā – A river in Bhā. LV. 10.

K

Kakudmat – A mt. in Śāl. D., LVI. 7.

Kaṅka (or Krauñca) – A mt. in Śāl. D., LVI. 7.

Kaṭāha – One of the nine parts of Bhā. LV. 5.

Kamboja – A country in the S. of Bhā. LV. 15.

Karṇāṭa – A country in the S. of Bhā. LV. 15.

Kaliṅga – A country in the S.E. of Bhā. LV. 14.

Kaśerumat – One of the nine parts of Bhā. LV. 4.

Kāmbhoja – A country in the S.W. of Bhā. LV. 16.

Kāraka (?) – A mt. in Kr. D., LVI. 13.

Kāverī – A river in Bhā. LV. 9; LV. 10.

Kāśi – A country in the E. of Bhā. LV. 13.

Kāśmīra – A country in the N.E. of Bhā. LV. 20.

Kimpuruṣa – One of the Varṣas; it is a part of J.D. and is to the south of Ilāvṛtavarṣa, LIV. 12; LV. 2.

Kirāta – A people to the E. of Bhā. LV. 6.

Kunti – A country in the middle region of Bhā. LV. 12.

Kumārī – A river in Śāka-D., LVI. 17.

Kumuda – A mt. in Śāl. D., LVI. 6.

Kumudvatī – A river in Kr. D., LVI. 14.

Kuru – (i) One of the Varṣas; it is to the north of Meru mt., LIV. 12; LV. 3;

(ii) A country in the middle region of Bhā. LV. 12.

Kuśa – One of the seven Dvīpas; it is surrounded by Sarpissamudra, LIV. 5; LVI. 8.

Kuśeśaya – A mt. in Kuśa-D., LVI. 10.

Kṛṣṇaveṇī – A river in Bhā. LV. 9.

Ketumāla – One of the Varṣas; it is to the W. of Meru mt., LIV. 13; LV. 3.

Ketumālā – A river in Bhā, LV. 12.

Kolāta – A country in the N.E. of Bhā. LV. 13.

Kramu – A river in Pl. D., LVI. 4.

Krauñca – (i) One of the seven Dvīpas; it is surrounded by Dadhisamudra, LIV. 5; LVI. 12.

(ii) A mt. in Kr. D., LVI. 13.

Kh

Khasa – A country in the N.W. of Bhā. LV. 18.

Khyāti – A river in Kr. D., LVI. 15.

G

Gabhastimat – One of the nine parts of Bhā. LV. 4.

Gabhastī – A river in Śaka-D., LVI. 17.

Gāndhāra – A country in the N. of Bhā. LV. 19.

Godāvarī – A river in Bhā. LV. 9.

Gomatī – A river in Bhā. LV. 9.

Gomeda – A mt. in Pl. D., LVI. 3.

Gaurī – A river in Kr. D., LVI. 14.

Gh

Ghana – A country in the S. of Bhā. LV. 15.

C

Candra – A mt. in Pl. D., LVI. 3.

Candrabhāgā – A river in Bhā. LV. 10.

Candrā – A river in Śāl. D., LVI. 7.

Cedi – A country in the E. of Bhā. LV. 13.

J

Jambū Dvīpa – One of the seven Dvīpas; it is surrounded by Lavaṇasamudra, LIV. 5; LIV. 11.

Jala-samudra – One of the seven oceans; it surrounds Pu. D., LIV. 6; LVI. 20.

Jīmūta – A country in the S. of Bhā. LV. 15.

Ṭ

Ṭaṅkaṇa – A country in the N.E. of Bhā. LV. 20.

T

Tāpī – A river in Bhā. LV. 9.

Tāmraparṇī – A river in Bhā. LV. 10.

Tāmravarṇa – One of the nine parts of Bhā. LV. 4.

Turaṣka – A country in the N.W. of Bhā. LV. 18.

Trigarta – A country in the N.E. of Bhā. LV. 20.

Tridivā – A river in Pl. D., LVI. 4.

D

Dakṣiṇāpatha – The southern region of Bhā. LV. 15.

Dadhisamudra – A sea surrounding Kr. D., LIV. 6.

Divāvṛta – A mt. in Kr. D., LVI. 14.

Dugdhasamudra – A sea surrounding Śāka-D., LIV. 6.

Dundubhi – (i) A mt. in Pl. D., LVI. 3.
(ii) A mt. in Kr. D., LVI. 14.

Dyutimat—A mt. in Kuśa-D., LVI. 10.

Draviḍa—A country in the S.W. of Bhā. LV. 14.

Droṇa—A mt. in Śāl. D., LVI. 6.

Dh

Dhūtapāpā—A river in Kuśa-D., LVI. 11.

Dhenukā—A river in Śāka-D., LVI. 17.

N

Nayarāṣṭra—A country in the S. of Bhā. LV. 15.

Narmadā—A river in Bhā. LV. 8.

Nalinī—A river in Śāka-D., LVI. 17.

Navarāṣṭra—The same as Nayarāṣṭra.

Nāgadvīpa—One of the nine parts of Bhā. LV. 5.

Nābhi—One of the Varṣas, LIV. 12.

Nārada—A mt. in Pl. D., LVI. 3.

Nāstika—A country and people in the W. of Bhā. LV. 17.

Niṣadha—(i) A mt. to the S. of Meru, LIV. 9;
(ii) A country in the w. of Bhā. LV. 17.

Nīla—(i) A mt. to the N. of Meru, LIV. 10.
(ii) A country in the N.E. of Bhā. LV. 20.

P

Pañcama[9]—A mt. in Kr. D., LVI. 14. (?)

Paṭaccara—A country in the middle-region of Bhā. LV. 12.

Payasvinī—A river in Bhā. LV. 10.

Payoṣṇī—A river in Bhā. LV. 9.

Pavitrā—A river in Kuśa-D., LVI. 11.

Pāñcāla—A country in the middle region of Bhā. LV. 12.

Padma—A country in the east of Bhā. LV. 13.

Puṇḍarīkavat—A mt. in Kr. D., LVI. 14.

Puṇḍarīkā—A river in Kr. D., LVI. 15.

Puṇḍra—A country in the S.E. of Bhā. LV. 14.

Pulinda—A country in the S.E. of Bhā. LV. 15.

Puṣkara—One of the seven Dvīpas; it is surrounded by the sea of sweet water, LIV. 5; LVI. 20.

Puṣpavat—A mt. in Kuśa-D., LVI. 10.

Plakṣa – One of the seven Dvīpas; it is surrounded by Ikṣusamudra, LIV. 5; LIV. 10; LVI. 1.

B

Bāhlīka – A country in the N. of Bhā. LV. 19.

Brahmaputra – A country in N.E. of Bhā. LV. 20.

Bh

Bhadrāśva – One of the Varṣas; it is to the E. of Meru, LIV. 12; LV. I.

Bhārata – One of the Varṣas; it is to the S. of Meru, LV. 2; LV. 4.

Bhīmarathī – A river in Bhā. LV. 9.

M

Mattagaṅgā – A river in Bhā. LV. 10.

Matsya – A country in the middle region of Bhā. LV. 12.

Madra – A country in the N. of Bhā. LV. 19.

Madhyadeśa – The middle region of Bhā. LV. 11, 12.

Manojavā – A river in Kr. D., LVI. 14.

Mandara – A mt. in Kuśa-D., LVI. 10.

Malaya – A mt. in Bhā. LV. 7.

Mahākeśa – A country in the N.W. of Bhā. LV. 18.

Mahānadī – A river in Bhā. LV. 9.

Mahānāsa – A country in the N.W. of Bhā. LV. 18.

Mahiṣa – A mt. in Śāl-D., LVI. 6.

Mahī – A river in Kuśa-D., LVI. 11.

Mahendra – A mt. in Bhā. LV. 7.

Māgadha – A country in the E. of Bhā. LV. 13.

Māṇḍavya – A country in the N.W. of Bhā. LV. 18.

Māthura – A country in the W. of Bhā. LV. 17.

Mūlaka – A country in the S.E. of Bhā. LV. 14.

Mūlika – A country in the N.W. of Bhā. LV. 18.

Meru – A mt. in J.D., LIV. 7; LV. 2.

Mleccha – A country in the W. and N. of Bhā. LV. 17; LV. 19.

Y

Yavana – A country and people to the W. of Bhā. LV. 6; LV. 17.

Yonitoyā – A river in Śāl-D., LVI. 7.

Yaudheya – A country in the middle region of Bhā. LV. 12.

R

Ramya (Ramyaka)—One of the Varṣas; it is to the N.W. of Meru, LIV. 12; LV. 3.

Rātri—A river in Kr. D., LVI. 14.

L

Lampāka (Lambaka)—A country in the N. of Bhā. LV. 19.

Lavaṇa—One of the seven seas; it surrounds the J.D., LIV. 6.

Lāṭa—A country in the S.W. of Bhā. LV. 16.

Lokāloka—A mt. beyond the Svādūdaka-samudra which surrounds the Pu. D., LVI. 21.

V

Vaṅga—A country in the S.E. of Bhā. LV. 14.

Varadā—A river in Bhā. LV. 8.

Vāmana—A mt. in Kr. D., LVI. 13.

Vāruṇa—One of the parts of Bhā. LV. 5.

Vitṛṣṇā—A river in Śāl-D., LVI. 7.

Vidarbha—A country in the S.E. of Bhā. LV. 14.

Vidarbhā—A river in Bhā. LV. 11.

Videha—A country in the E. of Bhā. LV. 13.

Vidyut—A river in Kuśa-D., LVI. 11.

Vidruma—A mt. in Kuśa-D., LVI. 10.

Vidhṛti—A river in Śāl-D., LV. 8.

Vindhyā—A mt. in Bhā. LV. 8; LV. 14.

Vipāśā—A river in Pl. D., LVI. 4.

Vimocanī—A river in Śāl-D, LVI. 7.

Vedasmṛti—A river in Bhā. LV. 8.

Veṇukā—A river in Śāka-D., LVI. 17.

Vaibhrāja—A mt. in Pl. D., LVI. 3.

Ś

Śaka—A country in the S.W. of Bhā. LV. 16.

Śatadrū—A river in Bhā. LV. 11.

Śāka—One of the seven Dvīpas; it is surrounded by Dugdha-samudra, LIV. 5; LVI. 15.

Śālmala—One of the seven Dvīpas; it surrounded by Surāsamudra, LIV. 5; LVI. 5.

Śikhī – A river in Pl. D., LVI. 4.

Śivā – (i) A river in Bhā. LV. 8;

(ii) A river in Kuśa-D., LVI. 11.

Śuktimat – A mt. in Bhā. LV. 7.

Śuklā – A river in Śāl-D., LVI. 7.

Śūrasena – A country in the middle region of Bhā. LV. 12.

Śṛiṅgin – A mt. to the N. of Meru, LIV. 10.

Śveta – A mt. to the N. of Meru, LIV. 10.

S

Sandhyā – A river in Kr. D., LVI. 14.

Sanmati – A river in Kuśa-D., LVI. 11.

Sarayū – A river in Bhā. LV. 9.

Sarasvatī – A river in Bhā. LV. 10.

Sahya – A mt. in Bhā. LV. 7.

Sarpissamudra – One of the seven Seas; it surrounds the Kuśa-D., LIV. 6.

Siṃhala – One of the nine parts of Bhā. LV. 5.

Sukṛtā – A river in Pl. D., LVI. 4.

Sukumārī – A river in Śāka-D., LVI. 17.

Sumanas – A mt. in Pl. D., LVI. 3.

Surasā – A river in Bhā. LV. 8.

Surāsamudra – One of the seven Seas; it surrounds Śāl-D., LIV. 6.

Sūta – A country in the E. of Bhā. LV. 13.

Saindhava – A country in the W. of Bhā. LV. 17.

Somaka – A mt. in Pl. D., LVI. 3.

Stananāga – A country in the N. of Bhā. LV. 19.

Strīmukha – A country in the S.W. of Bhā. LV. 16.

Strīrājya – A country in the W. of Bhā. LV. 17.

H

Hari – A mt. in Kuśa-D., LVI. 10.

Harivarṣa – One of the Varṣas; it is to the S.W. of Meru, LIV. 12.

Himavat – A mt. to the S. of Meru, LIV. 9.

Himācala – A mt. in the N. of Bhā. LV. 19.

Hiraṇmaya (Hiraṇvat) – One of the Varṣas; it is to the S.E. of

Meru, LV. 1; LIV. 12.

Hemakūṭa—A mt. to the S. of Meru, LIV. 9.

Hemaśaila—A mt. in Kuśa-D., LVI. 10.

References

1. *Mārkaṇḍeya P.*, 58. 7; 58. 15.
2. N. C. Bandyopadhyaya, *Economic Life and Progress on Anc. India,* I, pp. 32.
3. *Ibid.*, pp. 294, 295.
4. *IA.* XXII, pp. 169.
5. *Ibid.*, XXIII, pp. 1-6.
6. The reading is Andha(tha)kāraka. This may be taken as Andhakāraka or Atha+kāraka.
7. The reading is Vidyudabhrā. This cannot be taken as one name because in that case the number of the rivers in Kuśa-D. would not count seven as it has been found in all other cases.
8. A country commonly receives its appellation from its people. For example, the compounded word *Mahānāsa* (with a long nose), by which a country was known, indicates that there lived a kind of people who were famous for their long noses. The words *Aśvamukha* and *Mahākeśa* are of similar types. The Śakas, Sūtas, Videhas and Māgadhas also have imparted their appellations to the countries where they resided. Such terms are included in the lists of countries in the Purāṇa and therefore, in all such cases, they are described as countries. Whether such countries have borrowed their names from the people residing there is a subject left for further investigation.
9. It is doubtful whether the word *Pañcama* means 'the fifth', or it is the name of a mountain. But here it is taken as a mountain because otherwise the list of the seven mts. will not be complete.

13

Studies in Ancient Geography*

(*Mārkaṇḍeya Purāṇa*)

Harihara V Trivedi

Out of the eight Cantos (LIII-X) of the *Mārkaṇḍeya Purāṇa* containing geographical materials Canto LVII describes Bhāratavarṣa in detail with her mountain ranges, hills and rivers. Here are also mentioned the countries grouped according to its five main regions. Canto LVIII depicts India as resting on Viṣṇu in the form of a tortoise looking eastward, and distributes its various peoples over the several parts of his body. This Canto repeats many of the names mentioned in the preceding Canto, and preserves, unlike the preceding one, a nine-fold division of India.

In the following pages is given an alphabetical list of topographical names embodied in the Purāṇa (vide also *IHQ.*, IX, p. 471). The edition used by me is that of the Rev. Dr. K. M. Banerjea, and published in the *Bibliotheca Indica* in 1862. I have utilised Pargiter's translation and notes.

The following points in connection with the list should be noted:

1. Names occurring in Canto LVII are usually classed as countries as suggested by the word *janapada* (LVII. 33 etc.), whereas the names in Canto LVIII refer to peoples as is evident from the reading *janā madhyanivāsinaḥ* (LVIII. 9) and *janās saṃsthitāḥ* (LVIII. 37) etc. In the cases of names occurring in both the Cantos, they are styled as countries, and in such cases different figures of references are given.

---

* Continued from *IHQ.*, vol. IX, no. 2, pp. 478. For abbreviations used see *ibid,* pp. 471; other abbreviations are : Ś=Śaka; K=Kuśa; Km=Ketumāla; V=Varṣa; Par.=Pargiter's *Mārkaṇḍeya Purāṇa;* p=a people; e=a country; r=a river; l=a lake; mt=a mountian; o=an ocean.

Words denoting the eight quarters, such as N.W. etc., when otherwise not specified, must be taken as followed by the expression 'of Bhāratavarṣa.'

2. Words enclosed within small brackets show different readings, but this device has been resorted to only when the suggested name is alphabetically similar to a name preserved in the text, e.g., Andha (Andhra?).

3. Words used as descriptive epithets in the text are also noted as different names to avoid confusion and to make the list more exhaust Examples of this type are:

Agnījya, Ghoṣasaṅkhya, Aṅgulapramukha etc.

4. Names in square brackets are supplied from the tribal appellations, e.g., [Yaśomatī] – A river (LVIII. 46) from the mention of the Yaśomatyas as a people.

The Topographical information contained in the Mārkaṇḍeya Purāṇa

A

Akaṇin – p. in S., LVIII. 22.

Agnījya – p. in N., LVIII. 43.

Aṅgataka – p. in W., LVIII. 35.

Aṅgulapramukha – p. in Km. V., LIX. 14.

Añjana – (1) mt. in E., LVIII. 11.

(2) mt. to W. of Meru, LV. 10.

Atharva – c. in C.R., LVII. 33.

Adrija – r. rising from the Vindhya mts., LVII. 21.

Adhama – p. in N., LVIII. 44.

Adhrāraka – c. in E., LVII. 42.

Animadra – c. in N., LVII. 40.

Anīkaṭa – c. in W., LVII. 49.

Antargiri – c. in E., LVII. 42.

Antardvīpa – p. in N., LVIII. 43.

Antaśśirā – r. rising from the Ṛkṣa mts., LVII. 25.

Andha (Andhra?) – c. in S., LVII. 48.

Annaja – c. on the Vindhya mts., LVII. 55.

Annadāraka – p. in NE., LVIII. 51.

[Aparānta] – The Western Region, LVII. 49-52; LVIII. 34.

Aparānta – c. in N. (?), LVII. 36.

Abhisāra – p. in N.E., LVIII. 49.

U

Ujjihāna – p. in C.R., LVIII. 6.

Utkala – c. on the Vindhya mts., LVII. 53.

Uttamarṇa – c. on the Vindhya mts. LVII. 53.

Udayagiri – mt. in E., LVIII. 13.

[Udīcī][2] – The N.R., LVII. 35-42.

Udumbara – p. in C.R., LVIII. 9.

Udbhida – (1) c. in K.D., LIII. 25.

(2) c. in S., LVII. 48.

Urukarma – c. in N.W., LVIII. 40.

Uṣṇa – *c.* in Kr. D., LIII. 23.

Ū

Ūrṇa – c. in N., LVII. 41, 57.

Ūrdhvakarṇa – p. in S.E., LVIII. 16.

Ṛ

Ṛkṣa – One of the seven mt. ranges of Bhā., LVII. 10, 25.

Ṛṣabha – mt. in S., LVIII. 27.

Ṛṣika – p. in S., LVIII. 27.

Ṛṣikulyā – (1) r. rising from the Mahendra mts., LVII. 28.

(2) r. rising from the Śuktimat mts., LVII. 29.

Ṛṣyamūka – mt. in S., LVII. 14; LVIII. 24.

E

Ekapāda – p. in N.E., LVIII. 51.

Ekapādapa (oka)? – p. in E., LVIII. 14.

Ekaśṛṅga – mt. to S. of Meru., LV. 7.

Ekekṣaṇa – p. in W., LVIII. 36.

Elika – p. in S.E., LVIII. 17.

Au

Aukhavana – p. in S., LVIII. 26.

Aupadha – c. in N., LVII. 40.

K

Kaṅka – p. in C.R., LVIII. 8.

Kaccha – c. in S., LVIII. 28.

Kaṭaka – c. in S.E., LVIII. 18.

Kaṭhākṣara – c. in W., LVII. 50.

Kapila[3] – mt. to W. of Meru., LV. 9.

Kapilendra – mt. to N. of Meru., LV. 12.

Kambala – mt. range in Km. V., LIX. 12.

Karatoyā – r. rising from the Ṛkṣa mts., LVII. 25.

Karamodā – r. rising from the Vidhya mts., LVII. 22.

Karambhaka – p. in Km. V., LIX. 14.

Karūṣa – c. on the Vindhya mts., LVII. 53.

Karkoṭaka – A forest in S., LVIII. 21.

Karṇaprādheya – p. in S.W., LVIII. 31.

Karṇāṭa – p. in S., LVIII. 23.

Karmanāyaka – p. in S., LVIII. 26.

Karvaṭāśana – mt. in E., LVIII. 11.

Kala – p. in S.W. and W., LVIII. 31, 36.

Kaliṅga – (1) mt. to S. of Meru, LV. 6.

(2) c. in S., LVII. 46; S.E., LVIII. 16; and N. (?), LVII. 37.

Kaśeruka – c. in N., LVII. 39.

Kaśerumat – One of the nine parts of Bhā., LVII. 6.

Kākulālaka – p. in S.E., LVIII. 18.

Kāñcī – A town in S., LVIII. 28.

Kāpiṅgala – p. in C.R., LVIII. 9.

Kāpila – c. in K.D., LIII. 26.

Kāminī – r. in km. V., LIX. 15.

Kāmboja – c. in N., LVII. 38; LVIII. 30 (?).

Kālakoṭisa – p. in C.R., LVIII. 8.

Kālatoyaka – c. in N., LVII. 35.

Kālājina – p. in S., LVIII. 20.

Kālibala – c. in W., LVII. 49.

Kāverī – r. rising from the Sahya mts., LVII. 26; LVIII. 24.

Kāśī – c. in C.R., LVII. 32; LVIII. 14.

Kāśmira – c. in N., LVII. 41; LVIII. 49; W. (?), LVII. 52.

Kinnara – p. in N.E., LVIII. 48.

Kimpuruṣa – A part of J.D., LIII. 34, 36; LVI. 20, 22; LIX. 29; LX. 1.

Kirāta – p. along the eastern limit of Bhā, LVII. 8; in N., LVII. 40, 57; LVIII. 44; in S.W., LVIII. 31; in N.E., LVIII. 50.

[Kiṣkindhā] – c. on the Vindhya mts., LVII. 53; LVIII. 18.

Kīcaka – c. in N.E., LVIII. 48.

Kukkuṭa – mt. to W. of Meru., LV. 10.

Kuñjara – mt. in S., LVIII. 28.

Kuntaprāvaraṇa – A hilly country in N., LVII. 57.

Kuntala – c. in C.R., LVII. 32; S., LVII. 48.

Kunyatāladaha[4] – p. in N.W., LVIII. 39.

Kumāra – c. in Ś.D., LIII. 21.

Kumārī – r. rising from the Śuktimat mts., LVII. 29.

Kumuda – mt. in S., LVIII. 26.

Kumudvatī – r. rising from the Ṛkṣa mts., LVII. 24.

Kuru – A part of J.D., LIII. 35; LVII. 56; LVIII. 42.

Uttara-kuru, LIX. 18, 29; LVI. 18.

Kuruṭa – p. in N.E., LVIII. 51.

Kurumin – c. in W., LVII. 50.

Kururvāhya – p. in C.R., LVIII. 9.

Kulaṭa – p. in N.E., LVIII. 49.

Kulīra[5] – mt. to E. of Meru, LV. 4.

Kulya – c. in C.R., LVII. 32.

Kuśa – One of the seven D., surrounded by Sarpissamudra, LIII. 24; LIV. 6.

Kuśala – c. in Kr. D., LIII. 23.

Kuśottara – c. in Ś.D., LIII. 21.

Kusuma – c. in S., LVII. 46.

Kuhaka – c. in N., LVII. 41.

Kuhū – r. rising from the Himālaya mts., LVII. 17.

Kūṭaśaila – mt. in Bhā., LVII. 14.

Kṛtamālā – r. rising from the Malaya mts., LVII. 27.

Kṛtasmara – mt. in Bhā., LVII. 14.

Kṛpā – r. rising from the Śuktimat mts., LVII. 30.

Kṛṣṇa – mt. to the W. of Meru, LV. 10; in Km. V., LIX. 12.

Kṛṣṇā – r. rising form the Sahya mts., LVII. 26; LVIII. 25.

Ketumat – c. in Śāl. D., LIII. 27.

Ketumāla – One of the nine parts of J.D., LIII. 35; LIV. 14, 31; LVI. 15; LIX. 12, 17.

Kevala (Kerala?) – c. in S., LVII. 45, 53.

Kaikeya – c. in N., LVII. 37; LVIII. 42.

Kailāsa – mt. to S. of Meru, LIV. 24; LV. 8; LVIII. 41.

Kokaṅkaṇa (Kokanada?) – p. in W., LVIII. 35.

Koṅkaṇa – p. in S., LVIII. 21.

Kola – (1) mt. in S., LVIII. 23.
(2) p. in S., LVIII. 25.

Kolāhala – mt. in Bhā., LVII. 12.

Kośala – c. in C.R., LVII. 32, 54; in E. LVIII. 14; in S.E., LVIII. 16.

Kohalaka – p. in N., LVIII. 45.

Kaurañjaka – mt. range in Bhadrāśva V., LIX. 5.

Kauruṣa – Same as Karūṣa; Dakṣiṇakauruṣa, LVIII. 27.

Kauśikā – r. rising from the Himavat mts., LVII. 18; LVIII. 50.

Kramu – r. rising from the Vindhya mts., LVII. 23.

Krauñca – (1) One of the seven D., surrounded by Dadhi-Samudra, LIII. 24; LIV. 6.
(2) p. and a group of mts. in N., LVIII. 42.
(3) c. in S., LVIII. 23.

Kṣudravīṇa – p. in N., LVIII. 42.

Kṣurādri – mt. in W., LVIII. 34.

Kṣemaka – c. in Pl. D., LIII. 30.

Kṣemadhūrta – p. in N., LVIII. 47.

Kh

Khañjana – mt. in W., LVIII. 34.

Kharasa – p. in N., LVIII. 46.

Kharmaka – mt. in E., LVIII. 11.

Khasa (Khaśa) – (1) A hilly country in N., LVII. 56.
(2) p. in C.R., LVIII. 6; in E., LVIII. 12; in N.E., LVIII. 51.

G

Gaṅgā – r. rising from the Himavat mts. LVI. 1-5, 19; LVII. 16.

Gajāhvaya – p. in C.R., LVIII. 9.

Candreśvara – p. in E., LVIII. 12.

Carmakhaṇḍika – r. in N., LVII, 36.

Carmaṇvatī – r. rising from the Pāripātra mts., LVII. 20.

Carmapaṭṭa – c. in S., LVIII. 25.

[Citrakūṭā] – mt. in Bhā., LVIII. 23.

Citrakūṭā – r. rising from the Vindhya mts., LVII. 21.

Citrotpalā – r. rising from the Vindhya mts., LVII. 22.

Civiḍa – p. in N., LVIII. 43.

Cīnā – c. in N., LVII. 39.

Cīraprāvaraṇa – p. in N.E., LVIII. 52.

Culika – c. in N., LVII. 40.

Cūlika – p. in W., LVIII. 37.

Cedi – p. in S.E., LVIII. 16.

Caitraratha – A forest on mt. Mandara, LV. 2; LVI. 5.

Cola – p. in S., LVIII. 23.

J

Jaṭhara – (1) mt. to E. of Meru, LIV. 22.
(2) p. in S.E., LVIII 16.

Jambū – (1) One of the seven D., surrounded by Lavaṇa-Samudra, LIII. 32; LIV. 5, 6, 8-10; LVI. 19; LVII. 1.
(2) r. rising from Gandhamādana, LIV. 29-30.
(3) mt. in E., LVIII. 11.

Jayanta – One of the seven mt. ranges in Km. V., LIX. 12.

Jalada – c. in Ś.D., LIII.21.

Jalasamudra – One of the seven oceans, surrounding Pu. D., LIV. 7.

Jāguḍa – c. in N., LVII. 40.

Jārudhi – mt. to N. of Meru, LIV. 25; LV. 13.

Jīmūta – c. in Śāl. D., LIII. 27.

Jñeyamallaka – c. in E., LVII. 43.

Jyotiṣika – p. in C.R., LVIII. 7.

T

Takṣaśilā – A city in N., LVIII. 44.

Tamasā – r. rising from the Vindhya mts., LVII. 22.

Tāpasāśrama – p. in S., LVIII. 27.

Dh

N

Nāgadvīpa – One of the nine parts of Bhā., LVII. 6.

Nābhi – One of the nine parts of J.D., LIII. 34.

Nāmavāsaka – c. in S., LVII. 46.

Nārikela – p. in S.E., LVIII. 17.

[Nāsika] – A city in S., LVII. 51; LVIII. 24.

Nikaṭa – p. in S., LVIII. 20.

Nirvindhyā – r. rising from the Ṛkṣa mts., LVII. 24.

Niścīrā – r. rising from the Himavat mts., LVII. 18.

Niṣadha – One of the great mt. systems of J.D., LV. 5; LIV. 9, 22, 23; LVIII. 18.

[Niṣadha] – c. on the Vindhya mts., LVII. 54; LVIII. 18.

Niṣadhāvatī – r. rising from the Ṛkṣa mts., LVII. 24.

Nīpa – p. in C.R., LVIII. 6.

Nīla – (1) One of the great mt. systems of J.D., LIV. 9, 22, 23, LV. 12.

(2) mt. range in Bhadrāśva V., LIX. 4.

Nīhāra – A hilly country in N., LVII. 56.

Nūpī – r. rising from the Pāripātra mts., LVII. 20.

Nṛsiṃha – p. in N.W., LVIII. 39.

Naiśīka – c. in S., LVII. 48. (From Nāsika?).

P

Pañcadaka – p. in W., LVIII. 35.

Pañcaśaila – mt. to S. of Meru, LV. 8.

Paṭu – c. on the Vindhya mts., LVII. 54.

Pataṅgaka – mt. to S. of Meru, LV. 6.

Payoṣṇī – r. rising from the Ṛkṣa mts., LVII. 24.

Para – p. in S., LVIII. 25.

Parṇaśavara – p. in S.E., LVIII. 19.

Parṇaśālāgra – mt. range in Bhadrāśva V., LIX. 5.

Palāśinī – r. rising from the Śuktimat mts., LVII. 30.

Pallava – c. in N., LVII. 36.

Paśupāla – c. in N.E., LVIII. 48.

Pahlava – p. in S.W., LVIII. 30; N.E., LVIII. 50.

Pākhaṇḍa – p. in C.R., LVIII. 8.

Pāñcāla – p. in C.R., LVIII. 8.

Pāṇḍura – mt. to W. of Meru, LV. 10.

Pāṇḍya – p. in S.W., LVIII. 31.

Pārada – (1) c. in N., LVII. 37.
(2) p. in S.W., LVIII. 31.

Pāraśava – p. in S.W., LVIII. 31.

Pārā – r. rising from the Pāripātra mts., LVII. 20.

Pāri patra – (1) mt. to w. of Meru, LIV. 23; LV. 10.
(2) One of the mt. ranges in Bhā., LVII. 11, 20; LVIII. 8.

Piṅgala[8] – (1) mt. to W. of Menu, LV. 9.
(2) p. in N., LVIII. 45.

Piñjara – mt. to W. of Meru, LV. 9.

Pitṛsomā – r. rising from the Mahendra mts., LVII. 28.

Pīpāṭhaka – mt. to S. of Meru, LV. 7.

Pippalaśroṇi – r. rising from the Vindhya mts. LVII. 22.

Piśācikā – r. rising from the Vindhya mts., LVIII. 22.

Puṇḍra (Pāṇḍya?) – c. in S., LVII. 45.

Puṇya – An island near N. Kurus, LIX. 28.

Puruṣādaka – Cannibals dwelling on the Sea-Coast in E., LVIII. 1.

Pulinda – c. in S., LVII. 47; W., LVII 50.

Puṣkara – One of the nine D., LIII. 19; LIV. 5, 6.

Puṣkala – c. in N., LVII. 39; LVIII. 44.

Puṣpa – mt. in Bhā., LVII. 14.

Puṣpaka – mt. to N. of Meru, LV. 13.

Puṣpajā – r. rising from the Malaya mts., LVII. 27.

Pūrṇotkaṭa – mt. in E., LVIII. 13.

Pota – p. in Km. V., LIX. 14.

Paurava – p. in N.E., LVIII. 52.

Paurika – c. in S., LVII. 48.

Pravaṅga – c. in E., LVII. 43.

Pravijaya – c. in E., LVII. 43.

Prākara – c. in Kr.D., LIII. 23; in K.D., LIII. 25.

Ph

B

Bh

M

Ratnavat – mt. to S. of Meru, LV. 7.
[Rasā] – r. in N., LVIII. 42.
Rājanya – p. in N., LVIII. 47.
Rājaśaila – mt. to S. of Meru, LV. 7.
Rucaka – mt. to S. of Meru, LV. 6.
Rūpapa – c. in W., LVII. 50.
Raivata – mt. in Bhā., LVII. 14.
Rocana – mt. in Bhā., LVII. 13.
Rohita – c. in Śāl. D., LIII. 27.

L

Laṅkā – A city in S., LVIII. 20.
Lampāka – c. in N., LVII. 40.
Lambana – c. in K.D., LIII. 25.
Lavaṇasamudra – o. surrounding J.D., LIV. 7; LVI. 15.
Lāṅgūlinī – r. rising from the Mahendra mts., LVII. 29.
Lolana – p. in N.E., LVIII. 50.
[Lohita (Lohitya)] – r. in E., LVIII. 13.

V

Vaka[9] – p. in N., LVIII. 42.
Vaṅkṣu[10] – r. in Km. V., LIX. 15.
Vañjulā – r. rising from the Vindhya mts., LVII. 22.
Vaḍavāmukha – p. in S.W., LVIII. 30.
Vatsa[11] – p. in C.R., LVIII. 6.
Vadanadantura – p. in E., LVIII. 12.
Vadantika – p. in N., LVIII. 45.
Vanadāraka – c. in S., LVII. 48.
[Vanarāṣṭra] – c. of forests in N.E., LVIII. 49.
[Vanavāhya] – c. of forests in N.E., LVIII. 50.
Vanitāmukha – p. in S.W., LVIII. 30.
Vamana – p. in W., LVIII. 35.
Vaṃśakarā – r. rising from the Mahendra mts., LVII. 29.
Varāha – mt. to N. of Meru, LV. 13.
Varuṇoda – Same as Aruṇoda, LVI. 6.
Vardhamāna – (1) p. in E., LVIII. 14.
(2) mt. range in Km. V., LIX. 12.

Ś

Śāka—(1) One of the seven D., surrounded by Dugdha-Samudra LIII. 22, 30; LIV. 6.

(2) p. in Km., V., LIX. 14.

Śākabhava—c. in Pl. D., LIII. 29.

Śātaka—p. in N., LVIII. 46.

Śātaśṛṅgin—mt. to N. of Meru, LV. 13.

Śāntika—p. in W., LVIII. 34.

Śālmali—One of the seven D., surrounding by Surā-Samudra, LIII. 26, 28; LIV. 6.

Śālmaveśmaka—p. in W., LVIII. 35.

Śālva—p. in C.R., LVIII. 6.

Śikhara—mt. to S. of Meru, LV. 6; LVI. 9.

Śiprā—(1) r. rising from the Pāripātra mts., LVII. 20.

(2) r. rising from the Ṛkṣa mts., LVII. 24.

Śiva—c. in Pl. D., LIII. 30.

Śiśira—c. in Pl. D., LIII. 29.

Śiśirākṣa—mt. to W. of Meru, LV. 9.

Śītānta (Śītārta)—mt. to E. of Meru, LV. 4, 17; LVI. 6.

Śītoda—1. to W. of Meru, LV. 3; LVI. 14.

Śukti—mt. in S., LVIII. 24.

Śuktimat—One of the seven mt. ranges in Bhā., LVII. 10, 30.

Śuktimatī—r. rising from the Vindhya mts., LVII. 23.

Śubhra—p. in E., LVIII. 12.

Śūdra—c. in N., LVII. 36; LVIII. 31.

Śūrasena—p. in C.R., LVIII. 7.

Śūlakāra—c. in N., LVII. 40.

Śūlika—c. in N., LVII. 41.

Śṛṅgavat—mt. to N. and W. of Meru, LIV. 25; LV. 10.

Śṛṅgin—A great mt. system of J.D., LIV. 9.

Śailika—p. in S., LVIII. 20.

Śailūṣa—c. in S., LVII. 46.

Śaivāla—mt. range in Bhadrāśva V., LIX. 4.

Śoṇa—r. rising from the Vindhya mts., LVII. 21.

Śyāmaka—p. in N., LVIII. 47.

Śyāmā – r. in Km. V., LIX. 15.
Śrīparvata – mt. in Bhā., LVII. 15.
Śveta – (1) mt. range in J.D., LIV. 9.
(2) c. in Śāl. D., LIII. 27.
Śvetaparṇa – mt. range in Bhadrāśva V., LIX. 4.
Śvetodara – mt. to S. of Meru, LV. 7.

S

Sakṛtraka – A hilly country in N., LVII. 57.
Saṅketa (Sāketa?) – p. in C.R., LVIII. 8.
Sadānīrā – r. rising from the Pāripātra mts., LVII. 19.
Sabindu – mt. to E. of Meru, LV. 5.
Samūla – mt. to S. of Meru, LV. 7.
Saraja – c. on the Vindhya mts., LVII. 53.
Sarasvatī – r. rising from the Himavat mts., LVII. 16; LVIII. 7.
[Sarasvatī] – r. in W., LVII. 51.
Sarpissamudra – One of the seven seas, surrounding K.D., LIV. 7.
Sahasraśikhara – mt. to W. of Meru, LV. 10.
Sahya – One of the seven mt. ranges in Bhā., LVII. 10, 27, 34.
Sānumat – mt. to N. and S. of Meru, LV. 12, 6.
Sārgiga – p. in S.W., LVIII. 31.
Sārdana – p. in N., LVIII. 43.
Sāvitṛ – A forest on mt. Supārśva, LV. 2; LVI. 16.
Sinībālī – r. rising from the Ṛkṣa mts., LVII. 24.
Sindhu[14] – (1) r. rising from the Himavat mts., LVII. 16.
(2) r. rising from the Pāripātra mts., LVII. 19.
(3) c. in N., LVII. 36; LVIII. 30, 32.
Siṃhala – p. in S., LVIII. 27.
Sītā – r. flowing towards E. of Meru, LVI. 5-7; LIX. 7.
Sukaṅkavat – mt. to E. of Meru, LV. 4.
Sukumāra – c. in Ś.D., LIII. 21.
Sukhodaya – c. in Pl. D., LIII. 29.
Supārśva – mt. to N. of Meru, LIV. 20, 21; LVI. 16.
Suprayogā – r. rising from the Sahya mts., LVII. 26.
Sumīna – c. in W., LVII. 50.

Himavat—A great mt. system to S. of the Hemakūṭa mts., LIV. 9, 24, 26; LV. 8; LVI. 10; LVII. 18,59; LVIII. 32, 41; LIII. 36, 40.

Hiraṇmaya—One of the Varṣas of J.D., LX. 14.

Hiraṇya—c. in J.D., LIII. 34.

Hiraṇvatī—r. flowing in Hiraṇmaya, LX. 14.

Hūṇa—p. in N., LVIII. 45.

Hemakūṭa—A great mt. system to N. of the Himālaya mts., LIV. 9, 26; LVIII. 18.

Hematāraka—p. in N., LVIII. 46.

Haihaya—p. in W., LVIII. 34 †

References

1. This seems to be a compound (Par., pp. 374, n. §§).
2. I have taken names embodied in verses 38-39 of Canto LVII as included within the northern region and not in the northwest as Pargiter does, since this Canto preserves the fivefold traditional division of India.
3. Piṅgala is another reading (Par., pp. 279, n. ‡).
4. A compound (Par., pp. 375 n.).
5. I have taken the names of mts. contained in the list (LV. 4-5) as standing not to the east of Mandara as the text (LV. 4) reads, but to the east of Meru. Strictly speaking, the reading should be *Meroḥ Pūrveṇa* in view of the fact that the verses following it mention mountains standing to the south, west and north of Meru. This point is corroborated by the inclusion of the name Mandara in the same list.
6. The reading here is *Cakorāśca* which may be taken as *Cakora* or *Ca+kora*.
7. The reading is *Cakramuñja* which may be taken as one word or *ca+ kramuñja*.
8. See f.n. no. 3 above.
9. The reading is *Kuruvakāḥ*. It is not evident whether this is s compound or one single name.
10. The reading is Vaṅkṣuśyāmā. But Śyāmā as a river is again mentioned in the next line.
11. Pargiter reads Vatsa (child) and informs that it would be better to read *Vatsāḥ,* 'The Vatsas' (p. 351, 11.†).
12. This might also be read as *Vala+ avastha* (Par., p. 375, n. ¶)
13. Pargiter reads *Bāhyato narāḥ* which he translates, as 'the races of men outside' (p. 320). But this Canto mentions countries comprised within the five traditional regions and hence the mention of 'races outside' would be out of place here.

14. The reading in LVIII, 32 is *Sindhukālakavairatāḥ,* which is evidently a compound though its different elements are not intelligible (Par., p. 370, n. *).

15. This seems to be a compound name (Par., pp. 383, n. ‡‡‡).

† I must renew my deep obligations to Dr. N.N. Law, the editor of this Journal, for his valuable suggestions.

14

Place-Names in the Vāmana Purāṇa

(Alphabetically arranged)

Sibdas Chaudhuri

In the following pages a list of place-names and tīrthas found in the Vāmana Purāṇa has been given. The place-names noticed by Nundalal Dey (D), Bimala Churn Law (L), D.C. Sircar (S), and Pandurang Vaman Kane (K), in their geographical works, and by A.B. Keith (V) and V.R. R. Dikshitar (P) in their indexes, have been indicated by the letters D, L, S, K, V, P.[1] respectively.

In preparing this index the Vaṅgavāsī edition of the Vāmana Purāṇa has been followed.

Place names in the Garuḍa Purāṇa have been published in the *Indian Historical Quarterly.*[2]

Place names in the Vāmana Purāṇa

1. Agnikuṇḍa, [K_4. 730b; S. 220 (Agni Saraḥ-Kuṇḍa).]
   Tīrtha in Sarasvatī.
   (51)[3] 52b.[4]

2. Aṅga, [D. 7; P_1. 20; L. 42-4, 204-209; V_1. II; S. 83]
   A country in the East.
   (14) 44b.

3. Aṅgeya, [S. 27 people]
   In the East
   (13) 45b.

4. Añjana, [P_1. 34; D. 8; K_4. 733; L. 65]
   Mountain near Brahmagiri
   (65) 130b.

5. Adrika, आद्यान् वेशन् ...पर्वताशपिणस्तु...शशिखा द्रिकाः
   (13) 58b.

6. Anaraka, [K_4. 733a; P_1. 52]
Tīrtha under Kurukṣetra
(41) 22a, 23b.

7. Anūpa, [D. 8; K_4. 733b[3]; P_1. 61; S. 35, 214-5]
(Anūpā, river rising from Rkṣavat mt. K_4. 733b.)
Janapada in Vindhyamūla, (13) 56a.

8. Antaragiri, [D. 8; P_1. 64 (a tribe of East); L. 21, 209; S. 27 (North of Prāgjyotiṣa)]
In the East
(13) 44b.

9. Andhra, [D. 7; P_1. 69; L. 140; V_1. 23; S. 87-88]
A country in the S. of Bhārata.
(13) 13b, 50a.

10. Anna, [K_4. 733 (Annakūṭa, under Mathurā)].
Tīrtha,
(36) 63a.

11. Aparānta, [D. 9; P_1. 72; L. 12, 13; S. 264]
उत्तरपथवासिनः
(13) 38a.

12. Amara (kaṇṭaka) [K_4. 732a; D. 4; P_1. 81; L. 303; S. 34, 47]
Mountain
(65) 133b.

13. Amaravati, [D. 5; P_1. 82; L. 139]
(9) 9b; (10) 12b; (60) 36a.

14. Amlu, [K_4. 732b]
River in Kurukṣetra
(34) 7b (वर्षाकालवहाः)

15. Ayodhyā, [K_4. 736b; P_1. 95; L. 142; 67-9; S. 265]
A kingdom, (established by Kauśika)
(64) 62b.

16. Aruṇā, [K_4. 734b; D. 11; P_1. 101; S. 222 (Aruna)].
River.
(41) 32a, 43a.

17. Arbuyda, [K_4. 734a; D. 10; P. 111; L. 304; S. 33n4]
A Country (13) 18a.
Mountain Abu in the Aravati range in Sirohi state.
(90) 19b.

18. Alpeka Tīrtha. [Caitra-śukla-cāturdasyāṃ tīrthe snātvā *hyalepake*] (36) 46a.

19. Avakīrṇa, [K_4. 736a.]
Tīrtha under Kurukṣetra & Sarasvatī.
(39) 24b, 26a, 29a, 32a.

20. Avantī, [K_4. 736a; D. 13; P_1. 118; L. 304-308; S. 90]
Janapada in Vindhyamūla
(13) 56a.
Avantī Viṣaya, (83) 186 (city); (89) 25a; (90) 13a.

21. Aśmaka [D. 12; P_1. 123; 139; L. 142; S. 150ff.]
(1) City, (10) 56d.
(2) In Dākṣiṇātya. (13) 49b.

22. Aśvatīrtha. [K_4. 735b; D. 13]
(83) 26a.

23. Asi, [K_4. 734b; D. 12]
River under Varanasi.
(13) 28a.
(15) 53a.

24. Ahidevikā.
River rising from Ṛkṣa mountain.
(13) 26a.

"Ā"

25. Ānanda (also called Nandītara) [K_4. 732b].
In the East
(13) 46b.

26. Āpagā, [K_4. 733; D. 9]
River under Kurukṣetra
(36) 1b, 3a, 5a.

27. Ābhīra [D. 1; P_1. 164; L. 275-6; S. 91]
(1) Uttarāpatha-vasinaḥ, (13) 37b.
(2) In Dakṣiṇāpatha, (13) 48b.

28. Āraṇya(ka) [D. 10]
In Dākṣiṇātya
(13) 48b.

"I"

29. Indra-tīrtha [K_4. 758a]
(57) 92a.
(83) 7a.

30. Indra-dvīpa [P_1. 194; S. 66]
One of the nine parts of Bhārata
(13) 10a.

31. Irāvatī [K_4. 758a; D. 79; P. 1. 200; L. 86; S. 41]
A tīrtha, River (Modern Ravi)
(13) 21a; (57) 77a;
(79) 7b, 51b, 81a; (81) 1a;
(89) 6b (Airāvatī); (90) 5a.

32. Ilāvṛta [P_1. 202]
One of the varṣas
(13) 3a, 6b.

"Ī"

33. Īśvarī
River
(84) 6b.

"U"

34. Ujjayanta [K_4. 815a; D. 211; P_1. 212]
Girnar in Saurāṣṭra and near Dvārakā
Mountain
(13) 18a.

35. Utkala [D. 213; P_1. 214; L. 197; S. 100, 134ff.]
Janapada in Vindhyamūla
(13) 54a.

36. Utkrodhanī tīrtha,
(57) 97a.

37. Utpalāvati [K_4. 816a; D. 213; P_1. 221; L. 197]
River rising from Śuktimat mountain
(13) 32b.

38. Uttarakuru [D. 213; P_1. 217; L. 133; V_1. 84; S.9]
(84) 31b; (90) 22a.

39. Uttarāpatha [D. 214; P_1. 219; L. 12-13]
Inhabitants of,
(13) 37a-44a.

40. Uttamarṇa [S. 34]
Janapada Vindhyamūla
(13) 54b.

41. Udapāna [K_4. 814b]
(57) 92a.

42. Udaya [P_1. 222; L. 164-5, 196-7; 331-2]
Mountain,
(52) 46a; (57) 15a; (65) 76b; (73) 26a.

43. Uddālaka, [K_4. 815a. (Uddālakeśvara)]
Mountain
(52) 46b.

44. Ulūpī, [river rising from Pārijātra mountain]
(13) 24b.

45. Uśira,
River
(13) 21b.

"Ū"

46. Ūrṇa [S. 36, 300 (people)]
(13) 58a (ādayān deśān parvatāśrayiṇ) (a)

"Ṛ"

47. Ṛkṣa, [K_4. 736; D. 168; P_1. 260; L. 328; S. 49n3]
Mountain
(13) 14b; 28a (Rivers emanating from).

48. Ṛṣyamūka, [K_4, 797a; D. 169; P_1. 274; S. 293]
Hill, (13) 18a.

"E"

49. Ekalavta,[5] [S272 (people)]
Janapada in Vindhyamūla
(13) 54a.

"O"

50. Oghavati [K_4. 786b; D. 142; S. 46, 57]
River in Panjab
(13) 25a (rises from Pāriyātra mountain); (46) 50a; (57) 83a; (58) 115c; (62) 40b, 54b.

51. Ojasa, [K_4. 786]
Tīrtha under Kurukṣetra, probably same as Aujasa
(41) 6b; (90) 17a.

"AU"

52. Auśanasa, [K_4. 736a]
Tirtha on Saraswatī, same as *Kapālamocana.*
(39) 1a, 11b; (42) 24b; (57) 91a.

"K"

53. Kaṭāha, (Name of a Dvīpa, M. Williams' Dictionary p. 243c)
One of the nine parts of Bhārata
(13) 10b; (90) 34a.

54. Kanakhala, K_4. 762b; D. 88; P. 306; L. 89]
A mahātīrtha on the Gangaes near Haridvāra.
(4) 18b; (51) 52a; (57) 89b; (84) 38b.

55. Kanakekṣaṇam, [Prabhāvārthasahaṁ prādat kāṁcanā –]
River
(57) 81b.

56. Kanthāya,
Tīrtha,
(90) 28b.

57. Kapālamocana, [K_4. 763b; D. 90; P_1 309]
Tīrtha.
(3) 49b; (39) 14a.

58. Kapila, [P_1. 313]
Tīrtha.
(36) 14a.

59. Kapiladhārā, [P_1. 313; K_4. 764a; D. 90; L. 317]
under Amarakaṇṭaka.
(84) 24a.

60. Kapiahrada, [K_4. 764a.]
Tīrtha in Haridvāra.
(35) 24a.

61. Karkandha, [K_4. 764a]
Tīrtha (51) 52a.

62. Karṇā
River
(57) 82b.

63. Karatoyā, [K_4. 764b; D. 63; P_1. 320; L. 224; S. 95, 279]
River rises in Ṛkṣapāda.
(13) 26b.

64. Kalaśākhya-tīrtha, [K_4. 761a.]
(36) 18a.

65. Kalasvanā,
River rising from Sahyapāda,
(13) 31a.

66. Kaliṅga, [D. 85; P_1. 332; L. 156-9; S. 84, 137, 278]
In Madhyadeśa, (13) 36d.
In Dākṣiṇātya (13) 48a.

67. Kaśeruṇa dvīpa, [S. 5 (Kaserumat)]
(13) 10a.

68. Kaśerudeśa [P_1. 340]
(90) 12a.

69. Kāñcana,
River
(83) 2b.

70. Kāncanākṣī, [K_4. 762b]
River near Naimiṣa forest; one of Sapta Saraswati r.
(37) 18a, 28b; * (62) 54a. (65) 34b. * (83) 2b.

71. Kāñcīpurī, [K_4. 762b; D. 88; P_1. 345; L. 161; S. 279]
City
(13) 50c.

72. Kāmarūpa, [D. 87; P_1. 351; L. 226-8; S. 86, 273]
A mahātīrtha where Kāmakhyā resides, (84) 40b.

73. Kāmeśvara-tīrtha, [K_4. 762a Kāmeśwara-liṅga]
(34) 42b.

74. Kāmyakavana, [K_4. 762a; D. 88.]
(41) 30b; (42) 1a.

75. Karūṣa [D. 95; L. 225-6; S. 33 (Kārūṣa City in Vindhyamūla, Sahabad district in Bihar)]
(13) 54a.

76. Kālañjara, [K_4. 760b; D. 84; P_1. 361.2; S. 243]
Mountain
(6) 55c; (76) 14a, 25d; (84) 27b; (90) 27a.

77. Kālindī (Yamunā) [K_4. 761a; D. 85; P_1. 367; S. 39]
A tīrtha, River, (3) 8a; (6) 30a, 31a; (13) 20b; (57) 75a; (60) 17b, 40a; (63) 68b; (64) 10b. 12a; (65) 5b. 82a; (78) 88b; (79) 1a; (89) 24b; (90) 3a.

78. Kālī [K_4. 761a; D. 84; P_1. 368]
River flows through Saharanpur district., U.P.,
(57) 79a.

79. Kāverī, [K_4. 767b; D. 97; P_1. 369-70; L. 38, 162; S. 52, 280]
A river rising in Sahya mt., South India
(13) 31a.

80. Kiṃrūpa
Tīrtha,
(36) 27a.

81. Kiṁpuruṣa, [D. 100; P. 278; S. 63, 280 (people)]
One of the Varṣas,
(13) 5b.

82. Kikarava, [S. 280 (people)]
Janapada in Vindhyamūla,
(13) 54b.

83. Kiraṇā, [K_4. 768b.]
River,
(89) 5b.

84. Kirāta, [D. 100; P_1. 379; L. 98; V_1. 157; S. 95, 280]
East of Kumāra dvīpa;
(13) 12a.
(13) 58b. (ādyān deśān parvatāśrayiṇ)

85. Kiṣkindhā, [D. 100; P_1. 380; K_4. 768b; L. 21; S. 34]

(90) 17b.

86. Kuṇḍal(eśvara) [K_4. 772b (Under Narmadā or near southern gate of Śrīparvata); S. 31 (=Kuntala), 150ff., 282)]

In Madhyadeśa

(13) 36a; 50a. (Kundana)

87. Kuṇḍina, [K_4. 772b; D. 108; P_1. 389; L. 7; S. 153

(Capital City–modern Kauṇḍinyapura or the Wardka in the Chandur Taluk; amraoti dt., Berar).]

(84) 34b; (90) 24a.

88. Kuthaprāvaraṇa. [P_1. 390; S. 36n7 (Situated in the Himalayan region.)]

(13) 58a. (आद्यान् देशान् पर्वताश्रयिण)

89. Kubjāmr(aka), [K_4. 771; D. 105; P_1. 395]

Mahātīrtha,

(51) 51b; (79) 3b; (90) 3b.

90. Kumāra, [K_4. 772a; D. 106; P_1. 397; S. 30. 282]

(13) 11b; 59b (Kumāradvīpa), description of, 1-59.

91. Kumāradhārā [K_4. 772a; P_1. 399 (?)]

A river,

(90) 16b.

92. Kumārāda in Dākṣiṇātya,

(13) 47b.

93. Kumudvatī, [K_4. 772b; P_1. 401; S. 50]

A river rising in Vindhya.

(13) 29a.

94. Kuru [P_1. 406; L. 50; V_1. 166; S. 102, 282]

Country:

One of the Varṣas,

(13) 5a.

95. Kurukṣetra [K_4. 773a; D. 110; P_1. 406; L. 101; V_1. 169; S. 103]

Tīrtha,

(21) 21a; (27) 12b; (32) 1b, 24b; (33) 2b, 1b, 7a, 8b, 10a, 15a, 16b; (34) 3a-5b (7 forests in.); (36) 80a; (37) 23b, 29a, 31b, 35b; (39) 2a; (41) 13a, 15a, 20a, 21a; (42) 3a; (47) 39a (48) 23a, 33b; (50) Māhātmya; (57) 51b, 53b, 93b; (62) 40a; 56a, 57b; (69) 4b; (81) 2b; (84) 1b, (89) 1b, 53c; (90) 5a. (92) 40d.

96. Kulyā, [K_4. 772a; P_1. 410' V_1. 173; S. 22n 1 (People in m. Kulait region in upper Rāvī)]

River in Dākṣiṇātya,

(13) 47a.

97. Kuśa, [P. I. 412; S. 160ff.]

One of the Seven Dvīpas,

(11) 37b, 38a; (90) 42a.

98. Kuśasthala (under Mathurā) [K_4. 773a; D. 111; P_1. 414; S. 242n; 243 n.2. (*Same as* Kānyakubja city)] Kuśasthalī? City

(13) 51a; (76) 14c.

99. Kuśūdra, [S. 21n; 282 (people)]

In Madhyadeśa,

(13) 36a.

100. Kuhū [D. 105; K_4. 772a; P_1. 419; S. 41, n. 2 (=Kābul river=Kubhā of Ṛv), 282]

River sprung from Himālaya.

(13) 21a; (57) 80a.

101. Kurujāṅgala [D. 110; K_4. 773a; P_1. 407; L. 101; S. 21n3]

Sirhind in Punjab;

(3) 12a; (22) 42a; (23) 2b. निवासं वामनत्य; (33) 12a; (84) 3b, 17b; (89) 3b; (90) 48b, 17a.

102. Kurudhvaja,

City

(84) 22b.

103. Kulottaraṅka

Tīrtha

(36) 76b; (37) 4b.

104. Kṛtamālā [D. 104; K_4. 771a; P_1. 426; S. 52n 5 (=mod. Vaigai running past Maduri see *Caitanyacaritāmṛta,* ch. 9).]

River rising in Malaya (Śuktiman mt.)

(13) 32b.

105. Kṛtaśauca, [K_4. 771a; P_1. 428]

Mahātīrtha,

(90) 5b.

106. Kṛtasmara,
Mountain
(13) 18b.

107. Kṛṣṇavenyā (=kṛṣṇa-veṇā) [K_4. 770b; P_1. 453; D. 104; S. 51n7 (Veṇvā=mod. Veṇā, tributary of Kṛṣṇa: combined stream of the two is known as Kṛṣṇavenā etc).]
Same as Kṛṣṇā R. (S. 281).
River rising from Sahya mountain,
(13) 30b.

108. Kṛṣṇā [K_4. 770b; D. 104; P_1. 455; S. 281, 51n7 (same as above)]
River,
(78) 7b; (81) 9b; (90) 2b.

109. Ketumala [D. 99; P_1. 457]
One of the Varṣas,
(13) 4b.

110. Kedāra [K_4. 768a; D. 97; P_1. 458; L. 97; S. 13]
Tīrtha (origin & tīrtha māhātmya ch. 57, V. 8-15)
(36) 16b, 26b; (57) 97b; (60) 10b (orogin of); 11a, 16b, 17a; (79) 2b; (90) 3b.

111. Kerala [D. 98; P_1. 459; L. 163; S. 85-6, 280]
In Dākṣiṇātya,
(13) 47a.

112. Kailāsa [K_4. 760a; D. 82; P_1, 464; L. 87-88; S. 97, (Himalayan region to the north of Mānasasarovara), 278]
(43) 72a; (44) 3a, 21b; (58) 88c; (90) 33a.

113. Kokaṇaka
Mountain,
(13) 19a.

114. Kokāmukha [K_4. 768b; D. 101; S. 217ff]
Tīrtha,
(84) 26a.

115. Koṭītīrtha [K_4. 770a. D. 104; P_1. 465]
near Pṛthūdaka.
(36) 65b, 73a; (51) 53a; (84) 11a. 17a.

116. Kolāhala [K_4. 769a; D. 101; P_1. 467]
Mountain
(13) 16b; (65) 108b.

117. Kośala [D. 103; P_1. 468; V_1. 190; L. 99; S. 99 (=Mahā Kośala), 281]
A country,
(13) 55a (in Vindhyamūla)]; (37) 32a (in the north; Saraswatī flows by it); (64) 19b.

118. Kaunaṭa [K_4. 766b]
Tīrtha,
(51) 53a.

119. Kaurava in Madhyadeśa [S. 280 (=Kuru country)]
(13) 36c.

120. Kauśala in [P_1. 472]
(90) 29b.

121. Kauśika in Madhyadeśa [P_1. 474; S. 280]
(13) 36b.

122. Kauśikī [K_4. 767a; D. 97; P_1. 475, S. 42,
(River=mod. Kosi) 280]
(13) 22b; (34) 7b (वर्षाकालवहा), (36) 59a. 5b; (57) 77b; (65) 84b. 85a; (78) 5b (tīrtha).

123. Kriyā, [K_4. 770a; P_1. 481; S. 47]
River rising from Ṛkṣavat.
(13) 25b.

124. Krauñca, [K_4. 770a; D. 104; P_1. 484; V_1. 200; S. 163]
A mountain
(11) 38b; (58) 88d. 98a, 102b, 108a, 109a, 110a, 118b; (90) 43a.

125. Kṣīroda, [P_1. 490]
(35) 7a, 16b; (85) 5a; (60) 58a.

126. Kṣīrīkāvāsa [K_4. 771b.]
(84) 21b.

"Kha"

127. Khāsa- [D. 99; P_1. 498; S. 280 (people)]
A country,
(13) 57b. (आद्यान् देशान् पर्वतास्त्रयिण)

128. Kheṭaka- [D. 100 (Khaira on r. Vetravatī); P_1. 500; S. 280]
Uttarāpathavāsin
(13) 38a.

129. Khelliśa, [S. 280]
Janapada in Vindhyamūla,
(13) 55a.

"Ga"

130. Gaṅga- [K_4. 751b; D. 61; P_1. 501; L. 77, 152; V_1. 217; S. 172ff., 273]
River; A tīrtha,
(6) 4b; (34) 7a; (36) 64b; (42) 7a.

131. Gaṅgādvāra- [K_4. 751b; D. 62; P_1. 502; L. 33; S. 273]
Tīrtha, same as Haridvāra
(37) 36a; (39) 17b.

132. Gaṇḍakī- [K_4. 751b; D. 60; P_1. 507; L. 75; S. 42n3, 273]
Tīrtha, R. rises in Himālaya and falls into Ganges at Sonepur, Muzaffarpur dt., in Bihar.
(13) 22b; (57) 79a.

133. Gandhamādana [D. 60; K_4. 752a; P_1. 511; L. 76; S. 273]
Mountain.
(52) 19a, 21a, 43a.

134. Gabhastimat [P. I. 513; S. 5n]
One of the nine parts of Bhārata.
(13) 10a.

135. Gayā - [K_4. 752b; D. 64; P_1. 515; L. 219; S. 224ff., 274]
Tīrtha,
(33) 8a (Gayāśrāddha); (36) 50a; (37) 29b; (41) 8b; (79) 64a, 69b; (83) 4b; (90) 9b.

136. Gayā-Śiras [K_4. 752b; D. 65; P_1. 517; S. 227ff, 274]
Hill named after rājarṣi Gaya,
(32) 18b; (57) 89a.

137. Garuḍāsana,
(52) 46b.

138. Gāruḍa [K_4. 753b.]
Tīrtha,
(90) 4a.

139. Girivraja [K_4. 753b; D. 66; P_1. 535; L. 44; S. 24n6 (=Girjāk or Jalālpur city on the Jhelam)]

(84) 31b; (90) 26a.

140. Gokarṇa [K_4. 753b; D. 70; P_1. 544; L. 79, 153; S. 99 (Village in the Bāgmatī in Nepāl), 274; 11 (Kanare dt. Mysore)].

Mahā tīrtha,

(81) 5b; (90) 5b, 28a.

141. Godāvārī, [K_4. 753; D. 69; P_1. 546; L. 22. 378; S. 51n6, 274]

A river rises in Sahya mt., Western Ghat,

(13) 30b; (57) 75b; (65) 37b, 127b, 153a.

142. Gopta, [S. 274 (people)]

Janapada in Vindhyamūla,

(13) 54b.

143. Gomati [K_4. 754a; D. 70; P_1. 551; L. 80; V_1. 238; S. 41n3, 274]

A river

(13) 22a; (63) 61a; (83) 2b; (90) 31a.

144. Gomanta, [K_4. 754a; D. 70; P_1. 551; L. 22; S. 274]

Mountain

(13) 18b.

145. Govardhana [K_4. 754b; D. 72; P_1. 554; L. 21; S. 23n3 (near Nasik on Godāvarī river)]

A mahātīrtha, mountain

(13) 17b.

"Gha"

146. Ghaṭita,

(90) 33a.

"Ca"

147. Cakratīrtha, [K_4. 742a; D. 43; P_1. 570]

under Sarasvatī,

(7) 37b; (43) 11a; (57) 89a.

148. Cakriṇī [S. 269]

River rises in Ṛkṣapāda,

(13) 28a.

149. Caṇḍikeśvara [K_4. 742b.]

Tīrtha,

(51) 51b.

150. Candrikā [K_4. 743a; D. 47; S. 40n1]
River Candrabhāgā=m. Chenab
(12) 21a.

151. Campaka [K_4. 742b. (araṇya, tīrtha or varṣa;) D. 43; P_1. 589]
W.N. of Jambudvīpa
(13) 4b.

152. Campā [K_4. 742; D. 43-44; P_1. 589-590; L. 32, 44, 214; S. 27n5, 83 (city)]
(84) 12b.

153. Carmaṇvatī [K_4. 743a; D. 48; P_1. 592; L. 312]
Modern Chambal tributary of Jumna (S. 46n2).
River rises in Pārijātra,
(13) 24b.

154. Cītrakūṭa [K_4. 744a; P_1. 601; L. 20, 73, 313-4, D. 50; S. 270]
Hill, 65 miles S.W, of Prayāga, Banda Dist.
(13) 18b; (52) 47b.

155. Citrakuṭā [K_4. 744a; D. 50; S. 47n5 (either the same as Mandākin or a part of it)]
R. rising from Ṛkṣaparvata,
(13) 26a.

156. Citrā [P_1. 608; S. 270]
River rises in Himālaya (13) 22b.
River rises in Pariyātra (13) 25a.

157. Citrotpalā [K_4. 744a; D. 50; S. 48 n1 (R. Mahānadī below its junction with the Pyri or its branch)].
River rising from Ṛkṣapāda
(13) 26b.

158. Cauḍa,
In Dākṣiṇātya,
(13) 47a.

"JA"

159. Jamna [P_1. 627 (Janmeśvaram, M. 22.42)]
Tīrtha
(36) 28b, 39a.

160. Jambu Dvīpa [D. 80; P_1. 629; L. 9; S. 8, 9, 277]
(11) 33b, 41a; (13) 1b, 2a; (90) 42a.

161. Jambū nadī [K_4. 759a; P_1. 630; S. 277]
(18) 33b.

162. Jayanta [K_4. 759a; P_1. 635]
Tīrtha,
(51) 51b.

163. Jānuka, [S. 277]
In Dākṣiṇātya
(13) 47b.

164. Jyeṣṭhāśrama
Tīrtha,
(36) 69a.

"TA"

165. Takṣaka
Tīrtha,
(51) 53a.

166. Taṅgaṇa [D. 204; P_2. 2; S. 26n9 (=Upper Vitastā Valley, Hq. at Ṭaṅgaṇāpura, near Johimath, Garhwal dt. U.P.), 299].
(13) 57b (आद्यान् देशान् पर्वतात्रृषिणा)

167. Tamasā [K_4. 812a; D. 202; P_2. 10; L. 131; S. 47n7 =(Modern Tons), 298]
River rising from Ṛkṣpāda
(13) 26b; (57) 75b.

168. Tala,
(90) 37a.

169. Tāpī [K_4. 812b; D. 204; P_2. 13; L. 36, 330; S. 50n2, 299]
A river (=mod. Tapti) rising from Vindhya,
(13) 28b.

170. Tāmraparṇa [P_2. 16]
Island,
(13) 10a.

171. Tāmraparṇī [K_4. 812a; D. 203; P_2. 16; L. 192; S. 52, 299 *Mod.* Tāmravarī joins Chittur in Tiruveli dt.,

Madras, (S. 52n5.].
A river rises in Śuktimat
(13) 32b.

172. Tāmralipta [D. 203; P_2. 17; L. 263; S. 298 (same as Tāmralipti)]
in the East.
(13) 46a.

173. Tīrthanemi,
(57) 93a.

174. Tuṅgaprastha, [P_2. 28]
Mountain
(13) 17b.

175. Tuṇḍikera [P_2. 28; S. 35]
Janapada in Vindhyamūla,
(13) 56a.

176. Tumbara [D. 207 (Tumbura); P_2. 29 (Tumburā);
[S. 300]

177. Turaga [S. 300 (people)]
Janapada in Vindhyamūla,
(13) 55b.

178. Turaṣka [D. 207]
A country in the north of Bhārata
(13) 12b.

179. Tomara [D. 205; P_2. 37; S. 299 (Country)]
(13) 58b. (आद्यान् देशान् पर्वताशयिणा)

180. Toyā [K_4. 812b; P_2. 37; S. 299]
A river rising in Vindhya
(13) 29b.

181. Tośala [K_4. 812b; D. 205 (Tosali); P_2. 37; L. 195; S. 34n4;]
Dr. round the city of Tośālī (mod. Dhauli, Puri dt.)
Janapada in Vindhyamūla.
(13) 55a.

182. Trikūṭa [D. 205; P_2. 42; S. 189]
Hill,
(52) 47b; (84) 42b; (85) 4a ff. (Description); (90) 24a.

183. Trigarta [D. 205; P_2. 43; L. 131; S. 37n1 (=Mod. Jalandhar region)]
A country in the N.E. of Bhārata
(13) 58b. (आद्यान् देशान् पर्वताश्रयिणा)

184. Tridivā [K_4. 813a; P_2. 44; S. 299]
River rising from Ṛkṣavat,
(13) 27b.

185. Triviṣṭapa [K_4. 814a.]
Tīrtha,
(36) 43a; (51) 52b; (90) 32a.

186. Traipura [K_4. 813b; D. 205 (=Tripura); P_2. 54; 534n5 (people of Tripura or Tripurī)]
Janapada in Vindhyamūla
(13) 55a.

"D"

187. Dakṣatīrtha [K_4. 744b]
under Kurukṣetra
(46) 2a.

188. Daṇḍaka [samw as Daṇḍakāraṇya in Dākṣiṇātya) [K_4. 745a; D. 52; P_2. 65; L. 41; S. 271]
(13) 49a.

189. Daṇḍakāraṇya [K_4. 745a; D. 52; P_2. 65; L. 41, 280; S. 30N6]
Country,
(18) 28c, 34c; (39) 5a; (84) 43d; (90) 26b.

190. Daśārṇā [K_4. 745b; D. 54; P_2. 79; L. 314, 336; S. 47N4] (=mod. Dhasan)
River rising in mt. Ṛkṣa.
(13) 26a.

191. Daśāśvamedhika, [K_4. 745b; P_2. 79]
Tīrtha
(35) 49a.

192. Dākṣiṇātya, [P_2. 81; S. 271 (same as Daksināpatha)]
Countries in,
(13) 47-50.

193. Dāruvana, [K_4. 745a (same as Devadāru Vana); D. 53; P_2. 84]
(84) 32c.

194. Dāsārṇa [K_4. 745b; D. 54; L. 314; S. 150ff., 91 (Eastern Malwa)]
Country in Vindhyamūla,
(13) 54b.

195. Dugdhodā [S. 53 N3]
River rising in Sahya mountain
(13) 31b.

196. Durgandhā [S. 51 n2]
River rising in 'Vindhyapāda'
(13) 29b.

197. Durgā tīrtha [K_4. 748b; S. 31n7 (tributary of Sābarmatī), 51N2]
under Saraswatī
(42) 15b.

198. Durdhara [D. 58 (Durdhura); P_2. 102]
Mountain
(13) 16b.

199. Dṛḍaśṛṅga
Mountain
(52) 47a.

200. Dṛṣadvatī [K_4. 748a; D. 57; P_2. 110; L. 75; S. 41n4]
River,
(13) 22a; (33) 9a; (34) 8a (वर्षाकालवहा); (36) 48a, 59a.

201. Devadāruvana [K_4. 745. b; D. 54 (same as Dāruvana); P_2. 117]
(44) 34b.

202. Devahrada [K_4. 746a; P_2. 130]
(81) 14a.

203. Devikā [K_4. 746b; D. 55; P_2. 134; L. 74; S 41 n2 (=m, Deeg, tributary of Rāvī)]
River
(71) 5a; (78) 35a, 52a; (84) 7a, 12b; (90) 30b.

204. Devikā Devī. [P_2. 134]
(89) 7a.

205. Devī,
Tīrtha,
(35) 34b; (57) 96b.

206. Dviradapāvana tīrtha,
(57) 94b.

207. Dvaitavana [K_4. 748b; D. 58; L. 75]
(47) 56a.

"Dha"

208. Dharmāraṇya [K. 747 a (under Gayā); D. 56; P_2. 166]
(84) 12.

209. Dhātakī [S. 271]
River
(13) 21b.

210. Dhṛtapāpā/ Dhūtapāpā [K_4. 748a; D. 57; P_2. 174; S. 272]
A river. Tributary of the Ganges in Benaras region (S. 41n3)
(13) 22a; (57) 82b (Dhṛtapapa)

"NA"

211. Nakulagaṇa [K_4. 783b.]
under Kurukṣetra – tīrtha
(46) 2b.

212. Nadvāla [Irāvatī=nadvalā – Saṅgam, K4. 758a.]
(79) 51b.

213. Nandinī [K_4. 784a; P_2. 200; S. 287]
River rising in Pāriyātra,
(13) 24a.

215. Navarāṣṭra [P_2. 215; D. 139; S. 288]
Country
(90) 30a.

216. Narmadā [K_4. 785a; D. 138; P_2. 210; L. 36, 305. 323; S. 288]
A tīrtha, (7) 26d; (84) 24b; (90) 18b.
A river rises in 'Ṛkṣapada, (13) 25b; (42) 7b; (57) 75a.

217. Nalinī [K_4. 784; D. 137; P_2. 213; S. 288]
A river rises in 'Sahyapāda'
(13) 31b.

218. Nāgagiri [K_4. 783a; P_2. 217]
A hill under Gayā,
(13) 17b.

219. Nāgatīrtha [K_4. 783a; P_2. 219]
(57) 93b.

220. Nāgadvīpa [P_2. 219; S. 288]
(13) 10b.

221. Nāgahṛadatīrtha [D. 134]
(32) 24a; (36) 41.

222. Nisvarā
River
(13) 22b.

223. Nirāhāra [D. 141; P_2. 245; S. 288 (people)]
(13) 57b (आद्यान् देशान् पर्वताश्रयिणा).

224. Nirvindhyā [K_4. 786a; D. 141; P_2. 249; S. 50n2, 288]
River (mod. Newuj, tributary of Chambal)
rising in Vindhya and falling into Chambal
(13) 28b.

225. Niṣadha [K_4. 786a; D. 141; L. 325; P_2. 252; S. 288]
(13) 55a (Janapada in Vindhyamūla); (90) 13a.

226. Niṣadhā [K_4. 786b; P_2. 252; S. 288 (*also* Niṣadhāvatī)]
River rising in Vindhya
(13) 28b.

227. Nīla [K_4. 786a; P_2. 252]
Tīrtha
(84) 28a.

228. Nīlā [K_4. 786a. (Nīlotpalā); P_2. 259; S. 288]
River
(13) 21a.

229. Naimika [S. 287 (people)]
in Dākṣiṇātya
(23) 50a.

230. Naimiṣa [K_4. 783a; D. 135; P_2. 265; L. 41, 113; V_1. 460; S. 28]
Tīrtha
(3) 10a; (7) 37a, 38b, 39a, 41b; (8) 29b; (37) 8a, 24a, 28b, (39) 27a; (42) 3a; (63) 40b; (65) 34b, 75a; (83) 1b, 3b. (between Gomati & Kāñcananadī); (84) 11b; (90) 9a.

(*To be continued*)

References

1. L=Historical Geography of Ancient India, By Bimala Churan Law. Paris, Societe Aisatique de Paris, [1954] Printed in Calcutta v+354p., 24cm.

V= Vedic Index of names and subjects By Arthus Anthony Macdonell and Arthus Berriedale Keith. London, John Murray, 1912, 2 vols. (XVI+544; +592 pp.). [Reprinted by Motilal Banarasidas, Varanasi, 1958].

Indian Texts Series.

D= The Geographical Dictionary of Ancient and Mediaeval India. By Nundo Lal Dey. 2nd. ed. [Printed by C. Wollen at the British India Press, Mazgaon, Bombay.] London, Luzac & Co.1927. X+262P., 1 map, cm. Calcutta Oriental Series, No. 21. E. 13.

P= The Purāṇa Index, By V.R. Ramachardra Dikshitar. University of Madras, 1951-1955. 3 vols. 25 cm. Madras University Historical Series, no. 19. Printed at G.S. Press, Madras.

[Purāṇas indexed; Bhāgavata; Brahmāṇḍa. Matsya; Vāyu; Viṣṇu].

K= History of Dharmaśāstra (Ancient and Mediaeval Religious and Civil law in India). Bol. 4, sec. 4–Chapter 16–List of Tīrthas, pp. 723-827. Poona, Bhandarkar Oriental Research Institute, 1953.

S= Studies in the Geography of ancient & medieval India. By D. C. Sircar. Delhi, Motilal Banarsidass, 1960. 304 pp. 22 cm.

2. Vol. 37, part I, March 1961.

3. Chapter.

4. verse and line.

5. (ā) Name of the town, M. William's Dictionary p. 229a.

* { साऽमभ्यागता भद्रे स्नातुं पुणयां सरस्वती
नैमिषे का/नाक्षीन्तु विख्यातां धर्म्मामात्तरं । }

15

Place-names in the Vāmana Purāṇa

"P"

Sibdas Chaudhuri

231. Pañcavaṭa [K 4. 788. b.].
Tīrtha under Kurukṣetra, (41) 11a.

232. Pañcarūpa. [S. 289].
River (13) 20b.

233. Pampā [K_4. 787. a (tributary of Tuṅgabhadrā); D. 144; P_2. 286; L. 292; S. 289 (lake)] (90) 16a.

234. Payoṣṇī–[K_4. 790a; D. 156; P_2. 287; L. 326; S. 50N_2, 290].
A river identified with Pain or Pain Gaṅgā, tributary of Godāvarī (S. 50n. 2).
(13) 28b (rises in Vindhya mt); (63) 86c; (81) 10b; (89) 7a; (90) 7a.

235. Parṇāśā [K_4. 789. b; P_2. 300; D. 149; S. 45 N.3.
(=mod. Banās, tributary of Chambal in Rājasthāna)].
River rises in Pariyātra, (13) 24a.

236. Pallava [D. 144; P_2. 303; S. 289 (dynasty)].
Uttarapathabāsī. (13) 38a.

237. Pavanasya Hrada [K_4. 790. a].
Tīrtha, (37) 1a.

238. Paścimāśāṁ jānapada janāḥ.
(13) 51-53.

239. Pāñcāla–[D. 145; P_2. 308; L. 42, 50, 63, 115; V_1. 468; 514; S. 92, 289].
A country in the middle-region of Bhārata (14) 36 b; (83) 26 b; Pāñcālika, (90) 13b.

240. Pānikhyāta=Khāta [K_4. 788. b].
Tīrtha (36) 53a.

241. Pārijatra [K_4. 789a; P_2. 318; D. 149; V_2. 126;[1] 5289; 46 N. 6 (=Paripātra=W. Vindhyas together with Aravalli range)]. Mountain, (13) 15a, 25a (river emanating from); (83) 13 b; (90) 11b.

242. Pāvanī–[K_4. 790a; D. 155; S. 290; 59 N (= Irawadi)].
Eastern river rises in Pāriyātra, (13) 24a.

243. Pippalāla [K_4. 791a; P_2. 333; L. 182 (m. Pimpral)].
River rising from Ṛkṣapāda, (13) 27a.

244. Piśācikā, [K_4. 791. a; P_2. 335; s. 290].
River rising from Ṛkṣapāda (13) 26 b.

245. Puṣpgiri [K_4. 794. b; P_2. 367; D. 164; L. 22, 185] mt. (13) 18a.

246. Puṇḍra–[D. 161; P_2. 340; V.$_1$ 536; S. 291].
In Dākṣiṇātya, (13) 47a.

247. Pulinda [S. 103, 291; D. 161; P_2. 360; L. 184; V_1. 23, V_2. 8, 354].
A country in the Dākṣiṇātya. (13) 49a; (76) 25 (bet. Himādrāi and Kālañjara where Pulindas were given land).

248. Puṣkara–[K_4. 793 b; D. 163; P_2. 363; L. 41; S. 291].
One of the seven Dvīpas; (11) 39a, 42a, 46a, 47a, 48b; (13) 1a, (22) 19b; (37) 19a, 21a, 23a; (57) 90a; (65) 13b, 14b, 16b, 19b, (Puṣkara water), 31a. 40b, 52b; (83) 32b, (84) 12a; (90) 14b, 43b.

249. Pṛthūdaka, [K_4 793. a; D. 160; P_2. 387; S. 291].
Tīrtha on S. bank of Saraswatī, modern Pehoa.
(21) 21b; (22) 45d; (39) 16b, 19b, 29a.[2] (57) 88b; (58) 115b;[3] (50) 1c, 5b; (51) 54a, 74b, 73a; (62) 52d.

250. Pṛṣadhra, [S. 291].
In the East, (13) 46.

251. Paurika [P_2 395; S. 290].
In Dākṣiṇātya, (13) 49b.

252. Prajāmukha [K_4. 792. a.].
(90) 28a.

253. Pratiṣṭhāna, [K_4. 792, b; P_2. 411; D. 159; L. 183; S. 291].
City, mod. Paiṭhāna (21) 39a.

254. Prabhāsa–[K_4. 791b; D. 157; P_2. 422; L. 117, 293, S. 290].
A tīrtha, (57) 91b.

255. Prayāga–[K_4 792b; D. 160; P_2. 426; L. 117-8, S. 290].
A tīrtha, (3) 26b; (22) 18b; (51) 51a; (57) 99a; (83) 27b, 28a; (90) 1, 23b.

256. Pravaṅga [Identified with Aṅga by Pargiter Mārk. P., 325; D. 160; S. 291]. In the East, (13) 45a.

257. Prāgjyotiṣa [D. 158; P_2. 437. L. 252-3; S. 290].
In the East, (13) 46a.

258. Prācī Saraswatī, [K_4. 792a. (=Saraswatī, under Gayā) D. 158; P_2. 439]. River, (50) 4a.

259. Prācya, [D. 158; S. 172-3].
Same as Psrsii (S. 290).
Janapada, (13) 44b-46b.

260. Prāvijaya, [D. 160; S. 291].
In the East, (13) 45b.

261. Plakṣa–[P_2. 451; K_4. 791a; S. 290].
Tīrtha; one of the seven Dvīpas. (11) 36a, 44a; (90) 42b.

262. Plākṣāvataraṇa, [K_4. 791. b; V_2. 55^4] (90) 25a.

263. Pluṣṭa–[S. 36, 290].
(13) 58a.

"Pha"

264. Phalakīvana [D. 156. K_4. 790b.].
Tīrtha under Kurukṣetra, (36) 47a, 50b, 51a.

"Ba"

265. Badarikāśrama–[K_4, 737a; D. 15; P_2. 455; L. 69, S. 266].
A hermitage of Vyāsa, on Gandhamādana (S. 184).
(2) 42b; (3) 6a; (6) 4a (on the bank of the Gaṅgā). 8b, 23a; (8) 45b; (57) 96a; (65) 66b; (79) 4b; (90) 4a.

266. Balabhī, (D. 18).
(90) 34a.

267. Bahirgiri, [S. 27 N. 6 (North of Prāgjyotiṣa)].
In the East, (13) 44b.

268. Bahela, [D. 15].
(13) 55b (Janapada in Vindhya mt.).

269. Bāhudā, [K_4. 737. a; D. 16; P_2, 481; S. 41 N. 4 (also Bahudā), 266]. River, (13) 22a; (57) 78a.

Identified with (1) Dhavalā (M. Dhumela or Burhī[5] – Rāptī), tributary of Rāptī (2) Rāmgaṅga, near Kanauj.

270. Bāhyā, [K_4. 737. b.; P_2. 481; S. 266].

River rising from Sahya. (13) 31a.

271. Bāhlīka – [D. 15; P_2. 482; V_1 63[6]; S. 94, 266 (Bactria = Balkh)].

A country in the N. of Bhārata (14) 37b.

272. Brahma tīrtha, [K_4. 741. a; D. 40; P_2. 506].

(42) 28a.

273. Brahmasaras, [K_4. 741. a; D. 40; P_2. 512; S. 269 (holy pool)].

(32) 24a.

274. Brahmasthāna, [K_4. 741. a.; P_2, 513].

Tirtha, (37) 13b.

275. Brahmayoni, [K_4. 741. a.; S. 269 (= Gaya-śiras, hill)].

Tīrtha on Sarasvatī, (39) 23b; (57) 94a.

276. Brahmāvarta, [K_4. 741. a.; D. 40; S. 268 (district)].

(33) 9b; (35) 36a, 39a.

277. Brahmottara, [P_2. 519; S. 269 (district)].

In the East (13) 45b.

May be associated with the name Burma (Ś. 28 N. 5).

278. Brahmodumbara, [K_4. 741. b.].

Tīrtha, (36) 7b-10b.

279. Brāhmaṇī, [K_4. 740. b; D. 40].

River,(84) 32b.

"Bha"

280. Bhadrakarṇa [K_4. 738a; D. 31].

Tīrtha, (79) 6a; (90) 4b.

281. Bhadrakālī [K_4. 738a.].

Tīrtha, (57) 94a.

282. Bhadrā [K_4. 737. b; D. 31; P_2. 533; S. 266 (river)].

Tīrtha, (51) 52b.

283. Bhadrāśva – [P. 2. 535].

One of the varṣaṣ, (13) 3a.

284. Bhārata–[D. 32; P_2. 553. S. 267].
One of the varṣas; (13) 4a.

285. Bhārukaccha [K_4. 738. b; D. 32; P_2. 555; S. 267, 33 N 1 (=Bhṛgukaccha=Broach)]. (84) 12b.

286. Bhārgava [D. 32; P_2. 556; S. 28 N. 6].
In the East, (13) 45b.

287. Bhillivana,
(90) 24b.

288. Bhīmarathī–[K_4. 739a; D. 33; P_2. 564; L. 144. S. 51 N. 6 (= Bhīmā, tributary of Kṛṣṇā=Bhīmarathā)].
A river (13) 30b. (Rises in Sahy mt.); (57) 78b.

289. Bhṛgutuṅga [K_4. 739. b; D. 34; P_2. 582].
(90) 9a.

290. Bhogavardhana, [D. 33; P_2. 585 (People), S. 30. N. 9].
(reminds of Bhokardan Taluk, Aurangabad Dt.).
In Dākṣiṇātya, (13) 49b.

291. Magadha–[D. 116; P_2. 592; L. 42, 44-5, 208, 232-34; V_2. 116, S. 99, 284].
A country, (13) 46b; (90) 25b.

292. Māgadhāraṇya, [K_4. 775b.].
(3) 9a, (84) 11b, 35b.

293. Maṇimati [K_4. 779b; D. 126; P_2. 596. (River)].
Lake, (90) 7b.

294. Madgura [D. 115 (Madguraka=Modāgiri; Matsya P. 113); S. 27 N. 5 (=mod. Monghyr), 283].
In the East, (13) 44b.

295. Madana tīrtha.
(42) 10b, 14b.

296. Madra–[D. 116; P_2. 609; L. 105; V. 2. 123; S. 105, 283].
A country in the N. of Bhārata (79) 12a, Description of, 12a ff.

297. Madhunadī, [D. 115 (madhumatī, r.)].
(90) 8a.

298. Madhunandīnī [K_4. 775a.].
Tīrtha. River, (81) 16b.

299. Madhuvana [K_4. 774. b; D. 116; P_2. 613].
In Kurukṣetra, (36) 57b; (83) 31b; (90) 14b.

300. Madhuśravā [K_4. 775. a.].
River (34) 7b. (वर्षाकालवहाः); (39) 38a.

301. Madhūdakā [K_4. 774. b.].
River, (57) 80a.

302. Madhyadeśa –[D. 116; P_2. 614; L. 12; V_2. 125; S. 283].
The middle region of Bhārata (13) 51b; (14) 35b, 37a (countries in).

303. Manojavā (K_4.780a. P_2. 624).
Tīrtha, (36) 56b.

304. Manoharā [P_2. 625 (monohara)].
(River, (57) 82a.

305. Mantre [K_4. 780. a. (mantreśvara)].
(90) 24b.

306. Mandākinī [K_5. 779a, D. 124; P_2. 631; S. 285 47 N. 4].
River, near m. citrakūṭa and rising from Ṛkṣavat, (13) 26a; (34) 7a, (वर्षाकालवहाः) (57) 76b; (72) 44b.

307. Mandara [K_4. 779a; D. 124; P_2. 629; L. 21; S. 285].
A *mt.* in Kuśa D., Mahā *tīrtha,* (1) 11a; (2) 6a; (4) 2b, 18a; (13) 16b, (15) 56b; (51) 74d; (52) 2b, 46a, 64d; (53) 62d; (54) 37b, 77a; (58)18a; (62) 58b; (63) 1b, 12a; (66) 42b. 44b, 46a, 48a; (68) 4b; (69) 81b; 120b, 148a; (78) 17b.

308. Marmaka, [S. 286 (people)].
In Madhyadeśa, (13) 37a.

309. Marṣaka,
In the East, (13) 45b.

310. Malaya [K_4. 778b; D. 122; P_2. 644; L. 22, 172-3; S. 53 N.2 (Travancore hills and southernmost part of Western Ghats), 285].
A mt. in Bhārata, (13) 14b; (70) 76a; (71) 1a, 2a, 4a, 9a, 17a; (83) 16b; (90) 12b; (91) 20b, 48b.

311. Mahākauśī [K_4. 776.a. Mahākaśī; D. 117 (Mahākauśika. P_2. Mahākeśas.]. (84) 37b.

312. Mahākoṣī,
(90) 27b.

313. Mahāgaurī, [P_2. 650; S. 51].
River rises in Vindhya mt. (13) 29b.

314. Mahātala, [P_2. 651].
(90) 36b.

315. Mahānadī, [K_4. 776b; D. 117; P_2. 654. L. 22, 37, 235; S. 47 N. 2 (rises in Amarakantaka range, flows through Orissa into Bay of Bengal), 284].
A river rises in Ṛkṣa mt. (13) 25b; (57) 79b; (65) 105a; (76) 19a; 19e; (78) 6a; (83) 7b.

316. Mahāmeru śaila, [V_2. 141].
(72) 27b.

317. Mahārāṣṭra, [D. 118). P_2. 662; S. 87. 284].
In Dākṣiṇātya, (13) 48a.

318. Mahālaya [K_4. 776. a; D. 117. P_2. 663].
(90) 22a.

319. Mahāśaka, [S. 284].
In Dākṣiṇātya, (13) 47b.

320. Māhiṣmatī [K_4. 777. b; D. 120; P_2. 670; S. 90.
(=mod. Māndhātā, Nimar dt.), 284; L. 174, 305, 322].
City on Narmadā, (65) 136a; (90) 19a.

321. Mahī [K_4. 777.b; D. 119; P_2. 670; S 45 N4 (rises in Malwa, drains in Gulf of Çambay), 284].
River rising from Pāriyātrā, (13) 24a.

322. Mahī tīrtha, [K_4. 777. b; D. 119].
(84) 36b.

323. Mahendra [K_4. 777a; D. 119; P_2. 671; L. 22; S. 284, 54 N3 (Eastern Ghats)].
A mt. (13) 14b; (90) 11a.

324. Mahodarā [K_4. 777. b.].
River, (62) 54b; (90) 14a.

325. Mātṛi Tīrtha, [K_4. 781. a].
(35) 43b.

326. Mānasa – [K_4. 778-9; D. 123; P_2. 685; L. 111, 122; S. 285].
Tīrtha, (37) 18a (onc of 7 Saraswatī river); (57) 90b, 95a; (78) 2c; (90) 1a (lake).

327. Mālā – [K_4. 778. a; D. 121].
River in the East, (13) 46b.

328. Māhiṣika, [P_2. 701].
In Dākṣiṇātya, (13) 48a.

329. Miśraka [K_4. 781. b; D. 130].
Tīrtha in Mathurā, (36) 54a, 55b.

330. Mūṣikāda [D. 134; P_2 (Muṣika); S. 29 N 8 (people living on the banks of Muṣl)].
In Dākṣiṇātya, (13) 47b.

331. Mekala[7] [K_4. 781. b; D. 130; P_2. 728 (Mekalā); S. 33 N 9].
Janapada in Vindhyamūla, (13) 54a.

332. Meru – [D. 130; P_2. 736; L. 111, 175; S. 286].
A mt. in Jambu D. (9) 8 b; (13) 2 b; (21) 39 b; (24) 2b; (51) 31b;* (63) 17 b; (65) 42b, 43b; (77) 7b; (78) 2a, 84d;* (52) 53a.

333. Merumandara, [D. 130; P_2. 738].
Mountain (92) 18b.

334. Maināka [K_4. 778. a; D. 121; P_2. 740; V_2. 180].
Mountain (13) 17a; (58) 68b.

"Ya"

Yajñopavita,
(42) 4a.

335. Yamunā – [K_4. 824b; D. 215; P_3. 16; L. 34, 36, 135; V_2. 186; S. 304].
River, (3) 7b; (64) 9a, 47b, 49b; (42) 8a; (53) 11a; (78) 9a; (83) 28a; (90) 26a.

336. Yavana – [D. 215; P_3. 20; L. 136-7; S. 304, 24 N 1 (=Indo-Greek settlements in N.W. part of India & adjoining lands)].
Country and people to the W. of Bhārata (13) 12a.

"Ra"

337. Rantuka (K_4. 795. b.),
By the side of Saraswatī. (33) 2a.

338. Ramya (*Ramyaka*) – (P_3. 56).
One of the varṣas, in the W.N. of Meru, (13) 56 (52) 46a.

339. Ramyā, [S. 292].
River rises in Pāriyātra mt. (13) 25a.

340. Rasa [S. 292].
River (13) 216.

341. Rasātala, [D. 167; P_3 59].
(90) 35a.

342. Rāmahrada, [K_4. 795. a. (On the N. of Thāneśvar); D. 166].
(35) 1a, 15a.

343. Rudrakara, [K_4. 797. b.].
Under Kurukṣetra, (45) 30b; (46) 11b.

344. Rudrakoṭi, [K_4. 797. b; D. 171; P_3. 90].
Under Kurukṣetra and Saraswatī, (46) 51b.

345. Rudramahālaya, [K_4. 797. b.].
Tīrtha, (57) 98a.

346. Rudrahrada,
(45) 29b.

347. Revā–K_4. 796a; D. 168; P_3. 99; L. 238; V_2. 226; S. 293 (same as Narmadā)].
A tīrtha, river rises in Vindhya mt. (13) 29b, 81a.

348. Raivata[ka], [K_4. 794. b; D. 165; P_3. 100].
Mountain, (13) 18a.

"L"

349. Lāṅgalini, [K_4. 773. b; D. 113 (Lāṅgulinī); P_3. 119; S. 54 N2 (=mod. Lāṅguliyā running past Chicacole, Andhra)].
River rises from Mahendra mt. (83) 14a.

350. Lokoddhāra, [K_4. 774. b].
Tīrtha, (35) 21a.

351. Lohadaṇḍa–[P_3. 129; D. 115; K_4. 774. a.].
(90) 29b.

352. Lauhitya [K_4. 774. a; D. 115; P_3. 133; S. 283].
River=Brahmaputra, (13) 23a.

"Va"

353. Vaṅga–[D. 22; P_3. 135; L. 59, 267-9; V_2. 237; S. 84, 301].
A country in the S.E. of Bhārata Madhyadeśa (14) 36d, in Prayāgadeśa (14) 44b.

354. Vaṁśamūlaka tīrtha, [K_4. 817b].
(35) 16a.

355. Vañjulā, [K_4. 817. b; D. 23; P_3. 140; S. 302, 51 N. 7 (=mod. Mañjurā, Southern tributary of Godāvarī)].

River rises in Sūktimān mt. (13) 32b; (57) 76a.

356. Vañjulāvatī, [S. 302 (=Vañjulā)].

River rising in Ṛkṣa mt. (13) 27a.

357. Vadhūsarā, [K_4. 816. a; S. 301].

River, (13) 22b.

358. Varaṇā. [K_4. 818. a. (n. boundary of Banaras)].

(3) 27b; (15) 51b, 52b, 53a.

359. Varbara [P_2. 459; S. 102, 103].

In Madhyadeśa, (13) 36a.

360. Varāha, [K_4. 818. a; D. 23; P_3. 154].

mt. (52) 46b.

361. Valadantika [S. 301 (people)].

In the East (13) 45a.

362. Valgu Vāhinī, [S. 301].

River rises in Ṛkṣa mt. (13) 28a.

363. Vasiṣṭāpavāha, [K_4. 818. b.].

(39) 39a.

Vasupura,

(76) 14d.

364. Vāṅgeya, [P_3. 181 (Vāṅgas); S. 27 N. 5, 28 N. 2].

In the East, (13), 45a.

365. Vāṭadhāna, [D. 27. Mbh. Sabhā p., ch. 32; P_3. 185; S. 23].

In North India, (13) 37b.

366. Vātadhūma, [P_3. 186 (dhama)].

Mountain, (13) 17a.

367. Vāmanaka, [K_4. 817. b. P_3. 193].

Under Kurukṣetra, (36) 66b.

368. Vārāṇasī, [K_4. 618-42, 818a; D. 23; P_3. 197; L. 42, 46, 94, 208; S. 302].

A tīrtha, (3) 30a, 40a, 42d; (15) 50b, 57b; (51) 49a; (83) 29b; (87) 48a; (90) 15a.

369. Vārāha – [K_4. 818a; D. 23; P_3. 199; S. 302].

A tīrtha, (79) 5c; (90) 4a.

370. Vārisenā, [S. 302].

River rises in Sahya mt. (13) 31b.

371. Vāruṇa, [K_4. 818. b. (Vāruṇasrotasa); S. 302].

Tīrtha (13) 10b; (52) 46b.

372. Vāśilā,

River rises in Vindhya mt. (13) 29b.

373. Vāhā, [K_4. 816. b.; P_3. 211].

River, (57) 78a.

374. Vitaṇḍā,

River, (57) 77a.

375. Visastā, [K_4. 823. b; D. 40; S. 41 N. 1 (=modern Jhelam); 304; P_3. 224; V_1. 63; V_2 295].

River, (13) 21a; (81) 11b; (90) 7a.

376. Vidarbha–[D. 34; P_3. 225; L. 340-1; V_2. 297; S. 90, 303].

A country in the S.E. of Bhārata, (65) 35a. (King Suratha).

377. Vidiśā, [K_4. 820. b; D. 35; P_3. 227; S. 46 N. 3 (=mod. Bes or Besali falls into Betwa near Besnagar)].

River rising from Pāriyātra m. (13) 24b.

378. Videha–[D. 35; P_3. 229; V_2, 299; S. 94, 303].

A country in the E. of Bhārata (14) 46a; (90) 30b.

379. Vindhya [K_4. 821b; D. 37; P_3. 240; L. 19, 20, 36; S. 303].

A mt. (6) 56d; (13) 15a, 49a, 30a, (Rivers emanatfng from). (18) 21c, 23a, 26d. 28d, (19) 3b, 16c, 35b; (21) 4a; (54) 26b; (55) 29b, 75b; (56) 69a; (65) 109b; (83) 17b; (90)12b. 28b.

380. Vipāśā–[K_4. 821b; D. 38; P_3. 243; L. 134; V_1. 301[8]; S. 41 N. 2 (=m. Beas)].

A river, (13) 27a. (rises in Ṛkṣa mt); (57) 76b; (79) 6b (visited by Prahlāda); (83) 18a; (90) 4b.

381. Vimalā, [K_4. 821. a. P_3. 251; S. 303].

River, (37) 18a (one of 7 Saraswatis); (57) 82a.

382. Vimalodakā or Vimalodā

River; one of 7 Saraswatis in Gaṅgādvāra. (37) 18b, 36b; (62) 54a.

383. Virajā–[K_4. 822a; D. 38; P_3. 254; S. 303 (=Jāipur, Orissa)].

A mahā tīrtha; (22) 19a.

384. Viśamadrī, [S. 303].

River rises in Sahya mt. (13) 31a.

385. Viśākhayūpa, [K_4. 822. a; D. 39; P_3 263 (Viśākha)] (90) 6b.

386. Viśālā, [D. 39; K_4. 822. b.; P_3. 265; S. 303].

River in Gayā, Cont. of Saraswatī, (37) 30b; (57) 83b; (62) 54b.

387. Viṣṇupada, [K_4. 822. b.; P_3. 287; S. 304 (hill[9])].

Lake on Niṣadha mt. (39) 90a; (31) 87a.

388. Vītihotra, [S. 35 N 5 (people)].

Janapada in Vindhya, (13) 56a.

389. Vṛka, [D. 41; P_3. 302; S. 304 (people)].

In Madhyadeśa, (13) 36a.

390. Vṛtraghnī, [K_4. 824. a; D. 42; P_3. 304; V_2 320[10]; S. 45 N.2].

River rising from Pāriyātra, (13) 25a.

391. Vegasānu, [D. 28 (?)].

Mt. (52) 47a.

392. Veṇā, [K_4. 819. b.; D. 28; P_3. 315; S. 51 N. 7 (tributary of Kṛṣṇā)].

River rising from Vindhya, (13) 29a.

393. Vetra, [P_3. 316; S. 46 N. 3 (Vetravatī=m. Betwa, tributary of Jumna)].

River, (57) 80b.

394. Vedavatī, [K_4. 819. b; D. 28; P_3. 318; S. 302].

River, (37) 8b.

395. Vedasinī, [S. 302].

River from Pārijātrā mt. (13) 23b.

396. Vedasmṛti–[K_4. 819 b; D. 28; P_3. 321; S. 45 N. 1 (=m. Besulā, Malwa)].

A river (13) 23b.

397. Vaitaraṇī–[K_4. 817a; D. 18; P_3. 328; L. 37, 198, 267; S. 50 N. 4 (flows through Orissa into Bay of Bengal?)].

A River rising in Vindhya mt. (13) 56b, 29; (34) 6b, 8b; (36) 43b.

398. Vaidarbhā, [K_4. 816. b; D. 34; P_3. 329; V_2. 329; S. 301 (people)].

In Dākṣiṇātya, (13) 49a.

399. Vaidyuta–[D. 16; P_3. 331].
A varṣa in Śāl. mt. (13) 17a.

400. Vaibhrāja–[D. 16. (lake); P_3. 333; L. 265 (?)].
A mt. (13) 16b.

401. Vairāja, [P_3. 335; S. 301 (locality)].
(15) 60b; (77) 8b (city of Brahmā); (78) 25b.

402. Vaiśyaka,
In Dākṣiṇātya, (13) 48b.

403. Vyāsavana, [K_4. 824. b. P_3. 350].
(36) 56a.

404. Vyāsasthalī, [K_4. 824. b.].
Tīrtha, (36) 60a.

405. Vyoma tīrtha,[11] [K_4. 824.b].
(46) 1b.

"Śa"

406. Śaṅkhoddhāra, [K_4. 800. b; D. 177. P_3. 364 (Śaṅko)].
An island situated at s.w. extremity of the Gulf of Cutch. (90) 31a.

407. Śaka–[P_3. 354; L. 295; D. 174; S. 293].
A country in the Madhyadeśa, (14) 36c.

408. Śatadrū–[K_4. 803b; D. 182; P_3. 371; L. 30, 121. S. 40 N. 1 (m. Satlaj), 295].
A river (13) 21a; (89) 4ab.

409. Śatanandā,
Tīrtha, (57) 95b.

410. Śatasahasraka, (K_4. 803. b.).
Tīrtha under Sarasvatī, (41) 3a.

411. Śatika tīrtha, (K_4. 803. b.).
Under Sarasvatī, (41) 3a.

412. Śabara [P_3. 381 (?)].
In Dākṣiṇātya, (13) 48b.

413. Śaravaṇa, [D. 181; P_3. 389].
(90) 21b.

414. Śarā,
River rises in Pāriyātra mt. (13) 24b.

415. Śaśikha,

(13) 58b. (आद्यान दशान पर्व वाश्रयिणस्तु शशिखद्रेका:)

416. Śāka—[D. 172; P_3. 397: S. 293].

One of the seven Dvīpas, (11) 38c, 44b; (90) 43b.

417. Śākala [D. 173; S. 24 N 2 (Sialkot city); 105].

A city in Madradeśa, (65) 70b; (79) 12bff; 43a, 78a.

418. Śāk[12]yadhānakāḥ Uttarapatha Vāsinaḥ.

(13) 37a.

419. Śātadraba, [S. 295 (people)].

(84) 4ab.

420. Śālihotra Tīrtha, (37) 5b,

421. Śālūkini [K_4. 799. b.].

Under Kurukṣetra, (64) 3a.

422. Śālagrāma—[K_4. 799a; D. 174; P_3. 409; L. 187].

A tīrth near the source of Gaṇḍaki r. (35) 23a; (58) 80a; (84) 48a. (90) 44a.

Śāligrāma (same as Śālagrām).

423. Śālmalī—[D. 175; P_3. 411; S. 294].

One of the seven Dvīpas, (11) 37a; (90) 43a.

424. Śiprā, [K_4. 805. a; D. 187; P_3. 417; S. 296].

River rises from Pāriyātra, (57) 79b; (83) 19a.

425. Śivā—[P_3. 429; V_2. 381; K_4. 805. b; S. 296].

A river rises in Vindhya mt. (13) 28b.

426. Sitā [K_4. 805. a; D. 187; S. 58 N 9 (=Jaxartes or Syr Darya)].

River, (5) 2b; (57) 76a.

427. Suktimat—[K_4. 808b; D. 196; P_3. 438; S. 55 N 2 (=Śakti hills, Raigarh, Madhya Pradesh)].

A mt. (13) 14b; (52) 47a.

428. Śuktimatā [K_4. 809. a; D. 196; P_3. 438; S. 48 N 4 (=mod. Ken, tributary of Jumna, flows through Bundel-Khand)].

River rises in Ṛkṣa mt. (13) 27b.

429. Śukla tīrtha, K_4. 808. b; D. 196.

(On n. bank of Narmadā about. 10 m. N—of Broach); P_3. 443]. (46) 1a.

430. Śunī, [P_3. 450; S. 297].
River rises from mt. Śuktimat, (13) 33a.

431. Śudrāḥ uttarapatha vasinaḥ (D. 195).
(13) 38a.

432. Śurapura, [P_3. 456].
(90) 31b.

433. Śūrasena–[D. 197; P_3 457; L. 42 51; V_2. 122, 125^{13}].
A country in the middle region of Bhārata (79) 68b.

434. Śṛṅgavat, [P_3 460].
Mt. (52) 47a.

435. Śoṇa (river also called Hiranyavāha, rising in Mt, Ṛkṣa in Gondwana. [K_4. 806a; D. 188; P_3. 466; L. 128; S. 47 N 2].
Mahā tīrtha, (13) 25b; (84) 37a; (90) 24a.

436. Śrīkuñja, [K_4. 806.b].
Tīrtha under Saraswatī R. (37) 6b.

437. Śrī tīrtha, [K_4. 807. b.].
In Śalīgrama, (35) 23a.

438. Śrīparvata [K_4. 807. a; P_3 482].
(13) 19a.

439. Śvāvillomāpaha [K_4. 811. a.].
Tīrtha, (35) 47b.

440. Śveta–[K_4. 811a; D. 200; P_3. 495; L. 191 (?); S. 298].
A mt. to the N. of Meru. (21). 13b.
An island (25) 16a; (60) 56b.

"S"

441. Saptagodāvara, –[K_4. 801a: D. 178; P_3. 531].
A tīrtha, (63) 77b, 82b; (65) 55a, 75b, 78b, 110b, 134b, 136b, 164b; (85) 32a; (90) 23a.

442. Sapta Sārasvata, [D. 179; K_4. 801. b.].
In Kurukṣetra, (37) 17ab f (names); (38) 22a, 23a; (57) 92b; (72) 71b, 73a, 75b.

443. Samantapañcaka, [K_4. 799. b; D. 175. P_3. 536.
Same as Kurukṣetra. (22) 15b, 20a.

444. Saraka (K_4. 802a.)
Under Kurukṣetra, (36) 21b.

445. Sarayū–[K_4. 803a; D. 181; P_3. 553; L. 120; V_2. 433].

A river, (13) 23a; (57) 78b; (60) 43a; (83) 7b; (90) 27a.

446. Saraswatī–[K_4. 802b; D. 180; P_3. L. 14, 553; V_2. 434; S. 294].

A river, (2) 43b; (7) 42b; (13) 20b; (22) 13b; (32) 1b, 23a, 1-24 Saraswati māhātmya. (39) 19a, 20b; (40) 4ab, 6a, 12b, 13a, 16b, 18a, 22a, 23b, 27, 28b, 31b, 32b, 43a; (41) 4a. (32) 1b (passes through Kurukṣetra). (33) 2a, 9a, 11a, 20a. (34) 6b, 8b, 50b; (35) 37b; (37) 4b, 20ab, 21a, 22a, 23a, 26a, 27a, 29a, 30a, 32b, 34a, 36a, 37b, 38a; (42) 3b, 5b, 19a, 2ab; (43) 12b; (47) 45b, 57a; (49) 7b; (51) 52a; (53) 12b; (57) 51b; (60) 19a; (62) 54b, 55a; (63) 56a, 60a; (64) 34a; (69) 69a; (79) 5b; (84) 10b, 18b, 19a, 29a.

447. Saridvatī, [S. 295].

River rises in Sahya mt. (13) 30b.

448. Sahya–[K_4. 798a; D. 171; P_3. 576; L. 21. 186; S. 23 N 2 (W. Ghats excl. Travancore hills)].

A mt. (13) 14b, 32a (rivers emanating from); (83) 12b; (90) 11b.

449. Sannihatī, [K_4. 801. a. (on the n. bank of Saraswatī & near Dvaitavana; in Kurukṣetra; or another name of Kurukṣetra)].

(49) 6b. 21a.

450. Sārasvatāoy, [P_3. 589; S. 294].

River Saraswatī, (37) 18b.

452. Sinibāhu, [S. 296].

River rises in Vindhya mt. (13) 29a.

453. Sindhu, [K_4. 804. b; D. 186; P_3. 601; V_2. 450; S. 296].

River rises in Pāriyātra mt. (13) 23b; (42) 8b; (84) 11b.

454. Simhala–[D. 185; P_3. 603; S. 296].

One of the nine parts of Bhārata, (13) 10b; (90) 34b.

455. Sītāvana, [K_4. 805. a.].

Under Kurukṣetra, (35) 44b.

456. Sutala, [P_3. 619].

(In Pātāla) province.

Bali was made king there. (31) 71a. (90) 36a.

457. Sutīrtha, [K_4. 810. a.].

(35) 40a.

458. Sudāmā, [V_2. 454;[14] S. 297].
River from mt. Suktimat, (13) 33a.

459. Sudina, [K_4. 808. a.].
Tīrtha, (36) 63a.

460. Suprabhā, [P_3. 642 (Suprabhātā)].
River, Saraswatī. (37) 18a, 21b (Saraswatī name at Puṣkar); (62) 54a.

461. Suprayogā, [K_4. 809a., P_3. 642; S. 297].
River rises in Sahya mt. (13) 31a.

462. Surasā–[K_4. 809b; P_3. 660; S. 298].
A river rises in Ṛkṣa mt. (13) 25b.

463. Surāṣṭra–[D. 197; P_3. 663; L. 297-9; 305; S. 298 (90) 30a.

464. Sūrpāraka tīrtha [K_4. 809. b; D.; 197.; P_3. 683 Sopara, near Bassein, S. 31 N 6].
(90) 25b.

465. Suvarṇā, [D. 199 (?); P_3 669].
One of 7 Saraswatīs. (37) 18b.

466. Suhūhuka, [S. 297 (people)].
(13) 58a आद्या न देशा न पर्वताश्रयिण

467. Sūrya tīrtha, [K_4. 810. a].
(35) 26b; (43) 11b.

468. Saindhavāraṇya–(Sindhu) [D. 186; P_3. 692; L. 8; V_2. 473; K_4. 798. b].
(3) 9b; (84) 38a; (90) 31b (forest).

469. Somatīrtha, [K_4. 806. a; D. 188; P_3. 697; S. 297].
On the banks of Saraswatī, (37) 15a, (41) 4a; (43) 11b; (57) 91b; (83) 12b; (84) 20b.

470. Saugandhika vana, [K_4. 804. a; P_3. 701].
(47) 54b.

Saubhapurī,
(92) 61c.

Saurāṣṭra, [D. 183; P_3. 708; S. 295].
Country (79) 14a.

473. Sthāṇu tīrtha, [K_4. 808. a; D. 194].
(40) 3a; (42) 30a; (43) 1a. 11a. (45) 4b, 24b; (47) 1a, 39b, 59a, 61a; (48) 26b, 30ab. 35a; (49) 7a, 51a.

474. Sthāṇvīśvara, [K_4. 808. a. (m. Thāneswar, 25 miles S. of Ambala). D. 194] (44) 15a.

'Ha'

475. Haṁsapada [K_4. 755. a.].
Near Viśākhyūpa, (93) 6b.

476. Haṁsamārga, [S. 26 N 8 (=Humza, N-W Kashmir].
Country (13) 57b (आद्या न देशा न पर्वताश्रयिण:).

477. Hanumatsthāna [K_4. 755. a (Hanūmat tīrtha)].
Tīrtha, (37) 3a.

478. Harivarṣa, (D. 74; P_3. 752].
One of the varṣas. (13) 4a.

479. Hastināpur, (K_4. 756. a; D. 74; P_3. 762; S. 275].
City (90) 2b.

480. Hāṭaka [D. 74; L. 29. K_4. 756. b; P_3. 763].
Tīrtha, (65) 156a.

481. Hiṅgulaka, [D. 75 (Hingulā); S. 276].
Locality (70) 45d.

482. Himavat–[K_4. 756b; D. 75; P_3. 767; V_2. 503; L. 81; S. 276].
A mt. to the S. of Meru, (13) 23a (Rivers emanating from); (51) 14a, 24a, 32a; (52) 53a; (60) 8b; (81) 31c, 32b.

483. Himaśaila, [S. 276 (=same as Himālaya].
(50) 13a; (52) 15a, 17b; (76) 19b.

484. Himācala–[L. 81; S. 275 (=Himālaya)].
A mt. (58) 85b, 88c, 113a; (64) 8b; (82) 20b; (90) 8a.

485. Himādri, [D. 75; S. 276 (=same as Himālaya)].
(6) 55(d); (50) 13a; (52) 15a, 17b; (54) 11a; (56) 14b, 25d; (58) 86d; (64) 49b; (81) 27b.

486. Himālaya, (K_4. 756. b; D. 75; S. 276].
(2) 43a; (51) 24a; (52) 12b; (81) 23d.

487. Hiranmān, [D. 76; P_3. 768].
(13) 3b.

488. Hiraṇyapuram, [D. 76; P_3. 772].
(58) 44b.

489. Hiraṇvatī, [K_4. 756. b; D. 76; S. 276].
River (13) 20b; (34) 8a (वर्षाकालवहा:) (64) 16b, 19a, 34b, 46a; (90) 32a.

490. Hemakūṭa – [K_4. 756b; D. 75; P_3. 779].
A mt. (52) 46a; (90) 21b.

References

1. Paripātra, int.
2. Paripātra, int.
3. Paripātra, int.
4. Plākṣa Prasravaṇa.
5. (Rāptī), tributary 1 Rāptī (2) Rāmgaṅga, near Kanauj.
6. Balhika, a people.
7. Present Maikal range which is connecting link between the Vindhyas and Satpuras, stretches from the Khairagarh area (MP) to the Rewah region, – H. Ray Chaudhuri, *Studies in Indian Antiquities,* p. 134.
8. Vipāśa.
9. Vṛtraghna.
10. Vṛtraghna.
11. In Kīkaṭa (Gayā).
12. Śaṭhya.
13. Śurasenaka, people.
14. Sudāman

16

Situation of Rāvaṇa's Laṅka: *On the Equator*

V. H. Vader

At the Third Session of the All-India Oriental Conference held in Madras in 1925 Sirdar Madhavarao Kibe Saheb submitted a paper claming that the Laṅkā of Rāvaṇa described in Vālmīki's Rāmāyaṇa was located on a peak of the Amarakaṇṭaka mountain, which is an offshoot of the Vindhya and from which starts the Narmadā, which divides the continent of India into two parts, Northern and Southern. Professor Jacobi of Bonn admitted that this theory was superior to his, as regards the location of Laṅkā somewhere in Assam, when he edited Paumacariya which is a Jain version of the story of the Rāmāyaṇa. It is not a very old work. So also is the Daśaratha Jātaka which preserves the Buddhist version. The same topic formed the subject of a paper which the Sircar Saheb read at the Session of the First Oriental Conference held at Poona in 1919; but the paper submitted to the 3rd Oriental Conference concludes with a remark "the local information now supplied should leave no doubt that Rāvaṇa's Laṅkā was in Cental India."

Leaving aside the above two theories viz., Assam and Central India we may mention here the almost axiomatic theory that Ceylon was Laṅkā and Laṅkā is Ceylon. Many Oriental Scholars stick to this theory as a dead certainty.

We however propose to submit to the reader a new theory regarding the situation of Laṅkā, which is supported by more weighty and reliable evidence collected from our ancient Sanskrit literature and mostly from Vālmīki's Rāmāyaṇa. This fourth theory may be summed up thus :– "Laṅkā was the capital of the big island known as Rākṣasa Dvīpa situated in the midst of the Southern ocean. This Laṅkā was situated on the equator or the middle part of the earth. The distance between the Southern extremity of India and the Rākṣasa Dvīpa or Laṅkā was a hundred Yojanas i.e. about 700 miles."

First, we propose to quote authoritative evidences to show that Ceylon and Laṅkā were not the same nor was the Laṅkā city situated in Ceylon.

(1) Siṃhala Dvīpa is mentioned in Vanaparva and Sabhāparva of the Mahābhārata. Greek writers called Ceylon by the name Taprobane (Tāmraparṇa). Sahadeva, the Pāṇḍava conqueror of Southern India is said to have conquered Tāmra Dvīpa, Rāmaka Parvata, and despatched envoys to demand tribute from king Bibhīṣaṇa of Laṅkā. This Tāmra Dvīpa is of course the ancient name of Ceylon.

(2) In Vanaparva, chapter 51, it is narrated that Śrī Kṛṣṇa went to visit the Pāṇḍavas when they went into exile. Seeing the deplorable condition of the Pāṇḍavas, Kṛṣṇa gave vent to his feelings of anger against the Kauravas and is said to have expressed as follows : – "The prosperity of Dharmarāja at the time of the Rājasūya Yajña was so great that kings of all countries in India were offering services to him in any low capacity whatever, not even minding their position or prestige. The kings of Siṃhala, Barbara, Mleccha and Laṅkā were doing the work of serving food to the guests." Here the compiler of the Mahābhārata mentions Siṃhala and Laṅkā as separate kingdoms.

(3) Next in the Mārkaṇḍeya Purāṇa (chapter 58, verses 20-29), the Kūrma-vibhāga mentions the names of the countries of Southern India. Among the lists we read:

लङ्का कालाजिनाश्वैव शैलिका निकटास्तथा ॥ २० ॥
दक्षिणाः कौरुषा ये च ऋषिकास्तापसाश्रमाः ।
ऋषभाः सिंहलार्श्च व तथा काञ्चीनिवासिनः ॥ २१ ॥

These countries are said to be on the right side of the Kūrma. Here also we find Laṅkā and Siṃhala as separate countries.

(4) The Bhāgavata (5th skandha, chapter 19, verses 28-30) has enumerated the eight minor islands (उपद्वीप) of Jambu Dvīpa. It is said that

जम्बुद्वीपस्थ्य च राजन्र पद्वीपानष्टौ हेंक उपदिशंति सगरात्मजैरश्वान्वेषण इमां महीं परितो निखनङ्गिरुपकल्पितान् ॥ २९ ॥ तद्यषा स्वर्णप्रस्थश्चन्द्रशुल्क आवर्तनो रमणको मंदरहरिणः पांचजन्यः सिंहलो लंकेति ॥ ३० ॥

Here it is clear that the 7th उपद्वीप was Siṃhala and the 8th was Laṅkā.

(5) Varāha Mihira the great astronomer has mentioned in his सहसंहिता (chapter XIV) the names of the countries in Southern India.

अथ दक्षिणेन लङ्काकालाजिनणौरिकीर्णतालिकटा ॥ ११ ॥
काञ्ची मरुचीपट्टनचेर्यार्यकसिंहला ऋषभाः ॥ १५ ॥

It is stated further that the names are given in order, commencing from left to right. Anyhow we can say this much that Laṅkā and Siṃhala were away from each other.

(6) There are many passages in Sanskrit dramas and poetical works stating that Ceylon and Laṅkā were two different islands. At least it can be difinitely said that no reference from Sanskrit works has been yet offered which expressly says that Ceylon is the ancient Laṅkā. And it is quite likely that such a reference cannot possibly be discovered. We give below one of the passages in support of our statement from Bāla-Rāmāyaṇa, a Sanskrit drama in 10 acts by Poet Rājaśekhara. He lived in the 9th century A.C. He is said to have travelled throughout the length and breadth of India and his information may safely be believed to be quite correct regarding the geographical details he has offered. From the passage quoted below it will be clear that he meant for certain that Siṃhala (Ceylon) was different from Laṅkā. For example, in the 3rd act we find that a drama named "Sītā-svayaṃvara" was being staged before Rāvaṇa, the king of Laṅkā for his amusement. Among the kings assembled for seeking the hand of Sītā in marriage there is the king of Siṃhala, named Rājaśekhara. Rāvaṇa taunts him and says :–

रावण:-सिंहलपते किमिदं मन्दिह्यते। न च सन्देहदेहो वीरव्रतनिर्वाह:।

This means, if it means anything, that Rāvaṇa and the lord of Siṃhala were different personages.

Again in the 10th act while returning from Laṅkā to Ayodhyā with Sītā, Rāma first showed the city of Laṅkā and the place where he fought with Rāvaṇa. Bibhīṣaṇa was also their companion. He further showed her the Siṃhala Dvīpa on being questioned about it by Sītā :–

सीता—अखण्डिताखण्डलकोदण्डमण्डलप्रतिरुप: कतर: पुनरेष उद्देश:।

बिभीषण:—पश्यस्यग्रे जलधिपरिखं मण्डलं सिंहलानाम् चित्नोत्तसं मणिमयभुवा रोहणोनाचलेन॥

दूर्वाकाण्डच्छविषु चतुरं मण्डनं यहधूनां गात्नश्चांभो भवति गलितं रत्नतां शुक्तिगर्भम्॥

The very important thing to be noted in the above verse is that Bibhīṣaṇa does not mention anything about Laṅkā or himself in the above description of Siṃhala or Ceylon, because they had all left Laṅkā in the back ground and details about the same had been given to Sītā already. It clearly appears from the above verse that Siṃhala was a smaller island and the poet means that Laṅkā was situated to the south-west of Siṃhala.

If Laṅkā and Siṃhala were two different islands we must find out the exact situation of Laṅkā.

It has been stated above that Laṅka was at a distance of a hundred yojanas from the southern limits of India. The islands was 100 yojanas in length and 40 yojanas in breadth. The dimensions are certainly not applicable to Siṃhala. Professor S.B. Dikshit the author of the 'Bhāratavarṣīyabhūvarṇanā'says, "that Ceylon is Laṅkā" but the distance of a hundred yojanas as given in Rāmāyaṇa puzzles him and he seems to be uncertain about the identification.

Before we trace the path taken up by Hanumat when he first went to Laṅkā in search of Sītā, let us see whether there is any other evidence to prove that Laṅkā was away from Ceylon.

In the Vāyu Purāṇa, (Bhuvanavinyāsa, chapter 48), the author describes the six isles round about Jambu Dvīpa as follows : – (i) Aṅga Dvīpa, (ii) Yava Dvīpa, (iii) Malaya Dvīpa, (iv) Śaṅkha Dvīpā, (v) Kuśa Dvīpa, and (vi) Varāha Dvīpa.

The third in the above list viz. Malaya Dvīpa is further described in verses 20-30 of the same chapter. It is said about this island that there are many gold mines there and the population consists of several classes of Mlecchas. There is a great mountain named Malaya containing silver mines. Heavenly bliss is obtained on the mountain on every Parva or Amāvasyā day. The famous Trikūṭa mountain is also situated in this island. The mountain is very extensive and has several very beautiful valleys and summits. The great city called Laṅkā is founded on one of the slopes of this mountain. Its length is hundred yojanas while its breadth is 30 yojanas. To the east of this island lies a great Śiva temple in a holy place called Gokarna. The above description as clear enough to enable us to infer that Laṅkā Purī was on the mountain Trikūṭa, which was situated in the 3rd isle, Malaya Dvīpa, which was one of the six Upa-dvīpas of Jambu Dvīpa. This Malaya Dvīpa is nothing else but the present Maldives in the Indian Ocean. The Maldives are situated on the equator.

The above inference is fully corroborated and supported by the description of situation of Laṅkā as given by the great astronomer and mathematician Bhāskarācārya, a resident of Halebis Karṇāṭaka, (born 1037 Śaka or 1115 A.D.). He writes in the Golādhyāya, a work on Mathematics (Bhuvanakośa, 17) : –

लङ्का कुमध्ये यमकोटिरस्या: प्राक् पश्चिमे रोमकपट्टनं च ॥
अधस्तत: सिड्वपुरं सुमेरु: सौम्येऽथ यामे वड़वानलश्च ॥

The above verse means that Laṅkā is on or about the equator. Astronomers call the equatorial region by the name Nirakṣa i.e. 0^0 latitude Deśa. In the same chapter in verses 43-49 it is stated that Laṅkā Purī was on the equator and that there was a small difference in the longitudes of Avantī (Ujjain) and Laṅkā. At least such was the firm belief of Bhāskarācārya. The longitude of Avanti is 75^0 75'.

Now let us see whether the description about the situation of Laṅkā in the Rāmāyaṇa adds support to the above statement of Bhāskarācārya.

Sugrīva the all-India traveller *par excellence* while mentioning the geographical details to the south of the Kāverī says (Kiṣkindhā-kāṇḍa, sarga 41, verses 15-18) that "after crossing the Mahānadī Tāmraparṇī, which embraces the ocean as a young maiden, the gate of Pāṇḍya Deśa (कवाटं पांड्यानां) is to be reached and also the sea coast. The sea will have to be crossed over."

ततः समुद्रमामाद्य सम्प्रधार्यार्थनिश्चयम्। अगस्त्येनान्तरे तत्र सागरे विनिवेशितः ॥ १९ ॥
चित्रसानुनगः श्रीमान्महेंद्रः पर्वतोत्तमः। जातरूपमयः श्रीमानवगाढ़ महार्णवम्॥ २० ॥

These verses describe clearly that this Mahendra mountain is different from the one in the Kaliṅga province and that a side of this had entered in the ocean south-wards and was immerased in the waters of the ocean. Further on, in verse 23 we read that on the western side of this mountain at the other extremity, lies an island which extends over a hundred yojanas. (द्वीपस्तस्यापरे पारे शतयोजनविस्तृतः, compare verse 24: स हि देशस्तु वध्यस्य रावणस्य दुरात्मनः). Nothing can be clearer and we may safely infer that the abode of Rāvaṇa known as राक्षसद्वीप with its capital Laṅkā was in the westerly direction from the कवाट of पांड्यदेश or in other words, the southern extreme point on the coast of India. Siṃhala or Ceylon thus fails to answer the most crucial point of the above description.

In the same Kāṇḍa (sagra 60, verse 7) Sampāti says about the mountain where he along with the search party of Hanumat was seated before Hanumat flew over to Laṅkā दक्षिणस्योदधेस्तीरे विंध्योयमिति निश्चितः). It was from the top of this mountain that Māruti took his gigantic leap into the sky with a view to reach the island of Rāvaṇa.

The identification of पांड्यानां कवाटं with कवाटपुरम् or कपाटपुरम (Tamil) is an intelligent discovery by S. Krishnaswami Aiyangar.[1]

The Arthaśāstra of Kauṭilya has also referred to Tāmraparṇī Nadī and the Pāṇḍya Kavāṭa (Shamasastry's translation of अर्थशास्त्र, p. 86). Dr. S. K. Aiyangar says, "This पांड्यानां कवाटम्, a door-way of the Pāṇḍyas, is a fine commentary on the कवाटं पांड्यानाम् of the Rāmāyaṇa. The commentator of the Arthaśāstra explains it as a mountain known as Malayakoṭi in the Pāṇḍya country. It is rather of doubtful propriety that a place where pearls are found should be referred to as a mountain. It seems much more likely that the expression पांड्यकवाटम् means the doorway of entrance into the Pāṇḍya country from the sea, and the

Malaykoṭi of the commentator therefore would then be the promontory where the Western Ghats dive into the sea"[2]

The above details regarding the doorway of the Pāṇḍya Deśa clearly give us the idea that the southern cape of India, viz. Cape Comorin is the place meant here; for near this point the Mahendra mountain has dipped into the sea. From the details of the geograpny of South India as given by Sugrīva we are entitled to infer that the Rākṣasa Dvīpa, the abode of रावण was situated to the west of this mountain range.

We have several authorities to show that Laṅkā became immersed in the ocean owing to agitations of the waters soon after Rāma went back to Ayodhyā after the fight.

The present Maldives cover up the same position which once was covered by the Rākṣas Dvīpa. It extended from 6^0 north latitude down to 1^0 south of the equator lengthwise while its breadth was from $73\frac{1}{2}^0$ to 76^0 west longitude.

When the island was thus going under sea and became uninhabiable, some of the inhabitants might have come to colonize the ancient Tāmra Dvīpa or Tāmraparṇī, which was afterwards called the Siṃhala Dvīpa or Ceylon.

Even the geologists maintain that before the 4th millennium B.C. there existed a big continent in the Indian Ocean. Its extent lay from the south of Africa, eastward towards the south of America, to the south of India. In course of time this big continent became immersed in the waters and what portions we have now such as Malaya Dvīpa, Sychellis, Rodrigues, Chagoes, Mauritius, Madagascar, Java, Sumatra, Borneo, Ascension, Falkland, Graham, West An artica etc. are nothing but the mountain tops or plateaus of the old big continent. The Malaya Dvīpa or Maldives is the site of the Rākṣasa Dvīpa of Rāvaṇa with its capital Laṅkā Purī.

References

1. The Beginnings of South India History, p. 63.
2. *Ibid.*, p. 68 n.

17

Rāvaṇa's Laṅka located in Central India

M. V. Kibe

The earliest known history of the Indian people in an epic form is what is contained in the Rāmāyaṇa of Vālmīki. The language and metre of the work, which are nearer to the Vedic language than anything to be found in classical Sanskrit, point out the work to have been written in very ancient times. Indeed the writer claims it to be a contemporary work, and if the interpolations made in it, which are many and intermixed throughout the book, are deleted, what remains appears to be an authentic narrative, although subject to exaggeration here and there on account of its very nature as epic poetry. To the same reason is due the fact that it contains many riddles. Many of them have been successfully solved by that distinguished scholar Mr. C.V. Vaidya, M.A., LL. B., in his book entitled the "Riddles of the Rāmāyaṇa." But he too has failed to solve the toughest riddle in it, namely, the identity of Laṅkā, the capital of Rāvaṇa, with any site in modern countries. There was a time when it came to be believed that like Dvārakā of a later epoch it disappeared in the sea. But the question is so important that on its right solution depends the authenticity of the greater part of the history embodied in the epic.

The story of Rāma and Sītā is well-known. After Rāma had attained the age of maturity and was about to be installed as the heir-apparent, he was asked to go and live in the forest for 12 years. His younger brother Lakṣmaṇa and wife Sītā accompanied him. His adventures in the forests form the central theme of the epic. As commonly found in such narratives, it is full of adventures, into which the lapse of time has introduced elements of absurdity and exaggeration. They have so obscured history that doubts have been thrown on its authenticity, and some have gone so far as to assert that it is a myth of Nature.[1] Prof. Jacobi in his monumental work on the Rāmāyaṇa takes the hero to

Assam, which he calls Rākṣasa-sthāna (the abode of demons). The Indian astronomer Bhāskara (14th century) locates Rāvaṇa's Laṅkā, the destination of Rāma, on the equator in the ocean. Some identify it with an island near Sumatra, or Java. A few would locate it in the Arabian Sea on the west coast. Recently, however, some people have begun to place it in the Chhattisgarh District of the Central Provinces. But the most popular theory current in India for the last two thousand years is that Laṅkā is none other than Ceylon. The believers in this theory differ as to the route by which Rāma went to that island, one holding that he went through the middle of the Peninsula, and another asserting that he followed the East Coast.

It is not an uncommon phenomenon that when emigrants leaving their mother country go on founding colonies one after another, they carry with them to their new homes the names of places for which they have some attachment. From the places, which, as described in the preceding paragraph, claim the honour of being associated with Rāma's principal exploit, the theory set forth here receives confirmation.

There is, however, ample material in the earliest narrative of it, which, with the corroboration now made available by research, points to a place far nearer the country of Rāma's birth than the wild stories which later became current. Vālmīki's Rāmāyaṇa or the history of the exile of Rāma contains a plain narrative of facts, which has been laid under contribution for the writing of this paper.

From it, it is claimed that the site of Rāvaṇa's Laṇkā must be found in the Amarakaṇṭaka Mountains at the source of the Narmadā on the frontier between the Chhattisgarh Division of the Central Provinces and the Rewa State of the Central India Agency.

The Rāmāyaṇa of Vālmīki is not only the first and earliest history of the great hero, Rāma, but from the view-point of language and metre it is nearer to the Vedic Sūktas than anything found in the later Sanskrit literature. The story became so popular that not only the Mahābhārata but almost all the 18 principal Purāṇas and later works in modern Indian languages, among which Paumacariyam (published and edited by Prof. Jacobi), Tulasīdāsa's Rāmāyaṇa in Hindi, Kṛttivāsa's Rāmāyaṇa in Bengali, Moropant's 108 Rāmāyaṇas in Marathi and Pambam Rāmāyaṇa in Tamil are the most famous, have delighted to describe the beautiful and almost divine story, not to speak of several inferior versions of same in Sanskrit, and other works. Not only has not Vālmīki's work escaped interpolations to suit the later editions of the story, but they have been rendered by additions and exaggerations beyond recognition. Not only does the description in the Vālmīki

Rāmāyaṇa connected with Rāma's journey in forest and subsequently to Laṅkā preclude the possibility of its being so far away, as is indicated by the different places which claim the honour of being referred to in the history of the exploit, but, the other countries also which are described in it and which are equally wrongly identified with countries bearing the old names in modern times stand in the same position. As an example the identification of Videha, the kingdom of Janaka, the father of Sītā, with modern Bihar, can be cited. According to the Rāmāyaṇa (1, 69, 8) it was at a distance of four days' journey from Ayodhyā. This cannot justify the identification of Videha with modern Bihar. From Oudh it cannot but be at a greater distance than what is indicated by the above mentioned fact. No such army as is described in the Rāmāyaṇa, not even a chariot drawn by horses, could traverse the distance from Ayodya (Oudh) to Videha (Behar) in such a short time as is distinctly mentioned.

The data in the Vālmīki Rāmayaṇa are sufficient to identify Ayodhyā, from where Rāma started on his journey, and Citrakūṭa, where he was met by his brother Bharata, who came to him with the tidings of the death of their father Daśaratha, with the places bearing these names. The difficulty of identification commences with the further progress in the journey.

On leaving the last named place Rāma entered the Daṇḍaka forest. There he came across a colony of Ṛsis which was situated in an inaccesible place (3, 1, 1). Then he entered the forest and met with an adventure (3, 2). Here he saw a hermitage (3, 5, 4). He requested its owner to show him a suitable place for settling (3, 5, 33).

The Ṛṣi was about to die and so he directed Rāma to go to another Ṛṣī by name Sutīkṣṇa, in the neighbourhood (3, 5, 35). He desired him to follow the course of the Mandākinī which having its rise in the Citrakūṭa mountain joins the Jumna. Here there was a number of colonists who complained to Rāma of the harassment to which they were subjected by the fierce Rākṣasas (3, 6, 5). They described to him the extent to which their colonies, which were subjected to the harassment, had spread (3, 6, 17).

They were established on the area between the Pampā and the Mandākinī, and the Citrakūṭa mountain.

Being accompanied by the members of the colony, he went to the hermitage of Sutīkṣṇa after crossing the river (Mandākinī) (3, 7, 1). He stayed here for one night (3, 8, 1).

He then wandered over different places in the forest and returned to the same place after ten years (3, 11, 27). Here he was requested by the Ṛṣis to protect them from Rākṣasas which Rāma promised to do (3, 1, 34).

Here on enquiry Rāma heard that Agastya lived in the same forest (3, 11, 30 et seq.).

He is told that the hermitage of Agastya's brother was 32 miles to the south from there and Agastya's hermitage eight miles further to the south. He is advised that he should halt at the former place for the night and then proceed to the other place which was at the back (or end) of the part of the forest the next morning (3, 11, 37-42).

He goes to Agastya and asks him to show him a good place to live in (3, 13, 11).

He is pointed out a place 16 miles away near the Godāvarī, a place which was said to be not far away (3, 13, 18-21).

It was so near in the same Madhuka forest that he was told that he should go by the way on the north of the banyan tree and, getting on a hillock close by, see the Pañcavaṭī (3, 13, 25); Janasthāna was another name for it (9, 5, 69). It was Rāvaṇa's out-post (3, 21, 20). So Rāma settled there in order to keep his promise to the Ṛṣis (3, 10).

At Pañcavaṭī Rāma lived for nearly two years and from here Sītā was taken away by Rāvaṇa.

The above narrative makes it clear that Sutīkṣṇa's hermitage was not far away from Citrakūṭa, and from the former place Pañcavaṭī was only 48 miles.

Rāma had gone a-hunting at the time Sītā's abduction and Jaṭāyu tried to protect Sītā from the hands of Rāvaṇa. He was found to have been almost killed by Rāvaṇa, when Rāma returned. From the former he learnt the name of the abductor of his wife and the direction in which he had gone (3, 68, 9, 10 and 16). While going on to Pañcavaṭī, Rāma had seen a big bird perched on the banyan tree (3, 14, 1). This was Jaṭāyu, probably an aborigine.

Rāma went along that direction towards the south-west in search of his wife (3, 1 and 2).

Having gone six miles from Janasthāna (or Pañcavaṭī) he entered a forest by name Krauñca (3, 69, 5), and on going six miles eastwards he entered a valley (3, 69, 8-10), which was between the forest named Krauñca and the hermitage of Mātaṅga, who, before dying, told him to go to Sugrīva, who lived on a hillock on the banks of a reservoir named Pampā in the forest known after Mātaṅga. Sugrīva was the head of a tribe known as Vānaras, who being antagonistic to Rākṣasas was expected to help Rāma (3, 72).

Having stopped for one day on the way shown by Kabandha to the east of the hill (mentioned by him), he reached the western banks of Pampā (3, 74, 1, 3 and 4). Here was living a female hermit named Śabarī (3, 74, 4).

Then he saw Sugrīva, who was near the Ṛṣyamūka mount (4, 1, 130).

Rāma made friends with Sugrīva, who gave him tidings of his wife, who had been carried away by Rāvaṇa by that way (4, 6, 9).

Sugrīva had been driven away from home by his elder brother, Bālin (4, 6, 9 and 10), who lived at Kiṣkindhā, which was not at a great distance from the place (4, 12, 13 and 14). It was in a valley (4, 33, 1). From there he went to Pampā, near which was the mount Ṛṣyamūka (3, 75, 7).

It has been seen that Pañcavaṭī was only 48 miles from Sutīkṣṇa's hermitage, which itself was not at a great distance from Citrakūṭa. From Pañcavaṭī or Janasthāna he goes into the Krauñca forest at a distance of six miles in the south-west. Going on further six miles, he entered the valley in which he killed Kabandha. He told Rāma to go to Sugrīva who, it appears from the minute description given by Kabandha such as the road leading by a banyan tree and thence to the hillock from which Pampā and Ṛṣyamūka which enclosed Kiṣkindhā, and where Sugrīva lived could be seen, did not live far away, say another six miles. Therefore Kiṣkindhā was more than eighteen miles from Janasthāna or about 66 miles from Sutīkṣṇa's hermitage, or 96 miles, as will be shown later, from Citrakūṭa.

To the immediate south of Kiṣkindhā were the Vindhyas (4, 46, 17).

Sugrīva sent a batch of Vānaras under the leadership of Hanumat to the south (4, 47, 14). It began to search the deep valley of the Vindhyas (4, 48, 2).[2]

They lost their way. They were taken out of it by a nun who was living in it and who brought them on to the shores of the sea which was washing the base of the Vindhyas (4, 53, 3-5).

Here, when they were sitting ready to die, not knowing what to do, came to them the brother of Jaṭāyu, by name Sampāṭi (4, 56, 1-2). He told them that he had been living on the mountain Vindhya for a very long time (4, 58, 7).

He gives tidings of Rāvaṇa and Sītā, who, he says, are at a certain distance on the south banks of an island in the sea, on the shores of which they were sitting (4, 58, 20).

We find an indication of distance in the fact that he could see them, or rather the place where they lived, from the spot on which they were (4, 58, 29). It is emphasised in the same stanza that he could see what he was describing.

It was on this information that Hanumat, the leader of the party, made up his mind to leap or swim the distance. Hanumat swam this distance, through the air, after halting in the way.

It is then quite clear that Kiṣkindhā was on the northern slope of the Vindhyas which was at a distance of about 96 miles from Citrakūṭa, and Laṅkā to the south of the mountain in the sea. From the fact that Śabarī, who lived on the banks of the Pampā near Kiṣkindhā (3, 74, 4), can, as will be shown later, be said to have lived at a place within six miles of Amarakaṇṭaka, which is identified with Laṅkā in this paper, it was about 103 miles from Citrakūṭa.

Here the toughest problem arises. Mr. C.V. Vaidya, the learned author of the "Riddles of the "Rāmāyaṇa" and "Mahābhārata : a criticism," shows that even the Mahābhārata, which is next in authority to Vālmīki's Rāmāyaṇa, corroborates that Kiṣkindhā was to the north of the Vindhya mountain. Now the difficulty about there being no sea to the south of the Vindhyas can only be got over by agreeing to the view that what is described as sea here was only an expanse of water.

Assuming this theory for the sake of argument, luckily, there is actually such a place as indicated by the Rāmāyaṇa (vide Pioneer, July 27, 1908). There is a mystery hanging about it. At a distance of some 10 miles from the Pendra Road Station of the Bilaspur-Katni Branch of the Bengal-Nagpur Railway, there is a hill-top on which there is said to be a fort, which is called after Rāṇī Bakavali, a fabulous queen. It is visible from the spot known as Bhṛgu-Āśram about 2 miles distant from the source of the Narmadā. It is said that in the sixties of the last century Sir Richard Temple, then the Chief Commissioner of the Central Provinces, had attempted to reach it by crossing over the marsh, with which it is surrounded, by riding over an elephant, but as the animal got stuck up in the mud the attempt had to be abandoned. From this side of the marsh the fort looks as if submerged in a mist, which makes it appear to be at a greater distance than it really is. It is in fact a peak, just as Laṅkā is in the Rāmāyaṇa. The land which is marshy at present may have had water over it once. Local tradition says that there is treasure inside the fort. It may be the Laṅkā of Rāvaṇa.

Sutīkṣṇa's Āśrama, which Rāma was the first to visit after leaving Citrakūṭa, is identified with modern Sutna, which is a station on the E. I. Railway, the present head-quarters of the Political Agent in

Bhagelkhand and about 30 miles from Citrakūṭa as the crow flies. It is situated on a stream which has, even now, beautiful trees on its banks. Here Rāma lived for the ten years of his exile.

Rai Bahadur Hiralal, a distinguished archæologist, is responsible for the statement that Goda, which is the name given to the river at Pañcavaṭī, where Ramā lived for nearly two years and from where Sītā was abducted, is a common name for rivers in that part of the country. So it does not necessarily mean that Janasthāna should be located on the well-known river bearing that name, which has its source in the western Ghāṭs and falls into the Bay of Bengal.

From Janasthāna Rāma went to the Krauñca forest. Hereabout is Kenjuva, an offshoot of the Vindhyas. It may be identified with Krauñca.

In Śabarī dialect (Aboriginal Names in the Rāmāyaṇa by G. Ramdas Iyar, B.A., Journal of the Behar and Orissa Research Society, March, 1925) Jaitan means a place below the mountains just as Laṅkā means the high mountain. It is not difficult to hold that Janasthāna, which was in a forest, was with no habitation, as otherwise its meaning might imply the Sanskrit form of Jaitan. It was the advanced post of Rāvaṇa's army (3, 20, 22). Mr. Ramdas maintains that in Śabarī language Daṇḍaka means a place full of water.

Laṅkā itself was on the top of a peak known as Trikūṭa (5, 1, 2). In this paper it is proposed to identify it with a peak on the Amarakaṇṭaka mountain. According to Rai Bahadur Hiralal there is a peak called Āmrakūṭa (a place with mango trees) on the Amarakaṇṭaka mountain. It would not be difficult to identify the other two peaks as Śālakūṭa (Sal trees) and Madhūkūṭa (Mahua trees). Within seven miles of Amarakaṇṭaka there is a place called Śabarī Nārāyaṇa, after the hermit of that name mentioned in the Rāmāyaṇa (3, 4, 75). He met Rāma when he was on his way to and near Pampā or Kiṣkindhā (ibid.).

There also appears to be a striking phonetic similarity between the names Sālakaṭaṅkaṭa, the family name of Rāvaṇa and Amarakaṇṭaka. The inhabitants of these parts call themselves Rāvaṇa-vaṃśīs[3] and a song on Hanumat's exploits is sung with great zest by them. In that part of the Vindhya range in which is situated the Amarakaṇṭaka, and which is called the Kaimur range, there are traces of old habitations of men. In its caves are drawings of great antiquity.[4] This region, therefore, seems to have been connected with aborigines, and the tradition of Laṅkā may be traced to them.

There now remains the difficulty about Sāgara or the sea. In Sanskrit, according to Mr. Nundolal Dey, the word Sāgara includes a lake, a sea or an ocean. In these parts there are many lakes which are called Sāgaras.

Rai Bahadur Hiralal asserts that in some of these lakes pearls are found (Journal of Hindi Sammelan, vol. 14, 5).

Now the question remains as regards the tribes of Vānaras, monkeys, which inhabited the land between Janasthāna and Laṅkā, and the Rākṣ asas who lived beyond. That these two tribes had brotherly relations may be gathered from the mention in the Rāmāyaṇa that Hanumat, the companion of Sugrīva, introduced his name to Rāvaṇa, as that of a brother (5, 2, 51). It is said that Vānaras has a tail. Apart from the fact that in medical works evidence is available of men having tail, Mr. T.C. Hadson, in his "Naga Tribes of Manipur" describes a costume in which such a tail is added. The Rākṣasas too had different sorts of costumes (e.g., the ten heads of Rāvaṇa). But it is not the object of this paper to enter into that discussion. I have avoided any reference to the last canto of the Rāmāyaṇa as it is held to be an interpolation. Nor has any reference been made to the date of the Rāmāyaṇic events, which preceded the Mahābhārata War by about a thousand years.

The object of this paper has been to prove that the place-names in the Rāmāyaṇa are not fictitious and even today they can be identified with sites in existence. If, as is claimed in this paper, the hypothesis that the Laṅkā of Rāvaṇa was located on the now inaccessible peak of Amarakaṇṭaka; stands the test of criticism, it may lead some adventurous and enterprising person to survey it from the air.

References

1. Imp. Gaz., vol. I, p. 419.
2. On the word Vindhya Govindarāja's commentary observes:
   Vindhyapādapa ityanena Kiṣkindhāyā dakṣiṇato'pi Vindhyaparvataśeṣo 'stīti gamyeta.
   Here the party entered a valley which was full of trees and through which water was running and which was full of light (4, 15 and 20, 50).
3. Imperial Gazetteer, vol. XII, p. 323.
4. *Ibid.*, vol. XVI, p. 275.

18

Rāvaṇa's Laṅka

G. Ramadasa

Ceylon is popularly believed to be the home of the Rākṣasas of the Rāmāyaṇa. Sirdar M. Kibe has been trying, by adducing evidences from the Rāmāyaṇa, to locate it in Central India. In his article published in the Modern Review, 1914, he traced it to a hill near the Pendra station on the B. N. Ry., north-west of Bilaspur. His subsequent researches perhaps have led him to change it to Amarakaṇṭaka. He expounded this theory in his papers read in the 1st and 3rd sessions of the Oriental Conference held at Poona and Madras respectively. His arguments were all supported from the epic itself, and also by ethnographical and geographical evidences still to be found in the Central Indian hills.

But in the I.H.Q., vol. ii, pp. 345-50, Mr. V. H. Vader expounds a theory that Rāvaṇa's Laṅkā was situated on the equator. His arguments, supported by extracts from Sanskrit literature, to show that Laṅkā was quite distinct from Ceylon, are otherwise convincing, but do not prove what he says regarding its location.

He cites Vāyu Purāṇa in support of his conclusion and says (I.H.Q., vol. ii, p. 348): "In the Vāyu Purāṇa (Bhuvanavinyāsa, ch. 48), the author describes the six isles round about Jambu Dvīpa, as follows: (i) Aṅga Dvīpa, (ii) Yava Dvīpa, (iii) Malaya Dvīpa, (iv) Kuśa Dvīpa, (v) Śaṅkha Dvīpa and (vi) Varāha Dvīpa. The third in the above list, viz., Malaya Dvīpa is further described in verses 20-30 of the same chapter. It is said about this island that there are many gold mines there and the population consists of several classes of Mlecchas. There is a great mountain named Malaya containing silver mines. Heavenly bliss is obtained on the mountain on every Parva or Amāvasyā day. The famous Trikūṭa mountain is also situated on this island. The mountain is very extensive and has several beautiful valleys and summits. The great city called Laṅkā is founded on one of the slopes of this mountain. Its length is hundred Yojanas while its breadth is 30 Yojanas. To the east of this island lies a great Śiva temple in a holy place called Gokarṇa."

He asserts that this Malaya Dvīpa is the present Maldives in the Indian Ocean. But what about the Śiva temple to the east of these Maldives? Is the mountain there called Malaya? Are there any gold and silver mines in them? Without giving reasons he says: "this is fully corroborated and supported by the description of the situation of Laṅkā as given by the great astronomer and mathematician, Bhāskarācārya." He quotes the following :

Laṅkā kumadhye yamakoṭir asyāḥ prāk paścime romakapaṭṭ aṇañca/

Adhas tataḥ siddhapuraṃ suṃeruḥ saumye'tha yāme baḍavānalaś ca//

In his opinion this "verse means that Laṅkā is on or about the equator. At least such was the firm belief of Bhāskarācārya." But nowhere in the Rāmāyaṇa it is said that Rāvaṇa's town was situated in the middle of the earth. With regard to this astronomical Laṅkā the late Diwan Bahadur Swami Kannu Pillai says in his Indian Chronology as follows : "Now, as the moment of Sunrise depends on the latitude and longitude of each place, there should, strictly speaking, be as many 'pañcāṅgas' as there are places in India. Indian astronomers get over this difficulty by calculating time in the first place according to one central latitude and longitude, and then applying the necessary corrections in order to deduce the time for other places. The central latitude is the equator, and the central longitude is that of Ujjain (75^0 46'' East of Greenwich) where there was an ancient observatory. To combine the central latitude and the central longitude, they imagined an island, Laṅkā, in the Indian ocean, situated on the equator and having the same latitude as Ujjain. This Laṅkā is, of course, not Ceylon." It can neither be in the Maldives; for the astronomical Laṅkā is said in the Siddhāntaśiromaṇi to be on the same meridian as Ujjain:

Yal laṅkojjayinī puropari kurukṣetrādideśān spṛśan/

Sūtraṃ merugataṃ budhair nigaditā sā madhyarekhā bhuvaḥ//

As the Maldives lie between 72^0 and 74^0 E. long., the *rekhā* over any place in them cannot pass through Ujjain and the poles. In whatever way we consider, the identification of Rāvaṇa's Laṅkā with Maldives does not stand.

As a last support, Mr. Vader quotes from the Rāmāyaṇa (Kiṣkindhā, 41, 15-18) the directions given by Sugrīva to the Vānaras that were deputed to seek Sītā in the Southern quarter. "Sugrīva, the all-India-traveller *par excellence,* while mentioning the geographical details to the south of the Kāveri says that, after crossing the Mahānadī Tāmraparṇī, which embraces the ocean as a young maiden, the Gate of Pāṇḍya Deśa (Kavāṭam Paṇḍyānām) is to be reached and also the sea-coast. The sea will have to be crossed over." But when Rāma first asked, this "all-India-traveller *par excellence*" to tell him about the abode of Rāvaṇa, he replies that he does not know it (Kiṣkindhā, 7, 2). The commentators try to justify this by saying that Sugrīva said so because he was intelligent enough to see that Rāma would not help him if he had given the information. Even if we may agree to accept this justification, no reason can be offered for the following fact which clearly proves that Sugrīva knew nothing of the geography of the south. When Lakṣmaṇa went to Kiṣkindhā to chide its king for his lethargy, Tārā told him about the strength and defences of Rāvaṇa which information she gathered from Bālin (Kiṣkindhā, 35, 18). Had Sugrīva been aware of everything regarding Rāvaṇa, Tārā would have told Lakṣ maṇa that she had the information from Sugrīva himself. Had Sugrīva really known that Rāvaṇa's abode lay in the southern direction, he would not have sent searching parties to all the four quarters. Further his geographical knowledge does not seem to have been verified by those who had actually travelled in the southern direction. Sugrīva, while giving a description of the southern countries (Kiṣkindhā, 41, 8ff.), mentioned the Vindhyas with thousand peaks immediately to the south of the place where he sat, and the river Narmadā to the south of it; further south lay the Gate of the Pāṇḍya country, then the sea with the Mahendra mountain on it shores; beyond the sea, on the other side, was a dvīpa. He did not call this dvīpa Laṅkā but said that it was the country of Rāvaṇa. But it should be noted that none of the rivers, hills, islands or towns spoken of by Sugrīva was observed between the Vindhya mountains and Laṅkā by those that actually travelled in that direction.

The Vānaras led by Aṅgada and Hanūmāna proceeded southwards from Kiṣkindhā and entered the Vindhyas (ibid, 48, 2). They entered a cave there and then coming out of it reached the shore of the ocean (ibid, 53, 12). The surging ocean unexpectedly brought their path to an end and they sat helpless at the foot of the Vindhya mountains (ibid., 53, 16).

Sampāti, an inhabitant of that part of the Vidhyas, told them about Rāvaṇa and his abode. He even pointed to Laṅkā from that spot and the Vānaras might even have seen it. Hanūmāna flew to it, saw everything there and came back flying. Every object that the Vānaras had seen in their search in the Vindhya mountains is mentioned, but nothing is said of the river Narmadā that lies immediately to the south of the Vindhyas. Had this river been crossed, it would have been certainly mentioned.

The return journey from Laṅkā is described by Rāma to Sītā:

Divinely planned
And built by Viśvakarmā's hand,
Laṅkā, the lovely city rest
Enthroned on Mount Trikūṭa's crest. (Griffith)

As they were flying in the Puṣpaka Vimāna, they had a bird's eye view of the city of Laṅkā. It may be noted that attention of Sītā to the insular nature of the city is not drawn. Rāma showed the battle-field where both Vānaras and Rākṣasas lay dead, where Rāvaṇa fought and fell and where Mandodarī sat and bemoaned the death of her husband. Then Sītā was shown the shore of the sea on the side of Laṅkā where Rāma and the Vānara host slept after the sea had been crossed. The sea, the causeway built across it, the place where the sea-god had appeared before Rāma and the place where Vibhīṣaṇa had sought the protection of Rāma, were all shown. Then was shown Kiṣkindhā (Yuddha, canto 126, 24).

So between the sea-shore and Kiṣkindhā, Rāma had not had any opportunity of observing anything, for he led the Vānara host over the mountains avoiding, towns, hamlets and other human habitations (ibid., canto 4, 39). This was the reason why Rāma could not even show a single object between the sea-shore and the city of Sugrīva. From the accounts of these two journeys, one from Kiṣkindhā to Laṅkā and the other from Laṅkā to Kiṣkindhā, we see that even the river Narmadā is not mentioned. Thus it is assumed that Laṅkā lay to the north of the Narmadā valley.

The Vānara army is said to have observed, in their march, that the rivers were flowing in an unnatural way (ibid, śloka 60). This happened when the Vānaras went along that ridge which the modern geographers call the water parting. So, from Kiṣkindhā Vānara army marched along the top of the mountains that separated the rivers flowing northwards from those that flowed south-wards, and at last they reached the Mahendra mountain from the top of which they viewed the sea. This Mahendra cannot either be the famous hill of the same name in Kaliṅga nor the one said to be on the Indian coast opposite Ceylon.

Both in the Mārkaṇḍeya Purāṇa and Bṛhatsaṃhitā of Varāhamihira, Laṅkā is mentioned associated with Kāliñjar, a fort in Bundel-Khand :–

Laṅkā kālājināś caiva śailikā nikaṭās tathā/ (Mārkaṇḍeya Purāṇa)

Atha dakṣiṇena laṅkā kālajinasaurahkārṇatālikaṭāḥ// (Bṛhat J.)

From all these it is clear that Rāvaṇa's Laṅkā was not far off from the southern ridge of the Vindhya mountains.

Rāmāyaṇa tells us that Laṅkā was situated on the top of the Trikūṭ a mountain which according to the Vāyupurāṇa was in the Malaya-dvīpa. It is said that the chief mountain in this land was called Malaya. Matsya, Kūrma and Viṣṇu Purānas say that Krūṭamālā, Tāmraparṇī, Puṣpajā, Puṇyavatī and Utpalāvatī are the rivers that rise on the Malaya mountain. Of these Tāmraparṇī and Utpa lāvatī[1] are even to-day the rivers that flow through Orissa. The Malaya mountains are those that lie to the west of Orissa and the mountains of Ganjam and Vizagapatam are well-known by that name.[2] The highland which lies within the Mahānadī, Wainganga and the Godāvarī is named Malayadvīpa[3] in the Vāyupurāna. To the east of these hills lies a holy place called Gokarṇa. This Gokarṇa is the Mahendra mountain in Ganjam upon which still exists the great temple of Śiva. In ancient Kaliṅga copper-plate grants we often read *mahendrācalapratiṣṭhitasya gokarṇasvāminah*. Here among these hill tracts are found a variety of aboriginal tribes who are mentioned as Mlecchas in the Purāṇas. In the beds of many a river that flow through these hills gold sand exists which is a proof for the existence of gold mines in the valleys through which these rivers flow. In this region must Trikūṭā be located.

In the 5th Adhyāya of Revākhaṇḍa, a part of Avantikhaṇḍa of Skandapurāṇa, Narmadā is also spoken of by the name of Trikūṭī. Yudhiṣ ṭhira asks Markaṇḍeya why the river was called Trikūṭā:

kimarthaṃ narmadā proktā reveti ca kathaṃ smṛtā/

trikūṭeti kimarthaṃ vā kimarthaṃ bāluvāhinī//

In reply to this, the sage says (ibid., 6, 16f.); that because the river flows out of a mountain that has three peaks so is it called Trikūṭā; Matsya Purāṇa (ch. 185, 11f.) tells us that this Narmadā rises in the Amarakanṭaka. It is this Amarakanṭaka that is spoken of as the Trikūṭa in the Révākhaṇḍa. It is the biggest mountain (3493 ft.) in the Malaya hills; Laṅkā is said in the Rāmāyaṇa and the Vāyu Purāṇa to have been built on it. The existence of holy bathing places (tīrthas) after the name of Indrajit and Rāvaṇa, so far unknown to exist in any other part of India, is another evidence to prove that this was the site of Rāvaṇa's Laṅkā (Matsya, ch. 189, 3; ch. 190, 29). Above all, the very name Amarakaṇṭaka, a synonym for Devakaṇṭaka, an appellation of Rāvaṇa (Rāmāyaṇa, Yuddha, canto 127, 14), confirms the truth.

But in spite of all these evidences, one may not be satisfied at the absence of a sea or its signs around this Amarakanṭaka. Geological evidences there are none to show that a sea did exist here in ancient days. Yet the region in which this hill is situated is such that during the rainy season, it becomes water-clogged. "But between the hills . . . the soil is undermined by flood in the rainy season, and broken into innumerable holes and pitfalls, the surface water during the rains usually finding a readier method of drainage straight through the friable soil than by collecting in rivulets and streams, and finally making its way to the rivers" (Holdich's India, pp. 151-152). A sheet of water collected in pits and holes, if large enough, is known by the name of sāgara throughout India. Sirdar Kibe says that this has been the custom from ancient times. It may be one of such sāgaras that has been spoken of in the epic.

Ethnological evidences confirm the fact that in the neighbourhood of Amarakaṇṭaka was the home of the Asuras, a class to which Rāvaṇa asura belonged. "Colonel Dalton connects these Asuras (a non-Aryan Tribe of Chota Nagpur) with the Asuras who, according to Munda tradition, were destroyed by Singbonga (the sun). They believe in a god whom they identify with Singbonga," (Ling. Sur. of India, vol. iv).

As Vibhīṣaṇa, who was made the head of the Asuras, considered the kings of the Solar race as protectors, the modern Asuras consider the sun to be their god.

The Śavaras whom I identified with the Vānaras of the Rāmāyaṇa (Aboriginal Names in Rāmāyaṇa *JBORS.*, March, 1925; and Aboriginal Tribes in Rāmāyaṇa, *Man in India,* March-June, 1925) are found in the Saugor district, and Śavara mountains are found in the Shahabad district of Central India. The 'Oraon' identified by Rai Bahadur Sarat Chandra Roy with the Vānaras are found to the east of Bilaspur district of Chota Nagpur.

The Narmadā finds, such as Hacketts, Bhutra, Boucher, and a new locality for copper in the Narmada valley, are proofs of human habitation in the Narmadā region during pre-historic times. I may quote here a passage from the "Pre-historic India" of Dr. Panchanan Mitra determining the age of these finds.

"The change which has taken place in the Indian fauna since the period of the Nerbudda gravels consists in a substitution of animals with Malaya affinities for animals with European or African affinities . . . Dr. Falconer invariably spoke of those fauna as Pliocene as being a development of the Siwalik fauna in many respects and intermediate between them and our times. Though his opinion in question relating to the determination of vertibrate fossils, especially of India, is unassailable, his word "pliocene" has been the cause of much contention. Some would allow even 400,000 years or more when these bits were manufactured. But a few thousand years are of little account in the earliest palæolithic age where we have got to do more with geographical time of hundred thousand years than any lesser period. But the fact is important since much depends upon the lease of time granted for the first appearance of man . . . ".

Now in conclusion it may be said that, as there are geological evidences to prove that the Narmadā valley was one of the homes of man in prehistoric times, specimens of tribes described in the epic are still found in the Central Indian regions and as the geographical directions given in the Rāmāyaṇa and corroborated by the Purāṇas point out Amarakaṇṭaka to have been the Laṅkā, it may be asserted that the peak now called Amarkaṇṭaka got that name because the Laṅkā of Rāvaṇa was on it during the time when Rāma lived and ruled. No other place satisfies all the tests. Antiquarian researches may in future reveal more evidences in support of my conclusions.

Under the title of 'Ceylon and Laṅkā are different,' there appeared a small article in the Quarterly Journal of the Mythic Society Bangalore, vol. xviii, no. 1. The author contends that Laṅkādvīpa and Āmradvīpa mentioned in the Bodh-Gaya inscription of Mahānāman (Fleet's Gupta Inscriptions, no. 71) are two different places and do not refer to the same place as Dr. Fleet and General Cunningham thought. The first two lines of the verse in which the two names occur may be quoted here to make its interpretation clearer.

Āmradvīpādhivāsī pṛthukulajaladhis tasya śiṣyo mahīyān/

Laṅkādvīpaprasūtaḥ parahitaniratah san mahānāmanāmā//

It means Mahānāman, an inhabitant of Āmradvīpa, an ocean of a mighty family, born in Laṅkādvīpa. In the 2nd verse of this very inscription it is said, the disciples of Mahākāśyapa roamed at one time over the stainless country at the feet of the mountains of Lankā. Evidently the chief seat of Mahākāśyapa must have been this Laṅkā, and all the country around it is spoken of as holy (stainless). This Mahānāman (II) who was greater than his guru Upasena II, being born in Laṅkā, which must have been the chief seat of Upasena II, should not have left such a sacred place to inhabit one which had no name either for piety or for learning. It is groundless to think that a great preceptor like Mahānāman II should have left his place of birth, which had a great reputation for holiness for a place of no merit. This establishes that Laṅkādvīpa and Āmradvīpa are the two names of one and the same place. But where was that place?

In both the names the word 'dvīpa' is misleading; it is generally understood to mean an island; and Ceylon is, for unknown reasons, called Laṅkā. On these grounds Dr. Fleet identified both Laṅkādvīpa and Āmradvīpa with Ceylon. He thought that the island might have been named Amradvīpa on account of its resemblance in shape to a mango. This is a mere imagination. As far as I know, no Indian poet had ever thought the island to resemble an Āmra.

Poets play upon words, but at the same time give reasons for it. Amarakaṇṭaka was named Āmrakūṭa by Kālidāsa and immediately he explained the significance of the name by *channopāntaḥ pariṇataphaladyotibhiḥ kānanāmraiḥ* (Meghadūta, I, v. 18), i.e., the mountain was chiefly covered with wild mango trees.' This is the only place, in all India, that had a name suggesting its relation to the mango. Āmradvīpa of the inscription must, therefore, be the same as Āmrakūṭ a, for dvīpa and kūṭa mean the same thing.

It has already been pointed out that the plateau of Amarakaṇṭaka is full of places of pilgrimage, sacred to Śiva. All around this plateau are innumerable places which were once the centres of Buddhism, Jainism of Śaivism. Bilaspur, Pendra, Sirpur, Tewar, and Bhilsa are some of the places around the Amarakaṇṭaka hills. There are epigraphical and other evidences to show that several maṭhas were established in the Central Provinces and most of them were situated near the Amarakaṇṭaka. This vouchsafes the statement in the verse referred to above that the disciples of Mahākāśyapa once roamed over the stainless country at the feet of the mountains of Laṅkā.

This evidence further establishes the identity of Laṅkādvīpa with Āmradvīpa and of these two with Amarakaṇṭaka. Laṅkā was the name of the highland from which the two rivers, the Narmadā and the Mahānadī rise, and it was the chief abode of Rāvaṇa, the king of the Rākṣasas of the time of Rāma of the Ikṣvāku family of North Kośala.

References

1. Utkalāvati is only a corruption of Utpalāvatī. In Rāmāyaṇa Tāmraparṇī is called Mahānadī Tāmraparṇī.
2. Ganjam maliahs and Vizagapatam maliahs—Maliah is a corruption of Malaya. 'Malai' means 'a hill' in the Dravidian languages. The Eastern Ghats north of the Godavari Valley are called the Malaya mountains.
3. The word Dvīpa is misleading. It is generally understood to mean an island. But it appears to mean a land division. In Matsya, Kūrma and Viṣṇu Purāṇas, Bhāratadvīpa is said to be one of the nine divisions of Bhāratavarṣa. In Vāyupurāṇa Aṅgadvīpa is mentioned as one of the Upadvīpas. Aṅga is the name of a part of India around Bhagalpur. So it cannot mean an island. Again, Upadvīpas mean subdivisions and do not mean the islands near by.

19

Location of Kṛṣṇa's Capital Dvāravatī*

N. K. Bhattasali

In the present state of archæological exploration in India, archæological evidences (leaving aside those for the Indus civilization) for the political history of India prior to Buddha appear to be almost totally absent. We are fairly well-acquainted with the picture of northern India of Buddha's time. We see in it quite a number of kingdoms, large and small, with teeming and cultured population; and big towns and cities with numerous buildings in stone and brick, and citizens prosperous, energetic and gay; and merchants with fabulous riches. I hope no one will contend that all these had a past and they must have taken millenniums to develop. Why, then, are archæological evidences not forthcoming? Are archæological evidences of the existence of Indian kings and Indian civilization previous to thc 6th century B.C. totally absent? In answer, we must repeat the wail of the late Dr. V.A. Smith and say: – "Very little has been done yet to reveal the secrets of the most ancient sites in India." (*Early History of India,* 3rd ed., p. 31 fn.). The exploration of Girivraja, capital of Jarāsandha, was given only a preliminary handling by Sir John Marshall and the report published in the *ASIAR.,* 1905-6. In 1912-13, Mr. Jackson carried out some private reconnaissance of this pre-historic city and published the results of his survey with a map in the *ASIAR.,* 1913-14. This is all that archæology has done for this far-famed site so intimately associated with the heroes of the *Mahābhārata,* – a site pre-eminently suited for excavation and exploration, because it is entirely free from the obstruction of human habitations. Has any serious attempt been made to copy or decipher "the long rambling inscription" in curious shell characters in the Bawan Ganga defile, on the spot which is still pointed out as the arena on which Bhīma and Jarāsandha fought with each other? Even the publication of a faithful and accurate copy of this curious inscription and thereby placing the puzzle before the eyes of the students of

---

* Read at the Seventh Oriental Conference, Baroda, 29th December, 1933.

epigraphy, has not been considered a necessity. The only representation of this inscription available appears to be the small photograph published on p. 120 of Mr. Muhammad Hamid Kurashi's book on the monuments of Bihar and Orissa (*Archæological Survey of India,* New Imperial Series, vol. LI). The same story can be told of Indraprastha and other Paurāṇic sites.

In the absence of archæological evidence, we have no other course but to fall back on the Purāṇa literature for the location and identification of Purāṇic sites. The materials, though meagre and unsatisfactory, yield important information. In 'this paper, our object is to locate the site of Dvāravatī, (Dwaraka) – to which place the Yādavas migrated for safety from Jarāsandha's aggression, after having left Mathurā in a body.

That the present Dwārakā situated on the apex of the Kāthiāwāḍ peninsula is a rather modern place with plagiarised sanctity, is well-known. It is also well-known that Kṛṣṇa's Dwārakā was engulfed by the sea soon after his death, and the site is still known as Mūla-Dwārakā on the sea, about 22 miles east of Prabhāsapattana or Somnāth.

Our earliest and most trustworthy source of information regarding the location of Dwārakā is the *Mahābhārata,* in which there are certain indications which hardly fit in with the situation of Dwārakā on the sea-shore, about 22 miles east of Somnāth and about 60 miles south of the Raivataka or Girṇār Hills.

The first detailed notice of the migration of the Yādavas from Mathurā to Dvāravatī is to be found in the 14th Chapter of the Sabhāparva, where Kṛṣṇa recounts before Yudhīṣṭhira the oppression of Jarāsandha on the Yādavas and their consequent migration to Dvāravatī. The passage is worth quoting in extenso: –

इति सञ्चिन्त्य सर्व्वेस्म प्रतीचीं दिशमाश्रिता: ।
कुशस्थलीं पुरीं रम्यां रैवतेनोपशोभिताम् ॥
ततो निवेशं तस्याञ्च कृतवन्तो वयं नृप ।
तथैव दुर्गसंस्कारं देवैरपि दुरासदम् ।
स्त्रीयोऽपि यस्यां युध्येयु: किमु बृष्णिमहारथा: ।
तस्यां वयममितघ्न निवसामोऽकुतोभया: ॥
आलोच्य गिरिमुख्यं तं मागधं तीर्णमेव च ।
भाधवा: कुरुशार्द्दूल परां मुदमवाप्नुवन् ॥
एवं वयं जरासन्धादभित: कृतकिल्विषा: ।
सामर्थ्यवन्त: सम्बन्धाद्गोमन्तं समुपाश्रिता: ॥

त्रियोजनायतं सद्म त्रिस्कन्धं योजनावधि।
योजनान्ते शतद्वारं वीरविक्रमतोरणम्॥

* * * *

वयञ्चैव महाराज जरासन्धभयात् तदा।
मथुरां संपरित्यज्य गता द्वारवतीं पुरीं॥

A free translation of this passage is given below :–

"Having ruminated thus, we fled towards the west to the beautiful town of Kuśasthalī, the beauty of which was enhanced by the hill Raivataka. After having settled there, we repaired that fort of the place and made it invulnerable even to the gods. The women even can defend the place, not to speak of the great heroes of the Vṛṣṇi race. We are now living there and know no fear. Having observed the strong position of the great hill and thinking that we have at last escaped danger from the king of Magadha, my people are now exceedingly glad. Thus, suffering injury from Jarāsandha, we, though quite able to defend ourselves, have thought it discreet to take shelter under the Gomanta, i.e. Raivataka hill. The hill is three *Yojanas* in extent, has three peaks, each at the interval of a *Yojana,* and has 100 passes at the end of each *Yojana* where the gates are the valour of the heroes. Thus we, O Mahārāja, left Mathurā out of fear from Jarāsandha and went over to the city of Dvāravatī."

From this important passage, the following points stand out clearly:–

(i) Kuśasthalī and Dvāravatī are two names of the same town and it was under the shadow of the Raivataka or Gomanta hill, and protected by it.

(ii) The town existed even before the migration of the Yādavas and was evidently lying forsaken.

(iii) There was a very strong fort there, which the Yādavas repaired. With repairs, it became so strong that even women could fight under its protection.

(iv) The Raivataka hill was three *Yojanas* in extent. Taking four miles to a *Yojana,* the extent was about 12 miles. The extent of the Raivataka hill is given as 12 × 12 miles on modern Survey Maps also.

(v) There is no indication that this original Dvāravatī was on the sea.

This passage of the Sabhāparva is fairly conclusive and shows that the original Dvāravatī was situated very near the Raivataka hills. Certain passages in the Ādiparva also support this conclusion.

The Pāṇḍavas received possession of half their ancestral kingdom and settled in Indraprastha. Soon after, Arjuna had to go on a voluntary exile for breaking the conditions regarding visit to Draupadī. After visiting all the holy places of Eastern India, he wended his way towards the west by the coast of the Indian Ocean and ultimately arrived at Prabhāsa, the situation of which is well-konwn, on the southern coast of Saurāṣṭra. The Yādavas had already migrated there and were at that time settled in Saurāṣṭra, ruling with their capital at Dvāravatī. Kṛṣṇa had contracted a firm friendship for his cousin Arjuna when they met at the time of the *Svayaṃvara* of Draupadī. When news reached Kṛṣṇa that Arjuna was on an all-India tour and had arrived at Prabhāsa, he hurried there to meet him. After spending some pleasant time in this fascinating sea-side *tīrtha,* Kṛṣṇa took him to the Raivataka hill, where a charming residence had already been prepared for the reception of Arjuna. Thence he was taken to Dvāravatī, where he resided happily for a long time.

The Raivataka or the present Girnār hill is about 50 miles north of Prabhāsa-pattana or Somnāth. The site of the Dvāravatī-on-the-sea is only 22 miles direct east of Somnāth. If Dvāravatī at this period had been situated on the sea, Kṛṣṇa certainly would have taken him there first and then to the pleasure resort on the Raivataka. First going 50 miles northwards to Raivataka and then again returning more than the same distance to reach Dvāravatī is a curious peregrination and can only be explained by the fact that in approaching Dvāravatī from the south, Raivataka lay on the way, and so Kṛṣṇa made Arjuna halt there on one of its pleasure resorts. This movement of Kṛṣṇa and Arjuna from Prabhāsa to Raivataka and then to Dvāravatī certainly indicates that Dvāravatī at this period was not on the seashore, but near Raivataka.

The story of the abduction of Subhadrā appears to lead to the same conclusion.

The *Raivataka-Yātrā* or the festival of the visit to Raivataka takes place in the month of Phālguna in modern times. The festival seems to be as old as the *Mahābhārata* and we meet with a vivid description of it in the 220th Chapter of the Ādiparva. Palaces were erected in the dales and valleys of the Raivataka hill and stocked with all objects of enjoyment. The Yādavas, – men and women, young and old, gaily attired, streamed to the hill. Kṛṣṇa and Arjuna were also in the crowd and there the heart of Arjuna was captivated by the beautiful maiden, Subhadrā, half -sister of Kṛṣṇa. Arjuna, under the advice of Kṛṣṇa, resolved to carry to girl away forcibly and marry her. As the festival extended over a number of days, there was enough time and a fast courier was despatched to Yudhiṣṭhira at Indraprastha, asking for his permission to so bold a venture. The loving Yudhiṣṭhira of course promptly gave the permission and Arjuna made himself ready for the romantic adventure. The festival of the Raivataka-hill was still on and Subhadrā had gone as usual on a visit to the Raivataka. She had finished worshipping the sacred hill and was returning towards Dwārakā when Arjuna suddenly seized her, lifted her on his own chariot and started for Indraprastha, as fast as he could. The guards of Subhadrā immediately carried the news of the sensational abduction to Dwārakā and immediately the alarm clarion was sounded and a war-council of the Yādavas hurriedly summoned. On the advice of Kṛṣṇa, however, they decided to condone Arjuna's abuse of Yādava hospitality and marry Subhadrā to Arjuna.

Now, if Dvāravatī at this period had been situated on the sea, 60 miles south of the Raivataka hill, the whole episode would have been differently described. The abduction of Subhadrā just after she had finished her pious acts of worship on the Raivataka and was proceeding towards Dvāravatī, and the immediate carriage of the news to Dvāravatī show that the city must have been located at this period near the Raivataka hills.

But when we meet with Dvāravatī again in the Mauṣalaparva of the *Mahābhārata,* we find it undoubtedly situated on the sea. After the catastrophic Mauṣala strife and after the death of Kṛṣṇa and Balarām, Arjuna led the remnants of the Yādava hosts with the Yādava women and children out of Dvāravatī, and the sea engulfed it. So the present Mūla-Dwārakā appears to have been the second site of Dvāravatī and not the original site.

For purposes of historical investigation, the apocryphal *Harivaṃśa* is a rather confused literary source, undoubtedly later and less authoritative than the *Mahābhārata.* But even this book yields useful information.

A genealogy of the kings who reigned in Saurāṣṭra previous to the Yādava occupation is given in chapters X and XI of the *Harivaṃśa.* The progenitor was the Vaivasvata Manu. His son was Prāṃśu. Prāṃśu had a son Saryāti by name. Saryatī's son was Ānartta who gave his name to the whole country of Saurāṣṭra, so that it is also called the country of Ānartta. Ānartta's son was Reva, who is recorded to have inherited the kingdom of Ānartta's and the city Kuśasthalī or Dvāravatī. This would show that Dvāravatī existed before Reva's inheritance. Reva's son was Raivata, who gave his name to the famous Raivataka hill, now known by the name of Girnār. He was fond of music. The *Harivaṃśa* records that he took his daughter Revatī along with him and went over to Brahmaloka to listen to Brahmā's music. In his absence, his sons were driven out from Kuśasthalī or Dvāravatī by Rākṣasas and they were forced to take shelter in different countries. Thus Dvāravatī was left desolate and the valiant Yādavas, under the leadership of Kṛṣṇa, had no difficulty in occupying the capital and the country.

This account, shorn of Raivata's journey to Brahmaloka, (which may be only some place near about, famous as the seat of a reputed professor of music), sounds perfectly historical. It also agrees with the account of the *Mahābhārata* and explains how the Yādavas obtained possession of a ready-made city and had only to repair the strong fort there to convert it into a formidable stronghold against aggressors. That this Dvāravatī was close to the Raivataka hills is seen from the 112th, 113th and 115th chapters of the *Harivaṃśa,* which give details about the migration of the Yādavas from Mathurā. Unfortunately, there is a confusion in these passages between the Dvāravatī by the Raivataka hill and Dvāravatī on the sea. But there are some passages which can apply only to the Dvāravatī near Raivataka.

Kṛṣṇa, anticipating that Jarāsandha would not allow them to stay peacefully in Mathurā, was on the look-out for a new settlement. Garuḍa, his attendant, had informed him that the city of Kuśasthalī which belonged to Raivata and which had been taken forcible possession of by the Rākṣasas, was now lying forsaken, as the Rākṣasas had gone away. Garuḍa suggested that this city might provide a safe retreat for the Yādavas and he went with Kṛṣṇa's approval to reconnoitre the place. On his return, he reported favourably and suggested, –

रैवतं च गिरि श्रेष्ठं कुरु देव सुरालयम्।
नन्दनप्रतिमं दिव्यं पुरद्वारस्य भूषणम्॥११२।११०

"Do thou make the excellent hill Raivataka the house of gods, equal in excellence to paradise, the jewel beautifying the exit from your city."

This shows that the exit from Dvāravatī was guarded by the Raivataka hill.

When the Yādavas migrated from Mathurā and arrived in Saurāṣṭ ra, they met a vast country, sea-girt and with copper-coloured sand and soil: –

तत्र रैवतको नाम पर्वतो नातिदूरतः।
मन्दरोदरशिखरः सर्वतोऽभिविराजते॥
तत्रैकलव्यसंवासो द्रोणेनाध्युसितश्चिरम्।
प्रभूतपुरुषोपेत सर्वरत्नसमाकुलः।

विहारभूमिस्तत्रैव तस्य राज्ञः सुनिर्म्मिता ।
नाम्ना द्वारवती नाम स्वायताष्टापदोपमा ॥
केशवेन मतिस्तत्र पूर्यर्थे विनिवेशिता ।
निवेशं तत्र सैन्यानां रोचयन्ति स्म यादवाः ॥

"Not far was the hill Raivataka, looking fine with high peaks like the Mandara in all aspects. On that hill, thickly populated and containing all sorts of jewels, Droṇa lived for a long while and Ekalavya too. That king built a spacious pleasure resort there like a dice-board, and that received the name of Dvāravatī. Kṛṣṇa resolved to make that his city and the Yādavas also approved of garrisoning it." (112+27-30).

This passage certainly cannot apply to Dvāravatī-on-sea.

Chapter 115th of the *Harivaṃśa* describes the building of Dvāravatī by Kṛṣṇa. Chapter 155 again describes the building of Dvāravatī. The first description shows that Kṛṣṇa had practically finished building Dvāravatī, when he thought of Viśvakarmā as the proper architect for such a work. Viśvakarmā came and pronounced the place too cramped and wanted to reclaim spacious land from the sea and then build Dvāravatī. The second description gives the following boundaries for Dvāravatī.

On the east, the Raivataka hill.

On the south, the creeper-begirt forest of Pañcavarṇa.

On the west, a forest of small trees, looking like a rainbow.

On the north, the Venumān hills.

It is evident that Dvāravatī on the sea, which is sixty miles south of the Raivataka hill, can never have the Raivataka hill on the east. This can apply only to some city directly on the west of the Raivataka. And, the record of the building of Dvāravatī twice appears only to be a rather confused reflection of the fact that the Dvāravatī was originally situated near the Girnār hill and a second Dvāravatī was built on the sea afterwards.

Now let us take the aid of archæology and the accounts of Hiuen Tsang.

1. Hiuen Tsang (640 A.D.), records about the capital of Saurāṣṭra thus: – "Not far from the city is a mountain called Yuh-chen-to (Ujjayanta) on the top of which is a Saṅghārāma. The cells and galleries have mostly been excavated from the mountain side." Beal, vol. II, p. 269.

So, close to the Ujjayanta – Raivataka = Girnar hill, a city existed when Hiuen Tisang visited Saurāṣṭra.

SAURĀṢṬRA

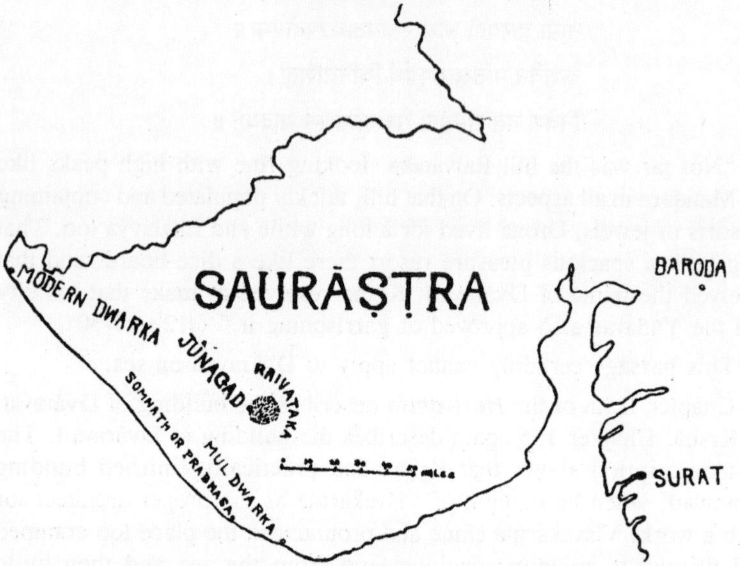

JUNĀGAḌ UNDER THE GIRNĀR HILL

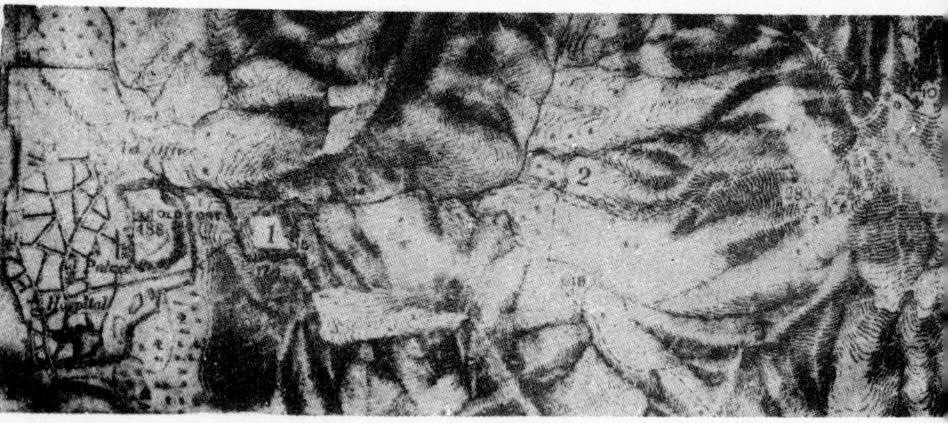

(1) The conical rock, about 12' high, with the Aśokan and other inscriptions, on the way to the Girnār Hill.

(2) The probable site of the Sudarśana lake.

(3) The Girnār peak.

2. The famous inscribed rock half-a-mile east of the walls of the city of Junāgaḍ, contains, as is well-known, the 14 Rock Edic's of Aśoka, as well as two well other inscriptions,—one, of the time of Skandagupta and the other of the time of the Śaka Satrap Rudradāman. These inscriptions (Fleet's *Gupta Inscriptions,* p. 56; *Epigraphia Indica,* vol. VIII, pp. 36ff.) tell us of a city near the site of these inscriptions. Rudradāman's inscription gives the name of the city as Girinagara, a name which still survives in the modern name Girnār, given to the hill Raivataka. This inscription recounts the interesting history that a large tank called the Sudarsana was formed at the time of Maurya Candragupta (313-290 B.C.) by damming up some streams rising on the Raivataka and these dams were strengthened at the time of Aśoka Maurya.

We know of only one city near the Girnār hills, and that is the present Junāgaḍ.

The antiquity of the place is written on its very face,—on its noble fort which goes by the name of Uparkoṭ and dominates the surrounding plains of Kathiāwāḍ. The discovery of an inscription of the time of the son of Rudradāman at the Uparkoṭ fort which begins: "Here, in Girinagara, ... ," (Burgess: *Report on the Antiquities of Kathiāwāḍ and Cutch,* p. 140) is an additional corroboration. Girinagara and Junāgaḍ must be identical and Prof. Altekar has also taken that view. (*'Ancient Towns and Cities in Gujarāṭ and Kathiāwāḍ,* p. 20).

I quote below two descriptions of the fort at Uparkoṭ.—

"The old citadel is built upon an elevation (cf. the name Girinagara), of the limestone which appears to cap over the granite at the base of the hills; and on which the city of Junāgaḍ is situated. The Uparkot is a noble specimen of eastern fortification, its walls being unusually high, with immense bastions. The materials for these have been taken from a wide and deep ditch, which has been scarped all round it. There is only one gateway and narrow entrance from the westward . . . . Lieut, Postans, *JASB.,* 1838, p. 874).

". . . . . The fort at Junāgaḍ, now known as the Uparkot. This fort lies on a most commanding position in the town of Junāgaḍ and about one and a half miles west of the holy Girnār hill. Its massive walls and strong defences must have made it a very formidable stronghold to attack before the days of artillery. From its walls, the whole country could be seen and in course of time, the town of Junāgaḍ came to be built round it, which in its turn was surrounded by a strongly fortified wall thus making the citadel doubly secure." (Wilberforce-Bell, *History of Kathiāwāḍ,* p. 55).

It has been shown that Junāgaḍ with its exceptionally strong fortification is the Girinagara of the Maurya times, standing a mile and a half west of the Raivataka hills. The history of the city thus goes from modern times to 300 B.C. Kṛṣṇa's original Dvāravatī, with its extraordinarily strong fortification, also stood west of the Raivataka. Though there is the difficulty of bridging the gulf of about a thousand years that separate Candragupta Maurya from Kṛṣṇa, it would not be wrong to come to the conclusion that modern Junāgaḍ, which was known as Girinagara in Kṣatrapa and Maurya times has been in existence from even remoter times and is the same city which the Yādavas occupied and knew as Dvāravatī.

And, very curiously, the present town of Junāgaḍ is actually shaped like a dice-board to which Dvāravatī is compared in the *Harivaṃśa,* with four elongated projections from a central square, – the northern, eastern and southern sides being clearly seen at a glance.

In Junāgaḍ, therefore, still stands almost in perfect condition a fort whose antiquity goes back to as early a time as that of the fortifications at Jarāsandha's capital Girivraja.

20

On the Washing Away of Dvārāvatī

H. V. Trivedi

In a short note published in the *Indian Culture,* II, 1, pp. 148-50, Mr. Dasharatha Sharma points out that Viṣṇu, who figures as a Yādava ruler in the *Mañju-śrī-Mūlakalpa*[1] (verse 608), is not a local chieftain as Jayaswal seems to have thought while writing his *Imperial History of India,*[2] but the great hero Kṛṣṇa of the *Mahābhārata.* In support of this theory, he refers to the washing away of Dvāravatī by the curse of Ṛṣis and to the destruction of the Yādavas in Kṛṣṇa's time, an event mentioned in the *Mahābhārata* and the *Bhāgavata Purāṇa,* and observes that this is the event which has been recorded by the author of the *MMK* in the following verse: –

यातवा वारवत्याश्च रिषिशापास्तमित्रा तदा।

कार्तिक: कार्तवीर्योऽसौ दशरथदाशरथी पुरा॥

While making these suggestions, Mr. Sharma seems to have overlooked the fact that the Yātavas of Vāravatī (Yādavas of Dvāravatī), whose mention is made in the above verse as destroyed by the curse of the Ṛṣis, are classed with ancient kings, and, as such, they seem to have been independent rulers; whereas those with Viṣṇu as one of them do not appear to have enjoyed that status; they are mentioned in the *MMK* as crownless (*mūrdhānta,* 'headless'), and, following this account, Jayaswal has rightly called them in his comments as constituting the Yādava republics.[3]

The *MMK* also mentions one Prabha as a Yādava ruler along with Viṣṇu; and if Viṣṇu is to be taken as the Epic hero, in the whole genealogy of Kṛṣṇa recorded in the *Mahābhārata* and elsewhere, with whom this king Prabha should be identified. That this Viṣṇu is a different personality from the well-known Epic hero, seems to have been known to the author of the *MMK;* otherwise he would have mentioned this ruler not as Viṣṇu, but as Kṛṣṇa, which is a more appropriate term to denote the same.

It has also been observed that in the *MMK* we find the use of the past tense and not of the usual future, and this has been taken to support the above identification. But in this connexion it may be pointed out that while mentioning the name of Viṣṇu the *MMK* has the use of the future (*rājā viṣṇunāmā bhaviṣyati*), and Mr. Sharma's observations cannot be said to be correct. Evidently the washing away of the place, as referred to in the *MMK,* should be taken as an event of the seventh century and not that of the time of Śrī Kṛṣṇa as Mr. Sharma observes.

References

1. Sanskrit text, revised by Ven. Rāhula Sāṅkṛtyāyana, p. 44.
2. *Op. cit.*, p. 25.
3. *Op. cit.*, p. 25.

Chapter 21

Ujjayinī was the Capital of the Later Aulikaras

V. V. Mirashi

While discussing the contents of two recently discovered stone inscriptions of *Mahārāja* Gauri – one from near Neemuch, dated in the V. S. 547 (A.D. 491), and the other, a fragmentary one, from Mandasor – I suggested that Daśapura, where king Gauri excavated a tank for the religious merit of his mother,[1] was probably his capital. In the Mandasor inscription the name of king Ādityavardhana is mentioned exactly as that of Kumāra-gupta I is mentioned in the so-called Mandasor inscription of Bandhuvarman. Ādityavardhana was, therefore, probably the suzerain of king Gauri. I further showed that he probably belonged to the Aulikara dynasty, which, for a long time, had been ruling from Daśapura (Mandasor). As his feudatory was at this time ruling from Daśapura, he himself must have had his capital at some other place. In this connection I drew attention to the following verse from the *Bṛhatsaṁhitā* (Chapter 85, verse 2) of Varāhamihira.

भारद्वाजमतं दृष्ट्वा यश्च श्रीद्रव्यवर्धनः ।

आवन्तिकः प्राह नृपो महाराजाधिराजकः ॥

This verse shows that *Mahārājādhirāja* Dravyavardhana, who flourished some time before Varāhamihira (A.D. 505),[2] was ruling from Avanti (Ujjayinī). His name ending in *vardhana* suggests that he belonged to the illustrious Aulikara family, which produced the redoubtable hero Yaśodharman-Viṣṇuvardhana, the vanquisher of the Hūṇa king Mihirakula. The aforecited verse from the *Bṛhatsaṁhitā,* which mentions *Mahārājādhirāja* Dravyavardhana of Avanti, suggests that like him, Ādityavardhana and Yaśodharman also might have been ruling from Avanti or Ujjayinī. This conjecture is corroborated by the Mandasor inscription of V. S. 589, which tells us that the country between the Vindhya and Pāriyātra (Aravali) mountains was being governed by Nirdoṣa, who was a *Rājasthānīya* appointed by Yaśodharman.[3] He evidently had his capital at Daśapura, where he excavated a large tank as recorded in his Mandasor inscription. This suggests that his suzerain Yaśodharman was ruling not from Daśapura but from some other place, which could have been only Avanti or Ujjayinī in view of the clear statement in the *Bṛhatsaṁhitā* that his predecessor king Dravyavardhana was an *Āvantika nṛpa* (a king of Avanti or Ujjayinī).

In a recent number of this Journal (Vol. XXXV, pp. 73 f.) Dr. D. C. Sircar has objected to some of my concusions. It is, however, a matter for satisfaction that he does not now feel doubtful about Ādityavardhana being an Aulikara king. He has raised the following objections to my conclusions: –

(1) The Later Aulikaras also ruled from Daśapura, because, firstly, all their inscriptions have been found at or in the vicinity of Mandasor and secondly, the Mandasor inscription of Gauri says that king Ādityavardhana was ruling from *daś-ādika pura* i.e. Daśapura.

(2) Dravyavardhana also, though he is called king of Avanti, may have had his capital at Daśapura; for Avanti was primarily the name of the country of which the capital was Ujjayinī and so may have included Daśapura.

(3) Even if we accept, for argument's sake, that Yaśodharman had his capital not at Daśapura but elsewhere, it certainly does not prove that Ujjayinī was his capital.

(4) The Mandasor inscription dated V. S. 589 does not mention that Nirdoṣa, who was appointed *Rājasthānīya* by Yaśodharman, had his capital at Daśapura.

(5) Even though Yaśodharman had his capital at Daśapura, he could have appointed Nirdoṣa a governor of the metropolitan district with his headquarters at the same capital.

We shall now take up these objections for examination.

(1) The objection that no inscriptions of the later Aulikaras have been found at or near Ujjayinī has not much weight; for only two records of these kings have been discovered so far. The evidence of one of them viz. the fragmentary Mandasor inscription of *Mahāraja* Gauri is doubtful, because, as Dr. Sircar himself has admitted, it is unsatisfactorily composed. The portion of the verse which is supposed to mention *daś-ādika pura* (i.e. Daśapura) does not suit the metre,[4] and the possibility of the reading being *pura-deśādikam* cannot be ruled out altogether, in which case there would be no reference to Daśapura at all. The second inscription is that incised on the pillars of

Yaśodharman at Mandasor.[5] I have shown that these pillars probably mark the site of the victory which Yaśovardhana gained over the Hūṇa king Mihirakula. So the evidence of that inscription also does not militate against the theory that Yaśodharman had his capital at Ujjayinī.

(2) Avanti was no doubt the name of both the country of Western Malwa as well as its capital Ujjayinī, but the expression *Āvantika-nṛpa* used in the aforecited passage of the *Bṛhatsaṁhitā* has to be taken in the sense of the king of the city of Avanti (i.e. Ujjayinī) and not of the country of Avanti. This has been clearly stated in the following extract from Utpala's commentary[6]:—यश्च शाकुनं भारद्वाजाख्यस्य मुनेर्मतं दृष्ट्वा श्रीद्रव्यवर्धनाख्यो महाराजाधिराजवंश-प्रसूत आवन्तिक उज्जयिन्या नृपो राजा प्राहोक्तवान्।

The correct grammatical form of the word meaning 'a king of the country of Avanti' is *Āvantya*[7] according to Pāṇini, IV, 1, 171 and 174. The word *Āvantika* used in Varāhamihira's verse is evidently formed like the word *Āyodhyika* used in the *Uttararāmacarita*[8] and means 'one residing in the city of Avanti or Ujjayinī.[9]

There is no evidence to show that the territory round Daśapura was included in the country of Avanti. Information regarding the exact boundaries of ancient countries are rarely available, but in the present case we are fortunate in having the following verse, which clearly distinguishes between the people of Avanti and those of Daśapura. While stating the countries where the different languages were spoken in ancient times, Rājaśekhara quotes the following verse[10]:—

गौडाद्याः संस्कृतस्थाः परिचितरुचयः प्राकृते लाटदेश्याः
सापभ्रंशप्रयोगाः सकलमरुभुवष्टक्कभादानकाश्च।
आवन्त्याः पारियात्राः सह दशपुरजैर्भूतभाषां भजन्ते
यो मध्ये मध्यदेशं निवसति स कविः सर्वभाषानिषण्णः॥

This verse clearly states that the Paiṣācī language was spoken by the inhabitants of Avanti, Daśapura and (the country round) Pāriyātra (Aravali mountain). This shows clearly that the country of Avanti did not include Daśapura. Dravyavardhana, who is described as a king of Avanti, could not therefore have been ruling from Daśapura.

(3) As shown above, Dravyavardhana, who was a predecessor of Yaśodharman, was ruling from Avanti or Ujjayinī. It is therefore very probable that Yaśodharman, who succeeded him and may have been his son, retained the same old capital. There is no evidence to show that he shifted the seat of his government to some place different from Ujjayinī, which has, from very ancient times, been noted as the capital of the Avanti country.

(4) The Mandasor inscription dated V. S. 589 does not, of course, mention explicitly that Nirdoṣa had his headquarters at Daśapura, but he was appointed *Rājasthānīya* of the country, extending from the Vindhya mountain in the South to the Pāriyātra in the North and to the Arabian Sea in the West. Daśapura is the only well-known ancient place in this region which is likely to have been his capital. His inscription at Mandasor supports this conjecture. His records have been found nowhere else.

(5) If Yasodharman himself was ruling from Daśapura it is very unlikely that he appointed a *Rājasthāniya* to govern the territory in which his own capital was situated. We have so far had no instance of a feudatory or a Rājasthānīya of an Emperor governing the territory round the latter's capital. If Nirdoṣa's was an exceptional case the burden of proving that it was so lies on those who make such a supposition.

There is thus no valid objection against my cojecture that *Ujjayinī was the capital of the Later Aulikaras including Yaśodharman.*

References

1. There is no ground for Dr. Sircar's conjecture that the mother had died at Mandasor, the capital of his suzerain.
2. In his *Pañcasiddhāntikā* Varāhamihira has taken Ś. 427 (A.D. 505) as the initial year for calcultaion.
3. *CII.,* vol. III, Nos. 33-34.
4. This portion of the verse has been read by Sircar as follows : जित्वा रिपुवलं संक्खे रम्यं पुर दशादि... । He proposes to emend it by reading संख्ये and पुरम्।
5. *CII.*, vol. III, pp. 154.
6. *Bṛhatsaṃhitā* ed. by Sudhakar Dvivedi, vol. II, pp. 1007.
7. The affix ञ्यङ् added to the name of countries ending in इ, which are also names of Kṣatriyas (e. g. Avantī) denotes both the senses of *apatya* and *rājan*. Later, the word came to be used in the sense of the people of the country also. The word आवन्त used in *Bṛhatsaṁhitā,* XIV, 33 is probably a mistake for आवन्त्य.
8. Cf. एषोऽस्मि कार्यवशादायोध्यिकस्तदानीन्तनश्च संवृत्त : *Uttararāmacarita,* Act I. The commentator घनश्याम says.अयोध्यासंबंधी आयोध्यिक: ।
9. It is noteworthy in this connection that Varāhamihira has used the same expression with reference to himself in his *Bṛhajjātaka* and it is well known that he was a resident of Ujjayinī. Cf. आदित्यदासतनयस्तदवाप्तबोध: कापित्थके सपितृलब्धवरप्रसाद: । आवन्तिको सुनियतान्यवलोक्य सम्यग्घोरां वराहमिहिरो रुचिरां चकार ॥
10. *Kāvyamīmāṁsā* (Gaekwad's Sanskrit Series, 1916), pp. 51

22

Early History and Archaeology of Kurukṣetra and Ambala Division*

R. C. Agrawala

I. Early Notices of Location and Extent

The realm of the ancient Kurus, over which Parīkṣit ruled, was very extensive indeed. The *Digvijaya Parva* of the *Mahābhārata* narrates[1] that it "extended from the border of the land of the Kulindas (near the sources of the Sutlej; the Jumnā and the Ganges) to that of the Śūrasenas and the Matsyas (in the Mathurā and the Bairāṭa regions respectively), and from the frontier of Rohtak (East Panjāb) to that of the Pañcālas (of Rohilkhand). It was divided into three parts, Kurujāṅgala[2], Kurus[3] proper and Kurukṣetra". Kuru kingdom and Kuru *janapada* were well known to Pāṇini (IV. 1. 172). The Kāśikā enumerates all the three different units of the Kuru country i.e. *Kuravaśca Kurukṣetraṃ ca Kuru-Kurukṣetram,*[4] *Kuravaśca Kurujāṅgalaṃ ca Kuru-Kurujāṅgalam.* (*India,* p. 54). According to Dr. V. S. Agrawala (*India,* p. 54): –

(i) Kuru-*rāṣṭra* proper was between the Gaṅga and the Yamunā rivers with its capital at Hastināpura;

(ii) Kurujāṅgala was equal to Rohtak, Hānsī and Hissār; while

(iii) Kurukṣetra was situated still to the north with its centre at Thānesar, Kaithal and Karnāl.

According to the *Taittirīya Āraṇyka*[5] (V. 1. 1.), the places bounding the region of Kurukṣetra were : – Khāṇḍava (to the south). Tūrghna (to the north), Pariṇāh[6] (to the west) etc. The same region has also been located[7] between the Sarasvatī and the Dṛṣadvatī rivers or between Tarantuka, Arantuka, Rāmahrada and Macakruka. This area was also irrigated by other rivers such as Aruṇā, Aṁśumatī or Indumatī, Āpayā or Āpagā, Kauśikī, Oghavatī, Hiraṇyavatī etc.

The other name of the place (i.e. *Samantapañcaka*), so often cited in the *Mahābhārata,* seems to denote the area of the region as 5 *Yojanas* on all the four sides. According to Hemacandra, the author of the *Abhidhānacīntāmaṇi*[8] (IV. 16), Kurukṣetra extended up to 12 *yojanas* i.e. *Dharmakṣetre Kurukṣetre dvādaśa-yojanāvadhiḥ*. Yuan Chwang, a Chinese pilgrim who visited India in the 7th century A.C., refers to the kingdom of *Sa-t'a-ni-shi-fa-lo* (Skt. *Sthāṇvīśvara,* modern Thānesar[9]) as about 7000 *li* in circuit and the capital 20 *li* or so[10].

II. Geography of the region in Mediaeval Inscriptions

The undated *praśasti* (of Mahendrapāla) from Pehoā (district Karnāl; *El,* I, pp. 242 ff.), describes Kurukṣetra (verse 3, p. 248) and the river Sarasvatī (verse 4, p. 248) in beautiful words:–

(i) "May the field of Kuru grant happiness, free from all pains, (that field) which is able to remove the impurity of sins of many kinds, that is inhabited by crowds of sages; who have destroyed the dense darkness (of ignorance) by gaining the knowledge of the self; (and hence) are filled with deep joy".

(ii) "And may that (beautiful) water of Sarasvatī's (stream) entirely cut your (bonds of) misery, (that water which is) a boat (for crossing the ocean of births), a chariot for travelling along the road of gods, a cloud such as appears on the destruction of world shedding copious showers on the fire of . . . the virtuous (and) a sun to destroy thick mud like darkness of a concatenation of virtuous diseases".

The same epigraph also refers to the names of three villages (Yakṣ apālaka, Gejjara and Pāṭala) assigned for the *bhoga* (the services) of the temple in the locality. It is of course not at all possible to identify these places.

The other inscription from Pehoā's Garībanāth temple is dated in *saṃvat* 276 and refers to the traditional name of the place as Pṛthūdaka[11] (*El,* I, pp. 184 ff; Cf. *JASB,* XXII, pp. 673 ff). It is also stated therein (line 14) that the place lay to the east of the river Sarasvatī. The Betmā grant (C. India), dated in *saṃvat* 1076 (=1020 A.C.) also states that a certain Bṛahmin (named Paṇḍita Della) had come from Sthaṇvīśvara to the village of Nālataḍāga (H.C. Ray, *Dynastic History of Northern India,* II, 1936, Calcutta, pp. 862).

The mediaeval epigraphs also refer to *Hariyānā* or *Hariyānaka* (modern Hariāṇā, comprising of the districts of Hissār and Rohtaka). The Delhi Museum inscription (dated 1328 A.C. in the reign of Muhammad Tughalak; *El,* I, pp. 93-5) furnishes the following information on this point:–

"There is a country called *Hariyānā,* a very h eaven on earth; there lies the city called *Ḍhillika* (modern Delhi) built by the Tomaras" (H.C.

Ray, *op cit.*, p. 1145). The Pālam Baolī inscription (from the village Boh'er, in the Rohtaka district) is dated in V. S. 1337 (=1280 A.C.) and states that the "land of *Hariyānaka* was first enjoyed by the Tomaras and then by the Cauhānas. It is now being ruled by the Śaka (i.e. Muslim) king etc.," (*Ibid*, p. 1146).

III. Early Associations

The Epic tradition connects the Puru-Bharata family with the kings of the Kurukṣetra region.[12] This association of the Bharatas with Kuru-land is also attested by the Vedic literature for the two Bharata princes (i.e. Devaśravas and Devavāta) happened to offer sacrifices in the land watered by the Āpayā, the Sarasvatī and the Dṛṣadvatī[13]. We are also informed in the *Brāhmaṇas* and the Epics that "Bharata Dauṣayantī made offerings on the Jumnā, the Ganges and the Sarasvatī. The territory indicated in these laudatory verses is exactly the region which is later on so highly celebrated as Kurukṣetra".[14] In fact the earlier history of Kurukṣetra is all shrouded in mystery. *It is proposed here, in the present paper, to throw some light on the history and archaeology of the region of Kurukṣetra and the territory bounding it (i.e. Karnāl, Ambālā, Hissār, Rohtak, Sonepat*[15]*, Pānipat etc., now included in the Ambālā Division of East Panjab).*

III A. Importance of the Area

(i) Indra killed the Vṛtra, near the Somatīrtha or Vedic Śaryaṇāvat.

(ii) Pururavas found his beloved Urvaśī here (*Śat. Br.*, XI. 5. 14).

(iii) Ancient sages performed the Vedic sacrifices and kindled the sacred fire at Kurukṣetra[16].

(iv) The Great War was fought here between the Pāṇḍus and the Kauravas.

(v) The famous battle of Tarāoṛī[17] was fought between Pṛthvī Rāja and Muhammed Ghori.

(vi) The Battle of Pānipat[18] was fought between Bābar and Ibrahim Lodi.

(vii) The Marathas were defeated at Pānipat at the hands of Ahmad Shāh Abdālī[19].

(viii) Even after the partition of India, millions of refugees were able to find shelter in the Refugee Relief Camp at Kurukṣetra. In fact Kurukṣ etra region has played a great role in the history of India. It had the privilege of witnessing the rise and fall of many kingdoms, some of which happened to be closely associated with the district of Kurukṣ etra.

(ix) It lay on the ancient trade route connecting the Western Panjab with Northern India[20]. It is interesting to note that the existing Grand-Trunk road, which connects Peshawar and calcutta, passes through Ambala, Kurukṣetra, Karnāl, Pānipat, Sonepat, Delhi etc. It has been narrated in the *Rāmāyaṇa* (II. 74. 11-5-cited in *Sārthavāha,* p. 16) that the ambassadors, deputed to bring Bharata from the Kekaya country, crossed the Ganges, reached the town of Hastināpur and then came to Kurukṣetra. It was here that they saw the *Vāruṇītīrtha* and crossed the river Sarasvatī. Then began their journey towards the Śaradaṇḍā[21] (i.e. the modern river Sirhind).

IV. Some Early Finds

(i) It was at Koṭalā Nihaṅg Khān (Rupar) in the Ambala district of E. Panjab that archaeological excavations[22] brought to light sufficient Indus Valley antiquities testifying to the extension of this culture towards the Gangetic plain. It is regretted that no such finds from the Kurukṣ etra region have been reported so far. Recent excavations at Rūpar have brought to light 5 habitation-phases beginning from 2000 B.C. to 1700 A.C. The discovery of grey and N. B. P. Wares here at Rupar is also any interesting indeed; (cf. *The March of India,* VI, no. 3, Delhi, 1953, pp. 12-16; *Ancient India, Bull. of Arch. Surv of India,* IX, pp. 123-6; *Indian Archaelogy* 1953-4 *A Review,* 1954, New Delhi, pp. 6-7 and plates; *ibid,* 1955, pp. 9-11, 59 for Indus Valley Culture in the region of Rupar).

(ii) Mr. B. B. Lal was able to discover certain pieces of the *Painted Grey-Ware*[23] (of about 800 B.C.) at various places of this area i.e. at Amīn (5 miles from Kurukṣetra), Rājā-Karṇa-Kā-Kilā at Kurukṣetra, Pehoā (ancient Pṛthūdaka, near Kurukṣetra), Pānipat etc. (*Ancient India,* X-XI, *op. cit.,* pp. 138-141).

(iii) D. B. Spooner (*ASR.,* 1922-3, pp. 89-90) opined that the ancient mound named Rājā-Karṇa-kā-Kilā at Thānesar might well date back from the Pre-Buddhist period. But he regretted about the utter absence of any material bearing upon the history of the region in those good old days. Spooner (*Ibid,* 1921-2, p. 46) also states that "Kurukṣetra is frequently alluded to in the Buddhist *Jātakas,* the most important reference to it being in the *Mahāsutasoma Jātaka*".

(iv) The famous Toprā (Ambālā district; *CASR.,* XIV, pp. 78 ff.) pillar[24] -edicts of Dharmarāja Aśoka bear testimony to the importance of this place as a stronghold of the Mauryan administration. The discovery of some uninscribed cast coins at Sugha[25] (ancient Srughna in the Ambālā Dist.) is also very interesting (*Report,* p. 24). These coins mostly bear a *caitya* on one side and a lion or an elephant on the other. Cunningham

(*Geography of Ancient India,* 1924, Calcutta, p. 397) reports that the area of Sugha, Māṇḍalapur, Būriā and Jagādharī has yielded coins ranging from the square punch-marked to the times of the Cauhān and the Tomara Rājās of Delhi. Thus he rightly asserts that Sugha, a site of the punchmarked coins, is at least as old as 500 B.C., if not 1000 B.C. Archaeological explorations and excavations at this site may push back this antiquity to a still earlier period. It is extremely essential to study the site with the help of a scientific spade. It is situated only 38 or 40 miles from Thānesar and stands on the high road leading from the Gangetic Doāb (via Meerut, Sahāranpur, Ambālā) to the Upper Panjab and commands the passage of the Jumnā river. It was by this route that Mahmūd of Ghaznī returned from his expeditions to Kanauj. Timur too visited this route while returning from his plundering campaign of Haridwār; and Bābar advanced to conquer Delhi by this side (Cunningham, *ibid,* pp. 396-8). For Sugha, also consult S. Beal, *Records of the Western Countries,* I, pp. 186 to 188 and f. notes; Varāhamihira's *Vṛhatsaṃhitā,* XVI. 21 and translation on p. 178 as edited by V. Subrahmanya Śāstrī, 1947, Bangalore City; *CASR.,* II, pp. 228-31; *ibid,* XIV, p. 134; Cunningham's *Geography of Ancient India,* 1924, Calcutta, pp. 395-398; *Dey,* p. 194. The recent excavations at Rūpar also yielded a small ivory seal inscribed with the word *Bhadapalakasa* in the *Brāhmī* script of the Mauryan period [*Indian Archaeology* 1953-4 *A Review, op. cit.,* p. 6].

The N. B. P. ware occurs at Panīpat (29^0 10´ North Lat and 75^0 56´ East Long) higher than the painted Grey Ware; [*Ancient India, op. cit.,* X-XI, p. 145]. It also occurs at Sonepat *(ibid).*

It has not yet been possible to study the early coins[26] from Thānesar or the neighbouring region of Kurukṣetra. Archaeological excavations in this area may help us in throwing some light on the early history of the locality. Following are some of the towns of the Ambālā Division as known to Pāṇini: –

(i) Kapisthala[27] (VIII, 3. 91) is modern Kaithal in the Karnāl district.

(ii) Śoṇaprastha is modern Sonepat ($28^0$59´ N. Lat, 70^0 1´ E. Lon).

(iii) Roṇī[28] (iv. 2. 78) is probably Roḍi in Hissar district.

(iv) Tauṣāyaṇa[29] (*Pakṣādigaṇa,* IV. 2. 80) is modern Ṭohānā, a place of historical and archaeological interest in Fatahbad tahsil of district Hissar.

(v) Śairīṣaka[30] (IV, 2. 80) is modern Sirsā, a sub-divisional headquarter in Hissar district.

(vi) Yugandhara[31] (i.e. Jagādharī, District Ambala).

(vii) Srughna (see fn. 21 above).

(viii) Kalakūṭa (IV. 1. 173) was probably modern Kalka in the Simla Hills (*India*, p. 54).

(ix) Gauḍapura (vi. 2. 100) is probably *Gauda-grāma* or Gurgaon in the south-east Panjab [*JUPHS.*, XVI (i), p. 42].

The Bharatas have been mentioned as an *āyudhajīvī saṅgha* by Pāṇini. Dr. Agrawala (*India*, p. 451) thinks that "it must be some old tradition, otherwise Pāṇini locates them in the Kuru region on the border land of the Udīcya and Prācya divisions of India. According to another *sūtra*, the Kurus lived under a regal form of government. It seems these Bharatas lived round about Kurukṣetra as a *saṅgha* in Pāṇini's time."

V. Post Mauryan Coins and Seals

Dr. Birbal Sahni happened to publish some Śuṅga antiquities from the Khokrākoṭa mound at Rohtak. They include a square terracotta seal (ordinary) and a round sealing baked in clay. Birbal Sahni[32] has given the following description of this important find :–

Size: –24 x 24 m.m.

Obv. There is an inscription from left to right–

(1) *bhadra mitra*

(2) *sya droṇīghā* (*ṭe*)

in the *Brāhmī* characters.

Rev. – Smooth and convex and it shows two perforations (indicated by arrows) where the string was probably attached to fix the sealing to an article, possibly a document sent to Rohtak.

Mr. Sahni quotes K. P. Jayaswal according to whom the owner of the sealing was "the Officer-in-charge of the pass over the *droṇī* (valley; Hindi *dūna*) which must have been in the Śiwālaks, probably identical with Dehrādūn." C. R. Singhal (***Bibliography of Indian Coins***, I, 1250, Bombay, p. 24) cites the remarks of Jayaswal (expressed in *JBORS.*, XXIII, p. 148) : "Bhadramitra evidently was the Yaudheya Officer-in-charge of the *dūna;* and the second line of the legend would better be read as ***droṇīpāla*** instead of ***droṇīghā*** (***ṭe***)."

A hoard of about 136 Yaudheya-coins was recovered from the village Panjya in Jaunsar-Bāwar area of Dehradun district in 1936. It was really interesting to observe the utter absence of the early Yaudheya coins in that hoard. On the other hand, the coins furnished by this hoard were closely associated with the Kuṇinda coins both in style and type (*JNSI.*, II, p. 109). In these circumstances it appears hardly plausible to consider

Bhadramitra of the Rohtak seal as a Yaudheya officer. Future discoveries are awaited to throw some light on the history and lineage of this Bhadramitra.

VI. Agāca Coins

Coins bearing the legends *Agodake agāca janapada* or *Agodakā agācaja* etc., were described by Allan (*op. cit.,* 1936, Introduction, pp. clvii-viii) in the uncertain category of the ancient Indian coins. Mr. Allah has also stated that a number of such coins was procured by Rodgers at Barwāllā. Mr. P. L. Gupta has tried to prove[33] that at Agrohā (Hissar) existed a tribe named *Agra* and that *Agāca* is the Prākṛt corruption of Sanskrit *Agreya*. *Agodaka* of the coins is the same as *Agrotaka* as found in an epigraph of 1328 A.C. (*El.,* I, pp 93 ff.). The site, about 13 miles from Hissar, yielded quite a large number of antiquities including stone fragments, terracottas, large size bricks etc. (*Report,* pp. 41-3)[34].

VII. A stone ball with ancient symbols

The excavations at the site of Rāja-Karaṇa-kā-Kilā brought to light a stone ball, weighing about 7 tolās of the Indian weight. D. B. Spooner (*ASR.,* 1921-2, p. 49) has furnished the following details of the same: – "There are sketched on it a number of sacred symbols including a pair of fish joined by a piece of string, a *swastika,* a *nandipada* – similar to the symbol which begins the Khāravela inscription, a rectangle with diagonals, a device consisting of two triangles joined at the apex, a circle, a three pointed star and what appears to be a *swastika* without the fourth arm. The exact purpose of these symbols is unknown". To me it appears that the peculiar ball, under reference, might have been used for weighting purposes at a time when coins having these very symbols were in frequent currency in the Indian markets. It is of course a conjecture and nothing can be said with definiteness at this moment.

VIII. Śuṅga Sculptures and Terracottas

(a) It is also essential to refer to a *yakṣa* statue from Palwal and illustrated by Dr. V. S. Agrawala in the *Journal of the U.P. Historical Society,* XXIV-XXV, p. 188, figure 4. According to Dr. Agrawala (*ibid*), "the statue consists of the head and bust of a colossal *Yakṣa* image of red sandstone. It was found at Palwal in Gurgaon District in 1914 and is now deposited in the Provincial Museum, Lucknow (0.107). The figure is wearing on the head a conical turban with tiered folds, big round discs in cloven ear-lobes, a double flat crescent-shaped torque, a flat triangular necklace, armlets with triple vertical projections and four heavy wristlets. The right hand is raised towards the shoulder and holds a conchlike tapering object, now mutilated. There are traces of a scarf looped on right elbow. On the back are shown pendant tassels of the necklace. The style of the turban, the torque and the necklace and the armlets with feathered projections seen in the side view, *all point to the image being an early Yakṣa type that may be assigned to the early Śuṅga period, about second century B. C.* The object in the right hand is unfortunately not very distinct and therefore the identification with Kubera is far from certain".

(b) Some interesting Śuṅga terracottas recovered from the excavations at Rūpar, have been illustrated by Dr. Y. D. Sharma in *Ancient India, op. cit.*, IX, p. 126, plate 50 A & B. They are able to throw a flood of light on the plastic art of the region during the Post-Mauryan period.

(c) About 5 miles to the S.S.E. of Thānesar lies the small village of Amīn,[35] situated on an ancient huge mound measuring about 2000 feet in length (from north to south), 800 feet in width and about 25 to 30 feet in height. This is considered to have been the traditional site of the *Cakra vyūha* where the armies were arranged at the time of the famous battle of Mahābhārata. The name Amīn seems to have been a contraction of Abhimanyu (son of Arjuna)-*kheḍa* (i.e. mound). It was here that two inscribed red stone rectangular pillars were discovered and are said to have been preserved in the Ṭhākurji shrine on the west bank of the tank called Sūraj-*kuṇḍa* (*ASR.*, 1921-2, p. 47; 1922-3 *ibid*, plate V. e.). No detailed account of these pillars has so far been furnished by any scholar. "They are carved on all the four sides and have no sockets for crossbars. They would thus appear to have supported some sort of a platform." Besides this, Mr. D. B. Spooner[36] (*ASR.*, 1921-2, p. 47) states that the "inscriptions on them are in the characters of the Kuṣāṇa period but are quite short and merely supply the names of their donors". But this dating by Spooner does not tally with the art of the times. In fact the depiction of the dress and the ornaments of the persons, so finely carved on these pillars, appears to have been the work of some Śuṅga artists. Dr. A Coomarswami[37] has also placed these pillars somewhere in the Śuṅga period. Following are the details of these sculptured posts under reference:—

(i) *Pillar to the left side*:—It depicts male person (in the *sthānaka mudrā*) who wears a typical Śuṅga turban[38] on the head, a necklace of 4 strings round the neck and a *dhotī* covering the lower portion of the body and coming up to the knees. This *dhotī* has been tightened with the help of a *kāyabandha* (waist-cloth). The standing person has caught hold of one of the ends of this *kāyabandha* in his left hand while the other end of it is hanging down below. The right hand is placed towards the right side of the chest and holds a lotus in it. He wears the long *karṇakuṇḍalas* in his ears but he appears bare-footed. From the looks of this person it appears that he is some *Yaksa* pondering over some problem out of great anxiety. The front portions of his arms, being somewhat covered by some cloth, do not depict any ornaments round this portion of his body. Just above the head of this person have been carved two full bloomed lotuses and around all this (i.e. the lotuses and the person) can be seen floral designs, along the rectangular edges of the slab; (cf. *JUPHS,* VI. 2, figure 17, p. 105, fn. where Dr. Agrawala considers the depiction of a *padma-pāṇi Yakṣa* on this pillar).

(ii) *Pillar to the right side*: —This piece too is very interesting for it seems to represent some amorous scene. It depicts a male and female standing bare-footed very close to each other. The lady wears the typical head-dress (i.e. a turban) of the Śuṅga times and looks at the male person (standing to her left) with a smiling face. Her left arm, placed round the neck of this person, touches his left shoulder. Similarly the right hand of the latter touches her left shoulder. The lady here wears three necklaces, the beads of which are clearly visible. She also puts on heavy *kuṇḍalas* in her ears. The breasts of the lady appear to be quite heavy. Both these persons are putting on *dhotīs* up to the knees. The ornaments, appearing in the front portion of the hands of the lady, have covered the entire portion from the elbow to the beginning of her palm. This reminds us of the existing fashion[39] of wearing bangles by the Rājasthāni ladies even now in the 20th century A.C. It is much more interesting to find that the lower portion of the legs of the lady (in the above Kurukṣetra panel) has also been covered by the rings which reach her ankles. She wears the *dhotī* in the current *Marāṭhī* style and there appears a girdle on the *dhotī* here; the beads of the girdle are quite visible. Above it has been tied a *kāyabandha* (round the waist), the ends of which are hanging down below. Her left leg has taken a turn behind her right leg and is placed on some object which looks like a stool or *ḍamaru.* Her right arm, stretching down below, is visible on one side. The male person holds a wine cup (in his left hand) which is placed near his chest but towards the left portion of the lady. The former here wears a necklace in the same fashion as put on by the person already cited in the first panel above. Dr. Agrawala (*ibid,* figure 12) is justified in tracing the depiction of *Yakṣa-mithuna* here.

IX. *Kuṣāṇa and Pre-Kuṣāṇa Finds*

(a) The excavations on the mound of Rājā-Karṇa-kā-Kilā at Thānesar yielded an Indo-Bactrian silver large coin of Hermaios (*ASR.,* 1922-3, p. 87). A hemidrachm of Apollodotus and one of Antimachus were also recovered by Rodgers at Jagādharī (*Report,* p. 24). The discovery of a hoard of quite a large number of coins 883 in number) of Menander from Sonepat is of course very interesting (cf. *Numismatic Chronicle,* London, 1872, p. 159). It is quite possible that this region too fell a prey to the attack of Menander who had penetrated as far as Madhyamikā (modern Nagarī, Chittaur district of Udaipur State) and Sāketa[40] (modern Ayodhyā, U.P.).

(b) The Kuṣāṇas, who ruled North India as far as Mathurā and Banaras, had also subjugated the region of the Ambala division. The Theh Polar[41] site (Karnāl district) yielded some rude imitations of those coins of Vāsudeva which were adopted by the foreign ruling chiefs of the Panjab towards the 3rd or 4th centuries A.C. (*ASR.,* 1930-4, pp. 143 ff). In one trench of the Theh Polar site were also found 2 debased copper coins bearing the figure of a Kuṣāṇa type of king at an altar (*ibid*). Besides this, some other antiquities[42] of this period, reported from Rājā-Karaṇa-[43]-kā-Kilā, include : –

(i) A terracotta sealing having a beautiful Indian bull on one side. This bull faces left. Above this animal appears a line of 5 minute letters "probably in the *Kharoṣṭhī* script" (*ASR.,* 1922-3, pp. 87-8). It is regretted that the sealing has not been illustrated by D.B. Spooner[44] in *ASR.,* 1922-3 cited just above.

(ii) Mr. Spooner (*ibid*) also refers to the large size bricks from the same place as belonging to the Kuṣāṇa period. They measure 14 to 14½ inches in length, 9 to 9½ inches in breadth and 2½ to 3 inches in thickness.

(iii) A terracotta votive-tank has been recovered in a broken condition but it depicts sufficient details bearing close similarity to similar finds from Texila, Ahicchatra, Kauśāmbi[45] etc. The corners of the Kurukṣetra votive-tank depicts one musician elevated on a platform; while the other is playing on a pair of cymbols while two others are playing on a flute and a tabor respectively. The fourth musician is a female and the musical instrument held in her hand cannot be determined with certainly (*ASR.,* 1921-22, p. 48). Another terracotta votive dish was found in a fragmentary condition (*Ibid,* p. 49).

(c) A fragmentary stone inscription (in the *Kharoṣṭhī* script), now preserved in the Lahore Museum, is said to have been recovered from Karnāl near Kurukṣetra. Dr. Sten Konow[46] has furnished the following reading of the same: –

Sidhi kri (*śa*) *vi* (*na*) *u* (*–putreṇa*)

lapotreṇa ae puka (*riṇi karavita*).

It refers to the construction of a pond (Skt. *puṣkariṇī*) by Kṛśakavi, the identification of Kṛśakavi being obscure.

(d) The region of Būriā, Sugha and Jagādharī has yielded several Kuṇinda coins of king Amoghabhūti who is said to have been a chieftain of the famous Kuṇinda tribe (*Report,* p. 24) in the early centuries of the Christian Era. Similar coins have also been procured at Karnāl in the Kurukṣetra region (*Proceedings of the Asiatic Society of Bengal,* 1875, p. 85; (cf. J. Allan, *Catalogue of the Coins of Ancient India in the British Museum,* London, 1936, p. ciii of the *introduction*).

(e) It was more than 75 years ago that Rodgers procured a unique coin from Rūpar (district Ambala) which bore the same legend in *Brāhmī* on one side and in *Kharoṣṭhī* on the other. Rodgers read the legend as *rājā ajamitra* on both the sides (*Report,* p. 38). He also states that there was the figure of an elephant on the obverse of it and of a man or woman on the reverse. Mr. Rodgers is of the opinion that "this coin is not at all like the *mitra* coins", found in abundance in the Uttara Pradeśa. It is regretted that the coin has not been illustrated by Mr. Rodgers. The existing coin of course adds one more name to the list of the rulers who issued a currency having the legend in *Brāhmī* on one side and in *Kharoṣṭhī* on the other. It is just possible that Ajamitra was some local ruler whose regime could not have lasted long. Perhaps he had issued his coinage imitating the coins of the Kuṇindas.[47]

(f) The ancient site of Rohtak also yielded a coin-mould which, according to Dr. V. S. Agrawala, was perhaps used to cast some coin of Huviṣka – the great Kuṣāṇa chief (*JNSI.*, XV i, pp. 68-9).

(g) Rodgers procured some coins of Gondophares and Amonghabhūti at Naraingarh (dist. Ambala; *Report,* p.28). Describing the copper issues of the foreigners, he states that they bear a king's head and some Greek letters on the obverse, while the figure of Pallas and some *Kharosṭ ḥī* letters on the appear on the reverse. These coins, according to Rodgers, weighed 30 grains.

(h) Cunningham (*CASR.*, p. 78) obtained 3 coins at Kapālamocana (Śiwālak hills) and one of these was "a small silver piece of the Indo-Sassanian type, with the letter *ma* between the two attendants at the fire altar". The remaining two copper coins were of Sāmantadeva. Rodgers procured a hemidrachm of Strato (helmeted king) and several coins of Menander in the bazars of Sāḍhaurā (Ambālā). He was informed by the local people that these coins had come from Kapālamocana, a place already referred to above (Rodgers, *Report,* p. 25).

(i) Two *Audumbara* coins and one coin of the Indo-Parthian ruler Soter Megas are some of the noteworthy antiquities from Rūpar [*March of India,* VI (3), pp. 12-16].

(j) Whitehead found a special type of the coins of Soter Megas in Delhi and Jagādharī and that variety was probably current in what is now called the S.E. Panjab [R.B. Whitehead, *Catalogue* of *Coins on the Panjab Museum Lahore,* I, p. 162 fn. 1].

(k) The discovery of some more Kuṇinda coins from Karnāl (*JASB*, XLIV, *p*. 82; *Proc. A.S.B.*, 1875, p. 85) is also to be noted.

(l) It was from the ancient site of Rāja-Karṇa-Kā-Kilā that a rare large round copper coin[48] was excavated by Dayā Rām Sāhnī about 25 years ago (*ASR.,* 1922-3, p. 87). It is regretted that it has not been published by Spooner in *ASR.,* 1922-23. The well defined incuse here appears to be similar to that on the well known Pañcāla series of coins. The name (on the Kurukṣetra coin) has been engraved in two lines and has been read thus:—*rajño Yajñajitasya.* The name of this *Yajñajita* is not available from any other source. According to Mr. Spooner, the script of the legend of this coin is of the second or third century A.C. Probably he was some local chief who might have risen to power for a little while, perhaps after Kuṣāṇa Vāsudeva II. He can also be placed somewhere in the period that followed the disintegration of the Kuṣāṇa regime towards the beginning of the third century A.C. In this connection it is essential to survey the political conditions of the East Panjab, Mathurā and Rājasthān before the beginning of the fourth century A.C.

On the basis of the early coin types of the Yaudheyas, it can be safely said that Kārtikeya was their *iṣṭadevatā.* Mr. P. L. Gupta[49] states that in the second and the first century B.C., they occupied the Haryāṇā (Skt. *Bahudhānyaka*) portion of the Panjab comprising Rohtak, Hissar, Sirsā, Karnāl and Gurgaon; and also the adjoining portion of the desert of modern Mārwār[50].

The Kuṣāṇa power was at its glory in the time of Kaniṣka and Huviṣka. That is why the Yaudheyas, a tribe closely associated with Rohītaka[51] (modern Rohtak, Ambala Division), were not in a position to raise its head in revolt against the foreign yoke.[52] It was somewhere in the middle of the second century A.C., that they revolted against the foreigners but were soon checked by Rudradāman—the famous Śaka Mahākṣatrap. In the opinion of Dr. A.S. Altekar[53], "the Yaudheyas made a second bid for independence towards the end of the second century A.D., came out successful in their venture and succeeded in freeing their homeland and ousting the Kuṣāṇas beyond the Sutlej. The coins of Kaniṣka III (180-210 A.D.) and Vāsudeva (210-240 A.D.) are not found to the east of the Sutlej; it is thus clear that they had lost all cis-Sutlej territories. On the other hand, the post-Kuṣāṇa coins of the Yaudheyas having legends in the characters of the third or fourth century A.D., are found in large hoards between Sutlej and the Jumnā, the homeland of the Yaudheyas, in the districts of Sahāranpur, Dehrādūn, Delhi, Rohtak, Ludhiana and Kangra". Yaudheya coins were also found at Abohar, Sirsā, Hānsi, Pānipat, Sonepat etc., and Rodgers (MSS. notes in Deptt. of coins, as cited by Allan, *op. cit.*, p. cli) also obtained some 4th century A.C. coins (class 6) at Hānsī and Kharkaundah near Sonepat. The evidence of the coin finds shows that the Yaudheyas occupied an area which may be roughly described as the Eastern Panjab (Allan, p. cli). Very recently, a unique Yaudheya copper coin was picked up from the top of the mound at Baghaulā in the district Gurgaon. It is a cast coin belonging to the second class of the Yaudheya series of coins [*JNSI.*, XIII (i), pp. 101-2 as discussed by O. Prufer].

It now appears that the foreigners were perhaps no longer ruling in the Ambala Division towards the beginning of the third century A.C. (Cf. Altekar, *op. cit.*, p. 21). It is also very likely that certain local ruler named Yajñajita (whose coin has just been cited above), after the fall of the Kuṣāṇas, gained power and issued coins in his own name for a short while. Perhaps the growing power of the Yaudheya tribe proved fatal to his existence.

R.B. Whitehead (*Numismatic Supplement*, 97, p. 1911) has described 21 coins found near Rūpar in the Ambālā district. "These coins are of mixed metal and weigh 190 grains. On the obverse there is a human figure copied from the Kuṣāṇa coins and the reverse bears a crude figure of an animal and some symbols. As these coins were accompanied by some copper coins of the White Hun Chiefs (Toramāṇa and Mihirakula), these are supposed to belong to about 5th century A.D." (C.R. Singhal, *Bibliography of Indian Coins*, 1, 1950, Bombay, p. 106).

Some earlier and later coins from the recent excavations at Rūpar have been illustrated in *Indian Archaeology 1953-4—A Review*, New Delhi, 1954, plate V.c.

(m) *Important Yaudheya Coins*:—The Yaudheya coin hoards from the following places of the region of Kurukṣetra are to be noted with great interest:—

(i) Sonepat[54] Hoard.

(ii) Karnāl[55] Hoard of 232 copper coins included the large variety of Yaudheya coins; showing a male deity holding a spear in the right hand and the left hand resting on the hip (Cf. V. A. Smith, *Catalogue of Coins in the Indian Museum of Calcutta*, I, plate XXI). Some coins of Kuṣāṇa Vāsudeva too were recovered from this very hoard.

X. Gupta Terracottas and Antiquities

(i) The region of Kurukṣetra has also yielded some very interesting Gupta terracottas which need to be described in detail[56] here: –

(A) Cunningham (*CASR.*, XIV, pp. 97 ff., plate XXVII lower half) excavated the broken part of a terracotta-plaque at the Asthipura site of Thānesar. On this plaque have been depicted two persons fighting with each other; their pose being very natural and charming. The upper portion of their bodies is quite naked while a *dhotī*-like object appears to have covered the lower portion. The folds of the drapery are of course quite visible. Besides this, there can also be seen a knot tied up (just below the naval portion) while one end of it is hanging down between the thighs. The man, to the left hand side, has caught hold of the arm of the other person. The latter wears a necklace, a fact which is quite unusual for the wrestlers at work. Usually the wrestlers do not put on such necklace as has been depicted in this plaque. Equally amazing is to note the long hair of one wrestler (to the left) and the curly hair of the other. The expression of pain on the face of the curly-haired[57] person is very well executed. It was probably a masterpiece of the Gandhāra art.

(B) Equally important is another terracotta plaque (from Peheoā[58], ancient Pṛthūdaka) which has been illustrated in *CASR* (XIV, plate XXVII, upper portion; *ibid,* p. 101). It is in a fairly well preserved condition and depicts some royal person sitting in the *sukhāsana* pose with his right hand placed on the right thigh. It appears that this person is sitting on some throne, the side portions and the back of which seem to have been shown a little here. He wears a full trouser (reaching up to the ankles). A full-sleeves shirt, in the upper portion of the body, covers the whole portion up to the beginning of the palms of the hand. Over this long coat appears a wrapper-like object which covers the upper portion of his arm and then hangs down below so as to cover the thigh portions too. The folds of the drapery here too suggest this plaque as having been executed under the influence of the Gandhāra art. Still more charming are the remaining details of the figure: –

(a) A round *tilaka* mark on the forehead.

(b) A crown (studded with circular jewels) on the head appears like the headdress worn by the court-judges.

(c) A fine jewelled garland appearing, not round the neck, but on the shoulders. It hangs on the chest so as to cover the naval portion altogether.

The left hand of the figure is completely broken; the eyes are open and there appear moustaches on the face. It is very interesting to note that the collar of the full sleeves coat (cited above) is round in shape.

(C) The mound known by the name of Rājā-Karaṇa-kā-Kilā (at Thānesar) also yielded some terracotta figurines and a small mould (height 2 inches and width 2 inches) which was perhaps used for preparing metal images of goddess Śrī. It is regretted that the back half of this mould has not been discovered. The remaining portion of course depicts the goddess seated on a full blown lotus and holding a flower in her right hand. Besides this, a male figure (height 3¾ inches; in a well preserved condition) has been depicted without clothing, "perhaps portrayed in the act of dancing" (Spooner, *ASR,* 1921-2, p. 48). Another terracotta relief (2¾ x 2½ inches) representing the lower half portion of a man and a woman (standing side by side) is also to be noted. The woman here is occupying the left portion as usual and both of them wear long-clothes. It is not yet possible to determine the theme of this relief (*CASR,* 1921-2, p. 48).

(i) Dr. R.C. Majumdar[59] has put forth a view that the East Panjab was perhaps included in the empire of Samudra Gupta. In his own words, "in the west it extended up to the Panjab, probably included its eastern districts between Lahore and Karnāl. From the last named (i.e. Karnāl) the boundary followed the Jumna river up to its junction with the Chambal . . ." M.S. Vatsa (*ASR.,* 1926-7, p. 233 plate XXIII f.) describes a rare gold coin of Samudra Gupta of the Battle Axe Type found along with 86 gold coins discovered at Mithathal in the Hissār district in 1915-16. Out of these[60] coins, 33 were of Samudra Gupta while the remaining were issued by the later Kuṣāṇa rulers of the Panjab (Cf. C.R. Singhal, *Bibliography of Indian Coins,* Bombay, I, p. 83). The discovery of this hoard (of gold coins) from the south-east Panjab is very important indeed. It is too early now to think that the armies of Samudra Gupta had penetrated as far as the Hissar district. The last king to be represented in this hoard is Samudra Gupta. The presence of only gold coins in the hoard suggests that the fellow who deposited the hoard was undoubtedly some wealthy person. He might have expired prematurely and so could get no time to take the coins out or to disclose the secret of their being hidden underneath the earth.

(ii) It was during his explorations and archaeological tour in the Panjab that Mr. Rodgers happened to acquire a gold coin of Samudra Gupta at Jagādharī (*Report,* p. 24).

(iii) It is equally interesting to note the famous Tushām[61] (Hissār) inscription carved in the huge rock in the characters of the Gupta period (J. Fleet, *Corpus Inscriptionum Indicarum,* III, pp. 269-70, plate XL facing p. 270). It throws a flood of light on the religious history of the place in the fourth century A.C. It contains a reference to the construction of a reservoir and a house for the use of god Viṣṇu by one *ācārya* Somatrāta, the great grandson of *Ārya Sātvata Yogācārya Yaśastrāta*. In the words of Dr. J. N. Banerjee (*Journal of the Indian Society of Oriental Art,* Calcutta, 1945, XIII, p. 56), "the wheel engraved about a foot below the last line of the inscription is evidently connected with it and is the wheel of Viṣṇu and not a Buddhist *dharmacakra* or a mere sun-symbol as Fleet has suggested".

(v) During his explorations in the Panjab, Cunningham was able to notice a stone inscription (on the walls of a Sikh Temple) at Kapālamocana in the Ambala district (*CASR.,* XIV, p. 77, plate XXV). This epigraph of two lines has been attributed to the Gupta period and furnishes the date as "when 165 years has elapsed in the month of Māgha". In case we take it to be dated in the Gupta Era, the date of the epigraph will come to 484 A.C. (i.e. 165+319). Some ornamental stones were also found by Cunningham here and they too have been assigned, by him to the same period.

(vi) A brass mask[62], inscribed in the characters of the 5th century A.C., is said to have been discovered in the temple of Laṭuśriya-Mahādeva at Rūpar (distt. Ambala). The small inscription of two lines has been read as: –

Śrī kuvilasya mitrā vasuputrasya devadharma.

XI. Some interesting Seals

The ancient site of Theh Polar (Karnāl) yielded some terracotta and copper seals and sealing too[63]. They resemble in technique, style, emblems and language with the coin-moulds found at Sunet[64] (near Ludhiānā) and described by Dr. Hoernle in the *Proceedings of the Asiatic Society of Bengal,* 1884, LIII, pp. 138-9.

(A) Some of the emblems on the Theh Polar seals are the human[65]-feet, *triśūla, cakra, padma,* bull, fire altar etc., and they are undoubtedly Brahmanical in nature. The bull, facing left, on one seal (*ASR.,* 1930-4, plate LXXXII, h) resembles that on the Yaudheya coins and coin-moulds from Rohtak. The name on the other seal, bearing an inscription ". . . . *bhadra* . . . . ." (*ibid,* plate LXXXII, k) needs to be compared with that of Bhadramitra from Rohtak and published by B. Sahni in *Current Science,* 1936, V, p. 81 ff. The third seal depicts the fire altar and an inscription *śri raja ma* (*ha*) *ta*.

(B) Of the copper seals found at Theh Polar, one bears a trident above the inscription[66] reversed and counterstruck. The latter is to be read (from right to left) as: – *Sammukhe kāśīśvarasya*[67] (*ibid,* plate LXXXII, I) in the characters of the later Gupta period. The other copper seal furnishes only *kāśiśvara* as the legend on it (*ibid,* plate LXXXII, g). The existence of the trident of course refers to its being purely Śaivite in nature.

XII. Later Gupta period

(A) D. B. Spooner (*ASR.*, 1922-3, p. 90) describes a stone slab (from Amīn) bearing a four armed seated figure of Gaṇapati with Śiva and his consort Pārvatī seated to his proper left. In Spooner's opinion, this sculpture was probably carved in the later-Gupta period. Besides this, there is not much of interesting material pertaining to the age preceding the accession of Harṣavardhana (seventh century A.D.). It was from Sirsā (Hissār) that certain early mediaeval inscriptions were recovered long ago (*EI.*, XXI, p. 293 ff.) and one epigraph of about the 5 or 6th century A.C. was also brought to light. The latter inscription refers to the valour of a certain ruler whose name and identity cannot be made out from the inscription.

(B) *Puṣpabhūtis of Thānesar*: –

The *Harṣacarita* of Bāṇa and the Sonepat Copper-Seal of Harṣavardhana (*CII.*, III, pp. 231-2) have also furnished the genealogy of the House of the Puṣpabhūtis of Thānesar. The first three rulers of this house (i.e. Naravarman, Rājyavardhan I and Ādityavardhan) were simply *Mahārājas*. It was Prabhākaravardhan (father of Harṣavardhan) who has been styled as *Mahārājādhirāja* for the first time. As he died shortly before Harṣa's accession to the imperial throne of Thānesar in 606 A.C., Dr. R. C. Majumdar (*The Classical Age,* 1954, Bombay, p. 97) is justified to place the commencement of Prabhākara's rule somewhere about 580 A.C. It would appear from all the contemporary sources, literary as well as archaeological, that the kingdom of Thānesar did not reach the pinnacle of glory till the last quarter of the 6th century A.C. The earlier history of the region of course remains shrouded in mystery. According to Dr. Majumdar (*op. cit.,* p. 97), "the first three kings, who flourished probably between 500-580 A.D., might have been feudatory chiefs, acknowledging the supremacy either of the Hūṇas, or of the Guptas, or both, at different times. It is also very likely that the Maukharis exercised supremacy over them for they did not claim the rank of the *Mahārajādhirāja* immediately after the fall of the Guptas and the Huṇas. It may be surmised that the dynasty really came into prominence after the death of Īśānavarman, and Ādityavardhan's marriage with a princess of the later-Gupta family probably marks a definite step in their rise to power and prominence. However all this is a mere speculation and no definite opinion is possible till more positive evidence is available".

The *Harṣacarita* refers to some poetical epithets[68] of Prabhākaravardhan of Thānesar, who was "a lion to the Hūṇa deer, a burning fever to the king of Sindhu, a troubler of the sleep of the Gurjara king, a fever to that scent elephant—the lord of Gandhāra, destroyer of the skill of the Lāṭas, an axe to the creeper which is the goddess of fortune (or sovereignty) of the Mālava". This much we know, about the Hūṇas, that just before his death, Prabhākaravardhan had despatched a military expedition to check the Hūṇa menace somewhere in the Uttarāpatha. His eldest son, Rājyavardhan was the leader of this expedition. Dr. Majumdar (*op. cit.*, p. 98) tries to locate the Hūṇa kingdom in the Northern Pañjāb. No sooner did Rājyavardhan proceed with his military operations, than the news of his father's illness reached him and he had to return to Thānesar immediately. In the meantime his father expired and his mother (Yaśomatī) burnt herself to death on the bank of the sacred river Sarasvatī which flowed near Thāṇesar. In fact the credit of the expansion of the Thānesar kingdom in the Northern India goes to Harṣavardhan. It is regretted that Yuan Chawang, who visited Thānesar in the 7th century A.C. and narrated a good deal about the social, religious and economic conditions of Thānesar,[69] failed to refer to the house of Puṣpabhūtis of the place.[70] Bāṇabhaṭṭa[71] has presented a very graphic view of the *Sthāṇvīśvara Janapada* which formed a part of the Śrīkaṇṭha country. We also learn from a later work, the *Ārya Mañjuśrī*[72]*-mūlakapla,* that Sthāṇīśvara formed a part of Śrīkaṇṭha and that the rulers of the place were Vaiśya by caste.

XIII. Thānesar region in Post-Harṣa Period

(i) The glory of Kurukṣetra perhaps faded with the transfer of the capital seat to Kanauj in the very life time of Harṣavardhan. The Khalīmpur copper plate informs us that the Pāla ruler Dharmapāla (770-810 A.C.) had installed the king of Kanauj in the presence of the various rulers of the Panjab including the petty chief of the Kuru country. These rulers have been described (in verse 12 here) as having bowed down before him respectfully with their diadems trembling. It will not be too much to deduce that the sway of Dharmpāla had perhaps penetrated as far as East[73] Panjab including the kingdom of Kīra (modern Kāṅgrā).

(ii) The influence of the Pālas could not have lasted for a longer period for it was rather impossible for them to control the N. W. borders of the country. It appears that the region came under the Pratihāras (of Kanauj) who were considerably powerful, just on the border of Delhi and the E. Panjab. The undated *praśasti,* recovered from Peheoā (ancient

Prithūdaka, about 16 miles from Thānesar), throws considerable light on the history of the region in the times of the Pratihāra emperor named Mahendrapāla (893-90 A.C.)[74]. The verses (6-19) of this inscription are able to furnish the geneaology of the rulers (of a local Tomara family) "who were apparently the feudatories of officials of the Pratihāra emperors. This inscription seems to show that these Tomaras were settled in the Karnāl area and were in the employ of the Pratihāra emperor Mahendrapāla. We may perhaps be allowed to guess that the members of the Jāula's family were resident of the area formerly known as the Delhi division of the Panjab.[75] Dr. H. C. Ray also states (*ibid,* p. 1148) that "the Tomaras were settled in the district round Delhi from at least the 9th century A.D. During the reign of Bhoja[76] (836-82 A.D.) and Mahendrapāla (893-97 A.D.) they came into the orbit of the mighty Pratihāra empire. But soon after, about the beginning of the 10th century A.D., as the Pratihāra power began to decline, a section of the tribe probably founded an independent principality round Delhi".

(iii) ". . . The king of Delhi, who tried to prevent Mahmud of Ghazni's sack of Thānesar[77] in 1041 A.D., was possibly a Tomara. Another occasion when the Tomaras appear to have come into conflict with the Yaminis, was when Majdūd (the brother of Maudid, 1040-9 A.D.), captured Thānesar and was waiting about 1041-2 A.D., at Hānsī for an opportunity to attack Delhi" (Ray, *op. cit.,* p. 1149).

(iv) Two years later, Mahīpāla (the *rājā* of Delhi) recaptured 'without difficulty' Hānsī, Thānesar and Kāṅgrā, inflaming the zeal of his troops by exhibiting to them at the temple in the last named fortress, a replica of the famous idol carried away by Mahmud now believed to have returned by a miracle to its former shrine[78].

(v) But after the final battle that ensued between Mohammed-bin-Sam and Pṛthvīrāja, the forts of Sarsutī, Hānsī, Samāna and Kohrām submitted to the Muslim conquerors in A.H. 588 (=1192 A.C.)[79].

(vi) Later on, Thānesar was invaded and bitterly sacked in the time of Sultan Sikandar Lodi.[80] Cunningham (*CASR.,* XIV, p. 96) has severely condemned this move of the Lodi emperor in the following words: – "Here we have the Mohammedan doctrines of the propagation of religion and plunder of the infidels, or God and Mammon joined together in the most naked and unblushing way".

(vii) After the fall of the Lodīs, the city of Thānesar appears to have remained undisturbed upto the time of Akbar, the great Mughal Emperor. The *Tabqāti-Akbarī* presents a vivid account of the great assemblage of the pilgrims on the banks of the sacred lake at Kurukṣetra.[81]

(viii) It was in the time of Aurangzeb, the great fanatic, that the shrine of Kurukṣetra is said to have been razed to the ground under the royal orders. This champion of Islam "built a castle on the island in the lake called Mughalpur from which soldiers could fire upon any venturesome pilgrim who came to bathe there" (*CASR*., XIV, p. 96).

* Abbreviations

CASR	=	Cunningham's *Archaeological Survey Report,* Calcutta.
Report	=	C. J. Rodgers, *Report of the Panjab Circle of Archaeological Survey,* Calcutta, 1891.
ASR	=	*Archaeological Survey of India* (Annual Report).
India	=	V. S. Agrawala, *India as Known to Pāṇini,* 1953, Lucknow University.
JUPHS	=	*Journal of the U.P. Historical Society,* Lucknow.
Dey	=	N. L. Dey, *Geographical Dictionary of Ancient & Mediaeval India.*
EI	=	*Epigraphia Indica.*
JBORS	=	*Journal of the Behar and Orissa Research Society,* Patna.
JNSI	=	*Journal of the Numismatic Society of India,* Bombay.

References

1. H. C. Raychaudhuri, *Political History of Ancient India* (=*PHAI*), 5th ed., Calcutta, pp. 21-2. He (pp. 22) thinks that it corresponded to modern Delhi, Thānesar and the Upper Gangetic Doab.
2. Probably the wild region of Kuru realm, stretching from the Kāmyaka forest (on the bank of the river Saraswatī) to Khāṇḍava near the Jumnā (*ibid,* pp. 22) In certain passages it indicates even the whole the country.
3. Probably located in the region around Hastināpur, near Meerut (*ibid,* pp. 22). The royal residence, according to Vedic Texts, was apparently Āsandīvat. Prof. Raychaudhuri (*ibid,* pp. 32) opines that "the city may have been identical with Nāgasāhvaya or Hastināpur but it is more probably represented by the modern Asandha near the Chitaṅg". But it should also be noted that Chitaṅg river has been associated with the Kurukṣetra region. Cf. *India,* pp. 54-5.
4. Cf. Monier Williams, *A. Skt. Eng. Dictionary,* 1899, Oxford, p. 294, *s. v.* Kuru.
5. Vināyaka Gaṇeśa Apte's Ed., 1926, Cf. *Vedic Index,* I, pp. 169-70; My paper *Kurukṣetra in Vedic Literature* in the *Journal of Indian History,* Trivendrum, April, 1955, pp. 85-90; cf. my paper in *IHQ,* March 1955, pp. 1-30 also.
6. Raychaudhuri (*op. cit.* pp. 22 f. n. 6) identifies it with the *Parenos* of Arrian (Indika, IV), a tributary of the Indus; Cf. Raychaudhuri, pp. 38 also for similar views.

7. In the *Mahābharata* and the *Purāṇās;* see my paper in the *Indian Historical Quarterly,* March, 1955, pp. 1-31 for details.
8. Bhāvanagar ed., Veer era 2441, p. 379; Cf. Cunningham's *Archaeological Survey Report,* Calcutta, XIV, pp. 87-91.
9. Another name for Kurukṣetra ($29^0 58'$ N. Lat., $76^0 50'$ E. Long).
10. S. Beal's *Records of the Buddhist World,* I, Book IV, p. 18. Alexander Cunningham (*The Geography of Ancient India,* London, 1871, pp. 328-9) however interprets 7000 *li* as equal to 1167 miles but he does not agree with this view of Yuan-Chwang.
11. Modern Pehowā, $29^0 59'$ N. Lat. and $76^0 35'$ East Long. about 17 miles from Thānesar. Painted grey ware has been found here too; cf. *Ancient India,* X-XI, New Delhi, p. 141.
12. *PHAI,* p. 23.
13. *R. Veda,* III. 23. 4, Maxmuller, *Hymns of the Ṛgveda,* I, 1877, London, p. 226.
14. *PHIA,* pp. 23-4, Cf. *ibid,* pp. 36-7 for the Kuru realm under Janamejaya, pp. 68-70; for the Kuru realm in the *Upniṣads;* pp. 133-4; for the Kuru land in the *Jātaka* and the *Jaina* literature etc.
15. i.e. *Śoṇaprastha* of Pāṇini. Places ending with *prastha* (Hindi *pata*) are confined mostly to the Kuru country and the region of the Himalayas watered by the Ganges. Cf. *India,* p. 67; *JUPHS;* XVI (i) p. 44; also *ibid,* p. 45 referring to a hill in Kurukṣetra.
16. *R. Veda,* IX, 113. 1; Cf. *CASR;* II, pp. 218-19; *Geography of Ancient India,* 1871, London, pp. 335-6; *Report,* p. 8.
17. Taräoṛī (तरावड़ी) is only at a short distance from Thānesar, cf. R.S. Tripathi, *History of Kanauj,* Banaras, p. 329.
18. Pānipat is ancient *Pāṇiprastha* – very near to Kurukṣetra on the Delhi-Ambala Railway line.
19. Cf. Moti Chand, *Sārthavāha* (Hindi), 1953, Patna, p. 14; *An Advanced History of India,* 1950, London, p. 549 as edited by Sarkar, Majumdar and Dutta.
20. There was another ancient route also. Fahien did reach Mathurā but Kurukṣetra did not fall on his way. Similarly Jīvaka Kumārabhṛtya, after his return from Texila, came via Bhadraṅkara (Siālkoṭ), Udumbara (Paṭhānkoṭ), Rohītaka (Rohtak), Mathurā etc. Cf. *Sārthavāha, op, cit.,* p. 142. The world conquest in the *Mahābhārata* refers to the expeditions to Sirsā, Rohtak etc., but not to Kurukṣ etra; Cf. *Sārthavāha, op. cit.,* p. 16.
21. In the words of Dr. Agrawala [*India,* p. 58] "the two names Śaradaṇḍā and Śarasvatī point to their being one and the same river. The latter formed the boundary between the *Prācya* and the *Udīcya* divisions of India and may be identified with the Dṛṣadvatī or Chitāṅg."
22. Cf. M. S. Vats, *Excavations at Harappa,* 1940, Delhi, I, pp. 476-7. It was in the years 1953-5 too that excavations were conducted in the college area at

Rūpar. Cf. Y. D. Sharma's paper in *The March of India,* Delhi VI (3), 1953, pp. 12-16; also *Indian Archaeology A Review,* 1953-4 and 1954-55, New Delhi, for more sites near Rupar.

23. Cf. B. B. Lal's paper on *The Painted Grey Ware of Upper Gangetic Basin,* in the *Journal of the Asiatic Society of Bengal (Letters) N.S,* XVI, 1950 p. 89 ff.; also *Ancient India,* X-XI, p. 138 ff. for such sites in the region of Hissar and Rohtak.

24. Now preserved in the Feroz Shāh's Koṭalā at Delhi. Cf. *Indian Antiquary,* XVII; *Epigraphia Indica,* II, p. 245 ff; *Corpus Inscriptionum Indicarum,* I, p. 119; D. C. Sīrcar, *Select Inscriptions,* I, Calcutta, 1942, p. 55ff. for the text of these pillar-edicts. Consult Elliot's *History of India,* London, III, pp. 250-1 about the account of the transfer of the pillar to Delhi in the time of Feroz Shāh Tughlak.

25. Srughna has also been referred to in the accounts of Yuan Chwang and the *Mahāmāyūrī;* Cf. *Sraughnaḥ* of Pāṇini (*India,* p. 431). Srughna was of course an important town in ancient days.

26. D. B. Spooner (*ASR,* 1921-2, p. 47) states that very ancient coins are said to have been found at Amīn (5 miles from Kurukṣetra) but no record of these coins is traceable. Amīn is situated at 29° 54′ North Lat. and 76° 52′ East Long. The Painted Grey Ware has been found here too [*Ancient India,* X-XI. p. 138].

27. *India,* pp. 71, 65, Cf. *Report,* pp. 19-30; Dey, p. 92.

28. *Ibid,* p. 71.

29. *Ibid,* p. 72., *JUPHS,* XVI (i), p. 49.

30. *India,* p. 72. It is situated on the north side of the dry bed of the river Ghaggar, having considerable ancient ruins and has also been referred to in the *Mahābhārata* (*JUPHS,* XVI (i), pp. 50-1; Dey, p. 181—referring to Vinaśana *tīrtha* near Sirsā; Cf. *ibid,* p. 256; *JUPHS,* XVI (i), p. 49.

31. Cf. Yugandhari of the *Mahābhārata.*

32. *Current Science,* V, Aug. 1936, p. 81 ff. Both are surface finds. Jayaswal has assigned second century B.C. as the probable date of this sealing.

33. *Journal of the Numismatic Society of India,* IV, p. 49ff; Cf. C. R. Singhal, *Bibliography of Indian Coins,* I, 1950, Bombay, p. 22.

34. For a detailed account of the excavations at Agrohā, consult H. L. Srivastava, *Excavations at Agrohā* (Punjab), *MASI,* No. 61, Delhi, 1952; Cf. *El,* I, p. 93; L. D. Barnett, *Bulletin of the School of Oriental and African Studies,* University of London, 1940, X, pp. 277-84; *JUPHS,* XVII (i), pp. 19-20.

35. There exists an ancient temple of Aditi and a Sūrya-*kuṇḍa* here. The ladies, who are desirous of having issues, like to bathe in this *kuṇḍa*. Cf. Cunningham's *Geography of Ancient India,* Calcutta, 1924, pp. 386; *ASR.,* 1922-3, pp. 89-90; *Report,* p. 14; *CASR,* XIV, p. 97ff.

36. He even thinks (*ASR,* 1922-3, p. 90) that these "two sculptured posts, in red stone of the Kuṣāṇa age, must have been imported from Mathurā".

37. *A History of Indian and Indonesian Art,* 1927, London. p. 32; cf. V. S. Agarwala, *JUPHS,* VI (2), figures 12, 17.
38. For typical head-dress as depicted in the Śuṅga art of India, consult Dr. Moti Chandra's book *Prācīna Bhāratīya Veśa Bhūṣā,* (Hindī), *Saṃvat* 2007, Allahabad, p. 66, figures 35 and 36.
39. Of course there are no bangles worn (by the lady of the Kurukṣetra panel under study) on the upper portion of the arm. For similar ornamentation in the Śuṅga period, consult *Prācīna Bhāratīya Veśa Bhūṣā, op. cit.,* figures 51-2 facing p. 73.
40. Cf. Patañjali's *Mahābhāṣya* (III, 2. 11) *arunat yavanāḥ sāketam aruṇad yavanāḥ madhyamikām.*
41. Theh Polar marks the ancient site (at Karnāl) on the south bank of the Sarasvatī river. There is simply a tradition that it was the abode of Muni Paulastya—an ancestor of Rāvaṇa (Cf. *ASR,* 1930-4, p. 143).
42. *ASR.,* 1922-3, pp. 87-8.
43. It is about 500 square feet at the top, 800 feet square at the base with a height of 30-40 feet. Cf. *ASR,* 1921-2, p. 48; *CASR,* II, p. 220. There is a large stepwell here of the Muslim period.
44. It will be really interesting if the Deptt. of Archaeology in India brings it to light at an early date.
45. During the excavations at Kauśāmbī in years 1949 and 1950, I was able to recover several pieces of this type from the Scytho-Parthian levels which appeared just below the surface near the ancient site marked by the famous Aśokan pillar at Kosam : consult *Ancient India, op. cit.,* IV p. 125 ff. and plates for the votive tanks and their distribution in India.
46. *Corpus Inscriptionum Indicarum,* II (i), Calcutta, 1929, p. 179.
47. As is evident from the bilingual legend of these coins.
48. Cf. also S.N. Chakraborty, *A Study of Ancient Indian Numismatics*, 1931, Calcutta, p. 207.
49. *Journal of the U. P. Historical Society,* XXIII, 1950, p. 171.
50. But no Yaudheya coin has so far been discovered in Mārwār at least. It is not possible to agree with the views of Mr. Gupta put forth on pp. 172-3 of the paper cited above.
51. The *Yaśastilaka* of Somadeva presents a vivid view of the Yaudheya country (Vol. I, Bombay, 1901, pp. 12-22 as edited by Paṇḍit Śivadatta). The *Mahābhārata* refers to Rohītaka as the capital of the *Bahudhānyaka* country. It was dear to Skanda-Kārtikeya, rich in cows and grains, and the people inhabiting the place were called the *Mattamayūrakas* (*Sabhā Parva,* XXXII. 4-5). For the antiquities from Rohtak, consult *Proc. Asiatic Society of Bengal,* Calcutta, 1881, pp. 70-2; *Current Science,* IV, 1936, p. 796; *ibid,* V, Aug. 1936, p. 81 ff; *JBORS,* XXII, pp. 51-62.
52. At this time they were living somewhere in the north-east Rājaputānā. For the coins of the Yaudheyas from Rohtak, consult Birbal Sahni, *Technique of*

Casting of Coins in Ancient India, Bombay, 1945, pp. 4-32; *JBORS;* 1936 XXII, pp. 51-62.

53. *A New History of the Indian People,* VI, 1946, Lahore, pp. 29; Cf. *ibid,* p. 21 for the independence of the E. Panjab from the foreign yoke in the beginning of the 3rd century A.C.

54. Allan; *op. cit.,* p. cli; Chakraborty, *op. cit.,* p. 220; Alexander Cunningham, *Coins of Ancient India,* London, 1891, p. 76 and *Geography of Ancient India,* London, 1871, p. 245.

55. *ASR,* 1230-4, p. 143 ff. These coins were recovered as a result of the excavations at the site called Theh-Polar.

56. They had not been described in detail by Cunningham who simply made a passing reference to these important relics. Similarly A. Coomaraswamy assigned them to an early age i.e. the Gupta period (cf. Coomaraswamy, *op. cit.*, p. 87).

57. The Gupta terracottas and sculptures depict the frequent use of curly hair; cf. *Nāgarī Pracāriṇī Patrikā,* Hindi, Banaras, *saṃvat* 1997, pp. 215-16 and plates.

58. Spooner (*ASR.*, 1921-2, p. 47) simply states that Cunningham obtained some excellent terracotta reliefs at Peheoā.

59. *A New History of the Indian People,* VI, 1946, Lahore , p. 144 and *The Classical Age,* Bombay, 1954, p. 9.

60. Out of this lot, 26 pieces were melted and only 69 coins could be recovered and deposited in the Lahore Museum.

61. It was discovered by A. Cunningham and has been referred to in *CASR.*, XXIII, 1887, Calcutta, p. 22 ff, plate XXVIII. Tushām is about 16 miles to the south of Hissār (*CASR,* V, pp. 137-40. Fleet *CII.*, III, pp. 269-70).

62. *Annual Progress Report of the Superintendent, Hindu and Buddhist Monuments of N. Circle, for year ending 1911*, pp. 18-19, Appendix D.

63. *ASR.*, 1930-34, pt. I, p. 143 ff. plate LXXXII.

64. *India,* pp. 72; *CASR.*, XIV, p. 65; *Journal of the Numismatic Society of India,* IV, pp. 47-8. The ancient name of the place was Sunetra (*Pāṇini,* Saṅkalādi *gana*). For coin-moulds from Sunet, consult Birbal Sahni, *Technique of Casting Coins, op. cit.*, pp. 32-7).

65. Represent the feet of Lord Buddha or Mahāvīra or Viṣṇu.

66. i.e. The trident is carved in the upper portion of the circular seal while the letters are in the lower portion.

67. The discovery of such seals here is very interesting in fact. H. L. Srivastava (*ASR.*, 1930-4, pt. I, p. 143 ff) dates one of these copper seals towards the 5th or 6th century A.C.

68. *The Classical Age, op. cit,* p. 97; cf. *Harṣacarita Eka Sānskṛitika Adhyayana* (Hindi), Patna, 1953, p. 63. For the coins of the Maukharis and rhe rulers of the Thānesar line, consult R. Burn, *JRAS,* London, 1906, p. 453 ff.

69. i.e. *Sa t'a ni shi fa lo* of Yuan Chwang. Consult S. Beal, *Record of the Buddhist World,* I, pp. 183-6 for a detailed account of the place as presented by this Chinese traveller.

70. From Thānesar Y. Chwang went to *Kiu-hoen-cha* after traversing a distance of about 100 *li* or 16–2/3 miles. The latter has been identified with modern Gunāna between Vyāsasthalī and Nisaṅga, about 17 miles S.S.W. of Thānesar. It was from the Gokaṇṭha monastery at Gunān that the Chinese pilgrim started his further journey to *Su-lu-kin,* i.e. modern Sugha as cited above (Cf. Cunningham's *Geography of Ancient India,* 1924, p. 395).

71. *Harṣacarita* (text only) as edited by P. V. Kane, Bombay, 1918, p. 43 ff. For translation consult the English edition of E.B. Cowell and F.W. Thomas, 1897, London, p. 79 ff. Cf. also *Harṣacarita Eka Sānskṛitika Adhyayana, op. cit.,* p. 56).

72. As edited by T. Gaṇapati Śāstrī, 1925, Chapter III, p. 626.

73. It is not possible to say whether Gandhāra (W. Panjab) had also accepted his suzerainty. Cf. R. C. Majumdar, *History of Bengal,* I, Dacca, 1943, p. 107.

74. *EI.,* I, p. 242 as edited by Bühler. Mahendrapāla here has been referred to as the paramount ruler.

75. H. C. Ray, *Dynastic History of Northern India,* II, 1936, Calcutta, pp. 1147-8.

76. The discovery of the Delhi fragmentary inscription of Bhoja from the Pāṇḍava-kā-kilā is also very interesting (Cf. *ibid,* p. 1148, f.n. 2). A 9th century stone inscription found at Sirsā (Hissar; *EI.,* XXI. p. 295) supplies the name Śrī Bhoja Deva without any royal honorifics. It is of course not possible to identify him with Bhoja Pratihara with definiteness.

77. For an account of M. Ghaznī's attack on Thānesar as given by Firishta, consult H. M. Elliot, *History of India,* London, II, 1869, p. 452 ff; H.C. Ray, *op. cit.,* pp. 1088, f.n. 3. Al-Utbi also referred to this event; consult Elliot, *op. cit.,* II, pp. 40-1; cf. *CASR.,* XIV, pp. 94-5; C.V. Vaidya, *Downfall of Hidu India,* 1933, Bombay, pp. 67-8.

78. Woolsey Haig, *Cambridge History of India,* III, 1928, Cambridge, p. 32.

79. *CASR.,* XIX, pp. 94-5.

80. Consult Elliot, *op. cit.,* IV, 1872, pp. 439-40 for the detailed account of the events at Thānesar.

81. Elliot, *op. cit.,* V, 1873, p. 318. This account needs to be compared with that furnished by Alberuni some centuries earlier (E. C. Sachau, *Alberuni's India,* II, 1910, London, p. 145). Abu Rihān, on the authority of Varāhamihira, refers to the bath at Kurukṣetra during the eclipses (Reinaud, *Memoire sur l' Inde,* p. 187–as cited by Cunningham in *Ancient Geography of India.*

23

Kurukṣetra in Later Sanskrit Literature

R. C. Agrawala

I. *Boundaries and Area*

(A) The ancient Kuru realm may be said to have comprised the region of Kurukṣetra, Sonepat, Amīn, Karnāl, Pānipat etc;[1] while Kurukṣ etra indicated the area between the Sarasvatī and the Dṛṣadvatī rivers: –

दक्षिणेन सरस्वत्या दृषद्वत्युत्तरेण च ।

ये वसन्ति कुरुक्षेत्रे ते वसन्ति त्रिपिष्टपे ॥[2]

उत्तरेण दृषद्वत्या दक्षिणेन सरस्वतीम् ।

ये वसन्ति कुरुक्षेत्रे ते वसन्ति त्रिपिष्टपे ॥[3]

Dr. B. C. Law (*op. cit.*, p. 28) proposes to identify this region with the ancient Kuru country which has also been mentioned in the *Lalitavistara*[4]. The region lying between these ancient holy rivers[5] was very sacred indeed. According to the *Śaktisaṅgama Tantra*[6], the Kuru country began from Hastināpura and lay to the south of Kurukṣetra and to the east of Pañcāla : –

हस्तिनापुरमारभ्य कुरुक्षेत्रस्य दक्षिणे ।

पञ्चालपूर्वभागे तु कुरुदेश प्रकीर्तितः ॥

The *Vāmana Purāṇa* (XXXIII. 8-9) too refers to the boundaries as depicted in the *Mahābhārata*. It was really a holy area called by the name of *Brahmāvarta*[7]: –

वासः पुंसां कुरुक्षेत्रमुक्तिरुक्ता चतुर्विधा ।[8]

सरस्वती दृषद्वत्योर्द्वयोर्नद्योर्यदन्तरम् ।

तं देवनिर्मितं देशं ब्रह्मावर्तं प्रचक्षते ॥[9]

The *Brahmarṣi-deśa,* according to Manu, included Kurukṣetra, the Matsyas, the Pañcālas, Śūrasenakas etc., and that it was quite different from *Brahmāvarta*: –

सरस्वती-दृषद्वत्योः देवनद्योर्यदन्तरम्।
तं देवनिर्मितं देशं ब्रह्मावर्तं प्रचक्षते ॥१७
कुरुक्षेत्रं च मत्स्याश्च पाञ्चालाः शूरसेनकाः।
एष ब्रह्मर्षिदेशो वै ब्रह्मावर्तादनन्तरम् ॥१८

[मनुस्मृति, II. 17-18]

Thus it is evident that *Brahmāvarta,* in the time of Manu, comprised the same region as has been called *Brahmāvarta* in the *Mahābhārata* and the *Vāmana Purāṇa.* But Manu seems to have included Kurukṣetra in the list of the countries forming a part of the *Brahmarṣi-deśa.* Does it mean that Kurukṣetra was something quite different from the region lying between the Sarasvatī and the Dṛṣadvatī rivers ?

(B) The country of Kurukṣetra was also situated between *Tarantuka, Arantuka, Rāmahrada* and *Macakruka*; and this *Kurukṣetra-Samantapañcaka* has been styled as the "Northern Altar of *Pitāmaha*" :–

तरन्तुकारन्तुकयोर्यदन्तरं रामह्रदानां च मचक्रकस्य च।
एतत्कुरुक्षेत्रसमन्तपञ्चकं पितामहस्योत्तरवेदिरुच्यते ॥[8]
तरन्तुकारन्तुकयोर्यदन्तरं रामह्रदानां च मचकुकस्य च।
एतत्कुरुक्षेत्रसमन्तपञ्चकं प्रजापतेरुत्तरवेदिरुच्यते ॥[9]

Guardian Yakṣas:–E. W. Hopkins [*Epic Mythology,* 1915, Strassburg, p. 149] states that Arantuka, Tarantuka, Macakruka[10] are the *Yakṣa*-gatekeepers[11] as well as the holy places bounding the holy land. According to the *Mahāmāyūrī* (57-58) the phrase *Yakṣendrau* included *Tarārka* and *Kutarārka.* These two *Yakṣas* seem to have been the same as Tarantuka and Arantuka of the *MB* cited above.

According to the modern *Māhātmyas,* relating to Kurukṣetra[12], the guardian-*Yakṣas* of the region of Kurukṣetra were as follows:–

(i) Ratna *Yakṣa* for N. E. Corner.

(ii) Arantuka *Yakṣa* for N. W. Corner.

(iii) Kapila *Yakṣa* for S. W. Corner.

(iv) Macakruka *Yakṣa* for S. E. Corner.

According to Alexander Cunningham [*CASR;* XIV, p. 89], "here 4 names belong to 4 *Yakṣas* (demons) who are said to have sung and danced with joy during the battle while they drank the blood of the slain".

Cunningham (*ibid;* p. 90) also tries to identify these corners when he states that "the S.W. corner is placed at Rāmray, 5 miles to the S.W.

of Jīnd where there are said to have been both a Rāmahrada and Kapila *tīrtha*. The S. E. corner is at Siṅkh, very nearly between Jīnd and Pānipat, on the bank of a stream which is said to be the old bed of the Rākṣī or the Dṛiṣdvatī. There is still a *Yakṣa-kuṇḍa* at Siṅkh. The N. E. corner is at Ratna-*Yakṣa* or Ratna *Jakkha* close to Pīpalī on the Sarasvatī. Lastly, the N. W. corner is at Ber or Baher to the W. N. W. of Kaithal where also there is a *Yakṣa-kuṇḍa* . . . Thus the estimate of the size of the region of Kurukṣetra agrees with the other name given in the *Mahābhārata* or Samantapañcaka on every side, 5 or 20 *Yojanas* all round the four sides".

According to Hemacandra[13], the area of Kurukṣetra amounted to about 12 *Yojanas* and that it was a very sacred place :–

गङ्गायमुनयोर्मध्यमन्तर्वेदि समस्थली।
ब्रह्मावर्तं सरस्वत्याः दृषद्वत्याश्च मध्यतः ॥१५
ब्रह्मावेदि कुरुक्षेत्रे पञ्चरामह्रदान्तरम्।
धर्मक्षेत्रे कुरुक्षेत्रे द्वादशयोजनावधि ॥१६

II. *Why the name was Kurukṣetra?*

It has been narrated in *SP.* (52-3) that *Haladhara* Balarāma once approached the gate of the Samantapañcaka *tīrtha* and enquired about the *Kurukṣetra-phalam* from the sages who replied thus:–"This Samantapañcaka is said to be eternal Northern Altar of Prajāpati and it was here that, in days gone by, the gods happened to perform a great sacrifice. The sage-king Kuru had cultivated this field for many days. Hence it came to be denoted as Kurukṣetra (i.e. Field of Kuru) after his name:–

प्रजापतेरुत्तरवेदिरुच्यते सनातन राम समन्तपञ्चकम्।
समीजिरे यत्रपुरा दिवौकसौ वरेणासत्रेण महावरप्रदः ॥
पुरा च राषिवरेण धीमता बहूनि वर्षाणि अमितेन तेजसा।
प्रकृष्टमेतत्कुरुणा महात्मनः ततः कुरुक्षेत्रमितीहपप्रथ ॥

[*SP.*, Sātav, ed., 53. 1-2]

महिम्ना तस्य कुरवो लेभिरे प्रत्ययं भृशम्।
तस्यनाम्नाभिविख्यातं पृथिव्यां कुरुजाङ्गलम् ॥३७
कुरुक्षेत्रं स तपसा पुण्यं चक्रे महातपाः ॥३८

[*Ādi-Parva*[14], 101. 37-8]

The *SP.*[15] further narrates that in days of yore, Kuru was engaged perseveringly in tilling the field. Requested by Indra he said–"those that will die on this plain shall proceed to the regions of bliss after being cleansed of their sins. Śakra, ridiculing this, went back to heaven. This happened repeatedly. Indra summoned the gods who asked him to stop Kuru by granting him a boon; if men by only dying there were to come to heaven without having performed sacrifices to us, our very existence would be endangered. Indra then came and they agreed that Kuru should not toil anymore but those that would die there, having abstained from food with all their senses awake and those that would perish there in battle, should go straight to heaven... etc". Similar views have also been propounded in the *Vām* (XXII. 20 ff.).[16] The *Vāyu Purāṇa* informs us that Ṛkṣa continued the line of Hastināpura and his grandson (Kuru) founded the city of Kurukṣetra [cf. D. R. Patil, *Cultural History from the Vāyu Purāṇa,* p. 12]. This Kuru was born from the womb of Tapatī, daughter of Sūrya [तपत्यां सूर्यकन्यायां कुरुक्षेत्रपतिः कुरुः *Bhāgavat,* IX. 22. 4.].

Even Alberuni was fully aware of the fact that Kuru gave his own name to Kurukṣetra. According to Alberuni, "another place of the kind (i.e. holy) is Tāneshar, also called Kurukṣetra, i.e. land of Kuru, who was a pleasant, a pious holy man who worked miracles by divine power. Therefore the country was called after him and venerated for his sake" [E. C. Sachau, *Alberuni's India,* 1910, London, p. 147].

A 14th century A.D. Jain work[17] too refers to the facts cited above. According to this work: –

..............कुरुर्नृपः ॥१

कुरुक्षेत्रमिति ख्यातं राष्ट्रमेतत्तदाख्यया ॥२

III. *Samantapañcaka and Rāmahrada*

Samantapañcaka of the *Ādi Parva* and *AP.* was "another name of Kurukṣetra, evidently a Bhārgava name. The people of India have forgotten this Bhārgava synonym; they remembered only Kurukṣetra – a name which has struck deep root into the memory of the people"[18]. It was here that Bhārgava Rāma, after extirpating the Kṣatriya race during the interval between the Tretā and the Dvāpara *Yugas,* made 5 tanks of blood dedicated to his forefathers[19]: –

स सर्वं क्षत्रमुत्साद्य स्ववीर्येणानलद्युति ।

समन्तपञ्चके पञ्च चकार रुधिरह्रदान् ॥४

स तेषु रुधिराम्भस्सु ह्रदेषु क्रोधमूर्च्छितः ।

पितृन्संतर्पयामास रुधिरेणेति नः श्रुतम् ॥५

तेषां समीपे यो देशो ह्रदानां रुधिराम्भसाम ।

समन्तपञ्चकमिति पुण्यं तत्परिकीर्तितम् ॥७

A similar story has also been narrated in connection with the (Rāmahrada at Kurukṣetra) in the *AP.* (III. 81. 22-3; *ibid,* 117.5 (ff.).[20] Dr. V. S. Sukthankar seems to be justified in identifying Rāmahrad with Samantapañcaka [*Annals*... ..., *op. cit.*, p. 20]. It was later on that the Great War of the *Mahābhārata* too was fought on this very spot[21] :–

समन्तपञ्चकं युद्धं कुरुपाणडवसेनयो: ॥

Bhāsa, the well known predecessor of Kālīdāsa, too refers to Samantapañcaka in his famous work–the *Urubhaṅgam.* Dr. V. S. Agrawala[22] is of the opinion that the place was so called for its circumference (*paridhi*) was about 5 *Yojanas* (cf. *vedi prajāpatereṣā samantāt pañca yojanā kurorvai yajñaśīlasya kṣetrametatmahātmanaḥ* in the *AP.*, Suk. ed., 122, verse 22). Dr. Agrawala also tries to identify Rāmahrada with Vedic 'Śaryaṇāvat'[23] which was also called 'Brahmasara' after some time.

The abode of the famous *Yakṣī* too was situated near the Rāmahrada [*AP.*, Suk. ed., 81. 19-20]: –

तत्रैव महाराज यक्षी लोकपरिश्रुता।

तां चाभिगभ्य राजेन्द्र पुण्यांल्लोकानवाप्नुयात् ॥१९

कुरुक्षेत्रं तद्द्वारं विश्रुतं भरतर्षभ: ।

प्रदक्षिणामुपावृत्य तीर्थसेवी समाहित: ॥२०

In chap. 129 of the *ĀP.*, the same *Yakṣī* has been addressed as a *Paiśacī.* It is very likely, as Dr. Agrawala also thinks, that she happened to have been the tutelary deity of some primitive tribe and that she lived on non-vegetarian diet. In *ĀP.* (chap. 129, verse 8), she has been described as putting on *ulūkhala* ornaments [cf. *ulūkhalai-rābharaṇaiḥ piśācī*]. It is simply interesting to find her designation *Ulūkhala-mekhalā* as narrated in the *Mahāmāyūrī*[24]. It is further narrated in the *ĀP* (chap. 129. 9-11) that she is said to have warned the pilgrims "not to stay there for more than a day." In case one liked to stay for the second night, he would find just the contrary to what he had met during the previous night there: –

उलूखलैराभरणै पिशाची यदभाषत।

युगन्धरे[२५] दधिप्राश्य उषित्वा चाच्युतस्थले।

तद्वद्भूतिलये स्नात्वा सपुत्रा वसितुमिच्छसि ॥९

एकरात्रमुषित्वेह द्वितीयं यदि निवत्स्यसि।

एतद्वै ते दिवा वृत्तं रात्रौ वृत्तमतोऽन्यथा ॥१०

अत्राद्द निवत्स्याम: क्षपां भरतसत्तम।

द्वारमेतद्धि कौन्तेय कुरुक्षेत्रस्य भारत ॥११

This led Dr. Agrawala (*op. cit.*, p. 20) to suggest that the above verses perhaps refer to the social conditions (of the Kurukṣetra region) in the second century B.C. It is of course evident that the holy tract had lost much of its sanctity by the time the above verses came to be composed [cf. E.W. Hopkins, *op. cit.*, p. 209].

IV. *Sthāṇvīśvara or Thānesar*

The Buddhist literature refers to two villages (of Kuru realm) which were said to have been visited by Lord Buddha himself. But these places[26] lay between the Ganges and the Yamunā. It is also interesting to find the use of the phrase *Kurukhetta*[27] in the sense of "the country of the Kurus" but the Pālī literature fails to throw any light on the history of Kurukṣetra in the contemporary times.

Yuan-Chuang, the famous Chinese pilgrim visiting India in the seventh century A.D., describes Thānesar as the westernmost boundary of the Buddhist Middle-country whereas the *Divyāvadāna* and the *Mahāvagga* (V. 13. 12) mention Thūna or Sthūna as its western boundary. This led S.M. Śāstrī[28] to identify these places with Sthāṇvīśvara, modern Thānesar (another name for Kurukṣetra). Dr. B. C. Law[29] too is of the same opinion.

St. Martin[30] has identified *Ostobalassara* [*Stobollosara*] of Ptolemy with Thānesar. Cunningham however thinks that Thānesar is Ptolemy's *Betang Kaiser* and suggests to read, *Satan-Aisara* to make the name approach nearer to Skt. *Sthāṇvīśvara,* the *Sa-ta-ni-shi-fa-lo* of Yuan Chuang.

The *Purāṇas* throw a good deal of light on the sanctity of the *Sthāṇu*[31] *Tīrtha* which was situated in the region of Kurukṣetra. That might have also given the name to the place: –

कुरुक्षेत्रे तु देवर्षे स्थाणुर्नाम महेश्वर: ।[32]

तदेव तीर्थमभवत् स्थानेश्वरमिति स्मृतम् ।

स्थानेश्वरमनुप्राप्य शिवसायुज्यमाप्नुयात् ॥[33]

According to the *Matsya Purāṇa* (XII. 31) there used to exist a *pīṭha* of goddess Bhavānī at Sthāneśvara [*sthāneśvare tu bhavānī*]. The *Vṛhatsvayambhu Purāṇa*[34] [as edited by H.P. Śāstrī] too furnishes the name of the place as Sthāneśvara: –

स्थानेश्वरेन युक्तं च वाग्मत्याञ्च विशेषत: ।

स्त्रियश्च मानुषाश्चापि तत्तीर्थे स्नानकारितम् ॥

The *Āryamañju śrī-mūla-kalpa* (III. – as edited by T. Gaṇapati Sāstrī, 1925, pp. 626) informs that the place was closely associated with the *janapada* named Śrīkaṇṭha: –

सप्तमघ्टशता त्रीणि श्रीकण्ठवासिनस्तदा।
आदित्यनामा वैश्यास्ते स्थानमीश्वरवासिनः ॥

The house of the Puṣyabhūtis was ruling at Thānesar before the accession of Harṣavardhana to the imperial throne[35]. Bāṇabhaṭṭa, in his famous work the *Harṣacarita* (Chap. III), presents a graphic view of the contemporary conditions as prevalent in the Śrikaṇṭha country and its prominent *janapada* named Sthāṇvīśvara. The Sanskrit text[36] runs thus: –

......''श्रीकण्ठो'' नाम जनपदः।......तत्रचैवं विधे नानारामाभिराम–कुसुम–गन्धपरिमलसुभगो यौवनारम्भ इव धर्मस्य कुङ्कुममलनपिञ्जरित (or मलनापञ्जरित) बहु महिषी सहस्त्रशोभितोऽन्तःपुर निवेश इव धर्मस्य, मरुदुद्धूयमानचमरीबालव्यजन शत (व्यजनधवलित) धवलित प्रान्त एकदेश इव सुरराज्यस्य, ज्वलन्मखशिखिसहस्रदीप्यमान दशदिगन्तः शिविरसन्निवेश इव कृतयुगस्य, पद्मासनस्थितब्रह्मर्षिध्यानाधीयामानसकल।कुशलप्रशमः प्रथमोऽवतार इव ब्रह्मलोकस्य, कलकलमुखरमहावाहिनीशतसङ्कुलो विपक्ष (or विक्षेप) इवोत्तर कुरूणाम् ईश्वर मार्गण सन्तापानभिज्ञ सकलजनो विजिगीषुरिव त्रिपुरस्य, सुधारससिक्त धवलगृहपङ्क्तिपाण्डुरः प्रतिनिधिरिव चन्द्रलोकस्य, मधुमत्तमत्तकाशिनी (or मधुमदमत्तकासिनी) भूषणरवभरितभुवनी नामाभिहार इव कुबेरनगास्य, स्थाणीश्वराख्यो जनपदविशेषः यस्तपोवनमिति मुनिभिः कामायतनमिति वेश्याभिः, संगीतशालेति लासकैः, यमनगरमिति शत्रुभिः चिन्तामणिभूमिरित्यर्थिभिः वीरक्षेत्रमिति शस्त्रोपजीविभिः, गुरुकुलमिति विद्यार्थिभिः, गन्धर्वनगरमिति गायनै विश्वकर्ममन्दिरमिति विज्ञानिभिः, लाभभूमिरिति वैदेहकैः, द्यूतस्थानमिति वन्दिभिः, साधुसमागम इति सद्भिः, वज्रपञ्जरमिति शरणागतैः, विटगोष्ठीति विदग्धैः, सुकृत इति परिणाम पथिकैः, असुरविवरमिति वार्तिकैः, शाक्याम्प्रम इति समिभिः, अप्सरपुरमिति कामिभिः, महोत्सवसमाज इति चारणैः वसुधारेति च विप्रैरगृह्यत ॥

यत्र च मातङ्गगामिन्यः शीलवत्यश्च, गौर्या विभवताराश्च, श्यामाः पद्मरागिण्यश्च, धवल-द्विजशुचिवदना मदिरामोदि श्वसाश्च, चन्द्रकान्तवपुषः शिरीषकोमलाङ्ग्यश्च, अभुजङ्गगम्याः कञ्चुकिन्यश्च, पृथुकलत्रश्रियो दरिद्रमध्यकलिताश्च, लावण्यवत्यो मधुरभाषिण्यश्च अप्रमताः प्रसन्नोज्ज्वलरागाश्च (or मुखरागाश्च), अकौतुकाः प्रौढ़ाश्च प्रमदाः ॥

यत्र च प्रमदानां चक्षुरेव सहगं मुण्डमालामण्डनं भारः कुवलयदउदामानि। अलक प्रतिबिम्बान्येव कपोलतलगतान्यक्लिष्टा श्रवणावतंसाः पुनरुक्तानि तमालकिसलयानि। प्रियकधा एव सुभगाः कणालङ्कारा अडम्बरः कुण्डलानि (or कुण्डलादिः)। कपोला एव सततमालोककारका विभवो निशासुमणिप्रदीपाः। निश्वासाकृष्टमधुकरकुलान्येव रमणीयं मुखावरणं कुलस्त्रीजनाचारो जालिका। वाण्येव मधुरा वीधा वाद्यविज्ञानं तन्त्रीताडनम्। ह्रासा एवातिशयसुरभयः पटवासा निरर्थकाः कर्पूरपांसवः। अधरकान्तिविसर एवोज्जवल-तरोऽङ्गरागो निर्गुणो लावण्यकलङ्कः कुङ्कुमपङ्कः। वाहव एव कोमलतमाः परिहासप्रहार-वेत्रलता निष्प्रयोजनानि मृणालनि। यौवनोष्मस्वेदविन्दव एव विदग्धा कुचालङ्कतयो हारास्तु भाराः।

श्रोण्य एव विशालस्फटिक शिलातलचतुरस्रारागिणा विश्रमकारण-निमित्तं भवनमणिवेदिका: ।कमललोभनिलीनान्यलिकुलान्येव मुखराणि पदाभरणकानि निष्फलानीन्द्रनीलनूपुराणि। नूपुररवादूता भवनकलहंसा एव समुचिता: सञ्चरणसहाया ऐश्वर्यप्रपञ्चा: परिजना: । तत्र च.........राजा पुष्पभूतिरिति नाम्ना बभूव ॥

The above text can be translated[37] thus: – "In such a country is a certain district (*janapada*), called *Sthāṇvīśvara,* blessed like the world's first youth, with sweet fragrance of lovely flowers in diverse pleasances bedecked, like the road to *dharma's gynaeceum* with many myriads of buffalos stained from rolling in saffron, whitened at its borders like a part of the celestial realm with Yak-tail flappers shaken by the winds; blazing to all the ends of heaven, like the encampment of *Kṛta* age, with thousands of flaming sacrificial fires; allaying all inauspicious signs like the *Brahma*–world's first descent by the meditation of Brahmarṣis seated in the posture of thought; thronged like a rival to the North Kurus with hundreds of great rivers uproarious with tumult surpassing Tripura as it were in having all its people unacquainted with the devastating might of Śiva's arrow, bright like the replica of the moon world. With rows of white houses plastered with stucco, like a claimant to the name of Kubera's city, oppressing the world with clanking ornaments of wine flushed beauties".

"Sages entitled it a hermitage, courtesans a lover's retreat, actors a concert hall, foes the city of death, seekers of wealth the land of philosopher's stone, sons of the sword the soil of heroes, aspirants to knowledge the preceptor's home, singers the *gandharva's* city, scientists the great Artificer's temple, merchants the land of profit, bards the gaming house, good men the gathering of the virtues, refugees the cage of adament, libertines the Rouge's meet, wayfares the reward of their good deeds, treasure-seekers the mine, quietists the Buddhist monastery, lovers the *apsara's* city, troubadours the festival congress, Brāhmaṇas the stream of wealth".

"There are women like elephants in gait, yet noble minded; virgins, yet attached to worldly pomp; dark, yet possessed of rubies; their faces are brilliant with white teeth, yet is their breath perfumed with the fragrance of wine; their bodies are like crystal, yet their limbs are soft as acacia flowers; they are unattainable by paramours, yet robed in bodies; wide are their beautiful hips, yet are possessed of thin waists; lovely are they, yet honeyed in speech; they trip not, yet have a bright, and captivating beauty; they are without curiosity, yet wedded".

"Their eyes are a natural *muṇḍamālā*-wreath, the garlands of lotus leaves are here a mere burden. The images of their curls in the convex of their cheeks are earpendants that give no trouble; *tamāla* shoots are a superfluity. The talk of their dear ones forms happy, ear-ornaments; rings and the like are but affection. Their cheeks alone give a perpetual sun-shine; for pomp only have they jewelled lamps by night. Tribes of bees attracted by their breath are their beautious veils, the duty of noble women, their hair nets. Their voices are alone their sweet lutes, harp-playing is but an irrelevent accomplishment. Laughs are their exceedingly fragrant perfumes needless is the camphor power. The gleam of their lips is a more brilliant cosmetic, saffron unguent is a worthless blot upon their loveliness. Their arms are the softest of playfully smiting wands, purposeless are lotus-stalks. Drops of the sweat of youthful warmth are their artful warmth as their artful bosom ornaments, necklaces but a burden. Their laps are broad squares of crystal slabs for their lovers; jewelled couches in their mansions a needless mean of repose. Bees clinging in greed for such lotuses are their resonant Foot-ornaments, useless are anklets of sapphire; domestic *kala-haṃsas,* summoned by the tinkle of their anklets are the unfailing companions of their walks; attendants are but the accidents."

"In that country, there arose a monarch named *Puṣpa-bhūti"*.

The Betma grant, dated in *V.S.1076* (=1019 A.D) states that a certain Brāhmaṇa named Paṇḍita Delha happened to come to village Nālataḍāga from Sthāṇvīśvara[38].

V. *Ancient Rivers of Kurukṣetra-region*

It was on the banks of the rivers Āpayā, Sarasvatī and Dṛṣadvatī that the Vedic sages and seers kindled the sacred fire[39]: –

दृषद्वत्यां मानुष आपयायां सास्वत्यां रेवदग्ने दिदीहे (*R. Veda,* III. 23.4). The *Mahābhārata* and the *Purāṇas* too bear testimony to the close association of these rivers with sacred region of Kurukṣetra. Not only that, some more names of the rivers of the locality have been alluded to. Most important references to the Sarasvatī and the Dṛṣadvatī have already been cited in the very beginning of the papers. Following are some of the remaining passages of sufficient importance: –

(i) वनानेतानि वै सप्तनदी: शृणुद्विजा: ।
सरस्वती नदी पुण्या तथा वैतरणी नदी ॥६
आपगा[४०] च महापुण्या गङ्गामन्दाकिनी नदी ।
मधुश्रवा अम्लु नदी कौशिकीपापनाशिनी ॥७
दृषद्वती[४१] महापुण्या हिरण्यवती नदी ।
वर्षकालवहा: सर्वा वर्जयित्वा सरस्वतीम् ॥८

[*Vām,* XXXIII. 6-8].

(ii) तत्र वैतरणी पुण्या नदी [*AP,* 18.70].

(iii) दृषद्वत्यां नरः स्नात्वा तपयित्वा च देवताः ।
अग्निष्टोमातिराजाभ्यां फलं विन्दति भारत ॥ [*ibid.,* 81.70].

(iv) Confluence of Kauśikī and Dṛṣadvatī: –
कौशिक्याः संगमे यस्तु दृषद्वत्याश्च भारत ।
स्नाति वै नियताहारः सर्वपापैः प्रमुच्यते ॥ [*ibid.,* 81.80].

(v) मानुषस्तु पूर्वेण क्रोशमात्रे महीपते ।
आपगा नाम विख्याता नदी सिद्धनिषेविताः ॥ [*ibid.,* 81.55].

(vi) Confluence of Aruṇā and Sarasvatī: –
तीर्थं देव्यायथकमम् सरस्वत्यारुणायाश्चसङ्गमम् लोके विश्रुतं
(*ibid.,* 81, 131-2).

(vii) एषा सरस्वती पुण्या दिव्या चोघवती नदी ।
एतद्विनशनं नाम सरस्वत्याविशां पते । [*AP.,* 130.3. Suk. ed.]

(viii) The *āśrama* of Dadhīci lay across the river Sarasvatī सरस्वत्याः परे पारे नानाद्रुमलतावृत्तम् ; *ibid,* 98. 12-7) and was surrounded by trees and creepers of various kinds. The Kāmyaka *vana* (forest) lay on the banks of the river Sarasvatī [*VP.,* 37.37, M. N. Dutta ed., 1896). M. N. Dutt even tries to identify the Sarasvatī with the Bhogavatī occurring in the *VP.* III, 13.20 (Suk. ed.).

Identification of the above Rivers: –

(a) According to Zimmer [cf. *Altindisches,* Leben, 18], the Vedic river Āpayā flowed very near to the Sarasvati river, either as a small tributary which flows past Thānesar or modern Indumatī further west; while Pischel [*Vedische Studien,* 1892, II, p. 218] assigns it to Kurukṣ etra. Cunningham [*CASR,* XIV, p. 89] even likes to identify the Āpagā with the Oghavatī river and opines that "Āpagā or Oghavatī is a branch of the Chitang which separates from the main stream a few miles to the west of Lāḍawā and flows past Palwala to Pabnāva where it is lost in the sands. Its whole length is about 25 miles". The *AP* (81. 55-7, Suk, ed.) refers to the Āpagā river as flowing to the east of the Mānuṣā *tīrtha*: –

मानुषस्तु पूर्वेण क्रोशमात्रेमहीपते ।
आपगा नाम विख्याता नदी सिद्धनिषेविता ॥५५

(b) According to the enumeration of the rivers in the *Ṛg Veda* (X. 75. 5), the Sarasvatī river comes between the Jumnā and the Sutlej (i.e. Yamunā and Śatudri respectively). The Indologists are of the opinion that the Sarasvatī is the same as Sarsuti which flows to the west of Thānesar and is joined in the Paṭiālā territory by a more westerly stream Ghaggar and passing Sirsā is lost in the desert at Bhaṭner; but a dry river bed (Hākṛā or Ghaggar) can be traced from that point to the Indus[42]. On the other hand, K. C. Chaṭṭopādhyāya[43] tried to prove "that in the earlier portions of the *Ṛg Veda,* the river Sarasvatī stands for the Indus and in the 10th *Maṇḍala* of the same work it denotes the Sarsutī in Kurukṣetra".

The *Śalya Parva* seems to suggest that the name Sarasvatī was given to seven rivers[44] called *Suprabhā, Kāñcanākṣī, Viśālā, Manoramā, Oghavatī, Sureṇu* and *Vimalodakā.* The *Sureṇu-Sarasvatī* is said to have appeared in Kurukṣetra as a result of Kuru's penance while the *Oghavatī-Saraswatī,* happened to come to that locality because of the severe austerities performed by sage Vasiṣṭha[45].

Cunningham likes to consider only 7 rivers of the region and omits the name of the Madhussravā and the Vaitaraṇī (*CASR.*, XIV. 89]. In his opinion, the Madhussravā denotes a pool while the Vaitaraṇī is identical with the Dṛṣadvatī or the Rākṣī. Cunningham also states that there is a place of pilgrimage in Kurukṣetra still called the '*Sapta-Sarasvatī*[46]' after the 7 ancient rivers of the region. As a matter of fact the Sarasvatī river was first of the Vedic rivers and its banks witnessed the development of the Vedic sacrifices (*Vedic Age,* 1951, London, p. 242).

(c) As regards the identification of the river Vinaśana, Dr. B. C. Law [*Geographical Essays, op. cit.*, pp. 86-7) is of the opinion that "Vinaśana was the traditional boundary and extremity of Āryāvarta and Madhyadeśa. In the *Ṛg Vedic* age, it was a mighty river and flowed into the sea [*Maxmuller, Ṛg Veda Samhitā,* p. 46]. It disappears for a time in the sand near the village of Chalaur and reappears at Bhavānīpura. At Bālchāpur it again disappears but appears again at Baṛā Kheṛā; at Urnai near Peheoā (ancient Pṛthūdaka) it is joined by the Mārkaṇḍā and the united stream bearing still name of Sarasvatī and ultimately joins the Ghaggar or Gharghar which was evidently the lower part of Sarasvatī".

(d) Dṛṣadvatī is a name given to the river which flows into the Sarasvatī after running parallel to it for sometime [*Vedic Index,* I, p. 374]. It was regarded to have been a very sacred river forming one extremity of the boundary of Kurukṣetra along with the Sarasvatī. The confluence (*saṅgama*) of Dṛṣadvatī and Kauśikī rivers was considered to be a very sacred spot indeed [*VP,* 81, 80, Suk. ed., as already cited above].

The Dṛṣadvatī has been identified by Dr. B. C. Law (*Geographical Essays,* p. 91) with "modern Chitang[47] (or Chitrang or Chautang) which runs parallel to Sarasvatī." Dr. Law also adds that "Elphinstone and Todd sought to identify it with Ghaggar flowing through Ambālā and Sindh but now lost in the desert sands of Rājaputānā [*JASB*, VI, p. 181] while Cunningham[48] (*CASR*, XIV, p. 88) found in it the river Rakṣī that flows to the southeast of Thāneśvara. According to the *Vāmana Purāṇa* (XXXIV), a branch of this river was Kauśikī[49]." Cunningham (*CASR.*, XIV, p. 88) even suggests that probably "Vaitaraṇī may be only another name for Dṛṣadvatī or Rākṣī, as it was the name of the mother of Rākṣasa".

A three year *Satra* (sacrifice) was performed at Kurukṣetra, on the very bank of the Dṛṣadvatī when the Paurava king named Adhisīma Kṛṣṇa, the Bārhadratha ruler Senajit and the Aikṣavāka ruler Divākara were in power[50].

According to the *Vāyu Purāṇa*[51] (LIX, 127-8) the original name of this river (Dṛṣadvatī) was "*Ratnāvalī*" but it came to be called the Dṛṣadvatī in the Kali age. The town called Vāyupura, was situated on its bank: – धर्मशालापि बहुला वायुस्थाने महापुरे। रत्नावली स्वर्गमयी गंगा चामृतवाहिनी। कलो दृषद्वती नाम महापातक नाशिनी[*Vāyu Purāṇa,* Ānandāśrama Granthamālā, p. 205].

(e) The *Ādi Parva* (suk. ed., chap. 3, verses 144 ff.) refers to Kurukṣ etra as having been situated on the bank of the river Ikṣumatī[52]. Takṣ aka (the great Serpent King) and Aśvasena used to line here in Kurukṣetra along the river Ikṣumatī[53]: –

तक्षकाश्वसेनश्च नित्यं सहचरावुभौ ॥१४०

कुरुक्षेत्रं चे वसतां नदीभिक्षुमतीमनु।

जघन्यजस्तक्षस्य श्रुतसेनेति यः सुतः ॥१४१

(f) It was on the bank of the Aṃśumatī river that Indra is said to have slain the demon called Kṛṣṇāsura [*Rg Veda,* VIII. 96. 13; *Atharva Veda,* I. 4. 1]. According to the author of *The Hindī Viśvakośa* (*op. cit.*, s.v. Kurukṣetra), "this river can well be identified with Aṃśumatī of the *Kurupradīpa* and Ambumatī of the *Vana Parva* (Chap. 81). It has also been stated in the *Vana Parva* that Sutīrhaka *tīrtha* was situated on the bank of the river Ambumatī.

VI. *Forests in the Kurukṣetra region*

The *Vāmana Purāṇa* (*op. cit.*, chap. XXXIV) furnishes the following names of the forests (*vana*)[54] in the Kurukṣetra region: –

श्रृणु सप्तवनानि इह कुरुक्षेत्रस्य मध्यतः।

येषां नामानि पुण्यानि सर्वपाप हरणानि च ॥३

काम्यकं च वनं तदा अदिति वनं महत्।

व्यासस्य च वनं पुण्यं फलकीवनमेव च ॥४

तथा सूर्यवनं स्थानं तथा मधुवनं महत्।

पुण्य शीतवनं नाम सर्व कल्पनाशनम् ॥५

(A) The Kāmyaka forest was situated on the bank of the river Sarasvatī [*AP.*, Suk. ed., chap. 6, verses 3-5] and was even visited by the Pāṇḍavas and Vidura :–

ततः सरस्वतीकूले[55] समेषु मरुधन्वसु।

काम्यकं नाम ददृशुर्वनं मुनिजनप्रियम् ॥३

.........काम्यकं वनमृद्धिमत् ॥५

Even *Dharmarāja* Yudhiṣṭhira had seen that forest [*A.P.*, 11. 11].

(B) The *Vanaparva*[56] presents a graphic view of the Dvaita-forest and enumerates every possible detail of the surroundings there: –

पुण्यं द्वैतवनं रम्यं विविशुर्भरतर्षभाः ॥१६

तच्छालतालाम्रमधूकनोप कदम्ब सजार्जुनकर्णिकारैः।

तपात्यये पुण्यधरैरुपेतं महावनं राष्ट्रपतिर्ददर्श ॥१७

महाद्रुमाणां शिखरेषु तस्थुर्मनोरमां वाचमुंदीरयन्तः।

मयूरदात्यूह चकोरसंघास्तस्मिन्वनेकाननकोकिलाश्च ॥१८

करेणुयूथैः सह यूथपानां मदोत्कटानामचलप्रभाणाम्।

महान्तियूथानि महाद्विपानां तस्मिन् वने राष्ट्रपतिर्ददर्श ॥१९

मनोरमां भोग[57] वतीमुपेत्य धृतामनां चीरजटाधराणाम्।

तस्मिन् तने धर्मभृतां निवारो ददर्श सिद्धर्षि गणनानेकान् ॥२०

The *Dvaita* forest was thus full of the *Śāla* trees [*VP.*, Suk. ed., III 26. 1 – तत्काननम्...सरस्वतीशालवनेषु तेषु]. It was here that the Pāṇḍavas had offered oblations to their ancestors (*ibid.*, 26. 2-3). The place became prosperous and continued to remain an abode of the sages and the Brāhmaṇas till the stay of the Pāṇḍavas there (*ibid.*, Chap. 27). It was from this forest that the Pāṇḍavas had left for the Kāmyaka *vana* (*ibid.*, 26. 28). There is of course no doubt that the Dvaita *vana* was very near to the river Sarasvatī (*ibid.*, 174. 21 सरस्वतीमुपेत्य निवासकामाः सरस्ततो द्वैतवनं प्रतीयुः) The *Vāmana Purāṇa* (*op. cit.*, XXII. 12-14) refers to the visit (of Urvaśī) to Dvaita-*vana*.

(B) The Phalakī *vana* was also very sacred (*AP.*, 81. 72-74):

यत्र देवाः सदा फलकीवनमाश्रिताः।

तपश्चरन्ति विपुलं बहुवर्षकम् ॥७२

In the words of Alexander Cunningham [*CASR.*, XIV, p. 91], "in the map it will be seen that the names of the Sūrya *vana* and Solan *vana* belong to the two outside forests and that a smaller *cakra* containing 7 forests might be made by leaving them altogether. This smaller space well would include all the famous places of pilgrimage as well as the great battlefield itself. On the west it would extend to farthest point of Pṛthūdaka[58] and on the south to Dāchor. And authority is not wanting for this smaller extent of the holy region as *kos* or *krośa* of the whole of N. W. India, from Delhi to Indus, is as nearly as possible 1 − 1/3 miles or 7040 feet, agreeing with the smaller valuation of 4000 cubits ... ... 5 *Yojanas,* forming the side of the holy region, would thus be reduced to 25 miles and the whole circuit to about 100 miles. This limitation would exclude both Kaithal and Jīnd, both of which I strongly suspect to have been added to *cakra* in recent times to gratify the Sikh Rājās of those places. There is a Rāmahrada near Rākṣī which is one of the 4 corners named in the *Māhabhārata,* 17 miles to the south of Thānesar, from which point the boundary will incline to southwest to Dāchor along the old bed of the Rākṣī."

VII. *Āśramas in and near the Kurukṣetra region*

The region of Kurukṣetra is also to be noted for the existence of various *āśramas* (hermitages) both inside and outside the *cakra* of Kurukṣetra.

(i) Reference to the Kāmyaka *vana*[59] has already been made above. Being situated on the very banks of the sacred river Sarasvatī, it was immensely dear to the sages and the *munis* [*AP.*, Suk. ed., chap. 6. 3]: –

तत: सरस्वती कूले समेषु मरुधन्वसु ।
काम्यकं नाम दद्दशुर्वनं मुनिजनप्रियम् ॥३

In fact it was abounding in everything that was good and sacred (*ibid.*, chap. 6, verse 5).

(ii) The Dvaita *vana* "was covered, at the end of the summer with *śālas,* palms, *kadambas, sarjas, arjunas, karṇikāras* clothed with flowers. The peacocks, *datyūhas, cakoras, varhiṇas, kokilas* sat on the top of the highest trees and emitted their sweet notes. In that forest, the king also saw the leaders of the elephant herds, gigantic like hills with temporal juice trickling down in the season of rut and accompanied by the herds of she-elephants. And approaching the picturesque Bhogavatī, he saw many ascetics of accomplished piety in that forest in the hermitages of pious and purified souls and wearing bark and matted locks." Such is the vivid description[60] of the environments in which the Hindu sages use to pass their time in severe austerities and penance.

(iii) The *Āraṇyaka Parva* (Suk. ed., chap. 98 12-18) furnishes equally with an interesting account of the Dadhīci's *āśrama* :–

देवाः नारायण पुरस्कृत्य दधीचस्याश्रमम् ययुः ॥१२
सरस्वत्याः परे पारे नानाद्रुमलतावृतम् ।
षट्पादोद्गीतनिनदैर्विधुष्टं सामगैरिव ।
पुंसकोकिलखोन्मिश्रं जीवं जीवकनादितम् ॥१३
महिषश्च वराहैश्च सृमरैश्चमरैरपि ।
तत्र तत्रानुचरितं शार्दूलभयवर्जितैः ॥१४
करेणुभिर्वारणैश्च प्रभिन्नकरटामुरवैः ।
सरोवगाढैः क्रीडद्भिः समन्तादनुनादितम् ॥१५
सिंहव्याघ्रैर्महानादान्नदद्भिरनुनादितम् ।
अपरश्चापि संलीनैर्गुहाकन्दरवासिभिः ॥१६
तेषु तेष्ववकाशेषु शोभितं सुमनोरमम् ।
त्रिविषपसमप्रख्यं दधीचात्रसमागमनम् ॥१७
तत्रापश्यन्दधीचं ते दिवाकरसमद्युतिम् ।
जाज्वल्यमानं वपुषा यथा रम्या लक्ष्म्या पितामहम् ॥१८

(iv) An extensive but important hermitage near Kurukṣetra has been alluded to in the *Śalya Parva.* It had the proud privilege of producing "two notable women hermits. There, leading from youth the vow of *brahmacarya,* a Brāhmin maiden was crowned with ascetic success and ultimately acquiring *Yogic* powers, became a *tapassidhā;* while another lady, daughter of a *kṣatriya,* a child not of poverty but of affluence, the daughter of a king (Śāṇḍilya by name), came to live there the life of celibacy and attained spiritual pre-eminence [R.K. Mookerjee, *op. cit.*, p. 335]. According to the narrative as given in the *Śalya Parva* [54. 1-12, edited by M. N. Dutt, translation, 1901], that hermitage was "overgrown with *madhuka* and mango trees and abounded with *plakṣas* and *nyagrodhas*[61]. It contained many *vilvas* and many excellent jack and *arjuna* trees. Here god Viṣṇu formerly practised austere penances and duly celebrated all the eternal sacrifices."

VIII. *Cults associated with Kurukṣetra region*

(A). *Yakṣas*: –

Reference to the *dvārapāla yakṣas* (i.e. Tarantuka, Arantuka and Macakruka) and the *Yakṣī* (i.e. Paiśācī) has already been made above. It is equally interesting to note the divine protectors of the Kuru-jāṅgala area as given in the *Vāmana Purāṇa* [XXII. 40-2]: –

तस्य क्षेत्रस्य रक्षार्थं ददौ स पुरुषोत्तम्: ।
यक्षं च चन्द्रनामानं वासुकिं चापि पन्नगम् ॥४०
विद्याधरं शङ्कुकर्णं सुकेशं राक्षसेश्वरम् ।
अजावनं च नृपातिमदादेवं च पावकम् ॥४१
एतानि सर्वतोभ्येत्यरक्षंति कुरुजाङ्गलम् ।
अमीषां बलिनोऽन्ये च भृत्याश्चैवानुयायिन: ॥४२

(B) *Goddesses*: –

There used to exist a *devī-pīṭha*[62] at Kurukṣetra पुण्येतीर्थे कुरुक्षेत्रे देवीपीठचंतुष्टये. The *Matsya Purāṇa* too throws some light on this problem when it refers to the abode of Bhavānī at Sthāneśvara (स्थानेश्वरे तु भवानी – chap. XII, verse 31) and of Devamātā on the Sarasvatī river (देवमाता सरस्वत्यां – chap. XII. verse 44).

(C) *Nāgas*: –

Takṣaka, the great *Nāga* king (*nāgarāja*) used to live in the Khāṇḍava *vana* in the beginning but when it was put to fire, he shifted to Kurukṣetra[63] and made his abode there: –

यस्य वास: कुरुक्षेत्रे खाण्डवे चाभवत्पुरा ॥१३९
तं नागराजमस्तौषं कुण्डलार्थाय तक्षकम् ।
तक्षकस्य चाश्वसेनश्च नित्यं सहचरावुभौ ॥१४०
कुरुक्षेत्रं च वसतां नदीमिक्षुमतीमनु ॥१४१

[*Ādi Parva,* Suk. ed., chap. 3, 139-41].

तक्षकस्तु न तत्रासीत् नागराजो महाबल: ।
दह्यमाने वने तस्मिन् कुरुक्षेत्रं गतो हि स: ॥

[*ibid,* Bombay ed. chap. 253, p. 422].

.........तक्षको भुजगोत्तम ॥१६
दाहकाले खण्डवस्य कुरुक्षेत्रं गतो ह्यसौ ।
न च शक्यौ युधा जेतुं कथंचिदपि वासव ॥१७

[*ibid.,* chap. 254, p. 424].

This led Dr. J. Ph. Vogel[64] to conjecture that the "original home of the cult of Takṣaka was Indraprastha from where it was carried northward to Kurukṣetra." Hopkins (*op. cit.,* p. 149) also remarks that "the connection with the *nāgas* as treasure-hiders appears in the description of the gatekeepers of the Nāga-Tīrtha at Kurukṣetra."

It is really interesting to notice some ancient *tīrthas* (in the region of Kurukṣetra) being even named after the *nāga* or *sarpa* cult. Not only that, some of the old names have been survived to this day: –

Nāgdu, 11 miles s. s. w. of Thānesar; cf. ancient *nāga*-tīrtha (*CASR*., XIV, pp. 97 ff.). The *VP.* refers to Nāgodbheda (*VP.*, 82. 113), Nāga *tīrtha* [*VP.*, 83. 45], Sarpadarvī *tīrtha* etc. The last one has been considered to be a very sacred spot, the most excellent of all the *nāga tīrthas*: –

सर्वदर्वो नागानां तीर्थमुत्तमम्।
आग्निष्टोममवाप्नोति नागलोकं च विंदति॥

[*VP.*, Suk. ed., 81, 12].

The Sarpadarvī *tīrtha* may be identified with modern Sapīdāna[65], very near to ancient Pṛthūdaka. Modern Saphīdān (सफ़ीदां or सफ़ीदों), identified Sarpadarpa and Nāgadamana *tīrtha,* was famous for 3 ancient *tīrthas* and temples (such as Nāgeśvara Mahādeva, Nāgadamanī Devī and Nāga-*kṣetra*) associated with Parīkṣita and his biting by Takṣaka *nāga*. Janamejaya is said to have established the above three *mūrtis* to avenge the Takṣaka *nāga* [*Indian Antiquary,* XXIII, pp. 298-300].

IX. *Persons associated with Kurukṣetra*

The old Vedic myths try to associate some important persons and personalities with the region of Kurukṣetra. It was here that: – (i) Pururavas found his beloved Urvaśī [*Śatapatha Brāhmaṇa,* XI. 5. 1. 4]; (ii) Indra killed the Vṛtras [*Ṛg Veda,* I. 84. 13]. The later Sanskrit literature too bears testimony to the close association of numerous persons, sages, kings, nāgas, *Yakṣas*... etc., with this area. Even foreign travellers, Chinese and Muslim, had the proud privilege of paying their visit to the place.

Following are some of the names[66] of the persons and personalities associated with Kurukṣetra in some way or the other: –

(1) Kuru – the sage-king, who gave the name to the place.

(2) Janamejaya performed a sacrifice here for a considerable period [*Ādi Parva,* 1906, Bombay ed., chap. 3, verse: – जनमेजयः परीक्षितः सहभ्रातृभिः कुरुक्षेत्रे दीर्घसत्रमुपासते].

(3) Combat between the Kuru chief and the *Gandharvarāja* took place at Kurukṣetra [*ibid.*, 109. 11-2], on the banks of the river Hiraṇyavatī [नद्यास्तीरे हिरण्यवत्याः].

(4) The two demons, named Sunda and Upasunda, after having

subjugated every nook and corner of the heaven, began to live in Kurukṣetra [*ibid.,* 230. 27 – कुरुक्षेत्रे निवेशमभिचक्रतु:].

(5) Bhārgava fought here at Kurukṣetra [*Śānti Parva,* P. C. Roy ed., 27. 7].

(6) It was the battle scene of the Great War (Mahābhārata War).

(7) The sages, the gods, the Brāhmins, the *gandharvas,* the *Yakṣas* etc., visited the place [*VP.,* Roy ed., 83. 5-8 and 108-9; *Vām.,* 57.51-3; *ibid.,* 89. 1-3].

(8) King Māndhātā performed the sacrifice here [*VP.,* Sāt. ed. chap. 126, Suk. ed., 126. 42] : –

तस्यैतद्देवयजनं स्थानमादित्यवर्चस: ।

तस्यपुण्यतमे देशे कुरुक्षेत्रस्य मध्यत: ॥

(9) King Mudgala used to live at Kurukṣetra: –

शिलोच्छवृत्ति-धर्मात्मा मुद्गल: संयतेन्द्रिय: ।

आसीद्राजन् कुरुक्षेत्रे सत्यवागनसूयक: ॥

[*VP.,* Sātav. ed., 260.3].

(10) Bhīṣma – Pitāmaha continued to lie on the bed[67] of arrows here (*Śānti Parva,* chap. 53).

(11) Yudhiṣṭhira had visited the holy place कुरुक्षेत्रमवतरत् – *Āśramavāsa Parva,* Sātav. ed., 19. 71; *ibid.,* 23. 16). It was from here that he left for Gaṅgādvāra (*ibid.,* 31, 37).

(12) It was the battle scene of the *Devāsurasaṅgrāma,* as a result of which all the gods and demons came to an end here [*ibid.,* 31.7]: –

देवाश्च दानवाश्चैव तथा देवर्षतोऽमला: ।

त एते निधनं प्राप्ता: कुरुक्षेत्रे रणजिये ॥

(13) King Sudarśana, a descendant of Manu, lived here along with his family [*Anuśāsana Parva,* Sātav. ed. 2, 40]: –

स गृहस्थाश्रमरत: तथा सुदर्शन ।

कुरुक्षेत्रेऽवसद्राजन्नोद्यवत्या समन्वित: ॥

(14) Balarāma gave away many gifts here [*SP.,* Sātav. ed., Chap. 55].

(15) Duryodhana and Bhīmasena fought at Kurukṣetra [*ibid.,*Chap. 55].

(16) We are informed in the *Kathāsaritsāgara*[68] of Somadeva that king Malayaprabha was the ruler of Kurukṣetra.

(17) Vairocana Bali visited this place [*Vām.,* 89. 1].

(18) The hill chiefs and other rulers from various parts of India

visited the place [*Śrīmad-Bhāgawat Puraṇa,* 82. 12-13, ed., by Govindadass, Mathurā, II, pp. 450 ff.][69].

(19) In the region of Sassala (1112-20 A.D.) three hill chiefs as well as the *Yuvarājas* of the Chiefs of Trigarta, Vallāpura; in all 5 Chiefs, met at one place in the beginning and visited Kurukṣetra[70] :-

वल्ह आनन्दराजश्च पंच संघटिता: क्वचित्।

प्रस्थानार्थं कृतपणा: कुरुक्षेत्रमुपागता: ॥ viii. 540

अर्कोपरागे प्राप्त: स कुरुक्षेत्रमवाप तम्[७१] । viii. 2220

(20) It was an abode of various gods [*Vām.,* XXXIII. 12].

X. *Kurukṣetra, as a place of Sanctity and Pilgrimage*

Kurukṣetra, situated between the rivers Sarasvatī and the Dṛṣadvatī, was regarded as a holy place as early as the time of the Vedic literature. It was here that the ancient Hindu sages had the proud privilege of kindling the sacred fire. This sanctity of Kurukṣetra was preserved for a considerable period. The later Sanskrit literature bears testimony to this fact i.e. :–

(1) It was the *Uttaravedī* [Northern Altar] of Prajāpati or Pitāmaha or Brahmā; a *devanirmita deśa; Brahmāvarta, Brahmarṣi-deśa* etc., as already discussed above. According to the *Jābāli Upaniṣad*[72], it was also called as *avimukta-kṣetra, brahma-sadana,* and *deva-yajña bhūmi.*

(2) The very sight of Kurukṣetra and the chanting of its name has got a great sanctifying effect: –

ततो गच्छेत् राजेन्द्र कुरुक्षेत्रमभीष्टितम्।

पापेभ्यो यत्र मुच्यते दर्शनात् सर्वजन्तव: ॥१

"कुरुक्षेत्र गमिष्यामि कुरुक्षेत्रे वसाम्यहं"।

य एवं सततं ब्रूयात् सर्वपापै: प्रमुच्यते ॥२

पांसवोऽपि कुरुक्षेत्रे वायुना समुदीरिता: ।

अपि दुष्कृतकर्माणं नयन्ति परमां गतिम् ॥३

[*VP.,* Suk. ed., chap. 81].

The verses also occur in chap. 81, verses 173-81 of the same *Parva.* The *Vāmana Purāṇa* [XXXIII 7-10] too corroborates the truth of this statement. The *Agni Purāṇa*[73] (109. 14) reproduces a verse from the *VP* (81. 2. Suk. ed.). It is equally interesting to note the following passage from the *VP* (*ibid.,* verse): –

मनाप्यभिकामस्य कुरुक्षेत्रे युधिष्ठिर।

पापानि विप्रनश्यन्ति ब्रह्मलोकञ्च गच्छति॥

(3) They who die at Kurukṣetra reach the Heaven: –

इह ये पुरुषाः क्षेत्रे मरिष्यन्ति शतकतो।

ते गमिष्यन्ति सुकृतांल्लोकान् पापवर्जितान्॥६

[*SP.*, Sātav. ed., 53. 6].

कुरुक्षेत्रं परं पुण्यं पावनं स्वर्गमेव च।

देवतैः ऋषिभिः जुष्टं ब्राह्मणैश्च महात्मभिः॥७

तत्र वै योत्स्यमाना ये देहं त्यक्षन्ति मानवाः।

तेषां स्वर्गे ध्रवोवासः शक्रेण सह मारिष॥८ [*ibid.*, 55. 7-8].

द्वारवत्यां कुरुक्षेत्रे योगाभ्यासेन वा मृताः।[74]

कुरुक्षेत्रमृतानां च पतनं नेव विद्यते। [*Vām.*, XXXIII. 6].

(4) Kurukṣetra is the most important of all the *tīrthas* on the earth: –

पृथिव्यां नैमिषं तीर्थमन्तरिक्षे च पुष्करम्।

त्रयाणामपि लोकानां कुरुक्षेत्रं विशिष्यते॥२०३

[*VP.*, 83., Roy ed.].

द्वापरे कुरुक्षेत्रं गङ्गाकलियुगे स्मृता।

[*ibid.*, 82. 91, Roy ed.].

पुण्यमाहु कुरुक्षेत्रं [*Śanti Parva,* Roy ed. 152. 9-10].

पुण्यतीर्थं सुसलिलं कुरुक्षेत्रं प्रकीर्तितम्।

[*Anuśāsana Parva,* Sāt. ed., 165 Chap., p. 1050].

पृथिव्यां नैमिषं पुण्यमन्तरिक्षे च पुष्करम्।

त्रयाणामपि लोकानाम् कुरुक्षेत्रं विशिष्यते॥

[*Matsya*[75] *Purāṇa,* 109. 3].

(5) Visit of Kurukṣetra proves very fruitful indeed and one acquires the merit of performing various Vedic sacrifices: –

गत्वा हि श्रद्धया युक्तः कुरुक्षेत्रं कुरूद्वह।

फलं प्राप्नोति च तदा राजसूयाश्वमेधयोः॥

[*VP.*, Suk. ed., 81.8].

Similar fruits are obtained by bathing and visiting different *tīrthas* (of Kurukṣetra region) such as: – Sarpadarvī, Varāha, Soma, Arantuka, Āpagā, Phalakī-*vana* etc., as stated in the *VP.*, chap. 81. Suk. ed. Sometimes *go-sahasra-phala* could also be accrued.

(6) Kurukṣetra is a befitting place for offering oblations to the

ancestors: –

गया प्रयागे गङ्गा च कुरुक्षेत्रं च नर्मदा
श्रीपर्वतः प्रभासश्च शालग्रामो वाराणसी।
गोदावरी तेषु श्राद्धं श्रीपुरुषोत्तमः ॥

[*Agni Purāṇa*, 117. 63-4].

It was here that Bhārgava Rāma, after having bathed at Samantapañcaka, had propitiated his ancestors.

(7) Bath at Kurukṣetra has got a sanctifying effect: –

कुरुक्षेत्रे समा गङ्गा अत्र तत्रावगाहिता ॥८९
पुष्करे तु कुरुक्षेत्रे गङ्गायां मगधेषु च।
स्नात्वा तारयते जन्तुः सप्तसप्तावरांस्तथा ॥९३

[*Vām.*, Sat. ed., 85 Chap.].

कुरुक्षेत्रं गङ्गा प्रभासं पुष्कराणि च ॥४८
एतानि मनसा ध्यात्वा अवगाहेत्ततो जलम्।
तधा मुच्यति पापेन राहुणा चन्द्रमा यथा ॥

[*Anuśāsana Parva*, Sāt. ed., Chap. 125].

यत्र तत्र कुरुक्षेत्रं नैमिषं पुष्कराणि च ॥१३
एतानि सर्वतीर्थानि कृत्वा पापैः प्रमुच्यते ॥१४

[Vyāsa[76] *Smṛti*, IV. 13-14].

स्नात्वाभिगम्य तत्रैव महापातकनाशनम्।
कुरुक्षेत्रस्य तद्द्वारं विश्रुतं पुण्यवर्धनम् ॥

[*Vām.*, XXXIV. 40].

सरस्वस्यां सन्निहित्यां स्नानकृद् ब्रह्मलोकभाक् ॥१५
पांशवोऽपि कुरुक्षेत्रे नयन्ति परमां गतिम् ॥१६

[*Agni Purāṇa*, chap. 109].

(8) A bath in the river Sarasvatī makes a man free from all his sins [*AP.*, Roy ed., 129.20]: –

सरस्वतीमिमां पुण्यां पश्यैकशारणामृताम्।
यत्र स्नात्वा नर श्रेष्ठ धूतपापत्मा भविष्यति ॥

The confluence of Aruṇā and Sarasvatī rivers too was quite famous (*ibid.*, Suk. ed., 81 131-2): –तीर्थं देव्या यथाक्रमम् सरस्वत्यारुणायाश्च सङ्गमं लोकविश्रुतम्।

(9) Kurukṣetra is a sacred place where sacrifices and penances are

to be performed: –

तस्यैतद्देवयजनं स्थानमादित्यवर्चसः ।

तस्यपुण्यतमे देशे कुरुक्षेत्रस्य मध्यतः ॥

[*VP.*, Suk. ed., 126. 42].

It was a *dharma-kṣetra* [land of piety]: – क्षेत्रं धर्मस्य कृत्स्नस्य कुरुक्षेत्रम् [*Śānti Parva*, Roy ed., 53. 23; cf. धर्मक्षेत्रे कुरुक्षेत्रे in the opening verse of the *Bhagavadgītā*]. It was a land of penance [कुरुक्षेत्रे तपःक्षेत्रे in the *Bhīṣ maparva,* Sāt. ed., 1. 2.]. A three-year *satra* was performed at Kuruks etra, on the banks of the river called Dṛṣadvatī [S. Pradhan, *Chronology of Ancient India,* 1927, Calcutta, p. 76]. King Kuru too performed the *yajña* here. Some other references to this land of sacrifices and piety too are very interesting: –

प्रजापतेरुत्तरवेदिरुच्यते सनातनं रा समन्तपञ्चकम् ।

समीजिरे यत्रपुरा दिवौकसौ वरेण सत्रेण महावरप्रदः ॥

[*SP.,* Sāt. ed., 53. 1].

समन्तपञ्चकं नाम धर्मस्थानमुत्तमम् [*Vām.*, XXII, 15].

कुरुक्षेत्रं पुण देशः [*ibid.*, chap. 99].

धर्मक्षेत्रे कुरुक्षेत्रे दीर्घसत्रं तु ईजिरे ।

नद्यास्तीरे दृषद्वत्याः पुण्यायाः शुचिरोधसः ॥

[*Vāyu Purāṇa,* Ānandāśrama Series, I. 14].

धर्मतीर्थं सुवर्णाख्यं गङ्गाद्वारमनुत्तमम् ।

[*Agni Purāṇa* 109. 16].

XI. *Kurukṣetra and Eclipses of the Sun and Moon*

Pilgrimage to Kurukṣetra, specially on the occasion of the Solar and Lunar eclipses was the harbinger of bliss and religious merit. Quite a large number of people, including the rulers and the sages, used to flock to the place to have a dip into the holy water of the sacred pools and lakes at Kurukṣetra. The place thus happened to attract quite a large number of visitors even in those good old days. The Sanskrit texts and the accounts of travellers visiting India bear testimony to the importance of pilgrimage to this place, specially during the lunar and solar eclipses. Some of the references are worth noticing here: –

(1) कुरुक्षेत्रे महापुण्यं राहुग्रस्ते दिवाकरे [*Matsya Purāṇa,* 199. 12, Calcutta ed., p. 318].

(2) According to the *Srīmad Bhāgavat Purāṇa* (edited by

Govindadāss, II, Chap. 82, p. 450 ff.), knowing that the Solar eclipse was at hand (सूर्योपराग: समहानासीत् कल्पक्षये यथा), people from all over the country assembled there before the scheduled time of the eclipse (verses 1, 2). They were extremely anxious to attain *puṇya* and so they observed fast, had their bath at Kurukṣetra and distributed garlands and cows among the Brāhmaṇas: –

तत्र स्नात्वा महाभागा उपोष्य सुसमाहिता: ।
ब्राह्मणेभ्यो ददुर्धेनूर्वास: स्रग्रुक्मभालिनी ॥

[*ibid.*, verse 9]

It is further stated (*ibid.*, verses 12-13) that the great assembly (at Kurukṣetra) on this occasion included even the rulers of various states and countries i.e. from Matsya, Uśīnara, Kośala, Vidarbha, Kuru, Sṛñjaya, Kambuja, Kekaya, Madra, Kunti, Ānarta, Kerala etc. Besides this, they had their relations too with them.

(3) *The Rājataraṅgiṇī* of Kalhaṇa [*op. cit.*, VIII, 2220] too informs us that the place was visited by the prince on the occasion of Solar eclipse (अर्कोपरागे प्राप्त: स कुरुक्षेत्रमवाप तम् etc.). A. Stein (*op. cit.*, II, p. 122) even states that "the eclipse of the sun in India took place on July 23 of 1134 A.D. It was visible at Thāneśvara." The solar eclipse occurred on the occasion of Koṭheśvara's meeting with Mallārjuna at Kurukṣetra [A. Stein, *op. cit.*, p. 171 f. n.].

(4) It is said that there was a solar eclipse on the eve of the battle of Kurukṣetra [S. N. Pradhan, *op. cit.*, p. 268].

(5) The *Vṛhat Saṁhitā* of Varāhamihira (V. 78; XI. 57) too refers to the eclipse and its effects at Kurukṣetra: –

(a) काश्मीरान् सपुलिन्द चीन-यवनान् हन्यात् कुरुक्षेत्रजान् ।
गन्धारानपि मध्यदेशसहितान् दृष्टोग्रह: श्रावणे ।
काम्बोजैकशफांश्च शारदमपि त्यक्तवा यथोक्तानिमानन्यत्र ।
प्रचुरान्नहृष्टमनुजैर्धात्रीं करोत्यावृताम् ॥ v ७८

i.e. "If an eclipse should occur in the Lunar month of Śrāvaṇa, the people of Kaśmīra, Pulindas, Chinese, Yavanas, those born in Kurukṣetra and Gandhāra, those living in the central tract, Kambojas and all whole-hoofed animals and also the grains of the autumnal season will suffer damage and perish. With the exception of those stated above, all those living elsewhere shall be happy and live in peace".[77]

(b) चित्रास कुरुक्षेत्राधिपस्य समादिशेत्तज्ज्ञ: ।
काश्मीरकाम्बोजौ नृपती प्रभाञ्जने न स्त: ॥ xi ५७

i.e. "When a malign *Ketu* eclipses or touches the star *citra,* people in the know should declare the exit from the world of the chief of Kurukṣ etra. If the star in question be *Svāti,* the two kings of Kaśmīr and Kamboja will cease to exist."[78]

(6) According to the *Vana Parva,* one attains the benefit of an *Aśvamedha yajña* by bathing at Sannihatī *tīrtha* modern Sannavaṭa, 9 miles south of Thānesar on the day of Solar eclipse.

(7) Alberuni too furnishes some information that he gathered (about sun and moon eclipses) on the authority of Varāhamihira. In his own words[79]: – "The *Saṃhitā of Varāhamihira* relates that in Thāneshar, there is a pond which the Hindus visit from afar to bathe in its water. Regarding the cause of this custom, they relate the following: – the waters of all the other holy ponds visit this particular pond at the time of an eclipse. Therefore a man, who washes in it, it is as if he had washed in every single one of all of them. Then Varāhamihira continues that – people say, if it were not the head which causes the eclipse of the sun and the moon, the other ponds would not visit this pond".

(8) The account of Abū Rīhān [Reinaud, *Memoire Sur l'Inde,* p. 287] too "records on the authority of Varāhamihira, that during the eclipses of the moon, the waters of all the other tanks visit the tank of Thānesar so that the bather in the tank, at the moment of the eclipse obtains the additional merit of bathing in all other tanks at the same time"[80]. In Cunningham's opinion, this notice by Varāhamihira, "carries us back at once to about 500 A.D. when the holy tank of Thānesar was in full repute".

(9) The Kulait plate of Somavarman, referring to Sāhilladeva of Mūṣaṇa race, relates that he "vanquished the Kīra troops of the lord of Durgar (Dugara) and their allies the Saumṭika who forced his suzerainty on the lord of Kulūta (Kullū) who was styled *Karivarṣa* because he undertook a pilgrimage to Kurukṣetra on the occasion of a Solar eclipse and made a gift of the elephants to the Sun-god who ensured the continuance of his family etc.[81]"

(10) *The Tabqāti-Akbarī* presents a vivid account of the assemblage of pilgrims on the bank of the holy lake at Kurukṣetra in A.H. 974 (=1567 A.D.): –

"When the emperor arrived at Thānesar, there was an assemblage of *jogīs* and *sannyāsīs* on the banks of a lake called Kurukṣetra. This is a sacred place of the Brāhmaṇas and on the occasion of the eclipses, the people of Hindustan flock thither from all parts to bathe. There was a great assemblage there on this occasion and people were bestowing their gifts of gold, silver, jewels and stuffs upon the Brāhmaṇas. Many of them threw themselves into water and the *jogīs* and *sannyāsīs* were gathering a rich harvest from their charity. In consequence of a feud which existed between these two sects, they came to the emperor seeking permission to settle it by fighting. The *sannyāsīs* were between 200 and 300 in number and *jogīs,* who wear only rags, were over 500. When the adversaries stood ready to begin the fray, by emperor's orders, some soldiers smeared their persons with ashes and went to support the *sannyāsīs* who were the weaker party. A fierce fight ensued and many were killed. Emperor greatly enjoyed the sight. At length, the *jogīs* were defeated and the *sannyāsīs* were victors" [H.M.Elliot, *The History of India,* London, vol. V, 1873, p. 318].

This is in nutshell a short account of Kurukṣetra as depicted in the later Sanskrit literature[82]

Abbreviations

CASR = *Cunningham's Archaeological Survey Report,* Calcutta.

Suk. = Sukthankara, V.S.

Vām. = *The Vāmana Purāṇa,* Veṅkaṭeśwara Press, Chap. 22.

MB. = *The Mahābhārata.*

VP. = *Vana Parva.*

AP. = *Āraṇyaka Parva.*

SP. = *Śalya Parva.*

References

1. B. C. Law, *Geographical Essays,* 1937, London, p. 132; cf. H.C. Raychaudhuri, *Political History of Ancient India,* 4th ed., Calcutta, p. 20.
2. *VP.,* 83. 4, P. C. Roy ed., Śaka year 1804, Calcutta.
3. *Ibid.,* verse 205, p. 226. They who reside in the region of Kurukṣetra really reside in heaven.
4. Written in the first or second century A.D.
5. Cf. सरस्वती-दृषद्वत्योरन्तरे कुरुजाङ्गले . . . etc., in *Vām.,* chap. 22, verse 47. The *Bṛhatkathākośa* of Hariṣeṇa [Bhāratīya Vidyā Bhavan ed., Bombay, 1943] relates to several stories connected with the Kuru-Jāṅgala country.
6. Cited in the *Hindi Viśvakośa,* V, 1922, Calcutta, p. 132.
7. Similar views have also been put forth by Manu; cf. the *Manu Smṛti,* II. 17; *Hindī Viśvakośa, op. cit.,* pp. 133-5.

   In the earlier history of India, the centre of civilization was tending to be localised in the land between these two rivers [*Cambridge History of India;*

I, pp. 116; also pp. 47, 120, 289, 307-8]. The close association of the Vedic poets with this region is a well-known fact [*Bulletin of the School of Oriental and African Studies,* University of London, VI, pp. 549-53; *Vedic Age,* 1951, London, pp. 245, 274, 251-2, 292, 319 etc.]

8. i.e. *VP.*, P.C. Roy ed., 83. 208, p. 227.
9. i.e. *SP.*, Sātavalekar ed., 53. 24. Note the phrase *prajāpati* here instead of *pitāmaha* of *VP.*, cf. प्रजापतेरुत्तरवेदिरुच्यते सनातनं रामसमन्तपञ्चकम् in chap. 53, verse 1 of *SP.*, *op. cit;* ब्रह्मवेदि: कुरुक्षेत्रं in the *Vām.*, XXXIII 15; उत्तरवेदि सा देवलोके प्रजापते in *SP.*, 55. 9.
10. Also read as Macakraka and Maṅkaṇaka.
11. The Macakruka *tīrtha* is said to have been guarded by *Yakṣa-Dvārapāla* [*VP.*, Suk. ed., 81. 7): –

    मचक्रुकं राजन्द्वारपालं महाबलम्।
    यक्षं समभिवाद्य गोसहस्रफलं लभेत्॥

    Cf. *ibid.*, 81. 13 for the Tarantuka, and chap. 171 for Arantuka. Arantuka has been called as 'Lord of the Yakṣas' (*Yakṣendra*) in *Vp.*, 81. 42: –

    ततो गच्छेत् राजेन्द्र द्वारपालमरन्तुकम्।
    तस्य तीर्थं सरस्वत्यां यक्षेन्द्रस्य महात्मन:।
    तत्र स्नात्वा नरो राजन्नग्निष्टोमफलं लभेत्॥

12. The *Kurukṣetra Tīrtha Nirṇaya,* cited in *CASR.*, XIV, p. 89.
13. In his *Abhidhānacintāmaṇi,* IV. 15-16, Bhāvanagara ed., Veer Era, 2441, pp. 379; cf. *CASR.*, XIV, pp. 87, 90-91 for the views of Cunningham.
14. i.e. *South Indian Text* as edited by Kṛṣṇācārya, 1906, Bombay, p. 183; cf. Roy ed., 94. 48-9; B.C. Law, *Tribes in Ancient India,* Poona, 1943, p. 24.
15. *Index to the MB.*, Sorensen ed., London, 1904, p. 442, chap. 53.
16. Cf. also the *Vāyu Purāṇa,* Ānandāśrama series, XCIX. 215. For Indra's ridicule of the holiness of Kurukṣetra, consult E. W. Hopkins, *op. cit.*, p. 136.
17. i.e. *Vividha-tīrtha Kalpa,* edited by Jinaprabha-sūri, Śāntiniketana, 1934, p. 94.
18. V. S. Sukthankar, *Annals of the Bhandarkar Oriental Research Institute,* Poona, XVIII, 1937, pp. 5-6.
19. *Ādi Parva,* Suk. ed., I. 2-12.
20. Cf. *Śānti Parva,* P. C. Roy ed., chap. 48, verses 3-14, p. 109.
21. *Ādi Parva,* Suk. ed., I. 2. 9; *ibid.*, I. 1. II.
22. *Hindi Hindustāna Weekly,* New Delhi, April 18, 1954, p. 19.
23. Cf. *Vedic Index,* II, p. 364; Cunningham's *The Ancient Geography of India,* 1871, London, pp. 331-2, 334-5; *ibid.*, 1924 ed., pp. 384-5.
24. As cited by Agrawala, *op. cit.*, p. 19. *Ulūkhala,* in the Sanskrit language, "is

a particular ornament for the ear" [Monier Williams, *A Skt-Eng, Dict.*, 1899, Oxford, p. 218].

25. Modern Jagādharī (in the Ambālā district of the E. Panjab) which is not very far from Thānesar (i.e. Kurukṣetra).

26. Rāhula Sāṅkṛtyāyana, *The Majjhima Nikāya,* 1933, Sarnath, p. 6 of the introduction, G. P. Malalasekera, *Dictionary of the Pāli Proper Names,* 1937, London, I, pp. 528-9; Rhys Davids, *Buddhist India,* 1950, p. 19.

27. i.e. Skt. Kurukṣetra. For the Pālī form consult Malalasekera, *op. cit.*, p. 642. King Jarāsandha is said to have resided in Kurukhetta (Cowell and Rouse, The *Jātaka,* VI, 1907, London, pp. 141). Kurukhetta also occurs in the commentary of the *Bṛhatkalpa Bhāṣya*—as cited by J.C. Jain in *Life in Ancient India as depicted in the Jain Canons,* 1947, Bombay, p. 324.

28. McCrindle's *Ancient India as described by Ptolemy,* 1927, Calcutta, p. 367; cf. Cunningham's *The Ancient Geography of India,* 1924, p. xliii of introduction.

29. B. C. Law's Works : *Geography of Early Buddhism,* 1932, London, p. 2, f.n. 2 and *Geographical Essays,* 1937, London, p. 40.

30. *McCrindle's* . . . ., *op. cit.*, p. 128; cf. *Encyclopaedia of Religion and Ethics,* XII, 1921, p. 261 and f.n. 2 of p. 261.

31. i.e. Śiva. It has also been narrated in the account of the Pañcavaṭa *tīrtha* that god Sthāṇu had himself appeared there [योगेश्वर: स्थाणु स्वयमेव वृषभध्वज:-*AP.*, Suk. ed., 81. 141-2].

32. *The Saura Purāṇa,* Ānandāśrama Series, Śaka year 1811, p. 276, chap. 67. 13-15. Cf. also *Vām.*, chapters 43 and 46; *CASR,* II, p. 217 about Sthāṇu *Tīrtha* where King Veṇa had dedicated a shrine to Śiva under the name Sthāṇu.

33. *The Liṅga Purāṇa,* Calcutta ed., Śaka year 1812, p. 52, chap. 36 verse 77.

34. *Bibliotheca Indica Series,* Calcutta, 1897, p. 261.

35. Cf. R. S. Tripathi, *History of Kannauj,* Banaras, p. 22 f.n. 1, 28, 30, 50, 55, 65, 789, 199.

36. The *Harṣacarita* as edited by pp. P. V. Kane, 1918, Bombay, chap. III, pp. 43-4. Cf. also V.S. Agrawala, *Harṣacarita eka Sāṁskṛtika Adhyayana,* Hindī, 1953, Patna, pp. 55-6.

37. Translation as given in the edition of E. B. Cowell and F. W. Thomas, 1897, London, p. 81 ff.

38. H. C. Ray, *Dynastic History of Northern India,* II, Calcutta, 1936, p. 862.

39. Cf. Maxmüller, *Hymns of the Ṛg Veda,* I, 1877, London, p. 226; *Vedic Index,* I, p. 374.

40. Cf. *AP.*, 81. 154, Suk. ed.

41. Cf. *Ibid.*, 88. 1-10 for the sanctity of the Sarasvatī and the Dṛṣadvatī rivers; cf. also *ibid.*, III. 6. 1 ff; *ibid,* chap, 129, verse 20.

42. *Vedic Index,* II, pp. 434-5; *CASR.*, XIV, p. 88, *ibid.*, II, p. 216; *Vedic*

Index, I, pp. 323-363; B. C. Law, *Geographical Essays,* 1937, London, pp. 86-7.

43. *Journal of the Department of Letters,* Calcutta, XV, as cited in the *Indian Historical Quarterly,* III, p. 663.
44. Cf. B. C. Law, *Geographical Essays* also.
45. Cf. *SP.*, Sātavalekar ed., 38, p. 258 ff., verses 27 ff. for *Sureṇu-Sarasvatī* and *Oghavatī Sarasvatī.*
46. For *Sapta-Sārasvata* in the *MB.*, consult *SP.* Sātav. ed., 38. 32 ff. and *AP.*, Suk. ed., 81. 97 ff.
47. Cunningham (*CASR.*, XIV, p. 89) states that the ancient names of several important rivers as Mārkaṇḍā, Nakaṭī, Chitang or Chatang etc., remain quite unknown so far.
48. He also states here that Kausikī-junction still exists near the village called Balu and the Rākhi (Rākṣī) river flows 17 miles to the south of Thānesar.
49. Cf. *Vedic Index,* II, p. 95, f.n. 9 quoting the river Kauśikī as a tributary of the Sarasvatī.
50. S. N. Pradhan, *Chronology of Ancient India,* 1927, Calcutta, p. 76.
51. Cf. Also Dr. D. R. Patil, *Cultural History from the Vāyu Purāṇa,* p. 275.
52. Also read as Ikṣuvatī, Īkṣumatī, Ikṣunadī etc.
53. *Ādi Parva*, 1906, Bombay, chap. 3, 140-1; cf. Suk. ed., verses 144-6.
54. Cf. *CASR.*, XIV, p. 91 also.
55. Cf. सरस्वती तीरे काम्यकं नाम काननम् in *AP.*, 37, 37.
56. Suk. ed., chap. 25. verses 13-19.
57. M. N. Dutt tries to identify Bhogavatī with the river Sarasvatī. This fact has already been cited above.
58. Modern Peheoā in the Kaithal *tahasīl* of the Karnāl district. It is about 16 miles west of Thānesar, Cf. *Imperial Gazetteer of India,* XX, p. 100.
59. Cf. *VP.*, 183; R. K. Mookerjee, *Ancient Indian Education,* 1947 London, p. 335.
60. The *VP.*, as translated by M.N. Dutt, 1896, p. 36, verses 17-20, chap. 25. The Skt. text has already been cited above.
61. The Vedic literature too refers to the growth of the *nyagrodha* trees in Kurukṣ etra [cf. *Aitareya Brāhmaṇa,* VII. 30, Bombay ed., Śaka year 1812].
62. D. C. Sircar's paper in *JASB.*, Calcutta, 1948, XIV, p. 14 citing the text from Yamala—as quoted in the *Tantrasāra,* p. 40.
63. Cf. E. W. Hopkins, *Epic Mythology,* 1915, Strassburg, p. 29.
64. *Indian Serpent Lore,* 1926, London, p. 205.
65. *Hindi Viśva Kośa* (s. v. Kurukṣetra) vol. V, 1922, Calcutta. There is a place now called Saphīdān in this area. Cf. *CASR.*, XIV, p. 97 ff.
66. Association of the *nāgas,* goddesses, *yakṣas* etc., has already been shown

above.

67. The ancient (mediaeval) temple at Kirāḍu (Jodhpur Division) presents an interesting and rare carving of Bhīṣma lying on the Bed of Arrows; cf. my paper in the *Śodhapatrikā,* Udaipur, March, 1954, p. 5; Stella Kramrisch, *Hindu Temple,* Calcutta, p. 407. plate LXXX.

68. N. M. Penzer ed., VI, London, 1926, p. 84 ff.

69. Cf. various *Purāṇas* referring to the visit of the chiefs and the rulers at the time of eclipses.

70. Kalhaṇa's *Rājataraṅgiṇī,* II, edited by A. Stein, VIII. 540 and 2220.

71. *The Rājataraṅgiṇī,* edited by Durga Prasad, Bombay, 1894, p. 191.

72. F. Otto Schrader, *The Minor Upaniṣads,* 1912, Madras, pp. 59-60. For Vedic literature, consult the following works such as *Ṛg Veda,* III 23. 4; *Pañcaviṃśa Brāhmaṇa,* II. 9, 4; *Taittirīya Araṇyaka,* V. 1. 1; *Śatapatha Brāhmaṇa,* IV. 1. 5. 13; *ibid.,* 1. 1. 2; *Maitrāyaṇī Saṃhitā,* II. 1. 4; *ibid.,* IV. 5. 9.; *Aitareya Brāhmaṇa,* VII. 30; *Jaiminīya Br.* II. 207 Caland ed., 1919, p. 303; *Śāṅkhāyana Śrauta-sūtra,* XV. 16. 11; *Kātyāyana Śrautasūtra,* XXIV, 6. 32: *Lāṭyāyana Śrautasūtra,* X. 19. 1. and 4; *Jābālī Upaniṣad; Tāṇḍya Mahābrāhmaṇa,* XXV. 13. 3 etc. Even the gods had the occasion of performing the *Yajñas* here.

73. R. L. Mitra's ed., Calcutta, I, 1873, p. 73.

74. *Padma Purāṇa* (*Pātāla Khaṇḍa*), chap. 93, Ānandāśrama Series, 1894, p. 648.

75. Calcutta ed., Śaka year 1812, p. 143.

76. *Smṛtīnām Samuccayaḥ,* Ānandāśrama Series, 1929, p. 367. This work (p. 387) also refers to the *Śaṅkha Smṛti* (127 ff.) according to which Kurukṣetra was a place fit for giving charity. Cf. *Kūrma Purāṇa,* Calcutta, 1890, edited by Nīlamaṇi Mookerjee. p. 719.

77. Translation of verse V. 78 as furnished by V Subrahmanya Śāstrī, *vāhamihira's Vṛhatsaṃhitā,* I, 1947, Bangalore.

78. *Ibid.,* translation of verse XI. 57.

79. *Alberuni's India,* II, 1910, London, p. 145 as edited by E.C. Sachau.

80. Alexander Cunningham, *The Ancient Geography of India,* 1871, London, pp. 334-5.

81. D.R. Bhandarkar, *A List of Inscriptions of N. India in Brāhmī and its Scripts from 200 A.D.,* p. 256.

82. The question of various *tīrthas* and localities in the region of Kurukṣetra has not been touched here. It will be taken up in a separate article.

The mediaeval lexicographer, Puruṣottama, identifies Vinaśana with Kurukṣ etra in his work the *Trikāṇḍaśeṣa* [*Age of Imperial Unity,* 1951, Bombay, p. 221 fn. 1].

Notes

67. The ancient [illegible] temple at [illegible] presents an interesting sculpture depicting [illegible] on the back of [illegible]; cf. [illegible] Madras 1934, p. 3; [illegible] plate LXIX.

68. N. M. Penzer [illegible] London 1926, p. 84 ff.

69. Cf. various Puranas referring to the [illegible] and the [illegible] at the [illegible] of things.

70. [illegible] Rg [illegible], edited by [illegible], VIII [illegible] and 21-27.

71. The [illegible], edited by Durga Prasad, Bombay 1894, p. 130.

72. T. [illegible], The Minor Upanisads 1912, Madras, pp. 55-63. For [illegible] consult the following works such as Rg Veda, III 23, 4; [illegible] [illegible] Vol. [illegible] [illegible] [illegible] p. 403 [illegible] XXIV, [illegible] and 4 [illegible] [illegible] the gods and the occasion of [illegible].

73. R. L. Mitra [illegible], I, 1871, p. 9 [illegible].

74. [illegible] ([illegible]) Sanskrit Series, 1894, p. [illegible].

75. [illegible] 1872, p. 162.

76. [illegible] Sanskrit Series (1929) p. 307. This work [illegible] [illegible] according to which [illegible] [illegible] 1890, edited [illegible] p. 716.

77. Translation of [illegible] translated by [illegible] [illegible], 1 1941, Bangalore.

78. [illegible] translation of verse XI 37.

79. [illegible], II 1900, London, p. 345 as edited by [illegible].

80. Alexander Cunningham, The Ancient Geography of India, 1871, London, [illegible].

81. D. R. Bhandarkar, A List of Inscriptions of Northern India [illegible] [illegible], p. 250.

82. The [illegible] of various works and [illegible] in the [illegible] [illegible] in a [illegible] article.

83. [illegible] and [illegible] [illegible] with [illegible] [illegible] this work the [illegible] 1971, Bombay, [illegible].

Historical Geography of India

Collection of Articles from the Indian Historical Quarterly

In 2 Vols.

These articles have been published in the Indian Historical Quarterly and the details of the articles is given below for reference:

Issue	Year of Pub.	Page Nos.	Page Nos. in the present book
Vol. 1 (1-2)	1925	130-136	293-298
Vol. 1 (3-4)	1925	456-463	299-304
Vol. 2 (1-2)	1926	27-38	305-313
Vol. 2 (1-2)	1926	232-249	315-328
Vol. 2 (3-4)	1926	515-536	329-345
Vol. 2 (3-4)	1926	720-737	347-360
Vol. 23 (1-4)	1947	320-322	361-363
Vol. 23 (1-4)	1947	65-68	365-368
Vol. 22 (1-4)	1946	309-315	369-376
Vol. 22 (1-4)	1946	228-229	377-379
Vol. 5 (1-2)	1929	119-124	381-385
Vol. 11 (1-4)	1935	771-778	387-394
Vol. 20 (1-4)	1944	1-8	395-402
Vol. 14 (1-4)	1938	747-756	403-411
Vol. 22 (1-4)	1946	277-285	413-422
Vol. 4 (1-4)	1928	169-178	423-431
Vol. 7 (3-4)	1931	741-742	433-434
Vol. 3 (3-4)	1927	728-732	435-438
Vol. 4 (1-4)	1928	44-56	439-448
Vol. 4 (1-4)	1928	234-242	449-455
Vol. 16 (1-4)	1940	105-117	457-466
Vol. 37 (1-4)	1961	183-188	467-472
Vol. 2 (3-4)	1926	655-656	473-474
Vol. 9 (1-2)	1933	588	475-476
Vol. 16 (1-4)	1940	827-837	477-484
Vol. 17 (1-4)	1941	236-240	485-489
Vol. 5 (1-2)	1926	341-346	491-496
Vol. 3 (3-4)	1927	518-529	497-508
Vol. 26 (1-4)	1950	118-128	509-518
Vol. 27 (1-4)	1951	250-254	519-523
Vol. 28 (1-4)	1952	135-141	525-531
Vol. 28 (1-4)	1952	249-256	533-540
Vol. 28 (1-4)	1952	350-359	541-551
Vol. 29 (1-4)	1953	56-63	553-560
Vol. 29 (1-4)	1953	121-128	561-569
Vol. 29 (1-4)	1953	276-285	571-579
Vol. 29 (1-4)	1953	378-386	581-589
Vol. 30 (1-4)	1954	148-153	591-596
Vol. 13 (1-4)	1937	521-526	597-601

Historical Geography of India

Collection of Articles from the Indian Historical Quarterly

Compiled by
P Mittal
Geeta Dua

Re-arranged with an Introduction by
Devendra Swarup

In 2 Vols.

Vol. 2

Originals
(an imprint of Low Price Publications)
Delhi-110052

Distributed by
D.K. Publishers Distributors (P) Ltd.
4834/24, Ansari Road, Darya Ganj,
New Delhi-110002
Phones: 51562573, 51562575, 51562578
e-mail: dkpd@del3.vsnl.net.in
visit us at: www.dkpd.com

Articles First Published in the Journal from 1925-1963
Collected and Published With an Introduction 2005

ISBN 81-88629-35-9 (Set)
ISBN 81-88629-37-5 (Vol. 2)

Published by
Originals
(an imprint of Low Price Publications)
A-6, Nimri Commercial Centre,
Near Ashok Vihar Phase-IV,
Delhi-110052
Phone: 27452453
e-mail: lpp@nde.vsnl.net.in
visit us at: www.lppindia.com

Printed at
D K Fine Art Press P Ltd.
Delhi-110052

PRINTED IN INDIA

Introduction

"A knowledge of space, no less than that of time, of geography, no less than that of chronology, is an indispensible prerequisite of any serious historical study." In fact, there can be no history without geography.

History of a people or civilization happens on the territory to which they belong or which they acquire through conquest or migration. Every historical event is connected with some place-name and therefore, when we read any ancient epic or modern book of history we come across names of rivers, mountains, towns, kingdoms, pilgrim centres, flora and fauna, climatic conditions etc. But many times we are not able to identify these place-names because, with the passage of time they have changed or new names have been superimposed upon them by foreign invaders and rulers. Here, historical geography comes to our help. It establishes a relation between ancient and modern place-names.

India is a vast country with a history going back to many millenia. Having passed through repeated foreign invasions, long periods of foreign rule and turbulence, she has been able to preserve a huge repository of literary, epigraphic and numismatic sources of its past. These sources are clothed in many classical and modern languages-Sanskrit, Pali, Prakrit, Tamil, Kannada, Telugu and other old regional languages. Besides these indigenous sources, the accounts of foreign invaders, travellers, scholars and ambassadors in their own ancient languages throw valuable light on our past. Sometimes we are puzzled to find the same place-name presented to us in different phonetic or linguist forms peculiar to different linguistic groups. So we find *Cholamandalam* transformed into *Coromandel*. Vedic river *Vitasta* being spelled as *Hydespes* by the Greek and Roman writers. Historical geography alone can unravel these puzzles. But it has been a very neglected subject in our country.

Some beginnings in the study of historical geography were made by Alexander Cunningham in the nineteenth century and were carried further by Indian scholars like Nundolal Dey, B C Law, D C Sircar and S B Chowdhary and some journals like Indian Antiquary and Indian Historical Quarterly conveyed their research articles, in a peace meal manner to interested readers. These journals ceased publication long back, therefore, much valuable and painstaking research done by the scholars of the old generation lies buried in their old files. Our best homage to the hallowed memory of these pioneers could be to compile and present their efforts to the inquisitive minds of the new generation. This book is a result of that craving.

The present book in two volumes presents 62 articles on the Historical Geography of India written by eminent scholars of the older generation. Their insightful wisdom and painstaking research reflected in these articles will guide us a correct understanding of the historical place-names connected with political as well as religious march of our civilizational history.

The articles have been arranged here is some topical order.

1. The first two articles penned down by H C Ray Chaudhuri and Vasudeva Sharan Agarwal respectively, clearly underline the importance and utility of the discipline called Historical Geography.

2. Subsequent articles present geographical data available in individual literary or epigraphic sources—such as Panini, Dharmashastras, Yadavapakasa, Agni Purana, Kalachuri inscriptions etc.

3. Next section brings together efforts by different scholars to identify and trace the history of specific historical places or pilgrimage centres. For example Sri Lanka of the Ramayana, Dwarka and Kurukshetra of the Mahabharata etc. These articles would show how scholars have strived to identify the location of an ancient place-name, and how they have sometimes arrived at quite different identifications.

4. In some articles the data about ancient ethnic groups or tribes such as ancient Tamils, Nagas, Chedis, Hunas, Yavanas, Kambojas etc. has been analysed.

5. Very useful data on fauna found in the Valmiki Ramayana and in the writings of Kalidasa has also been included in these volumes.

We hope that the material collected here will be found not only useful but inspiring for further reserarch in this important but neglected field of study.

Devendra Swarup

Contents

Plates

24

Rasātala or the Under-World

(*A forgotten country*)

N. L. Dey

Rasātala is not a myth; it is a forgotten country

Is Rasātala a myth, a creation of the poet's brain? Have the seven spheres of Rasātala below the earth been invented as a counterpart of the seven *Lokas* or worlds[1] above the earth. The name of Rasātala, or its synonym Pātāla, occurs in almost all the ancient Hindu works of importance, professing or pretending to give an account of historical events of ancient times. If Rasātala be an idle phantasm or a mere figment of the poet's imagination, the writers of different periods would not have tried to keep it alive. Rasātala has been peopled with serpents, demons, birds and animals, invested with the physical and mental qualities of a human being. Śeṣa Nāga, the king of the serpents, is described[2] as seated upon a throne with all the paraphernalia of royalty about him. His head is bedecked with a crown, his ears have pendants, and his arms extend up to his knees. He is clothed in black, and has, on his two sides, attendants waving the fly-whisks. He is also surrounded by his ministers and courtiers. He does not hiss, but talks like a human being, and talks wisdom like a veritable Veda-Vyāsa.[3] There were demons fearless, warlike, and generous. Bali, for instance, was so generous that he gave everything he possessed to the poor and the Brāhmaṇas[4]. They lived in cities, which in beauty could vie with any "city of heaven", containing houses, gardens and palaces; and Hiraṇyapura, the capital of the Daityas has been described as looking beautiful with roads and gateways specially prepared by Brahmā for the Dānavas[5]. The demons did not wander in forests and live in caves like the primitive man, but they possessed various amenities of civilisation. The Suparṇa (or Garuḍa) birds were human beings to all intents and purposes, except for their beaks and wings[6]. The Surabhis or the cowtribe lived in Rasātala, and they could speak like human beings and prophesy future events.[7] In spite of paucity of information we have enough evidence to conclude that Rasātala is a reminiscence of a primeval age when the Indo-Aryans lived with the Iranians in their ancient home in Central Asia called Ariana by Strabo, which is the Airyana-vīja of the *Avesta*[8]. This Airyana-vīja, which means the "Aryan seed," is evidently Azerbaijan or Azerbijan which was originally a province of ancient Media or "mad", as it was called the Uttara (north) Madra of the Purāṇas, and now a province of Persia. The river Daitya which flowed through it is the river Aras which divided Media from Armenia. Some authorities consider Media to be the original home of the Aryans.[9] Herodotus also says, "These Medes were called in ancient times by all people Arians[10]." Azerbaijan and the countries to the north were therefore known as Ārya of the Ṛg-veda and Hara of the Bible. In later times, the boundaries of Ariana were extended to the north of the valleys of the Oxus and the Jaxartes, and on the east, as far as the Indus[11], by conquest from the Scythians or Hunnic tribes who belonged to the Turanian race. There can be no doubt that either difference of opinion about religious matters perhaps when the schism regarding the supremacy of Varuṇa in the hierarchy of the gods originated as indicated by the promiscuous application of the words Sura and Asura to Varuṇa in the earlier portions of the Ṛg-veda[12], or the frequent inroads and depredations of the neighbouring barbarous tribes, or perhaps both, impelled the Indo-Aryans, the ancestors of the Hindus and the Pārsis, to migrate to the Punjab in India. They brought with them the memory of these invasions, wars, and oppressions, to which they were frequently subjected by the barbarous tribes surrounding the place where they lived with the Iranians. Daityas, Dānavas, Asuras, and Nāgas[13] are mentioned in the works of the Vedic period and in subsequent works down to the latest Purāṇa. Though the word "Rasātala" does not appear in the Vedas, yet the word must have been handed down by oral tradition, like the hymns of the Vedas, as the abode of the people called "Demons" and "Serpents". The word *Rasā* appears in the Ṛg-Veda[14], and the word *Rasātala* in the Rāmāyaṇa[15]. In the latter work, it is described as the abode of the Daityas, Dānavas, Surabhi cows, and Nāgas (Serpents) situated below the earth. But though placed below the earth, Rasātala does not appear then to have been divided into seven spheres, but the Rāmāyaṇa describes it as a flat country containing cities, palaces, lakes and mountains. In the Mahābhārata[16] and in subsequent works, we see it divided into seven spheres. The story of Rasātala has a substratum of truth, around which, has grown up a body of fiction in course of time. The real signification of the word has been lost, and the facts and concepts connected with the country and its people have been forgotten.

A whole country has been turned into a visionary land peopled by creatures of fantastic shapes, and uncouth descriptions.

Meaning of Rasātala

The lexicographical meaning of Rasātala is *adhobhuvana* that is "below the world". The place has evidently been divided into seven spheres in imitation of the seven spheres above the earth peopled by beings of different descriptions.

The Country of Rasātala

But in order to ascertain which country was meant by Rasātala, we must examine the word itself. *Rasātala* consists of two words *Rasā* and *Tala*. *Rasā* is mentioned in the Ṛg-veda[17] as the name of a river. It is the same as the Raṅghā of the *Avesta* which has been identified by Profs. Keith and Macdonell with the Jaxartes[18]. This identification is correct, as Rasā is evidently a corruption of Araxes, the classical name of the Jaxartes. Its identification with the Indus by Windischmann does not appear to be correct, as the river Indus was too well-known at the time of the Ṛg-veda[19] by the name Sindhu to be called by the name Rasā. The word *Tala* is the Sanskritised form of *Tele* which is another name for the Huns. Dr. J. J. Modi in his *Early History of the Huns* says, "the Huns were called Te-le or Til-le"[20]. The compound word *Rasātala* therefore means the country on the banks of the Jaxartes where the Huns resided. According to the Hindu works Rasātala has both a general and specific signification. In its general sense it means the whole region called "Rasātala" which is below the earth, and in its specific sense it means one of the seven spheres into which it is divided. As *Rasā* means the *world,* Rasātala in its general sense means the "world" or the country of the Huns, that is Tartary or Central Asia, including Turkestan; and as the name of a particular "sphere" or province of that country, it is the valley of the Jaxartes where the Huns resided. There can be no doubt that Rasātala originally meant the country of the Huns.

Confirmatory evidence from the Hindu works

The identification of Rasātala with Central Asia, including Tartary and Turkestan, is confirmed by the very works which place it below the earth. The Rāmāyaṇa[21] says that Rāvaṇa after conquering the Nāgas and Dānavas of Rasātala, emerged through the very hole through which he had entered it, and passed the night on the Sumeru mountain; in other words, Rasātala was close to the Sumeru mountain. The Mahābhārata[22] and the Matsya Purāṇa[23] distinctly say that Meru or Sumeru mountain is in Śākadvīpa. It is also stated in the Mahābhārata[24] that Garuḍa, who lived in Pātāla, having caught an elephant and a tortoise with his nails, wanted to eat them, and accordingly sat upon the branch of a Vaṭa tree (*Ficus Indica*). The branch broke. Some Bālakhilya (pigmy) ṛṣis were performing asceticism on that branch. In order to save the lives of those ṛṣis, Garuḍa took up the branch with his beak and flew to the Gandhamādana mountain where his father Kaśyapa was performing asceticism to ask his advice regarding a suitable place where he could eat the elephant and the tortoise with convenience. At the intercession of Kaśyapa the pigmy ṛṣis left the branch on the Gandhamādana mountain and went to perform asceticism on the Himālaya. Śeṣa, the king of the Nāgas, also started on a pilgrimage from Gandhamādana, and then visited Badarikāśrama in the Himalaya[25]. The Harivaṃśa also places Rasātala near the Gandhamādana and the Mandāra mountains[26]. The western portion of the Himālaya from Garwal was called by the name of Gandhamādana; hence Gandhamādana and the Himālaya were situated to the east of Sumeru Parvata, and there can be no doubt that Gàndhamādana was connected with the Sumeru mountain, which, as stated before, is in Śākadvīpa or Scythia, as one of its seven principal mounṭains. The Matsya Purāṇa[27] also says that Sumeru Parvata was bounded on the west by Ketumāla-varṣa, and according to the Mārkaṇḍeya Purāṇa, the Sakas or the Scythians resided in Ketumāla-varṣa[28]. Sumeru therefore is the Hindukush mountain, the Mount Meros of Arrian[29] situated near Mount Nysa of Niṣāda Parvata of the Purāṇas and Paropamisus of the Greeks[30]. Rasātala consequently must have been situated on the north and west of the Hindukush mountain, that is, it comprised the valleys of the Oxus and the Jaxartes.

Sapta Pātāla or seven spheres of Rasātala

The seven spheres into which Rasātala is divided are : Atala, Vitala, Nitala, Talātala, Mahātala, Sutala, and Rasātala. Rasātala being the country of the Huns, it is natural that its seven 'spheres' or provinces should be named after names of the Huns or rather of the tribes which dwelt in them. (1) *A-tala* derived its name from the *A-tele* or A-telites where the Asura named Bala (Belus of Babylon) resided[31]; (2) *Bi-tala* from *Ab-tele* or *Abi-tele* or Abi-telites, the word *Ab* being a corruption or abbreviation of *Abi-Amu* or the "river Oxus"[32], and Abtele means the Huns who lived on the shores of the Oxus. As the river Hāṭakī[33] or the Zarafshan, which is said to have its source in the Fan-tau mountain to the east of Samarkand near the Great Pamir, is in *Bi-tala,* it must have appertained to Transoxiana (*Māvar-ul-Nahr*) and formed a part of the kingdom of Bokhara. (3) *Ni-tala* from the *Neph-tele* or Neph-telites. In the Bhāgavata[34], the word *Pātāla* (the *Pātāla-tala* of the Devī-Bhāgavata) has been used for Ni-tala, and therefore the 'sphere' Pātāla was the same as Ni-tala. Pātālapura was originally the name of Aśma or

Oxiana, the capital of Sogdiana as we shall hereafter show. (4) *Talātala* is from the *To-charis*. The Asura Maya (Ahura Mazda of the Avesta), the Spiritual Guide of the Māyāvins, dwelt in this sphere[35]. Māyā and Māyāvins are the same as *Maga*[36] and *Magii* (the followers of the Zoroastrian religion). 'Maya' is a corruption of 'maga, or 'magus' who represents Ahura Mazda the architect of the universe, and hence Maya was the architect of the Asuras. The Magii were the "Śākadvīpī Brāhmaṇas brought to India by Śāmba[37] from Scythia. The Mahābhārata[38] mentions that the Brāhmaṇas of Śākadvīpa dwelt in Mṛga, which has been identified with Margiana, the country around Merv[39]. This sphere therefore comprised Margiana.

References

1. *Padma Purāṇa,* Sṛṣṭi-Khaṇḍa, ch. 22:—*Bhūloko'tha Bhuvarlokaḥ Svarloko'tha Mahar Janaḥ Tapah Satyañca Saptaite Devalokāḥ prakīrtitāḥ.*
2. *Harivaṃśa,* ch. 82.
3. *Padma P.,* Pātāla-kh., ch. I.
4. *Harivaṃśa,* ch. 220.
5. *Mahābhārata,* Vana Parva, ch. 172.
6. *Ibid.,* Udyoga, ch. 100.
7. *Ibid.,* Udyoga, ch. 101; *Mārkaṇḍeya P.,* ch. 21.
8. "The first of the good lands and countries, which I, Ahura Mazda, created, was Airyana-Vīja by the good river Daitya" *Vendidad,* ch. 1; see *Sacred Books of the East,* vol. IV, p. 4; Max Müller's *Sciencc of Language* (1873), vol. I, p. 227.
9. Dwight's *Modern Philology,* vol. I, p. 30.
10. *History of Herodotus,* translated by Rawlinson, vol. II, p. 145.
11. Hamilton and Falconer's *Geography of Strabo,* vol. III, p. 119 (Bk. XV, ch. II, 1).
12. *Ṛg-veda,* IV, 42; viii, 51, 9; Macdonell's *History of Sanskrit Literature,* p. 119.
13. For Nāgas, see *Śatapatha Brāhmaṇa,* II, 2, 7, 12; *Āśvalāyana Gṛhya Sūtra,* iii, 41.
14. *Ṛg-Veda,* I, 112, 12; V, 53, 9; X, 75, 6.
15. *Rāmāyaṇa,* Uttara, chs. 24, 25.
16. *Mahābhārata,* Udyoga, ch 101:—*Idaṃ Rasātalaṃ nāma saptamaṃ pṛthivītalaṃ yatrāste Surabhir mātā gavām amṛtasambhavā.*
17. *Ṛgveda,* I, 112, 12; V, 53, 9; X, 75, 6.

18. *Vedic Index,* Vol. II, p. 209; *S.B.E.*, Vol. IV, p. 3; Vambery's *History of Bokhara,* p. 5.

19. *Ṛg veda,* i, 122, 6; iv, 54, 6; iv, 55, 3; x, 64, 9.

20. *JBBRAS.*, vol. xxiv (1916-17), p. 565. Instead of *Til-le* Deguignes has *Tie-le* in his *Histoire. des Huns,* Tome ii, p. 282. *Til-le* therefore is a typographical mistake for *Tie-le.*

21. *Rāmāyaṇa,* Uttara, chs. 24, 25.

22. *Mbh.*, Bhīṣma, ch. II.

23. *Matsya P.,* ch. 121.

24. *Mbh.*, Ādi, ch. 30; Udyoga, ch. 100.

25. *Mbh.*, Ādi, ch. 36.

26. *Harivaṃśa,* chs. 218, 219.

27. *Matsya P.*, ch. 112, *vs.* 42, 43.

28. *Mārkaṇḍeya P.*, ch. 59.

29. McCrindle's *Ancient India as described by Megasthenes and Arrian,* pp. 179, 180.

30. Lassen's *History traced from Bactrian and Indo-Scythian Coins* in *JASB.*, 1840, p. 469 note.

31. *Bhāgavata,* V, ch. 24.

32. *Geography of Strabo,* Vol. I, p. 113, note 4; *JBBRAS.*, Vol XXIV, p. 565.

33. *Bhāgavata,* V, ch. 24.

34. *Bhāgavata,* V, 24, 7:—*Atalaṃ Vitalaṃ Sutalaṃ Talātalaṃ Mahātalaṃ Rasātalaṃ Pātālamiti.*

35. *Ibid.*, V, 24; VII, 10, 53:—*Māyinām Paramācāryaṃ Mayam śaraṇamāyayuḥ.*

36. *Kūrma P.*, Pūrva kh., ch. 49:—*Magāśca Magadhāścaiva mānasā mandagāstathā brāhmaṇaḥ ksatriyo vaiśyaḥ Śūdraścātra krameṇa tu.*

37. *Bhaviṣya P.,* Brahma Parva, chs. 73 ff.

38. *Mbh.*, Bhīṣma, ch. 11.

39. Rawlinson's *Five Great Monarchies,* vol. IV, pp. 25, 26 note: Bretschneider's *Mediæval Researches,* vol. II, p. 103.

25

Rasātala or the Under-World*

(A forgotten country)

Nundo Lal Dey

II

(5) *Mahū-tala* from the *Hae-tele* of Hae-talites, who under the name of Great Yuechi (Kushan) lived between the Jazartes and Chu rivers after the conquest of this tract[1]. Bokhara was a Hae-talite centre and in Bokharian language 'Haital' means 'a strong man'[2]. (6) *Su-tala* from the *Kidarites* or Su-tribes, who lived on the upper Jaxartes and the Oxus. King Bali was confined in Su-tala at Balkh which is a corruption of the Turkish word *Balikh* which means 'the residence of a king'. (7) *Rasātala* is the Sanskritised form of *Rasa-tele,* the velley of the Rasa or the Jaxartes, on the banks of which the Huns resided. This is the general name of the entire region called Rasātala, but with regard to the seventh sphere called Rasātala the *Mahābhārata*[3] says that the Surabhis, or Khorasmii of the classical writers, dwelt in this sphere; it therefore included Kharism or Khiva. We have already stated that for the sphere Ni-tala the *Bhāgavata* has got Pā-tāla, and it should also be stated that for the sphere Talā-tala, the *Viṣṇu Purāṇa* has got Gabhastimat, and Gabhasti appears to be the name of a river in Śākadvīpa[4] or Scythia, which is either the Murgab or the Jaxartes, most probably the former. In the *Sabdaratnāvalī* we have got Tala instead of Talā-tala, and Ta-la represents Tu-ho-lo of Hiuen Tsang, the country of the Tocharis[5]. For the seventh sphere Rasātala, some of the Purāṇas[6] have got Pātāla, but in the *Bhāgavata*[7] Rasātala and Pātala have both been mentioned as the names of two distinct and separate spheres, and Pātāla, as already stated, has been used for Ni-tala of the other Purāṇas. Pātāla is also used as a synonym for Rasātala as a general name of the entire region. Thus we see that Babylon was in Atala. Fan-tau mountain near the Great Pamir was in Bitala. Asma in Sogdiana was in Ni-tala, Margiana in Talā-tala. Bokhara in Mahā-tala, Balkh in Su-

tala, and Khiva in Rasātala. Hence it appears that the entire region of Rasātala was bounded on the east by the Great Pamir, on the west by the Babylonian empire or Śālmaladvīpa, on the north by the northern boundaries of the countries situated on the north of the Caspian Sea and the Jaxartes, and on the south most probably by the Indian Ocean which was the Southern boundary of Śaka-dvīpa.

Huns and Scythians were Turanians

It will be remarked that at least two of the spheres of Rasātala, namely Talā-tala and Su-tala, derived their names from the Tocharis and Su tribes who were Scythians and not Huns. But it should be stated that both the Scythians and the Huns were Turanians[8]. And most of the Śakas or Scythians were Hunnic tribes[9]. In fact both Herodotus and Strabo include all the Hunnic tribes under the general name of Scythians. The Tocharis, the Takṣaka Nāgga tribe of the *Mahābhārata* and the Takiuks of Scythia, are however stated to be Tak-i-uk Mogals by M. Deguignes[10]. Some of the tribes as the Messagetae were Huns[11], though according to Herodotus they were regarded as a "Scythian race"[12]. It should be here stated that in the 5th century A.D., the Huns lost the original name of Huns and began to be known as Turks, as one of their tribes of that name became very powerful. Later on the Mogul tribe of Huns under Jengiz Khan became very powerful, and this tribe gave its name to the whole nation[13].

Identification of the names of nāgas with those of Hunnic tribes Śeṣa and others

Rasātala has been principally described as the abode of the Nāgas, and the *Mahābhārata*[14] gives two lists of names of the principal Nāgas who lived there, and the *Padma Purāṇa*[15] also gives a list of their names. Though these names are stated to be names of individual Nāgas, yet it appears that each name represents a tribe of Huns. Śeṣa represents the "Sses" of Sogdiana[16], the capital of which was Marakanda or Samarkand[17] Vāsuki the Usuivis; Karkoṭaka the Kara-Kasak, the Kasaks were also called Kirghiz. They lived all over Central Asia; a dynasty of the tribe of Huns reigned in Kashmir after the Gonanda dynasty[18].

Takṣaka

Takṣaka, as stated before, represents the Tocharis, the Tak-i-uk Moguls who lived in Tocharistan or Bactria, after whom the whole country was called Turkestan. They are the Tuṣāras of the *Matsya Puraṇa*[19] and Tukhāras of the *Bṛhat-saṃhitā*[20] by Varāha-mihira. They were the inhabitants of the country Tu-ho-lo of Hiuen Tsang, which may phonetically represent Tur, and so indicate the origin of Turan, the region to which Wilford assigned the Tukharas[21]. Parīkṣit of the *Mahābhārata* was treacherously assassinated by a Takṣaka.

Elāpatra

Elāpatra represents the Ephthalites or the white Huns, from whom the word Pātāla, as the name of the seven spheres, has been derived and subsequently applied to the whole country of Rasātala. The Ephthalites were a most powerful tribe of Huns who lived in Rasātala or the valley of the Jaxartes, and who invaded India long before the time of Alexander the Great, and made settlements in the Punjab and in Sindh. They overran Persia and killed its king Firoz in a battle in 484 A.D. Their descendants also invaded India at the time of Skandagupta. The corruption of the two words *Elā* and *Patra* is *Alā* and *Pātā* respectively, and it is possible to conceive that the transposition of these two words might have led to the formation of the word *Pātāla*. There can be no doubt, however, that the word Pātāla has been derived from the Ephthalites, and it is confirmed by the fact that from the settlement of the Ephthalites in Sindh, who have been called Sogdoi[22] by Alexander's historians, the delta of the Indus was called Pātalene and its capital was called Pātāla[23]. The *Mahābhārata*[24], however, says that the word Pātāla means a "great fall" of water from the moon and other "watery heavenly bodies". This is of course a mythical interpretation. In the seventh century Hiuen Tsang mentions that the serpent Elāpatra lived in a tank on the north-west of Takṣaśilā at Hassan Abdul in the Punjab and obtained a share of the relic after Buddha's death[25]. The Ephthalites were also called Haetalites, and another of the seven spheres, Mahātala, has derived its name from them. In the Bokharian language "Haital" means a "strong man",[26] as stated before.

Ugraka and other Nāgas

Ugraka represents the Uigurs[27], Āryaka the Ariacæ[28], Sumukha the Kumüks[29], Tittari the Tatars, afterwards called Tartars[30], Aśvatara the Aspasians or Asis[31], and perhaps the Assakenoi of Arrian[32], Śālipiṇḍa the Salor, the oldest Turkoman tribe recorded in history[33]; Dadhimukha the Dahæ, a celebrated Scythic tribe who lived on the shores of the upper Jaxartes, after whom the whole of Central Asia was called the "country of the Dahis"[34]; Āpūraṇa, the Aparnis of Strabo[35], who lived in the 1st century B.C.; Kāliyas and Kālakeyas the Karas described as pitiless robbers and an exceedingly savage tribe of Turkomans[36].

Muṣakāda represent the Massagatæ, who, according to Herdotus, lived on the east of the Caspian Sea[37] beyond the Araxes[38] which is evidently the river Jaxartes, as it is said that Asia is bounded "on the north by the Caspian and the river Araxes which flows towards the rising sun.[39]" They were the Maśaka (Kṣatriya) of Śākadvīpa[40]. They have been included among the Su tribe of Scythians along with the

Tocharis and the Dahæ, but they were actually Hunnic tribes[41]. It is evident that after their name the province of Śākadvīpa, in which they lived, was called Maśaka, the Massagetai of Ptolemy[42]. The Massagetæ, which means the "Great Gete", were a very powerful race, and Cyrus king of Persia lost his life in a battle with their queen Tomyris and the greater part of the Persian army was destroyed. They were known by the name of Getes, – "Djetes," that is Jetes of Transoxania, – and also by the name of Jits or Jāts in India, and some of the Rajput clans claim descent from the latter[43]. At the time of the *Rāmāyaṇa,* many communities of Massagetæ had settled in the Deccan as has been allegorically described in the story of Jaṭāyu and his brother Sampāti. In fact Jaṭāyu is a contraction of Massagetæ or a variant of Gete. Jaṭāyu lived in Janasthāna and Sampāti dwelt in a cave in the Vindhya mountain in Mysore, which should not be confounded with its namesake in upper India[44], while the rest of the Deccan was interspersed with the settlements of Rākṣasas who were also Turanians and belonged to the Hunnic tribe. According to Herodotus, who flourished in the 5th century B.C., the Massagetæ were cannibals, as he mentions it among their customs : 'Human life does not come to its natural close with this people; but when a man grows very old, all his kinsfolk collect together and offer him up in sacrifice; offering at the same time some cattle also. After the sacrifice they boil the flesh and feast on it; and those who thus end their days are reckoned the happiest. If a man dies of disease they do not eat him, but bury him on the ground, bewailing his ill-fortune that he did not come to be sacrificed. They sow no grain, but live on their herds, and on fish, of which there is great plenty in the Araxes. Elsewhere Herodotus says, "The Scythian soldier drinks the blood of the first man he overthrows in battle"[45]. These were the customs of almost all the Scythic tribes though Herodotus speaks of cannibalism with special reference to the Massagetes only. Strabo also says that some of the Scythians were ferocious and were cannibals[46]. Herodotus himself, it appears, did not believer that the Massagetæ were a Scythian race; he, however, says that by many they were regarded as such, and in their dress and mode of living they resembled the Scythians[47]. It seems that like the Suparṇas and Surabhis of the Su tribe, some of the Massagetæ to which Jaṭāyu belonged, became early converts to the Aryan religion and subsequently became followers of Viṣṇu, as it appears from the fact that though Massagetæ, Jaṭāyu and his brother Sampāti have been stated as the nephews of Garuḍa being the sons of his brother Aruṇa[48] who belonged to the Su-tribe. As a Vaiṣṇava, Jaṭāyu gave up eating flesh, while his brother Sampāti manifisted some hankering after the flesh of the monkeys whom he saw from his cave at Vindhyācala where he resided, and perhaps for this provlivity his wings were said to have been scorched by Sūrya, the Sun-god, who is identical with Viṣṇu. As Garuḍa was the vehicle or charioteer of Viṣṇu and Aruṇa of Sūrya, so Jaṭāyu, on account of his conversion to Vaiṣṇavism, is said to have been an ally of Daśaratha, fought hard with Rāvaṇa and was killed by him, while Sītā was being abducted by him in the wilds of Daṇḍakāaṇya; and it was Sampāti who gave a clue to the monkeys as to the whereabouts of Sītā[49].

(*To be continued*)

References

* Continued from p. 136.

1. *JBBRAS.*, vol. xxiv, p. 568; Smiths *Early History of India,* pp. 218, 242.
2. *JBBRAS.*, vol. xxiv, pp. 567, 565.
3. *Mbh,* Udyoga, ch. 101.
4. *Viṣṇu P.*, ii, chs. 4, 5.
5. Beal's *Records of the Western World,* vol. I, p. 37 n.
6. *Agni P.*, ch. 120, vs. 1, 2.
7. *Bhāgavata,* V, ch. 24.
8. *JBBRAS.*, vol. IV, pp. 548, 564.
9. *JBBRAS.*, vol. IV, p. 563.
10. Tod's *Rājasthān,* vol. I, ch. 6, p. 60.
11. *JBBRAS.*, vol. XXIV, p. 562.
12. Rawlinson's *History of Herodotus,* vol. I, p. 103; see also M. Hue's *Travels in Tartary, Tibet and China,* vol. I, p. 237.
13. *JBBRAS.*, vol. XXIV, p. 558.
14. *Mbh.*, Ādi, ch. 35; Udyoga, ch. 102.
15. *Padma P.*, Sṛṣṭi, ch. 6.
16. *Geography of Strabo,* vol. II, pp. 240 note, 245.
17. McCridle's *Invasion of India by Alexander the Great,* p. 40.
18. Vambery's *History of Bokhara,* p. 103; Dr. Stein's *Rājataraṅgiṇī,* vol. I, bk. iv; Vambery's *Travels in Central Asia,* pp. 345, 368.
19. *Matsya P.*, ch. 121.
20. *Bṛhat-saṃhitā,* ch. 16.
21. Beal's *RWC.*, vol. I, p. 37 note.
22. McCrindle's *Invasion of India by Alexander the Great,* p.354.
23. McCrindle's *Ancient India as described by Megasthenes and Arrian,* p. 183 note.

24. *Mbh.*, Udyoga, ch. 98.
25. Beal's *RWC.*, vol. I, p. 137; vol. II, p. 41.
26. *JBBRAS.*, vol. XXIV, p. 565.
27. For the name see Prof. Max Müller's *Science of Language,* vol. I, p. 348.
28. *Ibid.*, I, p. 242.
29. *Ibid.*, I, p. 349. For *Sumukha* the *Padma P.* (Sṛṣṭi, ch. 6) has *Durmukha.*
30. *Ibid.*, I, pp. 349, 342; Sir Henry Yule's *Marco Poli,* vol. I, p. 12 note.
31. Tod's *Rājasthān,* vol. I, p. 61; McCridle's *Invasion of India by Alexander the Great,* p. 60.
32. McCridle's *Ancient India as described by Megasthenes and Arrian,* p. 180.
33. Vambery's *Travels in Central Asia,* p. 304.
34. *Farvardin Yast* (XIII), 144 in the *SBE.*, vol. XXIII; *JBBRAS.*, vol. XXIV, p. 548.
35. *Strabo.*, bk. XI, ch. viii, 2, trans. by Hamilton and Falconer, vol. II, p. 243.
36. Vambery's *Travels in Central Asia,* p. 304; *Mbh.*, Vana, ch. 100.
37. Rawlinson's *Herodotus,* bk. I, ch. 204. (vol. I, p. 104).
38. *Ibid.*, bk. I, ch. 20; vol. I, p. 103. Tod also says "We will merely add that the kingdom of the Great Gete whose capital was on the Jaxarted preserved its integrity and name from the period of Cyrus to the fourteenth century, when it was converted from idolatry to the faith of Islam". (*Rājasthān,* vol. I, p. 97).
39. Rawlinson's *Herodotus,* bk. IV, ch. 40 (vol. I, p. 302).
40. *Mbh.*, Bhīṣma, ch. 11.
41. *JBBRAS.*, vol. XXIV, pp. 548, 562.
42. *Mbh.*, Bhīṣma, ch. 11.
43. Tod's *Rājsthān,* vol. I, p. 97; Vambery's *History of Bokhara,* p. 174.
44. *Rāmāyaṇa,* Araṇya, ch. 49; Kiṣkindhyā, ch. 56.
45. Rawlinson's *Herodotus,* vol I, pp. 109, 312.
46. Hamilton and Falconer' *Strabo,* bk. VII, ch. III, 9 in Vol. I, p. 464.
47. Rawlinson's *Herodotus,* vol. I, p. 103, 108.
48. *Padma P.*, Sṛṣṭi, ch. 6.
49. *Rāmāyaṇa,* Araṇya, ch. 15; Kiṣkindhyā, chs., 56, 58.

26

Rasātala or the Under-World*

Nundo Lal Dey

III

Subāhu and other Su tribes

Subāhu, Śrīvaha, Surasa and Subala[1] represent the Su tribes of Scythians. It is mentioned in the Mahābhārata that while Nārada and Mātali went to Pātāla to seek a suitable bridegroom for the latter's daughter, they after visiting Hiraṇyapura went to the country of the Suparṇas, and then visited the country of the Surabhis[2]. The mention of Hiraṇyapura in Pātāla gives us some indication where to seek for it. Kaśyapa had thirteen wives; he had by his wife Diti two sons, Hiraṇyākṣ and Hiraṇya-kaśipu, who were the ancestors of the Daityas; and the sons by his wife Danu were called Dānavas. Hiraṇyapura was the capital of the Daityas and Dānavas. It will be observed that on the south-eastern side of the Caspian Sea. there was an ancient town called Hyrcania, which was the capital of the country of the same name; it was situated near the modern town of Astrabad. On the southern and western sides of the Caspian Sea and immediately to the east, according to some authority, to the north of Media was the country of the Kaspii or Kaspios. The Caspian Sea was called by the name of "Mare Caspium or Hyrcania" by the classical writers. The name of Hyrcania appears to be connected with those of the two brothers Hiraṇyākṣa and Hiraṇya-kaśipu, the "Ādi" or primitive Daityas who founded a royal dynasty[3], and the name of the Kaspii also appears to be connected with that of their father Kaśyapa. It is curious that the royal Scythians claim their descent from Colaxais[4], who is perhaps identical with Kaśyapa, the progenitor of the Daityas, Dānavas, Asuras, Nāgas and other Turanian tribes, who were, of course, non-Aryans. There can be no doubt therefore that the Daityas and Dānavas lived on the southern and western sides of the Caspian Sea and on the north and the east of the ancient country of Ariana. Hyrcania therefore was the Hiraṇyapura of the

Mahābhārata. From Hiraṇyapura, Nārada and Mātali went to the country of the Suparṇas[5] or Garuḍa birds. The names of all the clans which belonged to this tribe commenced with Su[6], and therefore they must have belonged to the Su tribe of Scythians. They evidently lived on the north of Hyrcania, and their country was separated from the latter by the river Atrik, the ancient name of which was Sarnius which is apparently a corruption of Suparṇa. Sarnius therefore separated the kingdom of Hiraṇyapura from the country of the Suparṇas. Hence the Suparṇas lived in Turkestan, including the Trans-Caspian district, bounded on the west by the Caspian Sea, on the south by the river-Sarnius, and on the north by the river Jaxartes. Strabo also mentions that on advancing from the south-east of the Caspian Sea towards the east, the nations to be met with were the Dahæ, Masaagetæ etc., who belonged to the Su tribe[7]. From the country of the Suparṇas, Nārada and Mātali went to the country of the Surabhis or the cow-tribe[8]. Surabhi is apparently the Sanskritised form of Khorasamii of the Greek writers. The country of the Surabhis therefore was situated on the north of the Oxus; it is now called Kharism or the Khanat of Khiva; it is also called Urgendj or Orgunje[9], which is the Urjaguṇḍa of the Matsya Purāṇa[10]. Strabo distinctly says that "the Khorasmii belong to the Massagetæ"[11] and therefore there can be no doubt that the Khorasmii or the Surabhis belonged to the Su tribe. It appears that Saramā, who was sent by Indra to ascertain the place where the cows robbed by the Paṇis and Parnis of Strabo, as the Dahæ were called, who lived on the eastern side of the Caspean Sea[12], had been kept concealed, was also a Scythian. Saramā apparently represents the tribe of "Sarmatians, who are Scythians" and who lived on the north of the Caspian Sea[13]. Su-parṇas and Su-rabhis, and Saramā, who is described as a 'fair' woman, belonged to the Su tribe of the Scythians, and it appears that they were the early converts to the Aryan religion. They were taken into the communities of Aryans, and to each converted tribe was assigned some particular duty. Thus the Suparṇa tribe became their charioteers, as Garuḍa, called also Suparṇa, was the charioteer of Viṣṇu, and his brother Aruṇa was the charioteer of Sūrya. Su-bāhu, which means 'one with beautiful arms as the same as Su-parṇa, which means 'one with beautiful plumage or wings'[14]. It appears that the Suparṇas were also called Śrīvaha[15] which means "beautiful". It has already been stated that Su-tala received its name from the Ki-darites. It cannot be ascertained whether the word *Śrī* is a corruption of *Ki-darites* or not, but there can be no doubt that *Su* stands for *Ki* of *Ki-darites,* as the Turanian *k,* or rather the non-Aryan *k* is equivalent to Sanskrit *s,* as *Sumukha* for *Kumiḳc, Surbhi* for *Khorasmii, Śālmala-dvīpa* for *Chal-dia.* It should be stated here that according to Drouin, the Kidarites were a Hunnic tribe different from the Ephthalites[16]. The Surabhi converts became the milkmen and soothsayers of the Aryans. According to Herodotus there were many people in Scythia who could foretell the future by means of willow wands, and it appears that the Surabhis were espacially endowed with power of prophecy[17]. It was purely a Magian prctice[18]. Surabhis were also called Surasa and Subala for supplying milk, and Vaśiṣṭha's 'cow', which evidently belonged to the Surabhi tribe, was called Subalā[19]. The Saramā coverts became door-keepers and watchmen[20] of the ancient Aryans. Saramā, according to the Bhāgavata, was one of the wives of Kaśyapa[21].

Names of Garuḍa

That the Suparṇas were early converts to the Aryan religion is confirmed by the fact that Dr. Spooner, was very much impressed "with the striking iconographical resemblance between the sculptured images of Garuḍa in India and the customary figure of Ahura Mazda in ancient Persian Art", and says that he found same relation between Garuḍa, the vehicle or Viṣṇu, and Garō-nmānem, the abode of Ahura Mazda in the Avesta[22]. Dr. Modi objects to this identification on the ground that one has to take the Avesta *n* for the Indian *d*[23]. But Dr. Spooner was correct in his identification, as his statement is confirmed by the Mahābhārata. Garuḍa, while carrying the elephant and the tortise with his nails, was invited by a Banyan tree (*Ficus Indica*) to sit upon its branch and eat them, and he was addressed "Oh Garut-man, you sit upon my extensive branch one hundred yojanas wide and eat the elephant and the tortoise"[24].

The Amara-koṣa and other lexicographies and the Padma Purāṇa[25] have got Garutmān as one of the names of Garuḍa[26]. The abode or paradise of Ahura Mazda named Garōnmānem[27] is also called by the names of Garōtmān in the Palhavi commentary of the Avesta[28], Garothmān by the Parsis[29], Garodmān[30] and Garō-demāna[31] in the Avesta. Garut-mān of the Mahābhārata and the Padma Purāṇa therefore appear to be identical with Garotman, Garothmān and Garoḍmān. But as the bird saved the lived of the Bālakhilya ṛṣis by holding up the broken branch with his beak, the ṛṣis bestowed upon him the name of Garuḍa for his power of bearing such an immense burden, and since that day he has called Garuḍa[32]. It is therefore clear that his foemer name was Garutmān and not Garuḍa. It is also related that while Garuḍa was carrying away *amṛta* or nectar in order ot release his mother Vinatā from her thraldom, Indra hurled at him his thunderbolt. It did him no injury whatever, yet in deference to the ṛṣis with whose bone the thunderbolt was manufactured, he gave up a feather which was so beautiful that the gods conferred upon him that title Suparṇa, and since that day he has been called Suparṇa and he became a friend of Indra[33], which perhaps indicated that in the religious schism he sided with the party of Indra. Garuḍa's name is mentioned in the Taittirīya Āraṇyaka[34]. This clearly proves that the Su tribes of the Scythians had become converts to the Aryan religion at a remote period, long before the Indo-Aryans migrated to the Punjab. Dr. Modi says, "The Su tribe, which was attacked (by the Huns), consisted of the different Turanian tribes, such as the Messagatœ, Tochari, and Dahæ, who lived on the frontiers of Persia on the shores of the Upper Jaxartes"[35].

Animal shapes of Scythian converts

It will be remarked that notwithstanding the inclusion of the Scythian coverts into the Aryan communities, some distinction appears to have been made between them and the true Aryans by ascribing to them some animal forms with a view to denote their Turanian origin. Thus the Suparṇas were considered as birds, the Surabhis as cows, the Saramās as dogs. To other Hunnic converts was given the shape of snakes.

Fight between the Elephant and the Tortoise

The episode of the fight between the *Gaja* and the *Kacchapa* that is the Elephant and the Tortise, as related in the Mahābhārata and the Purāṇas,[36] is an allegorical description of a protracted war between the people of Gazaka or Gaza – representatives of the Aryans, and the now extinct tribe called Kaspii (the Turanian Dānavas), till they were both exterminated by Garuḍa, (the Turnanian Huns). This is a traditional account of a war between the two races at a remote period before the Aryan migration to India. Gazaka or Gaza, as it was called, was the summer capital of Atropatene[37], modern Azerbijan, one of the two divisions into which ancient Media was divided, Atropatene being the eastern division. According to Pliny[38], the Kaspii lived on the north of Media along the Caspian Sea near the river Cyrus or the modern Kuru, on the southern side of Armenia and Albania. According to Strabo their country called Caspiana appertained to Albania[39], but elsewhere he designated them by the name of Caossæi and says that they lived to the east of Media[40]. There can be no doubt therefore that they lived on the eastern side of the Media but towards the north. The Kaspii were a famous tribe, as after their name the Caucasus mountain is called Mount Kaspius and the Hyrcanian Sea the Caspian Sea[41]. There can be no doubt that the country of the Kaspii adjoined Atropatian media or Azerbijan. The Kaspii have been described by Strabo[42] as a barbarous people who starved to death those among them who were above seventy years of age by exposing them in a desert place. They were a tribe of marauding bandits who never lost an opportunity to exact tribute from the Median kings[43]. It is very probable that the name of the Kaspii suggested the name of Kaśyapa as the progenitor of the Turanian race. In the Atharva-Veda Kaśyapa denoted a tortoise[44]. Gazaka was situated on the south-western side of the Caspian Sea and on the south-eastern side of lake Urumiya, and the fight between the Gaja and the Kacchapa is said to have taken place near the sea-shore, evidently the shore of the Caspian Sea. Garuḍa, after he had carried the Nāgas (serpents) on his back at the command of the latter's mother Kadru and at the request of his own mother Vinatā to *Ramaṇīyaka-dvīpa*[45] learnt at that place about his mother's thraldom to Kadru and also the means of her emancipation from her servitude. Garuḍa felt very hungry, and by the direction of his mother he devoured myriads od Niṣādas or fishermen on the sea-shore, but his hunger was not satisfied. He therefore went to his father who was performing asceticism on the north of the *Lauhitya Sāgara*[46] or the Erythræan Sea, and by his instruction he took up the elephant and the tortoise, which were of enormous size, with one of his claws and flew to a Baṭa tree (*Ficus Indica*) situated at *Alamba tīrtha,* to eat them. The branch broke and he flew away to a mountain elsewhere and there devoured the elephant and the tortoise[47]. But the Purāṇas go still further. They state that the elephant was very much presses in the fight, and in his despair he prayed to Viṣṇu to deliver him from his difficult position and Viṣṇu went to the spot on his vehicle Garuḍa, killed his enemy and saved him[48]. The Purāṇas, it will be remarked, thus preserve the Aryan origin of Gaja or the Elephant. It will be observed that the entire scene of the story is placed on the western side of the Caspian Sea, which is the Kṣīrasāgara of the Purāṇas, and the *Ramaṇīyakadvīpa* may be easily identified with the *country of Armenia* Ramaṇīyaka being a pleonastic form of *Ramaṇiya* or *Armenia,* and *Alamba* with *Albania,* the capital of the ancient province of the same name now called Shirwan, situated on the shore of the Caspian Sea, as is indicated by the word *tīrtha* attached to the name and by the distinct mention that the foot of the Baṭa tree situated in Alamba was laved by the waves of the 'sea'[49] which was evidently the Casipan Sea. The sence of the whole story therefore comprised Atropatian Media, Caspiana, Armenia and Albania, that is, most of the Trans-Caucasian States. Two facts may be deduced from the allegorical description of the fight. One is that the people of Azerbijan, the capital of which was Gazaka, and which in the language of the Avesta was called Āryavaijam, the supposed original home of the Aryans, were frequently subjected to the invasions and depredations of the barbarous nomad tribes by whom they were surrounded, and were in a constant state of insecurity. Hence it should be inferred that the principal cause of Aryan migration from Iran to India and the countries to the west was not so much for religious schism, as it has been generally supposed, though it may have been one of the causes; but was due to a feeling to escape from the oppression, cruelties and devastations of the barbarous tribes to a place of security where they could enjoy peace and the fruits of their labour in the fields. The other fact that may be deduced from the story is that Garuḍa, one of whose name was Śālmalī[50] or Chaldea, was originally an inhabitant of Chaldea[51] or Mesopotamia, and this is corroborated by the fact that his father Kaśyapa practised asceticism on the north of the Lauhitya (Red) or Erythræan Sea, which in the Pauranic language was called Ghṛta Samudra and which surrounded Śālmaladvīpa[52] or Chal-dea. It is also very probable that Kadru, the mother of the Nāgas, was a Kurd, Carduchi of the ancients[53] as her name indicates, that is a woman of Kurdistan, and that she was married to Kaśyapa ẉho was perhaps the same as Colaxais[54] mentioned by Herodotus as the progenitor of the royal Scythians. Hence it should be inferred that Chaldea was the original abode at least of the Su and other kindred tribes of Scythians, and that they were obliged to emigrate to the east of the Caspian Sea, most probably on account of the growing powers of the Semitic race, as is represented by the story of Garuḍa having carried his deformed brother Aruṇa on his back to the east across the Sea[55]. Garuḍa was a Chaldear or a Mesopatamian from his mother's side; this account for his and his brother Aruṇa's early conversion to the Aryan or Mithraic religion. From the cuneiform inscriptions of Boghaz-Keui and Tel-el-Amarna it appears that the Mitannians or Hittites of Northern Mesopotamia worshipped Mithra and Varuṇa so far back as 1500 B.C.[56] The Iranian Mithra and the Vedic Mitra being the Sun-god, it is very probable that Mitanni was the "Mitravana" of the Bhaviṣya Purāṇa[57].

Sanskrit names of serpents are almost all Hunnic names : Nāgas and other names

It is remarkable that almost all the generic names of the serpents in Sanskrit have been derived from the general and tribal names of the Huns and other Turanian races, as *Nāga* is a corruption of Hiung-nu[58] the original name of the Huns; *Sarpa* corresponds to the tribal name of *Sartaspa* or *Sarwya*[59]; *Uraga* to the *Uigurs*[60], who were the ancestors of the Usbegs. The word *Uraga* could not have been possibly derived from the Urogs, as the Ugric tribes were called after the dismemberment of Attila's Hunnic empire in 462 A.D., because the word existed before that year, and the Ugric tribes should not be confounded with the

Uigurs, an ancient Turkish tribe[61]. *Pannaga* is perhaps a combination of the two words *Parni*[62] (*Paṇi*) and *Nogāi*[63], the former being the name of a Scythic tribe which lived on the banks of the Jaxartes, and the latter lived on the north-east of the Caspian Sea.

Ahi is corruption of *Azi* of the Azi dynasty, the founder of which was Azi Dahāka which literally means (*ahi*) "the fiendish snake". He was a king of Chaldea. He built a palace called Kvirinta or the palace of the Stork in Babylon[64]. He was the counterpart of the Vedic Ahi[65] or Vṛtra, killed by Indra,[66] who was therefore called Vṛtrahan (Verethragna of the Avesta)[67]. The Ahi kings of Babylon belonged, of course, to the Semitic race, but according to the Ṛg-veda[68], Vṛtra's mother was Danu, and therefore he was a Dānava, and consequently he must have been a Turanian. The original seat of Azi myth was on the southern coast of the Caspian Sea[69]. The legend of Azi is localised only in Medic lands[70]. Though Ahi Dāsa is the Sanskrit from of Azi Dahāka, yet I leave it to the philologists to decide whether the word *Daṃśaka* (biter) has not any connexion with the same word Dahāka in its application to Ahi or snake, as Dasyu or Dāsa corresponds with the Iranian Dañhu.

(*To be continued*)

References

* Continued from p. 463 of Vol. I.

1. *Mbh.*, Ādi, ch. 35; Udyoga, chs. 101, 102.
2. *Ibid.*, Udoga, chs. 99, 100, 101.
3. *Bhāgavata,* iii, ch. 17; *Mbh,* Vana, ch. 101.
4. Rawlinson's *Herodotus,* Bk. iv, ch. 6 (vol. I, p. 289).
5. *Mbh.*, Udyoga, ch. 101, v. 1, *Ayaṃ lokaḥ suparṇānāṃ pakṣiṇāṃ pannagāśinam.*
6. *Ibid.*, Udyoga, ch. 101, vs. 2, 3: *Vaiñateyasutaiḥ sūta shaḍbhis tatam idaṃ kulam, sumukhena sunāmnā ca sunetreṇa suvarcesaā. Surucā pakṣirājena subalena ca mātale, vardhitāni prasṛtyā vai vinatākula kartṛbhiḥ.*
7. *Geography of Strabo,* vol. ii, p. 245, sec. 2, and note 2; *JBBRAS.*, vol. xxiv, p. 548.
8. *Mbh.*, Udyoga, ch. 101.
9. Vambery's *Travels in Central Asia,* p. 339; Burnes' *Travels in Bokhara,* vol. iii, p. 162.
10. *Matsya P.,* ch. 121, v. 46.
11. *Strabo,* bk. xi, ch. viii, 8.
12. *Ibid.*, bk. xi, ch. vii, 1.

13. *Ibid.*, bk. xi, ch. ii, 1.
14. *Mbh.*, Ādi, ch. 93.
15. *Ibid.*, Udyoga, ch. 101, v. 5.
16. *JBBRAS.*, vol. xxiv, p. 571 note.
17. Rawlinson's *Herodotus,* vol. I, p. 313 (bk. iv, ch. 67); *Mārkaṇḍeya P.*, ch. 21.
18. Rawlinson's *Five Great Monarchies of the Ancient Eastern World,* vol. iii, p. 130.
19. *Rāmāyaṇa,* Ād, ch. 52.
20. *Ṛg-veda* x, 14, 7-11; see Monier Williams' *Indian Wisdom,* p. 208.
21. *Śabdakalpadruma,* sv. *Kaśyapa.*
22. Dr. Spooner's *Zoroastrian Period of Indian History* in the *Journal of the Royal Asiatic Society,* 1915, p. 427, where he quotes the following passage from the *Vendidad :* – "I invoke Garô-nmānem, the abode of Ahura Mazda." See also Fergusson's *Nineveh and Persepolis,* p. 295 note.
23. Dr. J. J. Modi's *Ancient Pāṭaliputra* in *JBBRAS.*, xxiv, p. 530.
24. *Mbh,* Ādi, ch. 29.
25. *Padma P.,* Sṛṣṭi, ch. 44, *Tañ ca dṛṣṭvā Garutmāṃś ca praṇamya śirsā Harim.*
26. *Śabdakālpadruma, sv.* Garuḍa.
27. *Vendidad,* ch. 32 (150); *Yast,* iii, 1, 4; *S.B.E.*, iv, pp. 214, 215; xxiii, p. 43; *Visparad,* vii: *S.B.E.*, xxxi, p. 345.
28. *S.B.E.*, iv, p. 230 note.
29. *Ibid.*, vol. iv, p. 214 note; xxiii, pp. 317 n., 337 n.
30. *Gāthās,* Yasna, li, 15. Garôḍman means Home of Song, *S.B.E.*, vol. xxxi, p. 184.
31. *Rashn Yast* (xii), 37; *S.B.E.*, xxiii, p. 177.
32. *Mbh.*, Ādi, ch. 30.
33. *Ibid.*, Ādi, ch. 33.
34. *Tait. Ār.* X, 1, 6.
35. *JBBRAS,* xxiv, p. 548.
36. *Mbh.*, Ādi, ch. 29; *Padma P.*, Sṛṣti, ch. 44: –*Tiṣṭhantau vipulau tatra jighāṃsū Gaja-Kacchapau, aprameyau mahisatvau sāgarasthaikadeśataḥ.*
37. *Geography of Strabo,* vol. ii, p. 263.
38. *Ibid.*, vol. ii, p. 218, note 2.
39. *Ibid.*, vol. ii, p. 234.
40. *Ibid.*, vol .ii, p. 264.
41. *Ibid.*, vol. ii, pp. 226, 234.
42. *Ibid.*, vol. ii, p. 258.

43. *Ibid.*, vol. ii, p. 264.
44. *Vedic Index,* vol. I, p. 144; *Artharva-veda,* iv, 207; *Śatapatha Brāhmaṇa,* vii, 5, 1, 5.
45. *Mbh.*, Ādi, ch. 26.
46. *Padma P.*, Sṛṣṭi, ch. 44 :—*Tava tālas tapas tepe Lauhityasyottare tate.*
47. *Mbh.*, Ādi, ch. 30.
48. *Vāmana P.*, ch. 85.
49. *Mbh.*, Ādi, ch. 29.
50. *Amara-koṣa.*
51. *Bhāgvata,* v, 20, where it is said that Garuḍa lived upon the Śālmalī tree (*Bombax Malabaricum*) which gave its name to the division called Śālmala-dvīpa.
52. *Varāha P.*, ch. 89.
53. *Strabo,* Bk. xiv, ch. I, 24.
54. Rawlinson's *Herodotus,* Bk. iv, ch. 6.
55. *Mbh.*, Ādi, ch. 24, vs. 3, 4.
56. *Contemporary Review,* December, 1921, p. 767; Havell's *History of the Aryan Rule in India,* p. 41.
57. *Bhaviṣya P.*, I, 72, 4.
58. *JBBRAS.*, vol. xxiv, p. 544.
59. Tod's *Rājasthān,* vol. I, ch. 7, p. 104.
60. Max Müller's *Science of Language,* vol. I, p. 348.
61. *Ibid.*, vol. I, p. 366.
62. *Strabo,* bk. xi, ch. is, 2; vil. ii, p. 251. *Ṛgveda,* x, 108, 1.
63. Max Müller's *Science of Language,* vol. I, p. 348.
64. *S.B.E.*, vol. xxiii, pp. 60, 61; *Ābān Yast* (V), 29; *Rām Yast* (XV), 19, pp. 253, 254.
65. *S.B.E.*, vol. iv, Introduction, p. 28.
66. *Ṛg-veda,* I, 32, 1; III, 32, 11.
67. *Encyclopædia of Religion & Ethics,* vol. I, p. 792; *Bahrām Yast* in *S.B.E.*, vol. xxiii.
68. *Ibid.*, I, 32, 9; iii, 30, 8; see Max Müller's *Ṛgveda Saṃhitā,* vol. I, 97 note.
69. *S.B.E.*, vol. xxiii, pp. 60, 61.
70. *Ibid.*, vol. iv, p. 1 note.

42. Ibid., vol. ii, p. 240.

43. [illegible] vol. I, p. 14 [illegible] (1820) [illegible]
[illegible]

44. Ibid., [illegible]

45. [illegible]

46. Ibid., [illegible]

47. Ibid., [illegible]

48. [illegible]

49. Ibid., vol. iii, [illegible]

50. [illegible]

51. Ibid., [illegible] it is said that Chanda lived upon the [illegible] the [illegible] which gave its name to the division called [illegible]
[illegible]

52. Ibid., [illegible]

53. [illegible]

54. [illegible]

55. Ibid., [illegible]

56. Gentleman's Magazine, December, 1811, p. 502; [illegible]
[illegible]

57. [illegible]

58. [illegible]

59. [illegible]

60. Max Müller, Science of Language, vol. I, p. 148.

61. Ibid., vol. II, p. [illegible]

62. [illegible]

63. Max Müller, Science of Language, vol. I, p. 246.

64. [illegible]
[illegible]

65. [illegible] Introduction, p. 16.

66. [illegible]

67. [illegible]
[illegible]

68. [illegible]

69. [illegible]

70. [illegible]

[illegible]

27

Rasātala or the Under-World

Nundo Lal Dey

IV

Phaṇi derived from Paṇi

Phaṇi is derived from the word *Paṇi,* the name of a tribe mentioned in the Ṛg veda,[1] which lived in Vala in the bank of the river Vasā. It should, however, be mentioned that Mr. Nagendra Nath Vasu in his *Vaiśya-kāṇḍa,* states in one place that the Paṇis were a branch of the Aryan race,[2] and in another place that "the Paṇis could not have been non-Aryans, but they were Āryas or *Āryabhāvāpanna*' (endowed with the characteristics of Āryas).[3] He further says that they were traders, and lived in India; from India they went and founded the country known by the name of Phœnicia. Following Yāska, he derives from Paṇi the word "Fonik" (Phœnik), by which term the Phœnicians were known to the Greeks and Germans, and he further developed it into 'Vaṇik' i.e. the Vaiśya class of India.[4]

Paṇis were a non-Aryan tribe

Mr. Vasu has made many assumptions and his conclusions are not warranted by facts. He says that the Paṇis were Aryans, thought in the Ṛgveda they are called Dāsas or Dasyus.[5] Sāyaṇācārya and Mahīdhara, whom he has himself quoted, describe them as robbers and Asuras, that is as a non-Aryan race.[6] According to Mr. Vasu's own statement the Bhāgavata has mentioned them along with the Daityas, Dānavas, and other inhabitants of Rasātala.[7] It will be observed also that in the same Purāṇa the word Paṇi "has been used as a synonym for a thief, and Śrīdhara, the commentator of the Bhāgavata, refers to the Paṇis as "Vṛṣ alas" or Śūdras, and not as Vaṇiks or Vaiśyas.[8] Professor Max Müller and Dr. Macdonell, whom Mr. Vasu has cited as his authorities in connection with other matters on this subject, call them demons.[9] And Dr. Macdonell even goes so far as to say that the place called Vala on the Rasā, where the Paṇis kept the cows concealed, has been personified into a demon (Asura).[10] Mr. Vasu admits that the Paṇis lived on the bank of the river Rasā, which has been identified by Dr. Geiger with Raṅgha of the Vendidad. Drs. Keith and Macdonell have identified the river with the Jaxartes.[11] In fact Rasā appears to be a variant, or rather a corrupted form of Ataxes which, according to Herodotus[12] and Strabo,[13] followed through the country of the Massagetæ, or in other words, it has been corrected identified with the Jaxartes. That being so, it must be presumed that the Paṇis, who lived on the bank of the Rasā, were a tribe of the Huns, i.e. they were non-Aryans as stated by Sāyaṇa, Mahīdhara and the Bhāgavata. The Saramā story in the Ṛg-Veda further proves that the Paṇis never heard the name of Indra[14]; they asked Saramā, "What king of man is Indra, O Saramā?" Had they been Aryans they would not have certainly displayed such ignorance about Indra, and it further appears that "the land of the Paṇis does not seem to have fallen within the jurisdiction of the ruler of Div," in other worlds, they lived outside the Aryan country, and this is corroborated by *Ṛk* 5; "Fair Saramā, here are the cows in whose quest thou art running down to the *ends of Div,"*[15] and it also appears from verses 10 and 11 that the Paṇis were on the outskirts of the Aryan country at the time, and therefore Saramā advised them, "O Paṇis, remove yourselves further hence."[16] Moreover, the Devī-Bhāgavata distinctly states that the Paṇis lived in the sixth sphere called Rasātala.[17] It is often mentioned that one of their leaders was Śuṣṇa, and he is described by Dr. Macdonell as a "hisser" or "scorcher,"[18] that is, he possessed all the characteristic of a Nāga or serpent which hisses and throws out flames from its mouth as described in Buddhist works.[19] Ketu, another leader, is well known to have had the form of a snake. The leaders of the Paṇis, therefore, were Nāgas. The Paṇis were constantly at war with the Aryans, not because the priestly class of the latter stole their cows, as it has been said,[20] but because the Paṇis themselves stole the cows of the Aryans, which to the agricultural people formed the most valuable property. Had they been Aryan themselves, they would not have certainly done so. It has been further stated that the Paṇis tended cows and horses, and were traders.[21] The Scythic tribes were nomadic hordes; they did not live in houses and towns[22], and what Herodotus says regarding the Massagetæ applies to the Paṇis also that "they sow no grain, but live on their herds and on fish, of which there is great plenty in the Araxes. Milk is what they chiefly drink."[23] The Scythic tribes knew the art of getting increased milk by artificial means and the mares' milk constituted their chief article of food[24]. By the mistaken application of the Aryan root *Paṇa* to the Turanian word *Paṇi,* it has been sought to deduce that the Paṇis were traders in the modern signification of the word, and to evolve the word *Vaṇik* out of the Turanian word *Paṇi,* though we can understand that from the Aryan root *Paṇa* the Aryan word *Vaṇik* is derived. Hillebrandt says that by Paṇis "a real tribe is meant, the Parnians of Strabo, and that they were associated with the Dahæ (Dāsa)[25]. According to Strabo, the Parṇis were a nomadic tribe which lived on the bank of the Ochus, a tributary of the Oxus, and belonged to the well known tribe of Scythians called "Dahæ Scythæ" after whose name Central Asia was called *Dāhinām Dakhyunām,* "the country of the Dahæ"[26]. Paṇi, therefore, is evidently a corruption like all Sanskrit names of Nāgas, of the Turanian word Parṇi or its variant Paṇi. Mr. Vasu with a glow of patriotic feeling exults over the fact that the Vaṇiks went from India to Syria and founded a colony in Phœnicia which shed such brilliant lusture upon Assyrin, Babylon, Greece, etc. by its civilisation[27]. But Herodotus says, "This nation (the Phœnicians), according to their own account, dwelt anciently upon the Erythræan Sea, but, crossing thence, fixed themselves on the sea-coast of Syria, where they still inhabit. This part of Syria, and all the region extending from hence to Egypt, is known by the name of Palestine"[28]. The *Encyclopædia Britannica* also says that they originally lived on the Erythræan Sea and they settled along the Syrian coast. It further states, "The Phœnicians were an early offshoot from the Semitic stock, and belonged to the Canaanite branch of it...They called themselves Canaanites and their land Canaan; such is their name in the Amarna tablets, Kinahhi and Kinahni[29]." It is therefore clear that the Phœnicians lived on the Erythræan Sea, which by no dint of argument can be construded to mean India or any part of India; it meant either the Red Sea or the Persian Gulf[30], usually the latter. They belonged to the Semitic stock and to the Canaanite branch of it, and their language is called Northern Semitic[31]. Hence the "*Fonik*" (Phœnicians) were not an offshoot of the Paṇis of the Ṛg-Veda, who were Turanians, nor of the Vaṇikas of India, who are Aryans. It is possible that like other Scythic tribes, the Paṇis might have invaded India and founded settlements in the Panjab and other places, but that does not prove that they were the original inhabitants of India, as it has been sought to make out.[32] Mr. Vasu's statement that the word Paṇi (cheese) is derived from the name of the Paṇis[33] is as absurd as the word *dahi* (curd) is derived from that of the Dahæ, to which tribe the Paṇis belonged. The word *Phaṇī,* and not the word Phanik ('Fonik'), is derived from the word *Paṇi,* and *Phaṇī* means a Nāga as the Huns were called in ancient times, and the Paṇis lived in Rasātala or the valley of the Jaxartes.

Names of serpents in Sanskrit were borrowed mostly from the Turanian language

It will be seen therefore that all the generic names of serpents have been derived mostly from the tribal or generic names of the Huns.

Though the words Nāga, Uraga, Sarpa, Ahi, etc. appear to be very common words in Sanskrit, they were originally non-Aryan words absorbed in the Sanskrit language long before grammar as a science came into existence in its present form. The sly, deceitful and treacherous character of the barbarous hordes of Huns, who frequently attacked and subjected the Aryans to cruelties and oppressions in those very remote times when they were living in Ariana, must have led the latter to apply their names to the serpents which resembled them in character and nature of their work[34]. There cannot be any doubt that the original conception about these barbarous hordes was such, though by the lapse of time these Hunnic tribes by coming into frequent contact with Aryan civilisation, imbibed some form of religion from the Aryans and became their allies, for, during the Sūtra period we find the Nāgas invested with all the characters of demi-gods, though still imagined as retaining their ancient form of serpents, and a day called Nāga Pañcamī has been set apart as being sacred to them[35], when Manasā, the sister of Vāsuki, and other Nāgas are worshipped in various parts of India.

Śākadvīpa is the geographical name of Rasātala

Śākadvīpa, generally known as Scythia, is a geographical conception, whereas under the name of Rasātala, the Purāṇas and other ancient Hindu works give an ethnological description of the same region. Herodotus and Strabo, under the comprehensive name of Scythians, included in it all the Hunnic tribes known as Mongolic or Turkic[36]. The Persians use the work Śakā for the Scythians throughout their inscriptions[37]. The Indo-Aryans also use the word Śakā as a general name for the Scythians and the Huns; while describing Śākadvīpa they call its inhabitants Śākas and while describing Rasātala they call its inhabitant Śakas, and while describing Rasātala they call them Nāgas; in their later works[38] and inscriptions, we find that the Huns are called Hūṇas. They were called by different names by different nations of Europe and Asia. They were the Scythians of the Romans, the Sacæ of the Greeks, the Ephtalites or White Huns of the Byzantines, and Yue-chis of the Chinese[39]. According to the Mahābhārata[40] Śākadvīpa was surrounded by Kṣīra Sāgara or the Sea of Kṣīra (or Inspissated milk) which is evidently a corruption of the "Sea of Shirwan[41], as the Caspian Sea was called.

Ariana

It appears that Airyana-vāejo or Iran-vej was originally bounded on the north by the river—Araxes or Arras, on the cast by the Turanian countries, including Caspium and Hyrcania—the countries of the Daityas and Dānavas and other descendents of Kaśyapa, and also by

Śākadvīpa or Scythia—the country of the Nāgas; and on the west by Śālmala-dvīpa or Chal-dia, the Babylonian or Assyrian empire, the country of the Asuras or Assyrians who belonged to the Semitic race. The Aryans were frequently subjected to the inroads and oppressions of barbarous races by whom they were surrounded, and it is very likely that they lived in a constant state of warfare with their Turanian neighbours, who robbed them of their cattle, so necessary for agriculture, their only means of livelihood, as their very name Ārya, meaning "one who ploughs or tills," seems to indicate. Professor Max Müller says, "The Aryans would seem to have chosen this name for themselves as opposed to the nomadic races, the Turanians, whose original name *Tura* implies the swiftness of the horseman."[42] The Aryans, however, gradually extended their territory, both to the north and to the east, by means of conquest and brought most of the Scythic tribes to their subjection; and long before the Indo-Aryans migrated to Hapta Hendu[43], the Sapta-Sindhu of the Ṛg-Veda[44], and settled in the Panjab, their country had extended towards the east to the north of the Hindukush up to the sources of the Oxus and the Jaxartes. The story of Bali and Vāmana, an incarnation of Viṣṇu, which has its germ in the Ṛg-Veda, where Viṣṇu is said to have taken three steps[45], and in the Śatapatha Brāhmaṇa[46] where Viṣṇu is described as a dwarf, confirms this fact as Bali was confined in Sutala, one of the seven spheres of Rasātala, under the surveillance of Nāgas,[47] which indicates that they had by that time become the allies of the Aryans and had been brought under their civilising influence. It is also mentioned in the Rāmāyaṇa[48] that from Varuṇa's house in Rasātala, Rāvaṇa went to Bali's house and it should be borne in mind that in the division of the world Varuṇa had been assigned the kingdom of the west[49] so Rasātala must have been a country situated on the west. It also appears from the Saramā Hymn[50] that the boundary of the Aryan country extended to the north as far as the river Rasā or the Jaxartes, which at the time of the invasion of Alexander the Great also formed the boundary between the Persian empire and the barbarous Scythian tribes[51].

Religion of Scythic tribes

We can very well conceive that the habits, manners, and customs of the Scythians, at least of those who lived in the country washed by the Oxus and the Jaxartes, underwent a considerable change by coming into contact with their civilised Aryan conquerors. In course of time these Hunnic tribes became so much amalgamated with the Aryans that they gave up their nomadic habits, settled in towns, dwelt in houses and worshipped the Aryan gods[52]. In very early times the religion of the Huns was a sort of Mazdaism (*Maga-dharma* of the Bhaviṣya Purāṇa that is the religion of the Magii), or, in other words, a form of Mithraism, long before the advent of Zoroaster[53], the Asura Ṛṣi Jaruthas of the Ṛg-Veda[54], his full name being Zarathustra Spitama. It should be remarked that though Zoroaster was born in Ragh (modern Rae) in Media, or rather in Media Atropatene or Azerbijan[55], yet the scene of this religious activities has principally been placed in Bactria, especially in the court of Vitasa (Vishtaspa) or Gustasp, a king of the Bactrian dynasty of Kavja between the sixth and tenth centuries before the Christian era. Hence their subsequent religion must have been pure Zoroastrianism. Fire was the symbol of the Sun, and fire was the instrumental medium, by which offerings of worshippers were conveyed to heaven. The Purāṇas, therefore, describe the Śakas as Sun-worshippers,[56] and according to the Bhāviṣya Purāṇa, Sun-worship was introduced into India by Śāmba, son of Kṛṣna, from Śākadvīpa or Scythia[57] and by worshipping the god he was cured of leprosy. It is therefore no wonder that the Hindus should endow the Hunnic tribes in the valley of the Oxus with semi-divine power. It is said in the Vāyu Purāṇa that the Sun and the Moon were formerly the gods of the Asuras and that now they have been included among Suras or Aryan gods[58]. It is very probable that the Avestic and Babylonian 'Mithra' (Mith-Ra) and the Vedic 'Mitra' (Mit-Ra) and also the Avestic word 'Athro' the god of fire, and the corresponding Vedic word 'Rudra' (Rud-Ra) the "crying Sun" called "Āditya or Śiva[59] whose form is Fire which is the symbol of[60] the Sun, ('*Ra'* in Sanskrit, meaning Fire), are the later developments of the word '*Ra'* the Sun-god of the ancient Egyptians. Śiva, the later form of Rudra, has a serpent crest like that of *Ra* called *Uracus* in ancient Egypt as a symbol of majesty, holding a trident in his hand like the rod of Ra; the bull Nandi also is as sacred to him as the bull Apis was to Ra (Osiris). Rudra therefore appears also to have been originally an Asura god like the Sun and the Moon as stated in the Vāyu Purāṇa. Śiva was worshipped as Hāṭakeśvara Mahādeva in Pātāla[61]. But it cannot be affirmed definitely whether the Egyptian or the Chaldian civilisation is the earlier of the two until the exploration at Ur and the neighbouring towns Tel-el-Obeid and Eridu is completed. According to the Tel-el-Amarna tablets political marriage between Egypt and Chaldia were of frequent occurrence, which must have affected the religious system of both the countries. There is, however, no reasonable ground for holding in the absence of any strong evidence that Aryan civilisation was later than that of Chaldia or Egypt, as it has been asserted by some. The temple of the Moon at the mound of Mugheir, which marks the site of Ur of the Chaldees (Chaldians) of the Bible, appears to be the oldest temple in the world, containing an inscription dated 2630 B.C., and a well of the Second Dynasty of the early Sumerian period (3600 B.C.). The Devī-Bhāgavata says that the people of Śālmala-dvīpa were worshippers of the Moon god. Besides the temple of the Moon-god Nanna or Sin at Ur, temple of the Sun-god Shamash existed at Larsam and Sippara, and also a temple of the Water-god Ea existed at the mound of Abu Sharian or Eridu, twelve miles south-west of Ur, all these temples were in Southern Chaldia near the Euphrates[62]. But the words Sin, Nanna, and Urki, by which Moon-god is known at Ur,[63] have no affinity with the Avestic Māo, or the Sanskrit Māḥ or Soma, though the Chaldian 'Inzu' closely resembles the Sanskrit 'Indu'[64] neither does Shamash resemble the Avestic Mithra or Vedic Mitra, nor Ea the Babylonian Uru-w-na or Vedic Varuṇa. But these are questions of comparative religion which have not yet been decided. Mahārakkhita was sent to the convert the Turanians into Buddhism; at present the Turanians of Central Asia have adopted the faith of Islam[65]. Kaśyapa is said to have been the progenitor of the gods, daityas, dānavas, serpents, beasts, birds, yakṣas, rākṣasas and other living beings by different wives.[66]

Kaśyapa's wives

He is perhaps the same as Colaxais, the ancestor of the royal Scythians, as stated before. Kaśyapa had thirteen wives : Vinatā and Tāmrā were the mothers of the birds, Kadrū and Surasā of the Nāgas (Hiungnu) or serpents; Surabhi and Krodhavaśā of the beasts; Diti and Danu of the Daityas and Dānavas; Irā of the trees and plants; Khasā of the Yakṣas and Rākṣasas; Ariṣṭā of the Kinnaras and Gandharvas; Muni of the Munis and Apsarases, and Aditi of the gods. We have already stated that Garuḍa the son of Vinatā, was also called Śālmalī, from the fact of his being an inhabitant of Sālmala-dvīpa or Chaldia, which is very significant. His mother Vinatā was evidently an inhabitant of Sālmala-dvīpa and she perhaps represents the country of Biainas, the ancient name of Van – the Vanāyu of the Purāṇas, which now appertains to Armenia. 'Kadrū' represents Karduchi or Kurdistan, a country situated on the eastern side of the Tigris. Many of the Arabs still believe that the Kurds are Turanians, though they are now all Mahomedans. In fact, the Mahābhārata places the whole scence of the quarrel between Vinatā and Kadrū on the weatern side of the Caspian Sea. Tāmrā, the mother of the birds, used metaphorically to denote some Turanian tribes distinguised for the fleetness of their horses, represents Thamara, an ancient town on the Tigris in Mesopotamia on the present site of Kut-el-Amara[67]. Surabhi, the mother of the cattle, that is, of those nomadic tribes which tended cattle, sheep and horses and lived on their milk, represents the country of the Khorasmi or Kharism, modern

Khiva, on the northern-eastern side of the Caspian Sea. Krodhavaśā, the mother of the beasts with sharp teeth and claws, by which is meant those non-Aryan tribes which could attack their enemies and defend themselves from them when attacked represents Kardunias or Babylonia.[68] The word beast perhaps refers to the barbarous wolf-folk race of Num-Ma or Babylonia.[69] Diti represents the country of the Kaspii, which existended to the river Dāitya, the Avgestic name of the river Araxes of Armenia, or the modern Aras.[70] Danu represents a country or province situated on the river Udon (the modern Kuma) on the north of Albània in Sarmatia which was also the country of Saramā. It falls on the western side of the Caspian Sea. Perhaps the Dānus or Dānavas have given their name to the river Don. Surasā represents a country situated on the river Cyrus, the modern Kur which after flowing through Georgia, falls on the western side of the Caspian Sea; it divides Albanis from Armenia. Irā represents a country on the river Rha or the modern Volga, which falls on the north-western side of the Caspian Sea. She is said to have been the mother of trees and plants, which evidently mean nomadic tribes who had no house, but who lived in forests and jungles. Khasā represents a country on the Araxes of Scythia or the Jaxartes in fact, the word Khasā appears to be a corruption of Araxes. "Ariṣṭā," the mother of the Kinnaras or Kimmerii, who originally lived on the Caucasus, perhaps represents the Ust Urṭ plateau between the Caspian Sea and the Sea of Aral. The word Ariṣṭā is a transposition and corruption of the word Ust Urt, evidently a variation of *Ura Urṭu* meaning a *"highland"*[71]. Muni the mother of the Munis and Apsarases, represents the country of Mannai; called also Mannu, which formerly did not appertain to the kingdom of Van or Armenia. Mannai was situated on the northern and eastern sides of Lake Urumiah, the ancient name of which was Kapauta or Spauta Lake (*Sara*), which formerly appertained to Armenia. The inhabitants of the country were called Mannai or Minni[72], the Munis of the Padma Purāṇa; and perhaps the word *Apsaras* is an abbreviation or corruption of *Spauta sara* as probably the female inhabitants of Mannai were called. The name of Aditi, the mother of the Aryan gods Āditya[73], etc., is a negative term used in contradistinction to Diti, the mother of the Daityas; and Aditi was designed as a mother of the gods, because Āditya or Mithra, the Sun, and also the Moon were, as stated before, non-Aryan gods accepted as gods by the Aryans. Aditi, however, does not represent any country. It will be observed therefore that most of the tribes, which belonged to the Turanian race, dwelt originally on the western side of the Caspian Sea, and that almost all the names of Kaśyapa's wives represent the countries or their principal features, specially the rivers of the countries in which they lived. It will be borne in mind that these tribes were nomadic tribes, who dewlt on the banks of rivers for watering their cattle and for catching fish which was one of their staple food. From the story in the Mahābhārata that Garuḍa represented the Su tribe and carried his brother Aruṇa from the western side to the eastern side of the Caspian Sea, it appears that many of the Hunnic tribes, who dwelt on the western side of the Caspian Sea, must have migrated to its eastern side, not only on account of the growing power of the Semitic nations, but also to find food for themselves and fodder for their cattle and horses. In other words, they migrated from the *Atala* sphere to *Sutala, Vitala* and other spheres that is from Śālmala and Kuśa-dvīpas to Śāka and other *dvīpas* : or divisions of Central Asia. We do not know whether the Chaldian theogony is older than that of the Aryans, but it seems that the conception of Prajāpati Dakṣa, whose daughters were married by Kaśyapa, is a development of some of the attributes of the Chaldian god Marodach, the son of Ea, corresponding to the supreme Vedic deity Varuṇa, who was entrusted by the other gods with the creation of men and beasts[74]. The story in the Mahābhārata typifies Turanian migration to the east of the Caspian.

Other inhabitants of Rasātala

Besides the Nāgas, the other inhabitants of Rasātala, as it appears from the Purāṇas, were Dānavas, Daityas, Asuras, Rākṣasas, Yakṣas, Siddhas, Gandharvas and Kinnaras. The Brahmāṇḍa Purāṇa also mentions the aforesaid tribes as residing on the northern side of the Niṣadha Parvata, the Nysa of Arrian and the Paropanisos of Ptolemy, or the Hindukush range[75].

Dānavas

The Dānavas were the sons of Kaśyapa by his wifew Danu. Their capital was Hiraṇyapura, which was evidently Hyrcania near Astrabad on the south-eastern side of the Caspian Sea. The Dānavas were identical with the Dānus of the Avesta, and they belonged to the Turanian race, as they were called "Dānunam Turaṇām."[76]

Daityas

The Daityas were the sons of Kaśyapa by his wife Diti. They appear to be Turanians. The word Daityas is perhaps a corruption of Dūraékaéta mentioned in the Avesta along with the Dānus or Dānavas : "Grant us this. O good, most benevolent Ardvi Sūra Anāhita that we may overcome the assemblers of the Turanian Dānus, Kara Asabana, and Vara Asabana and the most mighty Dūraékaéta, in the battles of this world[77]". Being the descendants of Kaśyapa, they were most probably the tribe, now extinct, called Kaspii by Strabo, after whom the mountain called El Burz, the Durga-śaila of the Mahābhārata[78], on the southern side of the Caspian Sea, was known by the name of Mount Kaspios. If we are right in our conclusion that the Daityas were the Kaspii, then there is every reason to hold that the word *daitya* has some connection with "the good river *daitya*" of the Vendidad as the Araxes of Armenia was called at the time of the Sassanides[79], because the Kaspii, according to Strabo, lived on the banks of that river[80]. Prahlāda, the son of Hiraṇya-kaśipu and grandson of Kaśyapa, was a Daitya, and is said to have been the king of Pātāla, which indicated that the countries on the western side of the Caspian Sea were also included in Pātāla[81].

Asuras

The Asuras have been considered to be Assyrians. Long before the Aryans emigrated to India, Ariana seems to have formed a part of the Assyrian empire which was founded by Asshur, and the Aryans who remember the oppressions to which they were subjected, attached on odium to their name and associated with it all that is barbarous, tyrannical and cruel[82]. Asshur was the capital of the Assyrians in 1820 B.C., and Asshur was the name of their national deity. Rev. K. M. Banerjea says that the word 'Asura' was both and ethnic appellative for the Assyrian nation and also a denominational epithet for the followers of Ahura Mazda[83]. In the early hymns of the Ṛg-Veda[84] the term was applied to Varuṇa as a supreme deity and not as an enemy of the gods. The Asura Bala was an Assyrian, and he has been identified with Bel or Belus, the successor or Nimrod whose lofty temple or "Citadel" was situated in Babylon on the Euphrates[85]. It should also be stated that all the three terms Daityas, Dānava and Asura are promiscuously applied in the Purāṇas to any of the aforesaid non-Aryan tribes[86]. But it is very doubtful that the word *asura* could have been derived from the Assyrians who belonged to the semitic race, as we find that it was applied to all the Hunnic tribes who belonged to the Turanian stock. It is not at all likely that the ancient Aryans, who even in those early times distinguished themselves, their culture and civilisation, were unable to make any distinction between an Assyrian who belonged to the Semitic race and a Hun who belonged to the Turanian race. A Hun and an Assyrian must have differed widely from each other in their physical features, mode of dress, and manners and customs[87]. Neither the word *asura* was used in contradistinction to *sura,* as in later times it has been sought to make out, for the word *asura* is the same as *ahura* or *asshura,* the chief Assyrian deity, the prototype, according to Rawlinson, of the Itanian Ahura Mazda[88], hence no negative meaning can be attached to it. It is, however, very probable that the word *Asura* as applied to the Turanians; originally meant an inhabitant of Osrushna. The ancient country of Osrushna bordered eastwords on Ferghana, southwards on Kesh, northwards on Djadj and westwards or south-westwords on Sogdiana, in short Osrushna was the name of the eastern part of Transoxama, or rather of hte kingdom of Bokhara, commencing east of Samarkand running up to the Thienshan mountian,[89] comprising the Juzzak division[90] which is evidently the "Dizek (now Djizzak)" of Vambery. It was therefore a part of Rasātala or the valley of the Jaxartes. In the pre-hostoric period the predatory hordes of Huns most probably spread themselves from this region to different parts of Central Asia.[91] We can therefore very well conceive that from these inhabitants of Osrushna or Asuras, as they must have been called, their name was extended to all the Huns of Trans-oxiana and Turkestan, and in short, to all the people who belonged to the Turanian race. Burnes also thinks that the lands beyond the Jaxartes "may be safely fixed as the cradle of Scythian, Hun and Tartar inroad'. Hence the Assyrians were called 'Asura' as they lived in Assyria, and the Turanians were called 'Asura' as the original inhabitants of Osrushna. The word *Osiris* the name of the principal deity of the Egyptians, is perhaps a form of *Asura.* The term therefore found the general designation of all non-Aryan races and also of the worshippers of Ahura (Asura) Mazda of Iran.

(*To be continued*)

References

1. *Ṛgveda,* x, 108, 1; Max Müller's *Science of Language,* vol. I, p. 510.
2. *Vaiśya-kāṇḍa,* p. 8.
3. *Ibid.,* p. 13.
4. *Ibid.,* pp. 12, 13.
5. *Ṛgveda,* vii, 6, 3.
6. *"Paṇanti paradravyair vyavaharantī ti Paṇayo'surāḥ"*—Mahīdhara's commentary on the *Vājasaneyī-saṃhitā* (35, 1) : see *Vaiyśakāṇḍa,* p. 7; Sāyaṇa's commentary on the *Ṛg veda,* iii, 31, 5; x, 108.
7. *Vaiśya-kāṇḍa,* p. 7, citing *Bhāgavata,* iv, 24, 3 in correctly; see *Bhāgavata,* v, ch. 24.
8. *Bhāgavara,* v, ch. 9; see Śrīdhara's commentaries on verses 11 and 15 of the aforesaid chapter.
9. Max Müller *Science of Language,* vol. II, p. 510.
10. Macdonell's *History of Sanskrit Literature,* p. 114; see also *Bhāgvata,* v, ch. 24.

11. *Vedic Index of Names and Subjects,* vol. II, p. 209; *Sacred Books of the East,* vol. IV, p. 3.
12. Rawlinson's *Herodotus,* bk. I, ch. 201 in vol. I, p. 103.
13. Hamilton and Falconer's *Strabo,* bk. XI, ch. viii, 6 in vol. II, p. 217.
14. *Ṛg-Veda,* x, 108, 3.
15. *JBBRAS.*, vol. xx, pp. 247, 248–*Three Interesting Vedic Hymns* by Rājārām : *Imā gāva Sarame yā aichha pari Divo antāna subhage patanti.*
16. *Ibid.*, xx, p. 246.
17. *Devī-Bhāgavata,* pt. 8, ch. 20.
18. Dr. Macdonell's *History of Sanskrit Literature,* p. 114.
19. Watters' *Yuan Chwang's Travels in India,* vol. ii, p. 132; *Vinaya Piṭaka,* vol. I, pp. 24-35; *Surāpāna-Jātaka* in Cowell's *Jātaka,* vol. I, p. 206.
20. *Vaiśya-kāṇḍa,* pp. 11, 13.
21. *Vaiśya-kāṇḍa,* p. 8.
22. *JBBRAS.*, IV, p. 555.
23. Rawlinson's *Herodotus,* vol. I, p. 109; Yule's *Macro Polo,* vol. I, p. 252.
24. *Herodotus,* bk. IV, 2 in vol. I, p. 287.
25. *Vedic Index of Names and Subjects,* vol. I, pp. 357, 359, 472; *Ṛg-Veda,* vii, 6, 3, where Paṇis and Dasyus are mentioned together.
26. Hamilton and Falconer's *Strabo,* bk. XI, ch. vii; ch. viii, 2; ch. ix, 2; *Farvardin Yast* (XIII), 144 in *S.B.E.*, vol. xxiii.
27. *Vaiśya-kāṇḍa,* p. 14.
28. Rawlinson's *Herodotus,* bk. VII, ch. 89 in vol. ii, p. 153.
29. *Encyclopædia Britannica* (11th ed.), vol. XXI, p. 449.
30. McCrindle's *Commerce and Navigation of the Erythræan Sea,* pp. 1, 209 note. Śālmala-dvīpa or Chalidia (or Assyria), according to the Varāha Purāṇa (ch. 89) was bounded by Ghṛta Samudra or Sea of Ghṛta (or clarified butter) : Ghṛta Sea is a corruption of Erythræan Sea or Sea of Erythras.
31. Macdonell's *History of Sanskrit Literature,* p. 16.
32. *Vaiśya-kāṇḍa,* pp. 14, 19.
33. *Vaiśya-kāṇḍa,* p. 32, *Panir* is a Persian word, though derived from the common Sanskrit words *Pai* (Payas=milk) and *Nir* (nīra=water) meaning milk without water.
34. See Conolly's *Journey to the North of India,* vol. I, chs. vi-viii.
35. *Āśvalāyana Gṛhya Sūtra,* iii, 4, 1; *Vedic Index of Names and Subjects,* vol. I, p. 440; *Varāha P.*, ch. 24.
36. Max Müller's *Science of Language,* vol. I, p. 361; *Herodotus,* bk. IV, 1-7; *Strabo,* bk. XI, ch. vi.
37. Rawlinson's *Herodotus,* vol. ii, p. 146 note.

38. *Raghuvaṃśa,* IV, *v.* 68.
39. Vambery's *History of Bokhara,* p. 11.
40. *Mahābhārata,* Bhīṣma, ch. 11.
41. Sir Henry Yule's *Macro Poli,* vol. I, p. 59 note.
42. Max. Müller's *Science of Language,* vol. I, pp. 276, 277, 334; *S.B.E.*, vol xxi, Intro., p. xxi.
43. *Vendidad,* ch. 1, *S.B.E.*, vol . iv, p. 2.
44. *Ṛg-Veda,* iv, 28; Max Müller's *Humns of the Ṛg-Veda,* p. 286.
45. *Ibid.*, 1, 22, 17.
46. *Śatapatha-Brāhamaṇa,* XIV, 1, 1, 6; 1, 2, 5, 5.
47. *Harivaṃśa,* ch. 262.
48. *Rāmāyaṇa,* Uttara-kāṇḍa, chs. 23, 24.
49. *Harivaṃśa,* ch. 262.
50. *Ṛg-Veda,* x, 108, 5.
51. McCringle's *Invasion of India by Alexander the Great,* p. 40; *Strabo,* xv, ii, 8.
52. Max Müller's *Science of Language,* vol. I, p. 282.
53. *JBBRAS.*, vol. xxiv, p. 567; Burnes' *Travels into Bokhara,* vol. iii, p. 228.
54. *Ṛg-Veda*, vii, 1, 7; vii, 9, 6; x, 80, 3.
55. *S.B.E.*, vol. iv, Intro., p. xlviii; Rawlinson's *Seventh Great Oriental Monarchy,* p. 296.
56. *Agni-Purāṇa,* ch. 119 :–
    Magā Magadhamānasyā Mandgāś ca dvijātayah.
    Yajanti Śūryarūpaṃ tu Śākaḥ Kṣīrābdināvṛtaḥ. (21).
57. *Bhaviṣya Purāṇa,* Brahma, chs. 72-74; *Brahma P.* Pt. I, ch. 140.
58. *Vāyu Purāṇa,* ch. 68, *v.* 12:–
    Śarabho Śalabhaś caiva Sūryācandramasāv ubhau,
    Asurāṇāṃ Surāv etau Surāṇāṃ sāmpratāv ime.
59. *Kūrma Purāṇa,* pt. I, ch. 10; *Brahmāṇda P.*, ch. 28, *v.* 20.
60. *Ṛg-Veda,* I, 27, 10; vi, 50, 1; I, 98, 2.
61. *Devī Purāṇa,* ch. 8.
62. *Devī-Bhāgavata,* pt. 8, ch. 12; *Bhāgavata,* v, ch. 20. Maspero's *Dawm of Civilisation; Egypt and Chaldœe,* pp. 561, 648, 660. Mr. Wooley, who is now excavating the temple at Ur, calls it by the name of "The Temple of Nanna, the Moon-god". The Sumerians were a branch of the Turanian race. (*JASB.*, 1909, p. 418). The original inhabitants of Assyria and Babylon were Turanians.
63. Maspero, *op. cit.*, p. 654.

64. Maspero, *op. cit.*, pp. 637, 638.
65. Turnour's *Mahāwanso,* ch. xii; Vambery's *History of Bokhara,* p. 14.
66. *Padma Purāṇa,* Sṛṣṭi kh., ch. 6.
67. It appears that in early times Thamara was a common name of ladies in this part of the country. A reigning queen of Georgia, even in the 12th century A.D., was named Thamara (*As. Rev.*, 1923, p. 675).
68. Maspero's *Passing of the Empires,* pp. 140, 141.
69. H.R. Hall's *Ancient History of the Near East,* p. 200.
70. *Strabo,* bk. xi, ch. iv, 6; xiii, 6; xiv, 3, 4; ii, 15; *S.B.E.*, vol. iv, pp. 4, 5.
71. *Encyclopædua if Religion and Ethics,* vol. I, p. 793, s. v. *Armenia.*
72. Maspero's *Passing of the Empires,* pp. 55, 61, 820.
73. The word *Āditya* is not derived from *Aditi,* see *Varāha P.*, ch., 26; being Āditya's mother she was perhaps called Aditi. Prof. Max Müller also says, "Aditi is not a prominent deity in the Veda. She is celebrated rather in her sons the Ādityas than in her own person." (*Ṛg-Veda Saṃhitā,* vol. I, p. 231).
74. See Maspero's *Dawn of Civilization Egypt and Chaldæa,* p. 545.
75. *Brahmāṇḍa P.*, ch. 44.
76. *Farvardin Yast* (xiii), 38; *S.B.E.* (vol. xxiii, p. 189).
77. *Ābān Yast,* Yast V, 73 (*S.B.E.*, vol. xxiii, p. 71).
78. *Mbh.*, Bhīshma, ch. 11.
79. *S.B.E.*, vol. IV, pp. 4, 5.
80. *Strabo,* bk. XI, ch. iv, 6; ch. xiii, 6; ch. xiv, 3, 4; and aloso ch. ii, 15.
81. *Devī-Bhāgavata,* iv, ch. 8.
82. *Two Essays as Supplements to the Aryan Witness,* pp. 20-28.
83. *Ibid.*, p. 27.
84. *Ibid.*, pp. 7-9.
85. *Ibid.*, p. 26; *Herodotus,* bk. 1, chs. 181-183; *Strabo,* bk. xvi, ch. 1; *Bhāgavata,* v. ch. 24; Marshman's *Brief Survey of History,* p. 8.
86. *Mbh.*, Vana, chs. 170 f; Udyoga, ch. 99; *Vāyu P.;* ch. 68, v. 14.
87. For the physical features and manners of the Turks, see Elphinstone's *History of India,* p. 166 note.
88. G. Rawlinson's *Fifth, Sixth, and Seventh Great Oriental Monarchies,* p. 332.
89. Vambery's *History of Bokhara,* Intro., pp. xxiii, xxiv.
90. Burnes' *Travels into Bokhara,* vol. iii, p. 135.
91. *Ibid.*, p. 222.

28

Rasātala or the Under-World

V

N. L. Dey

Rākṣasas and Yakṣas

The Rakṣas or Rākṣasas and the Yakṣas are said to be the descendants of Kaśyapa by his wife Khasā.[1] Rāvaṇa, in his expedition to Rasātala, killed Vidyujjihva, the husband of his sister Sūrpaṇakhā, who is mentioned as a Rākṣasī.[2] The Rākṣasas evidently derived their name from the river Araxes, on the banks of which they originally lived. Most probably their original name was Arakṣa but like the Amardi who were called Mardi, a tribe which lived on the shore of the Caspian Sea, and like the Armenians who were called Rāmanīyakas, they were called Rakṣa instead of Arakṣa, by the elision of the initial *a*. They were very likely the tribe called Arachoti which lived close to the Massagetæ and the Bactrians, mentioned by Strabo.[3] Arachoti is evidently composed of *Araka* which is a corruption of Araxes and *ti* which is a contraction of *te-le* or *tie-le* meaning the Huns. There can be no doubt that the Araxes is the Jaxartes, as it flowed through the country of the Massagetæ who from all accounts lived on the banks of the Jaxartes.[4] Like the Massagetæ and other Scythic tribes the Rakṣas were cannibals.[5] The Rākṣasas are mentioned in the Avesta, where it is said : "Away, do I abjure the iniquitous of every kind who act as Rakṣas act."[6] The Rakṣas therefore were a Hunnic tribe, and were Turanians and not the aborigines of India as have been supposed by some writers. The Yakṣas were a tribe of Rakṣas, Rāvaṇa, the king of the Rakṣas, was a step-brohter of Kuvera, the king of the Yakṣas.[7] The Yakṣas apparently derived their name from the Yaxartes (Jaxartes), on the banks of which they lived with the Rakṣas. The Buddhist stories of Hārita-yakṣinī, who devoured the children of Rājagṛha, and of Vakula-yakṣa show that the Yakṣas were also cannibals.[8] They were proverbially black, which indicates that they were the "black or sun-burnt Huns of the north."[9] In the Indian folk-lore the Yakṣas are represented as the guardians of buried treasures like the 'Leprechauns" with their pot of gold in the fairy tales of Europe.

Siddhas

The Siddhas, who appear according to the Brahmāṇḍa Purāṇa[10] to have lived on the north of the Niṣāda or the Hindukush mountain, were undoubtedly the Sydracæ or Oxydracæ mentioned by Megasthenes and other writers,[11] who lived close to Mount Nysa, and are said to have been the followers of Bacchus who has been identified with Śiva.[12] They lived most probably near the source of the Oxus. Perhaps a colony of this tribe dwelt in the Punjab near Multan at the time of Alexander's invasion and were known as Sudrakas; they were the ally of the Mālavas or Malloi of the Greeks.

Gandharvas

The Gandharvas were not also the aborigines of India. They represent the Gandarians mentioned by Herodotus[13] and perhaps Gadha of the Avesta,[14] and Gadha is synonymons with Śaka or Scythian, and Śaka is a synonym for "a thief who carries off cattle." It is remarkable that in the Behistun inscription (516 B.C.), in the fifth year of the reign of Darius, Gadara is mentioned among his conquered countries. Gadara has been considered to be the same as Gandhāra or Gandharva-deśa.[15] It should be stated here that the Gandarians and the Dadicæ fought under one commander Artyphius, and not with the Indians under Pharnazathres, in the army of Xerxes.[16] Hence it is very probable that the Gandharvas were the Gandarian tribe of Scythians. According to Rawlinson, the Gandarians held Kabul and the mountain tract on both sides of the Kabul river as far as the upper course of the Indus.[17]

Kinnaras

The Kinnaras appears to be the Kimmerii of Strabo. With regard to this tribe Herodotus says: "The wandering Scythians once dwelt in Asia, and there warred with the Massagetæ, but with little success; they therefore quitted their homes, crossed the Araxes, and entered the land Cimmeria. For the land which is now inhabited by the Scyths was formerly the country of the Cimmerians."[18] They must have therefore lived on the northern side of the Jaxartes. The sculptural representation of a kinnara is the figure of a bird with the face of a human being, though it is often described as having the shape of a man with the face of a horse, perhaps in conformity with the idea conveyed by the term 'kin nara,' the literal meaning of which is "Is this a man ?" As the kinnaras were heavenly musicians, the figure of the bird perhaps represents their proficiency in singing, and the face of the horse, which represents a long face, indicates their Turkish origin. The Kimmerii originally lived on the Caucasus and they were considered to be an almost mythical race.[19] They evidently afterwards lived at the Ust Urt plateau in Kharizm, and "the inhabitants of Kharizm formerly had the fame of being proficients in the art of music."[20]

Bhogavatī

The names of towns, rivers, etc., mentioned in the Purāṇas confirm that Rasātala was Śākadvīpa or Scythia. In the Rāmāyaṇa[21] we find the names of the following towns and places: Bhogavatī, Aśma, Manimayi, Varuṇa-pura, Bali-ālaya and Kṣīrada-sāgara. The town of Bhogavatī was guarded by Vāsukī. The word *Bhogavatī* is the Sankritised form of *Bākhdhī* mentioned in the Avesta[22] which was the ancient name of Balkh, – the Bactria of the Greeks. It was the capital of Bactriana, which was subverted by the Scythians in 135 B.C.,[23] and it was called Um-ul-Bilad, "the mother of cities." It contained formerly many fine palaces and buildings of marble, the ruins of which existed at the time of Macro Polo in the 14th century A.D.[24] It is said to have been the ornament of all Ariana.[25] The opulence, prosperity and fame of Bhogavatī (Balkh) or Bactria was due to the fact it was the emporium of Asiatic commerce.[26] Bactria, according to Strabo, was also called Zariaspa, and it stood upon a river of the same name which emptied itself into the river Oxus,[27] and the river was evidently called Bhogavatī, the river Bactrus of Curtius, from the famous town situated upon it.[28] Burnes thinks that Zariaspa is a corruption Shahr-i-Sabz (Kesh) in the kingdom of Bokhara, the birth-place of Nadir Shah.[29] Bhogavatī is also called Pātalapura,[30] as it was the capital of the province of Pātāla. It is stated in the Mahābhārata[31] that Śeṣa Nāga, who represents "Sse" of Sogdiana, resided at this place. Pātāla, therefore, as a province, comprised both Bactriana and Sogdiana, the river Oxus flowing between them. Strabo also says that the Sacæ occupied Bactriana and Sogdiana,[32] as stated before. Burnes says, "Balkh boasts an antiquity beyond most other cities in the globe" and that its ruins extend over a circuit of about twenty miles.[33]

Aśma

The town of Aśma is the same as Aksu, the Oxiana of the Greeks. It was the head-quarters of the province of Vaksh or Aksu, situated between the river Oxus and its tributary called Vaksh or Aksu, the Ochus of Strabo, in the country of Sogdiana.[34] The river Oxus, which is the Okos of the Greeks, formed the boundary between Bactriana and Sogdiana. It derived its name from its tributary, the Vaksh or Aksu,[35] evidently called Aśma by the Aryans, and therefore in the Ṛg Veda[36] the Oxus is called Aśmanvatī from its tributary, just as it is called Bhogavatī Gaṅgā in the Purāṇas,[37] from its tributary called Bhogavatī or Bākhdhī river, the Bactrus of Quintus Curtius,[38] on which Bākhdhī or Balkh is situated. The river Aksu (Vaksh) is the Vakṣu of the Matsya Purāṇa,[39] Vaṃkṣu of the Bhāgavata,[40] Cakṣu of the Brahmāṇḍa Purāṇa,[41] Ikṣu of the Viṣṇu Purāṇa,[42] all these names being some forms or variants of Aksu. Aśma was the capital of Sogdiana, which was Rasātala proper, being situated in the basin between the Jaxartes (the Rasā of the Ṛg-Veda) and the Oxus, and Rasātala is the same as Pātāla. The name of Pātālapura was originally applied to Aśma, as it is said in the Vāmana Purāṇa[43] that "Aśmaka is the foremost city of Pātāla," and there cannot be the slightest doubt that the seat of government was afterwards removed to Bhogavatī (Bākhdhī) or Balkh which has since been called Pātālapura, for we do not hear of the name of Markanda or modern Samarkand, which was destroyed by Alexander the Great in the 4th century B.C.[44] in any of the ancient works of the Hindus. Aśma evidently existed before Markanda became the capital of Sogdiana. Though the Mahābhārata[45] does not mention the name of Aśma, yet it appears from a chapter of the Udyoga Parva that it refers to it by the name of Pātālapura, which does not evidently mean Bhogavatī, as the latter is mentioned elsewhere as a town different from Pātālapura.[46] It says that all the Brahmins of Pātāla were devoted to the performance of *Go-vrata* or the rites relating to *Go* or cow. It should be stated that the ancient names of Sogdiana appear to have been "Gau" and "Sughda", and it was the second of the sixteen localities created by Ahura Mazda.[47] The words "Sughda," "Sogd" and "Sogdiana were perhaps considered to have been the growth upon the word *Gau* or perhaps variants of the word *sughur* which in Turkish mean *cow.*[48] It is also related in the Vendidad[49] that Angra Mainyu, the evil spirit, thereupon counter-created the fly called 'Skaitya' which brings death to ox and cattle. Hence it will be remarked that *Go-vrata* is mentioned in connection with Pātāla in conformity only with its name of *Gau* which means a cow. It is also mentioned that near Pātālapura, fire is continually burning.[50] This, of course, refers to the spring of oil which according to Strabo[51] existed near the river Ochus which is identical with the river Vakhsh, or Aksu and it appears also that there are still petroleum wells in the country around Samarkand and Ferghana, the capital of which is Khokand.[52] All these circumstances show that Pātālapura of the Mahābhārata was Aśma, the capital of Sogdiana. Aśma was inhabited by the daityas called Kālakeyas. The Kālakeyas were the Kara-Asavana of the Avesta mentioned with the "Turanian Danus" (Dānavas) and "the most mighty Duraekatea" (Daitya) who were the enemies of the Aryans. The word Aśma mean a *stone* and the word *Asabana* means 'one who kills with a stone' (Asanban), the sling being, as it seems, the favourite weapon of the Danus (Yast, xiii, 38)[53]." Hence Asabana was a descriptive epithet of *Kara,* the Sanskritised form of which is *Kāla,* both the words meaning black, and there can be no doubt that from Asavana the name of the town Aśma was derived. The word *Kālakeya* is a pleonastic and derivative form of *Kāla* or *Kara.* These Kara-Asavanas or Kālakeyas were evidently Kara-niru which is another name for the Hiung-nu or Huns.[54] It is curious that in the ancient map of Sogdiana there is a town by the name of Petra Sogdiana which means the same thing as Aśma, the word *Petra* meaning *stone;* it was situated on the north of Oxiana. It should also be remarked that the Mahābhārata[55] in connection with another tribe of Huns named Nivāta-Kavaca relates that they were quite adepts in 'raining down stones unseen upon their enemies.' This evidently means that the Daityas or the Huns, as a class, were expert sling throwers. The Bhāgavata[56] distinctly says that the Nivāta-Kavachas and other Kālakeyas lived in the sphere called Rasātala. The derivation of the word *Pātāla* as given in the Mahābhārata[57] seems to be based on this idea. It says that *Pāta* means *fall* and *Akram* means *great;* therefore the word *Pātāla* means a "great fall," and the Mahābhārata interprets this as the melting of the Moon and other aqueous bodies in the shape of rain by the sound produced by Vedic students when chanting the Vedic hymns. This is of couse the esoteric meaning of the word *Pātāla.* But it seems that the "Great fall" or "Pātāla" meant great fall of stones like pattering rains showered upon the enemies by the inhabitants of Pātāla, that is, the Epthalites or Nephthalities, a powerful tribe of the Huns, who lived on or about the banks of the Jaxartes and who like other Hunnic tribes were proficient in hurling stones with their slings. Śāka-dvīpa is evidently the Sanskritised form of Sog-dia or Sog-diana, as Śālmala-dvīpa is of Chal-dia, though the term Śākadvīpa was applied to the whole region known by the name of Scy-thia.

Maṇimayī

Maṇimayī of Rāmāyaṇa is the modern Maymene. It is situated to the south-west of Balkh and to the south-east of Marv or Meru of Hindus and Meru or Maru of the Turks,[58] the capital of Margiana, – the Mṛga of the Purāṇas, and about half-way between Balkh and the river Murghab. It is twenty-two miles from Andkhuy. The ancient town of Nisaya or Nisa, one of the sixteen localities created by Ahura Mazda, was situated near Maymene.[59] The city of Maymene stands in the midst of hills and was a place of renowned strength.[60] From strategical point of view it must have been a great and natural strong-hold of the Huns in olden times before the modern ordnance was invented, and it was renowned for the bravery of its defenders. According to the Rāmāyaṇa, it was inhabited by the Daityas called Nivāta-Kavaca. *Nīvāta* is a corruption of Neph-tele, or the Nephthalites, which is one the general names for the Huns, and *Kavaca* is a corruption of Kaptchak of Deguignes, Kiptchak of Vambery, or Kipechak of Burnes. They were a wild and warlike nomadic tribe who had no home before the time of Jenghis Khan.[61] The word *Nivāta-Kavaca* therefore means the Kapchak Huns. Their original abode appears to have been Desht-i-Kipchak, or the "Steppes" or "Plain" of Kipchak, by which is meant that portion of the Turanian highlands which is immediately to the east of the Caspian Sea, and it appears that there is still a country by the name of Kipchak which appertains to the kingdom of Khiva.[62] The Mahābhārata also says that Arjuna conquered the Nivāta-Kavacas of Dānavapura situated on the shore of *Mahāsāgara* or the Great Sea, by which is evidently meant the Caspian Sea.[63] Vambery says, "The Kiptchaks are, in my opinion, the primitive original Turkish race," and their discendants claim that "Desht-i-Kiptchak as Turkestan is named in the documents of oriental history was conquered and peopled by their ancestors."[64] Maymene is still inhabited by the Uzbegs[65] who are mentioned to have their original home in Desht-i-Kiptchak[66]; at least they claim their connection with the Kiptchaks.[67] The Uzbegs are now in possession of Transoxiana, that is the tract between the Oxus and the Jaxartes.[68]

Varuṇapura

Varuṇapura was evidently Aornos, one of the two principal cities of Bactriana at the time of Alexander's invasion, the other city being Bactria or Balkh.[69] But it appears that at the time of the Rāmāyaṇa Varuṇapura was under the dominion of the Surabhis or Khorasmii.[70]

Bali-ālaya

Bali-ālaya or the house of king Bali was evidently Balkh, the ancient names of which were Bactria and Bākhdhī, the Bhogavatī of the Purāṇas. It is stated that the Turks about the second century B.C. subverted the Greek kingdom of Bactria, and erected an empire which lasted till the middle of the sixth century of the Christian era. The name of the capital was changed from Brctria into Balkh. The word *Balkh* is nothing but the old Turkish word *Balikh* which, according to the Turks, meant 'the residence of the sovereign, that is the capital.[71] *Bali-ālaya* has not only been evolved out of the word *Balikh,* that is from "the residence of a king" into "the residence of king Bali," but the further development of the story of Bali and Vāmana, which was extant during the Vedic period, appears to have been based upon this word at a subsequent period. That Bali-ālaya is the same as Bhogavatī appears to be confirmed by the Rāmāyaṇa. It is related that Rāvaṇa entered Rasātala or Pātāla through a hole, and the first city he entered was Bhogavatī, and after conquering Varuṇapura, he entered Bali-ālaya or "Bali's residence", and came out of Rasātala without going anywhere else through, the same hole, through which he had entered it.[72] Bālhīka of the Bhaviṣya Purāṇa[73] and of the Bṛhat-saṃhitā[74] is the same as Balikh or Balkh. Bāhīka has been abbreviated into Bāhīka in the Bhaviṣya Purāṇa.[75] Bali-ālaya or Bali-sadma is synonymous with Pātālapura; it became the capital of Pātāla after the seat of government was removed from Aśma or Akṣu. Balkh formerly covered a distance of five leagues; at present only a few heaps of earth mark the site of ancient Bactria.[76] Bactria or Balkh, that is, Bhogavatī or Bali-ālaya, is situated in the country called Tu-ho-lo- by Hiuen Tisang, it is Tukhāra or Tuṣāra of the Purāṇas[77] and Tokaristan of the Arab geographers.[78] Tokaristan or Turkestan therefore was the Sutala sphere of the Purāṇas, where king Bali is said to have been kept confined. According to tradition Zoroaster was slain at Balkh in the holy war between Iran and Turan[79]. It was one of the Haitalite centres.[80] In the middle ages Balkh became the capital of Islamic civilisation and was designated Kubbet-ul-Islam (the home of Islam) and Omm-el-Bul-dan (the mother of cities).[81]

Pātālapura

Besides Bhogavatī, the Mahābhārata mentions two other cities called Pātālapura and Hiraṇyapura and a lake called Vāruṇa-hrada in Rasātala. Pātālapura, as already stated, was originally the name of Aśma and afterwards of Balkh, which were the capitals of Pātāla. Patanti-nagara of Pātāla, mentioned in the Devī Purāṇa,[82] is evidently the same as Aśma; it was conquered by Asura Ghora, king of Kuśa-dvīpa.

Rāmaniyaka

We have already shown that Rāmaniyaka was Armenia. Romaka of the Bṛhat-saṃhitā is a corruption of Rāmaniyaka and the word still exists in Erzeroum (Arabic *Arzen-el-Roum*). The province of Van, which now appertains to it, formed in ancient time an independent kingdom and was known by the name of Biainas,[83] the Vanāyu of the Purāṇas. The Rohita Parvata of Śālmala-dvīpa appears to be Mount Ararat.

Hiraṇyapura

Hiraṇyapura is mentioned as the capital of the Dānavas called Nivāta-Kavaca and the Daityas.[84] It is, as we have already shown identical with Hyrcania, an old town near Astrabad on the south-eastern side of the Caspian Sea, in Mazenderan, the scene of Rustom's adventures against the "white Devas" or demons. The name of its king Hiraṇya-kaśipu represents the Kaspii who lived on the shore of the Hiraṇya or the Hyrcanian Sea.

Bhuṣkara or Puṣkara

The name of Bokhara has not been mentioned in any of the Purāṇas, as it did not become the capital of Tartary, that is the region between the Oxus and the Jaxartes, "the vale, called by the Romans, Transoxiana or Transoxania till the time of the Samanidus, when Emir Ismail removed the seat of his government from Marakanda, the modern Samarkand, the capital of Sogdia or Sogdiana, to this place which is 120 miles from Samarkand.[85] The ancient Iranian name was Jemu-ket or Jem-kot, which was changed into the Turanian name of Bokhara when the Turks invaded Transoxania, the first invasion having taken place, according to Sir Henry Rawlinson, in the year 700 B.C.[86] Elphinstone also thinks that the Turks had settled in Transoxiana long before the Christian era.[87] According to Dr. Spiegel *Bukhar* "is even now the Mongolian word for a Buddhist temple or a monastery."[88] *Bhuṣkara* is the Sanskritised form of *Bukhar;* it is mentioned in the Rājataraṅgiṇī; it was conquered by Lalitāditya, king of Kashmir, in the 8th century A.D. Puṣkara of the Matsya Purāṇa[89] is a corruption or variant of Bhuṣ kara. Puṣkara is mentioned in the Harivaṃśa as the place where Viṣṇu killed the Daitya named Madhu.[90] Perhaps Bokhara is referred to in the Bhaviṣya Purāṇa by the name of Taittiri-nagara or the city of Tartary.[91] But the ancient Iranian name of Jem-ket or Jem-kot (Jamakot) which, according to Abulfeda, "was considered as the eastern end of the habitable world" has been preserved by the Hindus and absorbed in their astronomical terminology as *Yamakoṭi,* signifying now the most eastern point of the world on the equator from the meridian of Laṅkā.[92] The ruins of Bykund (Baikuṇṭha ?), one of the most ancient cities in Turkestan, lie about twenty miles to the south of Bokhara which did not then exist.

Bibhāvarī

Bibhāvarī of the Bhāgavata[93] was *puri* or town of Varuṇa in Pātāla where Hiraṇyākṣa was killed. It appears to be a corruption of Bāveru of the Bāveru Jāṭaka,[94] Bamri of the Ṛgveda[95] and Bawri of the Avesta. Bāveru is the Sanskritised form of Babiru or Bapilu, the ancient name of Babylon as it appears from the Behistun inscription,[96] mentioned as Pripru in the Ṛg-veda.[97] From the inscription of Boghaz-Keui it appears that the Mittanians of Northern Mesopotamia (which included Babylon) worshipped Mitra and Varuṇa, who were also the gods of the Iranians and Indo-Aryans when they lived together in Ariana. Varuṇa was the prototype of Ahura Mazda as supposed by Professor Meyer.[98] *"Ilani Uru-w-na"* of the inscription, in the Babylonian language, means god Varuṇa. As Babylon contained the temple or "Citadel" and the tomb of

Bel or Belus, the Bala Asura of the Bhāgavata,[99] it was situated in the sphere called *Atala.* Belus was king of Babylon; it was he who first introduced the celebrated Chaldian astronomy into that city. There was trade connection between India and Babylon, and the trade routes have been described by Layard and Isidora of Charax.[100] Babylon is situated on the Euphrates, the Vivṛti of the Garuḍa Purāṇa, and Nivṛti of the other Purāṇas, which rises from the mountain called Nephates in which it has got its source. The Rohita mountain of Śālmala-dvīpa is perhaps the Sanskritised form of mount Ararat.

The Oxus

The rivers of Rasātala are the Oxus, the Jaxartes and the Zarafshan. The Oxus, which is also called Amudaria (*Amu* being a variant of *Aśma*), is the Aśmanvatī of the Ṛg-veda.[101] As a river of Śākadvīpa it is called Cakṣu, Vakṣu, Vaṃkṣu, Ikṣu and Sucakṣu in the Purāṇas,[102] all these names being variations of Akṣu, a great branch of the Oxus, from which the name of Oxus is derived.[103] The Oxus is called the Bhogavatī-gaṅgā and the Pātāla-gaṅgā of Rasātala, the former name it has received from a branch of the river called Bactrus on which Bākhdhī or Bhogavatī, the Bactria of the Greeks is situated[104] and it is called Pātāla-gaṅgā as it flows through the "sphere" or province of Pātāla, that is, between Bactriana and Sogdiana. The river was held in respect by the Hindus as it formed the principal trade-route for conveying large quantities of Indian merchandise to the Hyrcanian or Caspian Sea, whence through the Cyrus they were transported to the Euxine and the Mediterranian;[105] hence it was called "Gaṅgā" by the Hindus. The Oxus issues from the Sarik-kul lake in the Great Pamir, which by some authority is identified with the Anavatapta lake of the Buddhists, and hence can be no doubt that a branch of the river formerly flowed into the Caspian Sea through an ancient course which still exists, though it now falls into Lake Aral.[106]

The Jaxartes

The Jaxartes, which is also called Jaj (Djadj)[107] and Syrdaria, is the Rasā of the Ṛg-veda, the Raṅghā of the Avestā[108] the Araxes of Scythia, the Śīlā of the Mahābhārata,[109] perhaps the Gabhastī of the Purāṇa[110] and Sila of Megasthenes. Strabo mentions three rivers by the name of Araxes; the Araxes of Armenia,[111] the modern Aras on the northern boundary of Media, the Araxes of Persia,[112] the modern Bend-Amir, and the Araxes of Scythia.[113] The word *Jaxartes* appears to be a combination of the words *Jaj* and *Araxes* (of Scythia) in order to distinguish the latter from the Araxes of Armenia and the Araxes of Persia. From Syr-daria the Jaxartes is called Śīlā and Sītā, the word *Syr* being a corruption of *Su-Rasa*[114] (*i. e.* Su-Rasā), a local name of the

Jaxartes. It should be stated that Gabhasti may more properly be identified with the Murgab or "the river of Mṛga" or Margiana in Śākadvīpa. Araxes and Rasā are different forms of the same word. The Jaxartes rises in the same mountains as the Oxus, and falls into the sea of Aral.

The Zarafshan

The river Zarafshan, the ancient names of which are Sogd and Kohik, rises in the mountain called Fan-tau, perhaps the Phena-giri of the Bṛhat-saṃhitā[115] and flowing a little to the north of Samarkand and Bokhara, falls into the lake called Kara-kul also called "Dengiz" or sea by the Uzbeks. It is called the "blessed" river, and Zarafshan means "scatterer" or "distributor of gold."[116] It is the Hāṭaki-nadī of the Bhāgavata.[117] Hiraṇvatī-nadī of the Mārkaṇḍeya Purāṇa,[118] and Hiraṇyavatī-nadī of the Mahābhārata mentioned by Fausböll.[119] Hāṭakī, Hiraṇvatī and Hiraṇyavatī-nadī all mean the "golden river." Hāṭakī appears to be a corruption of Kohik. The Hāṭakīnadī is situated in the Bi-tala "sphere" of Rasātala.[120] The Kohik is the Polymetus of the Greeks, "a name imposed by the Macedonians, as they imposed many others, some of which were altogether new; others were deflections from the native appellations.[121] The river is called the golden river as it brings fertility to the soil over which it flows and helps in the luxurious growth of its crops. Samarkand, which became the capital of the great empire founded by Timur, was called the paradise of the world on account of its great beauty and fertility brought about by this river. Elphinstone also speaking of Transoxiana in which Sogdiana is situated says, "while it was in the hands of the Arabs, it seems not to have been surpassed in prosperity by the richest portions of the globe."[122] According to the Purāṇas,[123] Śiva was worshipped on the Hāṭ akī-nadī or Zarafsan by the name of Haṭakeśvara Mahādeva evidently by the Nāgas or Huns.

Meru Parvata

The mountain which is situated just on the outskirt of Rasātala is called Meru in the Rāmāyaṇa[124]; and Meru, according to the Mahābhārata,[125] is also the name of a mountain of Śākadvīpa or Scythia, the Mount Meros of Arrian and Megasthenes,[126] close to Mount Nysa or Niṣādha Parvata of the Purāṇas, that is, the Paropanisos mountain of Ptolemy, which is evidently a corruption of *Parvata Niṣādha*. It is therefore the Hindukush range.

Śyāma-giri

The Śyāma-giri is also mentioned as a mountain of Śāka-dvīpa. It is evidently mount Śyāmaka of the Avesta.[127] Both Śyāma-giri and Śyāmaka mean the "Black Mountain" and the mountain therefore is the Mustagh mountain, which means the Black Mountain.

Durga-śaila or Trikūṭa mountain

Durga-śaila[128] of Śāka-dvīpa, which means the "fort mountain," is evidently the same as the El-Burz which means "the Bastion mountain," and is situated on the southern side of the Caspian Sea; it is the Trikūṭ a mountain of the Bhāgavata.[129] It was Mount Kaspios of the Greeks named after the Kaspii, an extinct tribe, the Kacchapa of the Gaja-kacchapa story of the Mahābhārata. Both Śyāma-giri and Durga-śaila are part of Meru Parvata.

Kusesaya

The Kusesaya is the Caucasus mountain, which is a corruption of Koh Kosh (Kus) or the mountain Kus of Kuśa-dvīpa.[130]

Vāruṇa Hrada

Varuṇa Hrada (lake) has been correctly identified with the Caspian Sea.[131] It is mentioned both in the Rāmāyaṇa[132] and the Mahābhārata[133] as being situated in Rasātala. The Caspian Sea is the Hyrcanian Sea of Strabo,[134] but the Avestic name of Hyrcania is Vehrkāna. There can be no doubt that "Vāruṇa" of the Vāruṇa-Hrada is a corruption of "Vehrkāna or "Vār kāna,"[135] in other words, Vāruṇa Hrada is the Hyrcanian Sea; hence Vāruṇa Hrada could not have been derived from the name of the god Varuṇa. Though the legend makes it so, forgetting its true significance, the Caspian Sea is also called Mare Seruanicum or the Sea of Shirwan;[136] Seruanicum or Shirwan is evidently a corruption of Hyrcania, though Shirwan has been identified with Albania.[137] Shirwan has been further corrupted into Sarain, and the Caspian Sea is called the Sea of Sarain.[138] Kṣīrasāgara is the Sanskritised form of the sea of Shirwan; it is the sea of milk caused by the milk of the Surabhi cows (or Khorasmii), whose country Kharism (Khiva) is situated on the north-eastern side of the Caspian Sea. Surā-sāgara is the Sanskritised form of the Sea of Sarain. The Caspian Sea is also called Mahāsāgara in the Purāṇas. *Badku* generally called Baku on the west coast of the Caspian Sea is perhaps the *Baḍavā* of the Purāṇas, as it famous for its naphtha springs and mud volcanoes, the "perpetual flame" mentioned in the Mahābhārata as existing in Varuṇa-hrada; it appears to have been a place of Hindu pilgrimage and was called Mahājvālāmukhī.[139]

The Sapta or Seven Dvīpas and Seven Sāgaras

It should be stated here that according to the ancient Hindu works, the then known world, that is, the whole of Asia, was divided into seven Dvīpas, each Dvīpa being surrounded by a Sāgara. According to the Paurāṇic notion Sāgara did not mean Sea only, but also the ocean, sea, river or lake, as Dvīpa (Dvi-Apa) did not mean an island, but simply a division situated between two sheets of water, the original meaning of the term.[140] The seven Dvīpas are Jambu, Śāka, Śālmala, Puṣkara, Kuśa, Krauñca and Plakṣa; and the seven Sāgaras are Lavaṇa (salt), Kṣīra (milk), Ghṛta (clarified butter), Ikṣu (sugarcane juice), Surā (wine), Dadhi (curd) and Svādu-jala (sweet water).[141] For Plakṣa we have Gomeda in some Purāṇas[142] and Śveta-dvīpa in the Mahābhārata,[143] and for Svādu-jala we have Jala in some works.[144] (1) Jambu-dvīpa or India was bounded by the Lavaṇa (salt) Sāgara or the Indian Ocean.(2) Śāka-dvīpa or Scythia was bounded on its two sides by the Lavaṇa (salt) Sāgara or the Indian Ocean and by the Sea of *Kṣīra*[145] (milk), which, as stated before, is a corruption of the Sea of *Shirwan,* a name of the Caspian Sea[146]. The Caspian Sea therefore formed its northern boundary, while the Indian Ocean formed its southern boundary. Śāka-dvīpa was originally the Sanskritised form of Sog-dia or Sog-dia-na on the Rasā or Jaxartes, though the term was afterwards extended to the whole of Scythia. (3) Śālmala-dvīpa (i.e. the Sanskritised form of Chal-dia) had for its boundary the Sea of *Ghṛta*[147] which is clearly a corruption of the *Erythrean* Sea or the Sea of *Erythras,* which was either the Red Sea or the Persian Gulf, most probably the latter.[148] The Rohita Parvata of Śālmala-dvīpa seems to be the Mount Ararat. Perhaps the river Vidhṛti of the Garuḍa Purāṇa and Nivṛti of the other Purāṇas is the Euphrates, and the river Vitṛṣṇā the Tigris.[149] The Semetic Asuras, that is, the Assyrians dwelt in Śālmala-dvīpa. (4) Puṣkara-dvīpa or Transoxania was bounded by the *Ikṣu* (sugar-cane juice) Sea[150]. Ikṣu, however, is one of the names of the river Oxus.[151] The Matsya Purāṇa[152] also says that the river Śīlā or Jaxartes flowed through the country of Puṣkara. Puṣkara-dvīpa is the Sanskritised form of Bukhar-ia, which means the "country of the Buddhist monastery" or Bokhara, where *ia* stands for *dia,* Puṣkara being a corruption or variant of Bhuṣkara or Bokhara.[153] Puṣkara-dvīpa therefore commenced from the north of the Oxus which was the northern boundary of Śāka-dvīpa. The Turanian Asuras originally lived in Osrushna in Puṣkara-dvīpa.

References

1. *Padma P.*, Sṛṣṭi kh. 7: *Khasā tu yakṣarakṣāṃsi janayāmāsa koṭiśa.*
2. *Rāmāyaṇa,* Uttara, ch. 23.
3. *Strabo,* bk. xi, ch. viii, 8 (vol. ii, p. 248).
4. *Ibid.*, bk. xi, ch. viii, 6 (vol. ii, p. 247); *Herodotus,* bk. I, ch. 201; see also *Sacred Books of the East,* vol. iv, p. 3; Tod's *Rajasthan,* vol. I, ch. vi.
5. Hamilton and Falconer's *Strabo,* vol. I, pp. 299, 464.
6. *Yasna* xii in *S.B.E.*, vol. xxxi, p. 249.
7. *Rāmāyaṇa,* Uttara, ch. 13.
8. See *I-tsing,* bk. i, 9; Beal's *Records of Eastern Countries,* vol. I, p. 110 note; vol. ii, p. 191.
9. See *JBBRAS.*, vol. xxiv, p. 565.
10. *Brahmānda P.*, ch. 44.
11. *Strabo,* bk. xv, I, 8 (vol. iii, p. 76)
12. McCrindle's *Ancient India as described by Megasthenes and Arrian,* pp. 111 note.
13. Rawlinson's *Herodotus,* bk. vii, ch. 66 (vol. ii, p. 147).
14. *S.B.E.*, vol. xxiii, p. 161.
15. See my *Geographical Dictionary of Ancient and Mediaeval India* s.v. *Gandhāra.*
16. *Herodotus,* bk, vii, chs. 65, 66 (vol. ii, p. 145, 147).
17. Rawlinson's *Five Great Monarchies of the Ancient Eastern World,* vol. iv, p. 20.
18. Rawlinson's *Herodotus,* bk. iv, : ch. xi, 33 (vol. I, p. 291).
19. Maspero's *Passing of the Empires,* p. 342.
20. Conolly's *Journey to the North of India,* vol. I, p. 179.
21. *Rāmāyaṇa,* Uttara, ch. 23.
22. *Vendidad,* ch. I (*S.B.E.*, vol. I, p. 2).
23. Professor E., J. Rapson's *Ancient India,* p. 118.
24. Yule's *Marco Polo,* vol. I, p. 151.
25. *Strabo,* bk. xi, ch. xi.
26. Hamilton and Falconer's *Strabo,* vol. I, p. 23, note 2.
27. *Strabo,* bk. xi, ch. xi, 8.
28. Burnes' *Travels into Bokhara,* vol. ii, p. 211.
29. *Ibid.*, vol. iii, p. 6.
30. *Mbh.*, Udyoga, ch. 98.
31. *Ibid.*, ch. 102.

32. *Strabo,* bk. xi, ch. viii, 4; Hamilton and Falconer's *Strabo,* vol. ii, pp. 246, 240 note.
33. Burnes' *Travels into Bokhara,* vol. ii, p. 204.
34. Vambery's *History of Bokhara,* Intro., p. xxii, note I.
35. *Ibid.,* Intro., pp. xxii, note I; Dr. Modi's *Ancient Pāṭaliputra* in *JBBRAS.,* vol. xxiv, p. 520.
36. *Ṛg-Veda,* x, 53-8.
37. *Bṛhad-dharma P.*, Madhya, ch. 22, v. 50.
38. Burnes' *Travels into Bokhara,* vol. ii, p. 211.
39. *Matsya P.,* ch. 101, quoted in the *Śabdakalpa druma,* s. v. *nadī*.
40. *Bhāgavata,* v, ch. 17.
41. *Brahmāṇḍa P.,* ch. 51.
42. *Viṣṇu P.,* ii, ch. iv.
43. *Vāmana P.,* ch. 10, v. 56.
44. *Strabo,* bk. xi, ch. xi, 4.
45. *Mbh.*, Udyoga, ch. 98.
46. *Ibid.,* Udyoga, chs. 98, 102.
47. Vambery's *History of Bokhara,* p. 5.
48. Burnes' *Travels into Bokhara,* vol. iii, p. 216.
49. *Vendidad,* ch. 1 in *S.B.E.,* vol. iv, pp. 5,6.
50. *Mbh.,* Udyoga, ch. 98.
51. *Strabo,* bk. xi, ch, xi, 5.
52. *Contemporary Review,* October, 1921, p. 504.
53. *Ābān Yast* (v) 73, (*S.B.E.,* vol. xxiii, p. 71).
54. Beal's *Records of the Western Countries,* vol. I, p. 20 n; 37n.
55. *Mbh.* Vana, chs. 170, 171.
56. *Bhāgavata,* v, ch. 24.
57. *Mbh.,* Udyoga, ch. 98.
58. *Bṛhat-saṃhitā,* ch. 16, V. 38; Burnes' *Travels into Bokhara,* vol. iii, pp. 20, 31.
59. Vambery's *History oj Bokhara,* p. 5 note.
60. Vambery's *Travels in Central Asia,* p. 240.
61. Vambery's *Travels in Central Asia,* p. 397.
62. *Ibid.,* p. 342; Vambery's *History of Bokhara,* note 2; Deguignes' *Histoire des Huns,* vol. ii, pp. lxix; Burnes' *Travels into Bokhara,* vol. iii, p. 341.
63. *Mbh.,* Vana, ch. 166.
64. Vambery's *Travels in Central Asia,* pp. 382, 383.
65. *Ibid.,* p. 249.

66. Vambery's *History of Bokhara.* 244, note 2.

67. *Travels in Central Asia,* p. 345, note.

68. *Ibid.,* pp. 367; Elphinstone's *History of India,* pp. 264, 266.

69. McCrindle's *Invasion of India by Alexander the Great,* p. 39.

70. *Rāmāyaṇa,* Uttara, ch. 23; *Raghuvaṃśa,* 1, *v.* 80.

71. Vambery's *History of Bokhara,* p. 11.

72. *Rāmāyaṇa,* Uttara, ch. 24.

73. *Bhaviṣya P.,* Pratisarga, pt. iii, ch. 2.

74. *Bṛhat-saṃhitā,* ch. 18; *JSAB.,* 1838, p. 630.

75. *Bhaviṣva P.,* Pratisarga, pt. iii, ch. 3.

76. Vambery's *Travels in Central Asia,* p. 233.

77. *Mbh.,* Sabhā, ch. 31; *Bṛhat-saṃhitā,* ch. 16.

78. Beal's *Records of the Western Countries,* vol. I, p. 37 note.

79. *Encyclopædia of Religion and Ethics,* vol. I, p. 858.

80. *JBBRAS.,* vol. xxiv, p. 567.

81. Vambery's *Travels in Central Asia,* p. 233.

82. *Devī-purāṇa,* ch. 3.

83. Maspero's *Passing of the Empires,* p. 55.

84. *Mbh.,*Udyoga, ch. 97; *Śiva P.,* IV, ch. 4; *Padma P.,* I, ch. 6.

85. Vambery's *History of Bokhara,* Intro., p. xxvii, p. 66.

86. *Quarterly Review,* 1863. p. 491.

87. Elphinstone's *History of India,* p. 266.

88. Vambery's *History of Bokhara,* p. 14.

89. *Matsya P.,* ch. 120, p. 44.

90. *Harivaṃśa,* ch. 202; *Bhaviṣya P.* chs. 24, 25 (M.N. Dutt's trans., pp. 881, 884).

91. *Bhaviṣya Purāṇa,* Pratisarga Parva, pt. iii.

92. Vambery's *History of Bokhara,* pp. 2, note 2.

93. *Bhāgavata,* iii, ch. 17.

94. *Jātaka* (Camb. ed.), vol. vi, p. 83.

95. *JASB.,* 1909, pp. 407. *Ṛg Veda,* iv, 19, 9; *Śatapatha Brāhmaṇa,* xiv, 1, 1, 8, 14.

96. *JRAS.,* vol. xv, p. 9, 1692.

97. *Ṛg Veda,* I, 51; 1, 4.

98. *JASB.,* 1909, pp. 723, 724; *Contemporary Review,* 1921, Dec., pp. 767; *Strabo,* bk. xi, ch. xii, 3.

99. *Bhāgavata,* V, ch. 24.

100. Layard's *Nineveh and its Remains,* vol. II, pp. 413, 414; *Parthian Stations* by Isidora of Charax, translated by Mr. Wilfred Schoff.

101. *Ṛg-veda,* X, 53, 8.

102. Their names are mentioned in *Brahmāṇḍa P.,* ch. 51; *Matsya P.,* ch. 101; *Bhāgavata,* V, ch. 17; *Viṣṇu P.,* pt. II, ch. 4; *Kūrma P.,* ch. 46.

103. Dr. Modi's *Ancient Pāṭaliputra* in *JBBRAS.,* xxiv, p. 520.

104. *Bṛhad-dharma P.,* Madhya, ch. 22, v. 50; Burnes' *Travels into Bokhara,* vol. ii, p. 211.

105. *Geography of Strabo,* (by Hamilton and Falconer), vol. I, p. 113; vol. II, p. 243; Robertson's *America,* bk. I.

106. Beal's *Records of the Western Countries,* vol. I, pp. 12 note.

107. Vambery's *History of Bokhara,* p. 8.

108. Drs. Keith and Macdonell's *Vedic Index of Names and Subjects,* vol. II, p. 209; *JBBRAS.,* vol. xxiv, p. 532.

109. *Mbh.* Bhīṣma, ch. 11.

110. *Viṣṇu P,* ii, ch. 4.

111. *Geography of Strabo,* vol. ii, p. 217.

112. *Strabo,* vol. iii, p. 132.

113. *Ibid.,* vol. ii, p. 247; Rawlinson's *Herodotus,* vol. I, p. 302.

114. *JASB.,* 1911, p. 747.

115. Ch. xv, v. 20.

116. Vambery's *History of Bokhara,* Introduction, pp. xxxii, xxxiii; *Travels in Central Asia,* pp. 183; Burnes' *Travels into Bokhara,* vol. ii, p. 285.

117. *Bhāgavata,* v, ch. 24.

118. *Mārkaṇḍeya P.,* ch. 60.

119. *Mbh.* VI, 210: see Fausböll's *Indian Mythology,* s. v. *Garuḍa* but in *Mbh.* Bhīṣma P. ch. 8, the river Hairaṇvatī is mentioned.

120. *Bhāgavata,* v, ch. 24.

121. *Strabo,* bk. xi, ch. xi, 5.

122. Elphinstone's *History of India,* 4th ed., p. 264.

123. *Devī Bhāgavata,* pt. 8, ch. 19; *Devī,* chs. 82, 83.

124. *Ramāyaṇa,* Uttara, ch. 25.

125. *Mbh.* Bhīṣma, ch. ii.

126. McCrindle's *Ancient India as described by Megasthenes* and *Arrian,* pp. 152, 180.

127. *Zamyād Yast* (XIX) in *S.B.E.,*vol xxiii, p. 288, note 2 and 7; *Vendidad,* ch. I in *S.B.E.,* vol. iv, p. 7, note 8.

128. *Mbh.,* Bhīṣma, ch. ii.

129. *Bhāgavata,* viii, ch. 2.

130. *Varāha P.*, ch. 87; Thornton's *Gazetteer of countries adjacent to India.* s.v. *Hindoo Koosh.*

131. Mr. Shib Chandra Seal's *Āryajātir Ādinivāsa,* p. 7.

132. *Rāmāyaṇa,* Uttara, ch. 23.

133. *Mbh.*, Udyoga, ch. 97.

134. *Strabo,* bk. ii, ch. i, 15.

135. *Vendidad,* ch. I, 12 (41) in *S.B.E.*, vol. iv, p. 7, note 8.

136. Yule's *Marco Polo,* vol. I, p. 59 note.

137. *Geography of Strabo,* vol. ii, p. 217 note.

138. Yule's *Macro polo,* vol. ii, p. 424.

139. *Mbh.*, Udyoga, ch. 97; McCulloch's *Geographical Dictionary* s. v. *Baku; Asiatic Researches,* v, p. 41.

140. Bhāṣkarācārya's *Siddhānta-śiromaṇi,* Golādhyāya, ch. 3, *v.* 35.

141. *Devī P.*, ch. 3.

142. *Matsya P.*, ch. 122; see *Brahmāṇḍa P.*, ch. 63, *v.* 6.

143. *Mbh.*, Bhīṣma, ch. 12.

144. *Garuḍa P.*, Pūrva kh., ch. 54, *v.* 6.

145. *Varāha P.*, ch. 86. We have preferred to adopt the names of Dvīpas and the Sāgaras surrounding them as given in the Varāha Purāṇa as the Purāṇas are contradictory on these points.

146. Sir Henry Yule's *Marco Polo,* vol. I, p. 59 note.

147. *Varāha P.*, ch. 89.

148. McCrindle's *Commerce and Navigation of the Erythrean Sea,* p. 1, 309 note. Nearchos means by it only the Persian Gulf; see p. 222 note; also Maspero's *Down of Civilization,* p. 546.

149. *Garuḍa P.*, Pūrva kh., ch. 56, *v.* 7. Bitṛṣṇā appears to mean "what assuages thirst" that is fit for drinking, see *Strabo,* bk. xi, ch. xiv, 8.

150. *Varāha P.*, ch. 89.

151. *Viṣṇu P.*, pt. ii, ch. 4.

152. *Matsya P.*, ch. 110. The text appears to be corrupt: some editions have Pulikan for Pushkaran, comp. *Alberuni's India* (Dr. Sachau's ed.), vol. I, p. 261.

153. *Rājataraṅginī,* bk. iv.

29

Rasātala or the Under-World

VI

N. L. Dey

(5) The Kuśa-dvīpa was bounded by the Sea of *Surā* (wine) which is the Sanskritised form of the Sea of *Sarain* as the Caspian Sea was called.[1] The Sea of *Sarain* is perhaps a corruption of the Sea of *Shirwan* by which name the Caspian Sea was known; or perhaps the Sea of Surā is a corruption of the Sea of the *Surabhis* or Khorasmii, as they lived in Kharism close to the Caspian Sea[2]: at least the northern portion of the Caspian Sea was called the Sea of Surā. It should be stated here that both Surabhi and Surā (wine) rose from the Kṣīra Sāgara when it was churned by the gods and Asuras.[3] It is not likely that "Sarain could have been derived from Sari, the capital of Mezanderau, a very important trading town, which, however, is about nine hours' journey from the southern shore of the Caspian Sea. In the Varāha Purāṇa[4] Kuśa dvīpa is said to be bounded by the Sea of Kṣīra, which, as stated before, is the Sanskritised form of Shirwan, that is the Caspian Sea. Kuśa-dvīpa derived its name perhaps from the Kushans, a very powerful tribe of the Huns, who were also called the Great Yue-chis or Haitalite Huns,[5] and who lived between the Jaxartes and the Chu rivers.[6] Their country was called Kushan[7] which was included in this *dvīpa* or division. A section of this tribe called the Little Yue-chi occupied Kabul, and the famous Kaniṣka of Gandhāra belonged to this dynasty. It is however more probable that Kuśa-dvīpa derived its name from the mountain called *Caucasus* which is another form or corruption of Koh Kus or the "Mountain of Kosh" or Kuśeśaya mountain of the Purāṇas, included in this dvīpa (division). The word *Kuśa-dvīpa* still subsists in the name of *Circassia* (Cir-kosh-ia) and *Caucasia* (Koh-kas-ia). Kuśadvīpa appears to have been the original home of the Daityas and Dānavas. (6) Krauñca-dvīpa was bounded by the *Dadhi* Sāgara (Sea of Curd)[8] or the Sea of Aral which was most probably called the Sea of *Dahae* from a famous

Scythic tribe which lived on the Upper Jaxartes and evidently on the shore of this lake.[9] The whole of Central Asia was called after their name "the country of the Dahis"[10]. The Sea of Aral was also called Daria-i-Kharism, and it is stated that the Caspian Sea has communication with the Sea of Aral or in other words, the Sea of the Inspissated Milk communicates with the Sea of Curdled Milk.[11] The word '*Aral*' in Turkish means '*between*', that is, between the Jaxartes and the Oxus.[12] It is therefore a descriptive name. The Krauñca-ḍvīpa most probably derived its name from Kuchar, Koutcha,or Kucha which in ancient time constituted one of the four territories of Eastern Turkestan and an important Buddhist settlement. It was situated on the great caravan route between the East and the West.[13] (7) Plakṣa-dvīpa is also called Śveta-dvīpa[14] and Gomeda-dvīpa.[15] This Dvīpa is called Śveta, because the river Śvetā, now called the Swat, flowed through it and it comprised the Swat valley known in ancient times by the name of Udyāna. The inhabitants of this Dvīpa were worshippers of Viṣṇu,[16] of course, in his form of Buddha. It is called Plakṣa-dvīpa as it derived that name from a Plakṣa tree, now called Pilu tree (*Salvadora Persica*). It is recorded by Sung-yun that Buddha, when he visited Udyāna, planted there a Dantakāṣṭha (tooth-stick) which grew into a lofty tree. The Tartars called it Polu tree.[17] It is called Gomeda-dvīpa from the Gomeda mountain, as the Altai Range was called evidently from the Gobi desert, of which it formed the northern boundary, and a chain of this mountain traverses the desert on its western side. It was bounded on one side by the *Lavaṇa Sāgara* or the Indian Ocean[18] and on another side by *Svādu-jala* (sweet-water),[19] which is perhaps the Sanskritised form of *Tcha-dun,* a river of Mongolia, *Tchi* being a Turkish word for river. It also appears from the Bhāgavata[20] that the river Aṅgirā is evidently the river Angora which falls into the Lake Baikal in Siberia. Śvetadvīpa contained a *varṣa* (country) called *Uttara* (north) Kuru-dvīpa, the corruption of which is Kor-ia, which was situated on the south of the Northern Ocean.[21] There can be no doubt therefore that Plakṣa-dvīpa comprised all the countries to the north of India, including China, Mongolia and a part of Siberia. Some of the Purāṇas confound Plakṣa with Puṣkara-dvīpa. The seven principal *divisions* called "*Mahā-dvīpa*" in the Agni Purāṇa comprised sub-"dvīpas" or "Dias," which meant *countries,* as may be traced in Assuria (Ashur-dia), Armen-ia (Ramaṇa-[22] or Rāmaṇīyaka-dvīpa), Sarma-tia (Sarma or Saramā-tia or dia, the country of Saramā), Kor-ia (Kuru-dvīpa), Med-ia (Madra or Mad-dia), etc., where "ia" stands for "dia." *Asia* is a corruption of *aspa* (or *aswa*) and *dvīpa* (*dia* or *ia*); it means the region of horses, i.e. the home of the Turanian race, *Tur* implying the fleetness of a horse.

Similarly Arab-ia means the country of the Arabs, Mongolia the country of the Mongols. In short *dvīpa* or its corruption *"dia"* or *"ia"* when applied to a "Mahā-dvīpa" meant a *"division,"* when applied to a sub "dvīpa" in any Mahā-dvīpa, it meant a *"country."*

Names of Sāgaras are Turanian words absorbed in the Sanskrit language

It will be remarked that of the seven divisions into which Asia was divided, the Jambu-dvīpa (India) was inhabited by the Indo-Aryans. The Śākadvīpa, of which the northern boundaries were the Caspian Sea and the river Ikṣu or the Oxus, was inhabited by the Iranians and the Turanians, that is those Turanians who had come under the influence of Indian civilisation, and hence the Oxus was considered to be the "old boundary line between Iran and Turan."[23] Śālmala-dvīpa was inhabited by people who belonged to the Semitic race, which the remaining four divisions were exclusively occupied by nations who belonged to the Turanian stock. Excepting the name of *Lavaṇa*-(salt) Sāgara which surrounded Jambu-dvīpa, with the state of which the ancient Hindus were fully acquainted, the names of the other six Sāgaras were borrowed from the Turanian language and absorbed in Sanskrit and transformed into words which closely resembled the original words in sound, but were quite different in meaning, as *Shirwan* was changed into *Kṣīra* (milk), *Sarain* into *Surā* (wine), *Erythras* into *Ghṛta* (clarified butter), *Dahi* into *Dadhi* (curd), *Oxus* (Akṣu) into *Ikṣu* (sugarcane juice), and *Tcha-dun* into *Svādu-jala* (Sweet-water). The ancient Hindus cannot possibly have believed in such absurdities as oceans of Milk, Curd, Sugar, Cane-juice, etc. We must give them credit for possessing at least some amount of common sense. The names were records of old nomenclature; they underwent changes by lapse of time, and then ridiculous interpretations were put on them during the dark age of the Kali-yuga, showing symptoms that generally precede the downfall of a nation.

Identity of Rasātala and Scythia

It will be observed that notwithstanding the changes that have been brought about by the lapse of time in the names of places, rivers and mountains and the names of the inhabitants, both in Sanskrit and Turanian, of Rasātala and Scythia, the resemblance in the corresponding names in the two languages is yet remarkably striking, and the names are so considerable that their resemblance cannot be considered as merely accidental. It would not be reasonable to deny the identity of the two countries, especially when the inference based upon the resemblance of names is corroborated by various other facts and circumstances. Further researches will clear up many obscurities which still hang round several facts connected with the subject, and it is hoped that some of the hymns at least of the Ṛg-Veda, which have been interpreted by Sāyaṇa and other commentators as figurative descriptions of Nature when her elements are at tumultuous war or in serene repose, may be found possible to explain by the light of traditions of other nations who lived near the original home of the Aryans, as expressions of feelings of the human heart based upon facts and incidents of real life. According to Professor Weber the major portion of the Ṛg-Veda Saṃhitā was composed before the Aryan migration to India.[24]

Turanian or Hunnic settlements in India

It appears from the ancient Hindu works that even at a very remote period the Scythic or Hunnic tribes extended their inroads to India in search of food and fodder. They were a nomadic race, and did not till or cultivate land, but lived only upon milk and fishes, and the roots of some trees and the half-cooked flesh of animals. At the time of the Rāmāyaṇa, as stated before, we find the Massagetæ or "the Great Gate", as symbolised in Jaṭāyu, occupying Daṇḍakāraṇya, and nearly the whole of the Deccan was interspersed with Rākṣasa settlements. They were Turanians, and it is very probable that the language introduced by these races formed the basis of the "Tamulic or the language of the Deccan", one of the four classes into which Professor Max Müller has divided the Southern Turanian family of language.[25] The Rāmāyaṇa also mentions a colony of Yakṣas in the Himalaya and a tribe of Daityas under Madhu in Madhuvana or Mathura,[26] and it likewise speaks of Gandharva-deśa, the Gadara of the Behistun inscription, where a tribe of Scythic Gandarians must have established itself long before the Rāmāyaṇa was composed.[27] The Haihaya tribe lived on the bank of the Narmadā at the time of the Rāmāyaṇa.[28] They evidently belonged to the Hunnic tribe of Hui-he,[29] the ancestors of the Usbeks who had originally settled near Khotan, Kashgar, and other places. At the time of the Mahābhārata almost the whole of the Punjab, called Āraṭṭa, was occupied by Scythic tribes, especially by the Bāhīkas.[30] The Bāhīkas lived in the country of Madra, and therefore they were also called Madras. In short, according to Pāṇini and Patañjali Bāhīka was another name for the Panjab.[31] It appears that Bāhīka is an abbreviation of Bālhika of the Rāmāyaṇa,[32] and Bālhīka is the Sanskritised form of Balkh, the capital of Bactriana.[33] It is therefore clear that Scythic tribes from Bactriana occupied the Punjab at a very remote period. It appears also that the Suparṇa or Garuḍa tribe lived in Guzerat. From the story of Ulapī it appears that a Hunnic tribe lived at Gaṅgādvāra or Hardwar.[34]

There were Rakṣasa settlements also between Vāraṇāvata and Ekacakrā,[35] that is between Mirat and Itawah; and also in Magadha.[36] These tribes belonged to the Turanian race. There can be no doubt that at the time of the Mahābhārata many Hunnic tribes inhabited various parts of India,[37] and the snake-sacrifice of Janmejaya means only a compaign of extermination of the Nāgas or Huns to avenge the treacherous assasination of his father Parīkṣit by a Nāga of the Tochari tribe. It is stated that the first tribe whom Alexander met after leaving the great confluence at Uchh in Sindh, when he invadded India in the 4th century B.C. was the Sogdoi, whom Saint-Martin considers to be the same as Sogdians,[38] that is the people of Sogdiana or Sogdoi, the Chagzai of the Mahomedan historians, who must have invaded Sindh and settled there at least at the time of the Mahābhārata,[39] which classifies the people of Sindh with the Madrakas and other Scythic tribes in their manners and customs, and states that they are Mlecchas and irreligious and that they are natives of a sinful country. Sogdiana is the modern kingdom of Bokhara, and hence the Sogdoi of Sindh at the time of Alexander must have belonged to the Hunnic tribe called Ephthalites, and also Haetalites, who lived in the valey of the oxus and whose principal centres were Balkh, Bokhara and other places.[40] It is therefore evident that from the name of Ephthalite or Elāpatra of the Mahābhārata and Buddhist works, their principal town was called Pātāla (modern Hyderabad)[41] and the whole of the Indus Delta was called Patalene.[42] The Purāṇas[43] also refer to the Scythian inhabitants on the banks of the Yamuna, Gumti and Nerbuda. The nemes of Negapatam, Uragapura (modern Uraiyur or Trichinopoly), etc. indicate Hunnic settlements in Southern India. To an unbiassed mind many of the arguments advanced by Dr. Spooner in favour of the identity of the Mauryas with the Mauravas appear to be reasonable.[44] Maurava was the name of the people of Merv (Marv), and Merv is the ancient Margine or Marginia of Ptolemy,[45] and there is a close resemblance in sound between Maurya and Margine, and Merv according to some authorities was the "cradle of the Aryan race".[46] Magadha, according to Dr. Spooner, was peopled by the Magas or Magians of Scythia.[47] According to the Purāṇas, Magas, the Magi of Strabo, were the priest class, and the Magadhas formed the warrior class of Śākadvīpa.[48] The statement of Dr. Spooner appears to be confirmed by the Mahābhārata[49] which says that Pṛthu assigned Magadha to the Māgadhas for their residence, though the word "Māgadhas" there mean "panegyrists" which is the later application of the term, but it should be observed that the priest of Pṛthu was Śukrācārya, who was the Daitya-guru. Jarāsandha, king of Magadha, was an Asura.[50] The story of uniting the two parts of his body by a

Rākṣasī named Jarā at his birth is a figurative way of saying that he was born of a Hindu father by a Hunnic mother. Dr. Spooner has rightly come to the conclusion that the Śākya tribe of Kapilavastu, to which Buddha belonged, originally came from Śākadvīpa, as the custom of marrying one's own sister, as the ancestors of the Śākyas used to do, was prevalent among the Scythian and other non-Aryan races, especially those who followed the Zoroastrian religion.[51] Vistaspa, king of Bactria, married his sister Hutos, and the ancient Egyptians married their own sisters.[52] The word *Śākya* has evidently been derived from the word *Śaka*. Manu[53] mentions some tribes as *Vrātya Kṣatriyas* for the ruling class called "Rājanya" who were without the *Saṃskāra* or sacrament of the sacerdotal thread, which signifies that they were foreign non-aryan "warriors" admitted into Hindu community, that is, they were invested with the sacred thread after the expiry of the prescribed period of initiation, and he mentions among them Jhalla, Malla, Naṭa, Karaṇa, Khasa, Draviḍa and others. The Jhallas were the Jhala clan of the Rajputs who from their original settlement in Sindh migrated into Kathiawar (Surāṣṭra). They gave their name to the division called Jhalawar. The Mallas were evidently the Mallas of Kuśīnagara where Buddha died, and the Naṭas were the Nāṭa (or Nāya) clan of the Kṣatriyas of Kuṇḍagāma, a suburb of Vaiśālī, from which Mahāvīra, the founder of Jaina religion, hailed.[54] According to Dr. Satis Chandra Vidyābhūṣaṇa the Karaṇas were a Scythic tribe of Central Asia and were probably the inhabitants of Khaurana of Ptolemy,[55] The word *Karaṇa* and *Kuṣāṇa,* Kwei-shwang of the Chinese travellers, are according to Beal, only different forms of the same word.The Yue-chi king Kaniṣka was a Kuṣ āṇa, and his inscribed coins bear the legend of "Kanyski Korano". The Yue-chis were a tribe of the Turks.[56] The Karaṇas form a well-known Hindu caste and live in various parts of India; they have now become thoroughly Hinduised. The Karaṇas therefore were originally inhabitants of "Skythia" and were Śakas. According to Professor Monier Williams, the Khasas or Khasias are the representatives of "wild Tartar tribes" who marry their brothers' widows; they were perhaps the Cossei of Strabo. The Draviḍas or Dravidian races came from Central Asia, and their language shows that they were Turanians.[57] Prof. Monier Williams calls the Draviḍas "out-caste Kṣatriyas" by which he means "Vrātya Kṣ atriyas"[58] The peculiar custom by which property of the Dravidian races, as the Nairs, etc., of Malabar, Travancore, Cochin and other parts of Southern India, devolves upon the sisters' sons, if it be not the survival of their ancestral custom of marrying sisters at a remote period, indicates that the type of polyandry that prevails among the Nairs and others, is somewhat similar to that which prevailed among the early

Semites.[59] Ragozin also thinks that the Dravidians were Nāgas, not because they were Huns, but because the Serpent (Nāga) was their symbol of the Earth.[60] The story of Paraśurāma shows that the real Kṣatriyas of India were nearly extinct at the time of the Rāmāyaṇa by their constant wars with the foreign invaders and that the conquerers were afterwards admitted into the Hindu community as Vrātya (or spurious) Kṣatriyas in the place of those whose countries they occupied. During the Vedic period the Vrātyas were considered as nomads[61] which indicates that they were Scythians; other non-Aryan immigrants also settled in India. The Vrātyas were not Mulattos, as the word has been interpreted.[62] On account of these Hunnic settlements we have got counterparts of some cities and countries of Central Asia in India, e.g. for Bokhara we have Puṣkara in Rajputana, for Balkh Bālhīka or Bāhīka, for Media Madra.

Intermarriages

The long residence of the Scythic tribes in India brought them into close contact with the Aryans. Hence we find intermarriages taking place between these two different races at the time of the Mahābhārata. Yayāti married Śarmiṣṭhā, daughter of the Daitya Vṛṣaparvan, and Devayānī, daughter of Śukrācārya who was the priest of the Daityas and grandson of Hiraṇyakaśipu by his daughter Kāvyā.[63] Pāṇḍu married Mādrī, sister of Śalya, king of Madra, who belonged to the Scythic tribe of Bālhīka or Balkh. Bhīma married a Rākṣasī, and by her he had a son named Ghaṭotkaca[64]; and Arjuna married Ulapı, daughter of a Nāga[65]. Kaṃsa, king of Mathurā of the Bhoja dynasty, married Jarāsandha's daughters,[66] and Kṛṣṇa's grandson Aniruddha married Uṣā, daughter of Asura Bāṇa[67]. That such marriages have taken place between the princes and princesses of India with those of the Huns is a matter of history. A Śātavāhana prince named Gautamīputra Śātakarṇī, who was a Hindu, was married to a daughter of Mahākṣatrapa Rudradāman, who was Śaka; Yaśaḥkarṇa, king of Cedī, was married to a Huna princess Ahalladevī[68]. Such marriages and intercourse with Hunnic tribes must have influenced Hindu civilisation and produced very great changes in the manners and customs of the ancient Hindus. Many of the customs were modified, and many new customs and practices, borrowed from the Turanian races, came into existence. It is very probable that Rākṣasa and Gāndharva forms of marriage were adopted by the ancient Hindus, as the terms indicate, from the Scythic races; and the description of a Gretna Green marriage of the Turks, where the bridegroom was unable to pay the dower fixed by the parents of the bride, closely tallies with that of the Rākṣasa form of marriage.[69] Among the Tartars of Mongolia, though the match is arranged by the parents of the bride, and her "price" is settled by them, yet they make a show of fight and offer resistance to the bridegroom when he comes to their house to take away the girl betrothed to him to perform the ceremony at his own house[70]. The Gāndharva form of marriage is performed simply by exchange of garlands without any nuptial rite. It was a sort of Morganatic marriage, but the son was entitled to inherit the father's rank and property.

Association of Nāgas with the serpents

Centuries passed away from the time when the Aryans first migrated to India to the time of the composition of the Purāṇas. By that time the real significations of the terms *Nāgas* and *Rasātala* were quite forgotton. *Nāgas* became merely serpents and not Huns; and as serpents live in holes and consequently below the earth, Rāsatala where the Huns lived, that is the valley of the Jaxartes, came necessarily to mean the region below of earth or the *Under-world;* and as a logical sequence, when one desires to go to Rasātala, one must go to it through a hole as a serpent does. It was for this reason that the Rāmāyaṇa relates that Rāvaṇa in his expedition to Rasātala entered it through a hole near Mount Meru, and that Sāgara's sons entered it through a hole made by them at the mouth of the Ganges. Any hole anywhere on the surface of the earth was good for the purpose of entering Rasātala. The prince Kuvalayāśva entered Pātāla in pursuit of a daitya through a hole.[71] There was a tradition that these Nāgas lived near the banks of rivers; of course, the rivers were the Oxus and the Jaxartes; – this evidently led to the idea that Rasātala could also be entered through the beds of rivers. It is therefore that we find Akrūra entering the Nāga country or Rasātala through the Yamunā, Kuvalayāśva through the Gomatī and Cyavana through the Narmadā.[72] According to the Buddhist writers also the Nāgas lived not only below the earth, but also in lakes and rivers.[73] The association of the Huns or Nāgas, as they were called, with serpents, resulted not only in changing the meaning of Rasātala from the valley of the Jaxartes to the Under-world, where access was only possible from the surface of the earth through holes and crevices, but also in the division of the region into seven spheres, one above the other, so that the inhabitants thereof consisting of birds, beasts, reptiles and demons, who were inimical to one another, could live in peace and safety. By a further stretch of imagination, it was conceived that the rays of the Sun never penetrated into Rasātala which was below the earth, but that the whole region was illuminated by the brilliant flashes of light emitted by the gems which adorned the heads of the serpents.[74]

Ritter's view of Pātāla

The real meaning of Rasātala, the situation of the region, and the character of its people were forgotten in time. The seven *Lokas* or the worlds above the earth were subsequently invented, analogous to the seven spheres of Rasātala called "Sapta Pātāla" which were below the earth. This circumstance alone has served a good deal to put off investigation from the right track, leaving an impression behind that everything the ancient Hindus asserted which was not concerned with India was fictitious, especially when anything was limited to the mystic number "seven," which came to be regarded as the hall-mark of pure imagination. It was, however, Ritter only who thought that Pātāla was a country in the west and not a figment of the imagination, though he did not assign to it any definite place. He says, "Pātāla is the designation bestowed by the Brāhmaṇas on all provinces in the west towards sunset, in antithesis to Prasiaka (the eastern realm) in the Ganges-land: for Pātāla is the mythological name in Sanskrit of the Under-world, and consequently of the land of the west."[75] With regard to the inhabitants of Pātāla as Dānavas, Daityas and Rākṣasas, Mr. Pargiter says that the older Paurāṇic accounts treat them as men, whereas the later Brahminical accounts as demons.[76]

We have endeavoured to reclaim a lost and forgotten country, buried in the debris of time in the shape of traditions, legends, fables and superstitions. Some of the best European scholars, who consider that some of the narratives in the Rāmāyaṇa, the Mahābhārata and the Purāṇas, which embody many of the earlier traditions, as for instance, those regarding the seven Dvīpas, the seven Sāgaras, Rasātala, called also the "seven Pātālas," etc., are "wild ideas and absurd figments." But they are not to blame. The old Purāṇas mentioned by Manu and others,[77] which contained the accounts of the traditions, no longer exist. The Purāṇas, which are now extant and which have been adopted by Brāhmaṇas as their religious authority, are later compilations; they were composed and redacted when the traditions about the earliest occurrences had become distorted by lapse of time. This led their authors to interpret them in their own way and embellish them according to their own imaginary notions. Mr. Pargiter rightly observes with regard to ancient Indian historical tradition: "It is not to be put aside as wholly unworthy of attention, nor is it to be summarily explained by *prima facie* comments," especially as our knowledge of the most ancient times in India rests mainly on tradition.[78] We must avoid scepticism regarding the historical basis upon which the tradition is based, and at the same time we should avoid euhemerism, as it may lead to error. Independent evidence, if any, certainly does much to strengthen and confirm our conclusions. Besides traditions, which in many other cases have now-a-days been treated with greater respect by science itself, and which on many occasions serve as a clue and guide to real facts which lie at their basis, – the facts and circumstances adduced as evidence, together with a comparison of the physical features of the country and the condition of the people of Rasātala as described in ancient Hindu works with those of Turkestan or Tartary (both these names being synonymous with each other),[79] as recorded in the Avesta and in the works of travellers, go a great way to establish the identity of Rasātala with Central Asia. There is a strong resemblance in the names of towns, rivers, lakes, and mountains of Rasātala with those of Turkestan, and these resemblances could not have been the result of accidental coincidence, as for instance, we recognise Bhogavatī in Bākhdhi, Aśma in Aksu, Bali-ālaya in Balkh, Maṇimayī in Maymeni, Bibhāvarī in Bāveru or Babylon, Rāmaṇīyaka in Armenia, Alamba in Albany, Ikṣu in Oxus, Rasā in Araxes, Vāruṇa in Vehrkāna, Meru in Meros. There is a "golden river" in Rasātala (the Hāṭakī) and a "golden river" also in Central Asia (the Zarafshan). The names of the seven "spheres" or provinces of Rasātala correspond with the names of the Huns, or rather of the various sections of the Huns, who dwelt in Scythia. All these and other circumstances mentioned before could not have been the result of mere chance. Of course, traditions, facts and circumstances taken singly are not strong enough for the purpose, each of them being a link in the long chain of circumstantial evidence, but the cumulative effect of all of them considered together makes out a strong case in favour of that identity. Yet there remains much that should be cleared up, as time has distorted and transformed the names of places and people out of recognition, and dimmed the memory of ancient events as recorded in the traditions which have become susceptible of different interpretations from different points of view. Stripped of its grotesque verbiage, the story of Rasātala, as given in the Purāṇas, is founded upon traditional chronicles which again are based on a substratum of facts. Future researches will no doubt throw much light upon many things that remain obscure and explain many facts which have become blended and associated with the remote past, especially those which are connected with the original abode of the Aryans, which, notwithstanding the attempts of eminent scholars to elucidate them, are yet involved in considerable obscurity, as their conclusions on this point do not agree; but there can be not doubt that the places and peoples mentioned in ancient Hindu works, when correctly identified, will help a good deal in arriving at a right conclusion. According to the traditions of the

Turks, the earliest peopled portions of the earth were Balkh and Surukhs near Khorasan,[80] and according to the Avesta the first country created was Airyana Vaejo[81] on the river Dāitya. Merv, according to some authority, was the "cradle of the Aryan race."[82] The Mahābhārata[83] also appears to place the first inhabited portion of the earth in Pātāla or Central Asia, as it says that the egg, from which the great fire is to issue for the destruction of the world, yet remains there unhatched, implying that the other egg which produced the creatures had been hatched there before. It has been conjectured[84] by some scientists that "Mongolia of to-day and the adjacent territory had in ages past been the centre of disposal of animal life to other parts of the sacrifice of the earth." According to tradition[85] the original home of the Semites and other races was in Armenia. Much light therefore will be thrown on this point and other doubtful questions when the Hindu works will be clearly understood by future researches.

References

1. Sir Henry Yule's *Marco-polo,* vol. ii, p. 494.
2. *Mbh.* Udyoga, ch. 109.
3. *Viṣṇu P.,* pt. I, ch. 9.
4. *Varāha P.,* ch. 87.
5. Dr. Modi's *Early History of the Huns* in *JBBRAS.,* vol. xxiv, p. 568.
6. Vincent Smith's *Early History of India,* ch. x, p. 218.
7. *JBBRAS.,* vol. xxiv, p. 569.
8. *Varāha P.,* ch. 88.
9. *JBBRAS.,* vol. xxiv, p. 548.
10. *Farvardin Yast* (xiii) in *SBE.,* vol. xxiii; *JBBRAS.,* vol. xxiv, p. 548.
11. Vambery's *History of Bokhara,* p. 9 note.
12. Burnes' *Travels into Bokhara,* vol. iii, p. 163.
13. *Bower Manuscripts,* Introduction, pp. 1; Vincent Smith's *Early History of India,* p. 187.
14. *Mbh.,* Bhīṣma, ch. 12.
15. *Varāha P.,* ch. 89.
16. *Kūrma P.,* ch. 49.
17. *Travels of Sung-Yun* in Beal's *Records of the Western Countries,* Introduction, p. xcvi.
18. *Brahmāṇḍa P.,* ch. 52.
19. *Kūrma P.,* ch. 50.

20. *Bhāgavata,* V, ch. 20.

21. *Brahmāṇḍa P.,* ch. 44, vs. 37, 38; ch. 48, v. 12.

22. *Bhāgavata,* V, ch. 20, where *Ramaṇaka* is mentioned as a *varṣa* (country) in Śālmala-dvīpa.

23. Vambery's *History of Bokhara,* p. 11.

24. Weber's *History of Indian Literature,* p. 63.

25. *Science of Language,* vol. I, p. 334.

26. *Rāmāyaṇa,* Uttara, chs. 31, 74.

27. *Ibid.,* Uttara, ch. 113.

28. *Ibid,* Uttara, ch. 36.

29. For the name, see Prof. Max Müller's *Science of Language.*

30. *Mbh.,* Karṇa P., chs. 44. 45.

31. *Indian Antiquary,* vol. I, p. 22.

32. *Rāmāyaṇa,* Ayodhyā K., ch. 58.

33. *Bṛhat-saṃhitā,* ch. 18; *JASB.,* 1838, p. 630.

34. *Mbh.,* Ādi, ch. 214.

35. *Ibid.,* Ādi, chs. 155, 160.7. *Ibid.,* Ādi, chs. 155, 160.

36. *Ibid.,* Sabhā, ch. 16.

37. See Fausböll's *Indian Mythology,* p. 29.

38. McCrindle's *Invasion of India by Alexander the Great,* p. 354.

39. *Mbh.,* Karṇa P., ch. 41.

40. Dr. Modi's *Early History of the Huns* in *JBBRAS.,* vol. xxiv, pp. 562, 567.

41. McCrindle's *Invasion of India by Alexander the Great,* pp. 356. Pātāla has also been identified with Tatta and Minnagar (Burnes' *Travels into Bokhara,* vol. I, p. 27; Schoff's *Periplus*), Min or Ming being the name of a tribe of Usbeks. Min is also an Indian name for the Scythians (McCrindle's *Commerce and Navigaion of the Erythrean Sea,* p. 109 note).

42. Strabo, bk. XV, ch. I, 33; McCrindle's *Ancient India as described by Megasthenes and Arrian,* p. 183 note.

43. *Mārkaṇḍeya P.,* chs. 22, 23.

44. Dr. Spooner's *Zoroastrian Period of Indian History* in *JRAS.,* 1915, p. 406 f.

45. Bretschneider's *Mediæval India,* vol. ii, p. 103.

46. *JRAS.,* 1915, p. 407.

47. *Ibid.,* pp. 422-27.

48. *Kūrma P.,* Pūrva, ch. 49; *Strabo,* bk. xv, ch. iii, 13-15.

49. *Mbh.,* Śānti, ch. 59.

50. *Ibid.,* ch. 340.

51. *JRAS.,* 1915, pp. 438-40.

52. Maspero's *Dawn of Civilization,* pp. 50, 51.
53. *Manusaṃhitā,* x, 20, 22:–

    Jhallo mallaś ca rājanyād vrātyān nicchivir eva ca,
    naṭaś ca karaṇaś caiva khaso drāviḍa eva ca.

54. Dr. Hoernle's *Uvasagadasao,* p. 4.
55. *JASB.*, 1902, pp. 162, 163–S.C. Vidyābhūṣaṇa's *Vrātya and Saṅkara Theories of Caste.*
56. Beal's *Records of Western Countries,* vol. I, pp. 56 note 37.
57. Prof. Monier Williams' *Indian Wisdom,* pp. 312 note, Intro, p. xxx, note 2; *Śukranīti,* iv, 5, 98; Mr. E. J. Rapson's *Ancient India,* p. 29.
58. *Indian Wisdom,* p. 236, note 2.
59. *Encyclopædiā of Religion and Ethics,* vol. viii, p. 467.
60. Ragozin's *Vedic India,* p. 308.
61. *Vedic Index,* vol. I, p. 342.
62. *JASB.*, 1874, p. 254.
63. *Vāyu Purāṇa,* ch. 65.
64. *Mbh.*, Ādi, ch. 155.
65. *Ibid.*, Ādī, ch. 214.
66. *Harivaṃśa,* chs. 84, 90.
67. *Ibid.*, chs. 187, 188.
68. See Sir R. G. Bhandarkar's *Foreign Elements in Hindu Population* in *Ind. Ant.*, January, 1911, pp. 15, 21.
69. Burnes' *Travels into Bokhara,* vol. iii, pp. 37, 48; *Bhāgavata,* x, ch. 54.
70. M. Huc's *Travels in Tartary, Tibet and China,* vol. I, pp. 184, 185.
71. *Mārkaṇḍeya P.*, ch. 21.
72. *Devī-Bhāgavata,* iv, ch. 7.
73. *Yamunā* and *Ghaṭaka Jātakas* in Cowell's *Jātakas,* vol. I, p. 270; vol. iii, p. 174; vol. vi, pp. 44, 80.
74. *Bhāgavata,* V, ch. 34.
75. Quoted in McCrindle's *Ancient India as described by Megasthenes and Arrian,* p. 183 note.
76. Mr. Pargiter's *Ancient Indian Historical Tradition,* pp. 13, 290.
77. *Manu-Saṃhitā,* iii, 5, 232; *Chāndogya Upaniṣad,* vii, 1, 4; Professor Monier Williams' *Indian Wisdom,* pp. 492, 493.
78. Mr. Pargiter's *Ancient Indian Historical Tradition,* pp. 13, 14.
79. Burnes' *Travels into Bokhara,* vol. II, pp. 214, 221; cf. pp. 287, 295, 297; vol. III, p. 125, 210; *JBBRAS.*, vol. XXIV, p. 545.
80. Burnes' *Travels into Bokhara,* vol. ii, p. 206; vol. iii, p. 44; see also Marshman's *Brief Survey of History,* p. 10.

81. *SBE.*, vol. iv, pp. 4, 5.
82. *JRAS.*, 1915, p. 407.
83. *Mbh.*, Udyoga, ch. 98.
84. See Mr. R.C. Andrews' account of the Third Asiatic Expedition of the American Museum of Natural History in Asia (New York), 1923-24.
85. Chambers' *Encyclopædia,* vol. xxi, p. 643, s. v. *Semites.*

30

Identification of Kuntala and Aśmaka Countries

V. V. Mirashi

In a note of published in *IHQ.*, XXII, 309f. I pointed out that Kuntala in ancient times comprised not only the North Kanara District and parts of Mysore State and Belgaon and Dharwar Districts, but also the upper and central valleys of the Kṛṣṇā where the Rāṣṭrakūṭa king Mānāṅka and his descendants were ruling in the fourth and fifth centuries A.D. In his reply in this journal (XXIII, 65 f.) Dr. Sircar says that Dr. Fleet and himself had expressed practically the same view. If so, I would say, with Ānandavardhana, अयलसम्पन्नसमीहितार्थाः सम्पन्नाः स्मः (I have gained my object without any effort).

Dr. Sircar has, however, subsequently modified his statement. He says that the Kuntala country proper lay in the heart of the Kanarese area and only later on it signified the gigantic (?) Kuntala or Kanarese empire of later times. The only evidence that he has adduced to prove this view is that a record of the 11th century A.D. describes Vanavāsī as an ornament of the Kuntala country. I wonder how this proves that the country round Vanavāsī was the *original* Kuntala. It only shows that the district of Vanavāsī was included in the country of Kuntala in the 11th century A.D.

That Kuntala comprised what we now call the Southern Maratha country from very early times and not only in a later age should be clear from the evidence of the *Mahābhārata, Vāyupurāṇa, Daśakumāracarita, Bālarāmāyaṇa, Kāvyamīmāṃsā* and *Udayasundarīkathā,* detailed in my note. None of these works is later than the 11th century A.D., while some of them belong to a time not far removed from the age of Mānāṅka. Of the aforementioned works, the first three clearly show that Vanavāsī in early times lay outside the limits of Kuntala, while the others indicate that the northern boundary of Kuntala stretched to the Godāvarī. This was certainly not because the Kanarese empire of the Rāṣṭrakūṭas and Later Cālukyas extended to that river. In fact the empires of these dynasties extended much farther in the north and comprised Northern Mahārāṣṭra and Vidarbha also, but these latter countries are nowhere included in Kuntala. The Rāṣṭrakūṭas and Cālukyas are called rulers of Kuntala because their capitals Mānyakheṭa and Kalyāṇa were situated in that country between the Kṛṣṇā and the Godāvarī, more than two hundred miles north by east of Vanavāsī, the supposed heart of the Kuntala country. These rulers were called Karṇāṭa, because they spoke the Kanarese language. This does not prove that Kanarese was the language of the *whole* Kuntala country *in all ages*. Otherwise, Hāla, the author of the *Sattasaī* composed in the Māhārāṣṭrī Prakrit, who had his capital at Pratiṣṭhāna on the Godāvarī, would not have been called the lord of Kuntala.

Dr. Sircar asks, 'What can then be the objection if *śrīmat-Kuntalānāṃpraśāsitā* is translated 'the chastiser of the illustrious Kuntala people?'[1] The first objection is that Mānāṅka, who as shown above was ruling over Kuntala, cannot be supposed to have chastised his own people! Secondly, I would draw Dr. Sircar's attention to the difference in the wording of the two expressions *sa-Vidarbh-Āśmaka-vijetā* and *śrīmat-Kuntalānāṃ praśāstā* which occur in the description of Mānāṅka. There is evidently a contrast intended here between Vidarbha and Aśmaka on the one hand which Mānāṅka conquered and Kuntala on the other over which he ruled. The addition of *śrīmat* meaning 'glorious' or 'prosperous' to the name of Kuntala points in the same direction. Thirdly, I should like to know a single instance of □ *praśās* being used in the sense of the chastisement of a whole people.

Finally, Dr. Sircar says that Vatsagulma appears to have been sometimes a part of Aśmaka and sometimes a part of Vidarbha. I have already cited a passage from Rājaśekhara to show that Vatsagulma was included in Vidarbha. That the surrounding country was also included in Vidarbha would be clear from the description in the *Ganeśapurāṇa* that Kadambapura (modern Kaḷamb[2] in adjoining Yeotmal District) was situated in Vidarbha. I should like to know the evidence which indicates that the Vatsagulma country was a part of Aśmaka. That the Nanded-Nizamabad area (which Dr. Sircar takes to be ancient Aśmaka) lay immediately to the south of the Vatsagulma country is no argument. It is more probable that area also was like Vatsagulma included in Vidarbha. The identification of the Nanded-Nizamabad area with ancient Aśmaka is at best conjectural, being based on the uncertain equation of Paudanya or Potana with Bodhan near Nizamabad. No details about the situation of Potana available which could have enabled us to identify it with certainty. It appears more probable that Aśmaka lay directly to the south of Mūlaka (Aurangabad District) for the pupils of Bāveru who was living in Aśmaka are said to have gone to Pratṣṭhāna in the first stage of their journey to the north. If they had been staying in the Nanded-Nizamabad area they would have taken the route via Nāndīkaṭ a (Nāndeḍ) and Vatsagulma (Bāsim), instead of going to Pratiṣṭhāna (Paiṭhān) which lay at a considerable distance to the west. Aśmaka does not therefore appear to have been identical with the Nanded-Nizamabad area. The latter was under the direct sway of the Vākāṭakas of Vatsagulma and was evidently included in Vidarbha.

References

1. Dr. Sircar takes *Kuntalānām* in this passage to mean the people of Kuntala and refers to *Surāṣṭra* in verse 11 of the Junagadh inscription of Skandagupta as a similar case. Bur even in the latter passage *yo me praśīṣyān-nikhilān-Surāṣṭrān* (*G.I.*, p. 62) which Fleet translated as 'who shall govern all my (*countries of the*) *Surāṣṭras,'* the word *Surāṣṭrān* has to be taken to mean the country and not the people of Surāṣṭra, the sense being 'who shall govern my whole country of Surāṣṭra.' The plural number misled Fleet into supposing that there were several countries of the people called Surāṣṭras. In Sanskrit the names of countries are always used in the plural except when some word like *viṣaya* or *deśa* is added to them.
2. Kaḷamb even now contains a famous temple of Ganeśa under the name of Cintāmaṇi.

31
Kuntala and Aśmaka

D. C. Sircar

In *IHQ.*, XXII, pp. 30915, Prof. V. V. Mirashi has commented on my views regarding the identification of the Kuntala and Aśmaka countries (cf. *IHQ.*, XXI, p. 233 ff.). He has made an attempt to prove that "Kuntala in ancient times did not comprise only the North Kanara District and parts of Mysore, Belgaon and Dharwar Districts as stated by Dr. Sircar but that it extended much further to the north so as to include what we now call the Southern Maratha Country." Unfortunately Prof. Mirashi does not notice that practically the same view has been expressed by many other writers including Fleet (*Bom. Gaz.*, I, ii, p. 431) and myself (*Suc. Sāt.*, p. 215). The fact is that where other scholars would locate, according to evidence, the Kuntala country proper in the heart of the Kanarese area and distinguish between that land and the later empire (often called Kuptala) of the imperial Kuntala or Karṇāta, i.e. Kanarese, dynasties, Prof. Mirashi would place Kuntala proper in the Maratha country and would not distinguish the essential Kuntala country from the zigantic Kuntala or Kanarese empire of later times. If, in the days of Warren Hastings, the Benares District formed a part of Bengal, would it justify any one to identify Bengal with Benares or to locate Bengal in Benares? The name Vaṅgāla (Bengal) originally indicated a small district in southern Bengal; it was later used to signify the whole country comprising such ancient lands as Vaṅga, Samataṭa, Suhma, Tāmralipti, Gauḍa and Puṇḍravardhana. Can we locate the ancient Vaṅgāla country in any part of later Vaṅgāla (Bengal)?

Most of the questions raised by Prof. Mirashi in this connection were already answered by me in *Suc. Sāt.* (*loc. cit.*, footnotes) which appears to have escaped his notice. It will be clear from the following quotations from my work.

"Cf. a record of A.D. 1077....... 'In the centre of that middle world is the golden mountain to the south of which is the Bhārata land in which, an ornament....is Banavāsī.' Some other inscriptions also prove that Kuntala was the district round Banavāsī."

"Kuntala and Karṇāṭa are used as synonymous in the *Vikramāṅka-devacarita* by Bilhaṇa.[2] Vikramāditya VI has been called both *Kuntalendu* (or *Kuntalendra*) and *Karṇāṭendu*.....Vaijayantī, identified with Banavāsī, has been described as a *tilaka* (that is to say, the capital) of the Karṇāṭa country in the Birur grant of Viṣṇuvarman.....Karṇāṭa therefore signified the same territory as Kuntala or the country of which Kuntala formed a part.....The separate mention of Kuntala, Karṇāṭ a, Banavāsī, Māhiṣaka (cf. Mahiṣaviṣaya in a Kadamba grant), etc., some of the traditional lists may possibly refer to the fact that these names originally signified separate geographical units abutting on one another. Sometimes however one of them may have formed the part of another; cf. the case of Tamralipti which is mentioned in literature as an independent state, as a part of Suhma and also as a part of Vaṅga; also the case of Taxila (Raychaudhuri, *Indian Antiquities,* p. 186 f.) With the rise of Kanarese powers like the Cālukyas and the Rāṣṭrakūṭ as, the name Karṇāṭa (sometimes alos the name Kuntala) extended over a large part of western and southern Deccan. In the *Kaḷiṅgattuparaṇi,* the *Cālukyas* have been described as *Kuntalar,* 'lords of Kuntala' (literally, 'the Kuntalas,' indicating their Kanarese origin).....An inscription of Harihara II, dated in Śaka 1307.....says that Vijayanagara (modern Hampi) belonged to the Kuntala-viṣaya of the Karṇāṭa country."

Only a few words are required now to be added to the above. Vidarbha and Vatsagulma are separately mentioned in the *Kāmasūtra*. Prof. Mirashi thinks that the former incluced the latter and that they are separately mentioned according to hte Māṭhara-Kauṇḍinya *nyāya*. It will be clear from the extract quoted from my book that I would partially apply the same *nyāya* to explain the separate mention of Banavāsī and Kuntala in the *Mahābhārata* and the *Vāyu Purāṇa* on which Prof. Mirashi has taken his stand. The *Daśakumāracarita* and the *Kāvyamīmāṃsā* were composed in an age when the name Kuntala was often applied to the Kanarese empire of the Cālukyas and their successors (see *Suc. Sāt.*, p. 216, note 1), which usually included the Kuntala country proper. The separate mention of Banavāsī indicating Kuntala proper and Kuntala signifying the Kanarese empire in these works has nothing to do with Prof. Mitashi's location of the Kuntala country proper in the South Maratha country.

Prof. Mirashi suggests that the root *śās* or *praśās* means governing when the object is a territory and chastising when the object is a living being and that, in the passage *śrīmat-kuntalānāṃ praśātā,* the word *praśāsitā* means a ruler because the object of *praśas* in this case is not a living being out the Kuntala country. Unfortunately, he does not notice that, even if the distinction in the meaning of the verb is conceded, there is absolutely no reason why *Kuntala* (like *Surāṣṭra* in verse 11 of the Junagarh inscription of Skandagupta) should be taken in the sense of hte Kuntala country (an inanimate object) and not in that of the Kuntala people. What can then be the objection if *śrīmat-kuntalānāṃ praśāsitā* is translated "the chastiser of the illustrious Kuntala people"?

I do not subscribe to Prof. Mirashi identification of the Ṛṣika country with Khandesh. Sylvain Lévi rightly regards Ṛsika as the southernmost country in Gautamīputra Śātakarṇi's empire to the south of Aśmaka. According to the reading of the Hathigumpha inscription preferred by Barua and myself, the city of Ṛṣikanagara (capital of the Ṛṣika country) was situated on the Kṛṣṇabenā (Krishna). As regards his identification of Aśmaka with the Ahmadabad and Bhir Districts, it is certainly impossible for us to understand why the Nander-Nizamabad region lying immediately to the east of the area could not be incluced. I consider Ray-chaudhuri's identifications of Paudanya, the Aśmaka capital, with Bodhan in the Nizamabad District as exceptionally satisfactorily and suggest that even Ahmadabad-Bhir area or parts of it may have been included in the Aśmaka country and in the dominions of the Vākāṭakas of Vatsa-gulma. Nothing more can be said in the present state of our knowledge. We have to wait for further evidence. As however the Vākāṭakas of Vatsagulma are known to have ruled over northern Hyderabad, which is that ancient Aśmaka country proper according to many writers including Raychaudhuri and myself, they may have been regarded as the lords of Aśmaka. As regards the inclusion of Vatsagulma in Vidarbha, suggested by writers like Rājaśekhara (about the beginning of the tenth century), I may draw Prof. Mirashi's attention to what has been said about Tāmralipti and Takṣaśilā in the extract quoted from my book. Vatsagulma, like those localities, appears to have been sometimes a seperate state, sometimes a part of Aśmaka and sometimes a part of Vidarbha. It is well-known that Mūlaka or the land round Paithan in the Autangabad District was sometimes a separate country but was often regarded as a part of Aśmaka. For the expansion of Aśmaka, the readers may be referred to Raychaudhuri's *Pol. His.* cited in my paper in *IHQ.*, XXII, pp. 233-35.

In conclusion it may be pointed out that I am diffident in reading political history from fictions like the *Daśakumāracarita* exactly in the lines of Prof. Mirashi.

References

1. The tradition about Banavasi having been the capital of the Kuntala country was remembered even after the foundation of the Kuntala-Karṇāṭa (Kanarese) empire. For a tenth century record mentioning of Kuntala king residing at *Vanavāsa,* indicating the city as well as "exile", see *El.,* XXII, 132.
2. Note that the Cālukyas of Badami (*El.,* IV, 88, etc.) and Kalyani (ib, V, 16, etc.) were regarded as kings of Kuntala, while the Cālukya army was called the Karṇāṭaka *bala* (*IA.,*XI, 112, etc.). In Cola records like the Kanyakumari inscription (*El.,* XVIII, 27; vv. 69, 76), the Cālukya enemies of Rājendra I are mentioned as lords of the Kuntalas, while those of Virarājendra as kings of the Krṇāṭa family.

32

Were the Vākāṭakas the Rulers of Aśmaka?

V. V. Mirashi

In my article on the Rāṣṭrakūṭas of Mānapura.[1] I have shown that the Pāṇḍaraṅgapalli plates discovered in a village near Kolhapur describe Mānāṅka, the grandfather of the Rāṣṭrakūṭa king Avidheya in the following words :—

सविदर्भाश्मकबिजेता मानाङ्कनृपतिः श्रीमत्कुन्तलानां प्रशासिता।

This passage[1] states that the king Mānāṅka conquered Vidarbha and Aśmaka and ruled over the glorious Kuntala country. This Mānāṅka was the founder of the Early Raṣṭrakūṭa Dynasty. I further showed in that article that the Kuntala country where Mānāṅka was ruling comprised the upper Kṛṣṇā valley. Mānapura mentioned in the Unḍikavāṭikā grant[2] of Abhimanyu, another member of this dynasty, was founded by this Mānāṅka and is probably identical with Māṇ, the chief town in the Māṇ *tālukā* of the Sātārā District in the Bombay Presidency. These Early Rāṣṭrakūṭas who were ruling in the Kṛṣṇā valley were the contemporaries of the Vākāṭakas who were their northern neighbours and with whom they often came into conflict. One of these kings, probably Devarāja, was the Kuntaleśa (the lord of Kuntala) at whose court the famous Sanskrit poet Kālidāsa was sent as an ambassador by his patron Candragupta II Vikramāditya as stated in a *Kuntaleśvaradautya* and *Śṛṅgāraprakāśa*.[3]

Dr. D. C. Sircar, who has recently written on this subject, has put a novel interpretation on the expression *śrīmat-Kuntalānām praśāsitā*. He takes it to mean that Mānāṅka was the chastiser of the Kuntalas.[4] Further, he identifies this Kuntala country with the kingdom of the Kadambas. In a note recently published in this Journal,[5] he has suggested that Aśmaka which was one of the countries conquered by Mānāṅka was identical with the dominion of the Vatsagulma branch of the

Vākāṭakas. It is proposed to examine these identifications in some detail in the present article.

Let us first take the identification of Kuntala. As Dr. Sircar has shown, Mayūraśarman, the progenitor of the Kadamba family is, in some later records, represented as ruling over the Kuntala country which shows that the country round Vanavāsī (modern Banavāsi in the north Kanara District of the Bombay Presidency) was then included in Kuntaladeśa. But this does not mean that Kuntala did not comprise any territory to the north of the Kadamba kingdom. The boundaries of ancient countries have varied from time to time. As I have shown elsewhere, the Kṛṣṇā valley where Mānāṅka and his descendants were ruling was undoubtedly included in the Kuntala country. The following verse[6] which occurs in the Nilgund plate describes the Later Cālukya emperor Jayasiṁha II *alias* Mallikāmoda as ruling over the Kuntala country where flows the famous river Kṛṣṇavarṇā (i.e., the Kṛṣṇā which gets this name after its confluence with the Veṇā near Māhuli, 3 miles east of Sātāra) : –

विख्यातकृष्णवर्णो तैलस्नेहोपलब्धसरलत्वे।
कुन्तलविषये नितरां विराजते मल्लिकामोद: ॥

The Later Rāṣṭrakṭas[7] and Cālukyas[8] who ruled over the country watered by the Kṛṣṇā and its tributaries are described in contemporary records and Sanskrit works as rulers of Kuntala. The capital of the Later Rāṣṭrakūṭas was at Mānyakheṭa, modern Mālkheḍ in the Culbarga District of the Nizam's State, while that of the Later Cālukyas was at Kalyāṇ near Bidar in the Bidar District in the same State. Both these capitals are situated several miles north of the Kṛṣṇā. Mālkheḍ is about 250 miles, as the crow flies, north by east of Banavāsi and more than 50 miles north of the Kṛṣṇā. Kalyāṇa is about 50 miles almost due north of Mālkheḍ. According to Rājaśekhara Kuntala was included in Mahārāṣṭra.[9] The *Udayasundarīkathā* says that Pratiṣṭhāna, modern Paiṭhaṇ on the Godāvarī, was the capital of the Kuntala country.[10] This accords with the tradition that Hāla, the author of the *Saptaśatī,* an anthology in Mahārāṣṭrī Prakrit, rules at Pratiṣṭhāna in the Kuntala country.[11] The three Mahārāṣṭras of which Pulakeśin II became emperor, evidently after defeating the Kalacuris, were probably (1) Vidarbha comprising modern Berar and the Marathi-speaking parts of the Central Provinces and the northern districts of the Nizam's State, (2) Northern Mahārāṣṭra including Ṛṣika (Khandesh). Nāsikya (Nasik), Mūlaka (the country round Pratiṣṭhāna) and Aśmaka (modern Ahmadnagar and Bhir Districts) and (3) Southern Mahārāṣṭra or Kuntala.[12] These references will show that Kuntala in ancient times did not comprise only the

North Kanara District and parts of Mysore, Belgaon and Dharwar Districts as states by Dr. Sircar, but that it extended much further to the north so as to include what we now call the Southern Maratha country.

Some passages in early literature indicate, on the other hand, that in early, times the Kuntala country did not include the territory round Vanavāsī. The *Mahābhārata* and the *Vāyupurāṇa* mention Vanavāsī separately from Kuntala.[13] The *Daśakumāracarita* mentions in the eighth Ucchvāsa the ruler of Kuntala as a powerful feudatory[14] of the emperor of Vidarbha. He treacherously attacked his liegelord in the rear while he was fighting with the Vānavāsya (*i.e.*, the ruler of Vanavāsī) who had invaded the country of Vidarbha. As I have shown elsewhere,[15] the narrative in that chapter contains a reflex of the actual historical events which occurred in the last period of Vākāṭaka rule. It clearly indicates that the Vanavāsī Kingdom was different from Kuntaladeśa. In his Kāvyamīmāṁsā Rājaśekhara also mentions Vānavāsaka (i.e., the country round Vanavāsī) as different from Kuntala.[16] These references leave no doubt that at least in the period during which the Vākāṭakas and the Early Rāṣṭrakūṭas were flourishing the Kadamba kingdom was outside the country of Kuntala and the Kuntala comprised the upper and central valleys of the Kṛṣṇā. This is precisely the region where the Early Rāṣṭrakūṭas were ruling.

It may however be asked, 'How is Mānāṅka who ruled over this territory called the chastiser of the Kuntala?' The answer to this question is that expression *śrīmat-Kuntalanāṁ praśāsitā* does not denote any such chastisement. The root *śās* or *praśās* no doubt conveys both the senses of governing and chastising, but the former occurs when the object is some territory and the latter when it is a living being.

Notice, for instance, the following cases –

(A) Governing –

(i) सत्पुत्रः पार्थिवेन्द्रस्य प्रशशास धर्म्मेण मेदिनीम्। v.8

Vākāṭaka Inscription in Cave xvi at Ajaṇṭā.

(ii) सर्व्वेषु भृत्येष्वपि संहतेषु यो मे प्रशिष्यान्निखिलान्सुराष्ट्रान्।

Gupta Inscriptions, p. 59.

(iii) कुमारगुप्ते पृथिवीं प्रशासति। *Ibid.* p. 82.

(B) Chastising or controlling –

(i) राज्ञः प्रवरसेनस्य शासनं रिपुशासनम्। *Ibid.* p. 245.

(ii) प्रशासितारं सर्वेषाम्। *Manusmṛti, xii,* 122.

In the present case the object of *praśās* is the *Kuntala* country. Hence the correct meaning of the expression *śrīmat Kuntalānām praśāsitā* is 'the ruler or governor of the glorious Kuntala country.' That this was the intended meaning is also clear from the contrast in the two expression *sa-Vidarbh-Āśmaka-vijetā* and *śrīmat-Kuntalānāṁ praśāsitā*. The drafter of the record has prefixed the adjective *śrīmat* meaning 'glorious' or 'prosperous' to the name of Kuntala where the king Mānāṅka was ruling, whereas he has not done so in the case of the countries Vidarbha and Aśmaka which the king had conquered. This should leave no doubt that Kuntala was the homeland of these Rāṣ ṭrakūṭas of Mānapura.

We shall next take up the identification of Aśmaka. The passage from the *Suttanipāta* referred to by Dr. Sircar shows that Aśmaka lay to the south of the Godāvarī.[17] To the north of this country was Mūlaka the capital of which was Pratiṣṭhāna[18] (modern Paiṭhāṇ on the Godāvarī). The Nasik cave inscription of Puḷumāvi groups together Asika (Ṛṣīka or modern Khandesh) Asaka (Aśmaka or modern Ahmednagar and Bhir districts and Mūlaka (modern Aurangabad district).[19] The name of Mūlaka does not occur in later literature or inscriptions. The narrative in the eighth Ucchvāsa of the *Daśakumāracarita* mentions the rulers of Ṛṣīka and Aśmaka as feudatories of the emperor of Vidarbha, but is silent about Mūlaka. Aśmaka may therefore have extended in the north up to the Sātmālā range.

Dr. Sircar thinks that Aśmaka must have included southern Berar the capital of which was Vatsagulma. He has advanced two reasons for this view. The first is that the country of Vidarbha, of which the ancient capital was Kuṇḍinapura in the Amraoti District, lay on both the banks of the Varadā (Modern Wardhā) according to the *Mālavikāgnimitra*. He suggests by this that Vatsagulma was not included in either of these divisions of ancient Vidarbha. As a matter of fact Vatsagulma (modern Bāsim) lies only about 75 miles from the west bank of the Wardha and is north of the Pengaṅgā which forms the southern boundary of modern Berar. It was therefore undoubtedly included in Western Vidarbha. The statement in the *Mālavikāgnimitra* must not be taken quite literally. Just as there was some portion of Vidarbha north of Multan where the Wardhā takes its rise, similarly there was undoubtedly some territory of Vidarbha south of the confluence of the Wardhā with the Pengaṅgā which afterwards joins the Godāvarī. In the age of the Vākāṭakas Vidarbha was divided not by the river Wardhā, but by the Ajaṇṭā or Sātmālā range. The northern portion was under the rule of the elder branch of the Vākaṭaka family which had its capital first at Nandivardhana and later on at Pravarapura and Padmapura. The capital of the southern portion which extended to the Godāvarī was Vatsagulma. We need not therefore suppose that Vidarbha was confined only to the territory north of the Pengaṅgā.

The second and more important reason advanced by Dr. Sircar to support his view is that the people of Vatsagulma are distinguished from those of Vidarbha in some passages of Vātsyāyana's *Kāma sūtra.*[20] This appears, however to be an instance of *Māṭhara Kauṇḍinya-nyāya* explained and illustrated by Patañjalī.[21] Though *Vatsagulma* was included in Vidarbha, it is mentioned separately as its customs were in some respects different from those of the other parts of Vidarbha. An analogous instance is furnished by the Mahārāṣṭrakas and Dākṣiṇātyas who are mentioned separately in the *Kāmasūtra.*[22] Mahāraṣṭra being situated in South India, its inhabitants were included among the Dākṣiṇātyas, (Southerners), but they are mentioned separately as in some respects they had peculiar customs. Vatsaguḷma need not therefore be supposed to have been outside the limits of ancient Vidarbha.

An insuperable objection to the proposed identification of the Vatsagulma country with Aśmaka is the explicit statement of Rājaśekhara. In his *Kāvyamīmāṁsā* (p. 10) Rājaśekhara says –

तत्नास्ति मनोजन्मनो देवस्य क्रीडावासो विदर्भेषु वत्सगुल्मं नाम नगरम्।

This clearly shows that the territory round Vatsagulma was included in Vidarbha.[23] In his *Karpūramañjarī*[24] Rājaśckhara mentions *Vacchchhomī* (Sanskrit, Vātsagulmī) as a synonyam of the *Vaidarbhīrīti.* That Vatsagulma had become famous in ancient times as a centre of Prakrit literature is clear from such Prakrit *kāvyas* as *Harivijaya* which, as I have shown elsewhere,[25] was composed by the Vākāṭaka king Sarvasena of the Vatsagulma branch. Rājaśekhara's statement about Vatsagulma being included in Vidarbha is also corroborated by the narrative in the eighth *Ucchvāsa* of the *Daśakumāracarita* to which I have referred above more than once. As stated before, the narrative belongs to the last period of Vākāṭaka rule. It shows that six feudatory kingdoms of the south, including Aśmaka, owned the supremacy of the emperor of Vidarbha. This state of things existed only during and immediately after the reign of Hariṣeṇa, the last great Vākāṭaka emperor. All the events and topographical references in that narrative can be satisfactorily explained if referred to the period following the death of Hariṣeṇa.[26] We now know that Hariṣeṇa belonged to a younger branch of the Vākāṭaka family which reigned at Vatsagulma (modern Basim in the Akola District of Berar). This place must have continued as the royal capital during the reign of Hariṣeṇa's successor also. In that case Vatsagulma was not only included in Vidarbha, but was its capital. It was outside the limits of Aśmaka, for the ruler of the latter country is described in the narrative as a feudatory of the king of Vidarbha.

The foregoing discussion must have made it plain that the country over which the Early Rāṣṭrakūṭa king Mānāṅka was ruling was Kuntala and that the Vatsagulma country was comprised in Vidarbha which extended from the Narmadā in the north to at least the Godāvarī in the south.

References

1. *A.B.O.R.I.*, vol. XXV, pp. 36f. This reference to Kuntala was missed by the editor of the plates who read the words as *sāt-Kunta-dharāṇaḥ*. My reading has now been accepted by scholars.
2. *J.B.B.R.A.S.*, vol. XVI, pp. 88f.
3. *A.B.O.R.I.*, vol. XXV, p. 45.
4. *A New History of the Indian People,* vol. VI, p. 88, n.1.
5. *Ante,* vol. XXII, pp. 233f.
6. *Ep. Ind.*, vol. XII, p. 153. Dr. Barnett translates, 'Mallikāmoda is very illustrious in the land of Kuntala, which is famous for the (river) Kṛṣṇavarṇā and has a loyalty arising from affection for Taila (II)'. There is a beautiful play on the words, for which see *ibid.*, p. 144. Dr. Fleet says that Kuntala is well known as a general name for the Western Cālukya territory about the Ghauts.
7. Cf. Rājaśekhara, *Karpūramañjarī* (Harward Or. Series), Act. 1.

   आत्थे एत्थ दक्खिणावधे कुन्तलेसुं सअलजणवल्लहो वल्लहराओ णाम राजा। As I have shown elsewhere, this probably refers to the contemporary Rāṣṭrakūṭa king as the Rāṣṭrakūṭas were known by the *biruda* Vallabharāja.
8. Padmagupta in his *Navasāhasāṅkacarita* (I, 74) refers to the contemporary kings of the Later Cālukya Dynasty as *Kuntalendra*. Bilhaṇa also refers to the Later Cālukya kings as rulers of Kuntala. See *Vikramāṅkadeva-carita,* Canto, V., nos. 30, 47, 81, 84 etc.
9. See the following passage from Rājśekhara's *Bālarāmāyaṇa,* Act III :–

   हेमप्रभा—सिणिद्धसामलधणकुडिलकुन्दले कुन्दलेसरो एसो ता इमस्स दंसणोण सहलीकुर, पसइसमप्पभाणं णअणणिम्माणम्।

   सीता—जो मरहट्ठवरिट्ठो।
10. Cf. *Udayasundarīkathā,* कुन्तलेषु तटे गोदावरीति महासरित: प्रतिष्ठानं नाम नगरम्। p. 21 प्रतिष्ठाननगरपरमेश्वर: कुन्तलानामधीश्वरो राजा मलयवाहनो भवान्।
11. Cf. Bhuvanapāla's com. on the *Saptaśatī* (v. 1) – हाल इति शातवाहनस्य कुन्तलाधिपस्य नाम।

See also *Vajjālagga* v.468 – पुरिसविसेसेण सइत्तणाइं न कुलक्कमेण महिलाणं। सग्गं गए वि हाले न मुयइ गोला पइट्ठाणं ॥

12. Cf. Vaidya, *History of Mediaeval Hindu India,* vol. III, p. 254. It is noteworthy that Pulakeśin II who ruled over this territory is called the king of Mahārāṣṭra by Yuan Chwang.

13. Cf. *Mahābhārata,* Bhīṣmaparvan, Jambūkhaṇḍa, ch. 9, and *Vāyupurāṇa,* ch. 45, vv. 124-27.

14. Cf. *Daśakumāracarita* (B.S.S.), p. 138 अश्मकेन्द्रस्तु कुन्तलपतिमेकान्ते समभ्यधत्त। प्रमत्त एव राजा कलमाणि नः परामृशति। कियत्यवज्ञा सोढव्या। मम शतमास्ते हस्तिनां पञ्चशतानि च ते।...अयं च वानवास्यः परं मे मित्रम्। अमुनैनं दुर्विनीतमग्रतो व्यतिषक्तं पृष्ठतो प्रहरेम।

15. *A.B.O.R.I.,* vol. XXVI, pp. 20 f.

16. *Kāvyamīmāṃsā,* (G.O.S.). First Ed. p. 93, माहिष्मत्याः परतो दक्षिणापथः। यत्र महाराष्ट्र माहिषकाश्मकविदर्भकुन्तलक्रथकैशिकसूर्पारककाञ्चीकेरलक्रावेरमुरलवानवासक...प्रभृतयो जनपदाः।

17. *Suttanipāta,* Pārāyaṇavaggo, Vatthugāthā, 5, 2. सो अस्सकास्स विसये मूलकस्स समासने। वसी गोधावरीकूले उञ्छेन च फलेन च॥

18. *Ibid.,* v. 36.

19. *Ep. Ind.* vol. VIII, pp. 10f.

20. *Kāmasūtra* (Kashi Sanskrit Series), pp. 261, 268.

21. Cf. तद्यथा 'ब्राह्मणा भोज्यन्तां माठरकौण्डिन्यौ परिवेविषाताम्' इति। नेदार्नी तौ भुञ्जाते। *Mahābhāṣya* (N. S. ed.), vol. I, p. 113.

22. *Kāmasūtra,* p. 102.

23. It would rather seem that Vidarbha in the narrow sense meant Southern Vidarbha of which the capital was Vatsagulma, northern Vidarbha being called Krathafaiśika. Kālidāsa identifies the two, but Rājaśekhara distinguishes between them. See the passage from the *Kāvyamīmāṃsā,* cited above in n. 16.

    In his *Bālarāmāyaṇa* also Rājaśekhara gives the name *Krathakaiśika* ot Northern Vidarbha and mentions its capital Kuṇḍinapura. See *Bālarāmāyaṇa,* Act III, v. 50.

24. *Karpūramañjarī,* Act I, v. I.

25. *Ante,* vol. XXI, pp. 196f.

26. See my article 'Historical data in Daṇḍiniś *Daśakumāra carita*', *A.B.O.R.I.*, Vol. XXVI, pp. 26 f.

33

A Note on Rājagṛha

Helen M Johnson

In his monograph, "Rājagṛha in Ancient Literature."[1] Dr. Law intends to give an exhaustive study of Rājagṛha "from all the available literary sources, Brahmanical, Jain and Buddhist." But the only Jain source that he cites is Jinaprabhasūri's *Vividhatīrthakalpa,* a work dated by Winternitz between 1326-1331 A.D.[2] This work doubtless has the most detailed topographical description of Rājagṛha and its surroundings known so far in Jain literature, but for its early history and traditions we have a source almost 200 years earlier in that encyclopedia of all things Indian – the *Triṣaṣṭiśalākāpuruṣa-carita* of Hemacandra.

I have myself some years ago given a summary of Hemacandra's account of the history of the time in which Rājagṛha flourished.[3] At the time I wrote my article the *Mañjuśrīmūlakalpa* had not been printed.[4] Hence the *Triṣaṣṭi*⁰ was the earliest work in which I found the name Kuśāgrapura for Rājagṛha. Dr. Law also did not find the name in Pāli nor Ardhamāgadhī.[5]

Dr. Law decides that Rājagṛha was "just another name for the capital"[6] He discusses the account of Huen Thsang and Fa-Hien who speak of the 'old city' and 'new city' of Rājagṛha and he decides that they had confused the 'New Rājagṛha' with Pāṭaliputra, which was in fact the new Rājagṛha, or new capital of Magadha, as distinguished from the old Rājagṛha or Girivraja with its outer walls."[7]

As Dr. Law omits any reference to Hemacandra and as his account supports the Chinese in some respects, it seems advisable to call attention again to his statements about Rājagṛha. Notwithstanding the learning for which he was noted. Hemacandra can hardly be suspected of drawing his version from the Chinese. They must be two independent accounts going back to a well-established tradition and cannot be dismissed lightly.

Hemacandra says, in brief:[8] Prasenajit was king of Kuśāgrapura and was a powerful king. Among his numerous sons Śreṇika had distinguished himself and had been chosen as his successor, a fact which Prasenajit concealed. Because of frequent fires in Kuśāgrapura Prasenajit issued an edict that any one in whose house a fire occurred would be exiled from the city. As a fire subsequently occurred in the palace. Prasenajit felt bound by his own edict, left the city, and founded Rājagṛha. Prasenajit lived there and it was in Rājagṛha that Śreṇika became king. He came there from Veṇātaṭapura[9] where he had been living because of his father's apparent disfavour.

After Kūṇika-Ajātaśatru had been responsible for the death of Śreṇika, his father, overcome by remorse he left Rājagṛha and founded Campā.[10] Kūṇika was killed on an expedition[11] and his son Udāyin succeeded him. Pātaḷiputra was founded after the death of Kūṇika. Udāyin founded it to assuage his grief at his father's death, in imitation of his father's founding of Campā.[12]

There are, of course, differences in Hemacandra's and the Chinese versions, but they definitely agree that a new city was founded because of a fire and there is no reason to suppose that this new city was Pāṭ aliputra rather than Rājagṛha itself. The Campā which Kūṇika founded cannot be Campā, the capital of Aṅga. One of Śreṇika's sister-in-law was married to the king of Campā and Campā of the Aṅgas, which was still independent of Magadha in Hemacandra, was, of course, well-known to him.[13] Dr. T.L. Shah discusses the two Campās.[14] He does not use the *Triṣaṣṭi,*[0] but the *"Bharteśvar Bāhubali Vṛti"* which is not available to me. Apparently in that work Kūṇika rebuilt the Campā of the Aṅgas which had been destroyed in a war.[15] I cannot reconcile all of Dr. Shah's passages on the two Campās,[16] but in any case Hemacandra was not the only author who connected Kūṇika with the rebuilding or founding of a Campā.

References

1. Memoirs of the Archæological Survey of India, no. 58 (1938).
2. In his *History of Indian Literature,* vol. II, 121.
3. *JAOS.*, 45 (1925), 301 ff.
4. *An Imperial History of India (the Mañjuśrīmūlakalpa),* K.P. Jayaswal, Lahore, 1934.
5. Page 1 of the monograph.
6. p. 21.
7. p. 23.
8. Cf. T. L. Shah, *Ancient India,* I, 148 f.
9. *Triṣaṣṭiśalākāpuruṣacarita,* 10.6. 1-139.
10. *Triṣaṣṭi°* 10.12. 168-189.
11. *Triṣaṣṭi°* 10.12. 420-24.
12. *Triṣaṣṭi°* 10.12. 426 and Pariśiṣṭaparvan 6. 22-41, 177-180.
13. *Triṣaṣṭi°* 10.9 and *JAOS.*, 45, 306.
14. *Ancient India,* vol. I, Chap. V.
15. *Id.* I. 111 and footnote.
16. *Id.* I. 126.

34

The Karoura of Ptolemy

K V Krishna Ayyar

Writing about the year 150 A.C., Ptolemy mentions the following as the inland cities of Limyrike between the Pseudostomos and the Baris[1] : –

PASAGE, MASTANOUR, KOURELLOUR, POUNNATTA, where is beryl, KAROURA, the royal seat of KEROBOTHRAS, AREMBOUR, BIDERIS, PANTIPOLIS, ADARIMA, KOREOOR.

This royal seat of Kerobothras still remains one of the puzzles of ancient South Indian history; for according to the early classical writers the capital of this prince was MOUZIRIS which was also an entrepôt of trade and this city of MOUZIRIS is mentioned by Ptolemy as "an emporium" on the coast along with TYNDIS, the mouth of the river Pseudostomos, KOREOURA, BAKAREI, and the mouth of the river Baris.[2] This river, Pseudostomos, has been identified as the river PERIYAR, in the present Cochin state, and Baris as the KALLADA which pours its waters near Quilon in the Travancore state.

Among the classical writers Pliny is the first to make a definite reference to the ports and kingdoms on the west coast of South India. His *Natural History* was completed in 77 A.C., two years before his death. In it he says: – "From thence (Ocelis) they sail with the wind called Hippalos in forty days to the first commercial station of India named Muziris. . . . . . The ruler of the country at the time which I speak was *Coelobothras*" (according to another manuscript *Celobotras).*[3] In the *Periplus of the Erythræan Sea,* "written a little later after the death of Pliny between the years A.C. 80 and 89,"[4] we have as follow: – "Then follows NAOURA and TUNDIS, the first marts of LIMURIKE, and after these MOUZIRIS and NELKUNDA, the seats of government. To the kingdom under the sway of KEPROBOTRAS, TUNDIS is subject, a village of great note situate near the sea. MOUZIRIS which pertains to the same realm is a city at the height of prosperity."[5] The next writer to allude to these places is Ptolemy.

It is agreed on all hands that LIMYRIKE stands for DAMIRICE or Tamilakam, MOUZIRIS is Muyiricotta or Muyirikodu comprised within the limits of the present town of Cranganore and TUNDIS or TYNDIS is Kadalundi a few miles from Calicut. It is also certain that Kepro-Celo, and Cœlo-bothras is identical with the KERALAPUTRAS mentioned by Asoka.[6]

What were the limits of the territory of Keralaputra? Bishop Caldwell says:—"The name in Sanskrit, and in full, is *Keralaputra,* but both *Kera* and *Kela* are Dravidian abbreviations of *Kerala*. They are Malayalam, however, not Tamil abbreviations and the district over which Keralaputra ruled is that in which the Malayalam language is now spoken."[7] He confines, therefore, the dominion of Kerala-putra to the country west of the Ghats, to the narrow coast strip between the mountain and the sea. But *Kera* does not seem to have been an abbreviation of the Sanskrit Kerala; instead, *Kerala* itself seems to have been a variant of CHERA. "Cheraman," says Dr. Gundert,[8] "is the name of the whole dynasty of Chera or Kerala rulers; for these two names are the same, Kerala being only the Kanarese pronunciation as appears from the Deccan inscriptions of W. Elliott Esq. in which no Chera is associated with Pāndya but only a Kerala." Further, Pandit Saurirayan in the course of a learned article discussing the etymology of the words CHERA and KERALA says[9]:—"It is a well-ascertained fact that in Kanarese the initial palatals of Tamil words change as a rule into gutturals e.g.,

Tamil Cheyidan (He did)=Kanarese Geyidanu
Chevi (ear)=Kivi
Chenni (head)=Kenne

There are many instances as these and the same phonetic process was met by the Tamil word *Cheralam* and is naturally pronounced *Keralam*. Thus we can have no hesitation in saying that *Chera* is a contraction of *Cheralam* and that *Cherala* and *Kerala* are etymologically and historically the same."

Karoura, then, was the capital of the Chera ruler. Bishop Caldwell identifies this place with Karur, a few miles from Erode on the Erode-Trichinopoly branch of the South Indian Railway. "Karur," he observes[10] "is mentioned in Tamil traditions as the ancient capital of the Chera, Kera ot Kerala kings, and is generally identified with Karur, an important town in the Coimbatore district, originally included in the Chera kingdom . . . . . Ptolemy's word, *Karoura,* represents the Tamil name of the place with perfect accuracy." Following this lead, an attempt has been made to find in the "PUNTURAKKON,"(the lord of Puntura), one of the titles of the Zamorin, a reference to *Perindurai,* a village in the Coimbatore district and a station on the main railway line to Madras from the west coast and to trace the origin of his dynasty to some place on the banks of the Kaveri.

High as the authority of the learned bishop is, there are weighty reasons against his identification, CHENGUTTUVAN was the emperor of the Cheras when Ptolemy complied his geography. In the "CHILAPPATHIKARAM" and the "MANIMEKHALAI" two Tamil works composed in this period, the one by no less a person than the younger brother of the Emperor, the other by his protégé,VANCHI or TIRUVANCHIKULAM, figures the capital of the Chera ruler about a mile and a half from the *Mouziris* of the classical writers. After a critical examination of the geographical background of the *Chilappathikaram,* the fauna and flora of the country traversed by Chenguttuvan, the presents laid at the royal feet by his subjects, and the routes taken by Kannagi and the party sent in search of her, Mr. Ponnambalam Pillai had no doubt that the capital of Chera was Tiruvanjikkulam and not Karur in the Coimbatore district.[11] Further it is to Tiruvanjikkulam as the capital of the Cheras and the centre of learning and philosophy in the west coast that Manimekhalai, the daughter of the hero of the *Chilappathikaram* comes to find consolation.

Further the choice of such a town as Karur so far away from the sea is also opposed to the peculiar conditions of the Chera empire as the premier sea-power of the south in those days. The prosperity of the "three crowned kings" of the south depended on their seaborne commerce. It was for the convenience of trade that Karikala, the great Chola king, built a new capital at the mouth of the Kaveri and shifted his residence from the inland Uraiyur. The first two capitals of the Pandyan kingdom were situated, the one on the sea and the other at the confluence of the Tampraparni with the sea. And when this was submerged and the third capital, the present Madura, was founded on the banks of the Vaigai, KORKAI or KOLKHOI of the *Periplus* at the month of the Tampraparni became the commercial capital of the kingdom and the seat of the heir-apparent.

To the Cheras overseas commerce was no less important. The greatest wars of the Cheras had been probably those with NANNAN of Tulunad and his allies the KADAR-KADAMBA pirates. "Their particular service to civilization," it has been remarked, "consisted in their suppression of this post of piracy on the west coast which both the first Chera known to us and his son took so much pains to suppress, while other

Cheras perhaps subordinate chieftains did make substantial contribution towards achieving this object.[12]" The Tamil poet Paranar compares Chenguttuvan to a fisherman who constantly engaged himself on the sea to get rid of his enemies with a view to making the articles, coming over sea, available to those inside his own territory.[13]" Another Tamil poet, Nappalcaiyar, alludes to the Chera sea power in the following comparison of himself with other poets: –

> "No rival bard I sing ! We are little barks
> That sail not on the western main,
> Where Cheran's warlike fleets are seen."[14]

It does not stand to reason that Tiruvanjikkulam, consecrated by the installation of the PATTINIDEVĪ at which were present many kings including Gajabāhu of Ceylon, associated with the memories of the exploits of his ancestors, the trade centre of the empire in maintaining the security of which against the pirates his father lost his life and he himself spent the best part of his long reign, should have been lightly given up by Chenguttuvan, the contemporary of Ptolemy, in favour of a place which was situated in the north-eastern frontier of his empire and which has nothing to recommend it as an imperial capital and seat of government except the sanctity of the river on which it stands.

Too much has been made in the past of the accuracy of Ptolemy's geographical knowledge. Ptolemy compiled his account from various sources. He did not possess, as the author of the *Periplus* did, firsthand knowledge of the countries and towns which he mentioned in his geography. "Ptolemy's is a map of utter confusion," says Mc Crindle,[15] "out of which it is very difficult to extract in a few instances any definite conclusions. He misconceived the form and configuration of the Indian peninsula. He had to fit his data derived from various sources such as maritime and land itineraries based upon real experience into a framework to which they were wholly unsuited and this could be effected only by some Procrustean process or rather by a repetition of such processes concerning which we are left wholly in the dark."

The separate mention of MOUZIRIS and KAROURA as the emporium and the royal seat respectively can be explained, MOUZIRIS was the port, where ships were unloaded and KAROURA was the name of the place where the palace was situated – a mile and a half from the port. The earlier writers – Pliny and the author of the Periplus – did not make any distinction between the bazaar and the royal palace. The KAROURA of Ptolemy could not therefore have been the Karūr of

Bishop Caldwell; it must have been nothing else than Vanchi, the ancient capital of the Cheras in the neighbourhood of MOUZIRIS. The whole argument is clinched by the authoritative statement in the Tamil metrical dictionary, Tivakaram, that the modern name of Vanchi is Karur.[16]

References

1. Mc. Crindle, *Ancient India as described by Ptolemy*, p. 180.
2. *Ibid.*, p. 48.
3. Quoted in Logan, *Malabar Manual,* vol. I, pp. 250-251.
4. McCrindle, *The Periplus,* Introduction, p. 5.
5. *Ibid.*, pp. 131-2.
6. V.A. Smith, *Asoka*, p. 160.
7. *Comparative Grammer of the Dravidian Languages,* p. 95.
8. Quoted in Sangunny Menon, *History of Travancore,* p. 53.
9. *The Tamilian Antiquary*, vol. I, no. 4.
10. *Comparative Grammar of the Dravidian Languages,* pp. 96-97.
11. *The Tamilian Antiquary,* vol. I, no. 9: *The Origin of the Cranganore Temple*, p. 39.
12. S.Krishnaswamy Ayyanger, *The Beginnings of South Indian History,* p. 223.
13. *Ibid.*, p. 221.
14. Pope : *Purnanuru, The Tamilian Antiquary,* vol. I, no. 6, p. 66.
15. *Ancient India as described by Ptolemy,* p. 31.
16. *Gazetteer of the Malabar District*, p. 31.

35

The Antiquity of Paṇḍharpur

B. A. Saletore

Paṇḍharpur is one of the most celebrated spots in Mahārāṣṭra. The absence of any reference to this renowned place of pilgrimage in the *Rāmāyaṇa* and the *Mahābhārata* leads us to infer that in the days of the epics it was not reckoned as a holy centre.[1] It does not figure among the well known traditional holy places, *viz.*, Ayodhyā, Mathurā, Māyā (Hardvār), Kāśī, Avantī, Purī, and Dvārāvatī, which were considered to be the *sapta mokṣa-dāyikāḥ*. From this it may reasonably be concluded that Paṇḍharpur sprang into fame in comparatively recent times. Indeed, this sacred spot, as epigraphical evidence proves, was only a *paḷḷi* or *haḷḷi* (village) in the first quarter of the sixth century A.D., and it continued to be so until the ninth century A.D. But in the first quarter of the thirteenth century A.D., it gained considerable celebrity partly due to the activities of a remarkable saint and partly due to the patronage bestowed on it by a well known Karṇāṭaka monarch.

The original name of Paṇḍharpur was merely Paṇḍara. It has been opined that this name cannot be traced to a Sanskrit origin, and that, therefore, it must be Kannaḍa. Paṇḍharpur is only a Sanskritized form of the word Paṇḍara. The name of the god Viṭṭhaḷa likewise "does not appear to be a Sanskrit name, nor, though several attempts have been made, can the word be correctly traced to any Sanskrit root. The name is probably Kanarese." The same writer asserts that Paṇḍhari was the old name of the village.[2] But epigraphical records prove that Paṇḍarādri was the original name, the locality round about it being called Paṇḍarapaḷḷi or village of Paṇḍara. This is inferred from the Pāṇḍaraṅgapaḷḷi copper-plate of king Avidheya, which has been edited by Dr. Krishna of Mysore. The plate records a grant made by king Avidheya to a learned brāhmaṇa named Jayadiṭṭha, of the villages of Paṇḍaraṅgapaḷḷi along with Anevari, Cāla, Kandaka and Duddapalli (their location being given in detail). We may note the qualifications of the donee:Jayadviṭṭha was "learned in philosophy, of the same *gotra* as Bhārgava, installed in the great office of *upavid,* versed in the Vedic recitations, knower of the three *vidyās,* learned in the four *vedas,* most pious, who had the title preceptor of hundred brāhmaṇas, and whose speech was full of the eight qualities commencing with *vinaya* . . ." To him were granted the five villages named above, "with the eight kinds of wealth." The concluding lines of the same grant are the following: – "At the orders of the king, this was written by Devadatta, lord of Paṇḍarādri (*Deva-dattena Paṇḍarādrīśena*), in the sixteenth year of the reign, named Bhādrapada, on the fifth day of the dark half of Kārtika."[3]

From the above the following may be deduced:Firstly, the donee was a man of exceptional learning. Secondly, he is named after the famous god of the locality – Viṭṭhaḷa-Jayadviṭṭha. Thirdly, the locality is called by its original name Paṇḍara as well as by its Sanskritized form Pāṇḍaraṅga but is expressly stated to have been a *paḷḷi* or village. And fourthly, Devadatta, the scribe, is called lord of Paṇḍarādri, thereby suggesting that Paṇḍara or Pāṇḍaraṅga (the form Pāṇḍuraṅga being not noticeable as yet) was already a place of some importance inspite of the locality around it being called a *paḷḷi.* It is possible that the name Paṇḍarādri was given to the hillock itself on which the renowned temple of Viṭṭhoba stands.[4]

Dr. Krishna has assigned the above copper-plate to the earlier part of November A.D. 516. His arguments are perfectly sound.[5] Since the donee Jayadviṭṭha is called after the god Viṭṭhaḷa of the locality, and since we cannot conceive of a learned man like him living in an insignificant village, we have to assume that Pāṇḍaraṅgapaḷḷi must have already existed as a place of importance before the first quarter of the sixth century A.D. Our surmise is strengthened by the epithet given to the scribe Devadatta. He was *īśa* (lord) of Paṇḍarādri. Evidently we have to suppose that it was a hill (fortress?) of some consequence. If this is admitted, then, the name Paṇḍara may be traced to the Kannaḍa word *paṇḍe,* wisdom, suggesting thereby that before the installation of the image of Viṭṭhaḷa, that spot was already known for its learned men. Whatever that may be, the fact that Jayadviṭṭha is called after the celebrated god of Paṇḍharpur proves beyond doubt that the image of the god must have already been installed at least two or three generations before Jayadviṭṭha's time, *viz., circa* A.D. 460. We may reasonably date, therefore, the importance of Paṇḍharpur to the middle of the century A.D.

Sculptural evidence corroborates the above deduction. The image of the god is standing with its arms akimbo and hands resting on the hips, the left hand holding a conch and the right hand a *cakra* or discus. On the image are carved, but so slightly as to be hardly visible except on a close examination, a waist cloth, and round the waist a waistband or a *kamarband,* the end of which hangs on the right thigh. The ornaments consist of a necklace and in the long ears, earrings which touch the shoulders. It has been rightly remarked that the dress and ornaments of this image resemble the Udayagiri cave sculptures near Bhilsa which date from the beginning of the fifth century A.D.[6]

In the middle of the ninth century A.D., another famous Karnāṭaka monarch confirmed the grant recorded in the above Pāṇḍaraṅgapaḷḷi plate. This is proved from the short confirmatory grant engraved on the back of the third plate of the above Pāṇḍaraṅgapaḷḷi copper-plate. The ruler is called merely Sarbarasa, Lord of Kannavāḍa, Gaṅgavāḍa, Baḷeyavāḍa, Rerṇāḍāḷa, and Siyaḷāra. The epigraph only adds that it was made by his order and engraved by Śembaja of Śintarge. Dr. Krishna, to whom we are again thankful for editing this confirmatory grant, has identified the Sarbarasa mentioned in it with Amoghavarṣa I Nṛpatuṅga Deva, the famous Rāṣṭrakūṭa monarch whose kingdom stretched from the Kāverī to Central India. The absence of any *birudu* or title of Amoghavarṣa in the above grant, and the fact that he is called merely Sarva (Sarbarasa), which seems to have been his proper name, clearly indicate that confirmatory grant must have been inscribed soon after he came to the throne in about A.D. 815-20.[7]

One of the most remarkable names connected with the shrine of Paṇḍharpur is that of Nāmadeva, who has been assigned to the thirteenth century A.D. Another well known devotee of the god Viṭṭhaḷa was the Mhār Cokhāmela who is said to have lived in the same age (*circa* A.D. 1278).[8] No doubt these and the celebrated Jñāneśvara, who also belonged to the same century, spread the greatness of the god Viṭṭhaḷa all over the country.

But the patronage of kings was an essential factor in the evolution of a place from a mere *paḷḷi* into a famous place of pilgrimage of later days. The Karnāṭaka kings seem to have continued the tradition of bestowing their patronage on Pāṇḍaraṅgapaḷḷi. Here we may incidentally mention a ruler whose inscription has been noticed in the *Bombay Gazetteer.* In this work he has been wrongly stated to have been of the Devagiri Yādava line. Over two of the middle pillars in the temple is an old block 7´ 6´´ long, 1´ 2´´ broad and 9´´ thick. The beginning and the end of this inscription are hidden by a part of the pillar capital. The letters are not deeply incised and as the slab forms a part of the roof and is in the dark, the whole inscription can hardly be read without taking out the stone. The following details are given in the *Bombay Gazetteer* concerning the king who made the grant recorded in the inscription :—

(a) His titles:—*Pṛthvīvallabha, Mahārājādhirāja* and *Sarvarāja-cuḍāmaṇi.*

(b) He is said to have belonged to the Yādava line.

(c) The date is given as Śaka 1159 (=A.D. 1237).

(d) The inscription narrates that Someśvara Deva conquered the country round about and encamped at Paṇḍarige on the bank of the Bhīmarathī.

(e) The inscription further records a gift to the god out of the yearly presents from the people of Hiriyagarañja which has been identified with Pūluñj, a village about fifteen miles east of Paṇḍharpur.

The writer of the above notes maintains that since Siṅgahaṇa II of the Devagiri Yādava line ruled from A.D. 1209 to A.D. 1247, the date of this inscription falls within his reign; that Someśvara was another name of Siṅghaṇa II or of his son Jaitugi II; and that at Pūluñj a well-engraved inscription of Siṅghaṇa II has been found.[9]

The inscription mentioned cannot be referred to the Yādava king Siṅghaṇa II at all. But it belongs to the Hoysala king Someśvara Deva. The following reasons will make out point clear:—

The controlling *birudu* in the above list is what the writer states as *sarva-rāja-cuḍāmaṇi*. This is, we presume, a wrong reading for *sarvajñacuḍāmaṇi* which was a special *birudu* of the Hoysala king Someśvara Deva. It was not borne by the Yādava king Siṅghaṇa II whose *birudus* are thus given in a record dated A.D. 1217:—*samasta-bhuvanāśraya* (refuge of all the Universe), *śrīpṛthvīvallabha* (favourite of the goddess Earth), *mahārājādhirāja, rājaparameśvara, paramabhaṭ ṭāraka, Drārāvatī-puravarādhīśvara* (boon lord of Dvārāvatīpura), *Yādava-kula-kamaḷa-kaḷika-vikāsa-bhāskara* (sun in causing the lotus Yādava-kula to unfold), *Māḷavī-malla* (wrestler with Māḷavī), *ari-rāya-ūra-śella* (?), *Gurjara-rāya-vāraṇāṅkuśa* (an elephant goad to Gurjara Rāya), *Teluṅga-rāya-śiraḥ-kamalotpāṭana-punaḥ-athāpanācārya* (plucker of the lotus head of Teluṅga-Rāya and re-establisher of him). *Pannali-giri-durga-rajra-pañjara-vidravaṇa-pravīṇa* (melter down of the cage of adamant the Pannali hill fort), *Ballāḷa-rāya-rājīva-vana-vidh vaṃsana-mattebha* (a rutting elephant in destroying the lotus garden Ballāḷa Rāya), *śrīmat prauḍha-pratāpa cakravarti Rāya-Nārāyaṇa* Śrī Siṅghaṇa Deva.[10]

Someśvara Deva alone had the significant *birudu* of *sarvajña-cuḍāmaṇi*. But it must be said at the same time that he was also known by other similar *birudus* like *su-bhaṭa-cuḍāmaṇi,* as in A.D. 1235, or like *samyakta (samyukta) cuḍāmaṇi,* as in inscriptions ranging from A.D. 1236 to about A.D. 1245.[11] But of all these the *birudu sarvajña cuḍāmaṇi* or crest jewl of omniscience seems to have been the most correct form. This is proved again by epigraphs as well as by the testimony of his court poet Mallikārjuna. An inscription dated A.D. 1239 gives the following *birudus* to king Someśvara:—*śrīmat-pṛthvīvallabha,mahārājādhirāja, rājaparameśvara, paramabhaṭṭāraka, Yādava-kuḷaṃbaradyumaṇi* (sun in the sky of the Yādava kula), *sarvajña-cuḍāmaṇi* (crest jewel of omniscience).[12] Another record dated A.D. 1247 confirms the above *birudu*:it also calls the same ruler *sarvajña-cuḍāmaṇi.*[13]

Now, the fact of the king Someśvara Deva having had the *birudu* of *sarvajña-cuḍāmaṇi* is further corroborated by the court-poet Mallikārjuna in his great anthology of Kannaḍa poetry called *Sūkti-sudhārṇava.* We are once again indebted to Dr. Krishna for bringing to the notice of scholars a fresh copy of this Ms. from the library of Mr. Rama Das of Belur, Hassan District. In the 24th verse of the introductory part of this anthology, Mallikārjuna claims that Someśvara Deva became famous in this world by the work of Malla of Mallikārjuna himself: —

kṛtiyaṃ nirmisi munna mādariḷeyoḷ śrī-Harṣanuṃ Bhoja-bhūpatiyuṃ sat-kavi vajra hasta-nṛpanuṃ sarvajña-Someśana-unnati vettam dharegindu Malla-budhu-nindam.[14]

It is beyond doubt, therefore, that the Hoysala king Someśvara Deva gave a gift to the god at Paṇḍharpur in A.D. 1236.[15] Twenty years after the place was considered to be one of the holy spots in western and southern India. This is proved by an inscription dated A.D. 1255 which calls it 'the great Pāṇḍuraṅga.'[16]

The name Pāṇḍaraṅga has survived till the nineteenth century. In the *Viṭhoba-carita* or *Viṭṭhaḷa-carita,* composed by Veṅkaṭeśa Bhaṭṭa of Kundāpūru in Tuluva, dated A.D. 1830, it is narrated how a brāhmaṇa child about to be sacrificed for the attainment of riches, was saved by the interference of Viṭṭhaḷa of Paṇḍarinagara.[17] Evidently to the people of the Karnāṭaka it was still known by its ancient name Paṇḍari (or Paṇḍara).

References

1. The assertion that Paṇḍharpur was the same as Puṇḍarīka, Puṇḍarīkapura, Puṇḍarīkakṣetra, Puṇḍarīka-*tīrtha*, Pāṇḍupura, Tāpasāśrama, and the forest of Tāpasa, mentioned in the *Mahābhārata* and in other Hindu writings, is wholly untenable. Paṇḍharpur was not the same as the Puṇḍarīka-*tīrtha* spoken of in the *Mahābhārata* on the following grounds : – (1) In the list of *tīrthas* given in the *Vana Parva,* after Kindāna-*tīrtha* comes Kalaśi-*tīrtha,* and then Ambājanma-*tīrtha* which was to the east of Saraka. "One should next proceed, on the tenth day of the lighted fortnight, to the *tīrtha* called Puṇḍarīka. Bathing there, O King, one obtaineth the merit of the Puṇḍarīka sacrifice. One should next proceed to the *tīrtha* called Tripiṣṭapa that is known over the three worlds." *Vana Parva,* See. LXXXIII, p. 258 (Roy). None of these *tīrthas* can be located on the western coast of India. On the other hand, they seem to be places in the north somewhere in the Kedāra region. (2) Paṇḍharpur is not called Puṇḍarīka-kṣetra either in popular parlance or in literature of contemporary times. On Puṇḍarīka-kṣetra, and Pāṇḍupura, Dey gives the following references which are inaccessible to me : *Bṛhad Nāradīya Purāṇa,* Uttara. Ch. 73 where a *liṅga* of Mahādeva is said to have been established by Jaimini; *Caitanya, Caritāmṛta,* Madhya. Ch. 9.

   Paṇḍharpur was not the same as the forest of Tāpasa. The forest of Tapasa is located in the *Mahābhārata* in "the beautiful eastern country.". It is mentioned *after* Prayāga thus: – "In this direction, O foremost of kings, lieth the excellent asylum of Agastya, O Monarch, and the forest called Tāpasa, decked by many ascetics." *Vana Parva,* Sec. LXXXVII, p. 290 (Roy). In the literature of Mahārāṣṭra, as my colleague Professor Dāṇḍekar assures me, Paṇḍharpur is never called Tāpasāśrama. We have, therefore, to locate the *Tabosoi* of Ptolemy, which has been supposed to refer to Paṇḍharpur, anywhere but in or near Paṇḍharpur. On Tāpasāśrama, read *Bṛhatsaṃhitā,* XIV. v. 15; *Brahmāṇḍa Purāṇa,* ch. 49; *Vāyu Purāṇa,* ch. 45, v. 129; *Bombay Gaz.,* I. P. I., p. 511; Dey, *Geographical Dictionary of Ancient and Mediæval India,* pp. 147, 154, 161, 204. (2nd ed. 1927).
2. *Bombay Gazetteer,* XX, p. 423. Paṇḍara was a Kannaḍa name given to individuals. Thus, for example, in A.D. 1279 we have a Paṇḍara Lakṣmī Deva, see *Epigraphia Carnatica,* XI, JI. 30, p. 87. Pāṇḍaraṅga is the 'valiant' person who burnt Kiraṇapura, the residence of Kṛṣṇarāja, as mentioned in the Maliyapuṇḍi grant of Ammarāja II or Vijayāditya VI., the Eastern Cāḷukya king. *Epigraphia Indica,* IX, pp. 48-50.
3. *Mysore Archæological Report* for 1929, p. 198 seq.
4. Dr. Krishna writes that "as no hill of that name (Paṇḍarādri) is known, it (Paṇḍarādrīśena) may stand for Paṇḍarādhiśena." *Mys. Arch. Rep., ibid.,* p. 198, n. (2).
5. *Ibid.,* pp. 202-205.

6. *Bomaby Gaz.*, XX, pp. 424; *Mys Arch. Rep.* for 1929, p. 205; Smith, *His. of Fine Arts in India and Ceylon*, pp. 78-9. (Revised by K. de B. Codrington, 2nd ed, Oxford 1930). There is a sculpture of Viṣṇu or Kṛṣṇa or Pāṇḍuraṅga with arms akimbo but holding flowers or bags, in the south cell of the Lakṣmīnarasiṃha temple, constructed somewhere in the middle of the thirteenth century A.D., perhaps in the reign of the Hoysala king Someśvara Deva or Narasiṃha III. *Mys. Arch. Rep.* for 1931, p. 4.
7. *Mys. Arch. Rep.* for 1929, pp. 209-210; Rice, *Mysore and Coorg from the Inscriptions,* pp. 67, 71.
8. *Bomb. Gaz.*, XX, p. 418.
9. *Bom. Gaz.*, XX, *op. cit.* The writer of this article was one Mr. Santaram Vinayak Kanthak, Assistant Surgeon, Paṇḍharpur.
10. *EC.*, VIII., Sb. 135, text, p. 55. See also Sb, 276, 391, 398, p. 125, seq. 186, 188. These are but a few of the many inscriptions relating to Siṅghaṇa Deva II.
11. *EC.*, XI. Jl. 33, p. 235, Dg. 129, p. 188. The *birudu* in the original is given as *samyakta*. *EC.*, IV. Kr. 76, p. 316, Gu. 26, p. 16 in Tamil-Grantha characters; in Gu. 15, p. 95 it is given in the original as *samakta* which is evidently an error for *samyukta*. This epigraph has been assigned to *circa* A.D. 1245. See also *EC.* VII, Sh. 87, p. 99. The word *samyukta* has been invariably spelt as *samguktva*. It is interesting to observe that the *Mahāmaṇḍaleśvara* Tribhuvanamalla Pāṇḍya Deva, under the Western Cālukya monarch Tribhuvanamalla, was called *samyukta-cuḍāmaṇi* in A.D. 1107. *EC.*, XI, Dg. 128, p. 187.
12. *EC.*, VIII, Sb. 492, p. 220.
13. *EC.*, IV, Ch. 67, p. 2. This is in Tamil-Grantha characters.
14. *Mys. Arch. Rep.* for 1931, p. 88. Mallikārjuna also calls the ruler *sarvajña-cakri-Soma-nṛpāla*. Narasimhachar, *Karnāta Kavicarite,* I, 371. On Mallikārjuna praising his patron read, *ibid.*, p. 373 (Ist ed.).
15. Rice mentions an inscription in Paṇḍharpur which states that the same Hoysala king made a gift to the god (Viṭṭhaḷa) at Paṇḍharpur in Śaka 1159 (A.D. 1236), *Mys. & Coorg.*, p. 105. The reference is given to *Bombay Arch. Report* for 1897-8. Unfortunately this Report is not accessible to me. But I believe that the inscription mentioned by Rice is identical with the one I have discussed above. If Rice's surmise is correct, it seems to suggest that since the Seuṇas or Yādavas continued to make incursions in the north-west of the Hoysala Empire in the reign of king Someśvara (*Mys. & Coorg, ibid.*) the latter in order to propitiate the god made suitable grants to him.
16. *EC.*, V. Ak. 108, p. 157.
17. *Kavicarite,* III, p. 184. But unfortunately there is a printer's error on this page, and the story ends abruptly, For a succinct account of the story, see Kittel, in his Introduction to Nāgavarma's *Chandus*, pp. lxxvii, Mangalore 1875. *The Bom. Gaz.*, XX, p. 422, contains an inscription dated A.D. 1272 which records a gift to the same god by a Śrīpati Daṇṇa . . . ki (Śripati

Daṇṇāyaka ?). In the same page we have an abstract of what the writer says to be a Marāṭhi inscription purporting to be a gift to the same god by Pandit Hemādri. The date is given as A.D. 1276. But the remarks are by no means convincing. The Hemādri referred to here may have been Hemādri, king of Kalyāṇ, mentioned in a record dated A.D. 1268, *EC.*, XI, Dg. 36, p. 45.

36

Harikela and the Ruins at Maināmati[1]

D. C. Bhattacharya

No serious attempt seems to have yet been made by scholars to fix the position of the ancient kingdom of Harikela, though the Chinese accounts glorify it as containing the most celebrated seat of Buddhist learning in Eastern India next to Nālandā. The main site of this long lost university – practically the only one of considerable celebrity in Bengal proper – must be lying buried in one of the districts of Eastern Bengal entirely forgotten by the people.

In Julien's edition of *Hiuen- Tsang* (1858, vol II) there is an ancient map of Central Asia and India, originally published in Japan in 1710, which gives the position of Harikela to the south of Tāmralipta, east of Utkala and south-west of Samataṭa. This is against all other accounts. The earliest mention of Harikela, as far as available to us, is that by the Chinese traveller I-tsing in his second work – 'Memoirs of Eminent Priests who visited India'. A summary of this work is given in the Introduction to Beal's *Life of Hiuen Tsang*. Three of these priests came to Harikela, one of whom an aged Bhikṣu won the respects of the king of that place and was the pontiff of a Vihāra there; he died and was buried at Harikela, where he had collected a large number of Mss. and images. The account however, of another Chinese pilgrim named Wu-hing or Prajñādeva, the Dhyāna master, whom I-tsing actually met in India in the year 685 A.D. (Takakusu: Intro: xxxiii) gives some clue to the actual position of the kingdom. It appears that Wu-hing came to Harikela, which was 'the eastern limit of Eastern India,' starting by sea from Siṃhala towards the north-east. He remained there one year and thence went to Nālandā which is said to be about 100 *yojanas* from Harikela (Takakusu: p. xlvi, Dr. R.C. Majumdar in the *Pravāsī* for Āśvina 1331 B.S. p. 795) . The extent of I-tsing's *yojana* is uncetain, but an idea of thc distance between Nālanda and Harikela can be gathered from the fact that Tāmralipta, according to I-tsing, is more than 60 *yojanas* south (? south-east) from Nālandā on the one hand (Takakusu: p. xxxi, Watter's *Yuan Chwang,* vol. II, p. 190) and 40 *yojanas* south (? south-west) from the eastern limit of India on the other (Takakusu: p. xxxiii). Modern Tamluk is roughly 250 miles from Gaya and Harikela then would be about 400 miles from Gaya, taking us roughly to the eastern borders of the districts of Tippera and Noakhali in Eastern Bengal. Harikela's proximity to the sea indicated by Wu-hing's account precludes the possibility of its lying further up in the north. It should be considered in this connection that I-tsing does not apparently identify Harikela with Samataṭa which is also mentioned by him in the same works in his account of the Chinese traveller Seng Chi. I-tsing merely places Samataṭa in *East India* (Watters, vol. II, p. 188), implying that Harikela which is the eastern limit of Eastern India is further east from Samataṭa.

The other literary references to Harikela are scanty and practically useless for the purposes of identification. In the *Karpūramañjarī* of Rājaśekhara (900 A.D.) occurs the following passage in Act. I:– जय पूर्वदिगङ्गनाभुजङ्ग चम्पा-चम्पककर्णपूर लीलानिर्जितराढादेश विक्रमाक्रान्तकामरूप हरिकेली-केलिकारक अवमानित-कर्णसुवर्णदान (Nirn. Ed. p. 13). This simply eliminates the countries Rāḍha, Kāmarūpa and Karṇasuvarṇa for the identification of Harikela. Foucher in his *Iconographie* (vol. I, p. 200) reproduced the text of a lebel:– हरिकेल्लदेशे शिललोकनाथः from a Ms. dated 1015 A.D. The same Ms. gives another lebel as चन्द्रद्वीपे भगवतीतारा. So, Candradvīpa is more likely than not different from Harikela. In the *Ḍākārṇava* occur the following verses referring to Harikela:

राढी ढिंक्करी वङ्गाली खाडी च हरिकेलकी। चरित्तं हरिकेलञ्च मायापुरी श्मशानकम्।

(*Cat. of Buddhist Mss., A.S.B.*, pp. 92, 96)

If the process of elimination be allowed to operate here also, Harikela becomes different from the well-known country of Vaṅgāla i.e. East Bengal roughly. Yādavaprakāśa and Hemacandra identify Harikela with Vaṅga. This is too vague an identification to be of any practical use.

Harikela is mentioned in two important epigraphic records of Bengal. In the Rāmpāl plate of Śrīcandra (as well as in the Dhulla plate of the same king :– *Ins. of Bengal* , vol. III, p. 165) occurs the following verse (No. 5) :–

पुत्रस्तस्य पवित्रितोभयकुलः कौलीनभीताशयै
स्त्रैलोक्ये विदितो दिशामतिथिभिस्त्रैलोक्यचन्द्रो गुणैः।
आधारो हरिकेल-राजककुदच्छत्रस्मितानां श्रियां
यश्चन्द्रोपपदे बभूव नृपतिर्द्वीपे दिलीपोपमः॥

The late Mr. Majumdar took the verse to mean that king Trailokyacandra's kingdom was Harikela, 'including Candradvīpa which was the home territory of the dynasty.' (*ib.*, pp. 3). His translation of the last half of the verse is as follow: – 'He who was like Dilīpa became king in the 'Dvīpa' (island) to which is joined (the word) 'Candra' and was the support of Fortune goddesses (of other kings) smiling at (i.e. joyful on account of) the umbrella which was the royal insignia of the king of Harikela.' (*ib.*, p. 7). This interpretation seems to be wrong; for, the king Trailokyacandra is described by a well-known poetic conceit as becoming the lord of the Fortunes not certainly of other (vassal) kings but of the a famous king of Harikela, whose dominions passed to Trailokya or his immediate ancestors not apparently by lineal succession. In other words the first line simply means that Trailokya became the king of Harikela; the next line can, therefore, only mean that subsequently he became the king of another kingdom Candradvīpa. The comparison with Dilīpa may signify that he was the first of a new line of kings at Candradvīpa just as Dilīpa was in the *Raghuvaṃśam* of Kālidāsa. Anyhow the verse is a narration of the territorial dominions of king Trailokya-candra and it is very unlikely that a single territory should be mentioned here in two different names and in two different phrases in the same sentence. Candradvīpa has been included in Harikela by some scholars apparently relying on vague identification of Hemacandra; but as we have seen above this goes against the more definite evidence of I-tsing.

The next reference to Harikela is in the unfinished inscription of Kantideva, recovered from an old temple in Chittagong and now deposited in the Dacca Museum. Since the publication of the text of the inscription by us (*Modern Review*, Nov., 1922) we made thorough local enquiries into the history of the copper-plate and the full story of its discovery is given below. About the year 1915 the curious heavy thing apparently of stone was accidentally found and brought out from beneath the pedestal of God Rādhāmādhava in the main shrine of the old temple of Chittagong. It was awfully corroded and was first taken to the then Superintendent of the Chittagong Madrasa, who rightly found out that the inscription was not Persian or Arabic. It was then taken to the Head Clerk of the Bengal Bank, who is reported to have deciphered 5 letters (apparently the emblem on the seal) as 'Kākavāyasa' !! The late Mr. Satish Chandra Ghosh, the historian of Chittagong, took a pencil rubbing of the plate, which however was too imperfect for decipherment. The history of the temple where the plate was discovered goes back to the Moghul period. One Adhīnadāsa Vairāgī an upcountry ascetic founded the image of Rādhāmādhava and received

Devottara lands from Reja Khan, the then Governor of Chittagong by a *sanad* dated 23 Safar of the first regnal year of Emperor Shah Jahan III (1759-60 A.D.). Another large property was granted by Newajis Md. Khan. In the year 1126 *Maghi* (1764 A.D.) the huge properties stood in the name of Jagannāthadāsa Gossain (a disciple of Adhīnadāsa), the most famous *Mohunta* of the temple which went by his name for a long time. A long succession of Mohuntas lineally descended from Jagannātha ended with the death of Bālakadāsa in 1894 and the Managing Committee appointed a new Mohunta (who had no connection with the former Mohuntas) named Haragovindadāsa, whose disciple Rāmadāsa (1896-1926 A.D.) allowed us to examine the plate.

Rāmadāsa informed us that they have got a large property also in the Tippera district. An examination of the records preserved in the Tippera Collectorate elicited the fact that Mahārājā Kṛṣṇamāṇikya (1760-83 A.D.) of Tippera made a large gift of lands in and around the village named Jagannātha Uttar, only about two miles form the town of Comilla, to the above mentioned Jagannātha Gossain, for the worship of a deity named Narasiṃha (Cakra) established by that king in that village. The date of this grant is 5th Vaiśākha 1184 Tippera Era (April, 1774 A.D.). Jagannātha and the succeeding Mohuntas remained at Chittagong and arranged for the worship of the god Narasiṃha by appointing a local man there, who acted both as a priest and a clerk (*Gomastā*). In the year 1840 during the times of Mohunta Rādhikādāsa the *Devottara* lands of the god Narasiṃha were resumed by the reigning king of Tippera; but they were subsequently settled with Rādhikādāsa as a *Tāluka* with a fixed revenue. Rādhikādāsa soon after erected a brick-built temple for the god in the fifties of the last century. The village Jagannātha Uttar is now popularly known as *Itāllā* and the temple is still found there on a plot of slightly raised ground covering an area of more than 8 *Bighās*. This happens to be an ancient site with heaps of brickbats lying scattered over a wide area and is mentioned in old documents as the Mūḍā (hillock) of king Bhavacandra; a large tank on the south of the temple is also known as the Tank of king Bhavacandra ('Bhavacandra Rājār Dīghī'). According to a well-known tradition current in the locality king Bhavacandra and his whole family perished as the result of a tragedy in a pit full of flames and a large hollow in front of the temple, now being gradually filled up in course of time, is said to mark the place of that grim tragedy. The temple itself was finally deserted by the late Mohunta Rāmadāsa, who, owing to troubles with the people of the locality, removed the god Narasiṃha with other images and things to the temple at Chittagong. These things did not include the copper-plate under question as Rāmadāsa himself told us. But the respectable people of the locality near Itāllā testifies to the fact that in the temple at Itāllā there was deposited a copperplate inscribed in the Sanskrit language supposed to contain an account of king Bhavacandra. This plate was removed to Chittagong by Bālakadāsa Mohunta, son of Rādhikādāsa, who died in 1894. The plate while at Itālla was sought to be deciphered with the help of a Paṇḍit by Mahārajā Īśānacandra-māṇikya (1849-63 A.D.) of Tippera.[2] There is however no tradition regarding the find-place of the plate; but it can be reasonably supposed that it was probably discovered within this very *Mūḍā* during the erection of the temple by Rādhikādāsa. The close proximity of the district town of Comilla precludes the possibility of an antiquarian object lika a copper-plate coming to a small village mostly peopled by illiterate cultivators from any great distance. The fact that the possession of the plate remained with the above Mohuntas till the last and that a king of Tippera sent a Paṇḍit down to the village to decipher it without attempting to acquire it points to the same conclusion.

The Harikelā-maṇḍala or the kingdom of Harikela may under the above circumstances be identified with a tract roughly covering the southern part of the district of Tippera on the evidence of the find-spot of the plate. The ruins at Itālla extend up to a distance of about three miles to the north, in which there are three or four other small mounds (Muḍās). Itāllā is only a couple of miles to the north-east of the town of Comilla. About five miles to the west of the town is the famous range of small hills known as the Lalmai and Maināmati Hills, extending towards the south to a distance of about ten miles. The northernmost range Maināmati is a separate one and is a popular resort of towns-people. It contains in one hillock remarkable ruins evidently of an ancient palace and a temple. Thc Lalmai range begins only a small distance to the south and for a distance of about five miles to the south upto a hillock known as 'Koṭbāḍi' each and every one of its large number of peaks (Muḍās) is covered with a most remarkable set of ruins without its parallel, perhaps, anywhere in East Bengal. A large number of images was discovered in different parts of the range and the ruins of a fort were discovered in one of the hillocks along with a copper-plate of Raṇavaṅkamalla Harikaladeva of Pattikera dated 1141 Śaka (1220 A.D.). Some of the peaks are still associated with the names of ancient kings like Māṇikcānd, his son Gopicānd, Vijaya Rājā, Bhoja Rājā, Ānanda Rājā, Salban Rājā etc. Several large tanks as the foot of the hills on either side are also associated with ancient names. Though most of the ruins cannot be dated before the 10th century A.D., it is likely that far more ancient ruins are lying deeper below the surfaces. We are tempted by the nature and surroundings of this ancient site to hazard a conjecture that the ancient university of Harikela must be lying buried in this very range hills.

II

Since the above was written a more definite statement for the identification of Harikela was found in the following line of *Kalpadru-koṣa* (G.O.S., vol. I, p. 7): –

श्रीहट्टो हरिकेलिः स्याच्छ्रीहटोपि क्वचिद्भवेत्।

Strangely enough this very line with the reading Harikela for Harikeli has been traced in a lexicon named *Rūpacintāmaṇi* composed in 10 years and completed in 1515 Śaka (1593 A.D.) by one Yādavānanda Dāsa of Śrīhaṭṭa (Sylhet) (Ms. No. 1451 of the Dacca University, fol. 15a). There is no doubt that these two late writers must have come across some unknown but reliable authority to make such a clear statement. A corroboration of this statement has fortunately been traced by us in an earlier work. A fragment of a *Smṛti* work named *Kṛtyasāra* by Vāsudeva Kavikaṅkana-cakra-vartī (fol. 32 only) is in our possession. The author is a comparatively early writer and flourished, we believe, not later than the 15th century A.D. For, the latest work he cites is the *Ratnākara* (fol. 6a) and he quotes twice from an early work *Smṛtimañjūśā* (fol. 8a & 23a), which no scholar of Bengal and Mithilā after Śrīdattopādhyāya and Harinātha (*vide J.A.S.B.*, 1915, pp. 379-80, 387) has ever cited. His antiquity is also indicated by the manner of his reference to Aniruddha Bhaṭṭa, अनिरुद्धभट्टव्यवस्थया गौडीयाचार्य्यैः सन्ध्या कार्य्या। (fol. 16b). In this book in a section called रुद्राक्षमाहात्म्य the following verses are cited as from the *Liṅgapurāṇa*: – (fol. 28b)

त्रिपुरस्य वधे काले रुद्रस्याक्ष्णोऽपतंस्तु ये। अश्रवो विन्दवस्ते तु रुद्राक्षा अभवन् भुवि॥
रुद्रवामाक्षिसंभूतं रुद्राक्षं कामरूपके। दक्षिणाक्षश्रुसम्भूतं हरिकोलोद्भवं विदुः॥

The author adds the note 'हरिकोलः श्रीहट्टदेशः'. This identification is slightly in conflict with the evidence we have discussed above. We shall venture to suggest, however, for the consideration of scholars that a genuine tradition placing Harikela within the present Tippera district was recorded in the original sources of the above Harikela-Srīhaṭṭa texts, but the tradition was completely lost in course of time and the later authors adopted an easy but wrong reading and identification.

Hiuen-Tsang, as is well known, did not visit the countries to the east of Samataṭa but recorded the names of six kingdoms as he could gather at Samataṭa. The identification of these kingdoms has been a matter of great controversy among scholars. We are concerned here with the first named kingdom called 'Shih-li-ch'a-to-lo' which was situated to the north-east of Samataṭa according to 'the reading of all the texts, of the Life and of the Fang-chin' (Watters' *Yuan Chwang,* vol. II, p. 189), and not to the south-east as read by some. Watters and V. Smith surmised that it was situated somewhere in the Tippera district. The late Mm. Padmanātha Bhaṭṭācārya (*J.R.A.S.*, 1920, p. 1 f). stated that it was identical with Śrīhaṭṭa or modern Sylhet. It has, however, escaped the notice of all scholars that within the Tippera district itself a name corresponding to the Chinese 'Shih-li-ch'a-to-lo' is traceable in that of a small *Pargana* comprised of a number of villages very near the well-known village of Baḍ-kāntā. The name of this very small *pargana* is 'Śircāil' (शिरचाइल), sometimes written in a Sanskritised form as Śrīcāla. (*Rājmālā* by K. C. Siṃha, pp. 426, 441). In the rent-roll of Todar Malla the revenue is found as only 13,000 *Dams*. In W. Wroughton's *Report* dated the 12th of February 1788 the name is given as 'Serechaul' with a revenue of 2,200/-. It is described as a small *mahal* surrounded by Buldacaul, Dorely and Mehar, formed from jungle lands and with very poor and indigent proprietors. But the most important fact that has recently been found by us in old documents is that this Śircāli was the original name of Baldakhal or Bardakhat, one of the biggest parganas in the district of Tippera. We give below a short account of this important discovery. A large rent-free grant of the nature of *Madadmās* was made to one Saiyad Mahammad Ali, son of Saiyad Abul Faiz Razvi in the reign of Emperor Aurangzeb; the lands measured 200 *Bighās* within two villages (Korbanpur and Chapair) of the Pargana Bardakhat. A resumption case was instituted by Government in 1840 at Comilla when the proprietors submitted a large number of valuable documents, copies of which are preserved in the Tippera Collectorate (Register B. 1, No. 81). It appears that Mirja Md. Ibrahim, a former Zamindar of Bardakhat, partly dispossessed Saiyad Md. Askari, the daughter's son of the original grantee, when the latter went to Murshidabad with a large number of papers, including a Farman, Parwanas of Asad Khan, Azub Khan and Amir-ul-Umrah (i.e. Saistah Khan) and a Sanad of Mir Md. Sadeq Asadjang. The older papers are no longer available except a copy of the last mentioned Sanad of Sadeq, whose date, however, is lost. The name of the Pargana is clearly written in this Sanad as '*Siricāl oraf Baldākhāl*'. At Murshidabad Newajis Md. Khan (Shahmat Jung) granted a fresh Sanad to Md. Askari, dated 2 Rabi II, 1168 *Hijri* (January, 1755 A.D.). Here also the same phrase is found. There is no doubt that this description of the Pargana was borrowed from the older Sanads of the reign of Aurangzeb. So, Śircāil at one time formed a major portion of the district of Tippera and preserves the name of a very ancient kingdom which might have extended to the hills on the east and to the sea on the south. It subsequently merged into neighbouring kingdoms including Samataṭa till the name was almost completely lost. It is our conjecture that the early writers recorded the identity of Harikela with this Śircāil, whose ancient form was Śrīcaṭṭa, Śrīcaṭa or Śrīcattara (from Śrīcatvara) and we believe it better corresponds phonetically and topographically with the Shih-li-ch'a-to-lo' of Hiuen Tsang. In this connection we should refer to the following verse of the *Mañjuśrīmūlakalpa* (G. Sastri, p. 648): –

सिध्यते च तदा तारा यक्षराट् चैव महाबलः ।
हरिकेल-कर्म्मरङ्गे च कामरूपे कलशाह्वये ॥ v.900

Karmaraṅga seems to us to be the 'Kia-mia-lang-ka' of Hiuen Tsang which is to the south-east of Shih-li-ch'a-to-lo. If so, its mention along with Harikela and Kāmarūpa here makes it impossible to place it in Burma. In the Map given by Julien it is shown as an island to the immediate east of Samataṭa.

References

1. The first part of this paper was written for the Sixth Oriental Conference held at Patna in 1930; as the writer could not attend the Conference the paper was neither read nor published. *Vide Proceedings,* pp. xvii: the paper was entitled 'The lost kingdom of Harikela.' A copy of the paper was given on request to Mr. B. N. Sarkar B.A., C.E., sometime Hon. Secretary of the V. R. Society, Rajshahi, who briefly stated the subject matter of the paper in a paper by him, entitled 'Finger-posts of Bengal History,' published in the *IHQ.*, vol. VII, pp. 454. The paper is now published with a small addition at the end, as having a direct bearing on the remarkable discovery of archaeological relics at the Maināmati Hills in the Tippera District, which is bound to raise many a new problem for the historians to solve.
2. This important piece of news was gathered from Mr. Gagan Chandra Chakravarti of Pāchthupi (adjacent to Itāllā), who heard it from his father late Madan Mohan Chakravarti.

37

Identification of some Ancient Indian Place-Names*

Devasabhā-Dewas

J. N. Banerjea

Rājaśekhara, in his *Kāvyamīmāṁsā,* summarily indicates the five divisions of India by naming four towns viz., Bārāṇasī, Māhīṣmatī, Devasabhā and Pṛthudaka as the respective limits of the Eastern, Southern, Western and Northern divisions, the tract lying between these four places being described by him as the middle division (Madhyadeśa). There is no doubt about the location of the first, second and fourth of these towns; but with regard to that of the third, there is a great deal of uncertainty. S. N. Majumdar Sastri makes the following remark about it in his notes to his edition of Cunningham's *Ancient Geography of India* (p. 690): 'Devasabhā is a city on a mountain (not identified) referred to in *Arthaśāstra* as producing red sandal.' In the first and second editions of the *Kāvyamīmāṁsā* no suggestion is made about its identification, but in the third edition of the same (revised and enlarged by K. S. Ramaswami Sastri Siromani) we are told that 'Devasabhā may be identified with the mountainous parts of either the Dewas State or Udaipur where the Dhebar lake is situated.'[1] Several considerations lead one to lend support to the former of the two suggestions. First, there is a great deal of similarity in the two name forms. Dewas is the name of the curious twin states situated in the Malwa Agency, political charge of the Central India Agency, lying roughly between 22^0 24´N. and 75^0 77´E. It is also the name of the capital of these states; the auhor of the *Western States* (*Malwa*) *Gazetter* (vol. V, pt. A) informs us that the states as well as their capital derive their name from the hill of Dewas, probably a contraction of Devī vāsinī, which stands close to the capital. In the *Imperial Gazetteer,* vol. XI (p. 281), we are informed that Dewas town is situated between 22^0 58´N and 76^0 4´E., 1784 feet above sea-level, on the Bombay-Agra road, 24 miles from Lahore, and it lies at the foot of a conical hill, known as Cāmuṇḍā Pāhāḍ. A reference to the *Kāvyamīmāṁsā* will show that Devasabhā was not only the name of one of the janapadas of the western division (*Paśćāddeśaḥ*) but was also the name of one of the hills of the same. Majumdar Sastri's remark quoted above, that Devasabhā is a city on a mountain does not follow from Rājaśekhara's description of it. But what is of importance here is that as Devasabhā is the name of a town, a janapada as well as a hill, so also is modern Dewas which is not only a town but also the twin states as well as a hill. Another interesting factor to be noted in this connection is the marked similarity between the descriptions of the various janapadas of the western division in relation to Devasabhā as recorded in the *Kāvyamīmāṁsā* and the same of the modern towns and districts identifiable with some of them, in relation to Dewas. The constituents of this division are mentioned thus: *Devasabhā-Surāṣṭra-Daseraka-Travaṇa-Bhṛgukaccha-Kacchīy-Ānartt-Ārvuda-Brāhmaṇavāha-Yavana;* with the exception of a very few in this list, all the others have been identified correctly with modern place-names.[2] A reference to a good atlas will show that all these are to be placed to be immediate west, south-west or north-west of modern Dewas. It may be observed here that Rājaśekhara's naming of these janapadas does not seem to be in correct order, though it is certainly not so mixed up as the enumeration of the various constituent countries of the different divisions of India by the author of the *Bṛhatsaṁhitā*. The problem of this identification could be further satisfactorily solved if one could refer to the antiquarian remains of Dewas, if any, and if it could be shown that among the products of the Dewas states could be included some form of red sandal.[3]

Indrapura-Śvetavatālaya, Bhīmā-Bhīṣaṇā, Śivapura-Śiva in the Kāpiśa-Gandhāra Region

Indrapura has correctly been identified with Indor (Khera); the Indor copper-plate inscription of Skandagupta dated in the Gupta Year 146 records 'a perpetual endowment, by a Brahmin named Devaviṣṇu, for the purpose of maintaining a lamp in a temple of the sun at Indrapura or Indrāpura, i.e. the modern Indor, which is now the name of a large and lofty mound about 5 miles to the N.W. of Dibhai in the Bulandshahr district, U.P. But another Indrapura can be located far away from the Indor of Bulandshahr, in the Kāpiśa region (of modern Kafiristan) to the extreme north-west of India. In the *Mahāmāyūrī* list of the Yakṣas, the titulary divinities of particular localities of India, we are informed in verse 29, that Indra was the Yakṣa of Indrapura.[4] This Indrapura is mentioned along with such well-known localities of the extreme north-west of India such as Varṇu, Gandhāra, Takṣaśīlā and Chardaśaila,[5] and thus will have to be identified with some place in that region. Now, Hiuen Tsang informs us that about forty *li* (roughly 6 to 7 miles) south from the capital of Kāpiśa was situated the city of *Si-pi-to-fa-la-tzu*. Julien suggested *Sphitavaras* and St. Martin *Śvetavaras* as the Sanskrit base of the Chinese nameform. Watters appends the following interesting note to this passage of Hiuen Tsang, 'The last character *sse* cr *tzu* . . . . is probably a Chinese word in the sense of temple.' The other character may stand for *Śvetavat* one of the epithets of Indra the god who rides a white elephant. Thus, the name of the city would be Śvetavatālaya, the Abode or Shrine of Indra.[6] On the basis of Watters' interpretation of the Chinese name for a suburban city of Kapiśā, we would propose to identify it with Indrapura mentioned in the *Mahāmāyūrī*. Numerous instances can be quoted in which the same locality is described under various names which are synonymous in character; thus, Hastināpura, the capital of the Kurus, is referred to in indigenous literature in various ways such as Gajasāhvaya, Nāgasāhvaya; Pāṭaliputra, the capital of the Magadhan empire, as Kusumapura, Kusumadhvaja and Puṣpapura.[7] This proposed identification can be further supported by the evidence of the interesting coin device showing Indra enthroned in the manner of Zeus, but with the full or partial representation of his mount Airāvata before him, described in the coin-legend as *Kavisiye nagara devata,* used by Eukratides and a few Bactrian Greek and Scythian rulers of India in this region. This particular numismatic datum shows that Indra was the titulary deity of this place and thus effectively supplements the information supplied to us by Hiuen Tsang, as also the author of the *Mahāmāyūrī*.[8] Thus, this Indrapura-Śvetavatālaya is to be located very near the capital city of ancient Kapiśā, which has been located by Cunningham near modern Charikar, about 45 to 50 miles north of Kabul.

In the same *Mahāmāyūrī* list of the Yakṣas, we are told in verse 28 that Śiva was the Yakṣa of Śivapurāhāra and Śivabhadra was the one of Bhīṣaṇā (*Śivaḥ Śivapurāhāre Śivabhadraśca Bhīṣaṇe*). Śivapurāhāra, i.e., the *āhāra* (an administrative district) of Śivapura has not been identified. Sylvain Lévi rightly refers to the passage in the *Mahābhāṣ ya* on Pāṇini, IV, 2, 3, which mentions Śivapura as a village of the north (Udīcyagrāma).[9] But this does not help us in definitely fixing the locality. Cunningham noted in his account of Shorkot that according to the local Brahmins, the original name of the place was Śivanagarī or Sheopur (Śivapura), which was gradually contracted to Shor.[10] We could have attempted to identify with some justification the Śivapura of the *Mahāmāyūrī* with modern Shorkot on the basis of this local tradition recorded by Cunningham. But the latter will be topographically too far from the possible location of the Śivapura of the text and as Vögel has rightly shown from the Shorkot inscription (engraved round the neck of a metal cauldron) of the Gupta period (83 Gupta era) that the ancient name of Shorkot was Śibipura, the site of the capital of the well known ancient Indian tribe of the Śibis.[11]

So, we shall have to seek for the sites of Śivapura and Bhīṣaṇā far towards the north-west. Now, here also Hiuen Tsang comes to our aid. We learn from his *Si-yu-ki* (that section of Chuan II which deals with his peregrinations in Gandhāra), that he visited the shrine of Bhīmadevī, the consort of Īśvara-deva (Śiva) which was situated on the top of a high mountain about 50 *li* or so to the north-east (should be east-north-east) of Po-lu-sha, modern Shabazgarhi. Foucher correctly identified the Bhīmādevīparvata with the lofty peak of Karamar, 1030 metres high about 39 to 40 *li* east of Shahbazgarhi.[12] The Chinese traveller further informs us that there was a self-wrought image (Svayambhūmūrti) of dark blue stone of the goddess in the shrine on the summit and "at the foot of the mountain was a temple dedicated to the Maheśvara-deva in which the ash-smearing Tīrthikas (evidently the Pāśupatas) performed much worship." That these two shrines were very important ones in the seventh century A.D. and had long history before that period is fully proved by Hiuen Tsang's explicit statement that they were 'great resorts of devotees from all parts of India'. Moreover, their importance is further substantiated by the fact that Hiuen Tsang went out of his way to pay visits to these places which were in no way connected with Buddhism. In the *Mahābhārata,* we find a reference to a tīrtha named Bhīmāsthāna beyond Pañcanada, in the account of the various sacred places of India in the following lines: (here *tato* means from Pañcanada)

ततो गच्छेत राजेन्द्र भीमायाः स्थानमुत्तमम्।
तत्र स्नात्वा तु योन्यां वै नरो भरतसत्तम॥
देव्याः पुत्रो भवेद्राजन् रत्नकुण्डलविग्रहः।
गवां शतसहस्रस्य फलं प्राप्नोति मानवः[13]

This Bhīmāsthāna of the *Mahābhārata* beyond Pañcanada is evidently identical with the Bhīmā-devī shrine of Hiuen Tsang; what additional information we gather from this extract is that in the shrine was also situated the Yonitīrtha, a dip into its *kuṇḍa* being regarded as highly auspicious in character.[14] Now, this Bhīmāsthāna can justifiably be identified with the Bhīṣaṇā of the *Mahāmāyūri* text, (the terms being synonymous, a few observations made previously by me in connection with the location of Indra-pura in the north-west also applying in this case) and the Śivapura of the latter may be located at the foot of the hill. Foucher offers a very interesting suggestion that in the name of the present village of Shewa not very far from the foot of Karamar peak one may find the reference to the shrine of Maheśvara deva (Śiva) mentioned by the Chinese pilgrim.[15] It is our further suggestion that this modern site also marks the ancient one of Śivapura. It may well be presumed that populous cities once grew up round these shrines and the way in which the author of the Buddhist text refers to these localities leaves little doubt that these were contiguous to one another. It is true that there is no reference to the goddess Bhīmā in the *Mahāmāyūrī;* but it must be observed that the author refers only to the titulary gods in his long list and those of Bhīṣaṇā and Śivapura are one and the same, referred to as Śiva in the case of Śivapura and Śivabhadra in the case of Bhīṣaṇā.[16]

Po-Fa-To-Parvata

Hiuen Tsang tells us in his *Si-yu-ki* that he went north-east-wards for above 700 li from *Mou-lo-san-pu-lu* (almost unanimously identified with Multan) to the *Po-fa-to* country. The identification of this country has taxed the scholarship of many indologists but up till now no satisfactory solution of this problem has been arrived at. A brief summary of the various suggestions by a number of scholars is given here along with some additional observations on minc. Cunningham at first emended *po-fa-to* of the D text of *Si-yu-ki* (the *po-lo-fa-to* of other texts) into *So-lo-fa-to* and located its capital at Shorkot. But he subsequently gave up this view and placed it at Harappa in the Montgomery district of the Punjab. This latter suggestion of his was accepted by Dr. Fleet. V.A. Smith, in his notes on the itinerary of Hiuen Tsang appended to Watter's *On Yuan Chwang,* volume II, suggested that Po-fa-to indicated the region of Jammu, in the Kashmir State as at present constituted. Majumdar Sastri remarks that 'as Jummu is about 250 miles away from Multan, the identification of Smith cannot be accepted.'

Po-fa-to has rightly been assumed to be based on the Sanskrit *Parvata,* an early reference to which has been correctly found in Pāṇini, iv. 2, 143. The author of the *Mudrārākṣasa* speaks of one Malayaketu, the son of Parvataka, and the king of Parvata deśa which is presumably the same country as *Po-fa-to.*[17] In the Ghāṭiyālā inscription of the Pratihāra king Kakkuka we are told that he obtained great renown in the countrics of Travaṇī, Valla and Māḍa, amongst the Āryas, in Gurjjararātra, in the Laṭa deśa and in Parvata.[18] This Parvata is evidently the same as the

Chinese pilgrim's *Po-fa-to;* from this epigraphic datum it may be observed that the locality could not be far removed from the zone of activities of the Pratihāra king Kakkuka, and thus would lend some support to Cunningham's second identification endorsed by Fleet. The latest reference to Parvata we find in a 15th or 16th century A.D. inscription engraved on the upper part of the face of a pillar of the stone railing at Bodh-Gaya. The epigraphic record informs us that one sage Jinadāsa hailing from Parvata (*Parvatādāgata Paṇḍita Jinadāsa*) was responsible for some benefaction to the Bodh-Gaya shrine. B.M. Barua thinks that this Parvata may be the same as the Chinese traveller's *Po-fa-to,* but this identification also, if accepted, does not help us in fixing its location.[19]

Siṁhala, a place in the Deccan

J.C. Ghosh and M.V. Kibe discussed the problem of locating Laṅkā-Siṁhala somewhere on the border of or adjacent to the Madhyadeśa of the Buddhists.[20] Watters also drew the attention of scholars to the probability of locating the *Chih-shih-tzū kuo* or Siṁhala country mentioned by Hiuen Tsang in connection with his observations about the legend of Deva Pusa and Gaṅgādvāra in India, preferably South India.[21] There is a tradition recorded in the bardic tales of Mewar that Ratansiṁha, ruler of Mewar, married Padmiṇī, the daughter of Hamir Saṅkh of Siṁhala (cf. *Padumāvat*); this Siṁhala was identified with Ceylon by Todd (*Annals,* vol. I) as well as Gauri Sankar Ojha (*Rajputnekā Itihās*). Ojha discredits the story of Ratansiṁha's marriage with Padmiṇī on the ground that the Raja of Mewar could not have married the daughter of one Hamir Saṅkh who could not have ruled over Ceylon. S.C. Dutt in a Bengali article recently published in one of the issues of the monthly Bengali Journal, *Vicitrā,* has shown on the authority of a manuscript entitled *Udepur rājavaṁśāvalī,* finished about 1840 A.D. and now in the possession of the Royal Asiatic Society of Bengal, that there was a Siṁhala situated in Western India. We read in the folio 10 of the same manuscripts: –

> "राजा रतनसिंघजि.........समलद्वीप पाटन सहरमे
> चोहान राजसंध राज करतो हो जठ जाइने राजरी वेटी
> पदमनी ने परनी".........।[२२]

Dutt thinks that this Samaladvīpa is to be located in the kingdom of Anahilwara Pātan in Kathiwar Peninsula.[23] Rājaśekhara includes Siṁhala among the various constituent janapadas of the Dakṣiṇāpatha, such as *Mahārāṣṭra Māhīṣaka Āsmaka Vidarbha Kuntala Kratha Kaiśika Surpāraka Kāñcī Kerala Kaveramurala Vānavāsaka Siṁhala Coḍadaṇḍaka Pāṇḍyapallava Gāṅga Nāsikya Kauśika Kollagirivallāra.*

The editor of the *Kāvyamīmāṁśā* (third edition) in the Appendix I of the work distinguishes Siṃhala from Laṅkā and identifies the former with Ceylon while locating the latter island on the eastern side of the Peninsula beyond Travancore. But the express mention of Siṁhala by Rājaśekhara among the various countries of the Dakṣināpatha would preclude its location outside the Deccan Peninsula.

References

* Read in the second session of the Indian History Congress at Allahabad, October 1938.

1. *Kāvyamīmāṁsā,* 3rd. ed., Appendix I, pp. 294.
2. Surāṣṭra = Surat. We know from the Ghāṭiyālā inscription of the Pratihāra king Kakkuka that he attained a great renown in such countries as Travaṇī (referred to in Mātākisāl inscription as Tamani; the Jodhpur inscription of Pratihāra Bauka also mentions Travaṇī) Valla, Māḍa (Jaisalmer) etc. Arbuda = Mount Abu. Brāhmaṇavāha = Brahmanabad in Sind. Yavana = The tract further up the Indus valley, probably acquiring this name from the long settlement of the Greeks in this region.
3. *Daivasabheyaṁ raktaṁ padmagandhi* (*candanaṁ*); Kauṭilya, *Arthaśāstra*) p. 78.
4. *Journal Asiatique,* 1915, pp. 38.
5. Correctly identified by Sten Konow with Chaḍaśilā mentioned as a place-name in the copper-plate inscription of the year 134, found in the course of excavations at Kalawan, near Taxila. *Epigraphia Indica,* vol. XXI, pp. 253.
6. Watters, *Yuan Chwang,* vol. I, pp. 129.
7. Dr. Fleet mentions the interesting practice of the Pandits in reference to sampgaum and Ugar gol in the Belgaum district as Ahipura and Nakhapura; *Corpus Inscriptionum Indicarum,* vol. III, pp. 79, f.n. 2.
8. For my detailed observations on this coin device, cf. *Indian Historical Quarterly,* vol. XIV, 1938, Winternitz Number, pt. I. pp. 95-99.
9. *Journal Asiatique,* 1915, pp. 70.
10. *Archæological Survey Report,* vol. V, pp. 97.
11. *Epigraphia Indica,* XVI, 1921, pp. 16. The identification of Shorkot with the capital town of the Śivis, based on epigraphic data, finds corroboration from the classical source. Curtius definitely locates the town of the Siboi (Śibis) not far from the confluence of the Hydaspes and the Akesines a position very nearly agreeing with that of Shorkot.
12. Foucher, *Notes on the Geography of Gandhāra,* pp. 33. The Chinese pilgrim's 50 *li* in excess of 10 or 11 *li;* this excessive estimate has satisfactorily been accounted for by Foucher.

13. *Mahābhārata,* Calcutta edition, Vanaparva, Ch. 82, Verses 84-5.

14. Nandalal Dey in his *Geographical Dictionary of Ancient and Mediæval India,* 2nd edition, also notes the identity of Bhīmāsthāna of the epic with the Bhīmādevi shrine of the Chinese pilgrim, and finds a reference to the same shrine in the *Padma Purāṇa,* Svarga Khaṇḍa, ch. 11. But he did not utilise the useful information supplied to us by Foucher in definitely locating this shrine, and thus his indentification of it with Takht-i-Bahai is evidently incorrect.

15. Foucher, *op. cit.,* pp. 36.

16. It will not be out of place to note here that the epic reference to Bhīmāsthāna and its Yonitīrtha as well as Hiuen Tsang's mention of Bhīmādevï, her Svayambhūmūrti and the shrine of Śiva is of outstanding interest and importance from the religious point of view. We know Yonitīrtha is now situated at Kāmākhyā near Gauhati in Assam and her particular Bhairava is Umānanda a few miles distant from the Devī shrine there on the top of the hill. In the early centuries of the Christian era there was a similar Devī shrine in the heart of ancient Gandhāra with the adjacent shrine of the Bhairava (Śiva). Again, the self-wrought image of Bhimā of the place can be profitably compared with the principal object of veneration in the Kāmākhyā shrine, which though the public are not allowed to see it uncovered, seems to be also a virgin rock without any particular shape or form.

17. A few round copper coins with a bull on the obverse and a few symbols and a legend *Pavatasa* in early Brāhmī characters of the 2nd century B.C. on the reverse were found by Cunningham at Kauśāmbī, modern Kośam, near Allahabad; the form of the coin-legends does not necessarily prove that Parvata was the name of a person; it may as well be the name of a locality. But then the definite location of these coins at Kośam by Cunningham would militate against its being equated with Hiuen Tsang's *Po-fa-to.*

18. *Epigraphia Indica,* vol. IX, pp. 278-80. D.R. Bhandarkar who edited this inscription there, translated the passage—*Yena prāptā mahākhyatis tvavaṇyāṃ vallamāḍayoḥ! Āryeṣu Gurjjararāṭṭrāyāṁ Lāṭadeśe ca Parvvate*—as 'great renown obtained by whom in the countries of Travaṇi, Valla and Māḍa, amongst (the people known as) Ārya, in Gujjararāṭṭra and in Parvata in the Lāṭa country.' But he correctly translated it in his *List of North Indian Inscriptions,* pp. 7, where in a footnote he suggests that Parvata is perhaps identical with *Po-fa-to* mentioned by Hiuen Tsang.

19. B.M. Barua, *Bodh Gaya,* vol. II, pp. 73.

20. *Indian Historical Quarterly,* vol. V, pp. 355-6; *Annals of the Bhandarkar Oriental Research Institute,* vol. XVII, pp. 371 ff.; *Ibid.*, vol. XIX, pl. I, pp. 84-86. A locality somewhere near Amarakantaka, a place near Damoh in C.P. will mark the ancient site of Laṅka—Siṁhala according to Kibe and Ghosh respectively.

21. *On Yuan Chwang,* vol. I, pp. 321. "The *Chih-Shihtzū Kuo* or Siṁhala country of this passage has been taken to be Ceylon, the country generally so designated,

but it may be here the name of a country in India. Yuan Chwang, as will be seen hereafter, probably knew that Deva was a native of South India and not of Ceylon." See also in this connection *IHQ.*, VIII, pp. 99-100; IX. pp. 742, 745, 972f.; X, pp. 138f., 368f., 780f.

22. Prof. S.C. Dutt has kindly supplied me with all this information about Samala-Siṁhala. Now, Patan of the manuscript may also be identified with the modern locality of Patan near Jubbulpore where a sati record dated in 1361 V.S. was found; Hiralal pointed out that at about 1308 A.D., portions of the Damoh and Jubbulpore districts were being governed by a Mahārājaputra Vāghadeva, a Parihāra chief under the suzerainty of the Chauhāna kings. *Epigraphia Indica,* vol. XVI, pp. 11. Mr. J.C. Ghosh has kindly drawn my attention to this reference.

23. *Kāvyamīmāṁsā,* 3rd edition, pp. 93.

38

Origin of the name 'Bengal'

N. N. Das Gupta

How Bengal received its name as such is a question which in contrast with the degree of interest it does possess has called forth only a very few attempts at solution. In Bengali the term employed in modern times to denote the province is *Bāṅglā,* of which the English rendering is *Bengal,* denoting the Presidency round Fort William. Both words are of recent origin, neither having any claim to hardly a higher age than the 18th century A.D. The idea that palpably works in the popular mind is that the term *Bāṅglā* or *Bāṅgālā* is derived from *Vaṅga* which so frequently occurs in early and mediæval Indian epigraphs and literature, and the English have adapted it into their own language as *Bengal.* A statement made towards the close of the 16th century by Abul Fazl in his *Aīn-i-Akbari* is translated by Jarret as follows : "The original name of Bengal was *Bang*. Its former rulers raised mounds measuring ten yards in height and twenty in breadth throughout the province which were called *al.* From this suffix, the name Bengal took its rise and currency."[1] *Bengal* in the above translation is a misnomer; Gladwin in his translation of the same work maintains a semblance of truth by representing it as *Bungalah*[2], since the original has *Vaṅgāla*[3]. Erroneous as the notion that *Bāṅglā* or its English equivalent *Bengal* is derived from *Vaṅga* or *Bang* is, no less pretentious is the theory postulated some 33 years ago by as great and reputed a scholar as the late Professor Rakhal Das Banerji, who writing in a Bengali monthly said: "After the Muhammadan conquest the use of the word Vaṅga is found at one or two places, and even then the Western Bengal was denoted by Gauḍa, Lakṣmaṇāvatī or Lakhnauti, and the marshy Eastern Bengal by Bang or *diyār i Bang*. But shortly after Minhaj (-us Sirāj, the author of the *Tabaqāt Nāṣirī,* 1259 A.D.) Gauḍa and Vaṅga were designated as Baṅgālā instead of these names. Whence (the terms) Baṅgāla and Baṅgālā came to be introduced into the Gauḍīya language is difficult to say, but the supposition is that the word Baṅgālā came from the country where from the Sena kings hailed, the country from which the name *Vallāla* came. The Muhammadans and the Persian-knowing. Hindus even used to write it as Baṅgālā, but the English-knowing people in imitation of the mistake of the English write it as Baṅgālā instead of as Baṅgālā".[4] Our knowledge of the past of Bengal has since traversed a long way off this stage, and it would now be idle to indulge in controverting the fallacies that be in the statement point by point.

Much of the problem connected with the question disappears when we recall that there was in old Bengal a tract called Vaṅgāla. The Nālandā inscription of Vipulaśrīmitra, assigned to the first half of the twelfth century, records the death of a Buddhist ascetic, Karuṇāśrīmitra, when his house at Somapura (modern Pāhārpur in the Rajshahi district of North Bengal) "was burning (*being*) set on fire by the approaching armies of Vaṅgāla"[5]. An earlier reference to the name of Vaṅgāla occurs in the Tirumalai Rock inscription of Rājendra Coḷa I. The description of Vaṅgāla-*deśa* in it is that 'where the rain-wind never stopped' and from which its king Govindacandra (being attacked by the generals of the Coḷa monarch, *circa* 1025 A.D.) 'fled having descended (from his) male elephants'[6] This reference alone is apt to render ineffective the conjecture that the name Vaṅgāla came with the Sena kings. Still earlier is the reference to Vaṅgāla in the Goharwa inscription of Karṇadeva, the Cedi prince, whose great-great-grandfather, Lakṣmaṇarājadeva, flourishing in the first half of the ninth century, is said to have defeated the king of Vaṅgāla among others (*Vaṅgāla-bhaṅga nipuṇaḥ*)[7]. The name Vaṅgāla must have, therefore, been as old as at least the eighth century A.D.

Perhaps more important for our purpose is to muster together all the few available passages from literature and inscriptions that make mention of both Vaṅgāla and Vaṅga alongside, so as to bring forth that Vaṅgāla as a land is quite distinct from what is Vaṅga. In the *Tārikh-i Fīroz Shāhī* of Shams-i Sirāj' Āfif, the third *Mukaddama* relates the capture of fifty elephants and slaughter of one lac of the people of Bang (Vaṅga) and Baṅgāla (Vaṅgāla) by Fīroz Shāh in his battle with Shamsu-d-dīn.[8] Similarly, the *Ḍākārṇava, a* Tantric Buddhist work of 12th century or after, contains in the fifth chapter the names of the Devīs called after different districts or places of India, which include the names of both Vaṅga and Vaṅgāla.[9] Again in the *Hammīra-Mahākāvya* of Nayacānd Suri we have that the kings of Aṅga, Tilanga (Telang), Magadha, Masūra (Mysore), Kaliṅga, Vaṅga, Bhaṭa (Bhoṭ ?), Medapāṭa, Pañcāla, Vaṅgāla, Thamima, Bhilla, Nepāla, Ḍāhala and some Himalayan chiefs brought in obedience to the summons (of 'Alāu-d-dīn) their respective quotas to swell his invading army against Hammīra:

अङ्गस्तिलङ्गो मगधो मसूरः कलिङ्ग-वङ्गौ भट-मेदपाटौ।
पञ्चाल वङ्गाल थमीम भिल्ल नेपाल डाहल हिमाद्रिमध्याः ॥[१०]

Still again in the third *āśvāsa* (chapter) of the *Yaśatilaka,* written in 959 A.D. by the Jaina Somadeva under the Cālukya prince, Arikeśarin, a feudatory of the Rāṣṭrakūṭa Kṛṣṇa III. "while telling, in the story of Yaśodhara, about the vital importance to a king of the choice of ministers he makes, it is stated by way of illustration that, due "to the employment of unworthy persons, Karāla, king of Kerala, Maṅgala, king of Baṅgāla, Kāma, king of Kauśika, and Spliṅga, king of Vaṅga, could trace their ruin."[11] And apart from all these literary evidences there is also preserved to us at least one epigraphical testimony to demonstrate the difference of Vaṅgāla from Vaṅga; an inscription at Ablur says witrh reference to Vijjaṇarāya of the Kalacuri family that "having put down the Coḷa, having humbled Lāḷa, having deprived Nepāla of stability, having crushed Andhra to pieces, having made the Gurjara captive, having broken the greatness of the king of Cedi, having ground Vaṅga in a mill, and having fought the kings of Baṅgāla, Kaliṅga, Magadha, Paṭasvara and Mālava, the brave king Vijjaṇarāya has protected the whole circuit of the earth."[12]

The earliest reference to the Vaṅgas occurs in the *Aitareya Āraṇyaka* (II. I. I), and we need not doubt that the allusion is to a tribe of Bengal. In the *Mahābhārata,* as it is in the description of Bhīma's conquests in Eastern India, Vaṅga lay beyond Aṅga, to the south-east, and as such "must have comprised the modern districts of Murshidabad, Nadiya, Jessore and parts of Rajshahi; Pabna and Faridpur."[13] This tract, with further extension, to the south, the Vaṅgas seemingly continued to hold up till the days of Kālidāsa, as it appears from IV. 36 of his *Raghuvaṁśa:* "Having rooted out the Vaṅgas with great force who were haughty on account of their fleet of ships, he (Raghu) erected triumphal columns in the intervals between the streams of the Gaṅgā." In the Jaina *Bhagavatī,* fourth *upāṅga Pannavaṇā,* the nine groups of Āriyas included 'Tāmaliti Vaṅgāya', and if we take the expression in the sense of 'Tāmaliti (Tāmralipti) in Vaṅga' it would point to the south-western boundary of Vaṅga at times in or before the fifth century A.D., when the Jaina *upāṅgas* are believed to have been redacted. From the sixth or seventh century A.D., onwards, however, the land of Vaṅga became conterminous with a part of East Bengal, which is, generally speaking, bounded by the Brahmaputra on the west, by the Ganges on the south, by the Meghnā on the east, while on the north by the Khasia hills.[14] In some mediæval Vaiṣṇava works of Bengal, on the other hand, Śrīhaṭṭa or Sylhet is said to have been included in Vaṅga,[15] so that in the sixteenth century and thereabouts the north-easterly boundary of Vaṅga extended upto at least Sylhet, which is now incorporated in Assam.

The identification of the land of Vaṅgāla, as distinct an entity from that of Vaṅga, is neither too up-hill nor so embarassing a task. The Vaṅgāla-*deśa,* where according to the evidence of the Tirumalai Rock Inscription of Rājendra Coḷa I, "the rain-wind never stopped," is described in the *Deśāvalī-vivṛti.* a geographical work by Jagannātha Paṇḍita in the seventeenth century, as a tract in the vicinity of forest and sea.[16] In Macro Polo's description, "Bangala is a Province towards the South which upto the year 1290, when the aforesaid Messer Marco Polo was still at the court of the Great Kaan, had not yet been conquered; but his armies had gone thither to make the conquest. You must know that this province has a peculiar language, and the people are wretched idolators. They are tolerably close to India" (a province on the confines of India.)[17] Marco Polo's account of Bangala, indubiously Vaṅgāla, can only be applicable to the south-east Bengal including the Chittagongcum-Tippera region and not to Pegu, as Yule happened to conjecture.[18] This not only agrees perfectly well with the descriptions of the land as in the Tirumalai Rock Inscription and the *Deśāvalīvivṛti* but is also substantially corroborated by Ovington, who says, "Arracan is bounded on the north-west by the kingdom of Bengala, some authors making Chatigam to be its First Frontier city."[19] Ovington's account is based on that of Tosi (1669 ?), which in its own turn is "founded almost exclusively on that of Manrique."[20] Of Chittagong in the Sūbah of Vaṅgāla the *Aīn-i-Akbari,* too, says, "Chāṭgāon is a large city situated by the sea and belted by woods."[21] It is essential to note in this connection that Gopīcandra (Govindacandra), who figures in the Tirumalai Rock Inscription of Rājendra Coḷa I as a king of Vaṅgāla-*deśa* is represented also in the *Kāh-bab-ḥdun-ldan* of Tāranātha as a king of Vaṅgāla (and not of *Bengal* as has been resorted by the late Rai Sarat Chandra Das Bahadur), with his capital at Cāṭigrāma (Chittagong).[22] When Sarvānanda Vandyaghaṭīya in his commentary on the *Amara-Koṣa* (1159 A.D.) interprets the Sanskrit term *sidhma,* meaning dried fish, with the remark *yatra Vaṅgāla-vaccārāṇām prītiḥ*, it points to the same conclusion, for the common folks of the region under question, situated by the sea, relish dried fish (*śñuṭki māch*) much more than those of any other part of Bengal.

But Vaṅgāla can hardly be the same as Upa-Vaṅga of the *Vṛhat Saṁhitā* and some other old Sanskrit texts, as has been proposed by Dr. R. C. Majumdar[23], for Upa-Vaṅga even about 1600 A.D. when the *Digvijaya-prakāśa* was composed, denoted a part of the Gangetic delta comprising Jessore and certain other contiguous forestine tracts evidently of the Sundarbans. Equally, I beg to differ on obvious grounds from the suggestion of Prof. H. C. Raychaudhuri that the home territory of the Vaṅgālas lay in Bhāṭi, which is the name given to the low-lying flats of the Gangetic delta that border on the great estuaries.[24]

Besides the land or kingdom of Vaṅgāla (or Bengala), some of the early European travellers and writers have referred to a city also called *Bengola* or, more often, *Bengala.* In Blaev's Map[25], the city of Bengala is laid down opposite Chatigam, to the south-east, and as Blochmann informs us, the *Chart of the empire of the Grand Mogul* by N. Sausson (1652 A.D.) also locates the city at the same place.[26] To these we may add the evidence of Ovington who continuing says that "Teixeira and generally the *Portugese* writers reckon that (Chātigam) as a city of Bengala itself upon the same coast, more south than Chatigam."[27] In Rennel's Map the city is not given, while in his *Memoir* he states, "in some ancient books and maps we meet with a considerable city called Bengalla, but no traces of such a place now exist . . . . . ." But, at the same time, he admits candidly that "Bengalla appears to have existed during the early part of the past century",[28] the site of it being carried away by some natural catastrophe. Gastaldi's Map of Asia (1561 A.D.) wrongly places Bangala to the west of Catigam.[29]

Dr. James Taylor in his *Sketch of the Topography and Statistics of Dacca* liked to identify Dacca in Vaṅga with the city of Bengalla or Bengala in Vaṅgāla ![30] Similarly, the late R. C. Temple's assertion that the site of Lodovico di Varthema's 'City of Bengala' must have been Satgaon or an old bed of the Hughli river[31] is wholly wide of the mark, for Satgaon or Saptagrāma was a city of Rāḍha and not of Vaṅgāla. More ill-judged is the theory of Mr. Longworth Dames[32] who fixes on Gauḍa (Gaur), taken together with its subsidiary ports, viz. Satgaon or Sunargaon or both, as the place known as Baṅgāla in the very early part of the 16th century. It has been drawn into the efforts of J.J.A. Campos[33] to identify the city of Bengala with Chittagong, but only the few evidences cited above are apt to bespeak of an unmistakable distinction of the one from the other. There is, however, a pretty real sense in its identification with Dianga or Bandar on the left bank of the Karnaphuli river, as made by the Rev. H. Hosten, S. J.[34], and if it be not precisely true, it undoubtedly approaches well-nigh to the truth.

But whatever might have been the exact site of the once famous city of Bengala, we must cease to doubt its very existence, as Blochmann[35] did as early as 1873 A.D. Regarding Lodovico di Varthema, an Italian traveller of Bologn (1503 to 1508 A.D.), reports Garica de Orta[36] that he did not come to Bengal, but what Varthema[37] himself records is , "From Tarnassari (Tennasserim) we took route towards the city of Bangalla at which we arrived in eleven days. This city is one of the best that I had hitherto seen. Here there are the richest merchants ever met with." Early in the 16th century A.D. Barbosa also refers to this great city "with a good port".[38] From Orissa he goes on to Bengala.[39] In a geographical work of the same period, the *Sommerio de Regni,* etc. it is said that "the town of *Bengala* contains 40,000 hearths", while speaking of the rival port of *Satgaon* in West Bengal it says that it contained 10,000 hearths. Samuel Purchas (1626 A.D.) says that "Gauro the seat-Royall, and Bengala are faire Cities"[40] So also Methold designates Rajmahal and Bengalla as 'faire cities'.[41] Peter Heyleyn in his *Cosmographie in Four Books containing the Chronographie and Historie of the whole World, etc.,* London, 1652 A.D., menitons the following towns of Bengal: Bengala, Gauro, Catigan (Sāgaon), Texda (Tanda), Porto Grande (Chittagong) and Porto Pequeno (Hughli)[42]. According to Manrique, who sojourned about six years at Chittagong, one of the Twelve Bhūniyās was of *Bengala*[43], and as he mentions most of the other Bhūniyās by their respective cities as their seats of government, it is likely that in case of Bengala, too, he refers to the city, as against the sub-province of that name.

How old was this city of Bengala, there is no knowing. Dr. R. C. Majumdar[44] proposes, and with good grounds, that Baṅgāla, as a city of importance like Saptagrāma and Lakṣmaṇāvatī (Gauḍa), was known to the Moor traveller, Ibn Batuta. And as such the city was as old as at least the first half of the 14th century, if not earlier and perhaps much earlier still. Curiously enough, the Hindu and Muslim writers of India have stayed their hands from making any mention of this city.

In the letter, which constitutes the earliest Portugese account of 'Bengal', addressed to the king of Portugal on the 22nd December, 1518, Dom Joao de Leyma, a Portugese nobleman serving in India, writes: "Dom Joao, my Lord, spent the last cold season in Bengal (*sic*), where he wintered, ... At the bar of this river, my Lord, there are three fathoms of water at low tide, which swells from three to six fathoms at high tide. The city is said to be two small leagues from the bar. The city is big and populous but very weak. Here was Dom Joao for awaiting the monsoon for returning to India"[45] The *Bengal* of this letter is, I believe, no other than Vaṅgāla or *Bengala* of the later Portuguese, Dutch and English writers, and the big but weak city it refers to is also *Bengala* rather than Chittagong, and if so the river in question appears to have been not the Karnaphuli, but the Sangu river, south of Chittagong, on which stood Dianga, identified with Dakṣ iṇadāṅgā or Brāhmaṇadāṅgā[46]. It is indeed doubtful if we have any clear indication of the fact that the name Baṅgāl or rather Vaṅgāla was applied to the entire province of Bengal any time before Akbar's time when the Sūbah of Baṅgāl or rather Vaṅgāla was so constituted as to stretch right from Chittagong to Teliagarhi a pass between the Rajmahal hills and the Ganges, and in the few cases where it is believed to be so applicable.[47] It is only by close attention one may discover that they might be easily construced to yield that restricted sense in which Vaṅgāla had primarily been used. And even during and sometime after Akbar's reign *Bengala* continued to carry the conception of only a part of Bengal to the Portuguese. English and some other European sailors and writers in general. Thus Cæsar Frederick, the Venetian merchant (1563 to 1581 A.D.) says: "This island is called Sondiva (Sandvīpa) belonging to the kingdom of Bengala, distant 120 miles from Chatigan, to which place we were bound". Du Jarric wrote in 1599, "This country of Bengala, which comprises about two hundred leagues of seacoast, was inhabited partly by the native Bengalis, who were generally pagans, partly by Saracens, for the most part Patans of Parthians (Persians), ..."[48] In Samuel Purchas's *Description of India* (1626 A.D.) we also find, "The Kingdom of Bengala is very large, and hath of Coast one hundred and twentie leagues, and as much within Land. *Francis Fernandes* measureth it from the confines of the Kingdom of Ramu or Porto Grande (Chittagong) to Palmerine, ninetie miles beyond Porto Pequene (Hooghli), in all six hundred miles long."[49] When the pioneer English traveller in India, Ralph Fitch, who visited Bengal in 1586 A.D. wrote, "From Chatigan in Bengala, I came to Bacola (Bakla in Backerganj District) . . . .",[50] he evidently refers thereby to the land of Vaṅgāla. When, again, he speaks of 'Satagam (Saptagrāma) in Bengala',[51] and of Hugeli (Hooghli) as 'the place where the Portugals keep in the country of Bengala'[52] the region might well indicate a part of Bengal, just as we find it in the description of Francis Fernandes as referred to by Samuel Purchas. But when the same Ralph Fitch mentions Tanda (near Rajmahal) as a city that 'standeth in the countrey of Bengala'[53], it alludes past doubt to the province. There are evidences, however, that *Bengala* of the early Europeans had sometimes a much wider connotation than even that of the province. Thus according to a Dutchman who made a voyage to the Indies in December, 1603, "In all

Countrie of Bengalla (wherein Mesopotania is a Cheefe Cittie) are made all the stuffes that we Carrie to the Moloccos & are there to be had exceeding Cheefe, ... St. Thome & Cheramandalla (Coromandel) are also in Bengalla, ... There are many kingdomes in Bengalla, but the Cittie of Messopotania is the Cheeffest Citie . . . . . ."[54]. Again, in a Commission from the East India Company to Alexander Sharpie and Richard Rowles, dated March, 1607/8, we read, "Or (Our) desire is that such as shall be left there doe there best endevors to finde out trade at Mesopotania in the pte (port) of Bengalla Charemendall St. Thome or any other places fitt for trade."[55] Mesopotania of the above passages is, we are told, a blunder for Masulipatam[56] near the mouth of the Kistna in the Eastern Ghats. Far from being common as these references are, they prove nevertheless that *Bengala* or *Bengalla* at times before the 18th century denoted both sides of the Bay of Bengal, precisely as the *India* of the early Portuguese records denoted the Malabar coast.[57]

From the 18th century, or at best the last quarter of the 17th century, neither confusion nor ambiguity attends the use of the term *Bengala,* for with the final a thereof deleted, palpably through the phoneticism of the English who were then getting the upper hand of things in the province, *Bengal* became the abiding denomination of the region that once constituted the Mughal Sūbah of *Baṅgāl*. Thus the old kingdom of Vaṅgāla, embracing the south-eastern portion of the province, and having had at least during the mediæval age for its capital the 'faire' city known to the foreigners as *Bengala,* was destined ultimately to lend its name not only to the Mughal Sūbah but also to the British presidency, in two variant forms. The much older kingdom or tract of Vaṅga had nothing to do with the process of operation leading to the gaining ground of the proper name, *Bengal*. Nor there is any warrant to believe that *Bāṅglā* or *Bāṅgālā* by which the Bengalis now designate both their province and languge is a morphological transformation of Vaṅga or even directly derived from Vaṅgāla; the nomenclature is merely a convenient translation of the English *Bengal*.

References

1. *Aīn-i Akbari,* tr. by H. S. Jarrett, II, pp. 120.
2. *Ayeen Akbery,* tr. by Francis Gladwin, II, pp. 300.
3. *I.H.Q.*, XVI, 1940, pp. 227, n. 22.
4. *Mānasī,* 1320 B.S., *Āśvina,* pp. 771.
5. *Ep. Ind.*, XXI, pp. 98, 99-100, v. 2.
6. *Ibid.*, IX, pp. 233; *SII,* II, Nos. 67 and 68, pp. 98, 100.
7. *Ibid.*, XI, pp. 112, v. 8.
8. Elliot and Dowson, *History of India,* III, pp. 195.
9. *Buddha Gān-o-Dohā,* ed. H. P. Śastrī, pp. 251; *Bhandarkar Commemoration Volume,* 1917, pp. 251.
10. Ed Nīlakaṇṭha Janārdan Kīrtane, Bombay, 1895, pp. 95, *Canto* XI, v. 1.
11. *Śecond Report of Operations in Search of Sanskrit MSS in the Bombay Circle,* 1883-84, by Peter Peterson, pp. 38-39.
12. *Ep. Ind.*, V, pp. 249, 257, first pointed out by Prof. H. C. Raychaudhuri in the *Mānasī-o-Marmavāṇī* 1336 B. S. *Śrāvaṇa* pp. 701.
13. Pargiter, *J.A.S.B.*, 1897, pp. 97, and Map, Plate II.
14. Cf. Cunningham's *Ancient Geography of India,* ed. S. N. Majumdar, pp. 730, and *Arch. Surv. Ind. Rep.*, 1882, XV, pp. 145.
15. For instance, cf. the *Caitanya Maṅgala* of Jayānanda, pp. 11.
16. *Des. Cat. of Sans. MSS* in the As. Soc. Beng., by H. P. Śāstrī, vol. IV, 1923, pp. 54.
17. *Travels of Macro Polo,* ed. Sir Henry Yule, vol. II, 3rd ed., 1903, ch. LV, pp. 114-15 and pp. 128, n. 6.
18. *Ibid.*, ch. LIX, pp. 128, n. 6 and ch. LI, n. 2.
19. *A Voyage to Suratt* (1689), pp. 553-54.
20. *Bengal Past and Present,* Oct.-Dec. 1916, pp. 262.
21. Jarrett, *op. cit.*, pp. 125.
22. *Pag-Sam Jon-Zang,* Index, pp. xviii, and *J.A.S.B.*, 1898, pp. 20-28.
23. *IHQ,* XVI, pp. 237-38.
24. *History of Bengal,* vol. I, Dac. Uni., pp. 19.
25. *Theatrum Orbis Terrarum,* vol. II, Amsterdam, 1650, reproduced by Blochman in a reduced scale in *J.A.S.B.*, 1873, pt. I, pl. IV.
26. *J.A.S.B.*, 1873, pt. I, pp. 233.
27. *Op. cit.*
28. pp. 57.
29. *J.A.S.B.*, 1908, pp. 291 b.

30. Cal., 1840, pp. 92-93.
31. *Ind. Ant.*, 1933, pp. 45.
32. *Barbosa,* vol .II, 1921, Published by the Hakluyt Society, pp. 133-145.
33. *History of the Portuguese in Bengal,* Cal. 1919, pp. 77.
34. *Bengal Past and Present,* Oct.-Dec., 1916, pp. 262.
35. *J.A.S.B.*, 1873, pt. I, pp. 233.
36. Cf. *History of the Portuguese in Bengal,* (J. J. A. Campos), pp. 75.
37. *Travels of Lodovico di Varthema,*, etc. tr. by J. W. Jones and ed. by G.P. Badger, London, 1863, pp. 210.
38. *Ibid,* Intro, pp. cxv.
39. Cf. *Ind. Ant.*, 1923, pp. 133.
40. *Early Travels in India,* First Series, ed. J. Talboys Wheeler, Cal., 1864, pp. 1; also *Purchas His Pilgrims,* vol. V, pp. 508.
41. Cf. James Taylor, *op. cit.* pp. 92.
42. *J.A.S.B.*, 1913, pp. 415 n.
43. *Ibid.*, pp. 439.
44. *IHQ.*, XVI, pp. 230.
45. *Early Career of Kanhoji Angria and other papers,* ed. Dr. S.N. Sen, Cal., Uni. 1941, pp. 88 ff.
46. *J.A.S.B..*, 1893, pp. 233.
47. *IHQ.*, XVI, pp. 227.
48. *J.A.S.B.*, 1913, pp. 437.
49. *Op. cit.*
50. *Ralph Fitch,* ed. J. Horton Ryley, London, 1899, pp. 118.
51. *Ibid.*, pp. 100.
52. *Ibid.*, pp. 113.
53. *Ibid.*, pp. 111.
54. *The First Letter Book of the East India Company,* 1600-1619, ed. Sir George Birdwood, pp. 85.
55. *Ibid.*, pp. 261.
56. *Ibid.*, pp. 73, n. 10.
57. Dr. S. N. Sen, *op. cit,* pp. 89.

39

To the East of Samatata

P. N. Bhattacharya

In 1912 an incomplete set of copper-plates containing the record of a grant by Bhāskaravarman, the king of Kāmarūpa during the first half of the seventh century A.C., was discovered at Nidhanpur in the Pañcakhaṇḍa Pargaṇā of Sylhet. A point was raised whether or not Sylhet formed a part of Kāmarūpa at the time of Bhāskaravarman. While publishing the inscriptions, I tried to prove that Sylhet was not included in Kāmarūpa and one of the reasons I advanced was that Shih-li-ch'a-ta-lo, which had been identified with Sylhet (Śrīhaṭṭa) by Indian antiquarians, was separately mentioned as a country not visited by the celebrated Chinese pilgrim Yuan Chwang who, however, visited Kāmarūpa during the reign of this very king Bhāskaravarman.[1]

On this occasion I consulted Watters' Yuan Chwang, published by the Royal Asiatic Society, with maps and itinerary by Dr. V. A. Smith. There I found that Watters objected to change the locality of Shih-li-ch'a-ta-lo from N.E. of Samataṭa (as recorded by Yuan Chwang himself) to S.E. of that kingdom (as had been proposed by some other editors of the work) and the palce was identified by him as the Tipperah District[2], which identification was supported by Dr. V. A. Smith.[3] I saw that this identification went very near Sylhet which, as I have already stated, had always been looked upon as Shih-li-ch'a-ta-lo by the Indian savants.

This encouraged me to examine the localities of the other five kingdoms and in my first article "To the East of Samataṭa," I tried to demonstrate that (I) Shih-li-ch'a-ta-lo was Sylhet (Śrīhaṭṭa); (2) Kamo-lang-ka was the modern Tipperah District with Comilla as its headquarters; (3) To-lo-po-ti (or Tu-ho-lo-po-ti) was the Tipperah State; (4) I-shang-na-pu-lo was the Manipur State, which had Viṣṇupur as its former Capital; (5) Mo-ha-chan-p'o was the locality near Bhamo in northern Burma which had Sampenago as its whilom Capital; and Yen-mo-na-chou was Tampadeepa in the south-west of Mo-ha-chan-p'o.[4]

Not knowing Chinese in which the original records are written, and French in which the journals and books relating to researches in Indo-China are generally published, I proceeded with great care and caution and sent the manuscript of my article to Dr. V. A. Smith who was then living. He accepted my identifications.

M. L. Finot, the distinguished French antiquarian of Indo-China, published an article headed "Hiuen Tsang and the Far East," adversely criticising my article, in the same Journal, October, 1920. I wrote a reply to his criticisms and had it published as the second article under the same heading ("To the East of Samataṭa') in the Hindustan Review, July, 1924. *M.* Finot has come up again with an article, this time with a different heading – "Indo-China in the Records of Chinese Pilgrims", (Indian Historical Quarterly, Vol. II, no. 2) wherein he has written a rejoinder to my second article.

The present article which is the third with the same heading is an attempt to meet the great antiquarian's arguments.

M. Finot has raised a side issue:he objects to the spelling of the Chinese traveller's name as "Yuan Chwang," and says it should be "Hiuen (or Hsüan) Tsang." The alternative (Hiuan or Hsüan) shows indecision on his part. In fact, it is very difficult to transliterate Chinese names; our tongue fails to pronounce 'hs' and 'ts.' I adopted "Yuan Chwang" after consulting Watters' book, which I considered to be correct as it was published under the authority of the Royal Asiatic Society. In the present article also I stick to it. I think, however, we need not trouble much about the spelling of a name that cannot be put in any other language than Chinese with absolute correctness.

Now to the main issue, namely, the identification of the six countries heard of, but not visited, by the Chinese pilgrim. He came to India to know its people and places and to learn the scriptures. That he took care to take down notes of the six countries which he could not visit shows that the places belonged to India or to a region very near to India of which he had no previous knowledge. The south-eastern part of the Indo-Chinese peninsula was already known to the Chinese people, as that region was very near and at the same time easily accessible to them, especially by the sea route. It is, therefore, quite probable that these six countries were Śrīhaṭṭa, Kamalāṅka (Kāmlāk), Tipperah State, Manipur State, Northern Burma and South-Western Burma, which together formed a complete circle; and not Prome, Tenasserim (or Malay Peninsula), Siam, Cambodia, Annam and Yamunādvīpa (that has defied identification) that together made a parabolic curve, so the speak, ending in an unknown region, a point noted in both my previous articles,[5] but passed over by the learned critic.

Another point in my second article[6] was that I-tsing had visited none of the (six) countries mentioned by Yuan Chwang with the solitary exception of Shih-li-ch'a-ta-lo which was spelt exactly alike by both the Chinese travellers; and in my first article[7] I showed that Shih-li-ch'a-ta-lo of I-tsing must be Śrīhaṭṭa (Sylhet) and not Prome:but *M.* Finot, without sifting my arguments on the point, persists in identifying I-tsing's Lankasu, Shehopati (or Javapati), Pohnan (or Funan) and Lini with Yuan Chwang's Ka-mo-lang-ka, To-lo-po-ti, I-shang-na-pu-lo and Mo-ha-chan-p'o respectively, only to make confusion worse confounded.

I shall now proceed to deal with the countries one by one and, to meet *M.* Finot's arguments, shall in this article follow his order of enumeration. He has begun with Campā—his sheet-anchor. In his previous article, he was indignant that any other place than Annam should have gone by the name of Campā. This Annam is called Lin-i, which is the Chinese equivalent of Campā and *M.* Finot says that "the name Lin-i was never used by the Chinese for another State than Campā on the Annamese coast and by no ingenuity could it be located elsewhere".[8] *M.* Finot perhaps would have held a different view, if he had looked up the derivation of Lin-i. In the Abhidhānacintāmaṇi, Hemacandra Sūri gives the synonyms of the then celebrated towns of India and writes about Campā as follows:

Campā tu Mālinī—Lomapāda-Karṇayoḥ pūḥ.

i.e. Campā, Mālinī, Lomapādapūḥ and Karṇapūḥ (pūḥ=city) are the four names of the whilom capital of Aṅga. The Campā of Annam as a Colony inherited the synonyms of its mother City, and Lini is either Mālini, shorn of the first syllable (mā), or is derived from 'Lomapāda (Annamese Lömöp, Chinese Lin-i).[9] Hence wherever a colonial town or state bore the name of Campā,it would, in imitation of the mother City (or state), be called Lin-i by the Chinese; also, Mahā Campā (differentiated by 'Mahā' from the Annamese as well as the mother Campā in Behar) might be termed "the Lin-i of the Chinese",[10] and yet need not be the Annamese Campā. Dr. Takakusu of course locates I-tsing's Lini (as well as Mahā Campā of Yuan Chwang) in Annam; and in this he has only acquiesced in the hitherto established view of the Occidental Orientalists; but he has not said, as *M.* Finot does, that Lin-i or even Campā was a name of Annam.[11]

The next is I-shang-na-pu-lo—rendered Īśānapura, hitherto identified with Cambodia, because Īśānavarman ascended the throne of Cambodia about 600 A.C., and "dwelt in the town of Īshöna" says the Sueishu. Before that, the country was called Śreṣṭhapura and ruled by Śreṣṭ havarman, and Bhavapura when ruled over by Bhavavarman : so the custom apparently was that a king as soon as he ascended the throne used to give his name to the capital or to found a new capital after his name; and as soon as he died, a new king would come in and do the same. From Dr. Takakusu's notes[12] we learn that Īśānavarman conquered and took Funan (Eastern Siam) by 627 and that he was reputed as an enemy of Buddhism. From another account, however, we gather that Buddhism was introduced in Siam in 638 A.C. We may infer that when Yuan Chwang was taking note of the six countries on his way back from Samataṭa, which he visited by the year 643 A.C., i.e., almost at the conclusion of his sojourn in India, Īśānavarman, and with him his capital, as was the custom, was no more. It must therefore be proved that Īśānapura existed even after the demise of its founder, before the identification is accepted. I-tsing, writing of the place only a few years later, called it 'Funan' and not Īśānapura.

Moreover, if I-shang-na-pu-lo of Yuan Chwang was the same as this "Īśhōna (without "pura") of the Sueishu, then the wordings would not have been different and the same place would have been spelt and named alike, as was 'Shih-li-ch'a-ta-lo' by Yuan Chwang and I-tsing.

Then comes To-lo-po-ti. According to Yuang Chwang this was west of I-shang-na-pu-lo. *M.* Finot, interpreting 'To-lo-po-ti as 'Dvārāvatī,'[13] said in his first article: "To-lo-po-ti has not yet been located so definitely and nothing proves that Dvārāvatī occupied formerly the exact site of Ayodhyā; it may have been situated either in the neighbourhood of Ayodhyā, as Gerini thought, or at Lophburi as Pelliot suggested. * * * * * What alone interests us is the question whether Dvārāvatī corresponds roughly to Lower Siam and this fact is attested by the Old History of T'ang according to which the 'Water-Tchenla', i.e., Lower Cambodia, is bordered on the west by To-lo-po-ti."[14] In reply I wrote in my second article as follows: "If by Lower Cambodia is meant the southern half of Cambodia as represented in a modern Atlas, we find neither Ayodhyā nor Lophburi on the west or even north-west; and the western boundary is a sea rather than any land at all; even if what has been quoted by *M.* Pelliot from the Old History of T'ang is considered as authentic, I shall state here that there were many Dvārāvatīs in the Indo-Chinese Peninsula as was already stated by me in the previous article. Moreover, in order to establish that this To-lo-po-ti was what was mentioned by Yuan Chwang, it must be definitely localized and shown to have existed during the earlier half of the 7th century."[15] *M.* Finot, in his second article, takes no notice of this but now defines Lower Cambodia as the region lying south of Dongrek Mounts, which, in the modern Atlas, are the northern boundary of the whole Cambodia.

At any rate, if the whilom Cambodia extended considerably further north of these Dongrek Mounts, it ought to have been clearly stated and proved. No rejoinder has till now been vouchsafed to the latter part of my remarks. I should state here, that Yuan Chwang, who took care to say that Shih-li-ch'a-ta-lo and Ka-mo-lang-ka were on a sea and a bay respectively, did not even mention that I-shang-na-pu-lo and To-lo-po-ti were countries bordering on a sea or a gulf, though their alleged modern substitutes are so situated.[16]

The next country dealt with is Ka-mo-lang-ka. The attempt of the Orientalists to identify it with a region in the Indo-Chinese peninsula has an interesting history, of its own. Formerly it was identified with "Pegu and the delta of the Irāvatī."[17] As a result of this identification Shih-li-ch'a-ta-lo, the alleged Prome, became quite inland, and Ka-mo-lang-ka south rather than south-east of Shih-li-ch'a-ta-lo, and To-lo-po-ti (alleged to be Ayodhyā, lower Menum) south-east rather than east of Ka-mo-lang-ka. Then the position of Ka-mo-lang-ka was pushed further down and identified with Tenasserim.[18] This made Shih-li-ch'a-ta-lo (Prome) approach the sea below and put Ka-mo-lang-ka to the south-east rather than south of Shih-li-ch'a-ta lo and To-lo-po-ti to the east of Ka-mo-lang-ka fulfilling all the details of Yuan Chwang's description. But now Ka-mo-lang-ka is pushed further down and identified with a portion of Malayan Peninsula;[19] and To-lo-po-ti becomes more north-east than east in which side there is a gulf (the Gulf of Siam). And all this on the supposition that Yuan Chwang's Ka-mo-lang-ka is the same as I-tsing's Lankasu. The matter reaches the climax when a scholar like *M*. Sylvain Lèvi, in his work on "Austro-Asiatic" elements in the Indian names of places, explains the first part of the name as Austro-Asiatic pré-formante Kām which is to be found again in Kāmarūra, Kāmboja etc. "But," adds *M*. Finot quite pertinently "there still remains to be explained why in this particular case pré-formante Kām has separated from the organic element Lanka."[20]

M. Finot sums up thus: "If, therefore, it is likely that 'Ka-mo-lang-ka' and 'Langkiasu' are the same place, that is not quite certain; and should the Kāmalak-nagar, of which *M*. Vidyavinod finds traces in the vicinity of Comilla, finally turn up to have been a state of some importance, it would be possible to look there for the Ka-mo-long-ka of Hiuen-Tsang. However it is so far a mere name which gives but scanty ground for an identification."[21]

I am grateful to *M*. Finot even for this and must reiterate here what I stated in conclusion to my first article: "the region with which we have concerned ourselves here is as yet a virgin field for research, and if this our humble writing serves to invite the attention of the veteran antiquarians to work in this field, we should think ourselves amply rewarded."[22]

The next in *M*. Finot's order is Shih-li-ch'a-ta-lo. In order to identify it with Prome, the antiquarians are pleased to change N. E. in Yuan Chwang to S. E. Human beings are no doubt liable to errors and the Chinese pilgram was no exception: *M*. Finot has in his last article instanced one or two. The present case, however, is quite different. Watters, knowing fully well that N. E. was considered as a mistake by several antiquarians, says that north-east "is the reading of all the texts, of the 'Life,' and of the 'Fang-chih'."[23] Moreover, it is improbable that there should be a mistake, at a very outset, in taking notes of certain countries not visited by the pilgrim. In this case, therefore, the alteration is gratuitous, since, on the north-east, quite in contiguity of Samataṭa, there was a place "Śrī-haṭṭa" which as reported to and heard by the pilgrim was reproduced as 'Shih-li-ch'a-ta-lo.[24]

One of the grounds of Prome being not on the sea has now been removed by pushing it southwards so as to include the delta of Irāvatī that had so long been cosidered as part of Ka-mo-lang-ka. I mention this here for what it is worth. As regards another ground, viz., that the kingdom of Tharekhettara (=Śrīkśetra=the alleged Shih-li-ch'a-ta-lo) became extinct in 95 A.C., long before Yuan Chwang took note of the six kingdoms, *M*. Finot, who, in his first article stated that the above date occurs in the "Native Chronicles" whose records are of no value whatever, now brings forth "the highest authority of Burmese history" to support his own remarks. But unfortunately this authority has not helped him much; for he says "I am inclined to place the fall of Prome between the 5th and the 6th century".[25] Now, Yuan Chwang took note of Shih-li-ch'a-ta-lo in the middle of the 7th century—about two centuries after the fall of what is now alleged to have been Shih-li-ch'a-ta-lo.[26]

M. Finot has also stated that Shih-li-ch'a-ta-lo "located at Sylhet was cut out from the sea by that of Kamalanka."[27] I think I have said enough about this matter in both of my previous articles:the mention of "Sāgara" and "Nauvāṭaka" is found in copper-plates of Sylhet.[28] The reminiscence of the Sāgara is still left in the word "hāor" in the district; and an Englishman had to use compass as in a sea in his journey from Dacca to Sylhet : all this took place at a time far posterior to Yuan Chwang's visit. As to Kamalanka, I stated that "the Brahmaputra had its old channel terminated at a point which was then on the north-western boundary of old Tipperah and possibly this was then the head of an estuary that looked like a bay."[29]

If *M.* Finot looks to the geography of Dacca, Mymensingh, Sylhet and Tipperah, and compares Rennel's Map prepared a little over a century ago with the recent Survey maps, I am sure he will be impressed with the rapid changes in the configuration of this part of Bengal and also with the validity of my contention.

M. Finot has, last of all, dealt with Yen-mo-na-chou. 'Chou' means an island, a dvīpa; but what should 'Yen-mo-na' be has hitherto baffled the efforts of the antiquarians. 'Yen' is 'Jam' (cf. Jambu=Yenfo. So Yen-mo-na may be Jamuna. In searching for a word that ends in 'dvīpa', I find that 'Tambadvīpa'[30] is the very locality where, according to my theory, this last of the six kingdoms must have been situated. I consider this Tambadvīpa=the 'Tampadvīpa' of Mr. Taw Sein Ko[31] to be a corrupted Burmese form of Jambudvīpa (for Jamunadvīpa has no meaning). That Yuan Chwang wrote 'Yen-mo-na' was due probably either to the wrong (dialectic) pronunciation of his informer[32] or to the Chinese pilgrim's disbelief in the existence of a Jambudvīpa in that quarter.

Knowing the meaning and extent of "Jambudvīpa", I have no hesitation in agreeing with *M.* Finot that the Burmese knew its import.[33] But a Potentate possessed of only a small portion of the earth takes title of Mahī (or Pṛthivī) pati, or Shah Jehan (king of the world). He may as well style a part of his territory as 'Jambudvīpa' to feel as proud and glorious as the lord of Jambudvīpa.

This, however, is a side issue:let 'Yen-mo na-chou' mean some 'Dvīpa'; what we are concerned with is its location. Even in this matter I proceeded with caution. I asked for the opinion of Mr. Taw Sein Ko, an archeologist and a resident of Burma. He was kind enough to write as follows: "Your theory is that by Yen-mo-na-chou the Chinese traveller meant the southern half of Burma. You are perfectly entitled to hold your view and I am not disposed to oppose it."[34]

I would state in conclusion that controversy in a matter like this should be welcome as it is by discussion that truth comes out. Moreover "contest with great people", says our poet Bhāravi, "rather helps our way to progress" (samunnayan bhūtim . . . . varaṃ virodho'pi samaṃ mahātmabhiḥ).

References

1. Vide my article in the Epigraphia Indica, vol. xii, no. 13, p. 65f.
2. Vide Watters' Yuan Chwang, vol. ii, p. 187f.
3. *Ibid.*, p. 340.
4. Vide my article in the Journal of the Royal Asiatic Society, January 1920, pp. 1-19.
5. JRAS., January 1920, p. 18; and Hindustan Review, July 1924, p. 445.
6. Hindustan Review, July 1924, pp. 445-446.
7. Vide JRAS., January 1920, p. 6, footnote 2.
8. JRAS, October 1920, p. 450.
9. Vide Col. Gerini's Researches on Ptolemy's Geography, p. 235 et seq.
10. Watters' Yuan Chwang, vol. ii, p. 188, II. 2-3.
11. This is why I said in my second article that Dr. Takakusu "does not make the same allegation as put forward by *M.* Finot," which *M.* Finot condemns as inaccurate (vide IHQ., vol. II, no. 2, p. 254, footnote 2.)
12. Takakusu's I-tsing, pp. li-lii, footnote.
13. "But the characters seem to stand for Tālāpati, that is, Mahādeva" – Watters' Yuan Chwang, vol. ii, pp. 189. It also was recorded as Tu (or She)-ho-lo-po-ti (vide Watters' Yuan Chwang, vol. ii, pp. 189, footnote 3. Also M. Finot's article I.H.Q., vol. ii, no. 2, p. 261).
14. JRAS., October 1920, p. 450f.
15. Hindustan Review, July 1924, p. 444.
16. Tripurā and Maṇipur States are, as is well-known, inland countries.
17. Watters' Yuan Chwang, vol. ii, p. 189.
18. JRAS., October 1920 no. p. 447 and also I.H.Q., vol. ii, 2, p. 256 (*M.* Pelliot's view).
19. Vide IHQ., vol. ii, no. 2, p. 256, (*M.* Ferrand's and *M.* Cædes' views).
20. IHQ., vol. ii, no. 2, p. 257. We know for certain that in Kāmarūpa, Kāma has nothing of 'Austro-Asiatic pré-formante' in it.
21. IHQ., vol. ii, no. 2, p.257. The dispassionate readers, who would carefully of through my arguments (JRAS., January 1920, pp. 7-9) will not however think it a 'mere name' but will see that traces of a state (Karmanta) of some importance have already been found there which of course require further investigation.
22. JRAS., January 1920, p. 19.
23. Watters' Yuan Chwang, vol. ii, pp. 188-189.
24. *M.* Finot in a footnote (IHQ., vol. ii, no. 2, p. 259) says that this identification was made by Vivien de Saint Martin long before me. I do not claim any originality; in fact, as I have already stated, more than one Indian antiquarian

had said so. Only I have taken upon myself the task of demonstrating what has been a mere assertion heretofore.

25. I H Q., vol. ii, no. 2, In p. 259, footnote 2, *M.* Finot quotes G. E. Harvy's History of Burma where it is stated that "Prome was overthrown probably not long after A.C. 800." This however goes against the opinion of the "highest authority on the Burmese History" and so has been assigned a place in the footnote. It may however refer to a subsequent kingdom founded there.

26. I notice that *M.* Finot has quoted a saying of mine to apply it against me:I said "surely Prome was not left without any ruler after the extinction of the Tharekhettara kingdom." "All right," says *M.* Finot, "but why should not these new rulers have preserved the old name of Śrīkṣetra"? This is however the course of the world—"The old order changeth yielding place to new." Otherwise we should have still to use the name 'Tharekhattara; in lieu of 'Prome', and 'Campā' in lieu of 'Indo China.'

27. I H Q., vol. ii, no. 2, p. 259.

28. Recently my attention has been drawn to a verse in Jayānanda's "Caitanyamaṅgala", an old book on the life of Śrī Caitanya, wherein a description of a place in Sylhet (the birth-place of Caitanya's mother's father) is written: paścimete ḍhol samudra (a sea in the west). Jayānanda's Caitanyamaṅgala (Sāhityapariṣad's edition), p. 8.

29. JRAS., January 1920, p. 8.

30. Owing probably to a mistake in the copy of the extracts from the Northern Burma Gazetteer that I had, Tamba was written by me as 'Tambu' which *M.* Finot has taken as a quite change consciously made by me. The mistake was in a manner pointed out but not exactly corrected by Mr. Taw Sein Ko of the Archæological Department, Burma (vide JRAS, Jany. 1920., p. 18., fn. I).

31. JRAS., 1920, p. 18, footnote I.

32. "The names of places the pilgrims heard in conversation, were heard in local dialects" (Dr. Rhys Davids, Preface to Watters' Yuan Chwang, vol. I, p. vi).

33. In this connection I would invite attention to Col. G. E. Gerini's Synoptical Map prefixed to his "Researches on Ptolemy's Geography" in which Plakṣ a Dvīpa, Sālmali Dvīpa, Śāka Dvīpa and Krauñca Dvīpa, (i.e., the majority of the seven Dvīpas) are shown in the Indo-Chinese Peninsula.

34. Hindustan Review, July 1924, p. 445, fn. 2.

134. [illegible] and so, though their subscription to [illegible] of [illegible] that body [illegible] monastic [illegible]

135. [illegible], 1917, 225; [illegible] [illegible] testimony [illegible] whom his [illegible] was [illegible] probably nothing after [illegible]. This however goes against the opinion [illegible] on the [illegible] theory. And so has been assigned a place in the [illegible] to a [illegible].

136. [illegible] that [illegible] quoted a [illegible] and [illegible] with the [illegible] of the [illegible] Afghan [illegible] observed the [illegible] of [illegible] the course of these [illegible]. The old order [illegible] now [illegible] and [illegible] 'Caitya' [illegible]

137. J.A.S.B., vol. X, no. 6, p. [illegible]

138. Recently my attention has been drawn to a [illegible] appended a [illegible] on the [illegible] of [illegible] Cathedral [illegible] a [illegible] of a place [illegible] the open place [illegible] a [illegible] [illegible]

139. [illegible] January 1970.

140. [illegible] probably [illegible] who [illegible] was [illegible] in [illegible] [illegible] the [illegible] made by [illegible] [illegible] of the [illegible] Department [illegible] [illegible], p. 18.

141. J.A.S., 1929, p. [illegible], footnote 1.

142. [illegible] [illegible] Christianity, vol. [illegible]

143. [illegible]

144. Hindustan Review, July 1904, [illegible]

40

On the Antiquity of the Name "Kāsthamandapa or Katmandu"

P. C. Bagchi

According to the Nepalese Vaṃśāvalīs the ancient name of Kāṭmaṇḍu was Kāntipura. It was founded by king Guṇakāmadeva who ascended the throne in the Kali year 3824=724 A.D. Later on the 1595 A.D. the name of the city was changed into Kāṣṭhamaṇḍapa during the reign of Lakṣmī-Narasiṃhamalla. The legendary portion of the tradition says that a certain citizen had cherished the desire of building a temple with the wood of a single tree for the use of the wandering ascetics. During the procession of Matsyendranātha he suddenly discovered the *Kalpavṛkṣa* in person, got hold of him and asked for the boon. The *Kalpavṛkṣa* became pleased with him and he thus succeeded in building the temple with the wood of a single tree.[1] The said temple is still shown in front of the old palace of the Mallas at Kāṭmaṇḍu. It is still used by wandering ascetics.

Though it is pure legend the date 1595 A.D. had to be retained for want of further information about the name of Kaṭmaṇḍu. During my last stay in Nepal I came across a manuscript in the Darbar collection which contains some information about the name of the city.

It is the ms. of the *Lakṣahomavidhi* of Śaivācārya Tejabrahma. Its colophon runs thus:

श्रेयोऽस्तु, सम्वत् ५३१ वैशाख शिवनवग्यान्तिथौ लिखितं इदम् श्रीकास्तममन्डप नगरे श्रीभीमदत्त सोमशर्गणा लिखितमिदं ।[2]

The city of Kāstamaṇḍapa is no other than Kāṣṭhamaṇḍapa, the confusion made by the copyist being a very common one in the Nepalese manuscripts. The name Kāṣṭhamaṇḍapa, therefore, had come into use already in the Nepal era 531 i.e. 1411 A.D., 200 years before the time of Lakṣmī Narasiṃha Malladeva.

The name Kāntipura was also in use at that period as is evident from the colophons of mss.[3] Thus it seems probable that both the names, Kāntipura and Kāṣṭhamaṇḍapa were simultaneously in use during a certain period and subsequently the former became more popular and the latter fell into disuse.

References

1. S. Lévi, *Le Nepal,* I, pp. 52-54.
2. The Late MM. H. P. Śāstrī in his *Catalogue of Palm Leaf and Selected Paper Mss. belongining to the Durbar Library, Nepal* II, pp. 48 has also described these mss., but the colophon as given there contains a number of mistakes – *"Śrīyāstu saṃvat* 531 *Vaiśākhasya Śitanavamyāṃ tithau likhitamidaṃ Śrīkāstamaṇḍapa nagare Śrī-Bhīmadatta somaśarmāṇo-alikhit.*
3. See Śāstrī, *ibid.*, pp. 190 Pārthivārcana Cuḍāmaṇi (copied in 1715) Nepāle *bahupīṭ hamaṇḍitaśive Kāntipurī rājate;* pp. 196 Pūjākalpalatā (copied in 1669 A.D.) – "*Kāntapurīr rājā Pratāpamaller Guru Nārāyaṇa Bhāhuker puthi"*; pp. 233 Pitṛbhakti Taraṅgiṇī (copied in 1674 A.D.) – *Kāntipur nagare likhitaiṣā.*

41

Rāḍha or the Ancient Gaṅgā-Rāṣtra

N. L. Dey

Rāḍha is the ancient Gaṅgārāṣṭra

The word *Rāḍha* (pronounced *Rāḍh*) is a corruption of the Pāli word *Raṭṭha* or Sanskrit *Rāṣṭra,* an abbreviation of which is found in some geographical names such as Guj-rāt for Gurjjara-rāṣṭra, Mi-rāṭ for Maya-rāṣṭra, Su-rāṭ for Su-rāṣṭra. Hence *Rāḍha* is a corruption of *Rāṣṭra* meaning a country. The country therefore to which the general name of Rāḍha was applied and which was at once understood by this name must have had originally a specific name to which the word Rāḍha was attached, and we can very well conceive that the specific name was dropped for some very cogent reason, either on account of its extensive power or wide celebrity, simply to be understood by the general name of *Rāḍha.* The question is what was the real name of that country ? All authorities[1] agree that *Rāḍha* was, and still is, situated on the western side of the Ganges. Here we have some basis to proceed upon, and the clue to the name is supplied by the *Periplus of the Erythraean Sea,* which was written in the 1st century of the Christian era. The passage in which the name of the country occurs has thus been rendered by Mr. Wilfrid H. Schoff: "After these, the course turns toward the east again, and sailing with the ocean to the right and the shore remaining beyond to the left, Ganges comes into view, and near it the very last land toward the east, Chryse. There is a river near it called the Ganges, and it rises and falls in the same way as the Nile. On its bank is a market-town which has the same name as the river Ganges."[2] Commenting on this passage Mr. Schoff says "Ganges.—The name is applied in the same paragraph to district, river and town. By the district is meant Bengal."[3] Thus we find that in the 1st century of the Christian era there existed a country which was known by the name of "Ganges," a corruption of the word *Gaṅgā,* which extended to the Bay of Bengal; a river in it of the same name; and a town within it and upon the river, which was also called by the name of *Gaṅgā*. Ptolemy, who flourished in the 2nd century A.C. in the reign of Antoninus Pius, also speaks of a very powerful people called *Gangaridai* "who occupied all the country about the mouths of the Ganges," and he says that their capital was called *Gangé*.[4] Of course the country of the Gangaridai was called *Gaṅgārāḍha,* as the people generally derived their name from the country in which they lived. So here we have a distinct confirmation of the statement in the *Periplus* that there was a country on the bank of the Ganges (*Gaṅgā*) which was known by the name of *Gaṅgā-rāḍha,* or, properly speaking, *Gaṅgārāṣṭra* (the country of *Gaṅgā*), the capital of which was called *Gangé* or *Gaṅgā*. Megasthenes, who resided as an ambassador in the court of Candragupta in the 4th century before the Christian era, also says that the Gangarides were a powerful people, and that the final course of the Ganges passed through their country.[5] There can be no doubt therefore that there was a country on the western side of the river Ganges or Gaṅgā, which was called Gaṅgā-rāṣṭra. We can now un derstand that the specific name of *Gaṅgā,* as applied to the *country,* was originally dropped to avoid confusion, as that was also the name of the *river* which flowed through it, and likewise of the *market-town* which afterwards became its capital. Hence the word *Rāṣ ṭra,* or its popular form *Rāḍha,* came into vogue to indicate the name of the *country,* and in course of time when Gaṅgā-rāṣṭra became a powerful kingdom, the name of *Rāḍha* (or *Rāḍa*) as the name of the kingdom became stereotyped, and other countries also understood it by that name. The country of the Gangaridai, however, should not be confounded with that of the Prasii, the corrupted form of *Prācya* or Eastern, as the Magadha kingdom was called, though these two people were mentioned together by some of Alexander's historians[6] and though both these kingdoms were situated on the western side of the Ganges. They were two separate and distinct kingdoms, the capital of the former, according to Megasthenes, being Parthalis, and that of the latter, Palibothra or Pāṭaliputra which was situated on the upper Ganges. The southern boundary of Gaṅgā-rāṣṭra in the 1st and 2nd centuries A.C. was the Bay of Bengal.

Suhma, a division of Rāḍha

Though the early history of ancient Gaṅgā-rāṣṭra is lost in the mists of time and we have no sufficient materials for its reconstruction, yet from the stray facts which may be gleaned from the writings of ancient authors, Hindu and Greek, we can very well form an opinion regarding its extent, its influence and the power that it wielded: it maintained its supremacy and independence for several centuries before it was subjected to the Maurya empire. That the Gangarides or Gaṅgā-rāḍhīs were a powerful race has been attested by all Greek writers: their name has not only been associated with that of the Prasii, the brave men of the Magadha kingdom, but Megasthenes distinctly says that they always maintained a body of 60,000 foot-soldiers, 1,000 bowmen and 700 elephants. But the earliest mention of Gaṅgā-rāṣṭra that we have is in the writings of Jaina and Buddhist authors. The *Ācārāṅga Sūtra*[7] says "He [i. e. Mahāvīra] travelled in the pathless country of the Lāḍhas in Vajjabhūmi and Subbhabhūmi : he used there miserable beds and miserable seats." According to the commentators, Vajjabhūmi and Subbhabhūmi were the two divisions of Lāḍha, which, according to Professor Jacobi, "may be identified with the classical Rāḍha or western Bengal and Lāṭa of the Buddhists, the native country of Vijaya, the legendary conqueror of Ceylon. Subbhabhūmi is probably the country of the Suhmas, who are also indentical with the Rāḍhas."[8] There can be no doubt that Subbhabhūmi is the ancient Suhma. Thus we see that, at the time of Mahāvīra, the reputed founder of the Jaina religion, who lived in the 6th century B.C., Gangā-rāṣṭra had already come to be called by the name of Lāḍha or Rāḍha, or the modern Rāḍh, and that it had already conquered the ancient country of Suhma. It should be stated here that Suhma and Tāmralipta were two independent countries at the time of the Mahābhārata.[9] It appears that while Buddha was performing asceticism at Buddha Gayā before he attained the Buddhahood, two merchants Trapuṣa and Bhallika, who gave honey and articles of food to Buddha, came from Ukala or Utkala and arrived at a part called Suram where they hired five hundred carts to carry their merchandise. This part has been identified with a part of Tāmralipta or modern Tamluk.[10] *Suram* is evidently a corruption of *Suhma.* In the *Daśakumāracarita* Dūmalipta or Tāmralipta is also mentioned as being situated in Suhma.[11] It appears therefore that at the time of Buddha, Suhma had already conquered Tāmralipta so as to confer its name upon that maritime port. So we find that in the 6th century B.C., Gaṅgā-rāṣṭra or Rāḍha had already conquered Suhma and by its conquest acquired dominion in the ancient kingdom of Tāmralipta. There is nothing strange in the corruption of the name of Suhma in to Subbha and Suram, for we find Suhma called Sumbha in the *Mahābhārata*[12] and in the *Telapatta Jātaka.*[13] But it is curious that the Purāṇas, excepting the *Devī Purāṇa*[14] which is an Upa-Purāṇa, do not mention the name of Gaṅgārāṣṭra or Rāḍha, nor do we find the name of Rāḍha mentioned in the classical works before the 10th century A.C. The aforesaid works, evidently in their anxiety to preserve the ancient names of Suhma and Tāmralipta mentioned in the *Mahābhārata,* had studiously avoided mentioned the name of Rāḍha and in its stead had used one of the aforesaid two names. Nīlakaṇṭha, the celebrated commentator of the *Mahābhārata,* says "*Suhmāḥ Rāḍhāḥ*"[15], that is, Suhma is the same as Rāḍha. Rājaśekhara, who flourished in the 10th century A.C., was perhaps the first to use the name of Rāḍha in his *Karpūramañjarī.*[16] The *Prabodha-candro-daya Nāṭaka,*[17] which was written in the 11th century A.C., gives some account of Rāḍhāḥ. Buddha is also said to have visited Suhma and explained the *Janapada-Kalyāni Sutta,* while he was dwelling in a forest near the town of Desaka.[18]

References

1. *Śabdakalpadruma,* s. v. *Rāḍha;* Ānanda Bhāṭṭa's *Ballāla-carita* pt. II, ch. I.
2. *The Periplus of the Erythræan Sea,* p. 47, translated by Mr. Wilfrid H. Schoff.
3. *Ibid.,* p. 255.
4. McCrindle's *Ptolemy,* Bk. vii, ch. I, 81: *Indian Antiquary,* 1884, p. 365.
5. McCrindle's *Ancient India as described by Megasthenes and Arrian,* p. 135.
6. McCrindle's *Invasion of India by Alexander the Great,* pp. 221, 281, 310, 364.
7. *Sacred Books of East,* vol. xxii, p. 84.
8. *Ibid.,* p. 84 note.
9. *Mahābhārata* (P. C. Roy's edition), Ādi pp., ch. 113; Sabhā pp., ch. 30; Bhīṣma p., ch. 9: see also *Brahma Purāṇa.*
10. Kern's *Manual of Indian Buddhism,* p. 22, Dr. Satīs Ch. Vidyābhūṣaṇa's *Buddha-deva,* p. 143 note.
11. *Daśakumāracarita,* ch, vi.
12. *Mbh.,* Sabhā pp., ch. 30.
13. *Telapatta-Jātaka* (Cowell's ed.), vol. I, p. 232.
14. *Devī Purāṇa,* ch. 39.
15. Nilakaṇṭha's commentary on *v.* 25, ch. 30, Sabhā pp. of the *Mahābhārata.*
16. *Karpūra-mañjarī,* Act I.
17. *Prabodha-candrodaya Nāṭaka,* act ii.
18. *Telapatta-Jātaka* in *Jātaka,* vol. i, p. 232.

42

Raḍha or the Ancient Gaṅga-Raṣṭra

Nundo Lal Dey

II

Vajjabhūmi, the other division of Lāḍha mentioned in the *Ācārāṅga-sūtra,* is evidently a corruption.

Vajjabhūmi or Vijaya-bhūmi, which means the "country of conquest," that is where Mahāvīra, the 24th Tīrthaṅkara of the Jainas, made a "conquest of this passion" and became a "Jina" or conqueror and where he was called "Mahāvīra" or the Great Hero.[1] His great Ranunciation took place at a "Vijaya Muhūrtta" and he attained the Kevaliship at a "Vijaya Muhūrtta."[2] The *Ācārāṅga-sūtra,* which mentions the names of Vajjabhūmi and Subbhabhūmi as two divisions of Lāḍha, was composed in the 4th century B.C., that is, about two hundred years after Mahāvīra's death,[3] when, it is very probable, the word *Vijaya-bhūmi* had been corrupted into *Vajja bhūmi.* Its commentaries which were written not earlier than 876 A.C.,[4] that is, 1500 years after Mahāvīra's death, restored Vajja-bhūmi into Vajra-bhūmi. But it should be stated here that in Māgadhi-Prākṛta, in which language the *Ācārāṅga Sūtra* is written, *Vajra* assumes the form *Vayara,*[5] and in Pāli Vajira.[6] In the enumeration of countries in the *Matsya Purāṇa,*[7] which is one of the oldest of the Purāṇas, we find the name of a country called "Pra-Vijaya on the north of Suhma" (*Suhmottaraḥ Pravijayāḥ*). Some of the Purāṇas have "Brahmottarāḥ" instead of "Suhmottarāḥ[8] but "Brahmottarāḥ" is an obvious mistake for "Suhmottarāḥ" The prefix *Pra* of *Pra-Vijaya* has evidently been used either for the sake of the metre or for emphasising the word *Vijaya.* There can be no doubt that this Vijayabhūmi comprised the modern districts of Manbhum and Singbhum in the Chota Nagpur Division of the Province of Behar and Orissa. Manbhum is evidently a corruption of *Mānya-bhūmi* which means the "venerable country" and evidently derived its name from Mahāvīra, who was called the "Venerable Ascetic

Mahāvīra" on the attainment of Kevaliship in this district, as we shall show. The Paresnāth Hill, the eastern metropolis of Jaina worship, Abu in Rajputana being the western, is situated in this district. It was the scene of Nirvāṇa of no less than twenty Tīrthaṅkaras out of the twenty-four Tīrthaṅkaras of the Jainas, including Pārśvanātha, the twenty-third Tīrthaṅkara. It contains their cenotaphs or the *Samādhi-mandira,* for which reason the Hill is called by the Jāinas *Samet-śikhara* which reason the Hill is called by the Jāinas *Samet-śikhara* which is a corruption of *Samādhiśekhara.* Singbhum is a corrpution of *Siṃha-bhūmi,* which means "the country of the Lion." It also derived its name from Mahāvīra who was compared to a Lion[9] and whose symbol was the Lion (*Keśari-siṃha*).[10] The *Kalpa Sūtra,* which was written by Bhadrabāhu, the Jaina patriarch, who flourished during the reign of Maurya Candragulpta and died in 357 B.C.,[11] says "on the day called Suvrata, in the Muhūrtta called Vijaya, outside the town of Jṛmbhikagrāma on the bank of the river Ṛjupālika," Mahāvīra performed asceticism and became a Kevalin.[12] The river Ṛjupālika," or Ṛjupālukā as mentioned by Dr. Bühler, was also called Ṛjuvkula or Ṛjuālikā,[13] and it appears to be the ancient name of the river Barakar which rises in the central plateau of Chota Nagpur, and after flowing through the district of Hazaribagh, enters the district of Manbhum, and falls into the Damodar on the boundary of the district near Sankhtoria. From an inscription in a temple, about eight miles away from Giridih, dedicated to Mahāvīra, it appears that the name of the river, on which the original temple was situated but which is in a different locality, was Ṛjupālika, the present temple being erected with the materials of the old removed to this place. Hence it is very probable that the river Ṛjupālika is the modern river Barakar. Jṛmbhikargrāma[14] means the "village of Jṛmbhika." All circumstances indicate that the ancient Jṛmbhika of the 6th century B.C. is the modern Jharia. Mrs. Sinclair Stevenson in her *Heart of Jainism* says "Mahāvīra stayed in a place not very far from the Pārasnāth hills called Jṛmbhakagrāma" which was also called Jṛmbhilā."[15] Jharia is situated at a distance of 25 or 30 miles to the South of the Paresnāth Hill in the district of Manbhum. It is celebrated for its coal fields. If the weather be fair, Paresnāth Hill can be very clearly and distinctly seen from Jharia. Jharia is most probably the corruption of Jṛmbhilā. The religious sentiments of Mahāvīra, whose parents were the followers of Pārśvanātha, as well as his own earnest desire for the welfare of mankind, evidently prompted him to select a spot for asceticism not very far from the Pārśvanātha Hill, hallowed by the memory of the holy saints whose doctrines he had imbibed almost with his mother's milk, as the proximity and association of the sacred mountain would prove a source of the sacred mountain would prove a source of constant inscpiration and encouragment to him to save his fellow-creatures from the evils of existence which human beings are heir to. He selected a spot on the bank of the Ṛjupālika outside the village of Jṛmbhika where without hindrance or molestation, to which he was subjected during his twelve years' wanderings, he could perform his austerities and pursue his contemplation. It is very probable that the river Barakar, the ancient Ṛjupālika or Ṛjuvālikā, which means the "river with coarse sand," was much nearer to Jharia in the 6th century B.C. than it is now, as the rivers which are liable to sudden freshets, as the Barakar is, generally change their course through the breaks caused in their banks. The river Barakar is now about twenty miles away from Jharia. It is related in the *Kalpa Sūtra* that Mahāvīra spent one *Pajjusan* or rainy season in Paṇitabhūmi, which according to the commentators was in Vajjabhūmi.[16] This has not yet been identified.

Boundaries of Gaṅārāṣṭra

It will therefore be observed that Gaṅgā-rāṣṭra, or its abbreviations Rāḍha, Rāḍa, Lāḍha, Lāḍa, Lāṭa, Lāla, as stated in Hindu, Jaina and Buddhist works, was in the 6th century B.C. bounded on the east by the Ganges; on the west its boundary extended to the western limits of the districts of Manbhum and Singbhum, and on the south it was bounded by the Ocean. It also appears from the stories of Vijaya and Bhaddakacchana as stated in the *Mahāvaṃśa*[17] that at the time of Buddha's death, the southern portion of Lāla was very close to the ocean. The boundaries of Rāḍha varied at different periods till it was finally absorbed into the kingdom of Bengal. The *Prabodha-candrodayanāṭaka*[18] mentions Dakṣiṇa Rāḍha or Southern Rāḍh. This shows that before the 11th century Rāḍha was divided into Uttara (Northern) and Dakṣiṇa (Southern) Rāḍha. The portion on the north of the river Ajaya is the Uttara Rāḍha and it includes a part of the district of Murshidabad. The northern boundary of Rāḍha, therefore, extended to a portion of the Murshidabad district, Gaṅgā-rāṣṭra was not in existence in the 14th century A.C. Rāḍha included the modern districts of Hughli, Burdwan, Midnapur, Birbhum, Bankura, a portion of Murshidabad and other districts.

Gaṅgā-rāṣṭra before 5th century B.C.

The name of Gaṅga-rāṣtra or Gaṅgā-rāḍha, or its contracted form Gaṅgā or Gāṅga, Rāḍha, Rāḍa, Lāḍha, Lāḍa, Lāṭa, or Lāla, however, does not appear in the *Mahābhārata*. The reasonable inference is that the country did not come into existence, or rather the delta of the

Ganges in which the country is situated, was not formed till after the composition of the *Mahābhārata*. We have already stated that Suhma and Tāmralipta existed at that time. It is also clear from the route taken by Yudhiṣṭhira in his pilgrimage that the delta of the Ganges which contains the modern Rāḍh had not then been formed and the configuration of Bengal was then quite different from what it is now. This appears to be substantiated by geological evidence. According to the geologists the extension of the delta from the north to the present site of Calcutta took place twelve thousand years ago, but by a cataclysm, supposed to have been caused by a severe earthquake, there occurred a subsidence of Mis-Bengal, which had the effect of changing the courses of rivers, specially of the Ganges. We have no evidence or tradition when the subsidence took place, but Colonel F.C. Hirst has noted, and described the former land surface of Bengal in his *Report on the Nadia Rivers.*[19] There was, however, again a re-formation of the delta and emergence of the old depressed surface in some places; and Mr. Ravenshaw is of opinion that "it is not impossible that Calcutta itself may at that period (460 B.C.) have been not far distant from the mouth or one of the mouths of the Ganges."[20] Delta-building is indeed a very slow process. So making an allowance of six hundred years for the slow and gradual extension towards the south of that part of the delta which comprised the modern districts of Hughli and Burdwan on the north of Calcutta, as they appertained to the ancient kingdom of Gaṅgā-rāṣṭra or the modern Rāḍh, we may conclude that the country did not come into existence before the 11th century B.C., which is later than the period ascribed to the composition of the *Mahābhārata*. This part of the country, therefore, in the 5th century B.C. was a dense forest, like the modern Sunderbans, and was the abode of lions and other wild animals. In this wilderness lay the original site of the country afterwards called Gaṅgā-rāṣṭra, the Lāḷa of the *Mahāvaṃsa,*[21] which was written in the 5th century A.C., between Vaṅga and Magadha, there was only a caravan-route which joined the two kingdoms. Pāṇḍu Śākya, said to be a cousin of Buddha, fled from the Śākya country for fear of falling into the hands of Virudhaka, and, crossing the Ganges, founded a settlement which was close to the sea and the Ganges as the story of Bhaddakacchana indicates.[22] It also clearly shows that this part of the country in the 5th century B.C. was no man's land. This settlement was evidently called Pāṇḍuā in the district of Hughli after the name of its founder Pāṇḍu Śākya.[23]

Gaṅgā-rāṣṭra in inscriptions

Though there is no mention of Gaṅgā-rāṣṭra in any of the Purāṇas or in any classical work, yet we find the name and its abbreviated forms Gaṅgā, Gaṅga and Gāṅga mentioned in official documents an inscriptions. Professor Wilson in his Introduction to the *Mackenzie Collection,* remarking on Mr. Stirling's account of the Gaṅgāvaṃśī Kings of Orissa in the *Asiatic Researches*[24] says, "A few trifling matters may perhaps admit of correction, and an inscription procured since Mr. Stirling wrote, by Mr. Colvin, shows that Coraṅga was not the founder of the Gaṅga family, but that the first who came to Kaliṅga was Ananta Varman—also called Kolāhala, sovereign of *Gaṅgā Rāḍhi*—the low country on the right bank of the Ganges or Tamluk and Midanpore; this occurred at the end of the 11th century A.C., and from that till the beginning of the 16th century, the same family occupied the province of Orissa, the boundaries of their rule being extended or contracted variously at various times according to the personal characters of the princes themselves and of those to whom they were opposed."[25] It is, therefore, clear that even in the 11th century A.C., the kings of Gaṅgā-rāṣṭra were called kings of *Gaṅgā-rāḍhi.* Pliny, who lived in the first century A.C., mentions the *Macco-Calingœ* (which is a transcription of Majjka, or middle Kalingas) and the Gangarides-Calingæ as separate peoples form the *Calingœ* (that is, the people of Kaliṅga proper).[26] The Gaṅgā-rāḍhis were known as "Calingæ"[27] even at the time of Megasthenes in the 4th century B.C. General Cunningham also is of opinioin that the *Gaṅgarides Calingae* were one of the Tri-Kaliṅgas or Three-Kaliṅgas."[28] This appears to be confirmed by the legendary tradition recorded in the *Mahāvaṃsa*[29] about the foundation of the capital by Sīhabāhu. It is said that a king of Vaṅga married a daughter of the king of Kaliṅga, and by her he had a daughter named Suppadevī who eloped with a caravan chief who was proceeding to Magadha. In the wilderness of Lāḷa (that is, Rāḍha) she was chased and carried away by a lion to his den, where they lived together. She gave birth to twins, a son and a daughter. The son was named Sīhabāhu and the daughter Sīhasīvali. Sīhabāhu killed the lion and they all went to Vaṅga, where Suppadevī was married to her maternal uncle's son Anuro. After the death of the king of Vaṅga, Anuro succeeded to his kingdom, and Sīhabāhu (Sanskrit form Siṃhabābh) repaired with his sister to the wilderness where he was born, and, clearing the jungle, founded a city named Sīhapura (Sanskrit Siṃhapura) and became its king. He married his sister, and was the progenitor of a line of kings. It is, therefore, clear that being the descendants of a lion, they were of course unable to assume any patronymic, or claim an inclusion into any class; they were consequently known as people of Kaliṅga from Suppadevī's mother who was a princess of Kaliṅga. The story divested of its legendary feature shows that a branch of the kings of Kaliṅga founded a settlement, in Lāḷa or Gaṅgā-rāṣṭra, and established a kingdom, the capital of which was Siṃhapura. This circumstance evidently contributed to their being known as Kaliṅgas of Gaṅgā-rāḍha (*Gangarides Calingæ*). However, the name of Gaṅgā-rāḍhi existed in the 1st century. It appears from the Karhaḍ Plate and Deoli Plate inscriptions of Kṛṣṇa III of Śaka-saṃvat 862 and 880 respectively corresponding to 941 and 959 A.D. that the name *Gāṅgārāṣṭra* has been contracted or abbreviated into *Gaṅgā.*[30] These two inscriptions describing the conquests of Kṛṣ ṇa II, son of Amoghavarṣa or Nṛpatuṅga, state "his command was obeyed by the Aṅgas, the Kaliṅgas, the Gāṅgas, and the Magadhas." It will be remarked that Gāṅga has been placed between Kaliṅga and Magadha. The Pīṭhapuram Pillar Inscription of Pṛthvīśvara dated Śaka-saṃvat 1108 corresponding to 1185-86 A.D.[31] mentions the country as *Gaṅga,* and it is placed just before Kaliṅga. The Harihara Stone Inscription of 1147 A.D relating the exploits of Vīra Pāṇḍya Deva states "The mighty kings of Gaṅga, Kaliṅga, Vaṅga, etc., he causes to weep, so greatly do all people praise this Pāṇḍya bhūpaja."[32] So also the Belur Inscription of 1380 A.D. mentions "Aṅga, Gaṅga, Kaliṅga."[33] We have already states that the *Periplus of the Erythræan Sea* mentions the "country of Ganges" or Gaṅgā which of course means Gaṅgā-rāṣṭra. It should also be mentioned that Varāhamihira, who lived in the 16th century A.D., places Suhma which is synonymous with Rāḍha or Gaṅgā-rāṣṭra between Vaṅga and Magadha.[34] This indicates that the delta of the Ganges had considerably extended towards the south since the 5th century B.C., so the position of Gaṅgā-rāṣṭra was mentioned in later times with reference to Kaliṅga instead of to Vaṅga. Though the western Gaṅga kings who reigned in Mysore from the 2nd century A.C., are considered to be purely Mysorean in origin, yet it appears that they were preceded by a line of kings known as Raṭṭa kings, and the country over which they ruled was called Kongu.[35] The names of *Gaṅga, Raṭṭa* and *Kongu* (which is a corruption of *Gaṅgā*) raise the suspicion that these two lines of kings were originally connected with the country of Gaṅgā-rāṣṭra in northern India, which connection perhaps has not yet been discovered.

Capitals of Gaṅgā-rāṣṭra or Rāḍha

The most ancient capital fo Gaṅgā-rāṣṭra, of which we have got any record, is Sīhapura which is, as stated before, mentioned in the *Mahāvaṃsa.* Sīhapura, or properly Sīṃhapura, is the modern Siṅgur, now an insignificant village situated in the district of Hughli.[36] It was founded by Sīhabāhu, father of Vijaya who colonised Ceylon in the

5th century B.C., some years before Buddha's death, by clearing the wilderness. It was then near the ocean, and at one time the river Sarasvatī, an arm of the Ganges, used to flow by its eastern side. It is stated by Megasthenes that the capital of the "Gangarides" in the 4th century B.C. was at Parthalis,[37] which is perhaps a transcription or corruption of Pūrvasthalī, now a large village situated on the Ganges, about twenty miles from the town of Burdwan in the district of the same name. Parthalis, being on the eastern boundary of the Gangarides, must have been close to the sea at that time.[38] There can be no doubt that Pūrvasthalī, which is a very old village and certainly much older than Burdwan, was situated on the mouth of the Ganges, in the 4th century B.C. and its advantageous position in affording facilities to inland trade and commercial enterprise soon made it an entrepôt of commerce, and its importance was further enhanced when the capital of Gaṅgā-rāḍha was shifted to this place owing, evidently, to the insalubrious nature of the climate of Siṃhapura which was then situated in a low moist country on the sea-shore.

The third capital called Gāngē

The third capital of the Gangarides or the Gaṅgā-rāḍha is mentioned as Gāngē, which is evidently a transcription of Gaṅgā. It is mentioned in the *Periplus of the Erythræan Sea,* which was written in the first century of the Christian era, and also by Ptolemy who lived in the 2nd century. According to the latter it was situated on the third mouth of the Ganges. We can very well conceive that the extended area of the delta to the south of Pūrvasthalī acquired sufficient consistency and consolidation in the course of three centuries for the establishment of a market-town called Gāngē or Gāṅgā on the mouth of the Ganges, as in-coming and out-going vessels evidently felt inconvenience in going up and down in connection with their trade with Parthalis, and Gāngē became an emporium of trade: "through this place are brought" as recorded in the *Periplus of the Erythræab Sea*[39] "malabothrum and Gangetic spikenard and perals and muslins of the finest sorts, which are called Gangetic." But Pliny, who also lived in the first century A.C., states that Parthalis was the capital of the Gangaridæ Calingæ[40] or, in other words, Gāngē at that period did not become the capital of Gaṅgā-rāḍha. In the second century A.C., however, Ptolemy mentions "Gāngē, the royal residence."[41] In the second century, therefore, Gāngē became the capital of Gaṅgā-rāḍha. It appears that Gāngē had trade connections with Mouziris (modern Cranganore) and Nelkunda (near Kottayam, fifty miles away from Cranganore), and the commodities conveyed to these places were exported to Egypt and other countries, including the Roman Empire.[42] It should be stated here that the discovery of the passage from the Red Sea to India by Hippalus in the first century A.C. opened out to the Romans a good prospect of establishing a direct trade with India without the help of intermediaries. Thus Barygaza (Broach) in Guzerat and Mouziris in Malabar became the centres of Roman trade;[43] a great impetus was thusg iven to the development of the export trade of India. It should be remarked that Tāmralipta (modern Tamluk), situated in the district of Hughli, had been existing as a maritime port since the fifth century before the Christian era, and it was existing as such in the first and second centuries A.C. Though the latitudes and longitudes of Ptolemy are generally faulty, yet comparing the latitudes and longitudes of "Tamlites," and "Gāngē" as stated by him, these two places do not appear to be far distant from each other. The reason for the existence of a new port as Gāngē in the first century A.C. may, therefore, be found in the fact that the trade of Northern and Eastern India, as indicated by the names of the commodities exported from this place, had considerably increased and sought an outlet. This necessitated the establishment of a new port, as in those days the less dangerous and less expensive mode of transport to distant places and provinces was through waterways only, and it has been rightly observed by Mr. McCrindle with regard to Tāmralipti that "This place in ancient times was the great emporium of trade between the Ganges and Ceylon."[44] So a new market-town came into existence for the wider distribution of commodities, and its importance was further increased by its becoming the capital of the country.

Three conditions for identification of Gāngē

But the questions are where was this Gāngē and what is its modern name? Various identifications have been made by different authors, as Chittagong, Sonārgāon, Jessore etc.,[45] but they are not at all convincing as none of them conforms to the three conditions which are necessary for the identification of Gāngē, namely, that it must be situated in Rāḍha, that it must be situated on the Ganges, and that it must have been an emporium of commerce as described in Ptolemy's *Geography* and in the *Periplus of the Erythræan Sea.*[46] Most of these identifications were made on the erroneous assumption that the present tract called the Sunderbans existed with all its present places and the mouths of the Ganges in the first and second centuries of the Christian era. Being situated on the mouth of the Ganges in the first century A.C., Gāngē must be sought for on the south of Pūrvasthalī which was also near the mouth of the Ganges in the 4th century B.C., and being the capital of Gaṅgā-rāṣṭra or (in its contracted form) Rāḍha, it must have been situated on the *western* side of the Ganges. It could not have been Calcutta, as it is situated on the eastern side of the Ganges, and perhaps at that time it was in the midst of an ancient "Sundarbans." It could not have been Tāmralipta, as Ptolemy mentions both "Gāngē" and "Tamlites" in the same chapter.[47] Hence it must be sought for between Pūrvasthaliī and Calcutta to the south of the former.

(*To be continued*)

References

1. *Kalpa Sūtra* in S.B.E., vol. xxii, p. 263; Dr. Bühler's *Indian Sect of the Jainas,* p. 26.
2. *Ibid.,* pp. 257, 263.
3. *S.B.E.,* vol. xxii, Intro., p. xliii.
4. *Ibid.,* Intro., p. li.
5. The Rev. J. Stevenson's *Kalpa Sūtra,* appendix, p. 139.
6. *Pāliprakāśa* by Vidhuśekhara Śāstrī, p. 13 note.
7. *Matsya P.,* ch. 113, v. 44.
8. *Brahmāṇḍa P.,* ch. 49, v. 57.
9. *Kalpa Sūtra* in *S.B.E.,* vol. xxii, p. 261.
10. Dr. Bühler's *Indian Sect of the Jainas,* p. 71.
11. *Indian Antiquary,* vol. ii, pp. 265, 332; vil. iii, p. 153; Rice's *Mysore Inscriptions,* Intro., p. lxxxvo, pp. 302-3.
12. *Sacred Books of East,* vol. xxii, p. 263.
13. Mrs. Sinclair Stevenson's *Heart of Jainism,* p. 39 fn.
14. The Rev. Dr. Stevenson, in his *Kalpa Sūtra,* says "at the town of *Tṛmbhikagrāma,* outside the town, at a river called Ṛtuvālika." *Tṛmbhikagrāma* and *Ṛtuvālika* are evidently typographical mistakes for *Jṛmbhikagrāma* and *Ṛjuvālika* respectively in which J has been confounded with T.
15. Mrs. Sinclair Stevenson's *Heart of Jainism,* p. 38.
16. *Kalpa Sūtra, S.B.E.,* vol. xxii, p. 264, note 4. But it should be stated that other Jaina works have Paiśācabhūmi instead of Paṇitabhūmi (see Mr. U.D. Barodia's *History and Literature of Jainism,* p. 39 note).
17. *Mahāvaṃśa,* chapters vi, vii and viii.
18. *Prabodha-candrodayanāṭaka,* Act. ii.
19. *Prakṛti,* a Bengali Scientific Journal, vol. I, pp. 20, 21, edited by Dr. Satya Charan Law; Major (now Colonel) F.C. Hirst's *Report on the Nadia Rivers,* ch. iv.

20. Ravendhaw's *Memorandum on the Ancient Bed of the River Soane and Site of Pālibothra* in *JASB.*, 1845, p. 152.
21. Turnour's *Mahāwanso,* ch. vi.
22. *Ibid.*, ch. viii.
23. See my *Notes on the District of Hughli or the Ancient Rāḍha* in *JASB.*, 1910, p. 611.
24. *Asiatic Researches,* vol. xv.
25. *Mackenzie Collection* (2nd Ed.), p. 82.
26. General Cunningham's *Ancient Geography of India,* 519.
27. McCrindle's *Ancient India as described by Megasthenes and Arrian,* p. 135.
28. General Cunningham's *Ancient Geography of India,* p. 519.
29. Turnour's *Mahāwanso,* ch. vi.
30. *Epigraphia Indica,* vol. iv, p. 283, *v.* 15; vol. v, p. 193, *v.* 13–
Dvārasthāṅga-kaliṅga-gāṅga-magadhair abhyarccitājñaściram,
Sūnuḥ sūnṛtavāgbhuvaḥ parivṛdhaḥ śrīkṛṣṇarājo'bhavat.
31. *Epigraphia India,* vol. iv, p. 48.
32. Rice's *Mysore Inscriptions,* p. 70.
33. *Ibid.*, p. 222.
34. Varāha-Mihira's *Bṛhat-saṃhitā,* ch. 16, *v.* 1.
35. Rice 's *Mysore Inscriptions,* Intro., pp. cl, cli.
36. *JASB.*, 1910, p. 604.
37. McCrindle's *Ancient India as described by Megasthenes and Arrian,* p. 135.
38. *Ibid.*, p. 33.
39. Mr. Schoff's *Periplus of the Erythræan Sea,* p. 47.
40. *Indian Antiquary,* 1883, p. 365.
41. McCrindle's *Ptolemy,* Bk. vii, ch. i, secs, 80; 81: see *Indian Antiquary,* 1884, p. 365.
42. McCrindle's *Commerce and Navigation of the Erythraean Sea,* pp. 23, 25; Mr. Schoff's *Periplus of the Erythraean Sea,* pp. 205, 208, 217; Rennell's *Memoir of a Map of Hindoostan,* Intro., pp. xxxiv f.
43. Mr. Charlesworth's *Trade Routes and Commerce of the Roman Empire;* Mr. Schoff's *Periplus of the Erythræan Sea,* pp. 45, 227 f.
44. *Indian Antiquiry,* 1884, p. 364.
45. *Indian Antiquary,* 1884, p. 365.
46. See my *Early Course of the Ganges* in the *Indian Antiquary,* 1921, p. 16.
47. McCrindle's *Ptolemy,* Bk. vii, ch. 1, secs. 73 and 81.

43

Rāḍha or the Ancient Ganga-Raṣṭra

N. L. Dey

III

Gāngè is modern Saptagrāma

Ancient Gāngê, therefore, could be nothing else than the modern Saptagrāma.[1] Mr. Irving was nearer the mark than any one else in his attempt to find out the position of Gāngê. He says, "The town of Ganges, situated at no great distance from Calcutta, was a grand emporium for Bengal,"[2] but he does not identify it with any place. Saptagrāma, now called Sātgāon, is situated at a distance of two miles to the north of the town of Hughli, and it satisfies the three conditions mentioned above. It was situated on the Ganges at the point from which the Sarasvatī and the Yamunā branched off towards the south and the east respectively. The remains of ancient Saptagrāma are still to be found by the side of the Ganges and on the east bank of the Sarasvatī, through which once flowed the main stream of the Ganges.[3] Fragments of vessels have from time to time been exhumed from the silted-up bed of the Sarasvatī. From its very position Saptagrāma was eminently fitted for its being a trade distributory and an emporium of commerce. It maintained its position "from the Paurāṇic age to the beginning of the sixteenth century" of the Christian era.[4] It was situated in Rāḍha. It was "once a royal city and emporium of trade."[5] Saptagrāma means a cluster of seven villages; it is therefore a description of the place and not a name. It had a name of course before it comprehended within its boundaries seven villages, and it is reasonable to believe that it could not have started all at once a full-fledged town comprising seven villages and covering an area of fourteen miles.[6] The seven villages are Vāsudevapura, Vaṃśavāṭi Kṛṣṇapura, Nityānandapura, Śivapura, Sambachora and Baladghati.[7] Saptagrāma, therefore, had originally a name, however humble it might have been, and that name was *Gaṅgā,* the Gāngê of the *Periplus of the Erythræan Sea.* Saptagrāma was known to the Romans by the name of *Ganges Regia,*[8] and in *Ganges Regia* was preserved the ancient name of Saptagrāma, the *Gaṅgā* or "Gāngé, the royal residence" of Ptolemy. *Regia* means a "royal residence, capital," and *Ganges Regia* means "Gaṅgā, the capital," the adjunct *Regia* being necessary to distinguish it from "Gaṅgā, the country" and "Gaṅgā, the river," as stated in the *Periplus.* But it should be borne in mind that the Roman name of *Ganges Regia* does not refer to Sātgāon, as the seat of the Governors of Lower Bengal during the early period of the Mahomedan rule, for the Romans carried on a direct trade with India, as stated before, from the first century A.C., long before the establishment of the Mahomedan rule in India; it refers only to Gaṅgā as the capital of Gaṅgā-rāṣṭra. Sir William Hunter also says, "Sātgāon, the 'Ganges Regia' or ancient royal port of Bengal, lay upon its [Sarasvatī's] bank a short distance from the Triveṇī *Ghāt.*"[9] There can be no doubt that for the same reason, to avoid confusion, the town called Gaṅgā was also called *"Gaṅgā Bandar*" or the "Port of Ganges," or simply "*Bandar*" or the "Port," and the title of "Royal port" that was given to Saptagrāma was not a new distinction but a legacy inherited from the ancient *Gaṅgā Bandar.* The word *Bandar* still exists in its corrupted form in *Bandel*[10] which is about a mile of the north of Hughli town. It formed a part of ancient Saptagrāma. It contains a Roman Catholic Church, the oldest Christian Church built in Bengal by a Portuguese named Villalobos in 1597 A.C. Saptagrāma was visited in the hey-day of its glory by Fredericke, who in 1570 A.C. described it as a great centre of commerce. Kavikaṅkaṇa, who wrote the *Caṇḍī* in 1577, referring to Saptagrāma, says that the merchants of Kaliṅga, Trailiṅga, Aṅga, Mahārāṣṭra, Guzerat, Utkal, Draviḍa etc., and many other countries come to Saptagrāma with merchandise, but the Saptagrāma, merchants never go out of their town and they command the wealth of the world, and also such comforts at home as are procurable in Paradise.[11] The poet thus briefly but clearly described the opulence and prosperity of Saptagrāma, and the amenities of life which were enjoyed by its people. But the name of Saptagrāma is not mentioned in any of the Purāṇas. The name of Triveṇī, however, which is a quarter of Saptagrāma, is mentioned in the *Bṛhad-dharma Purāṇa*;[12] it is also alluded to in the *Pavanadūta*[13] which was written in the 12th century A.C. The reason is obvious. In the eyes of the philosophic and religious Hindus the sanctity of the name of Triveṇī was of far greater importance than the opulence and wealth of Saptagrāma, the emporium of commerce. Triveṇī, which means the "Three plaits" or the three rivers, Gaṅgā, Yamunā and Sarasvatī, is the counter part of Prayāga or Allahabad in the East. In Prayāga, the aforesaid three rivers unite and flow together, and, therefore, it is called *Yukta-veṇī*. In Treveṇī, the rivers separate and flow in different directions, and, therefore, according to Raghunandana,[14] it is called Dakṣiṇa (or Southern) Prayāga, and he explains it as"*Mukta-veṇī,* celebrated as Triveṇī in the southern country called Saptagrāma." *Mukta-veṇī* means where the rivers separate. Pliny[15] mentions Triveṇī as a great trading centre, and says that ships assembled near the Godāvarī and sailed to Treveṇī. The Rev. J. Long also says, "Tribeni was formerly noted for its trade: Pliny mentions that the ships assembling near the Godāvarī sailed from thence to cape Palinurus, then to Tentigalé, opposite Fulta, then to Tribeni and lastly to Patna. Ptolemy also notices Tribeni."[16] These ships were evidently bound for Sātgāon down the Sarasvatī, as it was two miles from Triveṇī. Mr. McCrindle while commenting on the word *Gāngê* in Ptolamy's *Geography of India* says "another Gāngê is mentioned by Artenidoros above or to the N.W. of Polibothra, and this Welford identifies with Prayāga, i.e. Allahabad, but Groskurd with Anupshahr."[17] We accept the identification of Wilford in preference to that of Groskurd, as, according to the Purāṇas, the Ganges is the most sacred in Prayāga, and so the name of Gaṅgā must have been extended to the town of Prayāga or Allahabad. This identification of the Gāngē of Artemidoros strongly supports our identification of the Gāngē of Ptolemy with Saptagrāma, the eastern quarter of which was Triveṇī, which is called *Dakṣiṇa* (*Southern*) *Prayāga* where the two rivers Sarasvatī and Yamunā separate from the Ganges, which is, therefore, deemed here to be as sacred as in Allahabad itself. At least this circumstance must have greatly influenced the selection of the same name for the "market-town" called *Gāngê* which afterwards came to be known as Saptagrāma. Owing to its antiquity, opulence, and reputation as an emporium of commerce, tradition has sought to invest Saptagrāma with the dignity of a pedigree town by ascribing its foundation to seven princes of Kānyakubja or Kanouj, and by assenting that it was the residence, and under the special protection, of the seven Ṛṣis who have given their names to the constellation called *Saptarṣimaṇḍala* or the Great Bear which revolves round *Dhruva Nakṣatra* or the Pole Star. The temple of the Ṛṣis existed near the Triveṇī-ghāṭ. Figures of Buddha engraved on a slab of stone affixed to the base of a pillar in a neighbouring mosque, and a broken statue of Pārśvanātha within the enclosure of Zaffar Khan's tomb, indicate that Triveṇī also passed through the usual stages of Jainism and Buddhism. There can be no reasonable doubt, therefore, that ancient Gāngē mentioned in the *Periplus* and in Ptolemy's *Geography* is the modern Saptagrāma or Sātgāon in the district of Hughli. Sātgāon declined when the Sarasvatī became deteriorated, and its ruin was completed when Hughli was declared to be a royal port in 1632.[18] It should be stated here that it was in Hughli that the first Bengali book was printed in 1778, and that book was Halhed's *Grammar,* the types of which were prepared by Sir C. Wilkins himself.[19]

Bhūriśreṣṭha, the capital of Rāḍha

The fourth capital of Rāḍha was Bhūriśreṣṭha or the modern Bhurset, now an insignificant village in the sub-division of Ārāmbāgh in the district of Hughli. It was so celebrated that it gave its name to a whole Pargana in that sub-division. The *Prabodhacandrodaya-nāṭaka,* a religious and philosophical play composed by Kṛṣṇa Miśra in the court of Kīrtivarman of Bundelkhand in the latter half of the 11th century A.C. mentions that Rāḍha, known also by the names of "Rāḍhā"[20] and "Rāḍhaka,"[21] was in the kingdom of Gauḍa, and in Rāḍhā there was a town called Bhūriśreṣṭha; and it described Rāḍha as a country.[22] It appears that Rāḍha appertained to the kingdom of Gauḍa at the time of Ādiśūra, but after the death of that monarch, Gauḍa was invaded and conquered by Dharma Pāla, king of Magadha, in the first half of the 9th century A.C., and Ādiśūra's son Bhūśūra was obliged to take refuge in Rāḍha which, however, was not invaded or subjugated by the Pāla kings of Magadha. Rāḍha continued to be an independent kingdom under the kings of the Śūra dynasty from Bhūśūra to Raṇaśūra (called also Anuśūra) for a period of over two hundred years from the 9th century to the latter part of the 11th century A.C.[23] That Rāḍha was an independent kingdom in the 10th century A.C. is confirmed by the Khajuraho inscription which enumerated Rāḍha as one of the independent kingdoms conquered by the Dhaṅga Deva, the Candrātreya (or Candella) king of Tejabhukti (Bundelkhand).[24] It also appears from the Tirumalaya stone inscription that Rājendra Coḷa (1012-1052 A.C.) defeated Raṇaśūra, king of Dakṣiṇa (or southern) Rāḍha and Mahīpāla, king of Magadha and Uttara (or Northern) Rāḍha. So it is very probable that the word Rāḍha after conquest of Dharmapāla was confined only to what is called Dakṣiṇa Rāḍha, mentioned in the *Prabodhacandrodaya-nāṭaka,* which is said to have been the abode of *Ahaṃkāra* or Pride.[25] Rāḍha and Gauḍa again formed a single kingdom at the time of Vijaya Sena, the father of Ballāla Sena of the Sena dynasty towards the close of the 11th century.[26]

Condition of the people

It appears from the writings of the Greek historians, the itineraries of the Chinese travellers and the Hindu works, especially those which were composed after the 4th century of the Christian era, that the people of Rāḍha were warlike, rich, prosperous and enterprising. They maintained a large standing army which bespeaks of their military prowess and constant preparation for war. There can be no doubt that during the Buddhist period, Tāmralipta or Tamluk became a great centre of education and training, and pupils from distant parts of India resorted to the Saṃghārāmas or monasteries of this place to receive instructions not only in religion, but also in various branches of learning bearing on the Buddhist religion. In later times, Saptagrāma, or, properly speaking, Triveṇī became one of the four Samājas, or renowned seats of Sanskrit learning, and men like Jagannātha Tarkapañcānana, the compiler of the *Digest of Hindu Laws,* Raghunandana Bhaṭṭācārya, the celebrated author of the smṛti works, and others flourished at this place, the other three Samājas being at Guptipara, Santipur and Nadia. There were thirty *tols* in Triveṇī alone. The *Kathāsarit-sāgara,* the *Bṛhat-kathā* and other works of a similar nature, though imaginary in many respects, give us some insight into the real condition of the people who lived at the time when they were composed, and from these works it appears that the merchants of Rāḍha as a class were very rich and prosperous. They not only sent their goods to several inland towns which were the centres of trade, but also their vessels visited distant parts of India, Suvarṇabhūmi (Burma) and Siṃhala (Ceylon), and in their voyages they touched at several islands which studded the Indian Ocean, where they sold or bartered their commodities. They even went to the Persian Gulf for trading purposes, notwithstanding the risks they incurred from the depredations of pirates who infested to ocean and the invasions of the barbarians who lived in the various parts of India and the islands they visited. The basis of pure morality upon which the Buddhist creed was founded gradually gave way to superstition and outward forms: and there was a reaction. The ideas which pervaded the Mahāyāna system of Northern Buddhism were amalgamated with those connected with the Brāhmaṇical cult of Yoga and Śaivaic mysticism with its worship of "female energies,"[27] or, to speak more precisely, there was an attempt to reconcile the Sāṅkhya system of Hindu philosophy[28] with the Mahāyāna doctrines of the Buddhists,[29] evidently with a view to find a basis of common creed for those who professed their faith in the Vedic religion and those who believed in the Mahāyāna doctrines of Buddhism.

Thus Tāntrikism came into existence which encouraged sacrifices and the performance of mystic rites for the attainment of wordly objects and salvation.[30] It has been rightly said that the main cause which contributed to the disappearance of Buddhism from the land of its birth was "undoubtedly the change in its own nature brought about by its attempt to absorb other beliefs and practices with which it came in contact."[31] Tāntrikism in Rāḍha has now been supplanted to a great extent by Śaivaism and also by Vaiṣṇavism since to advent of Caitanya (1485-1533 A.C.), whose religion has now taken a deep root in Bengal.

References

1. *JASB.*, 1910, pp. 614-616; *Indian Antiquary,* 1921 (*The Early Course of the Ganges*), pp. 16, 17.
2. Mr. Irving's *Commerce of India,* p. 84.
3. Rennell's *Memoir of a Map of Hindoostan,* p. 57 (See s. v. *Sātgong*): the river Sarasvatī is not mentioned, but it is called the "Satgong river"; *Imperial Gazetteer of India,* vol. v, p. 480; *Calcutta Review,* vol. xxi, p. 181; vol. vi, pp. 402, 403.
4. *Imperial Gazetteer of India,* vol. v, p. 481, S. V. *Hugli River.*
5. *Asiatic Researches,* vol. v; *Calcutta Review,* vol. xxi, p. 181, *The Grand Trunk Road—its Localities.*
6. *Sāhitya-pariṣat Patrikā,* vol. xv, p. 15, *Saptagrāma* by Mr. R.D. Banerji.
7. *JASB.*, 1910, p. 615.
8. *Asiatic Researches,* vol. v, p. 278.
9. *Imperial Gazetter of India,* vol. v, p. 481, S.V. *Hugli River.*
10. *Ibid.*, vol. ii, p. 57.
11. See *Calcutta Review,* 1891, p. 374.
12. *Bṛhad-dharma Purāṇa,* Pūrvakhaṇḍa, ch. 6.
13. *Pavana-dūta,* v, 33.
14. Raghunandana's *Prāyaścittatattva,* Gaṅgā-mahātmya, p. 100.
15. Pliny's *Natural History,* Bk. vi, ch. 19, translated by Philamon Holland.
16. *Calcutta Review,* vol. vi, p. 408—*The Banks of the Bhāgīrathī.*
17. *Indian Antiquary,* 1884, p. 365.
18. *Calcutta Review,* vol. vi, p. 404—*The Banks of the Bhāgīrathī.*
19. *Ibid.*, vol. xiii, p. 433.
20. *Prabodhacandrodaya-nāṭaka,* Act iv.
21. *Vārendrī-gauḍa-rāḍhakāḥ--Jyotistativa.*
22. *Prabodhacandrodaya-nāṭaka,* Act ii.
23. *JASB.*, 1910, p. 607.
24. Khajuraho Inscription, no. iv: *Epigraphia Indica,* vol. i, pp. 138, 140, *v.* 46. See also an inscription transcribed in *JASB.*, 1839, p. 173.

25. *Prabodhacandrodayanāṭaka,* Act ii (see *ante*).

26. Deopara Stone Inscription of Vijaya Sena in *Epigraphia Indica,* vol. i, p. 306; see also pp. 312, 313; also *Ep. Ind.,* vol. ii, p. 350.

27. L. Waddell's *Buddhism of Tibet,* pp. 13, 44.

28. Monier Williams' *Indian Wisdom,* p. 502,—"But in all probability, the Tāntrika doctrine owes its development to the popularising of the Sāṅkhya theory of *Puruṣa* and *Prakṛti.*"

29. Mr. D. T. Suzuki says in his *Outline of Mahāyāna Buddhism,* p. 138: "The Sāṃkhya philosophy is an avowed dualism and permits the existence of two principles independent of each other. Mahāyānism is fundamentally monistic and makes ignorance merely a condition necessary to the unfolding of Suchness (*Bhūtatathatā*). Therefore what the Sāṃkhya splits into two, Mahāyānism puts together in one."

30. *Mālatīmādhava,* Act v; *Bhāgavata,* v, ch. 9.

31. Earl of Ronaldshay's *Lands of the Thunderbolt,* ch. xii, p. 98.

44

Teliagarhi

S. S. Majumdar

Teliagarhi,* known as the key of Bengal, which stands hoary with age, on the Rajmahal hills near Sahibganj, has unfortunately failed to receive the prominence or attention it deserves. That it proved a veritable 'key' to Bengal's political problems throughout the ages has escaped the notice of the present day historians. The *Jahangir Nāmah* describes the fort of Teliagarhi as a burial ground, burial indeed of many a political ambitions. But physically too it bears many burials though the fort is too big to be described in the fashion of *Jahangir Nāmah.* A casual observer can only catch a glimpse of its central structure and satisfy himself with the idea that it is only as big as it can arrest the attention of his eyes but to a regular visitor of the site it reveals its real dimension now lying hidden under nature's vegetable vagary. In length it is two-third of a mile. The northern limit is a natural precipice just below which the swift-going Ganges flow. The area is bounded with a strong built rampart on all other sides barring a small portion on the south where the fort is embedded with mountains difficult to ascend. As we approach the area from the west we may yet see the rampart which has been described by *Ain-i-Akbari*[1] as a "raised stone wall extending from the Ganges to the mountains and this wall is considered to be the boundary between Bengal and Bihar." The translator of the *Seir-ul-Mutaqherin* writes that "Teliagarry is a fort that shuts up the passage into Bengal. It consists in a wall strengthened in towers, that extend from the foot of the hills to the rocky bank of the Ganges" but wrongly adds that "it has neither ditch nor rampart." As a matter of fact ramparts there are and we have just discussed about it. A deep natural ditch in the vicinity of its western wall is visible even to-day and perhaps Major Coote referred to this when he wrote : "a rivulet or water-course very hollow and impassable ran near the *phataks* or gates." For the purpose of defence, this frontier fort with the natural fortifications of the Ganges in the north and the hills in the south stood in no need of any more ditch.

The *Ain-i-Akbari, Khulasat-ul-Twarikh,*[2] and *Wakiat-i-Jahangiri*[3] have all measured the area of Bengal from Gaḍhi the western front to Chatgawn (Chittagong) on the east and this in itself proves that this 'Gate of Bengal' always carried an importance of its own. A close study of the descriptions of Gaḍhi in the *Akbarnāma, Tabakat-i-Akbari, Twarikh-i-Sher Shahi, Iqbalnāmah-i-Jahangiri, Al-Badaoni, Riaz-ul-Salatin* etc., will show that the authors one and all stress upon the strategic significance of its natural situation. The greatness of Gaḍhi lay on the fact that it was "the only passage to the countries of Gaur and Bengal, there being except by that gate no other way of entry or exit."[4] In the comment following the above quotation Elliott (vol. IV, 367 fn. 2) writes that the Gaḍhi is better known as Siclygully, properly Sankrigali,[5] the narrow pass about 8 miles north-west from Rajmahal. But this is a sad confusion between the two passes of Teliagarhi and Sakrigali (Sankarigali). The fact is that they are two distinct passes. The one that commences from the fort of Teliagarhi is known as the Teliagarhi pass and the other that ends at the promontary of the Rajmahal hills making a bid for the Ganges is known as the Siclygally pass and midway between them stands the Sakrugarh (Chikkoragarh).[6] As regards the role played by this pass in history in relation to Bengal we shall see from the sources of information of the Mughal period that it was always the theatre of decisive battles. But its history is not confined to the Mughal period only. Cunningham identified with Teliagarhi the lofty tower of Hieun Tsang's account and observed: "The pilgrim does not say what was the nature of the tower but from his description I gather that it must have been a Buddhist building, as its four faces were ornamented with panels filled with figures of saints, Buddhas and Devas. From the mixture of brick and stone in the building and its position on the northern frontier of the district and the south bank of the Ganges, I am led to think the tower was most probably situated at Teliagarhi itself."[7] I would like to draw the attention of all to some information of interest here:

(a) A stone pillar with small images of Buddha on its four sides has been recently found out in the fort area and is being worshipped by the Santals of the village lying close to the south-east corner of Teliagarhi.

(b) Just above the fort, on the top-most part of the mountains we have discovered a small stone structure built without mortar overlooking the surrounding area even miles off and curiously enough it goes by the name of 'Yogi-grah' among the Paharias living in the neighbourhood. Is it then out of the way to conclude in the light of the Buddhist stamps noticed by the renowned archæologist Cunningham and the relics recently discovered by me that the word "Yogi" carries with it the memory of its old existence as a Buddhist monastery which were so common in those days in Bihar?

The passes of Teliagarhi and Sakriagali were possessed by the Pīṭhipati Devarakṣita and a close guard of this front helped him in the revolt against his overlord Rāmapāla. I have already discussed in my paper "Pīṭhi and Pīṭhipatis" that the possession of this place by a revolting feudatory would prove fatal to the Pāla empire and hence the defeat of Devarakṣita at the arms of Mahana was a political necessity.[8] The discovery of the Janibagh inscription proves that the area was under the Pīṭhipatis for a long time after Devarakṣita.[9] The Vikramaśilā Vihāra which is identified with Patthalghatta, some ten miles off Teliagarhi, must have also been their possession till the powerful arms of Bakhtiyar Khilji and his son destroyed it, Mr. R.D. Banerji in his paper entitled "Lakṣmaṇasena" discusses about one of the three possible routes traversed by Bakhtiyar Khilji and says that "the third route (i.e. through the pass at Sahibganj) has been generally followed by the invaders of Bengal and most probably the first Muhammadan invader of Bengal also followed it."[10] The learned scholar has opined in his History of Bengal (in Bengali) that a successful guard of the pass of Taliagarhi would have checked the invader and the consequent history of Bengal would have been quite different.[11] The history of Bengal during the Pathan period had been that of a continuous tug-of-war between the local and the Imperial rulers but we do not find any direct reference to the part played by Teliagarhi. But that the fort was in existence towards the close of the Pathan rule can be proved from the well known *Caitanyacaritāmṛta,* a book written as early as 1582 A.D. The following reference appears in connection with Sanātana, the Private Secretary of Hussain Shah:

রাজবন্দী আমি গড়িদ্বার যাইতে না পারি
পুণ্যহবে পর্ব্বত আমা দেহ পার করি ।[১২]

As Sanātan bought off his release from the Imperial government he tried to steal his passage towards Benares. On his way he had to avoid the gate of Gaḍhi because a king's prisoner could have no free passage over there. Though the verses were composed nearly sixty years after the incident, it is definite that even during the time of Hussain Shah, the king of Bengal, Teliagarhi was an important post. We are now to move on to the histoy of Gaḍhi in the rôle of deciding battles.

Sher Shah, Mahmud Shah, and Humayun

In his attempt for a way into Bengal Sher Shah got his first real obstacle here at this pass. Mahmud Shah was then the Governor of Bengal. He found an enemy in the person of Makdum Alam, his own brother-in-law who again joined hands with Sher Shah. Makdum Alam soon lost his life. Sher Shah immediately drew his forces towards Bengal. "The nobles of Bengal guarding the passes of Teliagarhi and Sakrigali and for one month continued the fighting. At length the passes of Teliagarhi and Sakrigali were captured and Sher Shah entered Bengal, and Mahmud Shah, drawing his force, encountered the former, when a great battle ensued, Sultan Mahmud, being vanquished in the field, entrenched himself in the citadel, and sent a message to emperor Humayun in Delhi, seeking for help."[13] The fall of Teliagarhi opened the way for a triumphant entry of Sher Shah into Bengal. The empire was in danger and Humayun immediately hastened towards Bengal. But the resistance offered by Mahmud Shah at the passes of Teliagarhi and Sakrigali gave this definite lesson to Sher Shah that a close guard of the passes was a necessity. So he immediately sent Jalal Khan and Khawas Khan to defend the pass and to hold the emperor in check there. Emperor Humayun detached Jahangir Beg Mughal to capture Teliagarhi and Sakrigali. On the day that Jahangir Beg reached the place, just after he had dismounted, Jalal Khan and Khawas Khan, marching up quickly with an efficient force, attacked him. The Mughal forces, unable to cope were vanquished and Jahangir Beg getting wounded, in a helpless condition returned to the emperor's camp ('which must have been near Colgong'). But when Humayun himself marched up to Teliagarhi and Sakrigali Jalal Khan and Khawas Khan, seeing their inability to stand the emperor's onslaught, fled towards the hills and then to Sher Shah at Gaur. The Imperial army forcing its way easily through the narrow defile, marched up stage by stage.[14] Humayun entered Bengal and Sher Shah fled through the jungles of Jharkhanda. The victory of Humayun at the Garhi saved for a time his empire from the clutch of Sher Shah. The students of history all know the consequent facts. Sulaiman Karbani was appointed the governor of Bihar by Islam Shah, the son of Sher Shah, Karbani declared independence after the death of Islam Shah and consequently became the governor of Bengal. After the death of Sulaiman Karbani in 1572 A.D. the Afghan Sardars dethroned his son and placed Daud Khan on the throne. A man of very high ambition, Daud Khan began to establish himself independent of the Imperial government in Bengal and Bihar. Akbar was then the emperor and he made no delay to send Munim Khan against Daud. The general controlled the situation by annexing Patna. He was appointed the governor of Bengal and Bihar.

Daud vs. Imperial Army

"When Daud fled from Patna, he went to Gaḍhi.[15] Leaving aside trusty men there he proceeded to the town of Tanda. He made such efforts to strengthen the fort of Gaḍhi that in his vain idea it was impregnable. Khan Khanan marched against Tanda and arrived near Gaḍhi. As soon as the eyes of the terrified Afghans fell upon his army they fled and abandoned the fort, so that he obtained possession of Gaḍhi without striking a blow.[16] The road to Bengal was open to the Imperial army and so Daud fled towards Orissa. To cut the subsequent events short, we may only refer to the battle of Mogalmari where Daud suffered a defeat and promised to rule faithfully over Orissa. But when Munim Khan died and the Afghans of Bengal and Orissa revolted Daud took advantage of the anarchy and again strengthened his position at Rajmahal, 30 miles off from Teliagarhi. "Upon receiving this intelligence the emperor sent a letter to Subhan Kuli Turk to Khan Jahan, directing him to take with him all the Amirs and Jagirdars who had abandoned Bengal and to march against Daud . . . The Khan took the field and advanced into Bengal. He had an action with 3,000 men whom Daud had left in charge of Gaḍhi and took the place.[17] Khan Jahan (Hussain Kuli Khan), the governor of Bengal stormed the fort of Teliagarhi and Sakrigali, and by the delivery of first assault, slaughtered about 1,500 Afghans and advanced towards the site where Daud Khan was entrenched. Daud was captured and put to death. So the battle at Teliagarhi closed the career of Daud and decided the fate of Bengal in relation of the Imperial government.

The Secret Way

Akbar-nāma, while describing the preparations of the Imperial army against Daud Khan writes: "The Zamindars of the neighbourhood (of Teliagarhi) said that there was a secret way through the country of Teliraja, which though impracticable for beasts of burden, might be surmounted by active and intelligent horsemen... Manjum Khan was sent at the head of a brave and resolute detatchment by this route."[18] It is to be noted here that besides the main pass of Garhi there was a second secret way to Bengal. Here again we can quote to our advantage the verses from the *Caitanyacaritāmṛta* which refers to the same secret passage traversed by Sanātan in *c.* 1522 A.D.:

রাজবন্দী আমি গড়িদ্বার যাইতে না পারি,
পুণ্য হবে পর্ব্বত আমা দেহ পার করি।

* * * * * * * * *

তবে গোসাঞির সঙ্গে চারি পাইক দিলা।
রাত্রে রাত্রে বনপথে পর্ব্বত পার কৈলা ॥[19]

A local zamindar helped Sanātan with four 'paiks' who took him by the secret way over the hills.

Teliagarhi named after Teliraja?

One more point of interest needs be discussed here. In the same passage from *Akbar-nāma* we find that Teliraja was a zamindar of the vicinity. Is the fort of Gaḍhi named after some Teliraja? "Local tradition states that the fort is called after a Teli zamindar who was compelled by the Muhammadans to embrace Islam."[20] Taking the tradition and the reference in the *Akbar-nāma* into consideration we can conclude that the fort carries in its name the memory of some Teliraja of the neighbourhood.

Kakshals and the Gaḍhi

Let us go back to our topic. The problem of Bengal looked solved when Daud Khan was crushed and Akbar sent Muzaffar Khan to take over charge of the province after Khan Jahan. Shah Mansur was appointed to look after the affairs of the Jagirdars. He began with promulgation of strict measures. This, together with the imperial order of death on one Roshan Beg enraged the Kakshals so much that they resolved upon mutiny. Matters moved to an alarming situation. Muzaffar Khan sent his men for peace talks to Baba Khan but the latter replied with their arrest." Coincident with this the revenue officials of Bihar took away the Jagirs of Md. Masum Kabuli Arab Bahadur and all the amirs." This drifted matters to a climax and mutiny broke out." When the Kakshals confronted Muzaffar Khan Asi Masum marched to assist them and arrived to Gaḍhi. Muzaffar Khan then sent Kwaja Samsuddin Md. Kwaji with the detatchment and some guns to pass of Gaḍhi to arrest the progress of Asi Masum. But the latter had a strong force; he broke through Gaḍhi and attacked the Kwaja and defeated him."[21] The failure of the Kwaja at the pass of Teliagarhi brought sweeping success to the Kakshals. Had Masum been defeated there, he would have no chance to enter Bengal, from a junction with the Kakshals and all the countries of Bengal and Bihar would not have fallen into their hands. Akbar however sent a strong army under the able lead of Todarmall and as fortune would ultimately have it Gaḍhi fell into the hands of the royal troops and Bengal was regained at the place where it was lost. The pass of Teliagarhi once more showed how it decided the fate of Bengal.

Shah Jahan vs. Ibrahim

The next drama began when Prince Shah Jahan raised a rebellion against his father, forcibly annexed Burdwan and proceeded to fall upon Ibrahim Khan, the Subadar of Bengal. Ibrahim took his post at

Rajmahal. "Shah Jahan, convinced that in his situation delays were dangerous and that his success depended on prompt and vigorous measures, advanced by rapid marches towards the governor, who finding that the city of Rajmahal was incapable of standing a siege, retreated to the fortification of Teliagarhi, upon which were mounted a number of cannons served by vagabond Europeans . . . but not considering the place sufficiently secure, he entrusted the defence of it to one of his best officers, and encamped with his army on the opposite bank of the Ganges. Meanwhile Deriaw Khan, one of the Afghan chiefs in the army of Shah Jahan, won the assistance of some of the zamindars of Boglipore (Bhagalpur), secured boats and crossed the Ganges.[22] "When Ibrahim Khan found that the enemy had passed the river, he withdrew as many of his troops as could be spared from the defence of Terriagurhy; and being thus reinforced, advanced to meet the rebel chiefs."[23] Then began a great battle at Teliagarhi. The author of the *Riaz-ul-Salatin* gives a vivid description as to how one Syed Nurullah was ordered to form the van which eight hundred cavalry, how Ahmad Beg Khan formed the centre with 700 cavalry while Ibrahim Khan himself held the line of reserve with thousands of cavalry and infantry. In the long run Ibrahim got serious wounds and fell dead. "Roumy Khan, an engineer of Shah Jahan, had pressed forward the siege of Terriagurhy and at the time when battle was raging on the opposite bank he set fire to a mine which blew up twenty yards of the fortification and opened a breach, through which rebels rushed with impetuosity and put the greater part of the garrison to the sword. The capture of Terriagurhy and the death of the governor decided the fate of Bengal, and the authority of the prince was everywhere acknowledged."[24]

Aurangzeb vs. Shuja

The government of Bengal changed many hands after Ibrahim. Shuja, the second son the Shah Jahan came in. He changed the capital from Dacca back to Rajmahal and thus the importance of the passes of Teliagarhi and Sakrigali became once more doubly greater. When Shah Jahan fell ill his sons entered into internecine quarrels. In his attempt for the throne Shah Shuja suffered a defeat near Agra and retreated to Monghyr. His position at Monghyr also became insecure owing to the treachery played by Raja Bahroj of Kharagpur. The Raja secretly intrigued with Mir Jumla and showed the latter another route across the hills to the east of Monghyr. Shah Shuja was in the face of danger and he instantly sailed down his war vessels from Monghyr fort to Rangamati and Rajmahal and on the way fortified the passes of

Teliagarhi and Siclygalli."[25] So Shah Shuja thought of sealing the success of the enemy by shutting the gate of Garhi. Shuja "built a wall from the river to the southern hill barring the narrow plain through which the road ran" at Garhi[26] or at place named Rangamati (Lalmati) nearly four miles east of Teliagarhi.[27] The wall was constructed perhaps under the idea of giving a resistance there and controlling the Ganges. But Shuja had soon to evacuate the place, for, in the meantime, the Imperialists had avoided Teliagarhi and stolen a passage towards Rajmahal through Birbhum. Mir Jumla expected quite naturally that Shuja would concentrate at Garhi and he would fall upon him by a rear attack. The battle which was to be fought at Teliagarhi was fought and won by Mir Jumla on the other side of Rajmahal.

Sharfaraz vs. Alivardi

We need next pass on to the reign of Nawab Shujauddin. During his time two brothers named Haji Mohammad and Alivardi Khan became very prominent in the court. The latter was entrusted with the Government of Bihar in 1733 A.D. Sharfaraz Khan, son of Shuja, could not tolerate their eminence and when in 1739 he ascended the throne he was on the look-out for a plea. Meanwhile there was a conspiracy among Haji Mohammad, Jagat Seth and others to procure the Subadarship of Bengal, Bihar and Orissa for Alivardi. Sharfaraz detected the conspiracy and decided to bestow the Deputy-Governorship of Patna on his son-in-law Syed Muhammad Hassan in supercession of Alivardi Khan and the Fouzdari of Akbarnagar together with the command of Sakrigali and Teliagarhi passes on Mir Sharfuddin Bakshi in supercession of Ataullah Khan, son-in-law of Haji Mohammad.[28] Meanwhile Alivardi secured the allegiance of many generals and officers of army. Under the false pretext of waiting upon Sharfaraj Khan, Alivardi Khan marched swiftly, crossed the passes of Teliagarhi[29] and Sakrigali and reached the frontier of Bengal. At the instigation of Haji Mohammad, Ataullah Khan, the Foujdar of Akbarnagar had taken steps to prevent all movements of messengers and spies and to interdict all the intercourse through news-letters between Azimabad (Patna) and Bengal *via* the passes of Teliagarhi and Sakrigali until Alivardi had crossed through those passes. In consequence no news of Alivardi's movements had reached Sharfaraz Khan.[30] In the above debut Alivardi came out successful. We can have no better account than that of *Riaz-ul-Salatin* to reveal the unique part played by the passes in deciding a momentous battle. At a time when Alivardi was troubled by the Marathas in Bengal and the Pathans in Bihar this pass of Teliagarhi and Sakrigali helped him much as a base of operation and guard.

That the Britishers also fully realised the importance of the Teliagarhi pass is evident from the opinion of Colonel Scott, who, in his confidential scheme for the conquest of Bengal submitted to the Company, wrote, "500 disciplined troops might defend the pass against the whole power of Indosthan and secure us from that quarter."[31] The Colonel was confident that no invasion from Delhi could wreck their mission if they defended the pass of Teliagarhi. So we see that this pass played the same rôle in relation to Bengal as the Khyber did in relation to India for a considerable period.

References

* Read at the Third Indian History Congress, Calcutta. It is the history of the pass of Teliagarhi. By "Teliagarhi" people now mean the Fort and hence the title of this paper should be Teliagarhi, the Fort that decided the fate of Bengal.

1. *Āin-i-Akbari,* II, 28.
2. See *Tabakat-i-Nasiri,* 592 fn. and 593 fn.
3. Elliot , VI, 326.
4. Makhzan-i-Afghani, Mss. 202:Elliot IV. 367, fn. 2.
5. More properly 'Sankarigali.' See *Indian Culture,* V, No. 4.
6. *Ibid.*
7. *Reports, A.S.I.,* XV, 39.
8. *Indian Culture,* V, 379-83; *Proceedings Indian History Congress,* 1938, p. 141 ff.
9. *Ibid.*
10. *J. & P.R.A.S.B.,* 272-90.
11. *Bâṅglār Itihās,* II, 8 ff.
12. Krishnadas Kavirāja, *Caitanyacaritāmṛta, Madhyalilâ,* Ch. 20.
13. Stewart, *History of Bengal,* 120-21; *Riaz-ul-Salatin,* 138-39.
14. *Tezouh-al-Vakiat* (Tr. Stewart), 12; *Tabakat-i Akbari;* Elliot, V, 200 ff.; *Akbar-nāma,* Elliot, VI, 19; *ibid.,* (Beveridge). I. 328 ff. *Twarikh-i-Sher Shahi,* Elliot IV, 367, Briggs, II, 114 ff.; *Al-Badouni,* 457. *Riaz,* 141-42 all give the accounts of the above battle.

    Akbar-nāma, Elliot, VI, 19 calls it the 'town of Garhi' but the area of the fort is too insufficient to hold a town and does not bear any trace whatsoever of civil residence.
15. Dow, *Hindosthan* , II, 251 calls the above pass as 'Killagury.'
16. *T. Akbari,* Elliot, V, 381.

17. *Ibid.*, 397. Briggs, II, 246-48; *Akbar-nāma,* Elliot, VI, 44 ff.; *Riaz.*, 161-62.
18. Elliot, VI, 44 ff.
19. Krishnadas Kaviraj, *Caitanyacaritāmṛta,* Madhyalīlā, Ch. 20.
20. *Gazetteer, S.P.,* Ed. L.S.S.O. Malley, 1910, p. 285.
21. *T. Akbari, Elliot,* V, 416 ff.; *Al-Badouni,* II, 290 ff.
22. Stewart, *Bengal,* 227.
23. Stewart, *op. cit.*, 227.
24. *Ibid.*, 228ff.; Dow, *History of Hindosthan,* III, 66 ff.; *Iqbal-nāma,* 220-22; Elliot, 409 ff.; Khafi Khan, *Muntakhab-Riaz.*, 188-93.
25. *Riaz.*, 221 fn. 1. Stewart, *op. cit.*, 265.
26. Aquil Khan, 92.
27. *Alamgir Nāmah,* 534-36; 495; Sarkar, *History of Aurangzeb,* II, 241 ff.
28. *Riaz.*, 310.
29. Orme, *Hindosthan,* p. 30, vol. II, sec. I, calls it Tacriagully.
30. *Riaz.*, 311.
31. Unpublished Mss. in India Office.

45

History of Khaṇḍelā

K. C. Jain

At a distance of 28 miles from Sikar in Rajasthan stands the town of Khaṇḍelā. It is a place of great antiquity containing, as it does, ruins of old temples and monuments. The region round about Khaṇḍelā appears to be older than the Christian era. An inscription[1] of the third century B.C. of this place records that some body was killed by Mūla with a poisoned arrow and his memorial was set up by Mahīsa, one of his pupils. Its old names as known from the literary sources were Khaṇḍilla[2] and Khaṇḍelapura.[3] In the 16th century A.D., this town became well known by the name of Rāyasalāvāda after its famous ruler Rāyasāla. Its prosperity in early times is evident from the fact that some villages in the neighbourhood of Khaṇḍelā were once its wards and the Khaṇḍelavāla caste among the merchants and Brāhmaṇas originated from this place.

Khaṇḍelā appears to have been a great centre of Śaivism in early times. In the 7th century A.D., a Śaiva temple was in existence.[4] An inscription dated 644 A.D., records that Ādityanāga of Dhusara family[5] erected the temple of the God Ardhanārīśvara. The present temple of Khaṇḍaleśvara Mahādeva is built of old materials. That Śaivism was dominant at this place in early days at the time of the visit of Jaina *Ācāryas* for the propagation of Jainism, is known from the Jaina literary sources. Jinasenācārya in the line of the saint Aparājita is said to have converted to Jainism its Cauhāna ruler with his subjects who were formerly the followers of Śaivism.[6] When this incident took place is not definitely known. Probably, it happened in the eighth century A.D., because Khaṇḍelavāla caste is not known to be in existence before it. Its earliest mention is found in the inscription of 1197 A.D.[7] When these Khaṇḍelavālas increased in number, they formed *gotras,* after the names of villages, surnames etc. From a *praśasti* of the *Dharmaratnākara* written in 998 A.D., it is known that its author

Jayasena visited Khaṇḍalīka where he impressed the people by his teachings.[8] In 1287 A.D., Jinaprabha Sūri also came to Khaṇḍelapura which was then a great seat of Śaivism. He converted the people to Jainism by his preaching.[9] With a view to spreading Jainism, Brāhmaṇika, pupil of Bhaṭṭāraka Jinacandra of Mūlasaṁgha in 1461 A.D., paid his visit to Khaṇḍelapura where Śāha Gūrjara and Jagasī, sons of Pālhā got the *Vardhamānacarita* written and presented it to him for acquiring merit.[10]

Khaṇḍelā remained a holy place of the Jainas, and it is mentioned in the *Śakalatīrtha stotra* of Siddhasena Sūri, author of the 12th century A.D.[11] Probably Khaṇḍilla Gaccha among the Jainas was named after this place. Vīragaṇi, who lived in the 12st century A.D., was of this Gaccha. This literary association of Jainism with Khaṇḍela is also confirmed by the archaeological evidence. The *Sarāvagī* temple of this place is undoubtedly old but is dilapidated. It cannot be older then the tenth century A.D.[12] The old sculptures of the medieval times are also found.[13] In one sculpture, the principal and central figures are of a man and his wife. As there is a nimbus behind the head of each, these figures are most probably of king and queen. Originally, it seems to have belonged to some temple built by them. But it must have been a Jaina fane, as shown by the figure of a Jina with which the sculpture is surmounted. The lowermost part is occupied by a group of seven persons.

The early political history of Khaṇḍelā is still in the dark. It seems to have been ruled by the Nirvāṇa branch of the Cauhāna rulers. A certain king called Khaḍgalasena[14] is known to have ruled over this place but nothing is known about his time. From the *Hammīramahākāvya,* it is known that Hammīra, who ascended the throne in about 1282 A.D., started on *digvījaya* or conquest of all the quarters. On his return, he reached home passing through Puṣkara, Mahārāṣṭra, Khaṇḍilla, Champā and Karkarāla. From a *praśasti* of Kīrtistambha at Chitor, it is known that Mahārāṇā Kumbhā, who became the ruler in 1433 A.D., is said to have plundered the town of Khaṇḍelā with his large army. In 1461 A.D., Udayakaraṇa was ruling over this place as it is known from a *praśasti* of the *Vardhamāna-carita.*[15]

Rāyasāla was the most famous ruler of Khaṇḍelā. Originally, he was a Jāgīrdāra of Lāmbhī. He joined the imperial forces of Delhi against Afghan invasions at the advice of his minister Devadāsa of *Baniā* caste. He had the good fortune to distinguish himself by cutting down a leader of the enemy in the presence of the imperial general. He was introduced to Emperor Akbar who conferred upon him the title of

Rāyasāla Darabārī,[16] and granted him the districts of Revāsa and Kasulli then belonging to the Candellā Rājputs. It was the beginning of the greatness in the career of Rāyasāla. Scarcely, had he settled his new possessions, he was recalled to court to take part in an expedition against Bhatner. Fresh services obtained new favours and he received a grant of Khaṇḍelā and Odipur then belonging to the Nirvāṇa Rājputs who disclaimed to pay allegiance to the empire and gave themselves upto unlicenced rapine. Finding that, it would be difficult to expel the brave Nirvāṇa Rājputs, he took recourse to stratagem to occupy Khaṇḍelā. He accompanied Mānasiṁha against the heroic Rāṇā Pratāpa of Mewar. He was also in the expedition to Kabul against the Afghans. In all his enterprises, he obtained new distinctions.[17] The descendants of Rāyasāla using his name as patrynomic are styled Rāyasiloṭa.

After the death of Rāyasāla, his son Giradhara ascended the gadi. At his period, the Mughal empire was in the most disordered state and the mountainous region called the Mewat was inhabited by the daring and ferocious bandits called Mewas who carried systematic plunder even upto the imperial metropolis. In such a state of affair, the task of maintaining law and order was assigned to the chief of Khaṇḍelā who proved equal to the task and succeeded in exterminating the roving bands of the bandits. In recognition of his meritorious services, the Mughal emperor granted him the title of Rājā. After his death, his eldest son Dwārkadās succeeded in about 1600 A.D. He was a devotee of Narasiṁha and built the temple in his honour. He fought against the Khān Jahān Lodi, the great hero of the age in which he lived and was slain. He was succeeded in 1633 A.D. by his son Vīrasimha Deva who served with his contingent in the conquest of Deccan and was made the governor of Pernalla.

Bahadur Siṁh succeeded his father in about 1663 A.D. He was a contemporary of the great Mughal emperor Aurangzeb. As a result of the intolerant religious policy of the Mughal emperor, he left the imperial army. Aurangzeb sent his forces against Khaṇḍela with the object of exacting tribute and destroying the temples. At the sight of the royal army, Bahadur Siṁh abandoned his capital and did not resist the Mughal forces. Hearing this news, Sujana Siṁha, the Chieftain of Chapowlee, a descendant of Bhojarāja (the second son of Rāyasāla) resolved to protect the temple or to perish fighting. Sujana could not avert the inevitable and died in action for the ashes of his fathers and temples of the gods. The temple was razed to the ground, the idols broken to pieces and the fragments thrown into the foundation of a mosque erected on its ruins. Bahadur Siṁh continued to reside in an adjacent town. In course of time, when the Syed Brothers came to power, he regained his country. But an imperial contingent was permanently placed at Khaṇḍela and its expenses were borne by Bahadur.

From about the close of the 17th century A.D. we find the interference of the Kachāvāha rulers of Amber in the affairs of Khaṇḍelā.[18] In 1686 A.D., Rāma Siṁha, the Āmbera Rājā was asked by the Mughal authorities to settle some local trouble between Keśarī Siṁha, the fifth in descent from Rāyasāla and the Faujdar of Narnaul. In 1709 A.D., we find Amber intervening on a request from Delhi in connection with the incessant family feuds between the rivals Udaisiṁha and Dhirāja Siṁha, the former Keśarīsiṁha's brother and successor by adoption and the latter Keśarī Siṁha's nephew. In 1712 A.D. a mansab of 1000 personal and 700 horses was granted to Udaisiṁha by the emperor with parganas of Khaṇḍelā and Revāsā as his jagir.

As more formidable intervention by Sawai Jai Siṁha took place in 1718 A.D. Tod tells us that "he laid siege to the citadel called Udigarh". Udaisiṃha held out a month in this castle, he had constructed and called by his own name. Seeing his resources failing, he fled to Naru in Marwar and his son Sawai Siṁha presented the keys throwing himself on the clemency of the conqueror. He was well received and pardoned on condition of becoming tributary to Amber. He signed an agreement to pay annually one lakh of rupees. This account needs modification. It is incorrect to describe Sawai Jai Siṁha as the conqueror to whom Udai Siṃha became tributary. Dhirāja Siṁha in 1723 A.D. still called himself the servant of the emperor and it was to enforce Dhirāja Siṁha's claims upon the state that Jai Siṁha interfered. After achieving his object, the latter levied a lakh of rupees as *Kher Kharch* 'or military expenses from each of the *Panedaras,* realizing it by instalments during 1721, 1722 and 1723. A *peshakasha* was also taken but this seems to have been an imperial levy.

It is only from 1726 onward that we find regular collections taken from Khaṇḍelā by Sawai Jai Siṁha in his own right —the reason being that in 1725 A.D., he obtained the Ijāra for Khaṇḍelā and Revāsā from Delhi. Finally in 1813 A.D., the whole of Khaṇḍelā and Revāsā Parganā was seized by Lachmana Siṁha of Sikar.

Appendices

Appendix No. I

Inscription on the image in the Jaina temple of Jaipur.

1. खंडेलवालान्वय: स: १२६० श्रीमूलसंघे सा: राजदड़े सा जगमाहा पुत्र हरपति वैशाख सुदी १ शुक्ल।

Appendix No. II

Praśasti of Manuscript No. 16 in Ailaka Pannalal Digambara Jaina Saraswati Bhawan, Byawas.

वर्धमान चरित्र कर्ता हरिचन्द्र—स्वस्ति श्री सं: १५५८ वर्षे ज्यैष्ठ वदि १५ बहस्पति वासरे खंडेलपुर शुभ स्थाने रावत श्रीउदयकरण राज्ये श्री मूलसंघे बलात्कार गणे सरस्वती गच्छे नंदि संघे कुंदकुंदान्वये भट्टारक श्री पद्मनंदिदेवा तत्पहे भट्टारक श्री शुभ चन्द्र देवा तत्पट्टालंकार वादी चक्र चूड़ामणि भट्टारक श्री जिनचन्द्र देवा तत शिप्याय नीक्रद जोग्य प्रदत्तं॥ खंडेलवालान्वेय पाटनी गोत्ते सा: पाल्हा भार्या जाटी तत् पुत्र सा: गूजर जगसी इदं शास्त्रं लिखाप्य ज्ञानावरणी कर्म ययार्थं ज्ञानं पाजाय दत्तं। शुभं भवतु लेखक पाठकयो:।

Abbreviations

1	ARRMA	= Annual Report, Rajputuna Museum Ajmer.
2	JGPS	= Jaina Grantha Praśasti Saṅgraha.
3	KB	= Kharaturaccha Bṛihadgurvāvali.
4	GOS	= Gaekwads Oriental Series.
5	PRAS. WC	= Progress Report, Archaeological Survey, Western Circle.
6	URI	= Udaipur Rājya kā Itihāsa.

References

1. *ARRMA.*, 1935, No. 1.
2. *JGPS.*, pp. 3, See also HM IX, pp. 99.
3. *KB.*, pp. 96.
4. *ARRMA.*, 1935 No. 1
5. At present, the persons of this family call themselves Bhārgava Brāhmaṇas but in the 7th century A.D., they belonged to the Vaiśya caste.
6. It is known from the Vaṁśāvali of the Khaṇḍelavāla caste.
7. Inscription found in the Jaina temple of Jaipur. See Appendix No. 1 for the text.
8. *JGPS.*, pp. 3.

9. *KB.*, pp. 96.
10. Copy of *Vardhamāna Caritra in the Śāstra* Bhāṇḍāra at Beawar. Manuscript No. 16. See Appendix No. 2 for the text.
11. *GOS.*, LXXVI, pp. 156.
12. *PRAS.*, WC., 1910, pp. 57.
13. *Ibid.*, pp. 56.
14. *URI.*, pp. 307.
15. See fn. 10.
16. The name of Rāyasāla Darabārī will be found in the Ain-i-Akbari among the Mansabdārs of twelve hundred and fifty horses, a rank of high importance, being equivalent to that conferred on the sons of potent Rājās.
17. The details of Khandela's history, can be read at length in the fifth, sixth and seventh chapters of *AAR.*, II.
18. Report on the Land Tenures and special powers of Ṭhikanedārs of the Jaipur State, pp. 75.

46

Rohitāgiri of the Rāmpāl Copper-Plate

N. G. Majumdar

In the June issue of the *Indian Historical Quarterly* (pp. 313 342) Mr. Haridas Mitra has published an article on the unfinished Kedārpur copper-plate of Śrīcandradeva, for a critical edition of which, scholars are already indebted to Mr. N. K. Bhattasali of the Dacca Museum. Mr. Bhattasali first published a tentative reading of the text in the Bengali Journal *Pratibhā* (1326 B. S.) and later on (October, 1923) edited it in the *Epigraphia Indica,* vol. XVII, pp. 188-92.[1] It is most amusing to notice that Mr. Mitra has taken great pains to criticise the tentative readings given in Mr. Bhattasali's Bengali article and suggested textual emendations some of which are exactly those proposed by Mr. Bhattasali himself in the *Epigraphica* (as for instance, verse 3: नाम्रौ विशुडोच etc.).

Mr. Mitra's article contains statements unsupported by facts. One of these relates to the Rāmpāl copper-plate of Śrīcandra. Verse 2 of this copper-plate says that the Candras belonged to a family which originally ruled over 'Rohitāgiri.' The last letter of the word does not, however, occur in the original but is supplied by Prof. R.G. Basak *(Ep. Ind.,* vol. XII, pp. 138). Mr. Mitra finds himself unable to accept this reading and doubts whether Rohitāgiri could represent the actual form of the place name (*op. cit.,* p. 317 and p. 318). He observes that the metre of the verse being Śārdūlavikrīḍita the 3rd letter *tā* of the word, which is the 8th letter of the *pāda,* had perforce to be made 'long' and the 9th and 10th letters to be made 'short'. "It is not therefore certain," says he, "if the restoration should be रोहितागिरी.' Probably Mr. Mitra is not aware of the fact that *Rohitāgiri* occurs in at least three inscriptions, which come from Orissa. The plates of Gayāḍatuṅga (*JASB.,* 1909, p. 347 and 1916, p. 291) mention his grand-father, king Jagattuṅga as having immigrated from Rohitāgiri (*Rohitāgirinirgata*). As this occurs in a prose passage, the correctness of the form 'Rohitāgiri' is beyond all dispute. Again in a copper-plate of Vinītatuṅga II of evidently the same dynasty (H.P. Shastri, *JBORS.*, vol. vi, p. 238) it is mentioned, in a verse, that his grandfather Vinītatuṅga I came from a place which in MM. Sastri's transcript appears as *Rohitāśivi*. What actually occurs in the original is evidently *Rohitāgiri* the letter *ga* being easily mistaken for *śa* and the letter *ra* for *va*. That both the Candras of Eastern Bengal and the Tuṅgas of Orissa came from Rohitāgiri is a fact worthy of notice, although its real significance cannot be perceived at present. To prove that Rohitāgiri is the same as Rohtasgaḍh, we are, of course, not yet in possession of any definite data, but this identification may be provisionally adopted until a more suitable one is forthcoming. However it will be evident that there is absolutely no reason to doubt that 'Rohitāgiri' is the proper restoration of the word in verse 2 of the Rāmpāl copper-plate.

References

1. An article on this copper-plate will also be found in my forthcoming book entitled *Inscriptions of Bengal,* vol. III (pp. 10-13), which is being published by the Varendra Research Society, Rajshahi.

47

Udayapura-nagara

D. C. Sircar

There is reference to Udayapura-nagara in the inscription dated in the 28th year of Muhammad Shah, edited by me in the June 1931 issue of this Journal (vol. VII. pp. 410ff.) I could not identify it; but, the language of the 'Khaṭolā Bundelī' of Damoh, I suggested, was probably to be found somewhere in the Damoh, region. The town was situated in the Mālava subāh of the Mughals.

After going through that paper of mine, Mr. R. S. Saksena, Superintendent of Archæology of the Gwalior State, has written me saying, "Udayapur Nagar of the inscription is, in all probability, Udayapur town of the Gwalior State. It may also be safely assigned to the Damoh region of the Linguistic Survey, as the border of the State near Udayapur joins with that of the Saugar District (C.P.) in which Damoh is situated. Udayapur is a place of great antiquity dating back to the 10th or the 11th century A.D. and has still numerous ruins bearing Hindu and Moslem inscriptions."[1]

I also now think that Udayapura-nagara of the inscription should be identified with the town of the same name in Scindia's territory. It is now a decayed town in the Bhilsa District of the Gwalior State, 4 miles by road from the Bareth Railway Station on the G.I.P. Railway, and "possessing important and interesting archæological monuments." In his article in the *Indian Antiquary,* vol. LV. pp. 4ff. Mr. Saksena has spoken of "inscriptions on pieces of red sand-stone with raised letters" discovered at Udayapura. The epigraph, I had to deal with, is also a relievo and not an inscription, and is also on red sand-stone.

References

1. For a detailed account of Udayapura, see *Report of the Arch. Surv. of India,* vol. VII, p. 68 and vol. X, p. 69; *IA.*, LV, p. 4; *IHQ.*, vol. III, p. 715.

Uma-Maheswara

48

Schorer's Account of the Coromandel Coast

(Transl. by Prof. Brij Narain)

Sri Ram Sharma

[The following account of the Coromandel Coast was written by Ant. Schorer in 1616 in his retirement in Holland. It is preserved in the Dutch Archives at Hague. Professor Brij Narain translated the account into English when he visited Holland several years ago. The present writer has only indicated within bracket marks the identification of places, persons, commodities and institutions. Where the sense is not quite clear in the Dutch text, a few words have been put in within box brackets].

A short account of the coast of Coromandel, and the trade carried on there, chiefly at the Noble Company's factory at Masulipatnam, where I resided for seven years.

The coast of Coromandel extends from Menar (the gulf of Manaab) to the south of Narsapor, where the coast of Orissa begins. The Noble Company has 4 factories on the said coast namely, the first, on the way back from Ceylon, [at the place] called Tegnampatnam or Tieriepopelier (Tirupapuliyer), which is under the rule of the great Aya (Rai of Jinji), and is situated about 12 miles to the north of Negapatnam, which belongs to the Portuguese. There are about 5 persons in this factory. The trade that is carried on there consists in all kinds of cotton cloths, printed as well as woven. Saltpetre is also found there. Indigo is also grown there, but it is of very bad quality, and therefore it is little exported to other places. The commodities which are imported there are: pepper, nutmeg, cloves, sandalwood, *aglenhout,* lead, *speauter,* sulphur, alum, rawsilk from Aitchyn (Achin in Sumatra) and from China, also silk manufactures, but little in demand, musk, vermillion, quicksilver and camphor of China as well as Borneo, but that of Borneo is most in demand. Trade is done by means of Pardauws; 10 fanams are equal to 1 Pardauw, which is equal to about 2 Dutch gulden. A fannam is equal to 20 to 22 cassen, which is the smallest money. The weights used are bhaer, man and bissen, 1 bhaer is equal to 460 Dutch lbs; 1 man or tolam is equal to 23 lbs.; 1 biss is equal to 2−7/8 lbs. The merchants wishing to sell their goods must be guided by the course of the market, or the prices current, in Negapatnam. The duties levied there are 4% namely 2% on goods imported and 2% on goods exported, but it should be noted that the duties on exports must be paid in money; those on imports may be paid in the same goods that are imported. The inhabitants are for the most part of black or yellowish complexion, and are Hindus.

The second factory on the coast is at Paleaicatta (Pulicat), which belongs to one of the wives of king of Velour (Vellore). It lies 7 miles to the north of St. Thome, or Maliapore, which belongs to the Portuguese. In the said Paleaicatta, the Noble Company possesses a fort named Geldria, in which there is a house called Both. There are in this fort 72 men, merchants as well as soldiers, with 14 to 16 black people who have deserted from the other (Portuguese) side. There are also 18 guns, of copper as well as iron, 4 falaons, or bassen with 4 steenstucken. There are made all kinds of cotton cloths, woven as well as printed and they are much better (in quality) than in any other places on the whole coast particularly the printed (cloths), as the Portuguese have been there for a long time. The best Saye is available near about this place, used for dyeing red; there are also leaves of certain trees which are used for dyeing green. The goods mentioned on the preceding page are also imported there. The bhaer there is 480 lbs. and the man 24 lbs. or raetel. Trade is there carried on by means of pagodas, fanams and cassen. A pagoda is 15 fanam, and a fanam is 20 to 24 cassen. Every year some ships come there in February or March from the coast of Gangely (Ganges) or Orissa, laden with rice, butter and gengely seed and return in April or May, laden with salt and some spices. The duties levied there on goods exported and imported are 2 per cent. In addition to this each ship must pay 15 pagodas for permission to lie at anchor. The inhabitants are of black complexion and belong to the Hindu religion. There is also a river there where the Portuguese who live in St. Thome used to harbour such of their ships as were not very large.

Petapoly (Nirampatam), where [we have] the third factory, is 48 miles to the north of Paleacatta. It is under the jurisdiction of the King of Golcanda, but is ruled by a Hindu governor. The King farms to him the government of this place for a certain sum of money. There are 4 men in this factory. Very few ships, excepting those of the Dutch and the English come there. There are made all kinds of cloths, printed as well as woven. The red dye which is made there is very good. There is a small island in the middle of the river where the best Saye of the whole coast of Coromandel is found. The commodities imported there are the same as in the places mentioned before, excepting porcelain for which there is a larger demand there than in the other two places, the reason being that some Persian merchants live there who eat from porcelain-ware, but not the Hindus. The inhabitants are the same as in other places, and mostly belong to the Hindu religion. There are also Bramenes (Brahmans) there who may not eat anything that has life. They are very clever in making calculations, and [in dealing in] all kinds of commodities. There are [some] among them who understand astronomy very well. The bhaer there is equal to 500 lbs., the man 25 lbs., and the biss 3 – 1/8 lbs., the pagoda is equal to 16 fanam; 1 fanam is equal to 8 to 9 nevels; 1 nevel is equal to 4 to 5 taer cassen. The duty levied on imports is 3½ per cent, which must be paid in the same goods that are imported; and 3½ per cent on exports, which must be paid in money or in commodities on which the Governors are able to make the greatest profit. The English also have a factory there.

Masulipatnam, called by some Bander, which means a town, lies to the north in 16½ degrees. It is without doubt the most famous commercial town on the coast. It has been stated before that the Noble Company has a factory there. The Company has a hired lodge there in which 8 or 9 persons live. [Masulipatnam] has a river, but ships and yachts cannot conveniently come up the river as it has very little water and is very narrow. The ships which come there, namely our ships and those of the English, must anchor at about a mile from the land because [the water] is very shallow and the ground is very soft. The ships lie at anchor in 3 or 4 fathoms. The town is situated half a mile up the river. It is ruled by a Governor to whom land is farmed by the King of Golcanda. In addition [to the Governor] there is a Sabandar (Havaldar?), and a judge whom they call Chasi (Qazi), before whom all disputes are settled. The King of Golcanda maintains great state. When he comes, he is followed by a large crowd of people, some riding on horses, others being carried in Pallenguyns. He has a great number of camels and elephants. He himself sits on an elephant when he goes out. He is no warrior but he carries on great warfare with Meleik Amber (Malik Ambar), Lieutenant General of the Great Mogol, of Acha Baer (Akbar), in which he (the King of Golcanda) is assisted by two other kings, the one called Nisaem Schae (Nizam Shah) and the other Adulschae (Adal Shah). The forts which are on the land side are very strong, and well furnished with soldiers, victuals and all kinds of ammunition – particularly those situated on the enemy's frontier. It is said that the King's annual revenue exceeds all his expenditure by 19 tons of treasure, each ton being equal to one hundred thousand Pagodas. He gives much charity, particularly to Persians of high family but of small means; many of them come from Persia. So far as I know, he is as well as, if not better than, inclined towards us as towards the Portuguese, and that is also true of his subjects. But the worst (thing) that I know is that those who give the most presents are most respected, although for some time we were much in favour on account of the victories that we several time won over the Portuguese in different places.

Justice for the most part is administered by the Governor. The offence which is most often punished there is theft. Besides, the Governors much molest their subjects in order to extract money from them by fair or foul means: they must pay the King their annual rent; if they fail to do so, they are summoned before the King, who has them thrown before the elephants, unless they pay the sum they promised within such time as may be fixed. For this reason most of the Governors are Bramenes, or Hindus, and no Persians, because the King may not judge (i.e. punish) Persians, particularly those who are Sayed (Sayyid) or Mir (Pir) of origin, or in other words, descended from Muhammad, which is the religion of the King and most of his subjects. He has also many priests called Kahtiff, (Muftis?), living in his country and under his jurisdiction. They receive annually a certain amount of money for their maintenance, there are many of their churches in the town called Muschitt (Masjid), also in the villages both for travellers and inhabitants, because Muhammadans live throughout the whole country. The Hindus have also here and there some temples in the country, called pagodas, but because the land is mostly under the Muhammadans, many of their temples have decayed. Their priests or teachers are called Barmens who, as has been stated before, are very clever in all things. I have not seen the ceremonies observed in their temples. The ceremonies of the Moors are the same as those of the Turks, although there are some differences. There is a great difference between the religion of the Turks and of the Persians, although both follow the religion of Muhammed. The Muhammadans observe no special ceremonies in burying their dead. When a Hindu dies, the corpse is not buried, but thrown into the fire and burnt. Then their women come and spring into the fire with a cheerful countenance [and are burnt] with their dead husband. Friends throw wood and oil into the fire to free themselves from the pain as soon as possible. Women who do not do it are regarded as dishonourable, but all women do not have to do it as some (men) are buried. They marry very young. If the husband happens to die before reaching the age of manhood, the widow must not marry again throughout her life. Her hair is shaved from her head, all her ornaments are taken off from her body, and she must not wear fine dresses any more.

When Muhammadans die, their widows, if they desire, may marry again. The Muhammadans have four lawful wives, and in addition as many female slaves as they can buy, with whom, when they so desire, they also sleep and have children who are regarded as true born as the others. A Hindu marries only one woman, but when he has no children by her, with her consent, he may marry again in order to have an heir. The children of the Muhammadans, when they are old enough, learn to read and write. The children of some of the Hindus also learn to read and write. When they are old enough to enter a profession, it must be the same as that of their father or caste. In house-keeping they are very extravagant, particularly the Muhammadans, who are allowed to eat almost every thing except pork. They some times hold great feasts but may not drink wine, although there are many Hindus who may not eat anything that has life, chiefly the Bramenes and the Banjaenes, (Banyas=Jains) who follow the law of Pitagoras. The others eat almost everything, excepting beef. They drink nothing but water; some of their women, however, being ill or in child-bed, may drink wine. The inhabitants there are mostly black, and some yellowish; but others, for example, Persians, Arabians, Turks and Peguers, of which 4 nations living there, are white, but not of the same colour, as people of this country (Holland). The marriage state among them is well kept, but better among the Hindus who may have only two wives, and the Muhammadans have four, and in addition may have as many female slaves as they can buy. Notwithstanding this, they go to public women, of which there is a large number there. Muhammadans, when their children reach the age of manhood, before they are married, buy a female slave for them, so that they may go to public women. The children born of these female slaves are regarded as true-born children. The trade and traffic carried on there is great on land as well as water; the Muhammadans and Banjaenen carry on trade in various places on land as well as water, but the Hindus do not much go to the sea. Every year the ships go to the coast of Bengal, Arracan, Pegu, and Tennassery (Tennasserim), taking with them all kinds of cotton-cloths, glass, iron, cotton-yarn, white as well as red, tobacco and certain shells which are used as money in Bengal and Arracan. They also take with them some spices and sandalwood,and bring in return rice, butter, oil gingely seed, sugar, all kinds of woven cloths, some pretty knitted bed-covers (quilts), rubies, sapphires,. gumlac, black oakum, *benjeuyn,* raidx [rorī from China], gold, tin, *aglenhout, pausapon,* with which they dye red large pots which they call *martavan,* and a certain drink called *nypa.* These commodities are carried all over the coast, as far as Cochin. Further, their ships also go to Atechyn, Priamam, (Priaman in Sumatra), Queda (Kedah in Malay States) and Perae (Perak in Malay) taking with them all kinds of printed cloths and rice, bringing in return sulphur, camphor, silk, tin and some Guzerat cloths; also pepper from Priamam and some porcelain which they buy there from the Chinese. These commodities are again sold on the coast. Some ships also go to Ceylon and the Maldives, taking with them coarse cotton cloths and bringing from there coir, from which Indians and the Portuguese make ropes, and cocoa-nuts. Cocoa-nuts are found in certain places in the Maldives which are very good against poison. In my own time I have seen one sold for 200 larryns, each larryn being equal to about 9 stuyers. They bring from Ceylon cinnamon, finely woven mats, cocoa-nuts and some (precious) stones, which commodities are again sold on the coast, chiefly in Masulipatnam. Here trade is carried on by means of pagodas, each pagoda being equal to 15 fanam; 1 fanam being equal to 8 to 9 nevels. The smallest money used in the market is cassen, 70 to 80 being equal to 1 fanam (and) taer, each taer being equal to 4 small cassen. The goods produced or manufactured there are all kinds of cotton cloths, printed as well as woven, cotton yarn, cotton, iron, steel, and indigo. The best (indigo) is made in a place further inland called Negelwaensa and is sold by the littel, each littel being equal to 12 man of Masulipatnam, each man being equal to 24 Dutch lbs. The price of indigo is 28 to 39 pagodas per littel. The bhaer in Masulipatnam is 480 lbs., the man 24 lbs; the biss or 5 seers equal to 3 lbs. The Muhammadan ships which go from Masulipatnam to Bengal, Arracan, Pegu, Tennassery, Atchyn, Priamam, Queda and Perae, generally sail in the month of September, for if they wait longer, they run the risk of not being able to finish their voyage. The ship for Mecca generally leaves in January or at the end of December. Ordinarily our ships sail from the coast to Atchyn and further to Bantam in May, or in the beginning of June, because then the winds are blowing from the west. The ships from Masulipatnam go to Arrimogam, (Armagon) Paleacatta, St. Thome, Tegenapatnam, Porto Novo, Negapatnam and so on to Ceylon, and then as far as Cochyn. They start in the month of January. The commodities imported into Masulipatnam and the prices at which they were sold in my time are the following so far as I remember, for my books and papers are all at Masulipatnam: – Pepper, 25 pagoda per bhaer; Mace, 8 to 12 pagoda per man; Nutmeg, 33 to 60 pagoda per bhaer; Cloves, 5½ to 12 pagoda per man; Sandalwood, 100 to 120 pagoda per bhaer; *Aglenhout,* 7 to 9 pagoda per man; Lead, 17 to 20 pagoda per bhaer; *Speauter* or tintenago, 25 to 60 and 70 pagoda, per bhaer; Tin, 75 to 80 pagoda per bhaer; Sulphur, 20 pagoda per bhaer; Alum, 12 pagoda per bhaer; Haw Chinese silk, 40 to 45 pagoda per man; Twisted silk from China, 1 pagoda per seer; Untwisted silk (not so much imported as twisted) 1 pagoda per seer; Musls, 10 to 12 pagoda per seer; Vermillion, much in demand, but not imported in my time, Quicksilver, 20 to 25 pagodas per man; Camphor of Borneo, according to size and whiteness, 5 to 20 pagodas per seer; Chinese camphor, 4 pagodas per man.

All kinds of porcelain-ware are also imported, chiefly little things, and are sold at great profit, each according to its quality; and for this reason I am not quoting their prices.

Red crimson cloth, 6 pagoda per gass, gass being equal to 1¼ Dutch ell. Red Carmosynen Kerdeys, 2 to 2¼ pagodas per gass. Other colours of cloth as also of Kardeys are not much in demand, particularly black. Chinese velvet, 1 to 1¼ pagodas per gass; Chinese rolled damask, 5 to 6 pagodas per piece; Chinese plaited damask, 2¼ to 2½ pagodas per piece; Chinese gold-wire, 1 pagoda each paper; Chinese *armosynen,* 1¾ to 2 pagodas per piece, Chinese lacquer work is not much in demand. Some round closed boxes have been sold for ¾ to 1 pagoda per piece, but not many. Tortoise shell, 70 to 80 pagodas per bhaer; Tinsel was sold in my time at from 3 to 4 pagoda per man, but it was very much soiled. There is also a demand for pretty beer glasses made of crystal, 2 or 3 of which are sold for 1 pagoda. Pretty mirrors could also be sold, but it is to be noted that the glass should be pretty, if it is not so, they want another to be put into the frame. *Benjeuryn,* 6 to 8 pagoda per man; Wax, 2 to 2¼ pagoda per man; Sugar, 5 to 6 pagoda per bale, each bale weighing about 6 man.

The rubies brought there are sold according to their size, quality and weight; gold also; (in the same manner). Great number of rubies are carried from Masulipatnam far into the interior, even to Persia, where they are sold. For the most part gold is consumed in or round Masulipatnam. About 10 to 12 miles to the south of Masulipatnam there is a river there where the Muhammadans, Portuguese and also the Hindus build their ships, as wood, iron and other materials are available there in sufficient quantities, and wages are low. Shortly before I left Masulipatnam, an English ship, named the Globe, about 170 last, was covered there with an additional layer of planking. There are made there some coarse woven cloths of cotton, also printed [cloths], because many weavers live there and thereabouts; there are also many weavers on whole coast, also printers. There are some other craftsmen, as smiths, carpenters, goldsmiths, tailors, and a few other different crafts, but not so many as of those. The land roundabout Narsapor Petta, as also about Masulipatnam, yields much rice and various kinds of fruits, and there is an abundance of all kinds of animals. Butter and cheese are also made there. Good wheat is grown further inland from Masulipatnam. It is sold in Masulipatnam at 3 or 4 pagoda per bhaer; rice is sold at 1 to 1½ pagoda per bhaer; butter 7 to 10 fanam per man; an ox, 1 to 2 pagodas; a goat, 1 to 2 fanam; 60 to 70, sometimes 80 fowl for 1 pagoda; a pig 4 to 5 fanam; 80 eggs for 1 fanam, and other things correspondingly, because there is an abundance of all things also oranges and apples, lemons and all kinds of other fruits and fish. There is a little island in the river of Petapoly, where many spotted dear are caught, and are sold sometimes for 2 to 3 fanams, sometimes also for ½ pagoda. Roundabout Narsapor Petta, as also in other places inland, there are many deer, but not spotted, as in the river of Petapoly. There are also large numbers of elephants. There are many crocodiles in the rivers. Which sometimes do much damage to cattle when they are going along [the banks] of the rivers. Good material is available in Masulipatnam for making gun-powder; also ropes which are made from coir, of which some are sent every year to Bantam for ships which go to the Moluccas. Sail-cloth is also made there, but it is not so good as here (in Holland), but one may get along with it there and the Portuguese, the Muhammadans as also the Hindus, when they go from one place to another with their ships and commodities, use no other ropes and sail-cloth except those made there. In order to inflict losses on the Portuguese, in my judgment [subject to correction], it will be necessary to have some fast-sailing yachts well provided with guns and soldiers, as the Portuguese (ships) are now better equipped than before. They ordinarily sail from Cochyn (Cochin). Negapatnam and St. Thome in the months of August and September, to Bengal, Arracan, Pegu and Tennassery (Tenasserim), going along the coast, and return in March or April. So they must pass our ships, which are about this time under Ceylon where the Dutch ships ordinarily touch on the return journey. Some times the Portuguese come with their ships to Masulipatnam. The duties that they must pay there are 4 per cent on imports and 4 per cent on exports; so also the English. In addition, the Governor wants them to pay tschapadallaly, (broker-age), which amounts to 11 per cent, unless by means of presents they are able to get this duty [remitted ?]. The inhabitants of the place, the Muhammadans and the Hindus, do not pay it, for, a few years ago, the King remitted the duty, but, inspite of this, they must give presents to the Governor in order to get their goods earlier out of the Customs house. The Noble Company pays no duties there because Wemmer van Berchem has made a contract with the King of Golcanda to pay 3000 pagodas annually for goods imported as well exported. Still, when our ships arrive, one must give presents to the Governor, Sabandaer and other great lords in order to secure their friendship. It is otherwise difficult to trade there, particularly if one has not secured the friendship of the Governor.

This, my Noble Masters, is what is known to me about the coast of Coromandel, to the best of my recollection.

49

Notes on Schorer's Account of the Coromandel Coast*

C. S. Srinivasachari

(1) 'The great Aya' [in page 827, line 6.]. He was not the Nayak of Gingee, but a eunuch and a feudatory chief and had great influence with the then powerful Nayak of Gingee, Krishnappa Nayaka. The 'Aya' was, according to the evidence of the Dutch factors, of the time the person in whom the power of administration really vested. When the Nayak of Gingee gave a *cowle* to Jacob D. Bitter, promising permission to the Dutch to build a factory at Tegnapatam (now Fort St. David) in November 1608, the Aya assured the Dutch man that no toll would be levied on Dutch goods and that he would promote the work of construction of the Fort at Tegnapatam and secure dyers and weavers for the cloth required by them. It was the Aya that permitted the Dutch factors to remain on the coast against the wishes of the Raja of Candragiri, "the great king of Vijayanagar", who desired to help the Portuguese as against the Dutch and to get the Nayak of Gingee to his side in this matter. The Aya, however, kept a rigorous control over the movements of the Dutch; and the result was that the Dutch became anxious to secure a settlement at Tirumalipatam, *i.e.*, Tirumalairāyanpattinam on the coast between Tirupāpuliyūr and Negapatam and under the jurisdiction of the Nayak of Tanjore.

In the spring of 1610, Maertssen negotiated with "the great Aya" for a new contract which was actually concluded on the 29th March 1610, "between the Aya Tiere Wangelaye, Governor over the islands Tindamandalam (Tondaimandalam) on the one side and Arend Macrtssen and Pieter Gerritsz Bourgonjie on the other side." The Aya swore on his side to keep the contract with his Nayak, Christoppen Aya (Krishnappa Nayak). The Dutch should have within the fortress of Tirupāpuliyur, (a weaving village with a fortress temple about 2 miles from Tegnapatam up the river, gadilam) as a storehouse of ammunition and merchandise, the house called *Nota Calamatta Coin* and were to furnish the fort with a metal cannon and three iron guns. They should pay 2% import and export duties except for money, rice and other necessaries of the fort. The Nayak and the Aya should have the right to buy sulphur from the Dutch and they should compel the dyers and weavers to carry out their agreements with the Dutch and not permit other European nations to trade, without special papers from Prince Maurice. The Aya should be supplied with the goods that he desired to get from the Netherlands, at their cost price. The Dutch should not trouble ships sailing with the passport of the captain (native headman) of Tegnapatam. 'Thus the Dutch secured contractual confirmation for their possession of Tirupāpuliyūr and could use Tegnapatam as the harbour for it. Porto Novo (about a dozen miles lower down the coast also under the Nayak of Gingi who had fostered it) also stood open before them, but they did not establish a factory there immediately.'

After the conclusion of this treaty with the Aya, Maertssen went with a companion to Gingee from whose Nayak they took a letter to the Stadtholder of Holland wherein we learn that the Aya promised to keep the contract concluded now. The contract was later on sent to Vellore (the residence of Venkatapathi, Maharaja) from Gingee and was ratified by the Raya. Portuguese opposition, however, continued even after the news of the conclusion of the Twelve Years' Truce of Antwerp reached the Coromandel Coast at the end of 1610; and they offered 1,000 pagodas to the Aya, if he should drive the Dutch out of Tegnapatam; and in the sequel the latter had to pay 2000 rix dollars to the Aya for a continuation of their privileges and for the safety of Vander Meer, the head of the factory.

(2) Tirupāpuliyūr (line 7, p. 827) is situated two miles inland from the mouth of the Gadilam River on the north bank of which was Tegnapatam. It is at a much longer distance than 12 miles from Negapatam (p. 827). There is another port Tirumalairāyanpattinam, a few miles to the north of Negapatam, which might have been confused with Tirupapuliyur.

(3) *Pardauws* (usually known as *Pardaos* (lines 17-19, p. 827) is supposed to be a Portuguese corruption of the word, *Partab,* and was taken from the legend on some of the coins to which the name was applied. The Persian traveller, Abdur Razzaak who visited the West coast of India in 1443, makes 10 *fanams* equal to 1 *partab* and 2 *partabs* equal to 1 *varāha*. Ludovico Varthema, writing about 1545, says that 256 *cash* (*kassen*) was equal to 1 *fanam* and *20 fanams* equal to 1 *pradao,* which was "a gold ducat, smaller than the gold dinar."

Evidently the gold pagoda or *varāha* of Abdur Razzaak was the double *pagoda* of which some coins exist and the *pardao* (or partab) was a half-*hun* or *pagoda*. A *fanam* (Tamil *paṇam* from Sanskrit *paṇa*) was at first a gold coin in use, but latterly denoted a silver one. Usually 20 *faṇams* made a *pardao*. Latterly in Madras, late in the 18th century, 42 silver *faṇams* went to make 1 gold star *pagoda*, (*varāha*). A *faṇam* was worth from 2 to 3 pence. *Cassen* or *cash* was the name applied to sundry coins of low value; the word had been apparently derived from Sanskrit *karṣa,* equal to 1/400 of a tula, and became corrupted into 1 Tamil *kāśu*. The *cash* was the lowest unit of the monetary system of Madras till 1818. The Portuguese had long applied the term *cass* to the diverse small moneys of foreign systems. (Refers also to lines 25-26 on page 828).

(4) *Sabandar* (*Shahbandar*) (line 8, p. 830) is not the *havaldar.* The term literally means the 'king of the port', *i.e.*, Harbour-Master. The title was assumed by the officers in charge of Indian ports and was generally applied to chiefs in charge of the eastern ports. The Shahbandar was the chief authority with whom foreign traders and ship-masters had to transact business; he was also generally the head of the Customs Department. The term is usually rendered by European writers as *Xabander, Shabunder* or *Sabundar.* The title has now dropped out of in India; but it was applied till recently to the Consuls of the Persians. In the Malay States the Shahbandar was an important officer of the government. The term was sometimes applied even to officers in charge of inland towns, perhaps used to indicate the head of the merchants or master of their organisation. Thus Tavernier mentions the existence of a Shahbandar, in Golconda; and Warren Hastings in a letter of 1759, makes mention of *Shahbandar Daroga*. The Shahbandar was in charge of the port and port customs generally. Equivalent terms like Mīr Bunder and Sheikh Bunder seem to have been used elsewhere in other Islamic countries for the port officer.

(5) The term *khatiff* (line 10, p. 831) might probably be a corruption of *Khatīb* (Arab.=a preacher or reciter of the Khutba).

(6) *Larryn* (line 26, p. 833) or *Larin.* A coin that was in currency in the Persian Gulf and West Coast of India and also in the Maldive Islands. It was in shape like a small rod of silver, of the size of the pen of a goose feather. Six of such *larins* went to make up a *ducat* and one *larin* was equal to about half a *guilder.*

(7) The king of Velour (line 10, p. 828) means Maharaja Venkatapathi (1585-1614). Velour supplanted Candragiri as the chief royal residence from about 1606.

(8) *Armosynen* (line 12, p. 835). It is a kind of silk texture, usually black in colour, perhaps called so because originally associated with Ormuz, as it trade centre.

(9) *Aglenhout* (line 13, p. 833) perhaps means 'Eagle-wood.' This is an aromatic wood from Cambodia and has been referred to by the Portuguese writers as *Aguila* and known as also Agla-wood or Ugger-wood.

(10) *Saye* (line 22, p. 828) (i.e. *Sāya* or *Chaya*) known generally as chayroot which affords a red eye; it was also known as the 'Rāmeśwaram Root.' The colour was known to be fast and permanent. It was exported in quantities from several places in South India and at one time from Ceylon also; and it was used very largely on the coast for painting chintz cloth.

(11) The *Bhaer* or *Bāhar* (line 23, p. 825) (from Sanskrit *Bhāra*=load) was a weight used in large trading transactions varying from place to place and usually about 400 pounds *avoirdupois*.

(12) *Petapoli* (line 3, p. 829) is situated much more to the north of Pulicat than 48 miles (see *infra*, note No. 19).

(13) *Taer Cassen* (line 23; p. 829) is possibly the name for a silver coin known as *Tare* which was equal to *16 cash* and 16 of which made one *faṇam*. 8 *taeris* in Malabar in the late 18th century amounted to half a *faṇam*. The *tare* was generally worth hald a penny.

(14) *Benjeuyn* (line 12, p. 833) is *benjamin* or *benzoin,* a kind of incense derived from the resin of the '*styrax* benzoin' in Sumatra. It was called by the Arab traders as the "Frankincense of Java.'

(15) Martavan (line 14, p. 833) also known as Martaban, in the name given to peculiar pottery of very large size and glazed, made in that region, known also as Pegu Jars.

(16) *Nypa* (line 14, p. 833) is a Malay word denoting *arrack* extracted from the sap of a palm tree and usually exported from Pegu, Tenasserim and the Philippine Islands. In the Dutch languages the word *Nippen,* had come to mean "to take a dram."

(17) *Speauter* (line 13, p. 827) should be properly *spelter.* It is the Portuguese *Tutinaga,* Tamil *Tuttanagam* used in Indian trade and meant either zinc, pewter, or white lead of the Chinese.

(18) *Red Carmosynen Kerdeys* (line 7, p. 835) may probably refer to *Kersey,* an English word for a kind of woollen cloth, held by some, incorrectly however, to be a corruption of Cashmere by confusion of sound with Kersey. Valentijn (*Circa* 1626) makes mention of 2000 Persian ells of *Carsay.* It was principally manufactured in England.

(19) Petapoly (line 3, p. 829) (Nizampatam). Literally Peddapalli, meaning great village, changed by the English usage into Pettikpoly. Its Indian name is Arjumputnam. It is situated 193 miles to the north of Madras and 36 miles from Masulipatam west-south-west. It has been mentioned by Ferishta. The English commenced their trade here, for the first time on the eastern coast in 1611; the name of the place was changed to Nizampatam in 1679. An English factory was established here in 1621, dissolved in 1653 and again re-established in 1697.

Schorer's "Brief relation of the Trade of the Coromandel Coast, especially at the Factory at Masulipatam, where I resided in the service of the Hon'ble Company in the seventh Year" was given in its English translation and with notes by W. H. Moreland in his edition of *Relations of Golconda in the Early Seventeenth Century'* (Haklyt Society, 1931, Series II, Vol. lxvi, on pp. 51-65). Schorer was a commercial failure and was junior factor at Masulipatam in October 1609. He was sent to Bantam in disgrace after a few years. The seventh year mentioned in the title of his work is held by Moreland to be 1608, meaning the seventh year of the Dutch Factory's establishment at that place. He probably returned to Holland in 1615-16 and wrote or at least completed the relation either during the voyage or soon after arrival.

In the notes supplied by me to Schorer's account I have added additional notes for the benefit of the readers of the *Indian Historical Quarterly* and consequently based them on the account as given on pages 827-837 in the *I.H.Q.*, vol. XVI. The 'great Aya' whose full name as given in the records as Tiere (or Ciere), Wingelaya can be rendred into Ayya and Tiruvengadayya, Ayya being the shortened form of Tiruvengadayya. This has been suggested by Moreland.

Most of the points contained in the notes have been taken independently of Moreland and refer only to a portion of the terms etc., used in the 'Relation', as translated by Dr. Brij Narain and published by Prof. S.R. Sharma.

References

* (Translated by Prof. Brij Narain and contributed by Professor Sri Ram Sharma), in the *Indian Historical Quarterly*, vol. xvi, No. 4, December, 1940, pp. 827-837.

50

Mr. C. U. Wills on the Sambalpur Aṭhārāgarh

L. P. P. Sharma

The Sambalpur Aṭhārāgarh was an organisation with a history of its own. Major H.B. Impey the then D.C. of Sambalpur describes the Sambalpur Raj as a *cluster of 18 Garhs* (vide his Report entitled Notes on the Gurhjat States of Patna, prepared in 1863). He gives the following list of these garhs: –

1 Patna, 2 Sambalpur, 3 Sonepur, 4 Bamra, 5 Rerakhole, 6 Gangpur, 7 Bod, 8 Aṭhmallick, 9 Phuljhar, 10 Bonai, 11 Raigarh, 12 Baragarh, 13 Sakti, 14 Chanderpur, 15 Sarangarh, 16 Bindranawagarh, 17 Khariyar, 18 Borasamer.

Mr. C.U. Wills, I.C.S., in his paper on "The Rajput kingdoms of Mediaeval Chhattisgarh" (JAS. of Bengal, V, 1919) has tried to prove that the application of the term Aṭhārāgarh in the sense of the local traditions and authentic Govt. Reports is not historically correct. Mr. Wills is of opinion that the 18 garhs did not form a number of extensive states outside and around the state of Sambalpur proper, but they were the sub-divisions of a single state named Sambalpur. Thus according to him the Feudatory state of Patna, Sonepur, Bod or Baud, Sarangarh, Raigarh, Bamra etc. were excluded from the 18 Garhs of Sambalpur Rāj. In support of his point Mr. Wills produces two witnesses:

1. Mr. Motte who visited Sambalpur in 1766 A.D.

2. Prahlad Dube of Sarangarh C. P., author of a Hindi Poem entitled *Jaya-Candrikā*. Mr. Wills writes:

"Nor is Mr. Motte my only witness. It would be easy to disparage his testimony by saying that he was a mere European adventurer, probably ill-acquainted with the language of the country, who from the fact he never specified what was meant by the *Aṭhārāgarh* stands convicted of having made but superficial enquiries. But I have, by the courtesy of Rai Bahadur Hīrālāl, been given the translation of a poem composed by a certain Prahlād Dube of Sarangarh written in 1783 A.C. to commemorate the installation of one of the Rajas on the Sambalpur Gaddi. And this poem completely refutes those who regard the *Aṭhārāgarh* as a confederacy of states, and makes it clear that they were internal subdivisions held by local chiefs or lords as Motte would call them. This testimony is unimpeachable. It was prepared by a local poet for a public occasion and must be conclusive evidence on the point at issue"(page 224, para 48). Unfortunately Prahlād Dube's work in the original does not contain anything which might go to prove that the 18 Garhs of Sambalpur were only the internal subdivisions of a single state and not separate subordinate states with their own chiefs. The extracts from the Hindi poem "*Jaya Candrikā.*" of Prahlād Dube, as quoted by Mr. Wills, has not been properly understood and correctly interpreted. The lines quoted by Mr. Wills must be interpreted with reference to the context and it is then only that right conclusion can be drawn. Thus Mr. Wills' translates the passage "दुर्ग अठारह अमित छवि सम्बलपुर परसिद्ध" by "Sambalpur of unmeasured beauty was famous as 18 forts." Balbhadra Sai, one of its earlier kings, attacked the neighbouring state of *Bod* which both Kittoe and Impey count among the Aṭhārāgarh, But Balbhadra Sai makes his attack along with all his 17 forts, i.e., the chiefs thereof. So *Bod* could not have been one of them. He lays siege to the *Bod* king's capital for 11 long years without avail. At last the chief of Sarangarh is sent for and with his aid the *Bod* fort is captured. *Sarangarh* is thus excluded by the poet from the *Aṭ hārāgarh,* though Kittoe and Impey include it in their lists. Later, coming down to his own times, the poet tells us how the Dewan Akbar (mentioned by Motte, para 46) usurped the Raja's power and the Raja Jait Singh fled to Sarangarh and sought the help from Chhattisgarh and Patnā for: –

गढ़ सत्र[1] हके कोउ न अये। नमक छाँड़ि अकबर के भये॥

Not one of the 17 forts came to help him .Untrue to their salt they took the side of Akbar.

In the ensuing battle Sonepur comes to Jait Singh's help. This clearly excludes *Patnā* and *Sonepur* from the list of 18 forts. Also Bimbaji writes on Jait Singh's behalf to all the *Garhs* and all the 13 Dandpats, to Bengal, to Chandra, to Mandalla, to Patna and to Bamra. Thus we have a clear statement showing that neither Bod, Sarangarh, Sonepur, Patnā or Bamra were members of the local Aṭhārāgarh. This is sufficient to confute the lists of later writers. But the exclusion of Patnā puts the matter beyond all question. Patna was always not merely a member of the confederacy but with Sambalpur the head of it. If Aṭhārāgarh indicated any such confederacy it would be impossible to exclude the leading member. The conclusion of Mr. Wills is this: –

"A confederacy of states under Sambalpur and Patna did no doubt exist at one time or another, but it was never known as the *Aṭhārāgarh*. This term referred in Sambalpur as in Raipur, Ratnapur, Kālāhandi and Baster, to the internal organisation of the kingdom. But in the 19th century its real significance was forgotten while the memory of the confederacy of states survived, with the result that the term *Aṭhārāgarh* was misapplied. The title being an old one and its origin obscured by the gradual obliteration of the local system, it was easy enough to extend its significance so as to convey the idea that Sambalpur, for many ages, stood at the head of a large confederacy of adjoining states."

I am not going here to discuss Mr. Wills' investigation into the correct meaning of the term Aṭhārāgarh. What I wish to say is that the poet Prahlād Dube never meant by the term Aṭhārāgarh the 18 forts (or sub-divisions) within Sambalpur itself but by it he did mean the 17 adjoining states outside Sambalpur proper. The following quotations from the poem of Prahlād Dube will speak for themselves:

(1) सत्तह गढ़देसौ उमराव। तालगही मन दुंदज दाव॥
जब्बर बने अकब्बर राय। ताते यह बहुदूर तकाय॥

The local lords of the 17 forts adopted a dual policy. Akbar had grown very powerful and so all these people doubted the success of Jait Singh in regaining the throne.

(२) गढ सत्तहों उमराव ये। गहि रह्यो दून्दज दाव ये॥

If Sambalpur proper had 18 local and internal forts, why did the poet not mention it as such? By the use of the term गढ सत्तहों he did mean the adjoining states like Raigarh, Bargarh, Sakti, Sonepur, Phuljhar, etc. which were known by the general name Aṭhārāgarh although their number was not always 18 as in the reign of Balaram Deva, the 1st Mahārajā of Sambalpur.

(३) मँगी सूखपालै सोउको पठाये। तऊना दिरिब्रसिंह राजा सिधाये॥
पुनर भूप होना अविश्वास लागे। दबे सत्तहों दुर्ग देवान आगे॥

Again : The lord or Rāja of Raigarh, Drib Singh, wanted to have a palanqnin for his conveyance. It was duly sent, yet he did not come to Sarangarh. He was not sanguine of the success of Jait Singh and was afraid of Akbar Rai. All the 17 forts (leaving aside Sarangarh which was the 18th) were subdued before or were afraid of the Dewan Akbar Rai.

(४) अभयसिंह सुरपुर गए भैभय नर-पुर माइ।
कोस विलासै डगमगो बिन वैठे नरनाइ॥
बिनवैठे नरनाइ तखत शोभा नहिं पावै।
अष्टादश गढ़ दण्डपाट पन्द्रह अकुलावै॥

Abhaya Singh went to heaven (died). The people and city were under fear. The country of 120 kos (the Sambalpur Raj) began to tremble. In the absence of a king the throne was empty and was devoid of its beauty. All the 18 forts and 15 Dandpats felt uneasy.

(५) अकबर गर्ब दुहै रखो "गढ़ सतह" मम हाथ।
का मो पै अब करि सकै एक साह विसनाथ॥

Akbar Dewan took pride in the fact "the 17 forts are under my thumb. What care I for one man (lord of a single fort, Sarangarh), Sai Vishwanath; He can do me nothing."

Only this single *'dōhā'* is enough to prove the hollowness of Mr. Will's theory.

Prahlād Dube composed his poem "Jaya Candrikā" so late as 1783 A.C. It is quite possible that he would have based his poem upon earlier works both Vernacular and Sanskrit and other authentic records then available in the court of the Cauhān Rajas. We hear of a Sanskrit work named *Kośalānanda Kāvya,* composed by one Pandit Gangādhar Misra. A reference to this work is made in the "Gazetteer of the Orissa Feudatory States." It says (Page 285): –

"It appears from the Kośalānand, a local work on the history of the Patna Raj-family, that Baijal Deo, the 3rd chief from Ramai Deo was the most powerful chief, and extended his dominions far and wide. He fought with Ram Candra and Mahaling Gajpatis of Orissa for six years. Bamra was reduced to an annual tribute of 16 elephants, Gangpur, Bonai and other neighbouring states submitted without a fight, and Baud and Sirguza also submitted. It is said seventy-two chiefs were made tributary to Patna by Baijal Deo I. Dhenkanal was also subdued and the temple of the golden Mahadeo at Sonepur was built by him."

Unfortunately this local work "*Kośalānanda*" is now untraceable. If this work still exists and could be brought to light, the authenticity of the above statement could be tested.[2]

In 1924 I happened to come across a compilation in Oriya called चिकित्सामंजरी It is a treatise on medicine. The author is one Pt. Gopinath Sadangi, the court physician of Raja Chhatra Sai, who flourished in the beginning of the 17th century A.C. This work also mentions *"Aṭhārāgarh, 13 Dandpat."* In course of describing the state of Sambalpur the author speaks about the forts, population of the town etc.

The original lines in Oriya run as follows:

उत्कलदेशे महानदीतीरे सम्बलपुर अभिधा नगरे ॥ १ ॥
जहिं अछानी देवी समलाई सकल अर्थ सेवा कले देइ ॥ २ ॥
श्रीछत्रसाहि जहिं रे राजन क्षत्रियकुल कमल तपन ॥ ३ ॥
अठारागढ तेर दण्डपाट बत्तिस सहस्र बल मुराट ॥ ४ ॥
सीमा अटइ विशाशए कोश उपमा नाहिं जहि अन्य देश ॥ ५ ॥
नगरर नाम सम्बलपुर कोड़िए सहस्र बत्तीस घर ॥ ६ ॥

In the *Utkal* country on the bank of the Mahānadī there is a city named Sambalpur. Goddess *Samlāi* graces the town. She bestows everything upon those who worship and adore her. Like the sun to the lotuses of Kṣatriya family, there lives king Chhatra Sai. There are 18 forts and 13 Dandpats with an army numbering 32000. The boundary is 120 kos. No kingdom can be compared to Sambalpur Raj. In the city of Sambalpur, there are 20032 houses (the population of the city was then about 20032 x 5 = 100160).

I strongly believe that Prahlād Dube derived the materials for his poem not only from traditions but also from works like "Kośalānanda" and "Cikitsāmañjarī" referred to above.

I close the paper with a few official remark upon the "Aṭhāragarh, of Sambalpur.

"The origin of the tenures held by the Sambalpur Garhjat chiefs is not clearly known. The earliest authentic information we have of them is that they were first independent. Then they were held in subordination to the most powerful of their number, the Maharaja of Patnā. In later times the Maharaja of Patnā was forced to share his supremacy among the chiefs with his relative the Maharaja of Sambalpur. And this was the situation when they all fell under the Dominion of the Maharattas in A.C. 1755 as tributaries." (Reprint of Report on the Zamindars and other petty chieftains in C. P. by Richard Temple, p. 8.)

Two of the Garhjats which originally belonged to the Sambalpur and Patnā group, *viz.*, Baud and Authmallick, had previously in 1837 been transferred from the Superintendence of the Ranchi Agents to that of the Cuttack Tributary Mahals, with whom they still remain. Again at the transfer in 1861, two others, Gangpur and Bonai, remained with Chota Nagpur. Thus of the Atharāgarh 14 are within the jurisdiction of the C.P. and of these two, Sambalpur and Chanderpur are no longer managed by chiefs. There remain 12. But one, *viz.*, Baragarh, has been given to the chief of another, *viz.*, Raigarh. Therfore only 11 distinct chieftainship of the Sambalpur and Patnā group remain now attached as chieftainship to C. P. administration. They are: –

1 Patnā, 2 Bindrā Nāwāgarh, 3 Khariyār, 4 Bōrāsamber, 5 Phuljhar, 6 Sarangarh, 7 Sakti, 8 Raigarh cum Bargarh, 9 Bamrā, 10 Rerakhol, 11 Sonepur.

(Report on the Zamindars and other petty chieftains in C.P. by Richard Temple).

From local enquiries I gather that up till quite times several chiefs continued the practice of acknowledging the suzerainty of the Cauhān family of Patna or Samabalpur as their overlord by sending their representatives to *tie Rākhī* (Rakṣā-sūtra) to the Cauhān chiefs and of receiving due presents of cloth and pān (lāṭ-Bīrā) in return. This also shows that the states around and outside Sambalpur proper were once members of the *"Sambalpur Aṭhārāgarh."*

References

1. If according to Mr. Wills, the Sambalpur Raj included within itself 18 sub-divisions called garhs, why did not the poet Prahlād put it as अठारा गढ़ instead of गढ़ सत्रह। The facts is that Prahlād by गढ़सत्रह means the "subordinate 17 adjoining *garhs* (states)." Sarangarh itself, where Jait Singh was ruling, was the 18th.
2. Since writing this, I saw a palm leaf manuscript of "Kōśalānand" in Oriya characters with one Pandit Gopinath Panigrahi of Sonepur Raj. It was partly damaged.

51

The Ancient Tamils and the Nagas

C. S. Srinivasachari

The Geography of the Tamil Land

Tamilakam, the homeland of the Tamils, is regarded to have extended in olden days, east to west from sea to sea, and north to south from the hills of sacred Tirupati to Cape Comorin; but the tradition was that in still earlier times the land had extended further south which was swallowed up by a violent irruption of the sea. This region was called, in the *Periplus, Mares Erythræa* and by Ptolemy the Geographer as Limirike; and it was known as Damirike in the Peutinger Tables. These limits of the Tamil land were first given by Tolkāppiyar, an ancient grammarian, probably of the 4th century B.C.; and by Iḷangovadigaḷ, the reputed author of the *Chilappathikāram* (The Epic of the Anklet) and also by Sikandiyar, the author of a treatise on music.[1] The people of the west coast gradually differentiated themselves from the rest and developed a distinct language of their own – *Malayāḷam,* "a patois of Kodun- Tamil and Prākṛtic Sanskrit." But the Tamils made up for this loss in more directions than one, by colonising Northern Ceylon and more distant regions across the Bay of Bengal.

Racial elements in the population

Ancient Tamil grammarians classified men into three divisions, *Makkaḷ, Devar* and *Narakar* or *Nāgar*–which pointed to the existence of three types or races of people in the Tamil country, *viz.* the Tamils proper, the Aryan immigrants mostly Brahmins and the aboriginal Nāgas. The term *Nāgar* or *Nāga* seems to have been used in a rather broad sense. It was, according to one writer, applied to "all the aborigines, who used to inhabit the forests, the low regions and other unknown realms." There were Nagās in Northern India as well as in Southern India. The Nāgas of the south were supposed to be the original inhabitants of the land, to have preserved their racial individuality for a long time and to have supplied from their stock many of the ruling families of early times.

Nagas and Tamils connected in literary tradition

The earliest Pallava epigraphs give accounts of the connection of the Pallavas with a Nāga princess. The Velūrpaḷaiyam copper-plates, described in the Madras Epigraphist's Report for 1910-11, speak of Vīrakūrca, one of the early Pallava kings who preceded Siṃhaviṣṇu as "having acquired all the emblems of royalty on marrying the daughter of the Lord of Serpents—evidently a Nāga princess."[2] Tamil literary tradition makes prominent mention of the early Chola king, Kiḷḷi Vaḷavan who married Peelivaḷai, the daughter of the ruler of Nāganādu and of the son of this union[3] who was afterwards the ruler of the Tondaimaṇḍalam country about Kāñcīpuram (Conjeevaram). Apart from these examples of inter-marriage between Nāga ruling dynasties and later families that became prominent, we have instances which occur in Tamil literature and which bring out an amount of information of various importance about these so-called Nāgas.[4]

Theories as to the origin of the Nāgas

As already told there were Nāgas in Northern India also. Captain Forbes wrote in his book,[5] years ago, that when the Aryans settled in India they came in contact with two races, the Asuras, Rākṣasas, etc., who were savage; and the other, a people who lived in cities, and possessed wealth and who were known as Nāgas belonging to the "great Takṣak or serpent-race of Scythia." The Nāgas were according to this writer driven back by the advancing Aryans, " "carrying before them in their turn the feeble and scattered remnants of the black aboriginal race who were either exterminated or found a last refuge in the most inaccessible forests and mountains."[6] According to another opinion the Nāgas were a Tibeto-Burman race who were driven by some racial disturbances and movements from Central Asia to India through the passes on the north-east by way of Burma and the passes of Assam and the Lower Himalayas.

Filiation of the Nāgas of the South

Anyhow the peoples known by the name of Nāgas were a prominent non-Aryan race, most probably of Mongoloid descent, who were already settled in the northern parts of India, and later, either owing to Aryan migration or as a result of the operation of other causes, forced to expand into the Deccan, South India and Ceylon. How far the Nāgas of the South might have been of this race or different, is a matter difficult to settle and is discussed later.

Present-day relics of the Nāga element

We have got in the Rāmāyaṇa and in the Mahābhārata numerous references to Nāga towns and kings. In the Tamil country the Nāga name is preserved in places like Nagore, Nagappattinam (Negapatam) Nagerkoil, Nagalapuram, etc, as the names of sects or *gotras* among various classes in the Ganjam and Vizagapatam Districts, like the Dombs, the Bottadas, the Gadabas, the Porojas, etc. and as well as among the Kurnis and the Turiyands. Nāga is the name of a subdivision of the Gazula Kapus and the Koppala Velamas.[7] Rulers of the Nāgavaṃśa were numerous in the Deccan and around Nagpur; and they intermarried with the Sātavāhanas and the Pallavas. "Kings of the Nāgavaṃśa with the tiger-crest and the snake-banner were ruling at Cakrakūṭa and at Bhogavatī in the Bastar State in the Central Provinces even after the eleventh century A.D. Several of their inscriptions have been found and published."[8] The name Nāga may be pre-Aryan as applied to several tribes which were afterwards known by that appellation.

The Nāgas and their connection with serpents

The origin of the title cannot in all cases be traced to serpents or serpent-worship; for there were some tribes known by that name before the advent of the Aryans in whose language alone the word signifies serpents. But many of the Nāgas known to us were certainly serpent-worshippers. The head-covering of some of them was in the shape of the hood of the three-headed, five-headed, or seven-headed cobras. Among the sculptures of the Stūpas of Amarāvatī and Jaggayyapeta are figures of Nāga kings distinguished by the sheltering hood of a five or seven headed serpent at their back; while the figures of Nāgar pincesses were marked by a three-headed serpent; and those of ordinary Nāgas by a single-headed serpent.[9] "The artists who executed these sculptures with considerable labour and care seem to have imagined that the Nāgas partook of the nature of serpents and that their bodies were partly human and partly serpentine."[10] The sculptures and paintings found in the ancient Buddhist ruins of Ceylon representing the Nāgas as Dvārapālas etc. also exhibit the same features. Mr. Kanakasabhai Pillai, the talented Tamil scholar and author of *The Tamils 1800 Years Ago*, says that the Villavar and the Mīnavar (Bowmen and Fishermen) were the aborigines of South India being evidently part of a primitive race which was spread over the whole of India—tribes of the Bhīls and the Mīnas being still found in large numbers in Rajputana and parts of the Gujarat and the Canarese country.

Whether the Nāgas of the South were civilised or primitive

These barbarous primitive folk were conquered by the Nāgas, an immigrant race who were skilled in many arts and weaving in particular; and it was from them that the Aryans learnt the art of writing; and "hence Sanskrit characters are to this day known as Devanāgarī" (p.

45). These bold statements cannot hold good under a close examination. There is no caste or tribe in the Tamil country, bearing the names of Bhīls or Mīnas. The ethnic and other affinities of these races with the Tamils are not known and cannot be postulated with any approach to certainty. We know that many of the Nāgas known to Tamil literature were barbarous and not civilised at all. There are refernces to some of the Nāgas being even naked cannibals.[11] Nāga was the title assumed by a Veda (hunter) chieftain and also it was applied to of the father of the famous Śaiva saint, Kannappa Nāyanār. Nāga is a name familiar among the tribes of the Kallars and the Vettuvars. The Nāganādu as described in ancient Tamil books was a vast island situated to the east or the south-east of the Tamil country; the inhabitants of this region were regarded as half barbarous speaking a language not understood by the Tamil people. Hence it is not easy to accept the statement that all the Nagas were highly civilised. The theory that the Nāgarī alphabet was derived from the aboriginal Nāgas by the Aryans may be dismissed—the word Nāgarī being derived from *nagara* (a city) and the Devanāgarī being the alphabet used by the city-flok, according to Bühler and other eminent authorities.[12]

Srinivasa Iyengar on the Nāgas of the South

According to Srinivasa Iyengar, the name Nāga was given by the Aryans to any aboriginal tribe in South India and Ceylon. The Nāgas of South India were apparently distinct from those of North India. The former were aborigines while the North Indian Nāgas were descendants of "Turanian or Scythian immigrants from Central Asia belonging probably to the Mongolian race" (p. 29). He would conclude that the population of the Tamil contained three distinct elements, the Nāgas, the Dravidian Tamils and the Aryans; and the non-Aryan Tamils belong to the great Nāga-Dravidian race. The Nāgas had both a savage and a civilised element, the savage tribes having Negrito blood in them, and the latter being mixed (p. 377). "Apparently both the divisions of the Nāgas migrated to India when it was connected by land with Australia, the earlier tribes being driven to the interior hills and forests; and the later immigrants occupying the east coast from Cape Comorin to Vizagapatam and as far as Nagpur in the Central Provinces. These were the Vānaras and the Rākṣasas of Rāmāyaṇa. It is by no means easy when these races invaded India."(p. 377). Then followed the Dravidian Tamils probably from Western Asia migrating by the north-western passes long before the Aryans; and the Tamil tribes, particularly the Cholas and the Pandyas, had often to contend with the half-civilised Nāgas; while "the Cheras seem to have quietly taken possession of the country along the west coast almost uninhabited by any semicivilised section of the Nāga race."

Their fusion with the Dravidian Tamils

"In the east the close connection of the Nāgas and the Dravidians led to a fusion of races. In the west that could not have happened at so early a period. And I am inclined to think that the Nayars of Malabar and Travancore are not the modern representatives of the ancient Nāgas, but hybrid descendants of the original Nāga-Dravidians and the Aryans." This theory of Srinivasa Iyengar looks too complete, detailed and coherent to be all true; but some elements of it have been known or proved to be true. Thus the uncivilised Nāga element may be the Negroid pre-Dravidian element driven to the hills and submerged in the plains by the invading Dravidians, according to ethnologists like De Quatrefages, Topinard, Flower, Lydekker, etc. who speak of the Negrito element in the races of South India, especially noticeable in the aboriginal tribes.

The Negroid element in the Nāga

This Negroid element was probably of Lemurian origin, presupposing the existence of a Lemurian continent connecting Malaysia with Africa. The whole problem depends upon the exact scope which is given ethnologically to the terms pre-Dravidian and Dravidian and the ascertaining of the extent to which the Dravidians have absorbed and supplanted the pre-Dravidians.

The Nāga tribes in the Tamil land

There were several tribes of the Nāgas in the Tamil country described in literature like the Maravar, the Eyinar, the Oliyar, the Oviyar, the Aruvāḷar and the Parathavar. The Maravar as described in Kalithokai[13] were "of strong limbs and hardy frames, and fierce-looking as tigers, having long and curled locks of hair, and armed with the bow; bound with leather, ever ready to injure others, shooting their arrows at poor helpless travellers from whom they could rob nothing, only to feast their eyes on the quivering limbs of their victims."[14] The tribe was most numerous on the east coast between the Kaveri and the Vaigai rivers and was noted for its valour and bravery in fighting.

The Maravar

The Maravar were frequently recruited as soldiers into the armies of the Chola, Pandya and Pallava kings. In the *Purananūru*[15] we are given examples of Marava chieftains like Nalaikkiḷavanāgan who served the Chera and Pandya rulers as soldiers and ministers.

The Eyinar etc

The Eyinar and the Vedar (or Vettuvar) were "the most lawless of the Nāga stock." Raids of plunder and cattle-lifting were their chief occupation. One of the Eyinar chiefs, Dhirataran Murthi Eyinar, who was the chief of Viramangalam is referred to in the plates of Jatilavarman, a Pandyan ruler of the 12th century A.D.[16] Their descendants are now known as the Kallars and even now display traits of their old character.

The Oliyar

The Oliyar were another Nāga tribe who were conquered by Karikala Chola. A Mahabalipuram (Māmallapuram) inscription of the eleventh century A.D., being a copy of the conveyance, conveying a piece of land to the Varāhasvamī Temple at that place and issued in the 9th year of Rājendra Deva[17] (1050- 1062) mentions chieftains of the Oil Nāgas like Muvenda Velan, Chandrasekharan and Narayanan and also a Sanga Nagan and a Muguli Nagan.

The Oviyar: Were they of North Ceylon?

The Oviyar as described in the *Sirupāṇaṟṟuppadai*[18] one of the ten idylls of the Sangham were a tribe of Nāgas inhabiting the sea-coast; and their lord was one of several kings ruling Mavilangai (Great and Ancient Laṅkā). Their royal town of Āmūr was well-fortified and surrounded by a broad moat; and its approach was guarded by another fortified town on the sea-coast which is called by the commentator Eyilpattinam as well as by another fortress town called Velur.[19]

The Nāgas of Mantain

Mr. Rasanayakam, the talented author of the *History of Ancient Jaffna,* would identify these places with definite sites in the Jaffna country and particularly the town of Eyilpattinam with Māntai (Matota of the Sinhalese) which was a town of great antiquity and full of cunning artisans. He says,—"It is said that Viśvakarmā built an iron-fort at Mantai . . . The Nāgas of Māntai (Mātota) whose strong-hold was on the great highway of the merchant vessels which had to cross over to the Bay of Bengal from the Arabian Sea and vice versa developed into sea-pirates and lived by plundering and robbing unwary merchants."[20] He would identify this Nāga fortress with the Rākṣasa port into which mariners were inveigled by attractive women and plundered, according to Hiuen Tsiang and with the magnetic mountain of the mediæval Muhammadan writers which drew towards it all the iron-clad ships of the neighbourhood and wrecked them. The iron-fort at Māntai was euphemistically called in Tamil works as a magnetic mountain and was possibly the source of the belief which is so graphically described in the Arabian Nights. Sir Emerson Tennent in his *Ceylon* also mentions a writer of the 4th century B.C. who wrote of the loadstone attracting iron vessels among the group of islands called Maniolae (Maṇalūr and the dependent islands of the Jaffna Sea). Mr. Rasanayakam would say that Māntai was evidently conquered and destroyed by the Chola king Karikala; and since the Chola conquered Ceylon or at least the north-western portion of it called Taprobane (or Tāmra-parṇī) the Chola king came to be known as Chembian (Chembu=Tāmra); and no Chola earlier than Karikala was known by this title. Mr. Rasanayakam also attempts to prove that Māntai, known in Tamil literature as the Māntai of the Cheras (Kuttuvan Mantai) was probably conquered by the Chera Chenguttuvan of the *Chilappathikāram* fame from which time it must have come to be known as Kuttuvan Māntai.

They of Māvilangai

Malanka (Māvilangai) is thus identified by Mr. Rasanayakam with North-western Ceylon and associated with Nalliyakkodan, the hero-king of Āmūr, Eyilpattinam and Velur. Dr. S. Krishnaswami Aiyangar would say[21] that Māvilangai is not a country as was asserted by Mr. V. Kanakasabhai Pillai, but a town and most probably the port of Mamallapuram (in the vicinity of Madras). He would also say that the period of Nalliyakkodan is intermediate between that of Tondaiman Iḷandiraiyan of Kāñcī and that of Viṣṇugopa of Kāñcī who was defeated by the famous Samudra Gupta. In this conflict of views it is not possible for us to be sure of the kingdom of the Oviyar and of Nalliyakkodan. To strengthen his view of Nelliyakkodan being a Nāga king of North Ceylon, Mr. Rasanayakam brings in the evidence of a poet Nannāganar, who was evidently of the Nāga race and who sang of Nalliyakkodan and his Villi Ātan as kings of Malanka and Lanka respectively.[22] Besides the Nāga kings of Āmūr and Eyilpattinam, other Nāgas were supposed to have reigned at Kudirai Malai[23] on the west coast of Ceylon. Mr. Rasanayakam says that this place could not have been in the Western Ghats as asserted by some, and that it might be the Hippuros of the Greek travellers.

The Nāgas in North and West Ceylon

The Nāgas appear to have been confined originally to the western and northern part of Ceylon which was for many centuries known as *Nāgadīpa,*[24] while the Yakkhas who were apparently more numerous and powerful than the Nāgas inhabited the other portions of the island. It is clear that these were in some respects as civilised as the Nāgas and some of the Yakkha kings found their wives from among the Nāgas. Both the Nāgas and the Yakkhas gradually lost importance after the Aryan invasion and settlement of the land and in course of time, "lost their identity as they lost their power, and forming alliances with the new settlers, were thenceforth styled and known as *Sinhalese*".[25]

The Nāga kingdom in Nāgadvīpa

There was, according to Mr. Rasanayakam, a Nāga kingdom in North Ceylon continuously from the 6th century B.C. to the middle of the 3rd century A.D.; and even before the 6th century B.C. there was the tradition of the Nāgas ruling in the Island. He would even equate the story of Arjuna's marriage with the Princess Citrāṅgadā, the daughter of Citravāhana, the king of Manipuram, to mean that the Pāṇḍava hero married a Nāga princess of Manipuram (a name which was given at various times to Jaffna) and not a Pandya princess, as has been believed so long; and he would also quote evidence to prove that a portion of the mainland was in the days of the Bhārata War subject to the sway of the Nāga ruler of Manipuram; and that it is wrong to suggest that Citravāhana was a Pandyan.[26]

Coming to the topic of Nāgas, they appear to have risen to great power. The *Mahāvaṃsa*[27] gives us the names of the Nāga rulers of North Ceylon who became masters of the whole Island, like Mahallaka Nāga (*cir.* 135 A.D.), Cula Nāga (*cir.* 193 A.D.), Śrī Nāgas I and II who reigned in the second and part of the third centuries A.D. About this time the Nāgas of the Deccan also rose to great prominence; the Chūtu Nāgas succeeded to the power of the Andhra Sātavāhanas; and the Pallavas, intermarrying with the Chūtus, succeeded to their power in turn.

The Nagas and Buddhistic tradition

According to Buddhistic tradition, Nāga kingdoms flourished in Nāgadīpa (North Ceylon) and in Kelaniya on the west coast of the Island, even in the life-time of the Buddha. The story is given that Gautama Buddha visited Laṅkā on three distinct occasions, in the ninth month and in the fifth and eighth years respectively after he had attained Buddha-hood. On the second of these occasions he paid a visit to Nāgadīpa where Mahodara, the king of Nāgadīpa and Culodara his nephew and ruler of Kannavaddhamāna (Kandamādānam near Rameśvaram) were bitterly fighting for the possession of a gem-set throne, and the rival factions were supported by considerable forces on either side, Maniyakkhika, the ruler of Kelaniya being among them. The Lord Buddha appeared on the scene, settled the dispute and seated himself on the throne and preached to the rivals a sermon of reconciliation, as a result of which large numbers of Nāgas (to the traditional number of 80 crores) were converted to the faith. The jewel-throne sanctified by the Buddha's touch became an object of worship to all Buddhists who visited it from far and near. The Buddha came to the city of Kelaniya on his third visit to Ceylon whence he is said to have proceeded and left the impress of his feet on Samanakūṭa (Adam's Peak).[28]

Tamil confirmation of the tradition

The story of the Buddha's visit to Nāgadvīpa and of the sanctified gem-set throne is narrated in great detail in the Tamil epic *Manimekhalai.*[29] The scene of the episode is named Maṇi-pallavam in the Tamil work, which according to the equation of Mr. Rasanayakam is Jaffna—probably identical with the Nāgadīpa of the *Mahāvaṃsa.* Thus there were numerous Nāga settlements in the north and west of Ceylon on both sides of the Christian Era.

The Nāgas in the Chola region

In the *Chilappathikāram,* we are told that Kaverippattinam, the ancient Chola capital at the mouth of the Kaveri, was in more ancient times, famous as the capital of the Nāgas and the Nāganādu[30] which is also referred to in the sister epic of *Manimekhalai.* Thus the authors had some idea of the ancient Nāgas who preceded the Cholas in the basin of the Kaveri.

The Chola connection with the Nāgas

An early Chola king, Kiḷḷi Vaḷavan had a child by a Nāga princess, which was lost on its way from Manipallavam to the Chola country. This loss so much grieved the Chola king that he neglected to celebrate the annual festival to Indra at his capital; and the angry god punished him for his neglect by causing the sea to inundate and destroy the city. The date of this Chola monarch has been usually ascribed to the 2nd century A.D. Another Chola, Kokiḷḷi, is also said to have married a Nāga princess of North Ceylon and had a son by her of the name of Tondaimāndalan Iḷaṇtiraiyan who afterwords became the ruler of the region of Tondaimāndalan (the country round about Conjeeveram). Some say that Iḷantiraiyan was the son of Kiḷḷi; and he was so called because he was washed ashore by the waves (*tirai*) of the sea. Whether Iḷaṇtiraiyan was the son of Kiḷḷi Vaḷavan or Kokiḷḷi, he was the son of a Nāga princess of Ceylon. Kiḷḷi Vaḷavan, Chenguttuvan Chera and Gajabāhu of Ceylon are supposed to have been contemporaries on this basis of a supposed reference to them in *Chilappathikāram* (canto xxx). "Tondaimān Iḷantiraiyan was the progenitor of the powerful dynasty of the Pallavas.

The Pallavas and the Nāgas

This Nāga origin of the Pallavas is confirmed by the description given in the Velūrpaḷayam Plates[31] that the first member of the family of the Pallavas acquired all the emblems of royalty on marrying the daughter of the Lord of Serpents."[32] Thus the author of *Ancient Jaffna* would say, though it is a moot point whether sovereignty came to the Pallavas from the Chūtu Nāgas of the Deccan or the Nāgas of North Ceylon and whether there was not a hiatus between the time of Tondaimān Iḷaṇtiraiyan and the rise of the Pallavas.

He would then conclude that the dynasty was called Pallava because it derived its name from Manipallavam, the native place of Iḷaṇtiraiyan's Nāga mother. He also accepts that Pallava means a sprout or the end of a tender bough, and would say that "to observers sailing from India the peninsula of Jaffna would have appeared just like a sprout or growth on the mainland of Laṅkā." This is a very fanciful conclusion based on very slender evidence. The writer goes further and says that even in later times when the Pallavas claimed Aryan connections and filiation to the Bhāradvāja Gotra, they still traced their descent from Aśvatthāman through a Nāga Princess.

Submersion of Nāga and Tamil lands under the sea

We have also got the story of Tissa Rāja of Kelaniya witnessing the irruption of the sea swallowing up eleven-twelfths of his territory, including a large number of towns and fishing villages. It was perhaps at this period that the submersion of the 49 Tamil lands including the hill and the river Kumari took place as mentioned in Chilappathikāram.[33] "The river Pahruli and the mountain Kumari were submerged by the raging sea."[34] Nakkīrar's commentary on the *Ahapporuḷ* of Iraiyanār and the preface of Ilambūraṇar's Commentary on the *Tolkappiyam* contain similar descriptions of submersion. It was after the destruction of this region and of his capital at Kavādapuram, that the Pandyan king proceeded northwards and established a new kingdom with his capital at Madura. He proceeded higher up, having elbowed away the tiger and the bow (the crests of the Cholas and the Cheras) and planted his famous fish (the Pandyan crest) on strange territory. The submerged portion of Ceylon extended, according to theories as far west as Minicoy and the Maldives, (the Malaya Dvīpa of Indian geographers) where Rāvaṇa's Laṅkāpura was probably situated.

Conclusion

After this deluge Nāgadīpa became much diminished in size, leaving probably only the Jaffna Peninsula and a few adjoining islands; while Nāga importance on the mainland also diminished likewise. The Nāga connections of the Pallavas, and the Nāga character of the Aruvālar tribe living in the heart of the Pallava country show the continuity of Nāga influence on Tamil history. The filiations of Draviḍa Nāgas with those of the North would continue to form a vexed question until more light is thrown on the whole question.[35]

References

1. M. Srinivasa Iyengar, *Tamil Studies,* vol. I, (1914), p. 8.
2. p. 58, para (I) of the Report dated 28th July, 1911.
3. *Manimekhalai* ed. by Mahāmahopādhyāya V. Swaminātha Iyer, 1921, canto xxiv, ll. 54-55 and xxv, ll. 178 et seq.; and *Perumbāṇāṛruppadai* in *Patthuppāltu* ed. by Mm. V. Swaminatha Iyer (1918), p. 152.
4. That this legend is of an early date is proved by its existence in early epigraphic records.While the inscriptions of the Pallavas are unanimous in regarding Aśvatthāman, the son of Droṇa, as the progenitor of their line, they do not agree as to his wife and the name of his son. The wife is called in some inscriptions an *apsaras* and in others a *nīgī* (*vide* also J. Ph. Vogel, *Indian Serpent Lore,* 1927, p. 36).
5. *The Languages of Further India.*
6. As quoted in M. Srinivasa Iyenger's *Tamil Studies,* p. 28.
7. Thurston, *Castes and Tribes of South India,* vol. v, p. 134f.
8. *Epigraphia Indica,* vol. x, p. 25; and C. Rasanayakam's *History of Jaffna,* p. 6 (Madras, 1927).
9. V. Kanakasabhai Pillai, *The Tamils 1800 years Ago,* p. 40.
10. *Ibid.,* p. 40.
11. "The mountain inhabited by the naked nomads and Nāgas", *Manimekhalai,* canto xvi, 1 15.
12. M. Srinivasa Iyengar, *Tamil Studies,* p. 29f.
13. Edition of E. V. Anantarama Iyer (1925), vol. I, Palai c. iv, ll. 1-5; c. xv, ll. 1-2, pp. 29, 93.
14. Kanakasabai Pillai's translation as given in pp. 42 of his *Tamils 1800 years Ago.*
15. Edition of V. Swaminatha Iyer, stanzas 168, 179, pp. 269, 287.
16. Kanakasabhai Pillai, *op. cit.,* p. 43 and *The Indian Antiquary,* vol. xxii, p. 57.
17. No. 54 of 1890—dated in the 9th year of the king.
18. Edition of the *Patthuppāttu* (ten idylls) by V. Swaminatha Iyer (1918), p. 98, ll. 116-121.
19. *Ibid.,* ll. 151-153; notes on these lines—p. 117; also notes on ll. 171-173.
20. pp. 16-17.
21. Article on Mahabalipuram in the *Indian Antiquary,* vol. xlvi, p. 72.
22. *Ancient Jaffna,* pp. 24 and note *Puranānūru,* stanzas 176, 379.
23. General of the chieftains of Kudirai Malai like Eḷini and Koṛṛan are referred to in *Puranānūru,* stanzas 158, 168.
24. J. M. Senaveratna *The Story of the Sinhalese,* 1923, vol. I, p. 2.

25. Senaveratna, vol. I, p. 3.
26. *Ancient Jaffna,* pp. 33-44
27. List of kings, pt. I and ch. xxxvi.
28. Mahāvaṃsa I, *Rajavaliya,* a narrative of Sinhalese kings from Vijaya to Vimala Dharma Sūrya II. tr. by B. Gunasekhara, Mudaliyar (Colombo, 1900).
29. Ed. by V. Swaminatha Iyer, canto viii, ll. 43-63.
30. Ed. by V. Swaminatha Iyer, canto I, ll, 19,20.
31. Madras Epigraphist's Report for 1910-11, p. 59.
32. *Ancient Jaffna,* pp. 30-31.
33. Canto xi. ll. 18-20.
34. *Ibid.*, canto viii. commentary of Adiyārkunāilar on ll. 1, 2.
35. Vogel's *Indian Serpent Lore* recently published throws some light on the traditions existing about the Nāgas.

52

Hūṇs, Yavanas and Kāmbojas

S. B. Chaudhuri

The Hūṇas of Sanskrit texts plausibly stand for the famous Hūṇs of Central Asia, a fierce nomadic tribe who were known to the Chinese as Hiung-nu. The pillages and devastations committed by them caused wide-spread havoc in the early centuries of the Christian era. The very frequent references to the Hūṇs in the Epic and the Purāṇas indicate that they were quite familiar to Indian writers. The *Lalita-vistara* mentions also a Hūṇa-lipi.[1]

Towards the middle of the 5th century A.D. the Hūṇs, as M. Chavannes writes acquired great power in the basin of the Oxus[2]. A Hūṇ settlement on the Oxus was also known to Kālidāsa, a contemporary of Candragupta II (380-412 A.D.) Vikramāditya, for he places the Hūṇas on the banks of the Vaṅkṣu, the Oxus in Bactria[3]. Their first incursion into India was repulsed by Skandagupta (455-467 A.D.) as recorded in the emperor's Bhitarī inscription[4]. By the time of Varāhamihara (d. 587 A.D.) the Hūṇ settlement in India was fairly well recognised. They appear in the list of northern tribes furnished by the *Bṛhatsaṁhitā,* and the grouping and the context suggests that they were living near the Kulu Valley. The valley of the Upper-Sutlej adjacent to Tibet which was called Hundes, might have been the home of this tribe or a branch of them[5]. But in the early part of the sixth century A.D. the Hūṇs were also living in the traṇs-Indus region, as in the Christian topography of Cosmas Indikopleustes (c. 525 and 535 A.D.) it is expressly stated as follows: "The river Phīson (Indus) divides India from the country of the Huṇs".[6] Indian writers of the seventh century, however, associate the Hūṇs with the Punjab region. In the *Bārhaspatya Arthaśāstra,* a work not earlier than the 6th or 7th century A.D. the Hūṇ country is mentioned in conjunction with Kāśmīra. Bāṇa, the author of *Harṣacarita,* also refers to a Hūṇ principality of Uttarāpatha[7].

In the first half of the sixth century A.D. the Hūṇs enjoyed political power for a short period. Dr. D.C. Sircar thinks that the Eran inscription of the time of Bhānu Gupta (G. E. 191=510 A.D.) contains an allusion to the struggle between the Guptas and the Hūṇs in Central India[8]. This is supported by the evidence furnished by the Eran inscription of Toramāṇa (c. 500-515 A.D.)[9] which show that the Sāgar (Saugor) districts and presumably other northern region of the Central Provinces were under the rule of the Hūṇ Chie Toramāṇa. Toramāṇa had greatly raised the status of the Hūṇs. He struck 'solar type' coins in Brāhmī script which come mostly from Rajputana,[10] and he may have extended his rule even over a portion of the Punjab[11]. Toramāṇa was succeeded by his son Mihirakula (c. 515-535 A.D.)[12] who further enlarged the Indian dominions of his father. Mihirakula had his capital at Sialkot in the Punjab[13] and ruled over an extensive empire which stretched from the Himalayas.[14] But he was defeated by Yaśodharman, king of Malwa[15], and finally crushed, as seems very likely by the Gupta king Narasiṁha-Gupta Bālāditya[16].

Even after their defeat at the hands of Yaśodharman the Hūṇs maintained their hold over small principalities in the different parts of India where they ruled as local chiefs. Princes of Hūṇ tribe and Hūṇ royal houses are mentioned in the records of the Pratihāras, Paramāras, Cāhamanas, Cālukyas (Guzerat) and Pālas. Epigraphic sources indicate that at a later time the Hūṇ chiefs became the paramount lords of the whole country extending from near the Kota border to the precints of Bundi".[17] Some Paramāra records frōm Ujjaini[18] refer to Āvaraka-Bhoga (the country round the town of Agar north-east of Ujjain) and Hūṇamaṇḍala which proves the existence of a Hūṇ country in the mediaeval period in the very heart of Malwa. Hūṇ territories of this region later on passed under the possession of the Rajputs, and the Hūṇs similarly came to be known as one of the 36 Rajput clans.

The Hūṇs were later on absorbed into Hindu society and improved their social position. The Hūṇ Mihirakula was a devotee of Śiva[19]. Other records show that Hūṇ kings ranked with Indian Sovereigns and Hūṇ princesses married into the famous royal families. A Jaina work of the 12th century A.D. refers to a rājā of Hūṇadeśa who attended a *Svayaṃvara Sabhā* and sought the hand of a princess.[20] The Jubbalpur plates of Jayasiṁhadeva (1167 A.D.) records that the Kalacuri king Karṇa married a Hūṇ lady Āvallā devī by name.[21] The commentator of the *Raghuvaṁśa* (IV. 67-68) even calls them Kṣatriyas. Pargiter says "They appear to have been of light complexion, for their women are pictured as having made their cheeks pale red by beating them in grief".[22]

Mention of the mixed hordes of the Śakas, Yavanas and Kāmbojas occur very frequently in the *Mahābhārata*.[23] In Aśoka's edict[24] the

Yavanas are mentioned as Yoṇas in conjunction with the Gāndhāras and Kāmbojas as tribes living outside his territories whom he calls his 'borders'. There can be little doubt that by this name the Greeks were intended, who might have formed a small state on the north-west frontier[25] in a territory adjoining Gāndhāra but outside India[26]. Rapson was of opinion that these border tribes were not the subjects of Asoka, but Dr. Ray Chaudhury points out that they were included within the Rāja-viṣaya or the king's territory and that the real border peoples were the 'Greeks of the realm of Antiochos'.[27] Both in R.E. XIII and II Aśoka refers to the Yona king Antiyoka[28] who was a Greek prince. Aśoka's governor Tuṣāspha was a Yavana-rāja, a Greek prince, which indicates that potentates of these border tribes existed in his empire as feudatory chieftains. Very soon after the death of Aśoka the Yavanas emerged into importance in the political history of North-western India. The decline of the Maurya power was followed by a Yavana raid in Madhya-deśa. A passage referring to this in the Yuga Purāṇa section of the *Gārgīsaṁhitā* which runs thus: – "Then the viciously valiant Yavanas after reducing Sāketa, Pañcāla, Mathurā, will reach Kusumadhvaja . . .".[29] Demetrios the 'Indo-Greek contemporary of Puṣyamitra' (c. 187 to 151 B.C.) is perhaps mentioned in the Hāthīgumphā inscription (c. 1st century B.C.) of Khāravela as Yavana rāj(a) D(i)mi(ta)[30]. The Yavana invasion of India referred to in Patañjalis *Mahābhāṣya* who lived towards the middle of the second century B.C.; and also in the *Mālavikāgnimitra,* was obviously a Greek invasion in the time of Puṣyamitra, of either Demetrios or Menander.[31] Menander is identified with the king Milinda of Sagal (Śākala) mentioned in the *Milindapañha,* as a Yavana-rāja. But the Yavanas as a political power ceased to exist by the beginning of the second century A.D. We learn from the Nasik record of Queen Gautamī Balaśrī that her son Siri-Śātakani Gotamīputa destroyed the Yavanas, and also the Sakas and Pahlavas[32]. From some ancient texts we get a glimpse of the horror of Yavana raids. The passage of the *Gārgī-Saṁhitā* quoted above says that "all provinces will be disorder assuredly." In the Purāṇas it is stated that the Yavana king will follow evil customs and that massacring of women and children and killing of one another will be the normal feature of their life.[33] From the *Śukranīti* we learn that the Yavanas had all the four castes mixed together, did not recognise the authority of the Vedas and lived in the north and west[34]. The *Harivaṁśa* notes that the Yavanas shaved the whole of their heads[35]. The *Mahābhārata* records that they were very expert in shooting arrows : *Śaravānāsanadharā Yavanāśca prahāriṇaḥ*[36].

But the word Yavana does not merely refer to the Greeks and according to Otto Stein Yavana of early Indian inscriptions does not indicate Greek nationality.[37] D.R. Bhandarkar says that in early times Yavana always denoted the Greeks, but from the 2nd century A.D. onward it may have meant the Persians[38]. Another writer thinks that the word Yavana denoted the Arab traders, the Romans and Jews[39]. In later records Yavana stood for the Muhammadans. For instance, Viśvarūpasena is described as *'Garga Yavanānvaya-pralaya-kāla-rudra-nṛpaḥ,* in his Madanapara Grant[40]. The Yavana enemy who was defeated by Anaṅgabhima III (c. 1211 to 1238 A.D. of the Gaṅga dynasty of Orissa[41] was a Muhammadan invader. Other epigraphic references bear out that the Muhammadans were called Yavanas in the mediaeval period.

It has been seen that in Aśoka's edict the Yonas are grouped with the Kāmbojas. The *Rāmāyaṇa* combines them in a single appellation : *Kāmbojayavanāṁścaiva*[42]. In other passages of the *Mahābhārata* the Yavanas and the Kāmbojas having ordinarily as their companions, the Śakas are most often coupled together[43]. These allusions indicate that the Kāmbojas were mainly a northern or north-western race. The *Mahābhārata* also places them in Uttarāpatha along with Yavana and Gandhāra[44].

But unlike the Yavanas the Kāmbojas were an ancient people known to the Vedic texts. In early times the Kāmboja country was a seat of Brāhmaṇical culture[45]. Buddhism incorporated Kāmboja in the classical list of sixteen kingdoms, like Gandhāra, and the people are copiously referred to in other Pāli texts.[46] Kāmboja is also mentioned in Pāṇini's Sūtra, IV. 1.175. From the *Mahābhārata* we learn that they had a monarchical form of Government[47] and occupied a prominent position among the fighting powers of the Kurukṣetra War. The country of the Kāmbojas was known to the *Rāmāyaṇa* as Kāmbojaviṣaya[48]. In the time of Kauṭilya the Kāmbojas who had been organised into a corporation of warriors (Kṣatriyaśreṇī) lived by agriculture and trade[49] and were apparently living under a *Saṁgha* form of government. But is difficult to reconcile the different conflicting accounts regarding them. The people whose activities were conducted much in the same way like other Aryan tribes, as is clear from the notices made above, were again noticed with derision and contempt and treated as though they were degraded members of the Aryan stock if not altogether alien in race. The legend told in the *Rāmāyaṇa* about the origin of the Śakas, Kāmbojas etc., from the tail of a cow by Vaśiṣṭha is absurd but it is indicative of the contempt in which they were generally held. Dr. B.C. Law draws our attention to a statement of Pāṇini which speaks of the Kāmbojas as Muṇḍā or shavenheaded[50]. Strangely enough the *Harivaṁśa* has a reference to this; the legend runs that the Kāmbojas were compelled to shave the whole of their head like the Yavanas[51]. In the *Mahābhārata* they are even called Mlecchas and are said to have evil customs[52]. This is also supported by the evidence of a Jātaka story where the non-Aryan customs of a Kāmboja horde are hinted[53]. Like other Punjab races the Kāmbojas are stigmatised by Manu who says that they were Kṣatriyas originally, but became degraded through the extinction of sacred rites[54]. A passage states that they were valiant fighters : *Kāmbojā yuddha durmmadāḥ*[55]. The geographical location of this tribe has not been satisfactorily settled[56]. Zimmer on the authority of a passage in the *Vaṁśa Brāhmaṇa,* conjectures that the Kāmbojas and Madras lived not far distant in space.[57] The latter, presumably the Uttara-Madras, lived in the time of the *Aitareya Brāhmaṇa* beyond the Himalaya. The passage of the *Mahābhārata* which gives a clue to the home of the people runs thus: "*Karṇa Rājapuraṁ gatvā Kāmbojānirjitāstvayā Girivrajagatyāścapi*[58]. Rājapura has been identified with Rajaori to the south Kasmir and south-east of Punch[59], the Ho-lo-she-pu-lo of Hiuen Tsang[60]. Dr. Ray Chaudhuri says that the association of the Kāmbojas with the Gandhāras helps to establish this identity. No doubt this condition is satisfactorily accommodated in this location, but what about their association with the Yavanas which is too frequently noticed to be ignored? Dr. Ray Chaudhuri says that Hiuen Tsang's account of Rājapura and the neighbouring countries agree wonderfully with the Kāmbojas. This is hardly a convincing evidence, for tribes with 'rude violent dispositions' and of 'fierce and passionate temper', are frequently found in the pilgrim's account of trans-Hindukush regions (see the descriptions of Hamatala, Badakshan etc.). The inhabitants of these regions were the people who did not "properly belong to India" and were really 'frontier people.' Dr. Ray Chaudhuri's contention that on the west, Kāmboja must have reached out as far as Kāfiristan, is again opposed to all known facts about the geography and ethnography of this region. The cis-Indus and trans-Indus Valleys between Kasmir and Kafiristan was the home of many peoples such as the Darvas, Abhisīras, Uraśas, Kuhakas, Arimarddanas and Aśmakas. It is of course true that the same country very often happen to be the home of more than one tribe, but such a wide extent of the Kāmboja country seems improbable. Dr. Ray Chaudhuri also does not explain Girivraja of the above passage which in the north can only refer to the Kekaya city to the little Rājagṛha, Po-ho or Balkh of Hiuen Tsang's itinerary. Is it to be understood that Karṇa after vanquishing the Kāmbojas in Kashmir marched as far as Balkh, or is it hinted that Rājapura was near about Girivraja, that is, Rājagṛha, the city of Po-ho or Balkh the ancient Bactria?

The Kāmboja country was famous for its horses[61]. Other countries where horses of repute were found in ancient times were Samarkand[62], Tukhāristān[63], Khorāsān[64], Dranga[65], Vālhika[66], Cīna[67], Wakkān[68], Asvaka[69], Gandhāra[70], Vanāyu[71], Baluchistān[72], Sindhu[73], Arbuda[74], and Āraṭṭa[75]. It appears that excepting the last three, all these countries famous for the breed of horses were situated to the west of the Indus. The reference to the horses of the Kāmboja country unmistakably points to its location in the west far beyond the Indus and this is consistent enough with the association of the Kāmbojas and the Yonas, as border tribes of Aśoka's dominion which stretched as far as Peshawar on the west as the Shābazgarhi edict proves.

The Yona territory mentioned in the *Mahāvaṁsa* had its chief city at Alasanda. Geiger identifies Alasanda with the Alexandrian town built near Kabul[76], which according to Cunningham was in or near Opian, 50 miles to the north of Kabul. Very close to Opian, within six miles to the east, lay Begrām and Cunningham identifies it with the Karsana of Ptolemy and Kalasi of the Buddhist chronicles which is also mentioned as Alasanda, the capital of the Yona country[77]. The neighbouring regions of Afghanistan as we have already noted had the reputation for good horses and these features answer some of the requirements of the Kāmboja country. An evidence in favour of this hypothesis is obtained from the *Raghuvaṁśa*. Raghu after vanquishing the Pārasīkas (iv. 60f) marched against the rulers of Udicyadeśa (vs. 66) in course of which he reached the river Sindhu (vs. 67) which is a mistake for Vaṅkṣu, where i.e. in the Oxus Valley (Bactria) he had an encounter with the Hūṇas (vs. 68). The Hūṇs being overrun, Raghu set off towards the kings of the Kāmboja country (vs. 69) who being mowed down offered rich presents including horses (vs. 70) to Raghu. The locality thus indicated by all these notices point to Badakshan to the south-east of Balkh which is situated at the foot of Hindu-Kush on the Oxus basin. Raghu it is stated went up the Himalayas (vs. 71) after he had subdued the Kāmbojas. The Yona country Alasanda it may be noted lay on the other side of the Hindu-Kush.

The Kāmboja country of the North or North-West had, therefore, great reputation for horses. Kāmboja in the Monghyr Grant of Devapāla where his horses roamed about (v. 13) may refer to that country[78]. But the Irdā plate of the Kāmboja king Nayapāladeva[79] which may be placed in the latter part of the tenth century A.D. and the Bāngarh (Dinajpur) pillar inscription of the Kāmbōjā-nvayaja Gauḍapati which is referred to the same century shows that the Kāmbojas occupied a considerable portion of Bengal[80]. A Kāmboja country on the north-eastern frontiers of India is known to have existed[81]. Lüders' Inscriptions Nos. 176 and 472 refer to the gift of a monk Kābōja (Kāmbōja) from Nādinagara (Nāndinagara) at Sāñci Buddhist Stūpa. The monk was a Kāmboja of Nandinagara which might have been a place in the neighbourhood of Sāñci. In the *Agni-purāṇa* Kāmboja and Kāmbhōja are given as names of two places in the South and S.W. division respectively of India[82]. In the *Bārhaspatya Arthaśāstra* Kāmboja is grouped with Daśārṇa as one of the Mahāviṣayas. A branch of the Kāmbojas called Apara-Kāmbojas is also usually noticed.

Abbreviations

The abbreviations used in this paper are the following: –

AS = Arthaśāstra of Kauṭilya, Trans. by Dr. R. Shamasastry.

BR = Buddhist Records of the Western World by S. Beal.

CAGI = Cunningham's Ancient Geography of India, edited by S.N. Majumdar.

CII = Corpus Inscriptionum Indicarum.

CJ = The Jātaka, edited by Cowell.

CL = Carmichael Lectures by Dr. D.R. Bhandarkar.

DD = Geographical Dictionary of Ancient and Mediaeval India by N.L. De.

DHNI = The Dynastic History of Northern India by Dr. H.C. Roy.

DUHB = The History of Bengal, vol. I edited by R. C. Majumdar (Dacca University).

HV = Harivaṁśa.

IG = The Imperial Gazetteer of India, 1908.

MA = Ancient India, by Mc Crindle.

MM = Ancient India as described by Megasthenes and Arrian by Mc Crindle.

MP = The Mārkaṇḍeya Purāṇa, translated by Pargiter.

NHH = Notes on the History of the Himalaya of the N.W.P., India by E.T. Atkinson 1883.

NHIP = A New History of the Indian People, vol. VI, edited by Dr. R.C. Majumdar and Dr. A.S. Altekar.

PH = Political History of Ancient India by Dr. H.C. Roy Chaudhuri.

RT = Kalhana's Rājataraṅgiṇī edited by Stein.

SI = Select Inscriptions bearing on Indian History and Civilization, vol. I, edited by Dr. D.C. Sircar.

TAI = Tribes in Ancient India, by Dr. B.C. Law.

YC = On Yuan Chwang by T. Watters.

References

1. *IA.*, 1913, p. 266.
2. *Document sur less Toukiue occidentaux,* pp. 222-23. Also see Dr. Modi's *Early History of the Hūṇas in JBBRAS.*, XXIV, 562-67.
3. Mallinātha's (14th or 15th century) reading Sindhu is not correct in view of Vallabhadeva's (10th century) and Kṣīrasvāmin's (11th century) comments. See *JDL.*, IV, 107 ff. also K.B. Pathak, *IA.*, 1912, p. 265 ff.
4. *CII.*, III. 56, line 15. For a detailed account of this Hūṇ invasion in India, see *NHIP.*, VI. 193 ff.
5. *NHH.*, ch. II, p. 19.
6. *MA.*, p. 165.
7. Ch. v.
8. *SI.*, p. 336, fn. 9.
9. *Ibid.*, 396-7.
10. *Catalogue of the Coins in the Indian Museum,* Calcutta, vol. I, by V. Smith, pp. 232-33, 235-36.
11. This assumption is based upon the hypothesis that Toramāṇa Shāhi of the Kurā (Salt range, Punjab), inscription is the same as the Hūṇ Emperor Toramāṇa (*SI.*, p. 398, fn. 1 and 4).
12. Dr. R.C. Majumdar writes that there is hardly anything to show that Toramāṇa and Mihirakula were Hūṇs, on the contrary, the *Mandasor Inscription of Yaśodharman,* he says, even implies a distinction between Mihirakula and the Hūṇs. Dr. Majumdar agrees with Stein and Jayaswal in regarding Toramāṇa as a Kusāṇa chief who being allied with the Hūṇs led the Hūṇ hordes (*NHIP,* VI. 195-98).
13. Smith, *Cat. Coins,* I, p. 232; *SI.*, p. 395, fn. 1.
14. Cf. *Mandasor Stone-pillar Inscription of Yaśodharman* (*c.* 525-535 A.D.), vs. 6 (*SI.*, 394).
15. *Ibid.*, vs. 6-7.
16. *NHIP.*, VI. 199-201.
17. *El.*, XXVI. 85. N. L. De says that on account of Hūṇic settlements some place-names of India are found to be counterparts of Asiatic cities (Puṣkara-Bukhara). *IHQ.*, II, 730.
18. *El.*, XXIII. 102; *DUHB.*, p. 118, fn. 2.
19. Cf. *Gwalior Stone Inscription of Mihirakula* (vs. 3-4, *SI.*, 400-1, fn. 3 and p. 395, fn. 1.
20. *IA.*, IV. 113.
21. *El.*, XXI. 93.
22. *MP.*, p. 380.
23. *Mbh* (B)., i, 168. 37; iii. 43. 22; v. 19. 22; vi. 20. 13. The Yavanas were not presumably unknown to India even before Alexander's time. Pāṇini (5th century B.C.) refers to the writing of the Yavanas (*NHH.*, ch. II. p. 44).

Arrian's account of Nysa (which according to Dr. D.R. Bhandarkar was situated between the Kophen and the Indus) points to the existence of a Greek colony on the frontiers of India before the invasion of Alexander. It is also assumed on the basis of numismatic evidence that a Greek colony existed in some outlying province of India about 550 B.C. (*CI.*, 1921, pp. 29-32). See also Holdich, *The Gates of India,* pp. 19-22, 123-24, 128. Another writer is of opinion that the Yavanas were the Ionians of Sogdiana (*IC.*, II. 357-8).

24. *CII,* I. 10.
25. *Ibid.*, p. xxxviii.
26. *CL.*, 1921, p. 26ff.
27. *PH.*, p. 260.
28. *CII.*, I, 48.
29. Kern, *Bṛhat-saṁhitā,* Intro., p. 37. *et. seq.*
30. *EI.*, XX. 79-80, line 8.
31. *PH.*, p. 319. But the view is expressed that it is Demetrios who is to be identified with the Yavana invaders and not Menander who could not have been the contemporary of Puṣya-mitra (*PH.*, pp. 323-24).
32. *EI.*, VIII. 61.
33. Pargiter, *Dynastics of the Kali Age,* pp. 56 & 74.
34. Chapter IV, sec. iv, lines 74-5.
35. *HV.*, i. 14. 16.
36. VII. 117. 13. But the Yavanas later on exered considerable influence on the works of Hindu astronomy. The Indian astronomers write of the Yavanas as their teachers. See Kern's translation of *Bṛhat-Saṁhitā, op. cit.*
37. *IC.*, I. 343 ff.
38. *Ibid.*, 18; Bhandarkar, *ABRI.*, VIII 134 ff. Another writer distinguishes the Yavanas from Pārasikas (Dr. D.C. Sircar in *the Journal of Indian History* (vol. XIV, pt. i, April 1935).
39. *IC.*, II, 575-76. See *PH.*, 386, fn. 1 for early Roman connection with India.
40. *Inscriptions of Bengal,* pp. 132-139, v. 17.
41. *EI.*, XIII. 151, vs. 3.
42. iv. 43. 12.
43. *Mbh* (B)., vii. 18. 7.
44. XII. 207. 43.
45. *PH.*, p. 126. Dr. B.C. Law is of opinion that the Kāmbojas must have been a Vedic Indian people and not Iranian as has been supposed by some scholars (*TAI.*, pp. 1-2).
46. B.C. Law, *Some Kṣatriya tribes of Ancient India,* 1924, pp. 249-50.
47. i. 67. 32; ii. 4. 22; v. 165. 1-3.
48. i. 6. 22.
49. *AS.*, p. 407.
50. *TAI.*, p. 3.

51. *HV.*, i. 14. 16.
52. *MP.*, p. 318.
53. *CI.*, VI, p. 110.
54. X. 43-44.
55. *Mbh.*, vii. 117, 12.
56. For various theories on the location of Kāmboja, see *TAI.*, pp. 2-3.
57. *Ved. Ind.*, I. 84-85 & p. 138.
58. VII, 4. 5.
59. *PH.*, pp. 126-27.
60. *BR.*, I, p. 163.
61. *Mbh.*, vii. 35. 36; 119. 26; ii. 51. 4; Rām. i. 6. 22; IV. 165, *RT.*, I, p. 136; *Harṣacarita* (Trans. by Cowell and Thomas), pp. 50. In the *Mahābhārata* (ii. 49. 19 & ii. 51. 3) it is said that the Kāmboja country produced excellent blankets.
62. *BR.*, I, p. 32.
63. IV. 166, *RT.*, I, p. 136.
64. *DD.*, p. 242; *Harṣacarita* (trans. by Cowell and Thomas), p. 50.
65. *Ariaspae of Arrian*, Wilson, *op. cit.*, p. 155.
66. *Mbh.*, vii. 35, 36; 119. 26; *Rām.*, i. 6. 22.
67. *MP.*, p. 319.
68. *YC.*, II, pp. 279-80.
69. *MM.*, pp. 157-58.
70. *Mbh.*, ii. 51. 10.
71. *Mbh.*, vii. 35. 36; 119. 26; *Rām.*, I. 6. 22.
72. *IG.*, VI, p. 298. *Harṣa-carita,* op. cit..
73. *Rām.*, i. 6. 22; *Harṣa-carita, op. cit.; MP.*, p. 315; *BR.*, II, p. 272; *Ved. Ind.*, I, 43.
74. *MP.*, p. 289; IA., IV. 267; *Mbh.*, ii. 51 30.
75. *Harṣa-carita, op. cit.*
76. *Mahāvaṁsa,* Geiger's translation, p. 194.
77. *CAGI.*, pp. 32-33. In the Vajjayantī Yavana is identified with Huruṣkara (*IHQ.*, XIX, 216,) a name which seems to be unknown to ancient writers.
78. *DUHB.*, p. 118.
79. *EI.*, XXII, 154-55.
80. But the theory of a Kāmboja invasion is considered highly improbable (*DHUB.*, p. 134). The Kāmbojas of Bengal are, however, considered to be the same as the Kāmbojas of the North-Western Frontier. For other views on the subject see *ibid.*, 191.
81. *DHNI.*, I. p. 309. fn. 2.
82. *IHQ.*, IX, 470 ff.

53
Cedis

H. B. Chaudhuri

According to ethnographical tradition recorded in the Purāṇas, the central zone of India from Bihar up to Rajputana which lay skirting the banks of the Jumna belonged to the Vāsava kings, a sub-line of the Kaurava dynasty. A Kaurava prince called Vasa conquered Cedi and obtained the title *'caidyo paricara'*, the overcomer of the Caidyas[1]. He also extended his conquests in other directions, and then established each of his five sons in fine separate kingdoms. Thus the eldest son Bṛhadratha took Magadha, Pratyagraha repaired to Cedi, Kaśa or Kuśāmba evidently had Kauśāmbi[2]. Lalittha's share was Kārusa, and the fifth one is said to have taken Māthailya or Māruta, which in all probability must be the Matsya realm[3]. This tradition, therefore, links up the Magadhas, Karūṣas, Cedis, Vatsas and Matsyas into one ethnic and political group just as the belt of eastern peoples such as the Aṅgas. Vaṅgas, Kaliṅgas, Puṇḍras and Suhmas were grouped into another by a similar tradition. From a geographical point of view this position as outlined seems to be quite in order. The Great Epic furnishes a short list of Madhya-deśa janapadas which are described as lying particularly around the Kuku realm :[4]

Santi ramyā janapadā bahvannāh paritaḥ kurūna
Pāñcālāś Cedi Matsyāśca Śūrasenāh Paṭaccarāḥ
Daśārṇā Navarāṣṭrāśca Mallāḥ Śālvā Yugandharāḥ
Kuntirāṣṭraṁ Suvistirṇaṁ Surāṣṭrāvantayastathā.

This statement presents certain irregularities, for all these tribal janapadas were not situated encircling the Kurus from a regional point of view:Surāṣṭra, Avanti, and Daśārṇa lay far off from the Kuru realm, only the Śālva, Matsya, Śūrasena and Pañcāla janapadas were situated *'paritaḥ kurūn'.* The Cedi realm did not about on any point on the Kuru country, the janapadas of Matsya, Śūrasena and Pañcāla had shut out the Cedi country from the plains of Thaneswar and Delhi. But the Cedis were neighbours of the Pañcālas and Matsyas on the north and west respectively, and so the combination *Pāñcālāścedimatsyāśca* of the text cited above which puts the Cedis in close proximity to the Pañcāla and Matsya janapadas agrees well with the geographical setting. Again in the Great Epic the Cedis were invariably coupled with the Matsyas and Karūṣas their neighbours on the west and east respectively. Such combinations as *cedimatsyānāṁ* and *cedimatsya-kāruṣāśca* are often mentioned. Sometimes the Matsyas are omitted and replaced by the Kāśis resulting in groupings like *cedi-kāśī-kāruṣānāṁ* which are by no means rare. The collocation of names indicates that Cedi, Kāśi, Kāruṣa or Cedi, Matsya, Kāruṣa was a compact ethnic group. According to Purāṇic tradition, as noticed before, Cedi, Matsya and Kāruṣa along with Vatsa and Magadha formed one such group.

The Cedis were an ancient people and their country known as Cetiya was a janapada according to the Buddhist *Aṅguttara Nikāya*. From the *Mahābhārata* we learn that the Cedi country lay near the Yamunā. Early Jaina writers know the people as Āriyas and referred to the Cedi capital called Sottiyamai[5]. This Jaina tradition is in agreement with Buddhist tradition, for a Jātaka gives the name of the Cedi (Ceti) only as Sotthivatinagara[6]. The *Mahābhārata* has the form Śuktimatī[7].

It appears that the Jain, Buddhist and Epic accounts refer to one and the same place, and indeed Sotthivati has been found to be the same as Śuktimatī,[8] in the epic account. The name was perhaps derived from a river of same name which according to the Great Epic[9] was flowing by the capital of the Cedi-Viṣaya. The river Śuktimatī has been identified with the Ken and so the position of the Cedi capital points unequivocally to Banda or to some place in its neighbourhood[10] near the river Ken. The Cedi country corresponded to the region bounded by the plateau of Malwa and hills of Bundelkhand on the south and the Valley of Jumna on the north and north-east[11] thus roughly corresponding to the modern Bundelkhand region[12] which lies south-east of the Jumna from its junction with the Chambal[13] In this position the Cedis inhabited the vicinity of the Matsyas[14].

But in the mediaeval period the name was commonly used to designate a still more extensive tract stretching up to the banks of the Narmada on the south.[15] The mediaeval capital of Cedi-maṇḍala[16] was Tripurī[17], (purīṁ Tripurīṁ)[18] which was the same as Tewar[19], a village about 6 miles close to the Narmada[20] to the west of Jubbalpore (C.P.). The Amoda plates of the Haihaya kings Pṛthvideva I states that Kōkkala who became the lord of Cedi raided Karṇāṭa, Vaṅga etc., and made his eldest son the king of Tripurī[21]. In the *Abhidhāna-cintāmaṇi* we have again a reference to the city:Tripurī Cedīnagarī[22]. The people of Tripurī are mentioned in Purāṇic list as Tripuras as a people of the south-eastern division. The earliest reference to the people is perhaps to be found in same coins bearing the name Tripurī in Brāhmī characters of the 'late third or early second century B.C.' which go to prove the antiquity of the people. The coins are attributed to the ancient Tripurī on the Narbada, the capital of the Kalacuri dynasty[23]. The *Padma Purāṇa* describes the glory of the place where Mahādeva is said to have killed Tripurāsura.[24]

But mediaeval inscriptions refer to another territorial name called Dāhala-maṇḍala[25] the capital of which according to Alberuni was Tiaurī[26] i.e., Tewar. An inscription of A.D. 1038 connects Dāhala with Piawan a small valley, 25 miles to the north-east of Rewa[27]. Another inscription of a Dāhālīya-mahārājā has been found in Alha-Ghāt in Rewa.[28] In a different epigraph Dāhala-maṇḍala is described as situated between the Bhāgīrathī and the Narmada[29]. All these show that Dāhala-maṇḍala corresponded to the Baghelkhand Jubbulpore regions, extending down to the source of the Narmada on the south. The chief city was Tripurī, but mention is also made of Saubhāgyapura[30] which is the modern Sohagpur in the Rewa State. Modern Mandla, head-quarters of the district of the same name, 60 miles south-east of Jubbulpore was perhaps another city of this region. It was the Maṇḍalai of Ptolemy[31] and was a place of considerable antiquity. The old town of Maṇḍala was also called Maheshmatipura derived from Mahesa-maṇḍala.[32] The *Padma Purāṇa* has a reference to the place: *Narmadātaṭamāsthitaḥ nāmā Maheśvaraṁsthānam.*[33] The modern Maṇḍalā also stands 'in a loop of the river Narbada, which surrounds it on three sides.[34] Cunningham thinks that it was the original capital of the Upper Narbada Valley and afterwards supplanted by Tripurī.

It thus follows that excepting the Baghelkhand region, the Dāhalamaṇḍala was conterminous with the ancient Cedi janapada which was again synonymous with Tripurī. But it seems that in the mediaeval period these names were occasionally treated as convertible, for Hemachandra writes: *Traipurāstu Dāhalāḥ syuścaidyāste Cedayaśca.*[35]

The Cedi country was quite well-known in ancient times. A Jātaka states that it was rich in food and drink and was prosperous and strong.[36] In the Great Epic the Cedi country is described as *prabhūta dhanadhānyavān*[37] and also as:

Arthavāneṣ deśo-hi-dhanaratnādibhiryuktaḥ

Vasupūrṇā ca Vasudhā Vasa Cediṣu Cedivān.[38]

The Cedis are given unstinted praise. They were righteous, honest, cheerful and were not used to speak a lie even for the sake of a joke. They were loyal sons, devoted fathers and faithful pupils. They were fully sensible of the sufferings of the old and decrepit animals, particularly of cows.[39]

References

1. Pargiter, *Ancient Indian Historical Tradition,* p. 272, Caidya, as a form of the name is found in an inscription (*IA.,* VIII. 15-16. Cf. The Cetiya Jātaka, No. 422.
2. Tradition records the Kuru origin of the kings of Kauśāmbi, for the elder line of Kuru kings moved there when Hastināpura was threated by the erosion of the Ganges (Roychaudhuri, *Political History,* pp. 20 and 38).
3. Pargiter, *op. cit.,* pp. 118 and 294.
4. *Mbh.,* IV. I. 11-12.
5. *IA.,* XX, 375.
6. No. 422. Cowell's *Jātāka,* III. p. 272.
7. iii. 20. 50.
8. De., *Geographical Dictionary,* p. vii.
9. i. 63. 35.
10. Pargiter, *Mārkaṇḍeya Purāṇa,* p. 359.
11. Pargiter, *Mārkaṇḍeya Purāṇa,* p.359.
12. Bhandarkar, *Carmichael Lectures,* p. 52.
13. *Imperial Gazetteer,* IX, p. 68.
14. In one Jātaka (No. 547, *CJ.,* VI, p. 266) we read that a group of people left Jetuttara at breakfast time and in the evening came to the kingdom of Ceta. Jetuttara has been identified with Nāgarī.
15. Roychaudhuri, *Political History,* p. 109.
16. *EI.,* I. p. 50, v. 8.
17. *Archæological Survey of India,* Annual Report, IX, p. 98.
18. *EI.,* II, p. 3, v. 6.
19. In the Bilhari stone inscription of the rulers of Cedi, Tewer is mentioned as Tripurī (*EI.,* I. pp. 251-270, vs. 83-4).
20. A verse of Harivaṁśa places Tripurī near the Narmadā (v. 1983).
21. *EI.,* XIX, pp. 75-77.
22. *Abhidhāna,* p. 389. Hemacandra considered Cedīnagara as but another name of Tripurī which shows that in his time Tripurī passed off as Cedi.

23. *Catalogue of the coins of Ancient India*, by Allan, pp. cxl-cxli. Tripuri is commonly used as the name of a city but at one time it might have extended beyond the Narmada as far as the Maikāla Range (*Mbh.*, vi. 84. 9).

24. Svarga, ch. 7.

25. *EI.*, V. p. 16, lines 7-8. For various forms of the name see vol. II, p. 772, fn. 1.

26. *AI.*, I, p. 202, The *Rāsa Mālā* also refers to Tipera and the Dāhul (vol. II. p. 777).

27. *Archæological Survey*, op. cit., Vol. XXI, pp. 112-113. The inscription refers to Srimad Gāngeya Deva who is also mentioned by Rihān as Gāngec, of Dāhal whose capital was Piturī a mistaken form of Tripurī.

28. *IA.*, XVIII, pp. 213-214, lines 1-2.

29. *Dynastic History of Northern India*, vol. II, p. 763. A South-Indian inscription of SS. 1183 refers to Dāhala as lying between the Ganges and the Narmada (*JAHRS.*, IV, p. 152).

30. The Bilhari stone inscription, *EI.*, I, pp. 251-270.

31. McCrindle, *Ptolemy*, p. 168.

32. Cunningham, *Geography of Ancient India*, pp. 559-60.

33. Svarga, 7. 39.

34. *Imperial Gazetteer*, XVII, p. 170.

35. *Abhidhāna*, p. 381. See also *Trikāṇḍaśesa*, p. 31.

36. No. 547, Cowell, *op. cit.*, VI, p. 266.

37. i, 63. 8.

38. i, 63. 9.

39. *Ibid.*, vs. 10ff.

54

Concordance of the Fauna in The Rāmāyaṇa

Sibadas Chaudhuri

"As long as mountain ranges stand
And rivers flow upon the earth:
So long will this Rāmāyana
Survive upon the lips of men" –(Rāmāyana, i, 2, 40).

The *Rāmāyaṇa* has made such a name and fame that translations of it have been brought out in different languages of the East and the West, and thus abundantly fulfils the above prediction of the great Poet. 'Probably no work of world literature, secular in its origin, has ever produced so profound an influence on the life and thought of the people as the *Rāmāyaṇa.*' (Macdonell, *Ency. Rel. & Ethics*).

In this *Rāmāyaṇa* there are interesting questions that will suggest themselves to different scholars, according to their predilections and habits of investigation, for the solution of which, I hope, this concordance will prove to be a useful and effective tool.

In the absence of a critical and collated edition of the *Rāmāyaṇa,* like that of the *Mahābhārata* of the Bhandarkar Oriental Research Institute, Poona, it is very difficult to prepare a scientific index of the *Rāmāyaṇa*. Different readings are there in different recensions of the *Rāmāyaṇa*. To have incorporated all the references in different recensions into the concordance would have swelled its bulk inordinately. So while preparing this concordance, I have to lowed the Gauḍīya version of the *Rāmāyaṇa* only.* The aim of this concordance is to collect systematically materials and datas scattered over the vols of the epic to help the research scholars to reconstruct the history of human thoughts and institutions of the epic period.

In the following pages I have recorded the names of the animals referred to in the *Rāmāyaṇa*. Notices of animals in the Vedic literatures,

Mahābhārata (*Mbh*), and in the archaeological finds of identified animals in Harrappa and Mohenjodaro have been incorporated in the footnotes to facilitate and deepen the study of the different phases of Indian civilization. Definitions of the animals by Kṣīrasvāmin and Sarvānanda, commentators of the *Amarakoṣa,* † have also been noticed. For the transliteration and English equivalents‡ of the words Monier-Williams has been followed.

I tender my thanks to all scholars who have helped me in the preparation of this paper in various ways and whom I could not specifically mention here in consideration of space.

1. AJA = He-Goat; Ram.

   (AK. 152/217) अजति गच्छति व्यायामशीलत्वादजा

   Ādi – xvii (4a).

   Ayo – c (63a, 67a).

   Sun – xviii (32b).

2. AJINA = Black antelope's skin.

   (AK. 120/172) अज्यते क्षिप्यतेऽजिनम्

   Ādi – i (35b), xv (4a), lxxvi (3b).

   Ayo – ix (31a), xv (35b), xix (9a), xxviii (23a), xxx (14b), xxxiv (15b), lxxii (20a), xcvi (5a, 24b), civ (6a), cviii (24a), cx (2b, 3a).

   Ara – vi (6a), xxv (11b, 21a), xxxix (5a), xl (38a), xliv (13b, 33a), 1 (28b), liv (11a), lix (24a).

   Yud – cx (49a).

3. ANAḌUR-Ox, Bull.

   (A.K. 149/213) अनोवहत्यनड्वान्

   Ayo – lxxvi (30b).

4. AÑJANA = Name of an elephant of the West and South West Region;

   Ādi – vi (26a).

   Sun – iii (27b).

   Utt – v (4b), xxi (38b), xxiii (15a).

5. AṆḌAJA = Egg-born (i.e. bird, fish, snake, lizard).

   Ādi – ii (15a).

   Ayo – lxvi (2b).

   Kis – xliv (87c).

   Yud – lix (30a).

   Utt – xxiii (21b), lxiv (43a).

6. ANTARĪKṢA CARA = Passing through the atmosphere, e.g. Bird.

Ādi – xiii (29b).

7. AMBUJA = Aquatic Animal.

Utt – iv (18b).

8. AŚVA = Horse.

(AK. 129/184) अश्नुतेऽध्वानमश्वः

Ādi – i (101a), iii (8b, 13b, 140b), iv (65a), v (13b), xi (18a), xii (35b), xiii (2b, 28b, 31b, 34a, 35a, 40b), xiv (5c, 6c, 25b), xl (22b), xli (7b, 8a, 9ab, 13a, 14b, 16b, 18b, 28a, 29b), xlii (2b, 10ab), xliii (2a, 22a), xlvi (29a), lvi (4b, 7a), lxxix (8b, 21a), lxxx (3b).

Ayo – xii (11a, 25b), xiii (23b), xx (39b), xxvi (17a), xxxv (40b), xxxix (21b, 48a), xl (20b), xliv (11b), xlvii (22a, 23b, 24a), xlviii (20a), lxxii (23a, 25b), lxxiii (26b), lxxix (11a), xc (5a), xci (14b), xciv (22a), c (56a, 59a, 62a), cvi (9b, 12a), cviii (29a), cix (36a, 49a), cxi (45a), cxvi (42b), cxvii (9a), cxxvii (4b).

Ara – ix (19b), xxviii (27b, 30b, 38a), xxxii (17a), xxxiii (27b, xxxiv (33a), xxxv (2a), xl (22b), lv (16a), lvii (52a).

Kis – xxxix (14a), xliv (39b).

Sun – xi (10a), xli (25b), xviii (30b, 32b), xxvii (14a), xxxv (35b), xlii (27a, 38a), xliii (3b), lxxiv (11b, 48b), lxxviii (4b, 17b), lxxx (20b), lxxxii (18a), lxxxix (11b).

Yud – xviii (26a), xix (35a, 45b), xxx (6a), xxx क (10b), xxxvi (113a, 119a), xlv (18a, 20b), xlix (28b), l (11b, 27a), lii (18b), liv (26ab, 49a), lvii (1b), lix (41a), lxii (10b, 11a), lxvii (6b), lxviii (2b), lxx (47a, 48a), lxxi (1a), lxxiv (3a, 13a, 37a), lxxv (26a), lxxix (10b), lxxxi (18a, 19a), lxxvii (9a, 15a, 25a), xciii (46b), cx (33a), cxii (15a), cxiii (8a), cxiv (10ab).

Utt – vii (5b, 12a, 29b, 30a, 31a), xxvi (47b), xxix (41a), xlii (35a), xlix (20a), lii (1c), lxx (2a), lxxi (18c) xci (2a, 3b), xciii (9a, 19b, 20a), xcvii (13a, 14b, 25a), (6b, 7b, 15b, 17b), xcix (10a), cvii (2a, 3b), cxiii (18b).

9. AŚVATARA = Mule.

Utt – xxxi (22b).

10. AHI = Serpent, snake.

(AK. 38/58) अंहत्यहिः

Ayo – xlii (3b).

Sun – xxxviii (9b).

Yud – xxxvi (12b).

11. ĀŚIVIṢA = Venomous snake or serpent.

AK. 38/58) आश्यां विषमस्य, आशीस्तालुगता दंष्ट्रा तया विद्धो न जीवति

Ayo – VII (3a).

Ara – xxx (19a), xxxiii (31a), xxxiv (3b), xxxv (46b), xli (12b), lvii (27a).

Kis – v (23c), vii (23a), xv (27a), xviii (8b), xxii (21b).

Sun – ix (54b), xc (2a).

Yud – iii (39b, xix (24a), xxvii (15a), xxxक (37a), xxxvi (117a), l (7a, 18a), lvi (35b, 43a), lxviii (3b), lxix (5a), lxxi (32b), lxxv (17b), lxxvi (58a), lxxvii (25a), lxxx (51b), xci (17b), xcii (20b), xciii (21a).

Utt – xxxi (43c).

12. ĪHĀMṚGA = Wolf.

(AK. 85/125) ईहा मृगस्येवास्य ईहामृगः, ईहां मृगयते वा

Sun – xx (11b).

Yud – lxxx (69a).

13. UPTAKṢAKA = Name of a Nāga

Utt – xxi (23a).

14. URAGA = Snake.

(AK. 38/58) उरसा गच्छत्युरगः

Ādi – xxxiv (9a), xxxviii (15a), xlv (18a), lvi (9a), lvii (13b), lxix (9b).

Ayo – xix (1b), xxviii (11b), xli (23a).

Ara – ix (32b), xxxii (23b, 25b), xxxvi (29a), xxxvii (22a), lviii (8a), lxi (19a), lxxiii (3b).

Kis – v (31b), x (3a,/1a), (1), xxxiv (2a, 34a), xl (38a), xliv (17a, 54a, 56b, 67a), xlix (5a), liv (2b).

Sun – (18b), iii (59a), iv (14a), v (2b), vii (18a), xxiii (20a, 22b), xliii (19a), xlvi (7b), lv (5b, 9b, 16a), lix (12a), lxxi (4a), lxxv (32a), lxxv (32a), lxxxi (2a) xcvii (30a).

Yud – xvi (32b, 80a), xxv (34b), xxvii (18a), xxxiv (3a), xxxvi (121b), xl (38b), liii (48a), lix (36a), lxxi (16b, 30a), lxxx (66a), lxxxi (36c), lxxxiv (24b), lxxxviii (5a), xciii (32a, 40b, 47b), ciii (23a).

Utt – xv (19a), xxiv (4a), xxvi (25b(, xxvii (3b), xxxiii (17a), xxxvi (39a), xciii (3b).

15. URAGI = Female snake.

Ayo – ix (6b).

16. ULŪKA = Owl.

(AK. 86/127) उलति नेत्राभ्यां दहत्युलूक:

Ayo – cxxv (2a).

Ara – xx (19b).

Utt – lxiv (2b, 3a, 5b, 12bc, 26b, 29a, 33b, 49b).

17. UṢṬRA = Camel.

(AK. 152/127) उष्यते दह्यते मरौ—उष्ट्र:

Ayo – lxxii (25b), lxxxix (13c), c (55a, 63a, 75a).

Sun – xviii (30a), xxvii (18b), lxxviii (18a).

Yud – xxxv (15b), xxxvii (39a), xlv (20b), liv (25a).

Utt – vi (44b), xxxiii (37a), xxxvi (39a).

18. UKṢĀ = Bull or Ox.

(AK. 149/213) उक्षति उक्षा

Ayo – ix (45b).

19. ṚIKṢA = Bear.

(AK. 63&95/125) ऋक्ष्णोति हिनस्ति ऋक्ष: । अतएव भालूक:

Ādi – xx (5b, 10b, 19a), xxvii (13b), lx (12b).

Ayo – xxv (33b), xxvii (11b), xxviii (11b), liv (30a), cii (2a), cvi (3b).

Ara – liii (42b), lxiv (11b), lxxvi (17b), lxxvii (38b).

Kis – xxii (4b, 37a), xxiii (4b), xxvi (2b), xxviii (22a), xxxv (30a), xxxviii (34a, 52a), xxix (28a), lviii (5a), lx (15a).

Sun – xlviii (10b), lxiv (5a), lxxiv (63b).

Yud – iii (10ab, 29), vi (16a), vii (35b), xiii (1b, 30a), xv (18a), xvi (3b, 18b, 27b), xvii (21a), xviii (55b), xix (6a, 31a), xxix (34a), xxv (9b, 12a, 13b), xxxख (10a, 14a, 20b), xli (12c), xlvi (76b), liii (17c, 18a, 32a), lxiii (4a, 6a), lxv (20a), lxvi (5a, 11a), lxx (23a, 24a), lxxi (56a), lxxii (20b), lxxix (12b), xciii (71a), c (24a), cvi (8b, 14b), cxii (24b).

Utt – xx (19a), xlii (53b), xliii (6a, 11a), xliv (1a), xlvi (15b), xcviii (14b), cvi (5a, 11b), cxiii (36b, 38a, 40a, 47a), cxiv (18a), cxv (20a, 26a).

20. ṚIṢABHA = Bull.

(AK. 149/213) ऋषति णच छति ऋषभ:

Ādi – xiii (30b), xlix (3a).

Kis – xxi (38b), liv (6a).

Sun – xxvii (14), xxxiv (6b), lxxiv (24b).

Yud – xiii (2b), xx (3b), xcv (2b).

21. AIRĀVATA = A species of elephant. Name of Indra's elephant.

(AK. 10/15) इरावत्यध्वौ जात ऐरावत:

Ādi – vi (26b).

Ayo – xii (33b).

Ara – xxxvii (8b).

Sun – ii (29a), xii (31a), xv (16a), lxxiv (27b).

Yud – xxxviii (17b), xlix (5b).

Utt – xxxi (5a), xxxviii (95a, 96a).

22. AIRĀVAṆA = Name of Indra's elephant.

(AK. 10/15) इरावणोद्भव ऐरावण:

Ara – xx (25a), xlviii (7a).

to be continued

References

* Calcutta Sanskrit Series.

† Cf. (a) *Nāmaliṅgānuśāsanam :* ed. by K. G. Oka, Poona, 1913.

(b) The same, ed. by Hara Dutt Sharma & N. G. Sardesai, Poona, 1941. (*Indicated in the body of the Index* by AK. followed by the page marks of (a) & (b).

‡ Cf. *Nāmaliṅgānuśāsanam :* ed, Ganapati Shastri, Trivardrum, 1915-17. (*Indicated as* AS followed by page mark of the edition).

1. *Av.*, ix. 5, 1; *Ṛv.*, x. 16. 4; *Vāj. Sam.*, xxi. 9.
2. *Av.* v. 21. 7; *Ṛv.*, i. 166. 10.
3. *Ait. Brā.*, i. 14; *Av.*, iii. 11. 5; *Ṛv.*, x. 59. 10; *Śat. Brā.*, ii. 1, 4, 17; Mohenjo (Mackay), DK – 9238 (1).
4. *Sāṅ. Brā.*, iii, 7; *Sām. V Brā.*, 3. 1. 2; *Mbh.* (BORI), v. 77. 15a.
5. *Ait. Āra.*, ii, 6, 1; *Mbh.* (Beng.), xii, 348, 13492.
6. *Tait. Brā.*, iii, 12, 7, 5; *Mbh.*, (Beng.), ix. 50, 2879.
8. *Av.*, v. 17. 15; *Ait. Brā.*, vi. 35; *Sat. Brā.*, v. 5. 4. 35; *Ṛv.* iv. 32. 17; *Vāj. Sam.*, xxx. 13; *Bṛhad. Upa.* vi. 2. 13; *Chānd. Upa.* v. 1. 12; *Kāṭh. Saṁ.*, xvii. 13; *Mait. Saṁ.* i. 11. 6; Mohenjo (Mac.). DK – 4732; Mohenjo (Marshall). DM – 293; *Nighantu.*, i. 14; *Sāṅ. Āra.*, ix. 7; *Sāṅ. Srauta Sūtra,* xvi. 4. 5; *Tait. Brā.*, iii. 4. 7. 1; *Mbh.*, *Aśvamedhika Parva.*
9. *Ait. Brā.*, iii. 47; *Av.*, iv. 4. 8; *Jaim. Upa. Brā.*, i. 4, 4; *Sat. Brā.*, xii. 4. 1. 10; *Tait. Saṁ.*, vii. 1. 1. 2. 3; *Mbh.*, (BORI), ii, 9, 9a.
10. *Av.*, i. 27; *Bṛhad. Upa.*, iv. 4. 10; Harappa (Vats), 8157 (II), 12358, II; *Jaim. Brā.*, i. 9; *Kāṭh. Upa.*, ii. 6; *Sat. Brā.*, xi. 2. 6. 13; *Ṛv.*, vii. 104. 7.
11. *Ait. Brā.*, vi. 1.

12. *Mbh.*
13. *Mbh.* (BORI), ii, 9, 8a.
14. *Mbh.* (BORI), i. 4, 4b.
16. Harappa (Vats), I. 5893; *Ṛv,* x. 165. 4; *Av.*, vi. 19. 2; *Tait. Saṁ.*, v. 5. 18. 1; *Mait Saṁ.*, iii. 14. 4; *Vāj. Saṁ.*, xxiv. 23; *Mbh.*, (BORI), i, 60, 55a.
17. Mohenjo (Marshall), SD–1386; *Ṛv.*, i. 138. 2; viii. 5. 37; *Av.*, xx. 127. 2; *Vāj. Saṁ.*, xiii. 50; *Sat. Brā.*, i. 2. 3. 9; *Ait. Brā.*, ii. 8; *Tait. Saṁ.*, v. 6. 21. 1; *Kāṭh. Saṁ.*, xv. 2; *Mbh.*
18. *Ṛv.*, i. 168. 2; *Av.*, iii. 11. 8; *Vāj. Saṁ.*, xxi. 20; *Mbh.*
19. *Ṛv.*, v. 56. 3; *Jaim. Brā.*, i. 184; *Mait. Saṁ.*, iii. 14. 17; *Vāj. Saṁ.*, xxiv. 36.; *Mbh.*, (BORI), i. 60, 60b.
20. *Ṛv.*, vi. 16. 47; x, 91. 14; *Av.*, iii. 6. 4; *Tait. Saṁ.* ii. 1. 3. 2; *Vāj. Saṁ.* xxi. 22; *Pañca Brā.*, xiii. 5. 18; *Mbh.*, (Beng.), ii, 21, 812.
21. *Av.*, viii. 10. 29; *Pañca Brā.*, xxv. 15. 3; *Mbh.*, (BORI), i. 3, 174.
22. *Mbh.* (Beng.), i. 18, 1251.

55

Concordance of the Fauna in The Rāmāyaṇa*

Sibadas Chaudhuri

23. KAKUDA = Hump of a bull.

(AK. 201/291). कङ्कते कं कौति वा ककुदम्

Ayo – viii (42a).

24. KANKA = Heron.

(AK. 87/127). कङ्कते कङ्कः । के जले ह्वयति इति कङ्कः

Kis – lxii (56a).

Sun – vii (22a).

Yud – xvi (11a), lxiv (20a), lxxx (68a), xci (25a), xcv (68a).

25. KACCHAPA = Turtle.

(AK. 42/65). कच्छेन पिबति कच्छपः

Ara – xl (26a, 30b).

Kis – li (26a).

Sun – lxxx (19b).

Utt – vi (45a), xc (17a).

26. KADRU = Mother of Nāga (serpent).

(AK. 27/41). कन्दते कद्रुः

Ara – xx (29b, 32b, 33a).

27. KAPI = Ape.

(AK. 84/124) कम्पते चलति कपिः

(AS. 216) चलस्वभावात् कपिः

Ādi – i (78a, 83b).

Ara – lxxvii (75a, 76a).

Kis – 1 (13a, 14a, 17b, 31a, 32a), ii (25b), iii (24a), v (28b) viii (11a, 22a, 42b, 48a), ix (2b), xi (1b), xii (2a), xiii (43a), xvi

58a), liv (51b, 56a), lvi (13a, 44a), lvii (10a, 11a), lix (3b, 5b), lxi (10a), lxii (9a, 16b), lxiii (12b), lxvi (6b, 7a, 18b, 23b, 25a, 26a, 27a, 28b), lxx (22a, 26a), lxxi (46a), lxxiv (39c), lxxvi (42a), lxxvii (3b, 26a, 37a, 44b), lxxviii (9b, 18a, 28a), lxxx (6b, 36a, 40b), lxxxiii (47a, 95a, 99a, 139b, 140b, 154a, 174a), lxxxiv (16b, 35b), lxxxv (7a, 13a), cx (48a, 62b), cxii (16b), cxiii (58b).

Utt–xxiii (35a), xxxviii (55a), xl (18a, 20a), xlii (39b, 40a), xliii (16c, 18a, 20a).

28. KAPILĀ = Brown Cow.

'कपिला गोविशेष: ' इति हेमचन्द्र: ।

Ayo–lxxix (20a).

29. KAPOTA = Dove or Pigeon.

AK. 86/127. केन पवते कपोत:

Ayo–xi (4a).

Kis–xiii (22b).

Utt–vi (53a).

Sun–xciii (4a, 5b).

30. KAMBALA = A sort of deer with a shaggy hairy coat.

Utt–xxxi (22b).

31. KAMBU = Conch.

AK. 207/301. काम्यते कम्बु: शम्बुकेऽपि

Sun–xxxii (10a).

Utt–xxviii (12b), xxxi (8b).

32. KARABHA = Young elephant.

AK. 151/217. कं शिरो रभत उत्तम्भयति करभे बालोष्ट्र:

Utt–xxxviii (73b).

33. KARIN = Elephant.

Sun–xv (18b).

Yud–xxxv (9c).

Utt–vi (44a), vii (12a), xxxiv (12b), xxxviii (89a).

34. KAREṆU = Elephant.

AK. 196/282. के मूर्द्धि रेणुरस्य करेणु:

Ayo–ix (5a), xiii (23a), xxxix (35b), xli (17b), cxi (47a).

Kis–xiii (10b), xliv (44b).

Sun–xv (28b), xxiii (16b), xxvii (28a).

Yud–lxxiii (14b), xcv (6b), cxii (9b).

Utt–xxi (3b, 16b).

35. KALA-HAṂSA = Name of several speices of the Haṃsa bird or goose.

AK. 88/129 कलो मधुरवाग् हंस: कलहंस: ।

Kis – xxix (18a), li (12c).

36. KĀKA = Crow.

AK. 87/128. का शब्दं कायति ककते वा लौल्यात् काक: ।

Ayo – cv (40a, 41a, 42a, 43b, 45b, 46a, 47a, 48a, 50a, 56a, 57a, 58a).

Ara – iv (37a).

Sun – xxvii (34b), xxxvi (35b, 36a, 38b, 40a, 42b, 46b), xxxvii (4b), lxvii (29b, 30a), lxix (16b, 17b).

Yud – xi (35b), xxvii (34a), xxxb (13a), lxxx (68a), xciii (48a).

Utt – xxxvi (42a).

37. KĀDAMBA = A kind of goose with dark-grey wings.

AK. 88/129. कदम्बस्यायं संघचारित्वात् कादम्ब: ।

Kis – xiii (8a), xxvi (5a), li (12b), lii (39a).

Sun – lvi (1b), xiv (38a).

Utt – xx (20a).

38. KĀNANAUKAS = Monkey.

Sun – lx (12a), lxvi (7a, 12a).

Yud – xvi (19a), xxxi (17b), lxii (12b).

39. KĀRAṆḌAVA = Sort of Duck.

AK. 89/131. करणडो भवं कारणडं पञ्जरबन्धं वाति कांरण्डव:

Ayo – xxvii (18a), lii (33a), cxi (49a).

Ara – vii (3a), xii (14b), xv (42b), xxi (12a), lxxviii (15b), lxxx (27a), lxxxi (27b, 42b).

Kis – xxix (16b), xliv (30b).

Sun – ix (9a, 57a), xiv (39a) xvii (26a), lvi (1a).

Yud – lxxxiii (71a).

Utt – lxxxiv (4b).

40. KĪṬA = A worm or insect.

Ayo – xxv (32a), xxviii (14a).

41. KUKKUṬA = A wild cock.

AK. 128 कुगुञ्जारणेन कुटति कुक्कुट: ।

Sun – xv (41b).

42. KUÑJARA = Elephant.

AK. 183. कुञ्जौ कुम्भाधोगतौ दंष्ट्र वास्तोऽस्य कुञ्जरः । कुञ्जेषु रमते, डः ।

Ādi – xiv (37a), xxvii (13b), liv (19b).

Ayo – xi (26a), xx (4a), xxvii (11b), xxxvii (3b), liv (40a, 42c), lviii (7a), xci (17a, 20b), xciv (27b), cviii (9a), cix (27b), cxi (11b), cxvi (41b), cxvii (17a).

Ara – xv (4a), xxxii (29b), xxxiii (29b), xxxiv (17a), liii (43a).

Kis – ii (8a, 12b), xiii (10a), xxxi (16b, 21b), xxxvii (5a).

Sun – ii (15a), iii (16b, 17b, 28a), v (21a), vii (34b, 59a), xxvii (20a), xxxv (34a), xxxviii (4a, 33a), liii (12a), lix (16a), lxxviii (17a).

Yud – iv (10a), xvi (20b), xviii (53a), xix (10a, 34b), xxxiii (2b), xlv (11a), l (8a), lvi (46b, 52a), lxiii (12b), lxxviii (28a), lxxxiv (25a), cxi (13b), cxii (26a), cxiii (27a).

Utt – vii (11b, 50a), xxi (3b, 16b, 29b), xxx (7b), xxxi (13a).

43. KUÑJARĪ = Female elephant.

Ayo – lxxvii (7b).

44. KUMUDA = Elephant of the South West or Southern quarter.

Utt – xxx (7a).

45. KURARA = Osprey, species of eagle.

AK. 129. कुरति कुररः । कुर शब्दे, कुरेति शब्दं राति वा ।

Kis – xxix (16a), li (11a, 12a), lii (38b), lix (30a).

Yud – xv (11a)

46. KURARĪ- Female osprey.

Ayo – xxxix (44a), lxvii (16b), lxviii (43b), lxxxiii (28a).

Ara – xv (6b).

Kis – xviii (32a), xix (4b).

Yud – xxiv (12b).

Sun – xviii (49a).

47. KŪRMA = Turtle or tortoise

AK. 42/65. कुरति कुमूर्वति वा कूर्मः ।

Ayo – cxxv (15a).

Kis – xvi (35b).

Sun – lxxv (12b).

Yud – lxxiv (12a), lxxxiii (131a).

48. KOKA = Wolf.

AK. 85/126 कोकति गृह्णाति कवते याति बा कोकः ।

Ara – liii (42b).

Sun – xxvi (9b).

Yud – xxviii (18b).

49. KOKILA = Indian cuckoo.

AK. 87/128. कोकते चित्तं गृह्णोति कोकिल: ।

Ādi – ix (15a, lxvi (6a, 9a, 10a)

Ayo – xlix (2b), liv (42a), xcvi (6b), cv (12b, 13a).

Ara – lxxxi (10b, 26b).

Sun – xvii (8a), xviii (9b, 20b).

Yud – xv (10b).

Utt – xlv (11b), lxiv (1b).

50. KO-YAṢṬIKA = A small white crane, commonly called a *paddy-bird*.

AK. 131. की युजते कोयष्टिक: ।

AS. 245. कोयष्टिक: कोण्डेति ख्यात: ।

Ayo – liv (42a).

Ara – lxxx (23a).

Yud – xv (9a).

51. KRAUÑCA = Curlew.

AK. 129. क्रुञ्चति क्रुङ्। (क्रौञ्च) प्रज्ञादित्वादण्।

Ādi – ii (12b, 17b, 31b, 32b).

Ayo – cxi (49b).

Ara – xx (19a), xxii (16b), lxxviii (7a), lxxxi (43a).

Kis – li (11a), lix (30a).

Sun – ix (57a).

Yud – liv (19a), lxxi (23b), lxxv (18b).

52. KRAUÑCĪ = Female curlew.

Ādi – ii (14b, 16b, 30a).

Ayo – xxxviii (48b), lxxvii (32b).

Ara – xx (18a, 19a).

53. KṚKALĀSA = Lizard

AS. 226. कृकेन कण्ठेन लसति क्रीड़तीति कृकलास: ।

AK. 127. कृकं शिरोग्रीवं लासयति कृकलास: ।

Utt – xviii (5b, 29a), lv (18b, 19b).

54. KṚMI = Worm or insect.

AK. 127. क्रामति क्रि (कृ)मि: ।

Utt – xxv (12a).

55. KHAGA = Bird.

AK. 131. खे गच्छति खगः ।

Ādi – iii (57a).

Ayo – lvi (2a, 11b), xci (16b), xcvi (30b), xcviii (5b), cv (54a), cvi (3a, 29d).

Ara – xxiii (8a), xxix((9b), xxxvii (14a), lvii (6a), lviii (16a).

Kis – xliv (43b), lviii (4b), lxii (47a).

Sun – lxix (11a), xciii (5a).

Yud – xxvii (34a), lxxxiii (90b).

Utt – vii (21b).

56. KHAḌGĪ = Female rhinoceros.

AK. 125. खड्ति भिनत्ति खड्गः । खडगं शृङ्गमस्यास्तीति स्वड्गी ।

Ādi – xxvii (13b).

Ayo – xxv (33a).

(*To be continued*)

References

* Contd. from pp. 141 of vol. XXVIII, No. 2.

23. Harappa (Vats), I. 11510, II. 794, III. 739, V.J – 185, VI.J – 188; Mohenjo (Mackay), SD – 3137-u, DK – 9574-1; *Śat. Brā.*, (Kanva), i, 4, 1, 8; *Tait.*, *Brā.*, i, 4, 7, 1, *Mbh*.

24. *Sāṅkh. Āra.*, xii. 13; *Tait. Saṁ.*, v. 4. 11. 1; *Vāj. Saṁ.*, xxiv. 31; *Mait Saṁ.*, iii. 14. 12; *Sv.*, ii. 9. 3. 6. 1; *Mbh.*, (Beng.), i. 66, 2633.

25. Mohenjo (Mackay), DK – 3951, 6528-1; *Mbh.*, (BORI), i, 14, 60a.

26. *Śat. Brā.*, (Madh.), iii. 2, 4, 1; *Mbh.*, (BORI), i, 60, 66a.

27. Harappa (Vats), I. Pl. 16; III. 11625; Mohenjo (Mackay), DK – 8162; *Ṛv.*, x. 86. 5; *Av.*, iii. 9. 4; iv. 33. 11; vi. 49. 1; *Chand. Upa.*, i. 6. 7; *Tait. Saṁ.*, iv. 2, 10, 1.

28. *Mbh.*, (BORI), I. 49, 50; *Śat, Brā.*, XIV, 9. 4. 14; *Tait Āra.*, I, 9. 2.

29. Mohenjo (Mackay), DK – 5975 – L; DK – 12224 – U; SD – 2799 – U; *Ṛv.*, i. 30. 4; *Av.*, xx. 135, 12; *Mait. Saṁ,* iii, 14. 4; *Vāj. Saṁ.*, xxiv, 23. 38; *Mbh.* (BORI), XII. 141.

30. *Mbh.* (BORI), I, 31. 10a.

31. *Mbh.*

32. *Mbh.*

33. Mohenjo (Mackay), DK – 8324 – L; *Mbh.*

34. *Mbh.*

35. Mohenjo (Mackay). DK–4564; *Mbh.* (BORI), I, 60. 56.

36. *Kāṣikā,* IV, 1. 151, 49; *Ait. Āra.*, III, 2, 4; *Ṣad. Brā.*, 5, 8.

37. Harappa (Vats), II–5573; Mohenjo (Mackay), DK–11716-U; *Mbh.*

39. Harappa (Vats), I. 621; III. 4997; V. 11893; Mohenjo (Mackay), DK–9560-1; *Mbh.; Kāṣikā*, VI, 3. 119. 5.

40. *Av.*, ix. 4. 16; *Bṛhad-Up.*, vi. 1. 19; *Chānd. Upa.*, vi. 9. 3; *Kaus. Upa.*, i. 2; *Mbh.*, XIII, 117-9, 5728.

41. Harappa (Vats), II. 8300; Mohenjo (Mackay), DK–7896; *Vāj. Saṁ.*, i. 16; *Mbh., Kāṣikā,* II, 4. 31. 164; *Śat, Brā.*, I, 1. 4. 18; *Kāṇ. Śat. Brā.*, I, 1, 3, 2.

42. *Mbh.* (BORI), I, 31, 150; *Kāṣikā,* II, 1, 56, 11.

44. *Mbh.* (BORI), I, 31, 156.

45. Harappa (Vats), Seal–255; *Mbh.* (BORI), I, 31. 15a.

47. Harappa (Vats), Seal–426; Mohenjo (Mackay), DK–9683–1; *Mbh.* (BORI), I, 59. 40; *Av.*, IX, 4. 16; *Tait. Saṁ.*, II, 6. 3. 3, *Mait. Saṁ.*, III. 15. 3; *Vāj. Saṁ.*, XXIV, 34; *Śat. Brā.*, I, 6, 2, 3.

48. *Ṛv.*, vii. 104. 22; *Sv.*, v. 23. 4; viii. 6. 2; *Mbh.*

49. *Mbh.* (Beng.), v, 160. 5444; *Kāṣikā,* iv, 1. 4. 3.

51. *Tait. Saṁ.*, v. 5. 12. 1; *Mbh.*, vi, 51, 1.

53. *Tait. Saṁ.*, v. 5. 19. 1; *Mait. Saṁ.*, iii. 14. 21; *Vāj. Saṁ.*, xxiv. 40; *Bṛhad. Up.*, i, 5, 22; *Mbh.*, xiii, 132.

54. *Tait. Saṁ.*, v, 11. 1; *Mait. Saṁ.*, iii. 14, 11; *Vāj-Saṁ.*, xxiv. 30; *Mantra Brā.*, ii. 7; *Tait Āraṇ.*, iv. 36; *Śat. Brā.* v, 4. 1. 2; *Mbh.*, i, 1800.

55. *Mbh.*

56. *Mait. Saṁ.*, iii. 14. 21; *Vāj. Saṁ.*, xxiv. 40; Mohenjo (Mackay), DK–5863; *Mbh.*

56

Concordance of the Fauna in The Rāmāyaṇa*

Sibadas Chaudhuri

57. KHARA = Ass.

AK. 217. ख'राति खरति वा खरन्। खं शब्दं राति खर:।

Ayo – xxxix (13c), c (55a, 63a, 75a), cxvii (9a)

Ara – lvi (31a), lvii (49a).

Sun – xviii (30ab), xxvii (16a(, xl (5a), lxxviii (18a).

Yud – xi (38a), xxvii (26b, 28ab), xxxv (11c), xxxvii (39a), xliv (26b), xlvi (8c), xlviii (4b), liv (49a), lxxxviii (3a), cxiii (8a).

58. GAJA = Elephant.

AK. 127/183 गजति माद्यति गज:।

Adi – xx (10a), xlii (12b, 14a, 15a, 16a), xliii (7b, 9a, 10a, 11a), xlv (13b), lv (12a), lvi (4b).

Ayo – vii (30a), xii (11b, 33a), xx (23a, 41b), xlii (6a, 9a), xlviii (20a), lvi (20a), lvii (7a), lx (18a), lxv (20a), lxvi (13b, 15a), lxxii (23b), lxxiii (23a), lxxiii (23a), xciv (22a), xcvii (25a), c (7a, 31a, 55a, 56a, 75a), ci (15b, 30b, 35a, 39a), civ (19b), cv (10a, 59a), cvi (4a, 9b, 16b), cvii (18b)m cxi (45a), cxxvii (4b).

Ara – vii (7b), xv (6a), xx (25ab), xxv (2a), xl (30b), lvii (5ab), lxxvii (17a, 38b), lviii (21a, 22b), lix (35b), lxiii (32b), lxxvi (22a).

Kis – ix (43a), xiii (47a), xliii (14c), xliv (44b), lxii (61a).

Sun – iii (14ab, 20a, 21a), xi (13a), xii (25b, 30b, 31a, 33b), xiii (13a), xiv (36b), xviii (30a, 33c, 39b), xxi (17b), xxvii

(11ab), xxviii (1b, 15a), xlii (38a), lxxx (20b), lxxxii (18a, 24a, 32a), lxxxv (2a).

Yud – xi (43b), xiii (15a), xvi (56a), xxvii (13b, 27a), xxviii (13b), xxx (23a), xxxa (19b, 24b), xxxi (22b, 32b), xxxiii (3a), xxxv (8a, 13c), xxxviii (53a), xliii (28b), xliv (30a), xlv (20b), xlvi (83a), xlix (6b, 20a, 37a), l (10a, 13a, 33b), li (27a), lii (11a), liv (25a, 26ab), lv (13a), lvi (73c), lxiii (35b, 44b), lxxiv (23a), lxxvi (16b), lxxvii (22a, 27b, 28a, 29a), lxxxi (17a), lxxxvi (11b).

Utt – v (4b), vii (5a), xx (19a, 34a), xxi (45b, 66a), xxxiv (30b), lxiii (37b), lxx (2b, 21a).

59. GARDABHA = Ass.

AK. 217. गर्दति गर्दभः, गर्द शब्दे।

Ara – xxx (4b).

60. GARUTMAT = The bird Garuḍa.

AK. 7/10. गरुतः पक्षाः सन्त्यस्य गरुत्मान्।

Ara – xxxvi (6b).

Sun – ii (10b).

Yud – xxvi (26c), lxxxix (27b).

Utt – xxi (63b), xxxi (32a), xxxviii (77a).

61. GARUḌA = Crane, a vulture or an engle.

AK. 7/10. गरुद्भिर्डयते गरुड़ः।

Adi – xiii (28b).

Ayo – xli (23a).

Ara – xx (33b, 34a), xl (26b, 30a), xlv (30b)m lvi (30b).

Kis – x (6b), lix (17a).

Sun – i (32b), iii (59a), vi (1b), vii (40b), viii (14b), xxiii (22a), lxxi (3b), xcvii (30a).

Yud – xxvi (10b, 20a, 24b, 40c), xxxvii (2a), xl (38b), xlvi (32b), lxxi (30a).

Utt – vi (45a), vii (39a, 40a, 41a, 47a), viii (17b), xi (19a), xxi (41b), xxiii (14a, 18b), xxx (9b), xxxi (59a).

62. GO = Cow.

AK. 213. गच्छति गौः।

Adi – i (101b), ix (56ab, 57a, 58b), xvii (3b), xxviii (13b), xxix (4a), liv (10b, 13a, 22b), lxxiii (22a), lxxiv (24b, 27b, 28a, 29a, 30a), lxxv (1a), lxxvi (5a).

Ayo – ii (34a), xviii (36b), xxxii (9b, 23b, 40a, 42ab, 44a), xli (12a), xlii (18a), lii (20b).

Ara – xx (29a), xxix (28b).

Kis – iv (3b), xvi (33a), xxi (38b), xxii (30b), xxxiv (14a).

Sun – xv (27b), xviii (32b), xxxi (66a), xxxiii (22b), lxviii (17a), xc (9a).

Yud – vii (33b), xi (38a), xxiii (18b), xcv (2b), ciii (21a), cxiii (38a).

Utt – vi (44b), xxii (7a, 9a), xxv (17a), xxxi (19a), lv (8a, 10a, 12b, 14ab), lxiii (44b), cxv (22a).

63. GO-KARṆA = The deer antilope picta.

AS. 223. गोरिव कर्णोऽस्य गोकर्णः ।

Ayo – cxi (48b).

Kis – i (13a).

64. GO-PATI = Bull.

Ara – lii (4b).

65. GO-PUCCHA = A sort of monkey.

'गोपुच्छा गललाङ्गूलदीर्घा ये कपयः स्मृता' इति

Adi – xx (10b).

Kis – xxvi (2b).

66. GO-MĀYU = Jackal.

AK. 85/125. गां मिनोति मीनाति वा गोमायुः ।

Ayo – xci (18a).

Ara – xlvi (15b), lxv (2b, 3b, 4a, 9b).

Yud – xi (35b), xviii (55a, 57c), lix (29a), lxviii (22a), lxxvi (20a), xciii (48a), xcv (5b).

67. GO-LĀṄGŪLA = A black kind of monkey.

गो–लाङ्गूलः काकमुख वानर इति नारायणः । कृष्णमुखः कपिवां । (लो–टी)

Ayo – liv (30a).

Ara – xx (26b).

Kis – xxiii (4b), xxxv (30a), xxxviii (34a, 52a), xxxix (27ab).

Yud – iii (32c, 33b), xvii (20a), xxiv (34a), cvi (8b, 14b).

Utt – xcvii (14a).

68. GO-LĀṄGULĪ – Female of Go-lāṅgula.

गोलाङ्गुलीषु कृष्णरक्तासु वानरीषु। 'गोलाङ्गुल इति प्रोक्तः कृष्णरक्तंस्तु मर्कटः' इति रत्नमाला। गोपुच्छासु इति वा। (लो टी)।

Adi – xx (12a).

69. GṚDHRA = Vulture.

AK. 129. गृध्यति मांसं गृधः।

Adi – i (58b, 59a, 60a, 78a), iii (72b).

Ayo – xci (18a).

Ara – vii (2b), xx (1b, 19b), xxiii (4b, 9a), xxix (3b), liv (64c), lvii (10b, 37a, 38b, 39a, 40b, 42b, 53b), lviii (3b, 25a, 28b, 31b), lix (3b, 4b), lxxiv (12a, 14a, 24b, 29a, 31a), lxxv (1a, 18a, 21b, 22b, 23a, 27a, 28a, 32b, 40b, 41a).

Kis – xix (20a), lvii (1b, 6a, 9b, 13a, 14b, 18b, 20b, 23b), lviii (12a, 14b), lix (1b, 15a, 30b), lx (1a, 20ab), lxii (29b), lxiii (20a), lxiv (28b).

Sun – i (1a), xvi (26b), xxvi (34b, 41a), xxxii (26a), xxxvi (38b), lxxviii (20a).

Yud – xi (35b), xvi (11a), xviii (57c), xxvii (31a, 34a), xxxi (36a), xliv (44a), lix (29a), lxviii (22b), lxxvi (20a, 35b, 39a), lxxviii (11b), lxxx (68b), lxxxix (26a), xci (20a, 24a, 25a), xciii (48a), xcv (5b), cix (31a), cxi (28b, 29a, 31b, 35b, 36a, 44a).

Utt – vi (52a), xxxvi (42a), lxiv (3a, 5b, 7a, 12c, 22b, 26b, 27a, 28a, 33b, 49b, 50a, 51b, 55c, 59a).

70. GRĀHA = A rapacious animal living in fresh or sea water; any large fish or marine animal, e.g., crocodile, shark, Gangetic alligator, etc.

AK. 43/65. गृह्णाति ग्राहस्तन्तु नागाख्यः, विभाषा ग्रहः इति णः।

Adi – xlii (7b).

Ayo – lv (4a).

Kis – xli (21b), xliv (48b).

Sun – lxxiii (12b), lxxv (28a, 30a), lxxx (13a, 20a), xciv (12b).

Yud – liv (25b).

71. GRĀHĪ = Female marine animal.

Yud – lxxxiii (151c, 153a, 158b, 164a).

72. CAKRA-VĀKA = The Cakra bird. *Anas Casarca.*

AK. 88/129. चकते चक्रः। चक्रेति वाक्—आख्यास्य चक्रवाकः।

Ara – xv (3a, 42b), xx (20b), xxi (12a), lxxviii (15a), lxxx (27b), lxxxi (28a, 42b).

Kis – xiii (8b), xxix (19a), li (11b).

Sun – xiv (38b, 39a), xvii (25b).

Yud – lxxvi (38b), lxxxiii (71a).

Utt – xx (20a, 21a), xlv (14a), lxxxiv (4b).

73. CAMARA = A kind of ox called the Yak. *Bos Grunniens.*

AK. 86/126 चमति चमरः।

Ara – xv (4b).

Utt – vi (45b).

74. CILLIKĀ – Female of a cricket.

अन्तरीक्षस्थ कीट विशेषः

Adi – xxvii (12b).

75. CHĀGA – He-Goat.

AK. 152/217. छयति रोगं छागः।

Yud – lii (23b).

76. CHĀGALA = Goat.

AK. 152/217. छयति रोगां श्छागः, छागलश्च।

Yud = xix (42b).

77. JAṬĀYU = Name of the King of Vultures.

Adi – i (58b), iii (49a, 55a, 56b), iv (15a).

Ara – xx (1b, 34b, 36b), l (58a), lvii (5a, 10b, 33a, 36a, 39b), lviii (1a, 3b, 20a, 26b, 27a, 32a, 33c), lxxiv (10b, 23a, 24a), lxxv (21b, 26a, 36b, 40b).

Kis – lvii (2b, 9a, 15a, 18b, 21a, 22b, 23a, 24a), lviii (10a, 14b), lix (2a, 6b, 10b, 12a, 13a), lx (11b, 21a), lxi (5b, 7a, 18a, 19a, 20b).

Sun – i 53a), xxvi (35a), xxxii (16b, 25b, 28a), xci (54a).

Yud – cix (31b), cxi (31b).

78. JAMBUKA = Jackal.

AK. 125. जमति जम्बुकः सर्वभक्षत्वात्।

Kis – xix (20a).

79. JALA-KUKKUṬA = Water-fowl.

Kis – xiii (8a), li (12a).

80. JALA-KUKKUBHA = The aquatic bird Parra Jacana or Goensis.

Ayo – lvi (12b).

Utt – xx (20a).

81. JALA-CARĀ = Aquatic animal.

Adi – xiii (29b).

82. JALAJA = An aquatic animal, fish.

Ayo – lxii (32b).

83. JHILLĪKĀ – Female of a cricket.

AK. 88/130. झिल्ली वाद्यभेदस्तत्तुल्यशब्दा झिल्लिका चक्राख्या।

Ara – vii (4a).

84. ṬIṬṬIBHĪ = The Female of the bird Parra Jacana, or goensis.

AK. 90/131. टिट्टिशब्दं भाषते टिट्टिभ:।

Ayo – viii (41b).

Yud – lxxxiii (71b).

85. TAKṢAKA = Serpent.

Ara – xxxvii (12b).

Sun – lxxx (9b).

Yud – xxvii (62a).

Utt – xxiv (4a), xxxi (23a).

86. TARAKṢU = Hyena.

AK. 84/124 तरं क्षिणोति मार्गं रुणद्धि तरक्षुः।

As. 265. तरक्षु द्वयं स्वल्प व्याघ्र। अयं कुक्कुरप्रायो व्याघ्रपुच्छश्च।

तरन् प्लवन् क्षिणोति हिनस्तीति तरक्षुः।

Ayo – ciii (7a).

Ara – liii (42b).

Sun – xviii (33a).

87. TITTIRA = Francoline partridge.

AK. 90/131 तित्ति शब्दं राति तित्तिरि:।

Ayo – c (66b).

88. TIMI = A kind of whale.

AK. 42/64 तिम्यति तिमि: ।

Ara – xvii (23a), lxi (18a).

Kis – xliii (14c).

Sun – i (2b), xxxv (42a).

Utt – vii (7a).

89. TIRĪṬAKA = A kind of bird.

Ara – lxxx (23a).

90. TURAGA = Horse.

AK. 184. तुरं त्वरितं गच्छति तुरग:, ड: ।

Adi – xi (14b), xli (15b, 17b), xliii (14a).

Ayo – xxvi (19a), xliv (25a), lix (4a), cii (6a, 17a).

Ara – xxix (2a), xxxiii (32a).

Yud – xviii (53a), xxix (20a), xlix (68a), liv (25a), lviii (20c), lxxvi (27a), xci (30b), xcii (15a), cxii (10a).

Utt – xlix (2a, 12b).

91. TURAṂGAMA = Horse.

AK. 184. तुरं त्वरितं गच्छति तुरग:, ड: । (तुरङ्गम:) गमश्चेति खच् ।

Adi – xiii (1a).

Ayo – xliii (15a, 16a).

Sun – xlii (39a), liii (12b).

Yud – xix (12a), xxxv (1b), xliv (30a), xlix (20a, 74b, 76a), lxxvii (18b).

92. DANTIN = Elephant.

AK. 127/182. दन्तौ स्तोऽस्य दन्ती दन्तावल: ।

Ayo – xci (14b).

Utt – cxiii (18a).

93. DĀTYŪHA = Gallinule.

AK. 87/128-29. द्वितीयं तृतीयं वा रूपं वहति दित्यवाट्, तस्यापत्यं दात्यूह: ।

Ayo – liv (42a), lvi (12a), cxi (49a).

Ara – lxxxi (11b).

Kis – xiii (8b), xxvi (5a).

Yud – xv (9a, 11b).

Utt – xlv (14b).

94. DVIJA = A bird or any oviparous animal, appearing first as an egg.

AK. 89/131. द्विर्जायत इति द्विजः ।

As. 247. प्रथममण्डेन जायते, ततः शाबकेन। अतो द्विजः ।

Adi – lvi (10a).

Ayo – iv (14b), lxxiii (14c), xcviii (16b), ciii (4a, 16a), civ (11a), cv (3b).

Ara – lix (39a), lxviii (6a), lxxiv (10a), lxxv (27a), lxxviii (8ab), lxxxi (25b, 44a, 46a).

Kis – ix (24b), xli (9a), lvii (2a).

Sun – iv (5a), xiii (12ab), xvii (12a, 32a, 52a), xx (24b), xxxvii (40b), lvii (113a), lxix (12a), lxxiv (53b), lxxv (15b).

Yud – ii (26b), xi (43a), xvi (7b), xl (19b), lxxx (8b).

Utt – xxxix (6b), lxiv (2a).

95. DVI-JIHVA = Serpent. 'द्विजिह्वौ सर्पसूचकौ' इत्यमरः ।

Ayo – xlii (2a).

96. DVI-PA = Elephant.

AK. 127/183. द्वाभ्यां पिबति द्विपः ।

Adi – vi (26b).

Ayo – xxxix (42b), xlv (8b), xcvi (22a), ci (42a), ciii (13b).

Ara – xxx (27b), xxxiv (10b), xxxviii (5b), xli (3a), lix (41a), lxx (2b), lxxvi (17b), lxxviii (32a).

Kis – ii (8b), xv (29b).

Sun – iv (8b), xv (28b), xxxvii (19b), liii (2b), lx (7b), lxxiii (7a), lxxvii (23b), lxxx (19b), lxxxix (25b).

Yud – iv (2a), vii (34b), xxxi (10b), l (28a), li (85b), lvi (62b), lxx (6b), xci (14b).

Utt – vii (28a), xxi (24a).

97. DVĪPĪ = Tiger, panther, leopard.

AK. 84/124. द्वौ वर्णावीयते द्वीपोस्त्यस्य वा। तन्निवासित्वाद् द्वीपी ।

Ayo – ciii (7a).

Ara – liii (42a).

Yud – xi (38b).

Utt – vii (20b, 21a), xxxi (13a).

98. DHṚTARĀṢṬRĪ = Name of a daughter of Tāmrā, mother of geese and other water birds.

AK. 129. कृष्णैश्चञ्चु चरणै: । धृतराष्ट्रे—अमात्ये भवे धृतराष्ट्रा:, राज हंसेभ्यो न्यूनत्वात् ।

Ara – xx (18a, 20a).

99. DHENŪ = Cow which has lately calved.

AK. 151/216. धयत्येनां धेनु: ।

Adi – lv – (1a).

Ayo – xxv (8a).

Yud – viii (12b), cxiii (82a).

Utt – lv (9a, 11b, 13b, 22b).

100. NAKULA = The Bengal mungoose or Viverra Ichneumon.

Yud – xi (38a).

101. NAKRA = Crocodile.

AK. 43/65. न क्रामति नक्र: ।

Ayo – xxviii (15a), xlvii (3a), cxxiv (22a).

Ara – xvii (23a), xxvii (9a), lxi (18a).

Kis – xvi (36b), xliv (53b).

Sun – i (2b), xviii (29a), xxxv (42a), lxxii (13a), lxxv (28a), xciv (18a, 19a).

Utt – xxi (6a, 35c).

102. NANDINĪ = A kind of cow, mother of Surabhi.

Adi – lvi (17b).

(To be continued)

References

* Continued from p. 256 of vol. XXVIII, No. 3.

57. *Ait. Āra.*, iii. 2. 4; *Śat. Brā.*, v. 1. 2. 15; xiv. 1. 2. 17; *Mbh.; Kāśikā,* (72), 5, 1, 2, 17.

58. Harappa (Vats), IV. 10070; V. 1924; Seal 226-231; *Adbhuta Brāh,* (Ind. Stud. 1, 39). Mohenjo (Mackay), DK−8324−L; Seal. 57; Mohenjo (Marshall), DK−1212; SD−1683; *Mahābhāṣya,* 4, 2, 43; *Shaḍv. Brā.*, v, 3.

59. *Ṛv.*, iii 53. 23; *Av.*, viii. 6. 10; *Ait. Brā.*, iii. 34; *Tait. Saṁ.*, v. 1, 2, 1. 2; v. 1, 5, 5; *Jaim. Brā.* i., 57, 4; *Mahābhāṣya,* i, 1, 56, 136.

60. *Mbh.* (BORI), I. 29. 16a; *Sat. Brā.* VI. 7, 2, 6. *Kāśika,* (183). 8, 2, 9, 18; *Ṛv.* i, 164, 46; *Av.*, iv, 6, 3.

61. *Mbh.* (BORI), I. 15. 22a; *Tait. Āra,* x. 1, 6.

62. *Ṛv.*, i. 83. 1; *Av.*, i. 31. 4; *Vaj. Saṁ.*, xxi. 20; *Sāṅk. Śrauta Sūtra,* ix. 23. 4; *Śat Brā.*, ii. 4. 3. 13; *Tait. Saṁ.*, vii. 5. 3. 1; *Jaim. Up. Brā.*, i. 12. 4; *Tait. Brā.*, ii. 1. 1. 3; *Aśv. Śrauta Śūtra,* iii. 12. 2; *Gobh. Gr. Sūtra,* iii. 8. 7; *Mbh.* (BORI), l, 93, 8b, 14b.

64. *Mbh.*, xii, 4877.

65. *Kāśikā* (225) 5, 3, 107, 9, *Mbh.*, iii.

66. Shaḍv. Brā. v, 8; *Mbh.*

67. *Mbh.*, i, 2628.

69. *Ṛv.*, i. 118. 4; vii. 104. 22; *Av.*, vii. 95. 1; xi. 2. 2; *Tait. Saṁ.*, iv. 4. 7. 1; *Mait. Saṁ.*, iv. 9. 19; *Tait. Āra.*, iv. 29; *Mbh.* (BORI). I, 60, 55b.

70. Harappa (Vats), II. H−417; Seal-2430; Mohenjo (Marshall), HR-791; *Śat. Brā,* 3. 5, 3, 25; 6, 1, 25; *Mahābhāṣya,* 3, 3 156.

72. *Ṛv.*, ii. 39. 3; *Av.*, xiv. 2. 64; *Mait. Saṁ.*, iii, 14. 3. 13; *Vaj. Saṁ.*, xxiv, 22. 32; *Mbh.* (BORI), I. 60, 56b; *Kāśika,* 6, 3, 118, 6; 4, 2, 80, 9.

73. *Mbh.*, Mahābhāṣya, 2, 3, 36, 458.

75. Harappa (Vats), iii. Ah−29; Mohenjo (Mackey), DK−5951; Seal-430; *Ṛv.*, i. 162. 3; *Tait Saṁ.*, v. 6. 22. 1; *Vaj. Saṁ.* xix. 89; *Śat. Brā.*, iii. 3. 3. 4; *Mait. Saṁ.*, iii. 11. 2; *Mahābhāṣya, 2, 3, 61.*

77. *Mbh.*, i, 2634.

78. *Mbh.* (BORI), xii. 149. 103a.

79. *Mbh.*, iii, 9926.

82. *Mbh.*, ii, 94.

83. *Mbh.*, i, 2894.

84. *Mbh.* xii.

85. *Mbh.* (BORI), I, 3, 1196; *Tānd. Brā,* 25, 15, 3. *Sāṅkh, Gṛ,* iv, 18, 1.

86. *Tait. Saṁ.*, v. 5. 19. 1; *Mait. Saṁ.*, iii. 14. 21; *Vaj. Saṁ,* xxiv. 40.

87. *Tait. Saṁ.*, ii. 5, 1. 2; v. 5. 16. 1; *Vaj. Saṁ.*, xxiv. 30, 36; *Mait. Saṁ.*, ii. 4. 1; iii. 14. 1; *Kath. Saṁ.*, xii. 10; *Śat. Brā.*, i. 6. 3. 5; v. 5. 4. 6; *Jaim. Brā.*, ii. 154. 6.

88. *Mbh.*

90. *Mbh.*

92. *Ṛv.*, iv, 6. 8; *Tait. Brā.*, 3, 8, 9, 3; *Tait. Āra.*, 10, 1, 5, 16; *Mbh.*

93. *Tait. Saṁ.*, v. 5. 17. 1; *Mait. Śaṁ.*, iii. 14. 6; *Vaj. Saṁ.*, xxiv, 25. 39; *Mbh.*

95. *Śāṅ. Āra.*, 8, 7; *Mbh.*

96. *Kāśikā, iv, 1, 86, 12; Mbh.*

97. *Av.*, iv. 8. 7; vi. 38. 2; xx. 409. 4; *Mait. Saṁ.*, ii. 1. 9; *Mbh.* (BORI), I, 60, 63b.

98. *Tāṇ.*, *Brā.*, 26, 16, 3; *Śat. Brā*, 13, 5, 4, 22.

99. *Ṛv.*, i. 32. 9; i. 134. 4, ii. 2. 2; ii. 34. 8; vi. 135. 8; *Av.*, v. 17. 18; vii. 104. 1; *Tait. Saṁ.*, ii. 6. 2. 3; *Mait. Saṁ.*, iv. 4. 8; *Vaj. Saṁ.*, xviii. 27; *Śat. Brā.*, ii. 2. 1. 21; *Mahābhāṣya*, I, 4, 1, 300; 5, 4, 77, 440.

100. *Daiv. Brā.*, 2, 3; *Jaina. Brā.*, i. 545; *Kāśikā* (225), 5, 3, 107, 11; *Mbh.* (BORI), I, 2, 209b.

101. *Pāṇini*, vi, 3, 75; *Mbh.*

102. *Tait. Brā.*, 10, 1, 6, 16; *Mbh.* (BORI), I, 93, 16a.

57

Concordance of the Fauna in The Rāmāyaṇa*

Sibadas Chaudhuri

103. NALA=Species of reed. Amphidonax Karka.

Ara—lxxviii (9a).

104. NĀGA=Snake, serpent.

AK. 57. न-अगा नागा:

Adi—v (22b), xli (7b, 9a, 12b, 13a), xlvi (31b).

Ayo—xv (7b), xxv (27b, 30b), xxviii (13a), cviii (18b).

Ara—vii (32b), xx (29b, 32b), xl (14a), xliii (47b), xlvi (13b), xlviii (11c).

Kis—viii (19a), xviii (23b), xlii (3a).

Sun—vii (13a, 66a), ix (13b), xv (12a), xviii (5b, 30b), xlix (19a), lxxv (31a), lxxx (9a), xciv (12a).

Yud—iv (35a), xvi (61b), xix (50a), xxi (5a), xxiv (1b), xxvi (15c, 16a, 29a), xxxvii (55a) liii (61a).

Utt—vii (18b, 36b), xvi (10b), xxiv (18a), xxvii (4b), xxix (56a), xxx (7a), xxxi (23a), xxxii (6a), civ (8a), cv (29a), cxi (5a), cxv (13b, 20c).

105. NĀGA=Elephant.

AK. 127/183. नगे भवो नाग: । न-अगो वा ।

Adi—vi (25a), xxvii (24b), xxviii (2b, 6a), xli (22a) lxxix (21a).

Ayo—xxviii (7a), xxxii (9a), xl (9b, 20b), lxxvi (39a), lxxxix (13d), xc (3a), xcii (25c), cvi (12a, 29a), cvii (14b), cix (27a, 32b, 36a), cxi (47a), cxxiii (22d), cxxiv (20a), cxxv (22b).

Ara – xliii (4a), lxxviii (25a, 31a).

Kis – ix (35b), xxxi (22b, 23a), lx (15a), lxi (13c).

Sun – iii (19b), iv (13a), ix (20b), xxii (2a), xxxv (35b), xlii (38a, 39a).

Yud – vii (33a), xvi (41bc), xxxa (4a), xxxv (8c, 15b, 17c), xxxvii (39a), xlvi (13a), xlix (5a), lvi (57b), lxxv (la, 26a), lxxvii (4b), lxxx (21a), xciii (46b), cxii (9a), cxiii (28a).

Utt – x (19a), xix (10a), xxi (52a, 59a), xxxi (13b), xxxiii (37a), xxxvi (39a).

106. NĪLAKAṆṬHĪ = Pea-hen.

Sun – xi (23b).

107. PATAGA = A winged or flying animal, bird.

AK. 89/131. पतन्त्यनेनेति पत: पक्ष: । पतैर्गच्छति पतग: ।

AS. 247. पतन् उड्डयमानो गच्छति, पतग: ।

Adi – iv (53b), xliii (16b).

Ara – xxiii (8b), xl (27a, 32a), lii (15a), lvii (34b, 43a, 45b, 46b, 51a, 54b, 55a), lviii (23a), lxii (18a), lxxv (20c, 28b, 33b, 35a, 36a).

Kis – xliv (25b), lxii (38b), lxiii (11a).

Sun – v (32a), lxxxi (2a).

Yud – xvi (86a), xxvi (25b, 36a), xlvi (122a).

108. PATAṂGA = Any flying insect, a grasshopper, a bee, a butterfly or moth.

AS. 2. 243. पतङ्गद्वयं फड़िङ्ग इति ख्याते। "पतेरङ्गच् पक्षिणि" इत्यङ्गच्। पतङ्ग: ।

Adi – xiii (30a), xx (16b).

Ayo – xxv (32a), xxviii (14a).

Ara – xxxiv (13b).

Kis – lix (29a).

Sun – xxxviii (36b), lvii (27a), lxxxvii (10a).

Yud – xix (25b), xlv (33b), liv (53b), lxxvii (3b).

Utt – xxix (43b).

109. PATATRĪN = Bird.

AK. 89/131. पतत्राणि विद्यन्ते येषु ते पतत्रिण: ।

AS. 2. 247: (पतत्र) पत्रयोगात् पतवि-पविणौ । अत: इनि: ।

Uṇādi (Śveta), 4, 71, पतताति पतत्रि: पक्षी।

Ara – xxi (21b).

Kis – li (17b).

Sun – xliii (18a).

Yud – lxiv (20b).

Utt – xxviii (24b), xxx (24a).

110. PATTRA-RATHA = 'Using wings as a vehicle' – Bird.

AK. 89/ 131. पत्राणि पक्षा रथोऽस्य पत्ररथा: ।

AS. 2. 247. पत्रमेव रथ इवास्येति पत्ररथ: ।

Kis – xliv (93a).

Utt – vii (33b), xviii (25b).

111. PANNAGA = Serpent.

AK. 38/58. पद्भ्यां न गच्छति पन्नग: ।

Adi – iv (53b), xiv (19a).

Ayo – xv (6b), xci (12b).

Ara – xx (29b), xxvi (22b), xxviii (12a), xxxii (18b), xxxiv (16b), xxxv (12b), lv (3a), lvi (30b), lxiii (6b), lxxi (24a), lxxvi (22b).

Kis – v (8b), xvi (41b), xli (54a), xliii (53b), xliv (18a, 105b).

Sun – iii (39a, 44b), vii (46b), viii (26a), xviii (46b), xx (8b), xxii (29b), xxxi (55b), xlii (8a), xliii (21a), lix (12a), xciv (17b), xcv (21a), xcvi (1b).

Yud – iv (39b, 42a), vi (1b), xx (9b), xxvi (13a), xxxiv (22a) xxxv (18c), xxxvi (30a, 31a, 76a), xxxvii (2a, 27a), xlvi (32b, 121a, 140a), li (76b), lxviii (17b), lxxxii (1b), lxxxiv (30a), lxxxv (19a), lxxxvii (32a), ixxxix (27b), xcv (15a).

Utt – ii (8a), xxi (63b), xxiii (18b), xxvi (26a), xxviii (24b), xxxi (32a), xxxii (3a), xxxv (42b), xxxvi (30a, 39a), civ (16b, 21b).

112. PANNAGĪ = Female serpent.

Ara – xlv (18b).

Yud – iv (32b), ix (34b).

113. PARAPUṢṬA = Nourished by another, the Kokila or Indian Cuckoo.

Ara – lxxx (29a).

Ayo – lvi (13a).

114. PARABHṚTA=Nourished by another, the Kokila or Indian Cuckoo.

AK. 128. परभृतः काकी पृष्टत्वात्।

AS. 2. 234. विजातीयेन भृतः पृष्टः परभृतः।

Yud- xv (9b).

115. PAŚU='Animal'.

["पश"] इति सौत्रोऽयं धातुः। पशतीति पशुः चतुष्पदः।

—Uṇādi (Kātantra), 1, 15

Adi—v (5b), xiii (29a, 31a), lxiv (11b, 19a, 22b, 24b).

Ayo—xxxiii (19a), lxi (24b), lxix (22b), lxxxiii (36a), cix (22b), lviii (10b), lxiii (10b).

Yud—xl (14a), lxxiv (37b), xcvii (14a).

Utt—xxiii (38b), xxviii (48b), lxiii (44a).

116. PAKṢIN='Winged' creature. Bird.

AK. 131. पक्षाः सन्त्यस्य पक्षी।

Adi—xiii (30a), xxvii (12b), xxxiv (17a), xxxvi (15a), lvi (23a), lxxvi (10a, 11b, 13a).

Ayo—xxxiii (24a), xliii (33b), liv (9b, 13a), lv (20a), lvi (31a), lxii (14b), lxviii (22a), xcviii (4b), c (63a), ci (12b, 41a, 42b), cxi (50a), cxvii (9a).

Ara—v (5b), vi (9a), vii (3b, 5a), xii (13b), xv (3b, 43a), xxviii (29b), xxix (14b), xxx (6a), xl (35b), xliii (39a), 1(58a), liii (10b), lvi (48a), lvii (1b, 3a, 7a, 12a, 48a, 49b), lviii (2a, 14a, 29b), lix (6b), lxii (5b), lxiii (35a), lxv (14a), lxxv (3a, 24b, 34b, 35b), lxxvi (8b, 13, 18b), lxxix (21a), lxxxi (24b), xxi (5b).

Kis—xiii (11a, 20a, 46a,), xvii (9b), xix (20b), xli (10b, 31a), xliii (53a), xliv (18a), xlix (6a, 13b, 17b), li (16b), lvii (7a), lviii (5b), lx (7a), lxi (23a). lxii (3a).

Sun—ii (10b, 34b), iii (39a), vii (61a), xii (39a), xvii (xoa), xviii (9a), xxvii (34a), xxxvi (37a), xxxvii (2a), xliv (17a), lvii (73b), lxix (3b), xcvii (28a).

Yud—iii (35a), xi (40b), xxxi (17b), lxxvii (12b), lxxxiii (89b), lxxxiv (26a), xci (29a).

Utt—xviii (31b), xx (14a), xlv (11b), lxxxiv (1b, 5b), lxxxv, (17a), xciv (15a), xcv (8b), cvii (25a).

117. PUṆS-KOKILA = The male of the Indian Cuckoo.

AK. 128. कोकते चित्तं गृह्णाति।

Ayo – cxi (49b).

118. PUTRA-PRIYA = Name of a kind of bird.

Ara – lxxx (23b).

119. PŪRṆA-MUKHA = A species of bird.

Ara – xxx (23b).

120. PECAKA (Kṛṣṇa-) = Owl.

AK. 86/127. पचति पीयते वा पेचकः।

AS. 2. 229. पचय्येश्छन्दस्यमिपच्योर लिट्येत्वं वक्रव्यम। पेचकः।

Yud – xxvii (31b).

121. PṚṢATA = Spotted antelope.

AK. 86/126. पृषतो बिन्दुचित्रः।

AS. 2. 223. पृषिरञ्जिभ्यां कित् इत्यतच्। पृषतः। 'पृषतो विन्दुचित्रितः' इति माधवः।

Ara – lxxviii (13b).

Ayo – cii (2a), cxi (48b).

122. PRA-VĀLA (also bāla) = Coral.

AK. 155/221. प्रवलते प्ल (प्र)वते वा-अबधेरूर्ध्वं प्रवालम्।

Ayo – xc (17b).

123. PRĀNĪN = Animal, including man.

Adi – xli (29b).

Ayo – iii (20b).

Sun – lxxxiii (6b), lxxxix (17b).

Yud – lxi (28a).

Utt – x (16a, 20ab), xxv (9b, 16b, 21a, 22a), xxvi (33a, 41a), xxxviii (49b), lxxiv (4b), lxxix (7b), xc (13b), cvi (13a), cxi (16a).

124. PRIYAṂVADA = A bird.

Ara – lxxx (23b).

125. PLAVA = A kind of aquatic bird.

As. 2. 248. प्लवः पिल इति ख्यातः।

AK. 89/131. प्लवते प्लवः।

Ara – lxxviii (7a), lxxxi (43a).

Ayo – cxi (49a).

Kis – li (12c).

Sun – lxxxv (6b).

126. PLAVA-GA = Going by leaps or plunges, monkey.

AK. 84/124. प्लवैर्गच्छति प्लवगः।

AS. 2. 216 प्रवप्लवौ गतिविशेषौ। ताभ्यां गच्छतीति प्लवङ्गः प्लवगः।

प्रवङ्गः प्रवगश्च भुजङ्ग(म) भुजगवद् व्युतपाद्यौ।

Adi – iii (143b).

Kis – i (2a, 6a, 8b, 21a, 30a), iv (10a), ix (8a, 94a), xii (27a, 47b), xiv (21a), xvi (12b), xviii (12b), xxi (2a, 11b, 38a), xxiv (9b, 12b, 18a, 24a), xxviii (31a), xxx (16b), xxxiv (16b), xxxviii (3a, 6a, 38b, 39a, 48a), xl (15a), xli (32b, 66b, 71a), xlv (4ab, 5b), xlvii (4a), xlviii (8a), liv (20b), lvi (13a, 19a), lx (3a), lxii (28b), lxiii (9b, 25a), lxiv (29a).

Sun – i (35b, 89a, 92a), ii (48b), iii (70b), vii (1a, 14b, 32a), viii (15b), xiii (15a), xvi (45a), xxix (36a), xxxiii (18a, 21b), xxxv (31b, 39a), liii (6b, 17b), liv (18b), lv (6a, 18b), lviii (3a), lix (13a), lxi (11a), lxii (10b), lxxv (8b), xci (65a).

Yud – vi (22c), vii (26b, 27b), xiii (24b), xiv (17a), xvi (33a), xx (2a), xxii (1b), xxx (9a, 29a), xxxb (26b), xxxvi (112b), xlv (13a, 37a), xlvi (17a, 51b, 60b), xlix (56a), l (38a), lii (34b), liii (27a, 29b), liv (40b), lvi (18a, 21a), lxxvii (5a, 21b), lxxviii (12c), lxxxii (7a), lxxxiii (166a), xcix (28b, 39a), cx (54b), cxiii (2a, 27b).

127. PLAVAṂGA = Moving by jumps, monkey.

A.K. 84/124. प्लवैर्गच्छति प्लवङ्गः।

AS. 216. – see 126.

Kis – i (26b), iii (12a), xvii (6a), xviii (13b), xxi (3b), xxiv (43a), xxv (37a), xxxi (18a), xxxiv (17a), xxxvii (8b, 21b), xxxviii (38a), xxxix (39a), xliii (27b), xliv (37b, 68b, 128b), xlv (9a), xlviii (5b, 14c, 15a), li (2b, 22b), lii (40a), liv (21b), lvi (21a), lix (28a), lxii (12a, 29a), lxiii (18a), lxiv (24a).

Sun – i (1a, 9a, 19a, 37b, 47b), iii (7b, 65b, 71b, 73b), xxxv (33b), xxxvi (30a), xxxvii (1b, 2a, 22a), xliii (16a), liv (5b), lix (15b), lxi (10a) lxii (3b, 4b), lxv (25a), lxxiv (35a), lxxv (3b), xciii (2b), xciv (4a).

Yud – i (7b, 8b), ii (8b, 12a, 40a), iii (39b), vi (13b), xvi (37b, 46a, 58a, 95a), xvii (11a, 12a, 14a), xviii (49a), xix (7b), xxvi (41a, 45b), xxviii (7b, 20a, 39b), xxx (39b), xxxii (5b, 8a, 25b, 27b, 29a, 37b), xxxvi (60a, 102a), xlii (10a), xlv (9b), xlvi (20b, 48b, 555b, 112b, 114b, 115a), xlvii (11a), xlix (30a, 33a, 36a), l (45b), li (36b, 40a), liv (4a), lvi (84a), lix (2b), lxi (23a), lxii (3a), lxxi (57a), lxxii (2b), lxxiv (14), lxxvi (56a), lxxxii (12a), lxxxiii (73a), lxxxv (6b), xcviii (21b), xcix (16a, 17a, 32b), c (1a), cxi (3b), cxii (21b), cxiii (87a).

Utt – xxiii (5b, 40a), xxxviii (92a), xl (9a).

128. BAKA = A kind of heron or crane.

AK. 88/129. वक्ति बकः ।

AS. 2. 237. 'बक कौटिल्ये'।

Ayo – lxv (14b).

Yud – lxxxiii (71b).

(To be continued)

References

* Continued from pp. 359 of vol. XXVIII, No. 4.

103. *Mbh.*

104. *Śat. Brā,* xi, 2, 7, 12; *Āśval. Gṛ. Sūtra,* iii, 4, 1; *Mbh.* (BORI), 1, 2, 77; 1, 52, 14.

105. *Bṛhadāraṇyaka Up.*, i, 3, 24; *Ait Brā;* viii, 22; *Mbh.*, II, 360.

107. *Mbh.* (BORI), 1, 28, 22a.

108. *AV.*, vi, 50, 1; *Bṛhad. Up.*, vi, 1, 19 (Mādhyaṃdina, vi. 2, 14; Kāṇva, 2, 14); *Chand. Up.* vi, 9, 3; Uṇādi (Daṇḍanātha), II, 2, 56; *Adbhuta Brā;* vi, 5; *Mbh.*, v, 3933.

109. *Ait. Up.*, iii, 3, 3; *Av.*, viii, 7, 24; x, 10, 14; *Mbh.* (BORI), 1, 2, 77.

110. *Mbh.*

111. *Mbh.* (BORI), 1, 12, 2a.

112. *Mbh.* (BORI), 1, 92, 31a.

115. *Tait. Saṃ.*, iv, 2, 10. 1-4; *Kāṭh. Saṃ.*, xvi. 17; *Mait. Saṃ.*, ii. 7. 17; *Vāj Saṃ.*, xiii, 47-51; *AV,* iii, 10. 6; *Śat. Brā.*, ii, 8, 4, 16; *Pañc. Brā.*, x, 2, 7; Uṇādi (Daṇḍanātha), 2, 1, 30.

116. *ṚV.*, i, 48, 5; *AV.*, iv, 34, 4; xi. 5, 21; xii. 1. 51; *Kāth. Saṃ.;* xxxiv. 8; *Ait. Brā,* iv, 23; *Bṛhad. Up.,* ii. 5. 18.

117. *Uṇādi* (*kā*), 6, 46.

121. *Uṇādi* (*kā*), 3, 7,("पृषु वृषु") पृषतीति पृषतः कस्तूरीमृगः।
Uṇādi (Nārāyaṇa) :सिञ्चति रेतस्सेकं करोति पृषतः मृगः।

122. *Mbh.*

125. *Tait. Saṃ.*, v, 5, 20, 1; *Mait. Saṃ.*, iii 14, 15; *Vāj Saṃ.*, xxiv, 34.

58

Concordance of the Fauna in The Rāmāyaṇa*

Sibadas Chaudhuri

130. BALĀKĀ = Crane.

AK. 88/1 9 बलाहकान् कायति बलेनाकति याति वा बलाका।

AS. /240 स्वल्पबकजातौ बलाकाद्वयम्। 'वल वल्ल संवरणे'।

'बलाकादयश्च' (उ० ४।१४) इत्याकः।

Ara – lxxviii (15a).

Yud – lxxxiii (71b), xci (25a), xciii (48a).

131. BARHIṆA = Peacoke.

AK. 89/130. बर्हमस्यास्ति बर्हिणः, फलबर्हाभ्यामिनन्।

AS. 2/245. बर्हयोगाद् बर्हिणः।

Ayo – xlix (3a), lxv (14b), cii (18a).

Ara – viii (4a), xxvi (22a), liv (64b).

Sun – xvii (10b), liii (13a).

Yud – xv (9a), xlvi (105a), liv (19a), lxxxi (30a).

Utt – l (22b).

132. BIḌĀLA = Cat.

AK. 85/125. विशन्–आलात्याखून् विड़ालः, बिलालो वा। बिलान्यलति पर्याप्नोति वा, बिलति भिनत्ति–आखून्वा, विड् आलस्याशुचित्त्वाद्वा, विड आक्रोश इत्यस्माद्वा।

AS. 2/219. विड आक्रोशे।

Ara – liv (63c).

Utt – vi (53b).

133. BHADRA=A particular kind of elephant.

AK. 149/213. भन्दते भद्रः ।

Adi–vi (26a).

134. BHADRA-MANDA=A kind of elephant.

Adi–vi (27a).

135. BHADRA-MṚGA=A kind of elephant.

Adi–vi (27a).

136. BHARADVĀJA='Bearing speed or strength (of flight)'–A Skylark.

AK. 127. भरद्वाजापत्यं भरद्वाजोऽस्त्यस्य वा भरद्वाजश्चाटकेराख्यः ।

Ara–lxxx (23b).

137. BHĀSA=A bird of prey, Vulture.

Ara–xx (19a).

138. BHĀSĪ=Female vultures.

Ara–xx (18a, 19a).

139. BHUJAGA=Going in curves, i.e. snake.

AK. 38/58. भुजेन कौटिल्येन गच्छति भुजगः ।

Sun–ii (11b), v (34a), xv (17a, 19c), lxxv (29b).

Yud–cx (40a).

Utt–xlii (40b).

140. BHUJAGĪ=Female snake.

Ara–lxi (15b).

141. BHUJAṂGA=Serpent.

Ayo– xvii (1a).

Kis–v (16b), lxii (36a).

Sun–xi (13b), xxiv (26b, 27b), lv (17b), lvi (3b), lxxv (29b), lxxx (20a).

Yud–xlvi (91a), li (88b), liii (48a).

Utt–vi (44b), xviii (22b), xxiii (14a), xxxi (59a), xxxviii (114b).

142. BHRAMARA=A large black bee.

AK. 89/130 भ्रमति भ्रमरः ।

Ayo–lvi (13b), cxxv (9a).

Ara–lxviii (16a), lxxxvi (17a).

Kis – xlix (14b), li (30b).

Sun – xiv (24b), xviii (16b), xxii (35a).

Yud – iii (34a), xv (10a).

Utt – xlv (11a).

143. BHṚṄGA-RĀJA = Bee-king, species of large bee.

AS. 2/244. भृञ्जो गन् प्रत्ययेन भृङ्गः।

AK. 80/130 भृज्जति बिभर्त्ति वा भृङ्गः।

Ayo – cv (12a).

Ara – lxxxi (13a).

Sun – xvii (9a), xviii (20b).

Yud – xv (11a).

Utt – xlv (11b).

144. MAKARA = Marine monster.

AK. 64. माकुर्यात्किचिदिति त्रस्यन्त्यस्मान्मकर।

Ayo – xlvii (3a), cii (13b), cxxiv (22a).

Sun – ii (11a), vii (38a), ix (1a), xvi (23b), xxxii (29ab), lxxv (31a), xciv (5b, 11a, 13a, 18a, 19a), xcvi (18a).

Yud – lxxviii (6b), cix (15a).

Utt – vi (45a), vii (3b), xxi (6a, 35b).

145. MAṆḌŪKA = A Frog.

AK. 43/65. मण्डति मण्डते वा सरो मण्डूकः।

['मण्डूक: शोणभेकयो' रिति भूरि०]

Kis – xxxiv (23b).

Sun – lxxx (19b).

Utt – xxxi (9a).

146. MADHU-PĀ = A bee.

Utt – xxv (27b).

147. MAŚAKA = Mosquito, gnat, any fly that bites or stings.

Ayo – xxv (32a), xxviii (14a).

Utt – vii (3a).

148. MAHĀ-GAJA = Grown elephant.

Ayo – ix (5b), xxv (33a), lxxi (16b).

Utt – xx (30b, 34b, 37b).

149. MAHĀ-DHURYA = A full-grown draught-ox.

"गुरुभारवहनक्षमो बलीवर्दः।" (८८०)

AK. 214. (धुर्य इ०) धुरं वहति...।

Ayo – xi(10b).

150. MAHĀ-SARPA = Great snake.

AK. 58. सर्पति सर्पः।

Ayo – xx (2b).

151. MAHIṢA = Buffalo.

AK. 85/125. महति मह्यां शेते वा महिषः।

AS. 218. 'मह पूजायाम्'। अविमह्योष्टिषच् (उ० १।४४)। महिषः।

Ayo – xxv (33b), lxv (20a), c vi (4b), cviii (4b), cxi (48a).

Ara – xv (4b), lxxvi (17a).

Kis – xlix (13a).

Sun – xv (40a), xviii (30a).

Yud – xv (18a), xxxvii (31a, 78b).

Utt – xx (19a).

152. MAYŪRA = Peacock, cock.

AK. 73/130. मीनात्यहिं मयूरः।

AS. 245. 'मय गतौ।' मयूरनवकं मयूरे। 'खर्तिपिञ्जादिभ्य उरोलचा' (उ० ४। ९६)। मयूरः।

Ayo – xlvi (11b).

Ara – xii (15b), xxi (13a), lxxxi (14b, 15ab, 16a).

Kis – xxix (13a), xliii (37a).

Sun – xii (36b), xv (41b).

Utt – xviii (5a, 22a, 23c, 24a).

153. MAKṢIKĀ = A fly, bee.

AK. 88/130 मक्षन्ति रुष्यन्त्यस्यै मक्षिका।

Ayo – xxviii (14a).

Ara – liv (65b).

Kis – li (30b).

154. MĀRJĀRA = Cat.

AK. 85/125. आखुभ्यो गृहं मार्ष्टि मार्जारः।

AS. 2/219. 'मृजूशुद्धौ'। 'कजिमृजिभ्यां चित्' (उ० ३।१३२) इत्यारन्।

'मृजेर्वृद्धि: ' इति वृद्धि: । मार्जार: ।

Ayo – cxxv (2a).

Kis – i (16b), xxvi (2b).

Yud – xi (38b).

Utt – vii (21ab).

155. MĀTAṄGA = Elephant.

AK. 161/229 मा तङ्गति, मातङ्गापत्यंवा ।

Adi – xx (16a).

Ayo – ii (13b), xx (39b), lvi (16a), cx (15a).

Ara – xx (26a), lxx (26a) lxxxi (28b).

Kis-xxix (10b), xliii (13b).

Sun – iv (5b, 9b), v (32b), x (6b), xxiv (16ab), xlii (4b, 18a), lxxviii (4a).

Yud – iii (40a), vi (26a), ix (23a), xxxvii (2a), liv (49a), lviii (17b), lxiv (2b), lxx (1b), lxxiv (12a).

Utt – ix (20c).

156. MĀTAṄGĪ = Female elephant.

Ara – xx (23a, 25a, 27a).

157. MINA = Fish.

AK. 42/64. मांनाति मीन: ।

Adi – xlv (18a).

Ayo – ci (41b), cxxv (4b).

Ara – xxix (13a), lix (40a), lxi (19a), lxx (6b), lxxviii (9a).

Sun – lv (9b), lvi (2a), lxxiii (12b), lxxv (12b), lxxx (19a), xciv (13a).

Yud – cix (17b).

Utt – vi (45a), vii (7a), xx (28b), xxi (6a, 35b).

158. MŪṢIKA = Rat, mouse.

AK. 86/126. मूषेति मूषिक: ।

AS. 2/225. मुष्णातीति मूषिक: ।

Yud – xi (38a).

159. MEṢA = Ram.

AK. 152/217. मेषति वाशते मेष: ।

Adi – l (6a, 7a, 8a, 9b, 10b, 11a).

Ara – xvi (15a, 17a, 22b, 24b, 26a, 28b, 31b), xl (29b), xlvi (15b).

Utt – xxxviii (29b).

160. MṚGA = Deer, antelope.

AK. 85/126. मृग्यते व्याधैर्मृग: ।

Adi – iii (53a), viii (32a), xxxi (18b), xxxiv (17a), xxxvi (15a), lvi (23a), lxxvi (10b, 11b, 13b).

Ayo – ix (18b, 33b), xxiv (5a), xxviii (11b, 12b), lii (35a), liv (40a, 42c), lv (19b, 20a), lvi (16b, 22b, 23b, 25a), lxii (14b), lxv (19a, 20b), lxvi (12b), c (63a), ci (41a, 42b), cii (4b, 12a), civ (5a, 19a), cv (23b, 35a), cvi (3a, 29d), cviii (4b, 29c), cxi (48a).

Ara – i (34d), v (9b), vi (9a), vii (2a, 6a), xii (13b), xv)34c), xvii (15a, 17b), xviii (21b), xix (20a), xx (24a), xxi (12b, 16b, 21a), xxiv (18a), xxxvi (19a, 57b), xxxvii (14a), xli (26a, 27a), xliii (22a),xliv (7b, 17a), xlvii (13a), xlix (11b, 13b), l (1a,5a, 6a, 7a, 9a, 12ab, 15a, 16a, 18a, 20a, 21ab, 23a, 24b, 25ab, 26a, 27b, 28a, 30a, 31a, 37b, 39b, 40a, 42b, 44a, 46ab, 47a, 48a, 55a, 56a), li (1b, 3a, 8b, 9a, 12a, 14a, 15a, 16b, 24a), lii (14b, 22b), liii (42a), liv (25a, 55a), lix (41a), lx (4b), lxii (3b, 5b), lxv (1a, 5b, 14a, 20ab), lxvi (25b, 26c), lxix (6a), lxxiii (4b), lxxvi (8b, 18b, 19a), lxxvii (17a, 38b), lxxix (21a), lxxx (3b, 12a), lxxxi (13b, 28b, 45a, 48a).

Kis – xvii (16b, 17b, 18b), xviii (5b), xxvi (2a), xxix (20b), xlix (13a), lxii (36b).

Sun – xv (40a), xvii (8a, 49b), xviii (52a), xx (11a, 12a, 24b), xxviii (9a, 10a), xxxi (33a, 56a), xxxvii (24a), l (23b, 33b), lviii (12b).

Yud – xxviii (18b), xxxvii (31a), li (41b), lix (20b), lxxxiii (103a), lxxxiv (25a), lxxxix (17a), xciii (48a), cxi (23a, 24b).

Utt – xvii (21b), xxi (66a), xxxi (5a), cvii (25a).

161. MṚGA = Elephants with particular marks.

Adi – vi (26a, 27a).

Ara – vii (2a), xx (25b).

162. MṚGA = A forest animal or wild beast, game of any kind.

AS. 2/213. मृगा: पशव: ।

Adi – xxvii (13a), xxix (6a), lii (23b).

Ayo – xxv (34a), xxxiii (24a), xliv (3b), liv (9b, 13a), lix (9a), lxviii (22a)

Ara – xxi (5b).

Kis – i (13a, 16b), xiii (9b, 11a, 46a), xvii (9b), xix (20b), xxvi (6a), xliii (53a), xliv (18a), xlix (6a, 17b).

Sun – xii (39a), xvii (10a), xviii (9a, 18b), xxxv (29b), xxxvii (40b), xxxviii (2a), xlii (36a), xlvi (6b), lv (4b), lvii (113a), lxxiv (53b), lxxviii (21a), xcvii (28a).

Yud – xvi (7b), xxix (11b), lxxx (8b).

Utt – xii (4b), xx (14a), lxxi (13a, 14a), lxxxiv (1b), lxxxv (8a), xciv (9a, 10a, 14b, 15a).

163. MṚGA-VATĪ = Name of the mythical progenitress of bears and Srimars.

Ara – xx (22b, 24b).

164. MAṆḌA = A class of elephants. (See 133).

Adi – vi (27a).

Ara – xx (25b).

165. MṚGA-RĀJA = 'King of beasts', – Lion.

Ayo – xii (4b).

Kis – xviii (22b), xxvi (24b).

Sun – xvii (49b), lxiv (28a).

Yud – xxxv (9a), l (33b), lxxx (21a).

Utt – vii (11b).

166. MṚGĪ = (a) Female deer or antelope; (b) Name of the mythical progenitress of antelopes.

Ayo – xxxvii (9b).

Ara – lxvi (3b), lxxxi (45a), xx (22b, 24a).

Kis – xix (3b).

Sun – xv (60b), xviii (50a), xxi (18b), xxvi (9b), lxvii (31b).

Yud – xxiii (40b), ci (10b).

Utt – xxxii (10b).

167. MṚGENDRA = 'King of beasts', – Lion.

AK. 124 मृगाणां द्वीप्यादि-शशान्तानामिन्द्रः ।

AS. 2/113. मृगाः पशवः, तेषामिन्द्रो राजा मृगेन्द्रः ।

Ayo – xx (3b).

Kis – xiii (47b).

Yud – xxxv (15b).

168. MATSA = Fish.

AK. 64 माद्यति मत्स्यः, मच्छोऽपि।

Ayo – liii (39b), lxix (28b), xc (17b), xcii (1a).

Ara – xxviii (29a), xliii (47b), xlvi (13b), lxxviii (9b, 24b).

Kis – li (26a).

Sun – lxxx (19b).

Yud – lxxiv (12a).

Utt – xc (17a).

(*To be continued*)

References

* Continued from p. 63 of vol. XXIX, No. 1.

130. *Mait. Saṃ,* iii, 14, 3, 4; *Tait. Saṃ,* v. 5. 16. 1; *Vāja. Saṃ,* xxiv. 22, 23.

133-5. भद्रा हिमालयपर्वतजाताः, मन्दा विन्ध्यपर्वतजाताः, मृगाः सह्यपर्वतजाताः, तेषामन्वयैर्वंशैः। 'भद्रा मन्दा मृगाश्चेति विज्ञेयास्त्रिविधा गजाः। क्रमेण हिमवद्विन्ध्यसह्यजाः'। (रा०—टिप्पनी, १५७)।

137. *Adbhuta Brā.*, vi, 8, Apast.; *Mbh.*, Harivaṃśa.

138. *Mbh.*, Harivaṃśa.

143. *AV.*, ix. 2, 22; *Mait. Saṃ.*, iii. 14, 8; *Vāja Saṃ,* xxiv, 29.

144. *Tait. Saṃ.*, v, 5, 13, 1; *Mait. Saṃ.*, iii, 14, 16; *Vāja. Saṃ.*, xxiv, 35.

145. *Ṛv.*, vii. 103. 1; x. 166. 5; *AV.*, vii. 122. 2; *Tait. Saṃ.*, v. 4. 3; *Mait. Saṃ.*, iii. 13. 2; *Pañca. Brā.*, xii 4. 16; *Nirukta,* ix. 5; Moh. (Mac.). Seal 45; *Kaṭh. Saṃ.*, xiii. 1; xxi, 7; *Vāja. Saṃ.*, xxiv. 36; *Śata. Brā.*, ix. 1. 2. 20.

146. *Amara Kośa,* सिंहादिवर्गः, ३०

147. *AV.*, vii. 56. 3; xi. 3. 5; *Mait. Saṃ.*, iii. 14. 8; *Vāja. Saṃ.*, xxiv. 29; *Bṛbad. Up.*, i. 3. 24; *Chand. Up.*, vi. 9. 3.

151. *RV.*, viii. 58. 15; ix. 92. 6; ix. 87. 7; x. 28. 10; *Vāja. Saṃ.*, xxiv. 28; Harappa, Seal 229-40; Mohenjo (Mck) Seal 257, 279 ...; SD 3319 (u), DK 3907 (l) Mohenjo (Mar) HK 2974.

152. *ṚV.*, iii. 45 1; viii. 1. 25; *Mait. Saṃ.*, iii. 14. 4; Har. (Vats) A 317 (I), 5040 (II); Moh (Mac.) DK 7795 (I) *Vāja. Saṃ.*, xxiv. 23. 27.

153. *ṚV.*, i. 162. 9; i. 119. 9; *Bṛhad Up.*, iii. 3. 2; *ĀV.*, xi. 1, 2; *Praśna Up.*, ii. 4.

154. Harappa (Vats). Ac 317 Str. 2.

157. Harappa (Vats) 2391 (VI); Seal 427-8.

158. *Ṛ.V.*, i. 105, 8; *Mait. Saṃ.*, iii. 14. 17; Mohenjo (Marshall), VS 125; *Nirkuta,* iv. 5; *Vāja Saṃ.*, xxiv. 36.

159. *Ṛ.V.*, i. 43. 6; viii. 2. 40; *Vāja. Saṃ.*, iii. 59; xix. 90; *Śadv. Brā.*, i. 1; Harappa (Vats) Ab 616 (I), 8766 (III); Mohenjo (mac.) DK 9341; *AV.*, vi. 49. 2; *Tait. Saṃ.*, vii. 4. 12. 1; *Śara. Brā.*, iii. 3. 4. 18.

160. Mohenjo (Mac.) DK 6593, Seal 3; Mohenjo (Mac.) DM 55.

161. *Ṛ.V.*, i. 64. 7, iv. 16. 4; *Ait. Brā.*, viii 23. 3.

162. *Ṛ.V.*, i. 173. 2; viii, 1. 20; *AV.*, iv. 3. 6; x. 1. 26; *Ait. Brā.*, iii. 31. 2; *Tait. Brā.*, vi. 7. 10; xxiv. 11 .2; *Tait. Saṃ.*, vi. 1. 3. 7; *)ata Brā.* xi. 8. 4. 3.

59

Concordance of the Fauna in The Rāmāyaṇa*

Sibadas Chaudhuri

169. RAṄKU = Belonging to the Ranku Deer.

AK. 126. रमते रम्यते वा रङ्कुः।

Ayo – xiii (6b), xxx (14b), xxxii (8a), lxii (19a).

Ara – l (15b).

170. RĀSABHA = Donkey. Ass.

AK. 152/217. रासते रासभः, रासृ शब्दं।

Ayo – lxxi (15a, 19a), lxxii (25b).

171. RURU = Big black spotted deer.

AK. 86/126. रौत्ति रुरुः।

लो टीः रुरुर्म्मृगविशेषः।

Ayo – cxiv (33b).

Ara – lxxviii (13b).

172. ROHITA = Deer with stripes.

AK. 27/126. रोहिते, रौहितः, रक्तत्वात्।

Ara – lxxviii (9a).

173. VAÑJULAKA also VAÑJULA = A sort of bird.

Ara – lxxvi (13a), lxxx (23a).

Kis – xiii (8a).

174. VAḌAVĀ = A female horse.

AK. 129/185. वड़ं बलं हयं वा वाति वड़वा।

लो-टी। वड़वा अश्वा।

Ayo – lxvii (23b).

Kis – xl (49b, 50b).

Yud – ix (3b).

175. VANAUKAS = Animal, living in forest, e.g., Ape.

AK. 125. वने ओकोऽस्येति वनौका: ।

Kis – i (16a), xvii (50a), xviii (16b), xxi (5a, 38b), xxxvii (29a), xli (9b, 25b, 72b, 74a), xlii (16a), xliii (18b, 20b), xlv (8a), xlix (7b), l (13a, 19b), li (31b), liii (2a), liv (8b, 24c), lxii (30b).

Sun – i (84a), iii (8b), xvi (52b), xxx (19b), xxxi (42b, 48b, 71b), liv (22a), lxx (20a).

Yud – i (44a), ii (13a, 43b), iii (1a), x (35b), xvi (23b, 98a), xvii (32a), xxi (1a, 16a), xxvi (5a, 24b, 40b), xxvii (2a, 19b), xxviii (22a), xxx (34b), xxxa (31b), xxxb (5b), xxxi (8b, 45a), xxxii (15c, 20b), xxxvii (99b), xlv (11b), xlvi (93b), xlix (80a), lviii (3b), lix (7a), lxi (3b, 19a), lxii (1a), lxvi (10a), lxx (8b), lxxi (3a), lxxiii (34a), lxxvii (6a), c (36b, 38a), cviii (3a), cxii (20a), cxiii (61b).

176. VARĀHA = Boar, pig.

AK. 84/124 वरमाहन्ति वराह: ।

AS. 125. वरमाहन्तीति वराह: ।

Adi – xxvii (13b).

Ayo – xiii (7a), xxv (33a), xxvii (11b), xxviii (11b), xxix (4a), lii (27b), x (67a), cxi (48a).

Ara – xv (4b), xxxiv (32b).

Kis – i (13a), xliii (31b).

Sun – xv (40a), xviii (29a).

Yud – xv (18a), xxxvii (31a, 78b), lxxx (69b), ciii (13b).

Utt – vi (45b), xxxvi (39b).

177. VĀJIN = Horse.

AK. 89/184. वजति तच्छोलो वाजी, वजा: पक्षां अभूवन्नस्येति वा ।

AS. 247. वजत्यनेनेति वाज: । 'वज ब्रज गतौ' । घञ् । वाज: । तद्योगाद् वाजी ।

Adi – vi (2b), xi (11b), xvi (1a), lv (12a).

Ayo – xii (34a), xiii (23a), xx (41b), xxxviii (10a), xxxix (25c), lxxiii (23a), lxxxix (9b), xci (15a, 17a, 20b), c (7a, 31a, 75a), ci (15b, 34a, 39a, 42a), cv (59a), cvii (18b).

Ara – ix (5a, 10a), xx (29a), xxxiii (27a), xl (29b).

Sun—xxvii (20a), xli (3b), xlii (4b, 18a), xliii (16b), xlviii (4a, 33a), lix (16a), lxxxii (24a, 32a).

Yud—ix (23a), xi (43b), xix (48a), xxviii (14a), xxix (9a), xxx (23a), xlix (37a, 75a), l (4a), lii (11a), lxvi (14b), lxxix (23b, 34b), lxxv (1a), lxxviii (13c), xc (15a, 20a), xci (2a), xcii (16a), xciii (7a).

Utt—xix (10a), xlii (28b), xlix (4a), lxx (21a), x (1a), cvi (8a).

178. VĀNARA = Monkey. Ape.

AK. 84/125 वने रमते वनरस्तस्यायं वानरः, पक्षे नरो वा।

AS. 216 नर इव वानरः। वा शब्द इवार्थे।

Adi—i (64b, 66b, 67b, 69a, 71a, 72a, 73a, 77a), iii (17a, 69a, 70a, 72a, 104a, 111a, 133a), iv (26b), xx (6a, 8b, 9b, 10b, 12b, 18a, 21b).

Ayo—liv (30a), civ (19b), cv (24b, 26a).

Ara—xx (26a), lxi (5b, 8c), lxiv (11b), lxxvii (68a, 69b, 71a, 72a, 74a, 79a).

Kis—i (3b, 3b), ii (2a, 3a, 20a, 21b, 22b), iii (2a, 6b, 14b, 20b, 23a, 28b), iv (12b), v (13b, 23a, 27b, 30a), vi (2a, 8a, 23a), vii (1a), viii (15b, 31b, 34a), ix (7a, 23a, 67a, 69b, 71ab,77a, 97b), x (5a, 9a, 12a, 14a, 16a, 30a, 31a, 34a), xi (2a, 6a), xii (17a, 41b, 50a), xiii (4a, 33a, 34a), xiv (6a, 13a, 23a), xvi (3a, 36b), xvii (5a, 7a, 15b, 19a, 21b, 25b, 32b, 39a), xviii (1a, 7a, 9a, 12a, 15a, 21a, 30b), xix (4b,6b, 14b, 16b, 17b), xx (1b, 8a, 11a), xxii (3a, 4b), xxiv (17a, 21b, 24b, 28a, 30b, 31a, 35a, 34a, 40b), xxv (4b, 7b, 17a, 18a, 21a, 27a, 31a, 35a, 36a), xxvi (1a, 2b), xxvii (17b, 22a), xxviii (32a), xxx (7b, 9a, 20b, 23a), xxxi (2ab, 16b, 24b, 27a, 31a, 35b), xxxii (9b, 16a), xxxiii (7a), xxxix (5b, 19a, 20a, 27b, 32a), xxxv (13b, 29b), xxxvi (3b, 4a, 14b), xxxvii (6a, 7b, 10ab, 12a, 16a, 17ab, 19b, 23a, 24b, 26b, 27b, 30a, 33b, 34a, 35ab, 36a, 37b, 38a), xxxviii (1b, 10a, 26ab, 28a, 31b, 34b, 39b, 40b, 42a, 45a, 51b, 53ab, 55a, 56b), xxxix (14a, 15b, 17ab, 22a, 24a, 25b, 30a, 33ab, 34a, 36b, 38a, 41a, 42a, 43b), xl (1a, 3a, 4a, 12a, 15b, 16a, 17a, 27b, 36b, 47a, 48a, 58a, 67a), xli (1b, 23b, 24b, 38b, 43b, 46b), xlii (15c), xliii (4a, 8b, 24b, 25b, 27a, 52ab, 57b, 58a, 62a), xliv (1b, 2a, 3a, 5b, 6a, 18b, 27b, 58a, 115b, 125a), xlv (3b, 15a, 16a), xlvi (1a, 12a), xlvii (2a, 9b), xlviii (4b, 15b, 16a, 18a), xlix (22a, 27a), l (9b, 10a, 14a,

15b, 16b, 20a, 27b), li (8b, 21b, 35b), lii (2b, 17b, 27a, 31ab, 32b, 44b, 45b, 46a), liii (4b, 6b, 9a, 12ab, 22b, 23a, 25a, 27b), liv (1a, 7b, 9a, 16b, 23b, 24c), lv (6b), lvi (11b, 17a), lvii (5ab, 7b, 14c, 15b), lvii (22a), lviii (4a, 5a, 18ab), lix (1ab, 8a, 15b,16a, 27b, 32a, 34a, 39b), lx (7b), lxii (23a, 53b), lxiii (13b, 22a), lxiv (7a, 8b, 9a, 10a, 12a, 19b, 22b, 23b, 25a, 26a).

Sun – i (3a, 12b, 13a, 16a, 19b, 29a, 42a, 44b, 60a, 62b, 64a, 67a, 68b, 76a, 86b, 89b, 90a, 93ab, 95a), ii (2a, 4ac, 7b, 8ab, 42b, 47a), iii (2a, 28a, 32b, 53a, 54b, 60a, 69a, 74a, 75a, 80b), iv (1a, 2b, 3a), v (10a, 14a, 29a, 35b), vi (9a, 15a, 25b), vii (2a, 29a), viii (3b, 11a, 13b, 15a, 18b, 19a,,21ab), ix (24b, 28a, 60b), xii (19a), xiv (9b), xv (12a), xvi (2a, 11b, 23a, 49b), xvii (5a, 11b), xviii (21b, 26a, 68a), xix (10b), xx (22b), xxvii (18a), xxix (27a), xxx (13b), xxxi (28a, 37b, 41a, 46b, 47a, 59b, 61b, 62a), xxxii (1a, 2b, 21a, 50b), xxxiii (5a, 9b, 12a, 23a, 45b), xxxiv (4b), xxxv (4a, 16b, 30b, 43a), xxxvii (12b, 28b), xxxviii (5b, 36a, 46b, 47a), xxxix (5b, 8b), xlii (1a, 7a, 25b, 32a, 35b, 37b), xlv (1a, 21a), xlvii (5b, 7b, 8a), xlviii (29b, 34a), xlix (11a), l (24a, 32b), li (15b), liv (4a, 17a, 18a), lvi (5a, 10b, 18b, 20a, 28a, 33b, 36a). lvii (8a, 34a, 98a, 100b), lix (1b, 21b), lx (5b, 8b, 15b, 16a), lxi (3b, 4a, 19b), lxii (8a, 9a, 11a, 13a, 17b), lxiii (1a, 2a, 3a, 5a, 7b), lxiv (1a, 3b, 5b, 7ab, 9a, 14a, 15a, 18b, 19a, 21b, 23a, 26a), lxv (2b, 12a, 14a, 15b, 19a, 23b), lxvi (1a, 14b), lxvii (4a, 5b, 34a), lxix (1a), lxx (7b, 16a, 25b), lxxii (10a), lxxiii (17b), lxxiv (2b, 18b, 25ab, 26b, 29a, 30b, 31a, 32a, 39b, 42a, 43a, 44a, 47a, 63b, 64a, 65b), lxxv (1b, 6b, 7b, 18b, 21b, 25a, 26a), lxxvi (2a), lxxix (4b, 18a), lxxx (24b), lxxxi (2b, 4b, 10a, 11a), lxxxii (24b, 26b), lxxxiii (9a, 50b), lxxxiv (20b), lxxxv (3b, 4ab, 6b, 7a, 8b, 9a, 12a, 14a), xci (23b, 43o, 46ab, 47a, 52b, 53a), xciii (5b, 6b), xciv (2a, 3b), xcvi (15b, 20b), xcvii (3b, 5ab, 8a, 11b, 32b, 27a, 43a).

Yud – i (2a, 5a, 6b, 9b, 10a, 11a, 14a, 16a, 20a, 38b, 42b), ii (8a, 9a, 10a, 13b, 17b, 20a, 21b, 22b, 23b, 24b, 25a, 27c, 33a, 35b, 36a, 37b, 41a, 44b, 45a), iii (3b, 5a, 12b, 16b, 17b, 20a, 22ab, 26a,28b, 29a, 30b, 36b, 41b, 44a, 45a), iv (28c, 44a, 45b, 49a, 56b, 57a, v (2b, 24b), vi (4a, 5b, 13c, 20a, 2c, 23a), vii (19b, 24c, 29a, 35b), ix (10a, 16a), x (34a), xi (2a, 5a, 6b), xii (9a, 12a, 13a), xiii (1a, 3b, 30a,

31b, 32a), xiv (14a, 22a), xv (13a, 27b), xvi (3b, 20b, 24a, 27b, 36ab, 39a, 43b, 44b, 45a, 47a, 49b, 50b, 53b, 89b), xvii (1b, 4a, 9b, 10a, 16b, 26b, 27b, 28b, 29b, 30a, 31b), xviii (1a, 3a, 6b, 7b, 12a, 18a, 21a, 22b, 34a, 42a, 47a, 51a, 55b), xix (1a, 3a, 17a, 29a, 52a, 74b), xx (1b, 7a), xxi (7b, 8a, 19a, 25b, 29b), xxii (2b, 24b), xxiv (2b, 39a, 42b), xxv (4b, 5a, 6b, 9a, 12b, 13a, 24a, 40c), xxvi (1a, 4b, 15b, 42c), xxvii (1a, 3a, 29b), xxviii (1b, 3ab, 4a, 6a, 10a, 14b, 17a, 18a, 19b, 26a), xxix (5b, 14a, 23a), xxx (1a, 3a, 7a, 31b, 36b), xxxa (12a), xxxb (2b, 3b, 4b, 6b, 14a, 15b, 19b, 22a, 29b), xxxi (10a, 11a), xxxii (2a, 4b, 5a, 7a, 10b, 11a, 14a, 16a, 22b, 23a, 43a), xxxiii (5a, 44a, 46ab, 48ab), xxxiv (3b, 10b, 11a), xxxv (4b), xxxvi (9b, 17b, 18a, 27b, 30b, 31b, 38a, 40b, 43a, 44b, 61a, 64a, 70b, 84a, 100a), xxxviii (17b, 88a, 89a), xxxviii (4a, 6b, 32b, 33b, 34a, 37b, 38b), xxxix (21b, 22ab, 29c, 30a), xl (45a, 47b), xli (12ac, 20ab), xlii (10b), xliii (27a), xliv (17a, 38a, 39a), xlv (3b, 6b, 8a, 9a, 16a, 17a, 19a, 20a, 21a, 22a, 23b, 25b, 26ab, 27b, 35a), xlvi (3a, 4b, 6a, 11a, 13b, 14b, 23c, 26a, 29ab, 31a, 32a, 33b, 36b, 37b, 38a, 39b, 43a, 46a, 53a, 54a, 57a, 61b, 62a, 63b, 65b, 75a, 76a, 77a, 78b, 81a, 85b, 108b, 110a, 11a, 116a, 118b, 119a, 122b, 134b, 139a), xlix (31a, 34b, 42a, 43a, 44ab, 45b, 46b, 47a, 48b, 49c, 52b, 53a, 55b, 57b, 58b, 59a, 62b), l (17a, 36b, 37b, 51a, 52a, 53a, 54a), li (6b, 7b, 8a, 10b, 23b, 54b), lii (30a, 32a, 33b, 35a, 46b, 40b, 43a, 45b, 48a, 51a), liii (6a, 8b, 9a, 13a, 14a, 20b, 30b, 32a, 36a, 64a, 65a), liv (1a, 5b, 30a, 35a, 40a, 42a, 54b, 62ab, 63b, 64a), lv (9b, 16a), lvi (5b, 15a, 23b, 24a, 29a, 31a, 36a, 53a, 54a, 55a, 60b, 80a, 81b), lvii (8a), lviii (14b, 15a), lix (1a, 6a, 8a, 14a), lx (2a, 4b, 7b, 9a, 8b, 10b, 11a, 15a, 16c, 18b, 20c, 21a, 22a, 23b, 24b), lxi (1a, 4b, 5a, 10b, 11a, 22a), lxii (1b, 6a, 7a, 8b, 14a, 15a, 17b, 18b, 19a, 22a, 25b), lxiii (4b, 5b, 12a), lxiv (3b, 15b), lxv (28a), lxvi (9a, 11a, 16b), lxviii (4c), lxx (7a, 16b, 20b, 21b, 44a, 45a), lxxi (29a, 43a, 45b, 47a, 58a), lxxii (3b, 20b, 21a, 22a, 24b), lxxiv (8b, 9b, 10a, 11a, 13b, 15a, 16b), lxxvi (15a, 19b, 41b, 43a, 44b, 45b, 46b, 47b, 48a, 49b, 51b, 52a, 53b, 54a, 55a, 58b, 65b), lxxvii (2a, 8a, 11b, 18a, 19a, 23b, 30b, 41a, 43a), lxxviii (3a, 7a, 8a, 30a), lxxix (3b, 4b, 5a, 7b), lxxx (11a, 29b, 41a), lxxxi (22b), lxxxii (17a, 20a), lxxxiii (17b, 44b, 53a, 54b, 75a, 77a, 79a, 98ab, 105b, 107b, 120b, 135a, 142b, 143a, 148a, 171b, 172c), lxxxiv (2b, 4ab, 8a, 13b, 19ab), lxxxv (1b, 5b, 16a, 23a, 35b), lxxxvi (5a), lxxxvii (38a), lxxxix (33a), xcii (5a, 19b), xciii (61a, 62a, 71a), xciv (5ab, 9b), xcv (25a), xcvi (6b, 13a), xcvii (2a), xcviii (2b, 38b), c (14a, 15b, 24a),ci (11c, 21a), cii (14a, 34b), cvi (5b, 9b, 14b, 21b, 23a), cvii (14b), cviii (8a, 9a, 11a, 12a, 20b), cix (9b, 10a, 28a, 47a), cx (15b, 19b), cxi (41a, 42a), cxii (20b, 24a, 34a, 48b), cxiii (17b, 28a, 39b, 40b, 41a, 54a, 55c, 58a, 61a, 62b, 60a, 75b, 87c, 90a, 92a, 93b, 104a).

Utt – xvi (16b), xxiii (4a, 7b, 30a, 34a, 37a, 39a, 43a), xxxviii (50b, 61a, 63b), xl (7b, 11b, 12a), xli (17a), xlii (53a, 54b), xliii (13a, 21a), xliv (1a), xlvi (15b), xcviii (9a, 13b), xciv (7a, 11b), cii (7a), ciii (6a), cvi (5a, 11b), cxiii (36a, 38a, 40a, 44a, 46a, 47a), cxiv (18a), cxv (20a, 26a).

179. VĀNARI = Female ape.

Adi – xx (12b).

Kis – xxiv (29a).

Sun – i (14a), ii (14b).

Yud – ii (25b), li (66a), lxxvi (68a).

180. VĀYASA = A crow.

AK. 87/128. वय एव वायसः, प्रज्ञादित्वादण् (५।४।३८/२१०६), वयते बा।

Ayo – xci (18a), cv (55a).

Ara – liv (64a), lxxxi (23b).

Kis – xix (20a).

Sun – xxxvi (41a), lxvii (29a), lxix (2b, 5a, 8a, 9a, 12b), lxxviii (19a).

Yud – lix (29a), lxxvi (38b), xcv (5b), cxiii (8a).

Utt – xviii (5a, 31a).

181. VĀRAṆA = Elephant.

AK. 127/183 वारयत्यरीन्वारणः।

Ayo – xxviii (11b), xlvii (3b), lxv (21b), cii (6a, 10b), cviii (40a).

Kis – xxix (13a), xl (16a), xlvi (12a).

Sun – lvi (28a), lxxiv (8b, 33b), xcvii (11b).

Yud – xxxvi (27a), xlix (48a), l (2a, 13b).

Utt – vi (44a).

182. VIŚĀLĀKṢA = A screech-owl.

Utt – xxxi (22a).

183. VIHAGA = Sky-goer, a bird.

AK. 89/131. विहायसा गच्छति विहगः ।

Ayo – xlix (2b), lii (30a), lvi (16a), lxx (13a), cv (12a, 44a).

Ara – xvi (6b), xxix (13a), lvii (55c), lxxviii (26b), lxxx (3b, 24a, 25b), lxxxi (9a, 43b, 47a).

Kis – xliv (36b).

Sun – iii (59b), ix (8b), xiv (15a, 24a), xvii (7a, 8a, 11b, 32b), xviii (18b), xx (9b, 11a), lxix (9a), xcvii (14a).

Yud – xi (39b), xv (17a), lxxxiv (24b), lxxxix (27b).

184. VIHAṂGA = Bird.

AS. 247. "विहायस्ये विह च" इति खचो डित्वम् । विहङ्गः ।

Ayo – cv (13a, 40b), cxxv (4a).

Ara – lxxv (2a, 19a, 30a).

Kis – xxix (22b).

Sun – iv (13b), xi (17b), xii (21a), xiii (1b, 11b), xvii (40a), xxi (14a), xxxv (29b), xxxviii (29b).

Yud – xv (10a), xxxvii (41b), xliv (43b).

Utt – vi (45a), xviii (22b, 32a), xx (28b).

185. VṚKA = Wolf, jackal.

AK. 126. ईहां वर्कते—ईहा वृक एवैकदेशेन वृक इत्युक्तः ।

Ayo – cvi (29d).

Yud – xxvii (28a).

186. VṚŚCIKA = Scorpion.

AK. 86/127. वृश्चति वृश्चिकः ।

Ayo – xxv (32a), xxviii (9a).

Utt – xxviii (39b).

187. VṚṢA = Bull.

AK. 72/107. वर्षति मधु वृषः ।

Adi – iii (130a), xxxviii (9b).

Ayo – lxi (14a).

Sun – xi (3b), xv (27b), xc (8a).

Yud – xi (28b), cxiii (82b).

Utt – xxi (52a, 59a), xcvii (12ab).

188. VṚṢABHA=Bull.

Adi–xlix (3a).

Ara–lxxvi (26a).

Ayo–xxv (36a), xlii (11b).

Sun–xxxv (26b), xci (7a).

189. VYĀGHRA=Tiger.

AK. 84/124 व्याजिघ्रन् हन्ति व्याघ्रः । चित्रकायः पञ्चशिखरश्च ।

AS. 214. व्याजिघ्रतीति व्याघ्रः ।

Adi–xxvii (14b), xli (20b), xliii (17b).

Ayo–ix (45b), xxix (4a), xlii (13a), xliii (9a), xlix (8b), lii (8a, 20a, 27b), liv (33b), lviii (6b), lx (18a), lxxii (24a), lxxiii (16b), lxxv (28a), lxxxi (23a), xcvi (5b), xcix (25a, 33a), ci (2a, 23a, 27a), cvi (2b, 10a), cviii (11a, 13a), cx (13b), cxi (6a, 24a, 48b), cxii (18b), cxiv (6a), cxxiv (12b).

Ara–ix (24a), xx (26b), xxiv (21b), xliii (19a), l (20b), liii (42a), lix (41a), lxxxvii (38b), lxxx (11b).

Kis–i (13a), iii (5a), xliii (37a), lx (15a).

Sun–l (33b).

Yud–iii (39a), xix (61b), xxvii (27b), xxxii (33b), xxxv (15b), xlvi (31b), lxviii (31c), lxxiii (49a), lxxiv (7b), lxxx (68a), lxxxiv (19b, 25a), xcix (32a), cxiii (29b).

Utt–vi (45b), vii (20b), xxi (66a), lxiv (2a), lxxx (29b), xc (24b), cvii (25a).

190. VYĀGHRĪ=Tigress.

Ayo–ix (33b).

Ara–liv (53a, 57a), lxiii (36b).

191. VYĀLA=Snake.

AK. 38/58 व्याड़नं हन्तुमुद्यमीस्यास्ति व्यालः, अड़ उद्यमे ।

Ayo–cii (4b), cvi (5a).

Ara–i (14b, 34d), v (19b), vii (6a), xxi (1a), xxxvi (19a), liv (25a), lvi (21b(, lxxvi (6a).

Sun–xlii (36a), xlvi (6b).

Utt–xciv (15a).

192. VYĀLĪ=सर्पी

Ayo–ix (39b), xxxiv (9a), lxxv (17b).

Sun–xxvi (2b).

References

* Continued from p. 128 of vol. XXIX, No. 2.

169. *Ṛ.V.*, x. 68. 8; *AV.*, xi. 2. 25; *Vāja. Saṃ.* xxiv. 21. 34; *Śata. Brā.*, 1. 8. 1. 1.; *Kaus. Up.*, 1. 2; *Mait. Saṃ.*, iii. 9. 5; *Tait. Saṃ.*, ii. 6. 6. 1; *Chan. Up.*, i. 4. 3; *Bṛhad. Upa.*, iv. 3. 18.

170. *Ṛ.V.*, i. 34. 9; viii. 85. 7; *Tait. Brā.*, v. 1. 5. 7; *Śata. Brā.*, vi. 1. 1. 11; *Kauṣ. Brā.*, xviii. 1. Geldner, *Rigveda Glossar*, 149, suggests *mule* as possible sense in *Ṛ.V.*, iii, 53, 5.

171. *Tait. Saṃ.* v. 5, 19; *Vāja. Saṃ.*, xxiv, 27, 39; *Mait. Saṃ.*, iii, 14. 9; *Ṛ.V.*, vi, 75, 15; Mohenja. (Marshall)–SD. 2608.

172. *Red-horse*: *Ṛ.V.*, i, 94. 10; *Tait. Saṃ.*, I. 6. 4. 3; *AV.*, xiii. 1. I. *Pañc. Brā.*, xiv. 3. 12.

In some passages of *Ṛ.V.* (1, 14, 12 etc.) it denotes a *'red mare'*.

'Red doe'–in *Tait. Saṃ.*, vi, 1, 6, 5; *Mait. Saṃ.*, iii, 14, 11, 18; *Vāja. Saṃ.*, xxiv, 30, 37; *AV.*, iv, 4, 7; *Ait. Brā.*, ii, 33. 1.

176. *Ṛ.V.*, i. 61. 7; vii. 77. 10; ix. 97, 7; *AV.*, viii. 7. 23; xii. 1. 48; *Kāth. Saṃ.*, viii. 2; xxv. 2; *Mait. Saṃ.*, iii. 14. 19; *Tait. Saṃ.*, vi, 2, 4, 2; *Tait. Āraṇ*, 9, 4. Mohenjo (*Mck.*) DK. 9452 l; Mohenjo (Mar.) C. 3314; Har. (Vats) 163 (III) 2390 (IV).

177. *Ṛ.V.*, ii. 5. 1; ii. 10. 1; ii. 34, 7; iii. 53. 23; vi. 75. 6; x. 103. 10.

180. *Ṛ.V.*, i, 164, 32; *Ṣaḍ. Brā*, vi, 8; *Nirukta*, iv, 17.

181. *Ṛ.V.*, vii. 33. 8; x. 40, 4; *AV.*, v. 14, 11 (*Vāraṇī*).

182. *Tait. Saṃ.*, ii, 1, 8, 3.

183. *Tait. Saṃ.*, vii. 1, 1, 2; *Tait Brā.*, i. 8, 6, 3; *Śat. Brā.*, vi. 5, 2, 19.

185. *Ṛ.V.*, i. 42. 2; ii. 29. 6; vii. 38. 7; *AV.*, vii. 95. 2; xii. 1. 49; *Kāth. Saṃ.*, xii. 10; *Vāja. Saṃ.*, iv. 34 *Mait. Saṃ.*, iii. 14. 4; *Nirukta*, v. 21.

186. *Ṛ.V.*, i. 191. 16; *Śāṅk. Āra.*, xii, 27; *AV.*, x. 4. 9. 15; xii. 1. 46.

187. *Ṛ.V.*, x. 146. 2 (*vṛsā rava*–roaring like a bull); *Tait. Brā.*, ii. 5, 5, 6.

188. *Ṛ.V.*, i. 94. 10; vi. 46. 4.

189. *AV.*, iv. 3. 1; iv. 36. 6; vi. 38, 1; xii. 1. 49;... *Tait. Saṃ.* vi. 2. 5. 5; *Mait. Saṃ.*, ii. 1. 9.; *Ait. Brā.*, vii. 5. 3; *Chānd. Up.*, vi. 9, 3; *Kāth. Saṃ.* xvii. 2 *Yāja Saṃ.*, xiv, 9; xix, 10; *Śata. Brā.*, xii. 7. 1. 8. *Nirukta*, iii. 18. Harappa, J 55 (II), 3370 (iii) Seal 246, 248; Mohenjo (Mac) DK 977 (l).

60

Concordance of the Fauna in The Rāmāyaṇa*

Sibadas Chaudhuri

193. ŚAKUNA="A large bird, or a bird which gives omens".

AK. 89/131. शक्नोतीति, शकेरूनोन्तन्त्युनयः (उ० ३४९)

Adi—ii (18b).

Ara—vii (4a), lxxxi (20a).

Yud—xiii (8a), xv (20b), lxxiv (15b).

Utt—v (28b), xxi (10a),

194. ŚAKUNI=Bird. "It is used practically like *Śakuna,* but with a much clearer reference to divination. It was smaller than the *Śyena* or *Suparṇa,* gave signs, and foretold ill-luck".—(Keith : Vedic Index, ii, 347).

Ara—xv (41b), xvii (17b), lxxv (38b).

195. ŚAKULA=A kind of fish (perhaps, the gilt-headed).

AK. 42/64. शक्नोति गन्तुम् शकुलः। शकुलोऽत्र मत्स्यमाते।

Ara—lxxviii (9a).

196. ŚAṄKHA=Conch.

AK. 43/65. शं खनति शम्यति वा शङ्खः।

Ara—xx (27b).

Kis—xxxviii (33a), xxxix (19a), xliii (32b).

Sun—ix (12a), xi (2a), xii (22b), xxxii (41b), xciv (13a), xcv (20a).

Yud—xix (14b), xxvi (42b), xxxa (25b, 26a), xxxi (31b), xxxv (2a), xxxvii (37a, 39b, 41a, 50a), xliv (29b), xlix (25a), lii (13a), lviii (19a), ciii (13a), cix (17b), cxii (12a, 15b), cxiii (29a).

Utt—vii (9b, 10a, 11a, 12b, 16a, 24a, 37a), xxiii (7a).

197. ŚABALĀ = Spotted cow.

"शवलावर्णा गौः । इत्यमर भरतौ ॥"—(शब्दकल्पद्रुम, ५१८०)

Adi – liv (10b, 11b, 13b, 14b, 22b, 23b), lv (1b, 2a).

198. ŚARABHA = A kind of deer.

AK. 86/126. शृणाति शरभः ।

Yud – ii (35b), iii (44b), xvii (22a), xx (2b).

Utt – vii (20a), xxxi (13a).

199. ŚARĀRI = Heron.

AK. 88/129. शृणन्त्येनां शरारिः ।

AS. 240. शृणोते बाहुलक आरिः । शरारिः ।

Ara – xv (6b).

200. ŚALABHA = Grasshopper, moth, locust.

AK. 88/130. शलति शमं लभते वाग्नौ शलभः ।

Kis – xlv (1b), xlvii (1b).

Sun – xxxix (11a).

Yud – xvi (43b), xliv (38b).

Utt – vii (3a).

201. ŚALYAKĀ = Scaly fish.

Yud – xxv (18b).

202. ŚAŚA = Hare, rabbit.

AK. 86/126. शशति प्लुत्या गच्छति शशः ।

Sun – xxiv (16ab).

Utt – xxxii (14a).

203. ŚĀKHĀMṚGA = Monkey.

AK. 84/124, शाखा-संचारी मृगः शाखामृगः ।

AS. 216. शाखा-प्रसक्तो मृगः शाखामृगः ।

Ayo – ciii (7a).

Ara – liii (42a).

Kis – i (11a, 21a), xvi (26a), xvii (19b), xix (8b), xxv (1b).

Sun – i (36b), xcvii (14a, 16a).

Yud – ii (15b, 38b, 46b), iv (47b), xii (4a), xxxi (19b), liii (2b), lviii (14b), lxvi (5a), lxxvii (26a).

Utt – xli (23a).

204. ŚĀRDŪLA—Tiger.

'शार्दूल: शरभे व्याघ्रे श्रेष्ठे तूत्तरत: स्थित:' इति भूरि: ।

AK. 84/124. शृणाति शार्दूल: ।

Adi—li (17a), lxi (16b), lxviii (24a), xxxiv (4a, 7a), xxxvi (20b), xlii (13a), xliv (7b), xlv (35a), xlix (3a).

Ayo—xi (16b), xxvii (11b), xxviii (6a, 11b), xlii (2a), lxv (1a), ci (30a), cix (52a), cxi (33a), cxx (18a), cxxii (4b).

Ara—vi (3c), vii (2a), ix (25a), xxviii (20a), l (28b), lxxiii (13b), lxxvii (17a), lxxx (3b).

Kis—xviii (22b), xxvi (2a, 23a), xliii (53a), xlix (4a, 13b).

Sun—i (27b, 65a), ii (47b), iv (5b), v (34b), vii (1a, 9a, 59b), xii (27b), xviii (30a, 50a), xxiii (32b), xxxii (39a), xxxv (33a), lii (8b), lxx (25a), lxxiv (63b).

Yud—xvi (39a), xx (7a), xxix (12a), xxxa (18a), xxxii (33b), xxxvi (112b), xxxix (1a), xlvi (23c, 44b, 98a), l (35b), lii (42b), liii (24b, 30b, 36a), lxii (16b), lxiv (17a, 19a), lxx (22a), lxxxiii (29a, 44b, 121a, 139b, 154a), lxxxviii (2a), cii (16a).

Utt—vii (20b), xx (19a), xxi (29b), xxix (9a), lxxi (13a), lxxvi (2b), lxxx (26b, 28a), xc (17b, 21a), cxi (25a), cxii (11a).

205. ṢĀRDŪLĪ=Tigress.

Ara—xx (22b, 26b).

206. ŚIKHĪ=Peacock.

Ayo—lvi (12a), lxv (16b).

207. ŚIVĀ=Jackal.

AK. 85/125. शिनोति शिवाण **Incomplete word vol 29 page 381** दिनी वा, शृगलेऽपि स्त्रीलिङ्ग:, यच्छाश्वत:-शिव: कील: शिवा क्रोष्टा भवेदामलकी शिवा ।

Ara—xxix (6b, 12b).

Sun—lxxviii (20b).

Yud—xvi (11b), xxxa (29b), xliv (43a), lxxvi (35b), xci (24b).

Utt—vi (53c), ix (28a).

208. ŚIŚU-MĀRA=(a) Gangetic porpoise or dolphine—Delphinus Gangeticus. (b) Alligator.

Sun—xxvii (18a).

Utt—vi (44b), xxxvi (39b), xlv (18a).

209. ŚUKA=Parrot. Acacia Sirissa. Zizyphus Scandens.

AK. 129. शुको नीलत्वात्। शवतीत्येके। प्रियदर्शनोऽपि।

Ayo–liii (24b, 25a).

210. ŚUKĪ=Female parrot.

Ara–xx (18a, 21a).

211. ŚŪKARA (more correctly, *Sū-kara*)=Boar, Hog.

AK. 124. सूयतेत्यर्थं सूकरः।

AS. 215. शूचः करः शूकरः इति पृषोदरादित्वाद् धातुप्रदीपे तालव्य उक्तः।

Yud–xi (38b), xv (18a).

212. ŚŪKARĪ.

Sun–xviii (32b).

213. ŚṚGĀLA–Jackal.

AK. 125. असृगालाति सृगालः, सरति सृजति वा। (See also 207).

Ara–liv (62a).

Kis–xvi (36b).

Yud–lxxx (68b).

214. ŚYENA–Hawk, falcon, eagle, any bird of prey.

AK. 86/127. श्यायते श्येनः।

Ayo–xlvi (5b).

Ara–xx (19b).

Kis–lix (30b).

Yud–xvi (11a), xxvii (34a), lxviii (22a).

Utt–xv (5a).

215. ŚYENĪ=Female hawk.

Ara–xx (18a, 19b, 33a, 34b).

216. ŚVĀNA=Dog.

AK. 161/230. शवति श्वयति वा श्वा।

Ayo–lxxii (24b).

Sun–xxiii (32b).

Utt–vii (21a), lxii (14b), lxiii (1a, 2a, 12a, 27a, 34b, 39a, 47b).

217. ŚVĀPADA–Wild beast. Tiger.

"हिंस्र पशुः। इति हेमचन्द्रः। व्याघ्रः। इति शब्दरत्नावली॥"—श,क, ५६२६

Ayo – cvi (27b), cxii (7b).

Ara – xxx (32a).

Sun – xvi (55b).

218. ṢAṬ-PADA – Six- footed Insect.

AK. 89/130. षट् पदानि चरणा अस्य षट्पदः।

Sun – xiv (63a).

Yud – xv (8b).

219. SARPA – Snake.

AK. 38/58. सर्पति सर्पः।

Adi – xli (22a).

Ayo – vi (21a), xxviii (9a), xxxiii (24a), cviii (19b), cxxiii (3a).

Ara – xxxv (4b), xxxix (6b), lvii (27a).

Kis – xv (15b), xxxiv (23b), xli (53a, 54b).

Sun – iv (12a, 15a), v (13a), xxiii (22a).

Yud – xv (15a), xvi (30b), xxi (39b), xxvi (9bc), xliii (15b), li (53a) lxix (1b, 5b), lxx (39b), lxxx (70b), lxxxiii (3b), lxxxvii (29b, 33b, 36b), xci (13b), xcii (11b), xciii (3a).

Utt – vii (21b), xxiii (21b), xxviii (39b), lxiii (23a).

220. SARĪSṚPA = Reptile, snake.

AK. 38/58. कुटिलं सर्पति सरीसृपः, नित्यं कौटिल्ये गतौ (३।१।२३)/२६३४

इति यङ्।

Adi – xiii (30c).

Ayo – xxv (32b), xxviii (9a), lviii (6b).

Kis – lx (15a).

Sun – xxxiv (17a), lxxviii (16b).

Utt – xxvi (26c), lxiv (42b).

221. SĀRAṄGA – A kind of spotted antelope. Peacock.

AK. 128. सरति सारङ्गः, सह-आरङ्गति वा युथकाचारित्वात्।

"सारङ्गा हरिणाश्चातका वा। (रामायण तिलकम्)"

Ayo – lxv (14b, 16b).

Kis – xxix (22b).

222. SĀRAMEYA – Dog.

AK. 161/230. सरमायाः अपत्यं सारमेयः।

Utt – xviii (6b), xxv (12a), lxii (16a, 17a, 19a), lxiii (1b, 2b, 13a, 18b, 39b).

223. SĀRASA – Indian Crane. Bird in general.

AK. 88/129. सरसि भवः सारसो लक्ष्मणाख्यः ।

विलोनाङ्गो दीर्घजङ्घश्च ।

Adi – xxxvii (8a).

Ayo – xlvii (3b), civ (3a).

Ara – xv (3a), xx (20b), xxii (16b, 23a), liv (64c), lvi (45a), lxxviii (7a, 15a), lxxxi (43a).

Kis – xiii (8a), xxvi (5a), xxix (5b), xlix (5b), li (11a), lii (38b).

Sun – ix (57a), xvii (36b), xviii (20b).

Yud – xv (10b), xxxb (13a).

Utt – xx (20b), xlv (14b).

224. SĀKIK – A kind of thrush-like bird, Turdus Salica.

Ayo – liii (24a).

Sun – xv (35b).

Yud – xi (40a).

Utt – vi (53a).

225. SIṂHA – Lion.

AK. 84/124. हिनस्ति सिंहः ।

Adi – iv (19a), vi (23b), xii (21b), xv (5b), xx (10a), xxvii (13b), lxxix (10b).

Ayo – iv (25b), vii (30a), xxv (33a), xxvii (11b), xxviii (10b, 11b), xxix (4a), lii (27b), lviii (6b), lix (24a), lx (18a), lxi (25b), lxii (25ab), lxxv (31b), xcv (3a), ci (23a), civ (19b), cviii (21b, 25a), cxxv (23b).

Ara – vi (3c), vii (3b, 7a), xxiii (10b, 13a), xxv (13b), xxxiii (29b), xxxiv (12ab), xlii (24b), xliii (16b, 18a), lii (4b), liii (42a), liv (46ab, 55b, 62a), lvi (4b), lviii (8a), lix (41a), lx (11a), lxiii (4a), lxxvi (6a).

Kis – ii (7a, 12b), iii (5a), xiii (29a), xv (6a), xxi (38b), xxii (30b), xxvi (2a, 12b), xxxi (28b), xxxvii (23a, 24a), xliii (13a, 14a, 15b, 37a), xlix (4a), liv (6a), lx (15a).

Sun – i (1b), iii (4a), iv (5b, 8b), v (29a), vii (59a), ix (21a), xi (6a), xii (21a, 27b), xxiii (31ab), xxiv (23b), xxvi (14a), xxviii (1b, 9b), xxxi (62b), xxxiv (6b), xxxvi (62a), xxxvii (19b), xxxix (8b), xliv (17a), lv (14b), lxix (39a), lxx (25a).

Yud – ii (28b, 31a, 37b), iii (39a), vi (24a), vii (34b), xv (18a), xx (27a), xxvii (28a), xxix (12a), xxxa (18a), xxxb (23b), xxxi (10b), xxxii (13a, 33b, 40a), xxxv (2b, 16d), xxxvii (2a, 41a), xliii (15a), xlix (26b, 34b, 46b, 151c), li (6a), liv (39a, 46b), lix (7b, 20b), lxx (38a), lxxiii (38b), lxxiv (1b, 7b), lxxx (10a, 68a), lxxxiii (53a, 143a), lxxxiv (4b, 19b, 25a), lxxxv (1b), lxxxvi (11b), lxxxviii (2a), xciv (5b, 19b).

Utt – vii (20a, 41b, 45b, 50a), xx (15a, 19a), xxi (66a), xxiii (14a, 45b), xxviii (48b), xxix (45b), xxxi (5a, 9a, 13a), xxxii (10b), lxiv (2a), lxxv (31b), lxxxv (18b), xcix (17a), cvii (25a), cxiv (22b).

226. SIṂHĪ = Lioness.

Ara – liv (46b).

227. SUPARṆA = Any large bird of prey – vulture, eagle etc.

AK. 7/11 सुपर्णो हेमपक्षत्वात्।

रा–टी २–२५,२—"सुपर्णो विहङ्गमाः।"

Adi – iii (108b), xliii (16b, 23a, 24b).

Ayo – xxv (25a, 27b), cxvii (9a).

Ara – viii (3a), xxxiii (19b), xxxvi (33a), xl (14a, 27b, 36a), xliv (20b), xlv (18b), lxiii (6b).

Kis – i (15a), xv (25a), xviii (23b).

Sun – iii (62a), v (34b), xxii (29b).

Yud – xvi (35b), xxvi (17a, 19a, 25b, 36a, 40a), xlvi (140a), xlix (74a).

Utt – vi (60a, 62a), x (19a), xvi (10a), xxiii (40b), civ (8a), cxv (13b).

228. SURABHI = Cow.

AK. 26/302 सुष्ठु रभते सुरभिः।

Ayo – lxxvi (17a, 22a), c (55a).

Ara – xx (23a, 28a).

Utt – xxvii (20b).

229. SṚMARA = A kind of animal frequenting damp places (accord. to some the 'Bos Grunniens' or 'a young deer').

AK. 86/ 126 सरति सृमरः।

Ara – xx (24b).

Utt – vi (45b), xx (19a).

230. STOKAKA = Cātaka bird.

AK. 87/128 स्तोकं कायति वाशते याचते वा स्तोकक: ।

Ara − xxxv (28b).

(To be continued)

References

* Continued from pp. 285 of vol XXIX, No. 3.

193. *Ṛv,* iv. 26, 6; ix, 85, 11; *Av.*, xii, 1, 51; *Tait. saṃ.*, iii, 2, 6, 2; *Vāja. Saṃ.*, xviii, 53; *Nirukta,* iii, 18; *Kauṣ. Brā.*, vii, 4; *Mait. Upa.*, vi, 34.

194. *Ṛv.*, ii, 42, 2; *Av.*, x, 3, 6; *Tait. Saṃ.*, v. 5. 19. 1; *Vāja. Saṃ.*, xxiv, 40; *Mait. Saṃ.*, iii, 14, 21; *Kāth. Saṃ,* xxv. 7; *Ait. Brā.*, ii, 15, 12; *Sata. Brā.*, xiv, 1, 1, 31; *Chānd. Upa.*, vi, 8, 2.

195. *Av.*, xx. 136. 1; *Vāja. Saṃ.*, xxiii, 28; *Mbh.*

196. *Av.*, iv, 10, 1; *Bṛhad. Upa.*, ii, 4, 9; iv, 5, 10.

198. *Av.*, ix. 5. 9; *Tait. Saṃ,* iv, 2, 10, 4; *Vāja. Saṃ.*, xiii, 51; *Ait. Brā.*, ii, 8, 5; *Śata. Brā.*, i, 2, 3, 9.
"मृमेन्द्रविशेष: । अस्य लक्षणं यथा। अष्टपादूर्द्ध्वनयन ऊर्द्ध्वपाद चतुष्टय: ।
सिंहं हन्तुं समायाति शरभो वनगोचर: ॥ इति महाभारतम् ॥"— (शब्दकल्पद्रुम, ५१५७)

200. *Av.* (Paippalāda Recension), ix. 5, 9.

201. *Vāja. Saṃ.*, xxiv, 35.

202. *Ṛv.*, x. 28. 2; *Vāja. Saṃ.*, xxiii, 56; *Mait. Saṃ.*, iii, 14, 15; *Śat. Brā.*, xi. 1, 5. 3.

203. *Mbh.*

204. *Tait. Saṃ.*, v. 5, 11. 1; *Kāṭh. Saṃ.*, xii, 10; *Mait, Saṃ.*, iii, 14. 11; *Vāja. Saṃ.*, xxiv, 30; *Śata. Brā.*, v, 3, 5, 3; *Tait. Brā.*, i, 7, 8, 1; *Kauṣ. Upa.*, i, 2.

205. *Mbh.*

207. *Gṛ. Sū., Mbh.*

208. *Ṛv.* i, 116, 18; *Tait. Saṃ.*, v, 5, 11; *Av.*, xi, 2, 25.; *Mait. Saṃ.*, iii, 14, 2; *Vāja. Saṃ.*, xxiv, 30; *Tait. Āra,* ii, 19.

209. *Ṛv.* 1, 50, 12; *Tait. Saṃ.*, v, 5. 12, 1; *Mait. Saṃ.*, iii, 14, 14; *Vāja. Saṃ.*, xxiv, 33.

211. *Ṛv.*, vii, 55, 4; *Av.*, ii, 27, 2; *Mait. Saṃ.*, iii, 14, 21; *Vāja. Saṃ.*, xxiv, 40; *Chānd. Upa.*, v, 10, 2.

213. *Śat. Brā.*, xii, 5, 2, 5.

214. *Ṛv.* i, 32, 14; *Av.*, iii. 3, 4; *Tait. Saṃ.*, ii, 4, 7, 1; *Saḍv. Brā.*, iii, 8.

216. *Ṛv.*, i, 182, 4; *Av.* vi, 37. 3: *Pañc. Brā,* viii, 8, 22; *Śata. Brā.*, vi, 5, 2, 10 (*Śunī*); xii. 4, 1, 4; *Jaim. Brā.*, i, 51, 4; *Tait. Brā.*, iii, 4, 3, 1; *Vāja.*

Saṃ., xvi, 27, 5, 28; *Tait. Āra.*, vi, 3, 1; *Kāṭh. Saṃ.*, xvii, 13; *Mait. Saṃ.*, n. 9. 5.

217. *Av.*, viii, 5, 11; xix, 39, 4.

219. *Ṛv.*, x. 16, 6; *Av.* x, 4, 23; *Tait. Saṃ.*, i, 4, 6, 6; *Aita. Brā.*, v, 23, 22; *Śata. Brā*, xiii, 4, 3, 9; *Śaṇk. Śrauta Sū.*, xvi, 2, 25;

220. *Ṛv.*, x. 162, 3; *Av.*, iii, 10, 6.

222. *Ṛv.*, vii, 55, 2; x, 14, 10.

223. *Mbh.*, xiii, 736.

224. *Mbh.*

225. *Ṛv.*, i, 64, 8; *Av.*, iv, 36, 6; *Tait. Saṃ.*, v, 5, 21, 1; *Kāth. Saṃ.*, xii, 10, *Mait. Saṃ.*, ii, 1, 9; *Kauṣ. Upa.*, 1, 2.

226. *Tait. Saṃ.*, i, 2, 12, 2; *Vāja. Saṃ.*, v, 10; *Śata. Brā.*, iii, 5, 1, 21: *Mait. Saṃ.*, iii, 8, 5.

228. *Ṛv.*, i, 164, 20; *Av.*, i, 24, 1; *Tait. Saṃ.*, vii, 5, 8, 5; *Mait. Saṃ.*, iv, 9, 19; *Tait. Āra.*, iv, 29; *Jaim. Brā.*, ii, 4, 38.

230. *Tait. Saṃ.*, v, 5, 16. 1; *Mait. Saṃ.*, iii. 14, 20; *Vāja. Saṃ.*, xxiv, 39.

61

Concordance of the Fauna in The Rāmāyaṇa*

Sibadas Chaudhuri

231. HANUMAT=A particular sort of monkey. Simia Sinica.

Adi–i (78a), iii (62a, 70b, 75b, 81a, 84a, 85a, 88b, 21b, 114b, 127a), iv (22a), xx (20b).

Kis–i (5a, 18b, 23ab, 32a), ii (1a, 2a, 21b, 24a), iii (1a, 4a, 18b, 20a, 25b, 26a, 28a), iv (1a, 16a), v (1b), vii (14a), viii (33a), ix (99b), xiii (4a, 28b), xxiii (1b, 8b, 11a), xxiv (13b, 16a), xxv (3b, 8ab, 9b, 11a, 33b), xxviii (8b), xxxi (30b, 37a), xxxii (1a, 9a), xxxiii (13a, 23a), xxxvii (1b), xxxviii (17a, 21a), xxxix (22b), xli (2a, 80b), xlii (1a, 6a, 7a, 8a, 9ab, 15a), xliii (1a), xlviii (17a, 18a), xlix (1a), li (1a, 4a, 6a, 14a, 20b, 37a), lii (1a, 10ab, 28a), liii (1b, 9a), lv (1b, 2b, 5b), lvi (1a), lvii (6b), lxiv (4b).

Sun–i (14b, 38b, 58a, 97b), ii (1b, 2b, 4c, 5b, 9a, 33a, 42b, 48ab), iii (1a, 3b, 46b, 52b), v (21b, 22b), vi (3b, 7b, 14a, 22c, 27a), vii (1a, 2a, 9b, 13b, 21a, 36a, 39b, 65a, 69a), ix (1a, 33a, 44a, 59a), xii (2a, 5a, 15b, 48b), xiv (6b), xvi (7b, 14b, 16b), xvii (3b, 13a, 18a, 32b, 46a, 53a), xviii (2b, 37b, 39b, 55a, 73a), xx (22b), xxv (13a), xxix (1a, 36b), xxxi (1a, 27a, 62a), xxxii (4a, 42a, 49b), xxxiii (1a, 6a, 16b, 42b), xxxv (1b, 30a, 32a), xxxvi (10a, 25b, 71a, 76b), xxxvii (1a, 13b, 15a, 23b, 24a, 26a, 40a), xxxviii (22b, 25a, 27b, 31b, 35a, 38b, 45b), xxxix (1a, 9a, 10a), xl (5b, 6a, 11a, 20b), xli (6b, 11b), xlii (3b, 11b, 36b), xliii (1a), xliv (1a), xlv (7b, 9a, 15a), xlvi (1b, 13a, 15a, 19a), xlvii (10b, 14a), xlix (1a), l (10a, 12a, 16a, 20b, 21b, 22b), li (7a, 12b, 17b, 22b, 25b), lii (1b, 22b, 23a, 25a, 20b), liii (2a, 7a), liv (16b, 29a), lvi (5a, 7a, 9b, 14a, 20b, 23a, 28a,

29b, 32a, 35b, 37a), lvii (1b, 26b, 101a, 108b), lviii (1a), lix (1b), lx (8b, 9a, 16b, 17a, 18a, 19a), lxi (1ab, 2a), lxii (5b, 13b), lxiv (6a, 18b, 27b, 28a), lxvi (6a, 9a, 10b, 12a, 13b, 16a, 17b, 18b), lxvii (6b, 7a, 19b), lxviii (1a, 9b, 11a, 14a, 15b), lxix (1a, 39a), lxx (1a, 2b, 3b, 5b, 6a, 9a, 12b, 14b), lxxi (19b), lxxiii (1b, 4a, 5a),lxxiv (1b, 13a, 27b), lxxvii (1a, 3a), lxxix (1b, 3a, 5b), lxxxi (3a, 7a, 17b), lxxxii (6b, 11b), xci (47b), xcii (2b, 22a, 40b), xciv (5a), xcvii (3a).

Yud – iv (12b), vii (27c), xiv (11b), xvi (18a, 34a), xviii (9b, 19a, 31b), xx (3a), xxvi (7b), xxvii (29b), xxviii (31a, 33a, 34b, 35b), xxx (8b, 10a, 11a, 13a, 19b, 22b, 24b, 26b, 27b, 35b, 36b), xxxiv (11a), xxxvi (28a, 29b, 33a, 41a, 45b, 46a, 49a, 94a, 101a, 103a), xxxviii (39a), xlvi (14a, 16b, 19b, 58a, 66a), l (19b, 23a, 29b, 33a, 34b, 36a, 38a, 41b, 43b, 45a), lii (38a), liii (5b, 13b, 15b, 20b, 25b, 28b, 29a, 30a, 33b, 38a, 39a, 59a), liv (1b, 31a), lvii (8b, 12a, 15b, 16b, 19a, 20a), lxi (6a, 8b, 13a, 18a, 20b, 26a), lxii (2a, 7a, 9b, 20b, 26a), lxiii (2a, 4b, 5b, 6a, 12a), lxiv (7b, 9a), lxv (8b, 20b, 28a), lxvi (17a, 32a, 33b), lxix (13b), lxxi (56a), lxxii (2a, 3a), lxxiii (52b), lxxvi (61a), lxxxii (13a), lxxxiii (40b, 45a, 62b, 65a, 66a, 69a, 73a, 75b, 79a, 83a, 89b, 95b, 97a, 99b, 119b, 120b, 125a, 127a, 129a, 138a, 139a, 141a, 149a, 151a, 152a, 154a, 160a, 163a, 164a, 166a, 170b, 173a), lxxxiv (1a, 3a, 8b, 15b, 23a, 29b, 30b, 34a, 36a, 37a, 43b), lxxxv (7b, 9a, 13a, 20b, 26a, 27b, 33a, 34b), lxxxvi (1a, 3a, 4a), lxxxvii (11a), xcvi (12b), xcviii (3b, 21b), xcix (1a, 13a, 27b, 36a, 39a, 41b), c (4a), ci (7b), cii (13a), cix (18b, 19b, 23b), cx (20b, 39a, 41b, 45a, 46a, 54a, 60a, 61b), cxi (3a), cxii (18a), cxiii (39a, 87a, 90a, 95ab).

Utt – xxxviii (53b, 54b, 57b, 59b, 61a, 63a, 64a, 65b, 66a, 76a), xxxix (11b), xl (21b), xlii (41a, 44b), xliii (16a, 19b), xcviii (10a), cii (3a, 7a), cxiiii (43a).

232. HARI = Monkey.

AK. 312 हरति हरि: ।

Adi – i (74b), iii (86b, 92b), iv (31b), xx (17a, 20ab), lx (12a).

Ayo – cv (23a), cvi (3b).

Ara – xv (4a), xx (26a), lxxvii (73a).

Kis—xxxi (4b, 19a, 21a, 23c), xxxii (9a, 10a, 15a), xxxiii (2a, 20a, 33a), xxxiv (24b), xxxv (2b, 25a, 27ab, 28b, 32b), xxxvi (2a, 15b), xxxvii (4b, 5b, 11b, 16b, 32b, 34a), xxxviii (2ab, 4a, 7a, 8b, 9a, 11a, 21a, 25a, 27a, 32b, 35b, 51a, 55b, 58a), xxxix (11a, 13a, 18b, 25a, 31a, 37a, 40a), xl (49a), xli (1a, 5a, 6b, 7a, 8b, 63b), xlii (1b, 2b, 13a), xliii (1a, 6b, 16a), xliv (10a, 83a, 129a), xlv (1a, 17b, 18a), xlvi (18b), xlvii (1a), xlviii (7b), xlix (2a, 8a, 11a), l (1a, 21b, 22b, 28a), li (19b, 29a), lii (23b, 24b), liii (24a), liv (22b, 26a), lv (9a, 16b), lvii (1b, 3b, 8b, 24a, 28a), lviii (1a, 6b), lix (12b), lx (1a, 2a), lxii (29a), lxiii (24b), lxiv (4b, 6b).

Sun—i (7b, 10a, 12a, 25a, 26b, 27b, 30b, 33ab, 34b, 39b, 43a, 51ab, 65ab, 71a, 74b, 75a, 77a, 78a, 79a, 94a), ii (1a, 9a, 13a, 15a, 47b, 50b), iii (6a, 44b, 75b), v (3a), vi (26a), vii (30b, 56a), ix (23a, 25a, 63a), xi (20b), xii (10b), xiv (5b), xv (38b), xvi (40a, 51b), xix (1a, 33b), xxx (14a), xxxi (27a), xxxii (40b), xxxiii (6a), xxxv (15a, 20b, 41a, 48a), xxxvii (4a, 7a, 26b), xxxviii (34a, 37a), xxxix (1a), xlii (10b, 11a, 34b), xliii (6a, 10b), xlv (3a, 10a), xlvii (10a), xlviii (1a, 2b, 10b, 11b, 12a, 13b), l (10b), li (12a, 16b, 24b), lii (8a), liii (3a, 4a, 18b, 20b), liv (5b, 8ab, 19b, 24b), lv (10b), lvi (6ab, 8b, 21b, 32b, 35a), lvii (1b, 2b, 8b), lix (19b), lx (20b), lxi (1ab, 5b, 6b, 12b, 13a, 19a), lxii (11b, 12b), lxiii (7b, 10b, 12a), lxiv (1a, 17b, 20b, 22b), lxv (1a, 4a, 9b, 10b, 11a, 13a, 16a, 21b, 22ab, 24b), lxvi (8b, 14a), lxvii (1a, 6a), lxix (36b, 41b), lxx (4a, 6b, 17b, 22b), lxxi (15b, 17b), lxxii (11b), lxxiv (33b, 34a, 38b, 40b, 41ab, 46a, 66a), lxxv (20a, 23a, 24a, 27b), lxxxi (8b, 13b), lxxxii (27a), xci (49a), xcii (2b, 5a, 14a, 23a), xciii (1a, 15a, 16b, 17a), xciv (11a), xcvii (7a, 44a).

Kis—i (5a, 9b, 19a, 28b), v (31b), vi (21b, 24a), vii (12a), ix (65b), xii (27b), xiii (4b, 30a), xiv (5a), xv (6a), xvi (5b, 54b), xvii (2b, 33b, 45b), xviii (5a, 30a), xix (9b), xxii (10a, 19b, 37a, 38b), xxiii (2a, 4b, 5b, 10a, 11b, 12a), xxiv (11a, 25a), xxv (19a), xxviii (8b, 19b, 20a, 21a, 22a, 27b, 33ab), xxx (13a, 24b).

Yud—i (13b, 17a, 29a), ii (3a, 21b, 39a, 43a, 46b), iii (4b, 18a, 27a, 30a, 38a, 42b), iv (5b, 13a, 18a), v (1a), vi (7b, 8b, 9c, 19b), xiii (2a, 22a,), xv (1a, 12b, 16a), xvi (13b, 32a, 42b, 54b, 56b, 75a, 82a, 96b,) xvii (3b, 5b, 18a, 22c), xviii (14b, 16b, 17b, 23a, 24b, 29a, 45a, 58a), xix (3a, 8b,

18a, 69a, 73b), xx (6a), xxi (38b, 39b), xxii (2b, 23b), xxiv (5c, 36b), xxv (25a, 29a), xxviii (8a, 24a), xxix (16b, 18b, 22a, 25b, 26b, 28a, 29b), xxx (4b, 6b, 37a), xxxa (3a), xxxb (31b), xxxi (9a, 44a), xxxii (93a, 94a), xxxvi (10b, 11a, 13b, 47b, 48a, 53a, 120b), xxxvii (93a, 94a), xxxvii (93a, 94a), xxxviii (38a, 40a), xlii (6b), xlvi (16a, 34b, 44a, 56a, 57b, 67b, 68a, 70b, 71a, 76b, 80b, 83b, 118b), xlix (28a, 32a, 35b, 39b, 45a, 51c, 53b, 54b, 61a, 63a, 65a, 67a, 68b, 71a), l (18b, 35b, 50b, 51b), li (4b, 11a, 35a, 39a, 41a, 42a), lii (40a, 41a), liii (1a, 11a, 12a, 23b, 30b, 38b, 39a, 41a, 67a), liv (6a, 27a), lvi (52b, 56a), lx (5b, 17a), lxi (6a, 18a, 20ab), lxii (2a, 5a), lxx (42a), lxxi (14b, 55a), lxxvi (17a, 50a), lxxvii (1b, 7a, 20b, 28a, 30b, 38a, 46ab), lxxviii (17a, 30a), lxxx (5b, 75b), lxxxii (3a, 11a, 12b), lxxxiii (39b, 62a, 139b, 152a, 156b), lxxxiv (27b, 44a, 54a), lxxxvi (1b, 4b), xcii (2a), xcviii (7b, 8a, 10a, 24a), xcix (5a, 12a), c (45a, 53a), cii (31a), cvi (14a), cviii (5b, 17a), cx (11b, 25b), cxiii (95b).

Utt–xxiii (20a, 29a, 33a, 36b, 41a, 42b, 44a), xxx (28b), xlii (43b), xcviii (14a), cxiii (45a).

233. HAṂSA=Goose, gander, swan.

AK. 88/129–हन्ति गच्छति हंसः ।

Adi–xxxvii (8a), xlv (19b).

Ayo–xxvii (18a), xliii (22b), xlvi (11b), xlvii (3b), lii (33a), civ (3a), cxi (49a).

Ara–vii (3a), xv (6b, 42b), xx (20a), xxi (12a), lvi (45a), lxxvii (61a), lxxviii (7a), lxxx (27a), lxxxi (27b, 42b).

Kis–xiii (8a), xxix (16b), xliv (30b), li (11a), lii (38a), lix (31b).

Sun–ix (9a, 57a), xi (2b, 6a), xii (25a), xiii (7b), xiv (16a, 24b, 37b, 39a), xvii (26a), xviii (20b).

Yud–xxxb (13a), xlix (22b), lxv (25b), lxxxiii (71a), cx (59a), cxii (42b), cxiii (8a).

Utt–xviii (5b, 25a, 28a), xx (20a, 21b), xxx (10), xlv (14b), lxxxiv (4b, 10b).

234. HAṂSĪ=Female Goose.

Utt–xxxiv (13b).

235. HAYA=Horse

AK. 184–हयति याति हयः ।

Adi – vi (24ab), xi (12a) xiii (30b, 32a, 37a), xlii (23c, 24a), xliii (8b), xlv (13b), liv (21a), lxix (25b), lxxx (16b, 21b).

Ayo – xvi (13a, 16a, 22b), xxxix (47b), xli (15a), xlvi (5b, 11a), xlvii (6b, 8a), lvii (2a), lxx (3a, 6a), lxxxix (7a, 13d), xc (1a, 2b), xcvi (22a), xci (4a), c (55a), cii (13b), cvi (19a, 29a), cvii (13b), cxxiv (20a), cxxv (14a, 22a).

Ara – ii (3b), ix (10b), xxxii (15a), xxxiv (30b).

Kis – xliv (74b).

Sun – xx (6b), xli (7a), ix (20a).

Yud – vii (33a), ix (26b), xiii (15a), xviii (2a), xix (9a), xxvii (27a), xxxa (4a, 18a, 19a, 24b, 28b), xxxb (19b), xxxi (28b, 39c), xxxii (30b), xxxiii (3a), xxxv (12a), xxxvii (39a), xlix (7a, 15a, 48b, 52a, 54a, 66b), l (33a), lii (8b), lviii (24a), lxiii (44b), lxiv (22b), lxx (38b, 44a, 46a), lxxi (4a), lxxxvii (3a), lxxxviii (26a), xcii (26a), xciii (9a).

Utt – vi (44a), xxvi (7a, 8a), xxvii (35a), xxxiv (37a), xlix (19a), liii (16a), lxiii (21a), lxxvii (2b), xcii (20a), xciii (6b, 8c), xciv (2b), xcvii (18a, 21a), xcviii (3a, 16b), xcix (1b, 2a, 9a).

236. HARIṆĪ = Faminine of *Hariṇa,* which denotes 'gazelle'.

AK. 126 – ह्रियते गीतेन हरिणः । स्त्रियामणी ।

Sun – xvii (49b), xxv (43a).

237. HASTIN = Elephant.

'Having a hand', with *Mṛga,* 'beast', denotes in the *R.V.* and the *A.V.* the 'elephant'. Later the adjective alone comes to mean 'elephant'. – (Keith: *Vedic Index* : II, 501).

Adi – v (13b), lxxx (3b).

Ayo – ii (31a), xxxv (40b), lxxix (11a), c (59a), cviii (29a), cix (49b).

Ara – ii (3b), iv (34a), xl (22b, 26a), liv (63c), lv (16a).

Kis – ix (107a), xlix (13a).

Sun – iii (15b), xi (7b), xviii (30b), xxi (14b), lxxxiii (33b), xc (6a).

Yud – iii (23a, 28ab, 41b), xlvi (115b), xlix (28b), lxxiv (3a), cx (33a).

Utt – xxxi (5a), xlii (35a).

References

* Continued from pp. 386 of vol XXIX, No. 4.

233. *Ṛv.*, i, 65, 5; *Av.*, vi, 12, 1; *Kāth. Saṃ.*, xxxviii, i; *Mait. Saṃ.*, iii, 11, 6; *Vāja. Saṃ.*, xix, 74; *Tait. Brā.*, ii, 6, 2. 1; *Tait. Saṃ.*,v, 5, 21, 1.

235. *Ṛv.*, v, 46, 1; *Vāja. Saṃ.*, vii, 47.

236. *Tait. Saṃ.*, vii. 4, 19, 2; *Vāja. Saṃ.*, xxiii, 30; *Mait. Saṃ.*, iii, 13, 1; *Kāth. Saṃ.*, iv, 8; *Tait. Brā.*, iii, 9, 7, 2; *Av.*, vi, 67, 3.

237. *Ṛv.*, i, 64, 7; iv, 16, 14; *Av.*, xii, 1, 25; *Tait. Saṃ.*, v, 5, 11, 1; *Mait. Saṃ.*, iii, 14, 8; *Vāja. Baṃ*, xxiv, 29; *Pañc. Brā.*, vi, 8, 8; *Aita. Brā.*, iv, 1, 14; *Sata. Brā.*, iii, 1, 3, 4; *Chānd. Upa.*, vii, 24, 2; *Jaiṃ. Upa.*, *Brā*, iii, 22, 1.

62

On the Economic Geography of Kālidāsa

Krishnadeva Upadhayaya

It is not our endeavour here to propose any new indentification of the places occurring in Kālidāsa's works, but to show how the poet's description of flora and fauna of the different provinces of India are accurate.

In the *Raghuvaṃśa,* Canto IV, Kālidāsa describes in detail the achievements and military expeditions of the 'warlike son' of Dilīpa.

Kālidāsa says that Raghu on his victorious march reached the sea-shore on the eastern side of India which was darkened by exuberant growth of palm-trees.[1] This evidently refers to the palm-trees found in abundance on the sea-shore.

In connection with the people of Suhma[2] the poet speaks of them as having defended themselves by the adoption of the policy of canes.[3] It seems to be a reference to canes, the natural product of this sea-bordering district of the east.

He says that the inhabitants of Vaṅga[4] (eastern Bengal) were great experts in the art of navigation.[5] Bengal, as a matter of fact, possesses a network of rivers constantly replenished by the copious waters of the rains. The people of this province are by their natural inclinations devoted to the art of navigation. Even, to-day, the people of eastern Bengal enjoy the reputation of being expert sailors. Kālidāsa refers in this connection to the fact that the paddy plants when re-sown yield a rich harvest.[6] He describes village girls singing songs in the shade of sugar cane plants.[7]

Kālidāsa mentions paddy as the product of Bengal. The climate and soil of this province are suitable for the product of rice, and as a matter of fact, paddy plants grow here in large quantity.

Raghu marched from the east to the south through Utkal (Orissa) and reached the country of Kaliṅga[8] where his brave warriors drank the sweet juice of cocoanut.[9] The king of this country had a large number of elephants forming a part of his army.[10] Orissa and the country around it still abounds in elephants.

Cocoanut generally grows in abundance on the sea-shore and this was the case with the country of Kaliṅga[11] also. Even to-day on the south sea-side of India cocoanuts are found in large quantities.

The poet mentions that Raghu went from Kaliṅga to the southern countries through the sea-shore of Eastern Ghats and there he found the trees of betelnut with their fruits.[12] Areca or betelnut also is such a product which finds its favourable growth like palm-tree mainly on the sea-shore. Even to-day the sea-shores of the Coromandal Coast and Ceylon are famous for their product of betelnut and cardamom, etc.

The southern part of India is mentioned by Kālidāsa as the home of pepper and cardamom,[13] these being favourable products of the valley of the mountain Malaya (modern Nilgiris) the favourable haunt of green pigeons.[14] The poet also mentions the sandal trees[15] of this locality. These facts are amply attested by the economic geography of that part of the country. When this victorious hero marched further southwards the Pāṇḍyan king of that country offered him presents of the best of pearls collected from that part of the sea where the river Tāmraparṇī falls into it.[16] By mentioning this fact our poet refers to the ancient practice of pearlfishery which is still going on in the same manner near the port of Tuticorin below Tanjore. The sea at the mouth of the river is still considered to be one of the most important centres of pearl-fishery in the world which yields—as we are told by the experts—the most genuine and perfect specimens of these precious objects.

As regards the mountain chain of Southern India. This prince of Sanskrit poets mentions two mountains – Malaya and Dardura—which, he says, resemble the breasts of a woman.[17] We believe that this simile of Kālidāsa is quite appropriate owing to the height of these in the middle. Even in the *Mārkaṇḍeya Purāṇa* Malaya and Dardura are spoken of together. Hence with the identification of Malaya with the Nilgiris, it is but natural to suppose that Dardura meant that portion of the Ghats which forms the southern boundary of Mysore. The mountain Sahya (Western Ghats) is described like the hip of a lady.[18] This is testified by the shape of the Sahya mountain where it meets the Eastern Ghats about the Nilgiris.

The south-western part of India then comes for treatment at the hands of our poet. Kerala (modern Mālābār) abounds in datepalm and Tamāla trees.[19] The charming country even to-day captivates the heart of every traveller who happens to visit that part of southern India by its luxuriant tall, green palm and Tamāla trees.

After conquering the farthest southern countries of India the hero of our poet turns his attention to the Persians. There, he could not bear the flush caused by the wine in the lotus-faces of Yavana women.[20] This seems to be a reference to wine made by Persian women of grapes growing in that country. Kālidāsa adds that the country is surrounded on all sides by the beautiful bowers of vines.[21]

The western people are said to have fought with Raghu with their cavalry. In fact, this region is still famous for its superior breed of horses.[22] In the neighbourhood of this region on the north-western side in Kamboja[23] Kālidāsa has mentioned the growth of अक्षोट trees which were overpressed by the fastening chains of Raghu's elephants.[24] Even to-day the best walnut trees grow in this very part of our country.

Turning from the north-west countries of India our poet describes the victory of Raghu in the Himalayan regions. A very good piece of geographical information is furnished by Kālidāsa when he mentions that Raghu's armies took rest on those stone slabs which were made fragrant by the contact of the march of musk-deer.[25] Deer having musk in their navel are commonly found only in the interior parts of the Himalayas and even to-day the best musk comes from Nepal where these musk-deer are found in large numbers.

Kālidāsa mentions two main gifts of the Himalayas to the Indian people, viz., teak and cedar.[26] Himalayan regions abound in these two trees. The Himalayas are regarded as the home of teak trees. They abound also in the wild bamboos and birch trees[27] whose bark was in ancient times used as a writing material.

The power of observation of our poet was so keen that even the minutest things like the little phosphorescent herbs of the Himalayas did not escape his notice.[28] It is one of the special features of the Himalayas that they abound in phosphorescent herbs which glow during night. The expert botanists of modern times have noticed the presence in the Himalayas of such self-glowing phosphorescent plants.

Now after crossing the Himalayan regions Raghu crossed the river Lauhitya (the modern Brahmaputra) and came into the country of Prāgjyotiṣa[29] (the modern Assam). Here two things are particularly mentioned by our poet, and these are black Aguru trees[30] and mighty, wild, rutting elephants.[31] The forests of modern Assam still abound in the elephantine breed.

References

1. प्राप तालीवनश्याममुपकण्ठं महोदधेः ।–*Raghu.*, IV. 34.
2. सुह्म was situated to the west of Vaṅga, its capital being ताम्रलिप्त called also तामलिप्त, दामलिप्त, ताम्रलिप्ती, तमालिनी (Cf. हेमचन्द्र IV. 45). In times of महाभारत it seems to have included Western Midnapur only, as it is separately mentioned after ताम्रलिप्त (*Mbh.*, II, 30, 24, 26), but afterwards its extent was greater. नीलकण्ठ explains सुह्म by Rāḍha (*Mbh.*, II, 30, 16) which is undoubtedly the Western Bengal.
3. आत्मा संरक्षितः सुह्मैर्वृत्तिमाश्रित्य वैतसीम। –*Raghu.*, IV 35.
4. It was also known as Samataṭa or 'Plains'.
5. वङ्गानुत्खाय तरसा नेता नौसाधनोद्यतान्। –*Raghu.*, IV.
6. आपादपद्मप्रणताः कलमा इव ते रघून्।
   फलैः संवर्धयामासुरुत्खातप्रतिरोपिताः ।–*Raghu.*, IV. 37.
7. इच्छुच्छायानिषादिन्यस्तस्य गोप्तुर्गुणोदयम्।
   आकुमारकथोद्घातं शालिगोप्यो जगुर्यशः ॥–*Raghu.*, IV. 20.
8. उत्कलादर्शितपथः कलिङ्गाभिमुखो ययौ।–*Raghu.*, IV. 38.
9. नारिकेलासवं योधाः शात्रवं च पपुर्यशः ।–*Raghu.*, IV. 42.
10. [गजसाधनः] *Raghu.*, IV. 40.
11. Kaliṅga extended from the south of Utkala to the mouths of the Godavari. It did not extend beyond the Godavari, as its mouths are said to be in the possession of the Andhras. In the days of Daṇḍin its capital Kaliṅganagara was at some distance from the sea-coast, as he says, the king of Kaliṅga when taken captive by the neighbouring king of Andhra went out to pass some days at the sea-side.
12. ततो वेलातटेनैव फलवत्पूगमालिना।
    अगस्त्याचरितामाशामनाशास्यजयो ययौ–*Raghu.*, IV, 44.
13. *Raghu.*, IV, 47.
14. *Ibid.*, 46.
15. *Ibid.*, 48.
16. ताम्रपर्णीसमेतस्य मुक्तासारं महोदधेः।
    ते निपत्य ददुस्तस्मै यशः स्वमिव सञ्चितम् ॥–*Raghu.*, IV, 50.
17. *Ibid.*, IV, 51.
18. *Raghu.*, IV, 52.
19. *Ibid.*, 54, 56, 57.
20. यवनीमुखपद्मानां सेहे मधुमदं न सः ।–*Raghu.*, IV, 60.

21. विनयन्ते स्म तद्योधाः मधुभिर्विजयश्रमम्।
    आस्तीर्णाजिनरत्नासु द्राक्षावलयभूमिषु।–*Raghu.*, IV, 65.
22. *Ibid.*, IV, 62.
23. गजालानपरिक्लिष्टैरक्षोटैः सार्धमानताः। –*Raghu*, IV, 69.
24. In the Sabhā Parvan, the Kambojas are said to have been conquered by Arjuna along with the Daradas after the subjugation of Balkh (27. 22-3). As the Daradas now inhabit the valley of the Gilgit and Balkh is separated by the Hindu Kush, it is but natural to suppose that the Kambojas inhabited this mountain and its adjoining country.
25. *Raghu.*, IV, 74.
26. *Ibid.*, IV, 75, 76.
27. भूर्जेषु मर्मरीभूताः कीचकध्वनिहेतवः।–*Raghu.*, IV.
28. आसन्नोषधयो नेतुर्नक्तमस्नेहदीपिकाः।–*Raghu.*, IV., 75.
    Cf. भवन्ति यत्रौषधयो रजन्याम्–*Kumār.*, I, 10.
29. प्राग्ज्योतिष is identified with the eastern-most part of India comprising the Eastern Assam, the people of which country under the leadership of their king Bhagadatta played a conspicuous part in the Bhārata war, which explains the name thus–
    अत्रैव हि स्थितो ब्रह्मा प्राङ् नक्षत्रं ससर्ज ह।
    ततः प्राग्ज्योतिषाख्येयं पुरी शकपुरीसमा।
    Local tradition identifies Prāgjyotiṣapura with the modern Gauhati.
30. तद्गजालानतां प्राप्तैः सह कालागुरुद्रुमैः।–*Raghu.*, IV, 81.
31. तमीशः कामरूपाणामत्याखण्डलविक्रमम्।
    भेजे भिन्नकटैर्नागैरन्यानुपरुरोध यैः।–*Raghu.*, IV, 83.